Early New World Monumentality

UNIVERSITY PRESS OF FLORIDA

Florida A&M University, Tallahassee
Florida Atlantic University, Boca Raton
Florida Gulf Coast University, Ft. Myers
Florida International University, Miami
Florida State University, Tallahassee
New College of Florida, Sarasota
University of Central Florida, Orlando
University of Florida, Gainesville
University of North Florida, Jacksonville
University of South Florida, Tampa
University of West Florida, Pensacola

Early New World Monumentality

Edited by Richard L. Burger
and Robert M. Rosenswig

University Press of Florida
Gainesville · Tallahassee · Tampa · Boca Raton
Pensacola · Orlando · Miami · Jacksonville · Ft. Myers · Sarasota

Copyright 2012 by Richard L. Burger and Robert M. Rosenswig
All rights reserved
Printed in the United States of America on acid-free paper

First cloth printing, 2012
First paperback printing, 2015

Library of Congress Cataloging-in-Publication Data
Early new world monumentality / edited by Richard L. Burger and Robert M. Rosenswig.
p. cm.
Includes bibliographical references and index.
ISBN 978-0-8130-3808-7 (cloth: alk. paper)
ISBN 978-0-8130-6144-3 (pbk.)
1. Indian architecture—America. 2. Mound builders—America. 3. Indians—Dwellings. 4. Indians—Urban residence. 5. America—Antiquities. I. Burger, Richard L. II. Rosenswig, Robert M.
E59.A67E37 2012
977'.01—dc23
2012000881

The University Press of Florida is the scholarly publishing agency for the State University System of Florida, comprising Florida A&M University, Florida Atlantic University, Florida Gulf Coast University, Florida International University, Florida State University, New College of Florida, University of Central Florida, University of Florida, University of North Florida, University of South Florida, and University of West Florida.

University Press of Florida
15 Northwest 15th Street
Gainesville, FL 32611-2079
http://www.upf.com

Contents

List of Figures   vii
List of Tables   xi

Part I. Introduction

1. Considering Early New World Monumentality   3
   ROBERT M. ROSENSWIG AND RICHARD L. BURGER

Part II. North America

2. Early Mounds in the Lower Mississippi Valley   25
   JOE SAUNDERS

3. Shell Mounds of the Middle St. Johns Basin, Northeast Florida   53
   KENNETH E. SASSAMAN AND ASA R. RANDALL

4. Monumentality in Eastern North America during the Mississippian Period   78
   DAVID G. ANDERSON

Part III. Mesoamerica

5. Agriculture and Monumentality in the Soconusco Region of Chiapas, Mexico   111
   ROBERT M. ROSENSWIG

6. Early Olmec Wetland Mounds: Investing Energy to Produce Energy   138
   ANN CYPHERS AND JUDITH ZURITA-NOGUERA

7. The Origins of Monumentality in Ancient Guerrero, Mexico   174
   LOUISE I. PARADIS

8. Early Civilization in the Maya Lowlands, Monumentality, and Place Making: A View from the Holmul Region   198
   FRANCISCO ESTRADA-BELLI

Part IV. Intermediate Area

9. Monumental Architecture and Social Complexity in the Intermediate Area   231
   R. JEFFREY FROST AND JEFFREY QUILTER

Part V. South America

10. Early Mounds and Monumental Art in Ancient Amazonia: History, Scale, Function, and Social Ecology   255
    ANNA C. ROOSEVELT, J. DOUGLAS, B. BEVAN, MAURA IMAZIO DA SILVEIRA, AND L. BROWN

11. Why Do People Build Monuments? Late Archaic Platform Mounds in the Norte Chico   289
    JONATHAN HAAS AND WINIFRED CREAMER

12. Monumental Architecture Arising from an Early Astronomical-Religious Complex in Perú, 2200–1750 BC   313
    ROBERT A. BENFER JR.

13. Preceramic and Initial Period Monumentality within the Casma Valley of Peru   364
    THOMAS POZORSKI AND SHELIA POZORSKI

14. Monumental Public Complexes and Agricultural Expansion on Peru's Central Coast during the Second Millennium BC   399
    RICHARD L. BURGER AND LUCY C. SALAZAR

15. Agricultural Terraces as Monumental Architecture in the Titicaca Basin: Their Origins in the Yaya-Mama Religious Tradition   431
    SERGIO J. CHÁVEZ

Part VI. Conclusion

16. A West Asian Perspective on Early Monuments   457
    FRANK HOLE

List of Contributors   466
Index   471

Figures

1.1. Map of the Americas with location of sites presented in this volume 16
2.1. The locations of the Early Archaic Conly Site, the Middle Archaic mounds in Louisiana and Mississippi, and the Late Archaic site Poverty Point 29
2.2. Aerial view of Caney Mounds 30
2.3. Middle Archaic Evans points from Watson Brake 31
2.4. Zoomorphic bead from Monte Sano Mounds 32
2.5. Middle Archaic fired earthen objects 33
2.6. Significant Middle Archaic sites in northeast Louisiana 34
2.7. Topographic map of Watson Brake 35
2.8. 3-D model of Watson Brake earthworks 36
2.9. Topographic map of Frenchman's Bend Mounds 38
2.10. Topographic map of Hedgepeth Mounds 40
2.11. A plot of procurement sites near Watson Brake and Plum Creek Archaic 42
3.1. Map of the middle St. Johns Basin 55
3.2. Topographic map of Hontoon Dead Creek Mound and Live Oak Mound 59
3.3. Stratigraphic profile of trench in western slope of Hontoon Dead Creek Mound 60
3.4. Topographic map of sites along Silver Glen Run 63
4.1. Location of Archaic, Woodland, and Mississippian sites mentioned in the text 79
4.2. Traditional interpretation of mounds as green and covered with cropped grass, as seen at Cahokia 88
5.1. Map of the Soconusco and the land between swamps and a chronology chart for the Early and Middle Formative phases 114
5.2. Graph of total hectares of occupation in the Cuauhtémoc survey zone for the ten Early and Middle Formative phases 118
5.3. Map of Cuauhtémoc showing location of mounds 120
5.4. Ground stone patterns from Cuauhtémoc 126
5.5. El Sitio Axe and cleft and double line-break iconography from Cuauhtémoc 127

viii · Figures

6.1. Photograph of a large *islote* in San Lorenzo's northern plain 140
6.2. Map of the San Lorenzo region showing the principal permanent sites and identified *islotes* 142
6.3. Reconstruction of an *islote* showing the smoking of fish on a slatted stand placed above a sunken fire pit within a semi-enclosed structure 149
7.1. Map of Ancient Guerrero in the Early and Middle Formative Period 176
7.2. Ceremonial zone and precinct for Teopantecuanitlán 178
7.3. Ceremonial zone with two of the four monoliths at Teopantecuanitlán 180
7.4. One of the four monoliths at Teopantecuanitlán 180
7.5. Hydraulic work at Teopantecuanitlán 181
7.6. Oxtotitlán, Painting C-1, showing an important personage sitting on a throne 184
7.7. Oxtotitlán, Painting 1-D, showing a man standing near a jaguar 186
7.8. Oxtotitlán, Painting 7, showing a head in profile with a serpent mask over the mouth 187
7.9. Amuco Stele 189
7.10. Burials and Tomb 1 with corbelled arch at Coovisur 191
8.1. Map of the Maya Lowlands showing sites with Pre-Mamom ceramics and early architecture 199
8.2. Artist's reconstruction of vessels from the Holmul Pre-Mamom ceramic complex 203
8.3. Perspective view of three phases of construction in the ceremonial center at Cival 206
8.4. View of the landforms of the Cival area 206
8.5. Views from the west of the Middle Preclassic and Late Preclassic hilltop at Cival 208
8.6. Map of the ceremonial center at Cival showing all Late Preclassic architecture and the defensive wall 208
8.7. Profile of looters' trench in Triadic Group I at Cival, which cut through five construction stages of the platform dating to the Late Preclassic period 210
8.8. Comparison of combined volume of construction between the Middle and Late Preclassic periods at Cival 211
8.9. Artist's reconstruction of Cache 4 at Cival 213
9.1. Map of Guayabo de Turrialba 237
9.2. Causeway at Guayabo. Mound 1 in background and Turrialba Volcano in distance 239
9.3. Mound 1 and plaza/pool at Guayabo de Turrialba 239

9.4. Rivas–Panteón de la Reina site   242
9.5. Structure foundation and associated architecture at Rivas   243
10.1. Map of the Amazon   256
10.2. Rock painting panel, Serra da Lua, Monte Alegre, Brazil   263
10.3. Taperinha shell mound and surrounding site area   266
10.4. Formative pottery artifacts of the Zoned Hachure Horizon, Ponta do Jauari, near Alenquer, Brazil   273
10.5. Castanheira Site, Marajo Island, Brazil   274
10.6. Faldas de Sangay mound site, Ecuadorian Amazon   277
10.7. Incised and modeled jar, Faldas de Sangay   277
11.1. Examples of Andean monumental architecture   290
11.2. Map of Late Archaic sites with monumental architecture in the Norte Chico region   292
11.3. Reconstruction of platform mound and circular plaza complex at Norte Chico   293
11.4. Cerro Blanco 2, Fortaleza Valley   294
11.5. Caballete, Fortaleza Valley   294
11.6. Huaricanga, Fortaleza Valley   295
11.7. Vinto Alto, Pativilca Valley, profile of upper portion of Mound C, showing multiple construction phases   296
12.1. Late Preceramic monumental architecture at Buena Vista   315
12.2. Moisture, population density, and health measurements   320
12.3. Temple of the Fox and niched walls   332
12.4. Temple of El Paraíso del Valle and Temple of the Menacing Disk   333
12.5. Superimposed stairs and Temple of the Fox   337
12.6. Stairs to the platform of the Menacing Disk leading up from the Temple Paraíso del Valle   340
12.7. View of summer solstice sun rising over Rock A from the entryway of the Temple of the Fox   345
12.8. Drawing of Menacing Disk facing the WSSS   347
12.9. Gaze of Menacing Disk to WSSS, flanked by supernatural animals   348
13.1. Map of the Casma Valley showing the location of early sites   370
13.2. Plan of Sechín Alto Complex   371
13.3. Plans of Huaca A at Pampa de las Llamas-Moxeke and Mound of the Columns at Taukachi-Konkán   373
13.4. Plan of the site of Pampa de las Llamas-Moxeke   374
13.5. Views of the front and back of an Initial Period solid figurine found at Sechín Alto Complex   387

14.1. Location of U-shaped centers with monumental architecture in the middle and lower Lurín Valley   404
14.2. Aerial photograph taken in 1947 showing the large U-shaped center of Mina Perdida and the now-destroyed U-shaped center of Parka   405
14.3. Isometric reconstruction of the main staircase and entrance into the atrium on the central mound of Cardal   407
14.4. Low-altitude oblique photograph of Cardal showing U-shaped mounds and large central plaza area   408
14.5. Cross-section showing superimposed atria at Cardal   413
14.6. Balloon photograph of sunken circular patio with central ritual hearth at Cardal   414
14.7. Drawing of modular increments made to expand the right arm of Mina Perdida   416
14.8. Profile of looters' cut in the central mound at Mina Perdida showing superimposed staircase, fills, and other structures   418
14.9. Calibrated radiocarbon measurements from Mina Perdida, Cardal, and Manchay Bajo   419
14.10. Monumental dam built during the Initial Period to protect U-shaped center of Manchay Bajo   422
14.11. Inca offering of Spondylus shell and metal sheet left along central axis at Manchay Bajo   424
15.1. Map of the Copacabana Peninsula with an inset of the Lake Titicaca Basin showing all the temple sites mentioned in the text   432
15.2. Distribution of a selected sample of stone sculpture showing the "early" and "late" coexisting versions of the Yaya-Mama religious tradition in the Titicaca Basin and the "late" version extending into the Cuzco Basin   433
15.3. View from the Muruqullu temple site showing the distribution of stone-faced terraces to near lake shore and a narrow terrace on the right used as a path for people and beasts of burden   435
15.4. Satellite view of the excavated temple site of Muruqullu and surrounding steep hills and valleys extensively covered by terraces   436
15.5. Upper portion of stone-faced terraces near the excavated temple site of Huayllani   437
15.6. Excavated temple site of Ch'isi and surrounding hills and valleys extensively covered by terraces   440

Tables

2.1. Descriptive statistics for Middle Archaic mounds   27

2.2. Common taxa from Watson Brake and Plum Creek Archaic   44

5.1. Conchas phase architecture in the Soconusco   121

5.2. Conchas phase developments, material correlates and references   124

7.1. Noncalibrated radiocarbon dates for Teopantecuanitlán, Amuco, and Xochipala   177

12.1. Radiocarbon dates from Late Preceramic component at Buena Vista   316

13.1. Construction volume and labor calculations for Casma Valley mound sites   377

13.2. Rectangular plaza sizes at Casma Valley sites   379

INTRODUCTION

1

Considering Early New World Monumentality

ROBERT M. ROSENSWIG AND RICHARD L. BURGER

Monumental construction projects have always been a conspicuous reminder of past societies and thus have long been the subject of archaeological inquiry. Culture historians have cast their interpretive net across large areas and tried to explain why monumentality diffused from one region to another (e.g., Childe 1958, 70; Ford 1969; Griffin 1952; Tello 1943). Processual archeologists later shrank the geographical scale of inquiry to study monumental works in terms of local adaptation and sociopolitical organization (e.g., Renfrew 1973; Steponitis 1978; D. Wilson 1988). Postmodern archaeologists exploring agency and practice deemed the way past peoples experienced monumentality to be most important (e.g., Barrett 1994; Bradley 1998; Tilley 1994). Clearly these perspectives are not mutually exclusive in the questions they ask. However, none specifically address the issue of how and why large construction projects began. Diffusion cannot explain how things got started in the first place. And while particular forms of social organization can facilitate large work projects, they certainly do not necessitate that such endeavors will occur. Further, while specific historical conditions and the ability to coordinate people to undertake large labor projects obviously required specific cultural knowledge, this does not explain why monumentality is such a pervasive phenomenon in early cultures all over the world.

A comprehensive analysis of early monumentality incorporates a concern with labor and its mobilization as well as the longer-term impact of spiritual awe and political organization that can be both generated and naturalized by such undertakings. The large pyramids and impressive monuments that attract attention, as well as equally large but less conspicuous public works projects such as road or irrigation facilities provide a common starting point for a comparative study of the development of complex societies in the New World. Our goal in this volume is to compare early monumentality through a series of New World case studies that consider economic foundations as well as the lasting effects of large building projects. In this chapter, we provide a comparative starting point by considering two time scales from which to consider monumental construction projects. The first is the relatively short-term construction events that create architectural features. The second is the longer-term use of these features once they have transformed the landscape. Framing different temporal scales in such a manner is consistent with what has been called time perspectivism, the idea "that changes in the time scale at which we make observations change what we see and that varying time scales bring into focus different variables and processes that are not visible, or not so easily visible, at other time scales, thus requiring different sorts of concepts and explanatory principles" (Bailey 2008, 13).

Comparing Early Monumental Building Projects

In a much-cited article, Bruce Trigger (1990) employs the concepts of least effort and conspicuous consumption to argue for a cross-cultural meaning of the labor invested in monumental-scale public works. He observes: "Monumental architecture embraces large houses, public buildings, and special purpose structures. Its principle defining feature is that its scale and elaboration exceed the requirements of any practical functions that a building is intended to perform" (Trigger 1990, 119). This conspicuous consumption of human labor violates the principle of least effort, which is what gives monumentality salience cross-culturally. He continues by observing that "the most compelling demonstration of power is the ability of a ruler to consume some of the energy he controls for nonutilitarian purposes. It is because of this that monumental architecture constitutes a universally understood expression of power and also why the basic significance of monumental architecture and luxury goods is so readily apparent to archaeologists" (Trigger 1990, 125).

While this 1990 paper "aroused speculation that at last Trigger was about to become a processual archaeologist, [it] was written somewhat tongue-in-cheek" (Trigger 2004, 238). He explains that "by labeling my construction a 'thermodynamic explanation' I had, in mimicry of many early processualists who discussed anything other than subsistence behaviour, built into my argument without acknowledging it to my readers a non-adaptive, and hence a non-ecological explanation" (ibid.). Veblen's concept of conspicuous consumption is not thermodynamic but instead psychological. Trigger is therefore proposing a cross-cultural theory for the symbolic meaning of monumentality among early civilizations rooted in the biology of the human mind.

In the chapters that follow, authors explore less complex forms of cultural organization than those addressed by Trigger for his thermodynamic model, but ones that nonetheless undertook monumental building projects. Trigger's proposal to explain the cross-cultural meaning of monumentality has much to offer the study of the origins of such building projects. The pervasiveness of monumental building projects around the world "suggests that conspicuous consumption was universally equated with power in these societies ... [and this] ... runs contrary to what relativist cultural anthropology or postprocessual archaeology would predict. The creation of such structures was grounded not in reasoning that was specific to individual cultures but in cognitive and behavioural tendencies that are pan-humanly grounded" (Trigger 2004, 246).

Trigger's analysis of monumentality was used to examine fully developed secondary states and empires, but his formulation raises the question of how it all got started. In this volume we do not presume to provide a definitive answer as to why monumentality began. Instead, we present a series of case studies that document where and when some of the earliest monumental construction projects were undertaken in various regions of the New World. The early monumental building projects discussed in this volume were endeavors undertaken by groups of people over extended periods of time. But precisely how much labor was mobilized? What purpose(s) did it serve? And how did these societies differ from non-monument-building peoples that preceded and/or surrounded them? These are some of the questions that need to be answered if we are to better understand the origins of monumentality.

The "Utility" of Building Projects

The dichotomy between utilitarian and non-utilitarian labor specified in Trigger's thermodynamic model is not emphasized in this volume, nor is the division between building projects that are "utilitarian" (e.g., roads and administrative buildings) versus those that are "non-utilitarian" (e.g., stone monuments and temple mounds). Public works projects undertaken for "utilitarian" purposes, while perhaps not as conspicuous, can equally express the power of rulers that commission and/or coordinate such projects or the collective potential of the communities responsible for them. The ability to build roads, aqueducts, irrigation canals, or agricultural terraces (to name but a few utilitarian public works projects—see Frost and Quilter, Chapter 9; Paradis, Chapter 7; Roosevelt, Chapter 10) can reflect the power of rulers. Inca and Roman road systems and the walls around Uruk were signs of power that were as clear as any of the temples Sumerians built in their cities.

The utilitarian versus non-utilitarian dichotomy has the additional drawback of implying that "utility" was conceptualized in the same way in all societies or remained constant over time within a given society (see Benfer, Chapter 12). Even if we limit utility to mean economic utility, the dividing line is no more clearly drawn. For example, the number of square meters of domestic space in which most Americans live has steadily increased during the twentieth century despite a decline in average family size, but is the extra floor space non-utilitarian? More important, economic utility need not necessarily be assumed to be of greater importance than social or spiritual utility in the functioning of society. Each would have been necessary, especially among those societies with weak central authority and little means of coercive control. Large temples or public monuments can awe foreigners and reassure residents, thus serving important social functions. Think of the Statue of Liberty or the Arc de Triomphe—it would be hard to argue that these emblematic national monuments serve *completely* non-utilitarian purposes. Or that Big Ben is *simply* an oversized public timepiece. Our approach to monumentality therefore does not discriminate on the basis of function and includes all large-scale work projects.

Monumentality as Evidence of Power

The comparative perspective adopted in this volume attempts to elevate analysis above that of a single case. Monumental construction projects can be undertaken by nonhierarchical societies or can potentially serve nonhierarchical functions within hierarchical societies. It is ill advised to equate the existence of a single characteristic such as monumentality a priori with the presence of political power or the social hierarchy that often accompanies such authority (Arnold 1996; Gibson 2004, 256–258). Haas and Creamer (Chapter 11) propose that their chapter "diverges from others in this volume by proposing that *all* monumental architecture requires leadership and centralized decision-making." There is little doubt that large public works projects require organization that extended beyond the household group and that such organization has the potential to be used to establish and maintain an elite sector of society. However, it is not *necessarily* the case that such organization reflects social stratification or political hierarchy. This is discussed by Sassaman and Randall (Chapter 3) and Saunders (Chapter 2) for the Archaic period in the U.S. Southeast. Roosevelt (Chapter 10) reviews similar ideas for the Archaic in Amazonia, as do Burger and Salazar (Chapter 14) for the Initial Period Lurín Valley and Chavez (Chapter 15) for the Yaya-Mama religious tradition in the Lake Titicaca Basin. Each of these chapters proposes that factors other than social stratification can explain early public works projects.

In addition to the relationship between large construction projects and sociopolitical organization, another unwarranted assumption is an a priori relationship between monumentality and the subsistence economy. This consideration is important due to the long-standing assumption that the workers undertaking public works projects needed to be provisioned by intensive agriculture and that a great deal of organization is required. Rosenswig (Chapter 5) argues that this assumption accurately describes the Soconusco region of southern Mexico, where intensification of food production and a network of conical mounds occur together beginning at approximately 1000 cal. BCE along with a clear increase in the degree of social stratification (see Rosenswig 2007, 2010). However, other cases of early monumentality presented in this volume preceded intensification of the subsistence base by many centuries (Benfer, Chapter 12; Haas and Creamer, Chapter 11; Sassaman and Randal, Chapter 3; Roosevelt, Chapter 10).

It is best to seek independent evidence of the function(s) of monumental features, the presence of social hierarchy, and the existence of food production so as to not construct circular arguments. A large conical mound at a site center should not in itself be used to argue for the existence of an elite priestly-chief class that organized the labor of others and depended on stable crop production to feed a subservient work force. However, if independent evidence of rulers exists (using mortuary patterns, iconography, etc.) along with evidence that the mound served a distinct function (by documenting trash comprising different types of objects than other contexts at the site and/or distinct features) and the society depended on agriculture (using isotopes and fauna and flora remains), then such a model may be reasonable. Illuminating comparisons may then be made with societies that built equally big mounds but where evidence of social stratification or agriculture (or both) is lacking. This is particularly instructive when comparing these relationships among multiple cases, as we do here.

Circular reasoning when interpreting monumental architecture has been widespread. Renfrew's (1973, 1974) well-known classification of Neolithic chiefdoms provides one example of this. The Neolithic societies that built mounds in southern England were classified as chiefdoms because they built large barrows. Renfrew (1973, 554) used the same barrows as evidence of food redistribution and centralized control and for his conclusion that such control was vested in an individual. Further, the spacing of these barrows, particularly in the west Salisbury Plain, suggested to him that each mound defined the territory of a separate chiefdom (Renfrew 1973, 544, Figure 1). Renfrew still considered societies that lacked the expected mortuary evidence of social differentiation (ibid., 556) to be chiefdoms, but of a newly defined "group-oriented" variety (Renfrew 1974, 75–77). Renfrew's argument is hampered by his assumption that building a mound is necessarily evidence of an individual (or limited group of individuals) exercising political power and controlling a territory. According to this logic, a society was a chiefdom because it built a big mound and it built a large mound because it was a chiefdom. As Jon Gibson (2004, 258) argues in relation to Archaic mounds and political complexity in the southeastern United States: "You simply cannot use mounds to prove the existence of the very phenomenon they are assumed to represent, at least not their presence or absence." We agree.

Energetic Baseline

Regardless of the utilitarian versus non-utilitarian nature of large building projects or the hierarchical versus nonhierarchical nature of the societies that created them, energy expenditure provides a baseline with which to compare one case to another. Descriptions of each society's largest or most impressive monument remain anecdotal, but energetic calculations, in contrast, provide a comparative framework for assessing the "cost" of structures relative to each other within a site or total construction programs from one community or society to another.

Individual structures or monuments and entire sites can be compared to each other in terms of labor costs required for their construction. Labor estimates (generally derived from volume of fill in the case of platforms, roads, mounds, etc.) function best when comparisons are made in relative terms (Kolb 1997, 269). This is because calculations of the durable archaeological remains do not account for the labor expended on related tasks that do not leave material traces, such as quarrying stone and preparing materials, transporting earth and stone, provisioning workers with food and water, laying out architectural plans (possibly associated with astrological considerations), building wooden scaffolding, and constructing temporary earthen ramps. Calculations of construction efforts in relative terms can subsume such extra costs within the resulting labor estimates. Elliot Abrams's (1989, 1994) detailed ethnoarchaeological estimates for the procurement and transport of various construction materials as well as building techniques provide a reasonable baseline for relative labor estimates.

In cases where the quantity of labor required to build a residence *can* be accurately reconstructed and the maximum number of people who would have lived in that residence are taken into account, differential social power can be inferred, since nonresidents would have had to be recruited to make up any labor deficits. As Abrams and Bolland (1999, 268) state: "If social power is defined in part by differential access to a compliant human labor force, then the ability for some households to access (through some mechanism) relatively large numbers of people in the construction of their residence is a direct consequence of differential power." Thus, monumental domestic residences are one of the most straightforward indicators of unequal political power and social ranking (e.g., Evans and Pillsbury 2006; Lyons 2007; Rosenswig and Masson 2002).

Labor expenditures for nonresidential buildings or monuments, in contrast, have a less direct or necessary relationship to political power. This is especially true for societies where residential differentiation (or other clear indicators of social stratification) is not documented to exist. In such cases, there is no necessary reason to interpret large construction projects as being controlled by rulers. However, when coercive labor conscription (or evidence of social stratification) is documented, a more convincing case can be made for similar elite power being exercised in the mobilization of labor for public works projects. Again, rather than begin by assuming the political implications of monumental work projects, it is more productive to evaluate this as one possibility on a case-by-case basis. Energetic estimates provide a comparative baseline between cases when reviewing other indicators of political power and social hierarchy (or their absence) but do not speak to issues of function or meaning.

Temporal Control of Monumental Building Projects

Although the quantity of labor expended in monumental construction projects provides an energetic baseline with which to compare individual cases, it does not reflect the crucial variable of the duration of time over which the labor was expended. If a mound required one million person-days to construct, it could have taken one million people a day to build it or one person a million days (Aaberg and Bonsignore 1975; Clark 2004, 192–193). The importance of this distinction is similar to the use of both number of identified specimens present (NISP) and minimum number of individuals (MNI) statistics by faunal analysts. As with faunal analysis, the process of aggregation becomes of utmost importance. Within what blocks of time (aka archaeological phases) were particular construction episodes carried out? There are, to be sure, practical limitations to these minimum and maximum numbers. One million people could not physically work on a mound simultaneously. Nor is it realistic to propose that one Noah-like individual (or a series of single individuals) toiled at the task for one million days. If a construction project was completed during a single archaeological phase, this usually provides a temporal limit on the order of a few centuries. Furthermore, within a temporal phase, stratigraphy often allows finer resolution based on the number of construction episodes that are documented. When interpreting the construction projects that often loom large, one of the most important questions to ask is whether it was a single event, two or three events, or a gradual process of incremental expansion (e.g., Blitz and Livingood 2004). This is unlikely to be evident from surface inspection, and determination will require an excavation strategy designed to study this question.

A relevant example is provided by the detailed redating of Silbury Hill, the Late Neolithic mound in Wessex (Bayliss, McAvoy, and Whittle 2007). Silbury Hill rises 30 m from the ancient ground surface and at its base measures 160 m in diameter. The mound was formed by three building episodes, but there was disagreement over whether this was carried out during the course of a decade or over the period of a generation or two (Bayliss, McAvoy, and Whittle 2007, 29). By running a series of AMS dates, including samples of mosses retrieved from the surfaces of turves, and interpreting them within a Bayesian statistical framework, Bayliss, McAvoy, and Whittle (2007, Figure 6) propose that the mound was likely built over a 300-year period during the first part of the second millenium BCE. Therefore, if the (very rough estimate) of 300,000 m³ of mound fill is divided by 300 years, then Silbury Hill could have been built with approximately 1,000 m³ of fill moved each year. The implications of this are significantly different than if 300,000 m³ of fill were moved in a decade two. Likewise, Cyphers and Zurita-Noguera (Chapter 6) argue that at San Lorenzo, prior to the site's emergence as a major center, 1.3 million m³ of fill was moved over the course of numerous centuries as "a long-term effort well within work capacity of the early population and thus a task that did not require centralized coordination." Temporal control of the rate of construction projects is thus key to inferences of political hierarchy and/or social control.

Multiple construction episodes at the same site or of the same mound do not, however, diminish the significance of the undertaking. A mound (or other monumental-scale architectural feature) is likely to remain a focal point on the local landscape and as such is bound to be important over the long term. Resurfacing the top of a 30-meter-high mound such as Silbury Hill would reinforce its importance even if relatively little additional fill were added by such renovation. The political implication of mound maintenance is a separate issue and is dependent on who is organizing the public work project. In the context of a mobile foraging society, voluntary labor expended for the common good is a reasonable default assumption (e.g., Saunders, Chapter 2; Sassaman and Randall, Chapter 3). In contrast, when similar quantities of fill are moved in the upkeep of a mound located in the capital of a powerful centralized polity (e.g., Estrada-Belli, Chapter 8; Pozorski and Pozorski, Chapter 13), it is equally reasonable to assume that the exercise of political authority may have played a role. However, making this distinction can be contentious, as is illustrated by the differing interpretations of contributors in this volume. Haas and Creamer (Chapter 11) argue that the Late Preceramic mounds in Norte Chico illustrate political hierarchy, and Pozorski and Pozorski (Chapter 13) see a similarly early phenomenon in the Casma Valley, where inland and coastal sites culminated in the hierarchical Sechin Alto polity during the Initial Period. In contrast, Burger and Salazar (Chapter 14) do not see hierarchical relations among Initial Period sedentary food producers on Peru's central coast. These divergent interpretations are not in conflict if Initial Period political organization is not assumed to have been homogeneous throughout the region and a mosaic of political systems existed.

The Built Environment

Architecture, monuments, and other features built by human toil enclose behavior and so create a built environment within which activities occur at the household, village, and regional levels. In Amos Rapoport's (1990, 2006) terms, "systems of settings" structure "systems of activities," and so architectural form and layout reflect and reinforce cultural norms and values. Manuel Castells (1983, 311) also argues in relation to modern cities that "spatial forms . . . will be produced by human action, as are all objects, and will express and perform the interest of the dominant class according to a given mode of production." Adam Smith (2003, 32) defines larger-scale landscapes in similar terms as "encompassing not only specific places and moments but also the stretches between them: physical, aesthetic, and representational." He observes "In spatial terms, landscapes are not simply built out of a collection of practices but simultaneously constrain the possibilities for practice. By remaining within a given set of spatial parameters, practices reproduce not only the spaces themselves but also the social structures and political regimes that these spaces support" (Smith 2003, 72).

The built environment can reflect and (equally important) can reinforce existing social and political relations. The built environment generally creates a "political aesthetic" (sensu Smith 2000), and in the case of stratified societies, this aesthetic acts to naturalize the elites' elevated standing. Put simply, this commonsensical observation is that the form, arrangement, and size of architecture at a site as well as its distribution across the landscape reflects the social and political functions it serves. Architecture (including pyramids, walls, roads, irrigation systems, etc.) constrains and directs human movement and thus imbues it with the power to remake social norms (Love 1999). Once constructed, the built environment naturalizes existing social and political organization by structuring the movement of people, activities, goods, and ideas (e.g., Barrett 1999; Burger and Salazar 1991; Fisher 2005; Johansen 2004, 326–328). The long-term result is to create lasting focal points on the landscape that later people remember and use to emphasize the antiquity of their claims to legitimacy (e.g., Dietler 1998; Pauketat 2007, 199; Sassaman 2005).

Changing architectural practices are thus a productive place to begin exploring changes within the societies that constructed them. Transformations of the form and arrangement of coordinated work projects can be expected to reflect evolving social and political norms (e.g., Joyce 2004;

Low 2000, 105–118; Rosenswig and Masson 2002, 229–230). Particularly relevant to early examples of monumentality in a region are the cultural implications of first undertaking large building projects and creating a built environment like nothing that had previously existed at a particular site or across a larger area (Estrada-Belli, Chapter 8; Rosenswig 2010, 126–128, Chapter 5).

Local Built Environment

In a Zen rock garden, the spaces between the rocks are equally as important as the rocks themselves. Similarly, spaces created between and around mounds need to be understood along with the architectural features that produce them (Hillier and Henson 1984; Low 2000; Rautman 2000). Lewis, Stout, and Wesson (1998, 11) note that "architecture is composed of two basic elements, mass and space. . . . It is unproductive to view plazas merely as residual spaces around which structures are raised." While mounds and the structures atop them may be the domain of individuals or limited groups of people, the spaces they formed tend to be where the majority of people experienced their lives. The creation of culturally defined space thus seems to be why U-shaped mounds were built in both Florida (Sassaman and Randall, Chapter 3) and Peru (Burger and Salazar, Chapter 14). The impetus in both cases may have been less to create the mounds and more to create the space in between. To approach monumentality more comprehensively, significance must also be attributed to the cultural remaking of spaces created by road systems, defensive walls, irrigation canals, commemorative statues, and so forth. Consideration of the symbolic information expressed by monumental constructions in the production of social relations has long been part of anthropological interpretation (e.g., Blanton 1994, 79–114; Ferguson 1996; Lawrence and Low 1990; Love 1999; Moore 1996; Parker Pearson and Richards 1994; Siegel 1999; Steadman 1996, 64–72; Wilk 1983, 112–115; P. Wilson 1988, 134–135).

Regional Built Environment

The discussion of the built environment above focused mainly on centers of human habitation and their layout and use. But any single location is often also part of a system linked to other locales through ties of marriage and exchange and other social relationships. At a larger geographic scale, a site and its architecture can be more fully understood in relation to the other sites that surround it with (and without) their own monumental features. The relationship of such a regional-scale built environment to the natural environment has been termed landscape archaeology by some (e.g., Ashmore and Knapp 1999; Ucko and Layton 1999). The landscape perspective is basic to most contemporary regional settlement survey projects and, as Kanter (2008, 57) astutely points out, has much in common with historical ecology. Both focus on human interactions with the environment, and vice versa. Those that focus on ideational aspects of inhabiting a region call what they do landscape archaeology (e.g., Bender 2002; Tilley 1994), whereas those who are more inclined to address economic and functional relationships between humans and their environment label their work historical ecology (or socioecology) (e.g., Balée and Erickson 2006; Barton et al. 2004). At the local level, it is significant that focal points are created and redefine how people moved through sites. The same is true at a larger spatial scale because a series of monumental features would result in a remaking of the regional built environment. Early monumentality thus remade how regions were navigated both physically and cognitively, and such changes were embedded in evolving political and social structures of people inhabiting the region.

The interpretation of ashmounds created by Neolithic (3000–1200 BCE) agro-pastoralists in southern India provides an example of a regional built environment and the long-term use of these constructed features (Johansen 2004). More than 100 ashmounds, measuring as much as 10 m in height and covering up to almost 5,000 m^2, are known from the semi-arid area around three major, slow-moving rivers near the Karnataka–Andhra Pradesh border. They are "comprised of stratified deposits of decomposing, burned and vitrified cow dung and other culturally modified soils bearing a variety of artifacts" (Johansen 2004, 309). The lower sections of these mounds built up accretionally due to mundane activities such as penning cattle and storing and disposing of dung. The upper part of the mounds were also formed incrementally by piling up dung and regularly burning it at a low temperature as well as less frequent burning events that vitrified deposits up to one meter thick. Together, the "activities involved in ashmound construction, use and maintenance . . . were structured, repetitive, cyclical, and public" (Johansen 2004, 325). Over time, these ashmounds reached monumental proportions and a series of them were created across a defined region. Placed at prominent locations in the flat and arid environment, these mounds provided permanent focal points that marked communities. During the subsequent Iron Age (1200–400 BCE), dependence on agriculture increased dramatically and, just as significantly, ashmound construction decreased. Nonetheless, the Iron Age use of Neolithic ashmounds is well documented, as is the building of megalithic constructions on and around these earlier ashmounds. In this way, Neolithic monuments marking important locations on the landscape constituted a historical legacy that was incorporated into the Iron Age built environment. The former were locations of site cohesion, whereas the latter use of the same features functioned to express newly emerged power.

For states and empires, such a regional perspective entails defining territorial extents as well as relationships with neighboring polities. For the majority of societies addressed in this volume, the relationship between neighboring polities engaged in projects of monumental constructions is not necessarily as simple. Are similar features, such as large mounds, meant to demarcate different territories, as Renfrew (1973, 1974) proposed for the British Neolithic? Or did they signal shared cultural unity and perhaps differentiation from surrounding peoples who did not build monumentally? Large construction projects are what bring the essays in this volume together, and exploring such alternative interpretations is one of the main goals of this book. Each chapter is written by scholars with first-hand knowledge of the early New World monumentality they describe and provides a substantive contribution with new data and/or syntheses.

Differences across the New World

This volume brings together sixteen essays: three from the southeastern United States, four from Mesoamerica, one from lower Central America, one from the tropical lowlands of South America, five from Andean South America, and a comparative discussion of Old World developments. The authors each discuss monumentality based on their respective theoretical perspectives. However, by explicitly approaching monumentality both in terms of initial labor organization and longer-term effects of large construction projects that transform the landscape, this volume provides a comparative perspective.

One of the hemisphere-wide patterns that these essays highlight is how early the first monumental construction projects were undertaken in areas of the southeast United States and South America compared to how relatively late such developments occurred in Mesoamerica and lower Central America. This is particularly noteworthy when contrasting the earliest large mounds in each region to other developments such as dependence

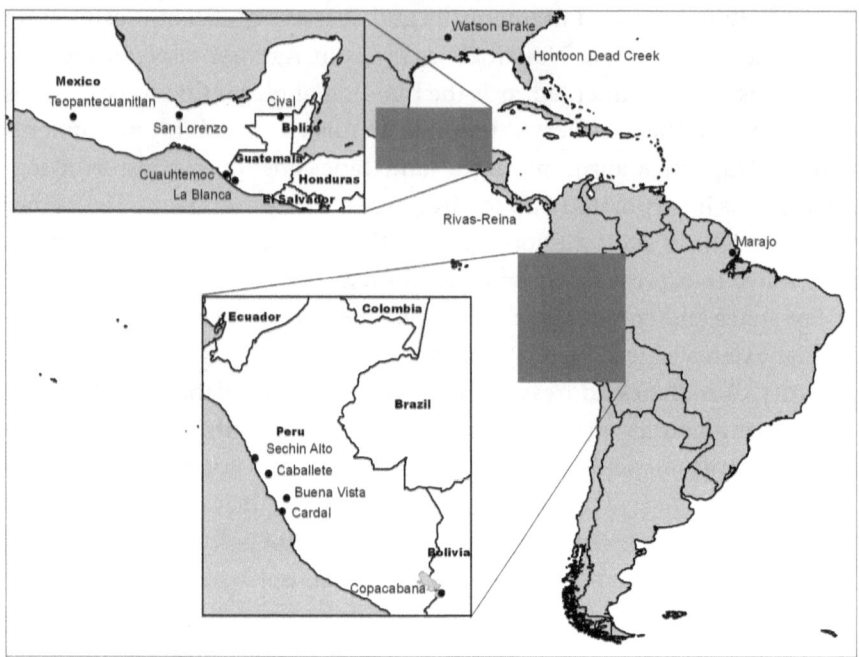

Figure 1.1. Map of the Americas with location of sites presented in this volume.

on food production or the origins of sociopolitical hierarchy. Preceramic peoples with little evidence of large permanent settlements or dependence on intensive agriculture came together to build huge mounds on the Pacific coast of Peru by 3000 BCE and in the southeastern United States by 5000 BCE during each region's Archaic period. In contrast, large mounds were not built in Mesoamerica until aproximately 1000 cal. BCE, nearly a millennium after ceramic-using villages of agriculturalists were first established in some parts of the region (Estrada-Belli, Chapter 7; Paradis, Chapter 8; Rosenswig, Chapter 5). Monumental sculptures of powerful rulers were carved and transported to San Lorenzo before this and an amazing 14–18 million person-hours of labor was required for earth-moving projects to construct terraces as well as fill in and level the San Lorenzo plateau (Cyphers and Zurita-Noguera, Chapter 6). However, virtually no pyramid mounds were built in Mesoamerica until after the San Lorenzo polity collapsed. Therefore, while Early Formative (~1900–1000 cal. BCE) construction projects in Mesoamerica required the organization of labor (i.e., the short-term time scale discussed previously), they did not transform the local landscape by providing long-lasting focal points (i.e., the longer-term time scale). In contrast, in the southeastern United States and in South

America, conical mounds were part of the local landscape that later peoples used and reinterpreted (Anderson, Chapter 4; Pozorski and Pozorski, Chapter 13; Roosevelt, Chapter 10).The numerous case studies presented in this volume document a diversity of social and political trajectories that are paralleled by the many roles that monumental architecture played in shaping, expressing, and reinforcing the structure and character of these distinctive cultural and social formations.

The examples from the Soconusco region and the Lurín valley provide a particularly illustrative comparison both in their similarities and in their differences (and provided the initial motivation for assembling this volume). Rosenswig (Chapter 5) argues that the first system of conical mounds emerged at the top three tiers in the Soconusco settlement hierarchy during the Conchas phase (1000–850 cal. BCE) along with a significant increase in the reliance on food production as well as a greater degree of social stratification. Burger and Salazar (Chapter 14), in contrast, propose that in the first system of large U-shaped mounds are documented at similarly sized sites in the Lurín valley by the end of the Initial Period (1800–800 BCE) along with a significant increase in food production but with an absence of social stratification. Large mounds and agriculture emerged together in both cases, but hierarchy is observed in one case and not the other. The Peruvian Initial Period pattern seems to have employed the long-standing tradition of building large mounds to create a stable political phenomenon. In contrast, the La Blanca polity in the Soconusco seems to have been a relatively short-lived experiment where conical mounds were used to define political centers as one of numerous strategies to establish a new level of social stratification and political hierarchy in the region. The La Blanca experiment was abandoned after a century or two, in contrast to the Initial Period Lurín valley centers that were occupied for a millennium.

As the essays in this volume show, monumentality is a cross-culturally relevant practice that provides a productive starting point for comparisons of cultural developments between regions. This assemblage of wide-ranging examples of New World monumentality is far from comprehensive. Each reviewer and commentator on the volume since the 2006 session of the Society for American Antiquity in Puerto Rico has had suggestions for additional cases or regions to include. Our geographic coverage certainly does not encompass the full range of monumentality in the Western Hemisphere. We have tried instead to provide depth of knowledge rather than completeness of coverage—an intensive, not an extensive, survey strategy. Further, the focus on the American continents is itself a rather arbitrary limitation driven by our research experiences. There is nothing that necessarily unites New World monumentality beyond geography, and comparisons to the Old World are productive, as the examples in this introduction and Frank Hole's contribution (Chapter 16) illustrate. Rather than presenting clear conclusions, this volume provides a starting point for future comparison. We hope that you will find this beginning as stimulating as we have in assembling these essays.

References Cited

Aaberg, S., and J. Bonsignore
1975   A Consideration of Time and Labor Expenditure in the Construction Process at the Teotihuacán Pyramid of the Sun and the Poverty Point Mound. In *Three Papers on Mesoamerican Archaeology,* edited by J. Graham and R. Heizer, pp. 40–78. Contributions of the University of California Archaeological Research Facility 24. University of California, Department of Archaeology, Berkeley.

Abrams, Elliot
1989   Architecture and Energy: An Evolutionary Perspective. *Archaeological Method and Theory* 1:47–88.
1994   *How the Maya Built Their World.* University of Texas Press, Austin.

Abrams, Elliot M., and Thomas W. Bolland
1999   Architectural Energetics, Ancient Monuments and Operations Management. *Journal of Archaeological Method and Theory* 6:263–291.

Arnold, Jeanne E.
1996   The Archaeology of Complex Hunter Gatherers. *Journal of Archeological Method and Theory* 3:77–126.

Ashmore, Wendy, and A. Bernard Knapp (editors)
1999   *Archaeologies of Landscape: Contemporary Perspectives.* Blackwell, Oxford.

Bailey, Geoff
2008   Time Perspectivism: Origins and Consequences. In *Time in Archaeology: Time Perspectivism Revisited,* edited by S. Holidaway and L. Wandsnider, pp. 13–30. University of Utah Press, Salt Lake City.

Balée, William, and Clark L. Erickson (editors)
2006   *Time and Complexity in Historical Ecology: Studies in the Neotropical Lowlands.* Columbia University Press, New York.

Barrett, John C.
1994   *Fragments from Antiquity: An Archaeology of Social Life in Britain, 2900–1200 BC.* Blackwell, Oxford.
1999   Chronologies of Landscape. In *The Archaeology and Anthropology of Landscape: Shaping Your Landscape,* edited by Peter J. Ucko and Robert Layton, pp. 21–30. Routledge, London.

Barton, C. Michael, Joan Bernabeu, J. Emili Aura, Oreto Garcia, Steven Schmich, and Lluis Molina
2004   Long-Term Socioecology and Contingent Landscapes. *Journal of Archaeological Method and Theory* 11:253–295.

Bayliss, Alex, Fachtna McAvoy, and Alasdair Whittle
2007   The World Recreated: Redating Silbury Hill in Its Monumental Landscape. *Antiquity* 81:26–53.
Bender, Barbara
2002   Time and Landscape. *Current Anthropology* 43:S103–S112.
Blanton, Richard
1994   *Houses and Households: A Comparative Study*. Plenum Press, New York.
Blitz, John H., and Patrick Livingood
2004   Sociopolitical Implications of Mississippian Mound Volume. *American Antiquity* 69:291–301.
Bradley, Richard
1998   *The Significance of Monuments: On the Shaping of Human Experience in Neolithic and Bronze Age Europe*. Routledge, London.
Burger, Richard L., and Lucy C. Salazar
1991   The Second Season of Investigation at the Initial Period Center of Cardal, Peru. *Journal of Field Archaeology* 18:275–296.
Castells, Manuel
1983   *The City and the Grassroots*. University of California Press, Berkeley.
Childe, V. Gordon
1958   Retrospect. *Antiquity* 32:69–74.
Clark, John E.
2004   Surrounding the Sacred: Geometry and Design of Early Mound Groups as Meaning and Function. In *Signs of Power: The Rise of Cultural Complexity in the Southeast*, edited by J. L. Gibson and P. J. Carr, pp. 162–213. University of Alabama Press, Tuscaloosa.
Dietler, Michael
1998   A Tale of Three Sites: The Monumentalization of Celtic Oppida and the Politics of Collective Memory and Identity. *World Archaeology* 30:72–89.
Evans, Susan Toby, and Joanne Pillsbury
2006   *Places of the Ancient New World*. Dumbarton Oaks Research Library and Collection, Washington, D.C.
Ferguson, Thomas J.
1996   *Historic Zuni Architecture and Society: An Archaeological Application of Space Syntax*. University of Arizona Press, Tucson.
Fisher, Christopher T.
2005   Demographic and Landscape Change in the Lake Pátzcuaro Basin, Mexico: Abandoning the Garden. *American Anthropologist* 107: 87–95.
Ford, James A.
1969   *A Comparison of Formative Cultures in the Americas: Diffusion or the Psychic Unity of Man*. Smithsonian Institution Press, Washington, D.C.
Gibson, Jon L.
2004   The Power of Beneficent Obligation in First Mound-Building Societies. In *Signs of Power: The Rise of Cultural Complexity in the Southeast*, edited by J. L. Gibson and P. J. Carr, pp. 254–269. University of Alabama Press, Tuscaloosa.
Griffin, James
1952   *Archaeology of Eastern United States*. University of Chicago Press, Chicago.

Hillier, Bill, and Julienne Hanson
1984 *The Social Logic of Space*. Cambridge University Press, Cambridge.
Johansen, Peter G.
2004 Landscape, Monumental Architecture, and Ritual: A Reconsideration of the South Indian Ashmounds. *Journal of Anthropological Archaeology* 23:309–330.
Joyce, Rosemary A.
2004 Unintended Consequences? Monumentality as a Novel Experience in Formative Mesoamerica. *Journal of Anthropological Method and Theory* 11:5–29.
Kanter, John
2008 The Archaeology of Regions: From Discrete Analytical Toolkits to Ubiquitous Spatial Perspective. *Journal of Archaeological Research* 16:37–81.
Kolb, Michael J.
1997 Labor Mobilization, Ethnohistory, and the Archaeology of Community in Hawai'i. *Journal of Archaeological Method and Theory* 4:265–285.
Lawrence, Denise L., and Setha M. Low
1990 The Built Environment and Spatial Form. *Annual Review of Anthropology* 19:453–505.
Lewis, R. Berry, Charles Stout, and Cameron B. Wesson
1998 The Design of Mississippian Towns. In *Mississippian Towns and Sacred Spaces: Searching for an Architectural Grammar*, edited by B. R. Lewis and C. Stout, pp. 1–21. University of Alabama Press, Tuscaloosa.
Love, Michael W.
1999 Ideology, Material Culture and Daily Practice in Pre-Classic Mesoamerica: A Pacific Coast Perspective. In *Social Patterns in Pre-Classic Mesoamerica*, edited by D. G. Grove and R. A. Joyce, pp. 127–154. Dumbarton Oaks, Washington, D.C.
Low, Setha M.
2000 *On the Plaza: The Politics of Public Space and Culture*. University of Texas Press, Austin.
Lyons, Diane E.
2007 Building Power in Rural Hinterlands: An Ethnoarchaeological Study of Vernacular Architecture in Tigray, Ethiopia. *Journal of Archaeological Method and Theory* 14:179–207.
Moore, Jerry D.
1996 *Architecture and Power in the Ancient Andes: The Archaeology of Public Building*. Cambridge University Press, Cambridge.
Parker Pearson, Mike, and Colin Richards
1994 Ordering the World: Perceptions of Architecture, Space and Time. In *Architecture and Order: Spatial Representation and Archaeology*, edited by Mike P. Pearson and Colin Richards, pp. 1–37. Routledge, New York.
Pauketat, Timothy R.
2007 *Chiefdoms and Other Archaeological Delusions*. Altamira, Latham, Maryland.
Rapoport, Amos
1990 Systems of Activities and Systems of Settings. In *Domestic Architecture and the*

Use of Space: An Interdisciplinary Cross-Cultural Study, edited by S. Kent, pp. 9–20. University of Cambridge Press, Cambridge.
2006 Archaeology and Environment-Behavior Studies. *Archaeological Papers of the American Anthropological Association* 16:59–70.

Rautman, Alison E.
2000 Population Aggregation, Community Organization and Plaza-Oriented Pueblos in the American Southwest. *Journal of Field Archaeology* 27:271–283.

Renfrew, Colin
1973 Monuments, Mobilization and Social Organization in Neolithic Wessex. In *The Explanation of Culture Change: Models in Prehistory*, edited by C. Renfrew, pp. 539–558. Duckworth, London.
1974 Beyond a Subsistence Economy: The Evolution of Social Organization in Prehistoric Europe. In *Reconstructing Complex Societies: An Archaeological Colloquium*, edited by C. B. Moore, pp. 69–95. Bulletin of the American Schools of Oriental Research 20.

Rosenswig, Robert M.
2007 Beyond Identifying Elites: Feasting as a Means to Understand Early Middle Formative Society on the Pacific Coast of Mexico. *Journal of Anthropological Archaeology* 26:1–27.
2010 *The Beginnings of Mesoamerican Civilization: Inter-Regional Interaction and the Olmec*. Cambridge University Press, New York.

Rosenswig, Robert M., and Marilyn A. Masson
2002 Transformation of the Terminal Classic to Postclassic Architectural Landscape at Caye Coco, Belize. *Ancient Mesoamerica* 13:213–235.

Sassaman, Kenneth E.
2005 Poverty Point as Structure, Event, Process. *Journal of Archaeological Method and Theory* 12:335–364.

Seigel, Peter E.
1999 Contested Places and Places of Contest: The Evolution of Social Power and Ceremonial Space in Prehistoric Puerto Rico. *Latin American Antiquity* 10:209–238.

Smith, Adam T.
2000 Rendering the Political Aesthetic: Political Legitimacy in Urartian Representations of the Built Environment. *Journal of Anthropological Archaeology* 19:131–163.
2003 T*he Political Landscape: Constellations of Authority in Early Complex Polities*. University of California Press, Berkeley.

Steadman, Sharon R.
1996 Recent Research in the Archaeology of Architecture: Beyond the Foundations. *Journal of Archaeological Research* 4:51–93.

Steponitis, Vincent
1983 *Ceramics, Chronology and Community Patterns: An Archaeological Study of Moundville*. Academic Press, New York.

Tello, Julio C.
1943 The Discovery of the Chavin Culture in Peru. *American Antiquity* 9:135–160.

Tilley, Christopher
1994   *A Phenomenology of Landscape: Places, Paths and Monuments.* Berg, Oxford.
Trigger, Bruce G.
1990   Monumental Architecture: A Thermodynamic Explanation of Symbolic Behaviour. *World Archaeology* 22:119–132.
2004   Settlement Patterns in the Postmodern World: A Study of Monumental Architecture in Early Civilizations. In *The Archaeologist: Detective and Thinker,* edited by L. Vishnyatsky, A. Kovalev, and O. Scheglova, pp. 237–248. St. Petersburg University Press, St. Petersburg.
Ucko, Peter J., and Robert Layton (editors)
1999   *The Archaeology and Anthropology of Landscape: Shaping Your Landscape.* Routledge, London.
Wilk, Richard R.
1983   Little House in the Jungle: The Causes of Variation in House Size among Modern Kekchi Maya. *Journal of Anthropological Archaeology* 2:99–116.
Wilson, David
1988   *Prehistoric Settlement Patterns in the Lower Santa Valley, Peru.* Smithsonian Press, Washington, D.C.
Wilson, Peter J.
1988   *The Domestication of the Human Species.* Yale University Press, New Haven.

II

NORTH AMERICA

2

Early Mounds in the Lower Mississippi Valley

JOE SAUNDERS

The rich and diverse environment in north Louisiana provided the economic foundation for establishing and maintaining a sedentary settlement pattern that eventually transformed preferred camp locales into residential sites. Mound construction began shortly thereafter, ca. 3700 cal. BC, and ended 1,000 years later. Limited excavations at many of these residential/mound sites identified little evidence of significant differences in the economy and society of the pre-mound and mound occupations.

The earthworks (Connaway, Brookes, and McGahey 1977; Gagliano 1967; Gibson 2000; Gibson and Shenkel 1988; Peacock et al. 2010); Saunders et al. 1997, Saunders et al. 2005; Saunders, Jones, and Allen 2010) and shellworks (Sassaman 2008; Sassaman and Randall, this volume) in the Lower Mississippi Valley are among the oldest in North America. Earthwork construction began around 3700 cal. BC, and perhaps as early as ca. 5000 cal. BC, although the evidence for an earlier origin is tenuous (Gibson 1996; R. Saunders 1994). The adaptation of local populations to the abundant riparian resources preceded this monumental achievement. Residential sites and a fisher-hunter-gatherer economy were well established by 5000 BC (Girard 2000; Girard et al. 2005). Once established in the Early Archaic, the riparian mode of production sustained mound-building cultures during the Middle Archaic (3700–2700 cal. BC), the Late Archaic (ca. 2700–700 cal. BC), and into the early Woodland (ca. 700 BC). Then monumental architecture in the Lower Mississippi Valley ended abruptly ca. 2700 cal. BC (Gibson 1996; Saunders 2010) and did not resume until 1,000 years later with the Poverty Point Period (1700–1200 cal. BC; Connolly 2000; Gibson 2000, 2007; Kidder 2006; Ortmann 2010).

The Middle Archaic monumental architecture in the southeast is not as complex or elaborate (see Sassaman and Randall this volume) as their Meso- and South American counterparts in this volume. The builders appear to have been egalitarian, localized fisher- or hunter-gatherers who did not engage in trade, and they built mounds while others in the same region did not. A comparable degree of complexity in both architecture and economy was later achieved at Poverty Point, approximately 1,000 years after the last Middle Archaic mound was completed (Kidder and Sassaman 2009).

The Middle Archaic societies were part of the panarchaic culture, perhaps reminiscent of Caldwell's (1958) primary forest efficiency, which shared fundamental technologies such as hot-rock cooking (Thoms 2008) and stone bead production (Crawford 2003). Within that backdrop, mound building and other stylistic attributes became localized in their distribution to the point that mound building was an autonomous act for each community.

We know a great deal about the early mound builders of the Lower Mississippi Valley, including the size, shape, construction sequence, and configuration of their monumental earthworks. We know the mounds were the residential base for foragers tethered to ecotonal settings with aquatic, riparian, upland, and lithic resources. We know that trade was rare and we know when monumental architecture started and when it ceased, but we don't know why.

Statistics

To date, 16 mound sites have been radiometrically dated to the Middle Archaic period (Figure 2.1). The summary statistics of the sites are extremely sparse. Middle Archaic research has focused on establishing the age and stratigraphy of the mounds, and fortunately that can be accomplished with coring and test-unit excavations. The unfortunate consequence is that beyond site chronology, site layout, and mound stratigraphy, very little is known about activities that occurred at the mound sites.

In 1994 (1994a, Table 2:92), Russo listed 60 possible Archaic mound sites in the Lower Mississippi Valley (5000 BC–1200 cal. BC). R. Saunders (1994, Table 1:120, 122) compiled data on 25 of the possible Middle Archaic mound sites in southeast Louisiana. Only four of the 25 sites had been radiometrically dated to >2700 BC, but the chronometric data from these sites were inconsistent (Brown and Lambert-Brown 1978; Gagliano 1967; Manuel 1979; Neuman 1985; and R. Saunders 1994), leaving only a few voices accepting

Table 2.1. Descriptive statistics for Middle Archaic mounds

Site	Mound Shape	Mound ID	Stages	Height	Length	Width	Rank
Banana Bayou	Dome	A	2	2	30	30	1,800
Belmont	Conical	A	1	11	50	53	29,150
Caney Mounds	Dome	A	1	1.8	25	20	900
Caney Mounds	Conical	B	2	2	45	30	2700
Caney Mounds	Dome	C	2	2.9	22	20	1,276
Caney Mounds	Dome	D	2	3.1	38	30	3,534
Caney Mounds	Dome	E	1	2.7	30	25	2,025
Caney Mounds	Dome	F	1	1.7	42	45	3,213
Caney Mounds	Causeway?						
Denton, MS	Dome	A	1	1	45	30	1,350
Denton, MS	Dome	B	1	1	25	30	750
Frenchman's Bend	Conical	A	3	3.6	60	45	9,720
Frenchman's Bend	Dome	B?	1.2	30	25	900	
Frenchman's Bend	Dome	C	1	1.5	40	43	2,580
Frenchman's Bend	Dome	D	1	0			
Frenchman's Bend	Dome	E	1	0			
Frenchman's Bend	Ridge?	B/C?	1	0			
Hedgepeth	Conical	A	2	6	70	45	18,900
Hedgepeth	Dome	B	1	2.1	35	46	3,381
Hedgepeth	Dome	C	1	0.8	22	32	563
Hedgepeth	Dome	D	1	1.3	25	17	553
Hedgepeth	Dome	e	4	2.45	28	20	1,372
Hedgepeth	Dome	F	1	0.9	23	19	393
Hedgepeth	Ridge	B/C	1	0			
Hornsby	Conical	B	2	1.2	27.4	27.4	901
King George's Island	Ridge	D/C	1	0			
King George's Island	Conical	A	1	2.6	35	35	3,185
King George's Island	Conical	B	1	3.2	35	40	4,480
King George's Island	Dome	C	1	1.8	22	25	990
King George's Island	Dome	D	1	2.2	45	30	2,970
King George's Island	Dome	E	1	1.6	10	25	400
King George's Island	Ridge	A/B	1	0			
King George's Island	Ridge	A/D	1	0			
Lower Jackson	Conical	A	1	3	35	35	3,675
LSU Campus Mds.	Conical	A	1	5	40	40	8,000
LSU Campus Mds.	Conical	B	1	4.9	36	36	6,350
Monte Sano	Conical	A	4	5	45	45	10,125
Monte Sano	Dome	B	1	2.5	36	36	3,240
Nolan	Conical	A	3	6.5	50	50	16,250
Nolan	Dome	B	3	3.3	45	40	5,940
Nolan	Dome	C	3	3.9	0		
Nolan	Dome	D?		3.1	30	25	2,325
Nolan	Causeway?	A/C	2	2.1			2400
Riser	Dome	A	1	1.5	40	40	

(continued)

Table 2.1—Continued

Site	Mound Shape	Mound ID	Stages	Height	Length	Width	Rank
Stelly	Dome	A	2	1.5	50	30	2,250
Stelly	Conical	B	2	4.3	40	45	7,740
Stelly	Conical	C	2	5	50	48	12,000
Watson Brake	Conical	A	6	7.25	62	60	25,970
Watson Brake	Dome	B	4	2.6	35	30	2,730
Watson Brake	Dome	C	2	1.3	22	20	572
Watson Brake	Dome	D	4	2.3	30	38	2,622
Watson Brake	Dome	E	1	3.8	52	48	9,485
Watson Brake	Dome	F	2	1.9	20	10	380
Watson Brake	Dome	G	1	1.3	7	5	46
Watson Brake	Dome	H	1	1.3	10	10	130
Watson Brake	Dome	I	3	2.4	40	32	3,072
Watson Brake	Conical	J	3	3.2	45	36	5,184
Watson Brake	Dome	K	1	0.5	2	3	3
Watson Brake	Dome	L?	1	1.5	22	10	330
Watson Brake	Causeway	A/B	1	0			
Watson Brake	Causeway	B/C	1	0			
Watson Brake	Causeway	D/E	1	0			
Watson Brake	Causeway	G/H	1	0			
Watson Brake	Causeway	K/A	2	0			
Watson Brake	Causeway	J/K	2	0			
22LI504	Conical	A	5?	2	22	21	924

the antiquity of the Louisiana mounds (Gibson 1994; Gibson and Shenkel 1988; Jeter et al. 1989; and Neuman 1984) and one mound site in Mississippi (Connaway, Brookes, and McGahey 1977). Over the past 15 years, 11 additional mound sites have been radiometrically dated to >2700 BC, bringing the total to 16 sites with 53 mounds and 13 causeways. The breakdown of the number of mounds per site is as follows: five with one mound, four with two mounds, three with three mounds, two with five mounds, one with six mounds, and one with eleven. The existence of Middle Archaic mound building is no longer questioned (Figure 2.1, Table 2.1).

The mounds are conical (n = 17) or dome-shaped (n = 36) and measure between .5 m to 8 m in height. The tallest known Middle Archaic mound is conical, as is the tallest mound on each multimound site. Dome-shaped mounds tend to be smaller (2.0 m vs. 3.6 m). The mounds and causeways are single-stage or multiple-stage structures. The developments of A horizons in the multistage earthworks show that the intermediate surfaces were stable for extended periods of time, perhaps as long as 100–200 years.

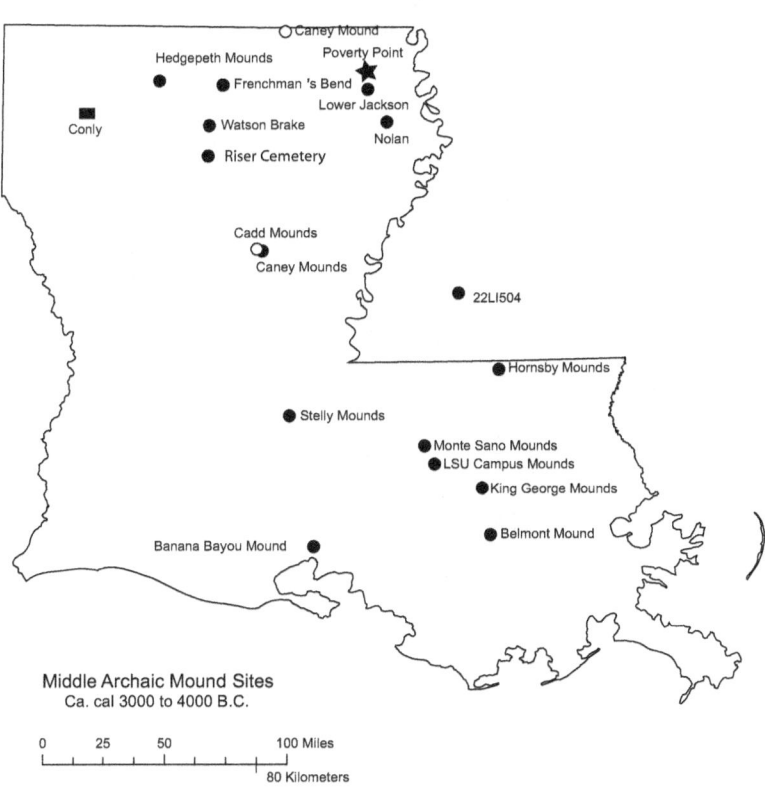

Figure 2.1. The locations of the Early Archaic Conly Site, the Middle Archaic mounds in Louisiana and Mississippi, and the Late Archaic site Poverty Point.

The recovery of artifacts from the A horizons shows that the serial surfaces had been occupied. Since none of the buried mound surfaces had evidence of human interments, it is difficult to argue that the intermediate surfaces were for burials. The sterile fill between the buried soils do not appear to be capping events as described by Sassaman and Randall (this volume, "capping events . . . may signal the 'death' of a location"), since subsequent stages were added to many of the existing mounds and newer mounds to the sites. Instead, the larger mound sites may have been active for up to 1,000 years.

There is one Euclidian fact that may elucidate the morphology and function of conical mounds. The surface area on the top of the mound is diminished with each stage, so fewer people could simultaneously participate in activities on the mound. It is interesting that this trend differs from

Figure 2.2. Aerial view of Caney Mounds. White arrow points north.

mounds in Chiapas, where platform mounds were elevated to incorporate larger numbers of people (Rosenswig this volume).

Four of the largest earthworks appear to form an enclosure around a central "plaza." Sassaman and Heckenberger (2004) argue for an a priori layout of the site that places the mounds, including the tallest mound, parallel along a terrace escarpment to create the illusion that the mounds are taller. The second-tallest mound, the backset mound, is placed at a point perpendicular to and in line with the terrace mounds to create the extent of a "plaza" on the landscape (Figure 2.2).

Material Culture

The material culture of the early mound builders is rather bland, consisting of a few stone beads, bannerstones, notched points, and fired-earthen objects. Stone or ceramic vessels did not exist, so hot-rock cooking technology was used. By count, weight, and volume, fire-cracked rock dominates every assemblage. Cobbles were heated for processing food; the heating and cooling caused the stone to fracture and shatter. Experiments (Jones 1997) have demonstrated that the use life of a cobble was one cycle of heating and cooling. The consequences are at least twofold: the massive quantities

Figure 2.3. Middle Archaic Evans points from Watson Brake.

of fire-cracked rock generated thus provide a high profile for identifying residential sites, and the proximity of cobble outcrops was an important variable in the location of residential sites. In addition, Middle Archaic folk relied almost exclusively on local raw material for lithic production, an additional incentive for establishing residential sites near gravel outcrops.

Middle Archaic stylistic attributes are the notched Evans projectile point, stone effigy beads, and fired earthen objects. The Evans point (Figure 2.3) distribution includes southern Arkansas, extreme northeast Texas, and all of Louisiana, except for the parishes east of the Mississippi River (Jeter et al. 1989; Saunders and Allen 1998). Of the nine Middle Archaic mound sites west of the Mississippi, the Evans point has been recovered from six of them, suggesting that the Evans point was a "cultural boundary" during the Middle Archaic.

Effigy beads are a Middle Archaic phenomenon. The beads, most often made of red jasper, occur in a variety of zoomorphic forms (Figure 2.4). A recent study of more than 60 beads (Crawford 2003) shows them to be widely distributed in the Lower Mississippi Valley, with a higher frequency in northwest Mississippi and eastern Louisiana. Specimens have been found at four Archaic mound sites, leading some to suggest that mounds and effigy beads may be associated (Blitz 1993). The lapidary technology associated with the zoomorphic beads has been recorded in western Mississippi and eastern Louisiana (Connaway 1981; Connaway, Brookes, and McGahey 1977; Gibson 1968; Johnson 2000).

Trade during the Middle Archaic is marginal. Local pebble chert is the raw material used for making stone tools. A significant trait of the

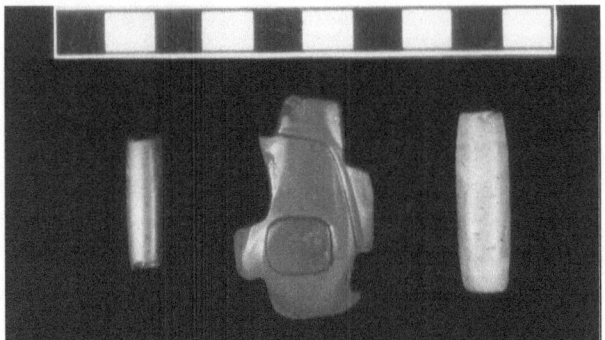

Figure 2.4. Zoomorphic bead from Monte Sano Mounds. Photograph by Karl Kuttruff.

subsequent Late Archaic period is extensive trade, culminating with the Poverty Point culture (Jackson and Jeter 1991; Jeter and Jackson 1994).

The final Middle Archaic stylistic attribute is fired-earthen fired earthen objects (Saunders et al. 1998). They probably represent a very brief cultural horizon, occurring only in six contiguous parishes in northeast Louisiana ca. 3600–3200 cal. BC. The most common shapes of the objects are cubes, blocks, balls, and pucks that average a diameter of 4–5 cm (Figure 2.5). Their purpose is unknown.

The Beginning (6000 cal. BC).

The Conly site (Figure 2.1) in northwest Louisiana provides the first known evidence of a shift from a presumed mobile, generalized exploitation strategy of the Early Archaic (8000–6000 cal. BC) to a more sedentary, selective exploitation strategy of the Middle Archaic.

Conly is located in the floodplain of the Red River, with tertiary uplands to the east and relict channels of the Red River to the west (Girard 2000; Girard et al. 2005). Eight radiocarbon assays from four features suggest that the site contained a series of encampments spanning 500 years.

Deer and fish were the focus of the people's diet (Scott and Jackson 2000; Jackson and Scott 2001). A sample of 5,446 NISP fragments identified twelve taxa common to each feature: opossum, cottontail and swamp rabbit, gray squirrel, white-tailed deer, box turtle, bowfin, gar, largemouth buffalo, channel catfish, blue catfish, and finfish. Seven taxa were present in four of five pit features: fox squirrel, raccoon, softshell turtle, bullhead, flathead catfish, freshwater drum, and sunfish. Crawfish, mussels, and aquatic snails also were commonly consumed. Flora included hickory nuts and

Figure 2.5. Middle Archaic fired earthen objects.

acorns from adjoining uplands and the surrounding floodplain. Seasonal indicators suggest year-round use of the site.

The abundance of fire-cracked rock attests to the processing of foods at the site. Evidence of stone tool manufacturing is sparse. Instead, tools were transported to the site and refurbished or discarded.

Four burials were recovered from the site (Girard 2000; Girard et al. 2005). Two were adult, one was a child, and the other could not be determined. Radiocarbon assays from Burial 1 and Burial 2 do not overlap, suggesting that the two burials are associated with separate site occupations.

Location, Location, Location

The intensive occupation of sites that predate many of the Middle Archaic mounds demonstrates the continuity between the Early and Middle Archaic folk. The sites were used for generations before the mounds were built. As at Conly, fishing, hunting, and gathering sustained the premound inhabitants. Then, for some unknown reason, monumental architecture began. Qualitatively, a shift in site perception occurred, but the very limited excavations have not isolated plausible reasons for the shift. Take away the monumental earthworks, and the Middle Archaic occupations would hardly be discernible from the Early or Late Archaic sites. The construction of earthworks does not appear to have altered the economic strategy or social structure.

Northeast Louisiana Sites

Most of the current research on the Middle Archaic has taken place in northeast Louisiana (Figure 2.6). Four sites provide the best opportunity

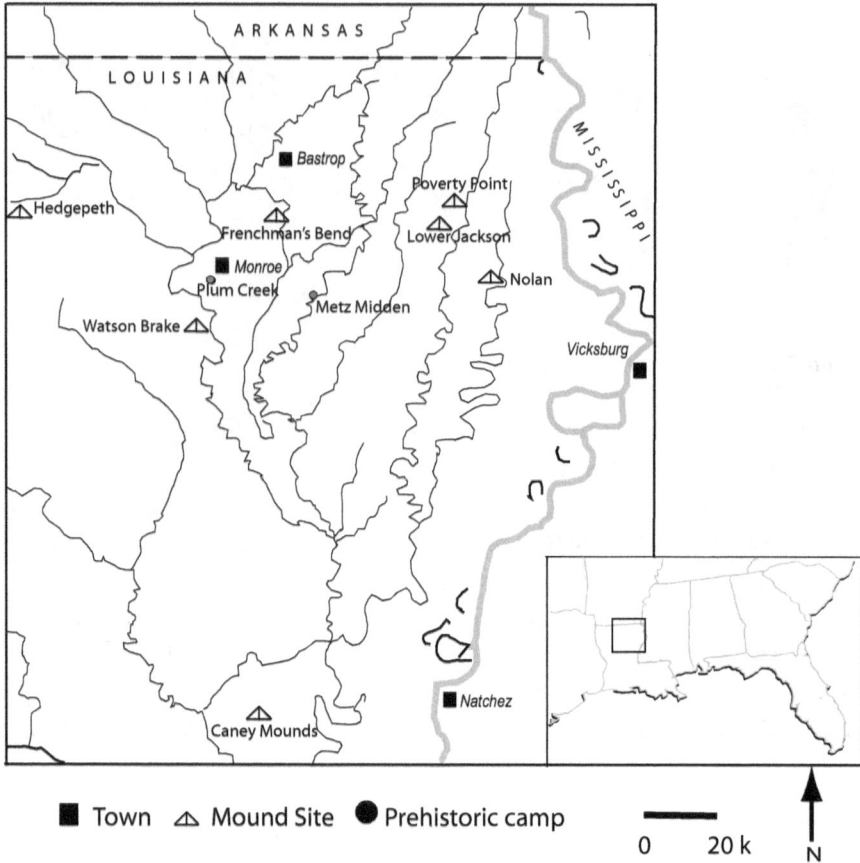

Figure 2.6. Significant Middle Archaic sites in northeast Louisiana.

to study the origins of monumentality. Much of the excavation, coring, site survey, and off-site survey have been done by the same individuals, thus providing continuity to the research design, field methods, and interpretation of the data. In particular, Watson Brake, Frenchman's Bend Mounds, Hedgepeth Mounds, and Plum Creek Archaic (a non-mound site) will be discussed.

Watson Brake (ca. 3500–2700 cal. BC)

Watson Brake is the most complex earthwork yet identified in the Middle Archaic. Research at Watson Brake has produced 30 radiometric assays and 1.7 metric tons of artifacts, mostly gravel and fire-cracked rock (Johnson 2000; Jones 1983; Saunders, Allen, and Saucier 1994; Saunders et al.1997; Saunders et al. 2005) (Figure 2.7).

Early Mounds in the Lower Mississippi Valley · 35

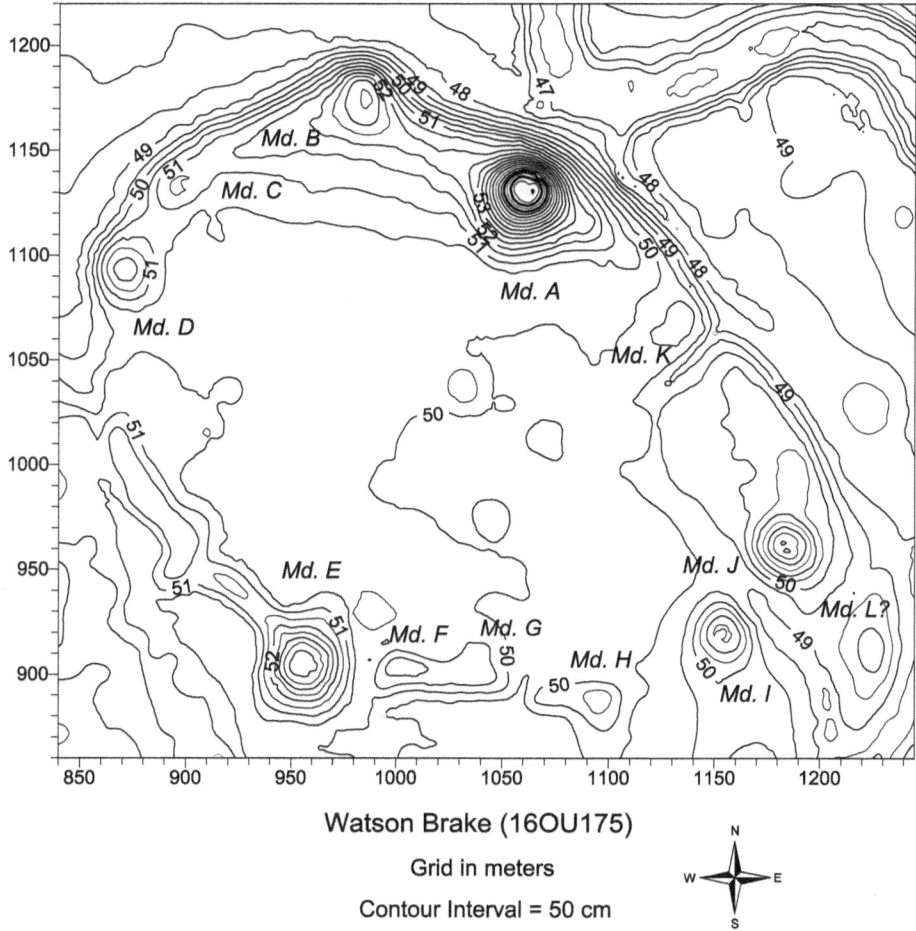

Figure 2.7. Topographic map of Watson Brake.

The site is built along the edge of the Pleistocene terrace, creating an illusion that the mounds are 5–10 m taller above the small tributary of Watson Brake. The site is composed of 11 earthen mounds and six connecting causeways that form an oval with its long axis oriented east-west, dividing the site into a north and south half (Figure 2.8). A probable (subject to verification) 12th mound lies outside the enclosure east of Mound J here; otherwise the cultural origin of each mound has been verified by test-unit excavations and/or coring. Cores from causeway sections consistently show them to be cultural features as well. The only natural topographic feature on the site is the large rise in the center of the enclosure (Figure. 2.8).

Figure 2.8. A 3-D model of Watson Brake earthworks.

The mounds are conical (A, I, and J) and dome-shaped (B, C, D, E, F, G, H, and K). Mound A on the north side is the largest in volume and in height, and Mound E on the south side is the second largest in volume and height. The smallest, Mound K, may be an accumulic midden deposit and not a mound. The morphology of the southwest corner of the earthworks suggests that an additional mound may exist.

The oval shape of the enclosure is in part determined by the morphology of the Pleistocene terrace. Mounds I, J, K, A, B, C, and D are built along the terrace edge, following the northern arc of the escarpment, while the trajectory of Mounds E, F, G, and H completes the enclosure.

Initially, it was thought that site construction was accretional. Test-unit excavations into the submound surface of Mounds A, B, C, and D uncovered a dense midden. It was apparent that the site location of Watson Brake had been occupied for perhaps hundreds of years before the mounds were built. In contrast, soil cores from Mounds E, F, G, and H and their associated causeways did not have submound middens. Furthermore, these mounds were built in single stages, whereas the "north" mounds A, B, C, D, I, and J were built in multiple stages. The "south" mound architecture seemed simplified and rushed. However, a ca. 3510 cal. BC radiocarbon assay from a thin lens of charcoal on the submound surface of Mound E matched the charcoal assay of ca. 3440 cal. BC under Mound A. It became apparent that the construction of the two mounds took place at the same time, and thus the placement of the two largest mounds in opposite halves of the oval was planned from the start.

The causeways are not so predictable. Segments between Mounds J and K and K and A are two-stage earthworks. The segments on each side of Mound A are single-stage structures covering truncated surfaces, the geomorphology of which is not yet understood.

Residential activities took place on the mounds and causeways, but the distribution of the activities was not uniform. A higher density of artifacts existed on the north side of the earthworks, the site earthworks nearest to the gravel outcropping from the Pleistocene terrace—an application of least effort. The earthworks on the south side of the site had a much lower artifact and gravel density.

The enclosed area was virtually artifact free. An array of 37 auger probes were excavated in the enclosure to assess the artifact density. Augers next to the earthworks recovered as many as 82 artifacts and averaged 48, while augers in the enclosure averaged three artifacts, most of which were microdebitage, or micro-fire-cracked rock (Saunders 1994, 46). Apparently, daily activities did not occur in the enclosure. But the reason for that may be a consequence of the site's topography rather than human behavior. It is not uncommon to find 5–10 cm of standing water in the interior after a hard rain or during the wet season, so the low occurrence of artifacts in the enclosure may be related more to comfort than to a sacred/profane dichotomy in site usage (Durkheim 1947 [1912]).

Excavations revealed few features, with the most common being sequential stages of mound (and occasionally causeway) construction. The lithic assemblages associated with the living surfaces on each stage of construction are fairly redundant: projectile points (only 24 completed bifaces), biface reduction, flake cores, and drills. The only exceptions were a flint-knapping workshop near Mound K and a bead workshop in Mound D with 55 drill preforms and 87 microdrills. The most common and widespread tool was the microdrill (n = 154), but only eight beads in various stages of production were recovered, suggesting that finished beads were removed from the site.

Frenchman's Bend Mounds (3400–2700 cal. BC)

Frenchman's Bend Mounds may have five mounds (Figure 2.9). When the site was first investigated, Mound E had been partially leveled and

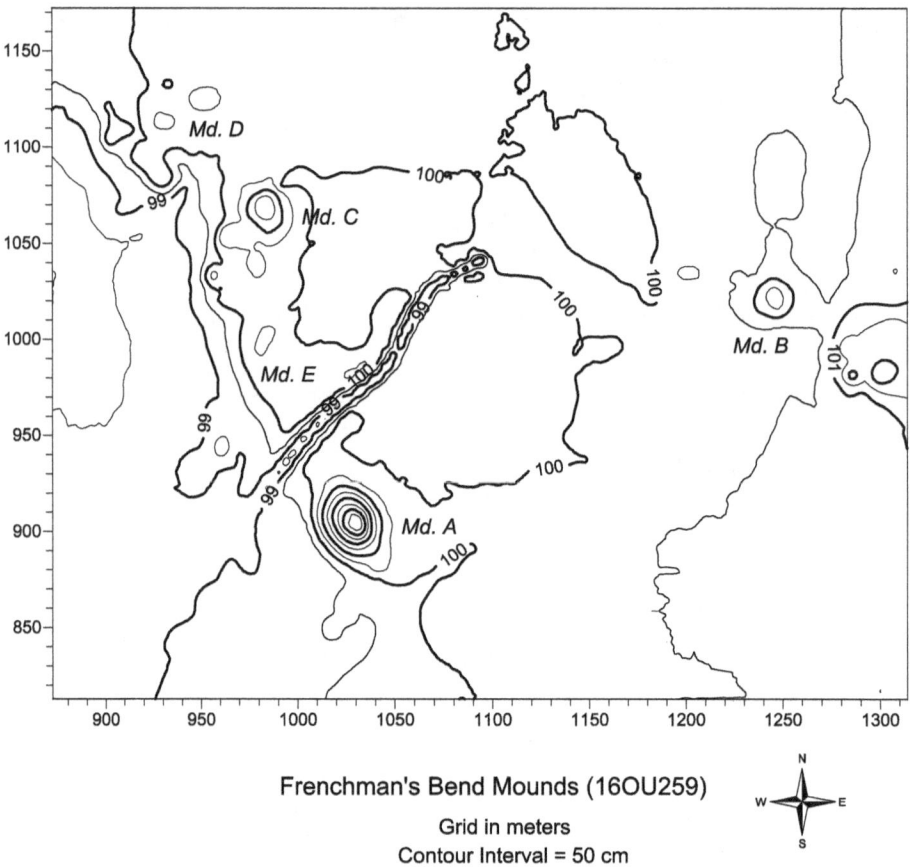

Figure 2.9. Topographic map of Frenchman's Bend Mounds. N-S trench is modern.

a bulldozer trench had cut through the center of Mound A, the largest mound. A preliminary topographic map of the site may have defined a causeway and a sixth mound northwest of Mound B (Saunders 1993). Unfortunately, neither the possible sixth mound nor the causeway could be verified before they were leveled by the housing development that now encompasses the site. Mounds A, C, D, and E have been verified; attempts to core Mound B failed, so this mound has yet to be confirmed.

Mound C has one stage of mound fill (155 cm) that covers three successive floors or platforms. Each floor varies in thickness, and the surfaces of the floors are unevenly fired and stained with an organic veneer. The first floor (the deepest one) lies on top of the intact A horizon of the Pleistocene terrace. One posthole and one probable posthole extended through the three floors.

The southeast corner of the test unit exposed a cylindrical-shaped hearth 30 cm in diameter and 30 cm deep. The hearth extended through the three floors. It is not known if the floors were built around the hearth or if the hearth was excavated through the floors. Charcoal from the hearth dates to ca. 4610 cal. BC. However, the organic veneer on floors 1 and 2 (which are stratigraphically older than the hearth) was determined to be ca. 3520 cal. BC and ca. 3610 cal. BC in age, placing the age of the hearth in question.

Mound A is a 2.5 m conical mound built in at least three stages. As noted, a bulldozer trench had been excavated through the center of the mound. Looters' excavations in the bulldozer trench exposed a cylindrical hearth. Its shape and dimensions were virtually identical to the hearth under Mound C. Charcoal from the hearth provided an assay of ca. 2740 cal. BC.

Mechanical and hand excavations in the bulldozer trench identified two stages of mound construction above the submound surface. The uppermost stage was composed of a secondary deposit of mottled sediments, fauna, flora, and fire-cracked rock. Beneath it was fine sandy loam with a light scatter of charcoal between the interface of the two stages. It covered a deposit of yellow silt loam 1–2 cm thick that was laid over the original submound surface and abruptly ended at a line of three postholes perpendicular to the trench. The postholes were 10–12 cm in diameter and 20–25 cm deep. The configuration suggested a floor and a standing structure. The posts had been removed before the mound was built. A horizon 10 cm thick with fire-cracked rock and debitage covered the Pleistocene terrace surface. Submound charcoal dated to ca. 3275 cal. BC.

A submound posthole pattern similar to the one at Frenchman's Bend Mounds was recorded at the Middle Archaic site Monte Sano Mounds. Salvage excavations uncovered a 10 × 11 m rectangular posthole pattern under Mound A (R. Saunders 1994). An 8.5 × 6.5 × .45 m earthen platform was built over part of the posthole pattern. Two earthen domes were built in turn on the small platform mound. Two charcoal samples from one of the domes dated to ca. 5030–5500 cal. BC. The antiquity of the two samples remains problematic.

Hedgepeth Mounds (3100–2700 cal. BC)

Hedgepeth Mounds is a group of six mounds and a single causeway (Figure 2.10) built on a Pleistocene/Early Holocene terrace above Bayou D'Arbonne, a major tributary of the Arkansas River of the time (Saunders and Allen

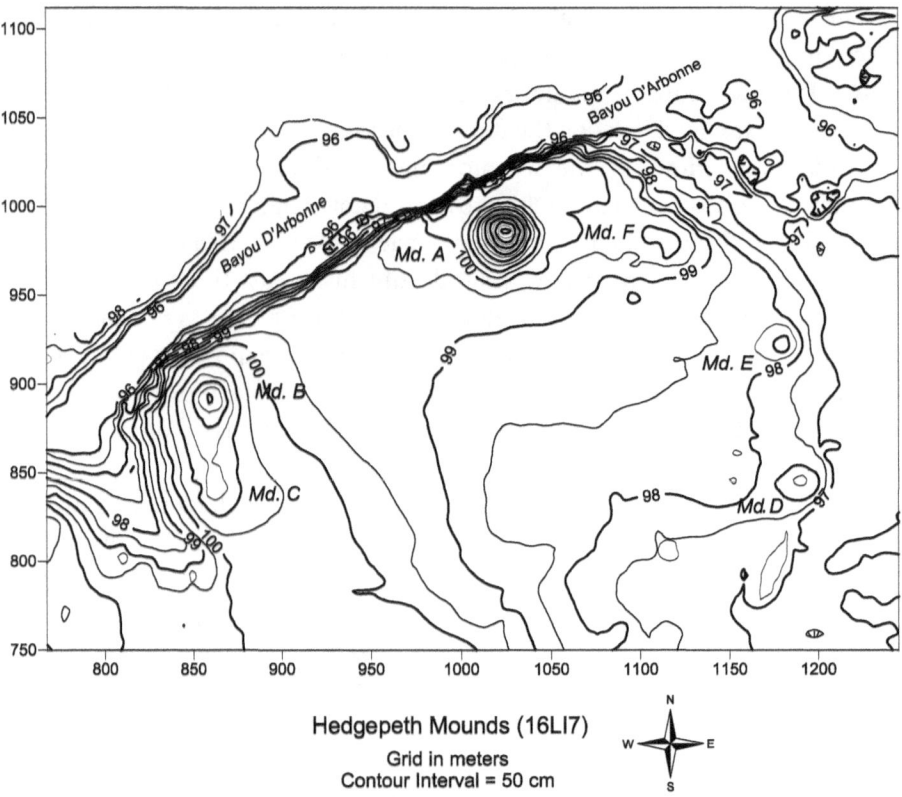

Figure 2.10. Topographic map of Hedgepeth Mounds.

1994). The configuration of the mounds most closely resembles the oval enclosure at Watson Brake (Saunders, Jones, and Allen 2006). The largest monumental feature is a two-stage conical mound with a small earthen platform mound in its center, reminiscent of the submound structures at Mound C at Frenchman's Bend Mounds and in Mound A at Monte Sano Mounds. The other Hedgepeth Mounds are small one-stage (B, C, and F) and two-stage (D) mounds and a possible four-stage mound (E).

The density of fire-cracked rock is the lowest among the larger mound groups. This is most likely related to the lack of river cobbles in Bayou D'Arbonne. So instead of cobbles, local ironstone from the Tertiary uplands was used for heating/cooking. Unlike chert cobbles, the ironstone can be reheated many times, thus the smaller number of fire-cracked rock fragments on the site.

Unlike the other Middle Archaic sites in northeast Louisiana, there is marginal evidence of trade for novaculite, a tool stone found in central to southern Arkansas. Perhaps the north-central Louisiana location of Hedgepeth Mounds is close enough to the novaculite outcrops to be "local." Only chips have been found, suggesting that the novaculite is from sharpening tools brought onto the site.

Hedgepeth Mounds may be the youngest Middle Archaic mound site. A hearth under Mound A (2870 cal. BC) and assays from Mounds D (Saunders, Jones, and Allen 2007) and E (Saunders, Jones, and Allen 2006) suggest that site occupations ended ca. 2700 cal. BC.

Settlement Pattern

A peculiar thing about Watson Brake is the persistent lack of evidence for small encampments near the earthworks, the adjoining uplands, the backwater swamp, and the Watson Brake drainage area along the north site of the site and its confluence with the Arkansas River of that time. The fauna unequivocally show that each of these environments was exploited, with an emphasis on backwater and main channel riparian species (Jackson and Scott 2001). Surveys in each respective habitat have recorded 105 archaeological sites (see Saunders, Jones, and Allen 2007), but none of them contains an artifact density remotely equal to the density recorded in the premound middens or the earthworks at the Watson Brake site.

The lack of short-term encampment sites in the uplands cannot be attributed to poor ground visibility. Most of the sites were recorded in clearcut areas, where ground visibility approached 100 percent. Upland areas in pasture or pine were shovel tested to compensate for poor visibility. Surely marginal sites were overlooked, but the artifact density of sites that were recorded was extremely low, two to three artifacts from four to five shovel tests (Saunders, Jones, and Allen 2007). The south shoreline of Watson Brake swamp was shovel tested and push probed, but again, only low-density sites were found (Saunders, Jones, and Allen 2006). Collectively, the accumulation of sites recorded in upland and riparian areas next to Watson Brake consistently point to a foraging model of residential hunter-gatherers (Binford 1980; Taylor 1964). Resources were gathered daily, transported to the residential site (Watson Brake), processed, and consumed.

Seasonal indicators suggest year-round use of the site (not to be confused with a year-round occupation of the site). The data show a trend of residential redundancy of the earthworks. The greatest density of artifacts at Watson Brake, Frenchman's Bend Mounds, Hedgepeth Mounds, Caney Mounds (Saunders et al. 2000), Lower Jackson (Gibson 1989; LaBatt in

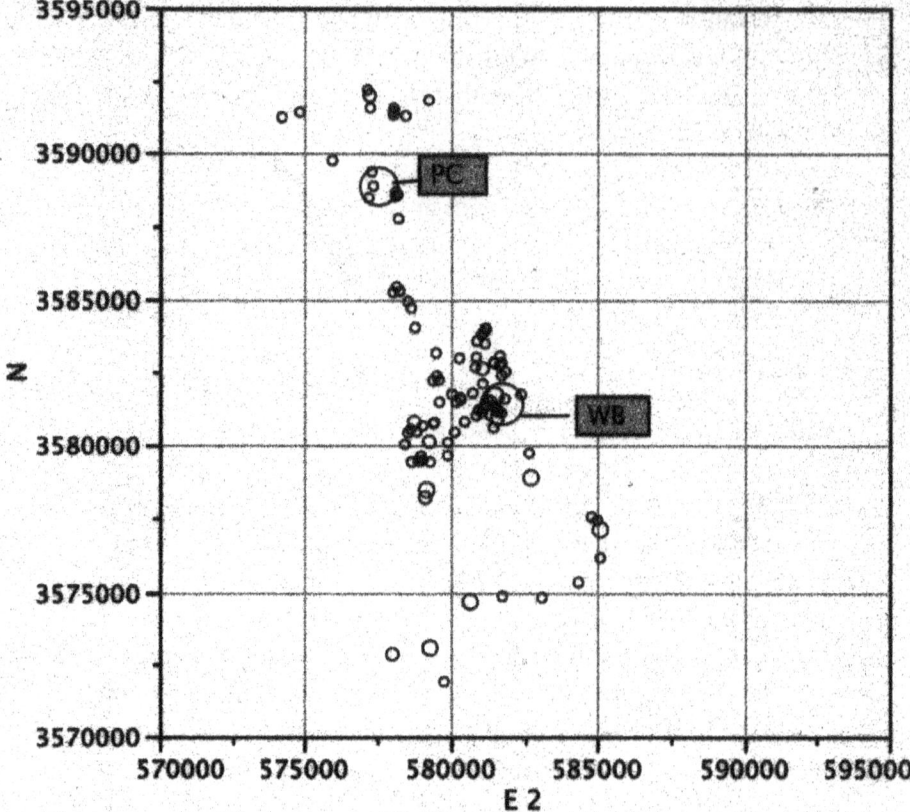

Figure 2.11. A plot of procurement sites near Watson Brake and Plum Creek Archaic.

Saunders et al. 2001), Stelly Mounds (Russo and Fogleman 1994), and King George Island Mound was on the earthworks (Vasbinder 2005).

People consumed the same array of food and resided at the same location before, during, and after the mounds were built. Artifacts associated with the procurement of resources were discarded in off-site areas around Watson Brake (Dunnell and Dancey 1983; Saunders 1992). Recognizable clusters or concentrations of artifacts were rare. None were large enough to suggest short-term campsites, which one would expect if neighboring bands coalesced seasonally to refurbish or expand the earthworks.

The distribution of 105 Archaic sites within a 10 km radius of Watson Brake is illustrated in the bubble graph above). Each bubble is a site, and the size of the bubble is proportional to the number of dart points found at that particular site (Figure 2.11). The pattern is a classic base camp/procurement pattern for hunter-gatherers (Binford 1980; Sampson 1985;

Saunders 1992; Silberbauer 1981; Taylor 1964; Yellen 1977). Artifacts associated with the procurement of plants, animals, and fish were discarded in their area of use, and the bounty of these activities was transported to the base camp/mounds for distribution and consumption among members of the society.

The off-site data from Watson Brake seem to fit a forager settlement pattern, one that is tethered to the same location during the premound and mound occupations. However, the apparent lack of residential mobility is not tied to a particular resource necessary for survival, as postulated by Binford and Taylor; instead, it is the opposite. The diversity and abundance of resources available to the community appear to be what promoted residential stability and autonomy.

Diet

The residents of Watson Brake were fishers, hunters, and gatherers. Main channel, tributary, backswamp, and riparian habitats were the focus of their economy, supplemented by flora and fauna from the floodplain, the natural levee, the terrace, and the upland.

Substantial faunal assemblages were recovered from Watson Brake (Jackson and Scott 2001) and Plum Creek Archaic (Sheffield 2003), a residential site approximately 12 km northeast of Watson Brake. That site had a small midden/mound on the Pleistocene terrace above the confluence of Cheniere Creek and the Arkansas River. Substantial gravel deposits outcrop at the base of the terrace, and a dense scatter of fire-cracked rock, cores, projectile points, and fired earthen objects extends west from the terrace edge in an area of approximately 75 × 350 m. The ecotonal setting of the site is the same as for Watson Brake. The obvious difference between the two sites is the absence of substantial earthworks at Plum Creek Archaic.

The Watson Brake faunal assemblage is from Stage 1 fill and the sub-mound midden of Mound B. Charcoal from the sub–Mound B midden has an assay of ca. 3780 cal. BC. Stage I dates to ca. 3400 cal. BC (Saunders et al. 2005). The Plum Creek Archaic fauna are from a single-component burned-rock midden (Saunders and Jones 2002; Sheffield 2003). Charcoal from a small pit feature has an assay of ca. 3730 cal. BC.

The NISP count for the Watson Brake sample is 16,049 (Jackson and Scott 2001) and 23,372 from Plum Creek Archaic (Sheffield 2003). The ecotonal setting of the sites is apparent with the 24 taxa the two sites share (see Table 2.2). Fish comprise the largest number of taxa. A nonparametric

Table 2.2. Common taxa from Watson Brake and Plum Creek Archaic

Taxa	Common Name	Family	Watson Brake	NISP	Plum Creek	NISP
Meleagris gallopavo	Turkey	Aves	wb	31	pc	8
Anatidae	Duck	Aves	wb	4	pc	2
Chelydridae	Snapping turtle	Reptile	wb	22	pc	3
Kinosternidae	Mud/musk turtle	Reptile	wb	26	pc	2
Terrapene carolina	Box turtle	Reptile	wb	33	pc	10
Trionychidae	Softshell turtle	Reptile	wb	46	pc	47
Nerodia sp.	Water snake	Reptile	wb	14	pc	8
Rana/Bufo sp.	Frog/toad	Amphibian	wb	6	pc	8
Pomoxis sp.	Crappie	Pisces	wb	18	pc	147
Amia calva	Bowfin	Pisces	wb	507	pc	98
Lepisosteidae	Gar	Pisces	wb	1,064	pc	713
Ictiobus sp.	Buffalo	Pisces	wb	105	pc	1,413
Aplodinotus grunniens	Freshwater drum	Pisces	wb	486	pc	1,083
Catostomidae	Sucker	Pisces	wb	227	pc	1,290
Ictalurus furcatus	Blue catfish	Pisces	wb	23	pc	105
Ictalurus nebulosus	Brown bullhead	Pisces	wb	2	pc	8
Ictiobus bubalus	Smallmouth buffalo	Pisces	wb	21	pc	34
Didelphis virginianus	Opossum	Mammalian	wb	8	pc	3
Odocoileus virginianus	Whitetail deer	Mammalian	wb	306	pc	124
Procyon lotor	Raccoon	Mammalian	wb	12	pc	2
Sciurus carolinensis	Eastern gray squirrel	Mammalian	wb	15	pc	9
Sciurus niger	Eastern fox squirrel	Mammalian	wb	7	pc	2
Sylvilagus aquaticus	Swamp rabbit	Mammalian	wb	5	pc	16
Cricetidae	Mouse/rat	Mammalian	wb	2	pc	6

Mann-Whitney U Test of NISP counts of the shared taxa show that the relative abundance of procured animals is not significantly different at the two sites. The two samples also share 18 of 24 mussel taxa and the aquatic gastropod *Campeloma* sp. To paraphrase an old Cajun poet "nothing was safe in the Arkansas River."

The NISP counts by taxonomic class show the dominance of Pisces at both sites. At Watson Brake, fish make up 70 percent of the sample; at Plum Creek Archaic the percentage is approximately 82. At both sites, mammals are the second most significant component: approximately 15 percent at Watson Brake and four percent for Plum Creek Archaic. Large mammals and deer compose about 55 percent of the Plum Creek Archaic mammalian fauna, compared to 71 percent at Watson Brake. The Watson Brake diet was more diverse; it also has 33 unique taxa, of which 12 are fish, 10 are small mammals, four are birds, six are reptiles, and one is an amphibian. Plum

Creek Archaic has ten unique taxa, including four reptiles, four fish, one amphibian, and one mammal.

The small sample from Frenchman's Bend Mounds contained alligators (Delahoussaye in Saunders et al. 2009) largemouth bass, bowfin, catfish, gar, and sunfish. Mussel shell species numbered 15, plus *Campeloma* sp. pond, musk, and soft-shell turtles. Raccoon and deer bones were also identified (see Russo in Saunders 1993).

Excavations by Russo at Stelly Mounds in north-central Louisiana identified 834 NISP which were composed of gar, catfish, shad, suckers, freshwater drum, sunfish, bony fish, nonvenomous snakes, small and large mammals, and hickory and pecan (Russo and Fogleman 1994). The consistency in the Middle Archaic diet is notable.

The End

When mound construction began in the Lower Mississippi Valley remains a matter of contention among southeastern archaeologists. The disagreement revolves around the legitimacy of the two very early Monte Sano Mound dates from Mound A. The end of Middle Archaic mound building is becoming more clearly defined. New radiometric data indicate a sudden and widespread cessation of mound building (Arco et al. 2006; Kidder 2006; Saunders 2010) in northeast Louisiana. The clustering of the ten youngest dates from seven mounds at four sites is remarkable. The median probability for seven of the ten samples falls between 2884 cal. BC and 2739 cal. BC. Equally remarkable is that the cessation of mound construction may have lasted up to 1,000 years (Gibson 1996; Saunders 2010), or until the emergence of the Poverty Point culture (1700–1200 cal. BC). The cause for the apparent hiatus is unknown. Certainly climate change deserves consideration (Hamilton 1999; Kidder 2006; Sampson 2008). However, if the hiatus was caused by a change in the environment, the event must have been catastrophic to have affected all the mound sites in the eastern half of Louisiana. Evidence for that magnitude of change has not been found, although it has yet to be actively sought.

The "synchronous" event may be better understood as a social phenomenon. The abandonment of an ideology or change in ethos can occur simultaneously within a diverse range of environments. Also, the absence of environmental change would be consistent with the documented continuity in economy from the Early to Late Archaic periods—before, during, and after mound building. Perhaps the urge or need for monumental architecture abated and remained dormant for 1,000 years. To date, not one mound site dating to the Late Archaic (2700–1700 cal. BC) has been identified in the Lower Mississippi Valley.

Conjecture and Discussion

The descriptive overview of Middle Archaic monumental architecture has shown that there is a great deal of variability among the earthworks of the early mound builders. Mound building was not monolithic. Each mound site was a unique expression by that society. The earliest construction of earthworks in the Lower Mississippi Valley appears to have been made by autonomous societies. Practically speaking, it is difficult for 16 Middle Archaic mound sites spanning 1,000 years of prehistory in three subregions of Louisiana (southwest, southeast, and northeast) and two in Mississippi not to look autonomous.

But there must have been some communion among the autonomous societies because there are too many shared traits that cross the vast expanse of the Lower Mississippi Valley, and there is no evidence of other monuments being made elsewhere. If all of the Middle Archaic mounds were spontaneous creations, would they not occur spontaneously elsewhere as well? Much like diffusion, spontaneity is not the answer (Rosenswig and Burger this volume).

A preferred explanation is that the late Early Archaic adaptation to the riverine environment established an economy capable of sustaining residential sites (Girard 2000; Girard et al. 2005). Native economies established residences of choice that eventually became the tethering points of their societies. The diversity and richness of the fauna, flora, and local lithics reduced the need for mobility and trade. Any one of the communities could have initiated mound building, and the only noticeable difference would be the mounds themselves. Archaeological evidence of environmental or social change preceding or following mound building is negligible. What is measurable had not changed significantly. The society that had established the community was the same society that built the mounds.

The procurement site density suggests a low population for the largest site, Watson Brake. Thus, one would expect a smaller labor pool for the one- and two-mound sites. Yet their planning and labor initiated a Lower Mississippi Valley tradition of monumentality that recurred with different cultures (Poverty Point) at different times (Late Archaic and Woodland periods), but the economic strategy remained the same. The earthworks at Poverty Point are a local and indigenous phenomena (Gibson 2007), as are the early Woodland mounds (Kidder 2006). Monumentality did not signify the directional development in stages of cultural historical evolution (Russo 1994b). Mound building was an iterative mechanism adopted and abandoned by societies of varying complexity, economy, and antiquity.

Our knowledge about the Lower Mississippi Valley continues to grow (Arco et al. 2006; Gibson 1996, 2000, 2007; Girard 2000; Girard et al. 2005; Kidder 2006; Kidder, Ortman, and Arco 2008; Saunders 2010; Saunders et al. 2005). We no longer can assume that monumentality marked the start of a mound-building continuum extending throughout the prehistory of the Lower Mississippi Valley. Instead, it appears that there was a series of building events punctuated by a hiatus between the Middle Archaic and Poverty Point periods (Gibson 1996, 2007; Saunders 2010) and one between the Poverty Point and Early Woodland periods (1200–900 cal. BC; Gibson 1996, 2007; Kidder 2006; Kidder, Ortman, and Arco 2008).

References Cited

Arco, Lee J., Katherine A. Adelsberger, Ling-yu Hung, and Tristram R. Kidder
2006   Alluvial Geoarchaeology of a Middle Archaic Mound Complex in the Lower Mississippi Valley, U.S.A. *Geoarchaeology* 21(6):591–614.
Binford, Lewis R.
1980   Willow Smoke and Dog's Tails: Hunter-Gatherer Settlement Systems and Archaeological Site Formation. *American Antiquity* 45:1–17.
Blitz, John G.
1993   Locust Beads and Archaic Mounds. *Mississippi Archaeology* 28:21–43.
Brown, Ian W., and Nancy Lambert-Brown
1978   Lower Mississippi Survey Petite Anse Project. Research Notes No. 5, Peabody Museum, Harvard University, Cambridge, Massachusetts.
Caldwell, Joseph R.
1958   *Trend and Tradition in the Prehistory of the United States*. Illinois State Museum, Springfield.
Connaway, John
1981   The Keenan Bead Cache: Lawrence County, Mississippi. *Louisiana Archaeology* 8:57–71.
Connaway, John M., Samuel O. Brookes, and Samuel O. McGahey
1977   The Denton Site: A Middle Archaic Occupation in the Northern Yazoo Basin, Mississippi. Archaeological Report No. 4, Mississippi Department of Archives and History, Jackson.

Clark, John E., Jon L. Gibson, and James Zeidler
2010   Searching for Agriculture, Population Growth and Other Enabling Conditions. In *Becoming Villagers Comparing Early Village Societies*, edited by M. S. Brandy and J. R. Fox, pp. 205–245. University of Arizona Press, Tucson.

Connolly, Robert P.
2000   An Assessment of Radiocarbon Age Results From the Poverty Point Site. *Louisiana Archaeology* 27:1–14.

Crawford, Jessica
2003   Archaic Effigy Beads: A New Look at Some Old Beads. Master's thesis, University of Mississippi, Oxford.

Dunnell, Robert C., and William S. Dancey
1983   The Siteless Survey: A Regional Scale Data Collection Strategy. In *Advances in Archaeological Method and Theory*, Vol. 6, edited by M. Schiffer, pp. 267–287. Academic Press, New York.

Durkheim, Emile
1947 [1912]   *The Elementary Forms of Religious Life*. Free Press, Glencoe, Illinois.

Gagliano, Sherwood M.
1967   *Occupation Sequence at Avery Island*. Coastal Studies Series No. 22. Louisiana State University Press, Baton Rouge.

Gibson, Jon L.
1968   Cad Mound: A Stone Bead Locus in East Central Louisiana. *Bulletin of the Texas Archaeological Society* 38:1–17.
1989   Digging on the Dock of the Bay(ou): The 1988 Excavations at Poverty Point. Center for Archaeological Studies Report No. 8, University of Southwestern Louisiana, Lafayette.
1994   Before Their Time? Early Mounds in the Lower Mississippi Valley. *Southeastern Archaeology* 13:162–186.
1996   Ancient Earthworks of the Ouachita Valley in Louisiana. Technical Reports No. 5, Southeast Archeological Center, Tallahassee, Florida.
2000   *Ancient Mounds of Poverty Point: Place of Rings. Native Peoples, Cultures, and Places of the Southeastern United States*. University Press of Florida, Gainesville.
2007   "Formed from the Earth at That Place": The Material Side of Community at Poverty Point. *American Antiquity* 72(3):509–523.

Gibson, Jon L., and J. Richard Shenkel
1988   Louisiana Earthworks: Middle Woodland and Predecessors. In *Middle Woodland Settlement and Ceremonialism in the Mid-South and Lower Mississippi Valley: Proceedings of the 1984 Mid-South Archaeological Conference, Pinson Mounds, Tennessee, June 1984*, edited by R. C. Mainfort, pp. 7–18. Archaeological Report No. 22. Mississippi Department of Archives and History, Jackson.

Girard, Jeffery S.
2000   Regional Archaeology Management Unit 1: Eleventh Annual Report. Report on file at the Louisiana Division of Archaeology. Northwestern State University, Baton Rouge, Louisiana.

Girard, Jeffery S., Nathanael Heller, J. Phillip Dering, Susan L. Scott, H. Edwin Jackson, and Gary L. Stringer

2005   Investigations at the Conly Site, a Middle Archaic Period Settlement in Northwest Louisiana. *Louisiana Archaeology* 32:5-7.

Hamilton, Fran E.

1999   Southeastern Archaic Mound: Examples of Elaboration in a Temporally Fluctuating Environment? *Journal of Anthropological Archaeology* 18:344-355.

Jackson, Edwin, and Marvin Jeter

1991   Late Archaic Settlement and Poverty Point Connections in the Lowlands of Southeast Arkansas: An Initial Assessment. *Mississippi Archaeology* 26(2):33-55.

Jackson, H. Edwin, and Susan L. Scott

2001   Archaic Faunal Utilization in the Louisiana Bottomlands. *Southeastern Archaeology* 20(2):187-196.

Jeter, Marvin D., and H. Edwin Jackson

1994   Poverty Point Extraction and Exchange: The Arkansas Lithic Connections. *Louisiana Archaeology* 17:133-206.

Jeter, Marvin D., Jerome C. Rose Jr., G. Ishmael Williams, and Anna M. Harmon

1989   Archeology and Bioarcheology of the Lower Mississippi Valley and Trans-Mississippi South in Arkansas and Louisiana. Research Series No. 37. Arkansas Archeological Survey, Fayetteville.

Johnson, Jay K.

2000   Beads, Microdrills, Bifaces, and Blades from Watson Brake. *Southeastern Archaeology* 19(2):95-104.

Jones, Reca

1983   Archaeological Investigations in the Ouachita River Valley, Bayou Bartholomew to Riverton, Louisiana. *Louisiana Archaeology* 10:103-169.

1997   Replicating Fire-Cracked Rock. Paper presented at the 25th Annual Meeting of the Louisiana Archaeological Society, Alexandria.

Kidder, Tristram R.

2006   Climate Change and Archaic to Woodland Transition (3000-2500 cal. B.P.) in the Mississippi River Basin. *American Antiquity* 71(2):195-231.

Kidder, Tristram R., Anthony L. Ortman, and Lee J. Arco

2008   Poverty Point and the Archeology of Singularity. *The SAA Archaeological Record* 8:9-12.

Kidder, Tristram R., and Kenneth E. Sassaman

2009   The View from the Southeast. In *Archaic Societies: Diversity and Complexity across the Midcontinent,* edited by T. E. Emerson, D. L. McElrath, and A. C. Fortier, pp. 667-696. State University of New York, Albany.

Manuel, Joseph O., Jr.

1979   A Radiocarbon Date from the Hornsby Site (16SH21). *Louisiana Archaeological Society* 6(1):18-19.

Neuman, Robert W.

1984   *An Introduction to Louisiana Archaeology.* Louisiana State University Press, Baton Rouge.

1985   Report on the Soil Core Borings Conducted at the Campus Mounds Site (16EBR6) East Baton Rouge Parish, Louisiana. Technical Report. Museum of Geoscience, L.S.U., Baton Rouge.

Ortmann, Anthony L.
2010 Placing the Poverty Point Mounds in their Temporal Context. *American Antiquity* 75(3): 657–678.
Peacock, Evan, Philip J. Carr, Sarah E. Price, John Underwood, William L. Kingery, and Michael Lilly
2010 Confirmation of an Archaic-Period Mound in Southwest Mississippi. *Southeastern Archaeology* 29(2):355–369.
Russo, Michael
1994a A Brief Introduction to the Study of Archaic Mounds in the Southeast. *Southeastern Archaeology* 13(2):89–92.
1994b Why We Don't Believe in Archaic Ceremonial Mounds and Why We Should: The Case from Florida. *Southeastern Archaeology* 13(2):93–108.
Russo, Michael, and James Fogleman
1994 Stelly Mounds (16SL1): An Archaic Mound Complex. *Louisiana Archaeology* 21:127–158.
Sampson, C. Garth
1985 Atlas of Stone Age Settlement in the Central and Upper Seacow Valley. *Memoirs Van Die Nasionale Museum Bloemfontein,* No. 20. Bloemfontein, Republic of South Africa.
2008 Middle Archaic Mounds in the American Southeast and the Onset of Mid-Holocene El Nino/ENSO Events: Is There a Connection? In *Man-Millennia-Environment,* edited by Zofia Sulgostowska and Andrzej Jacek Tomaszewskii, pp. 133–145. Institute of Archaeology and Ethnology Polish Academy of Sciences, Warsaw.
Sassaman, Kenneth E.
2008 The New Archaic, It Ain't What it Used to Be. *The SAA Archaeological Record* 8:6–9.
Sassaman, Kenneth E., and Michael J. Heckenberger
2004 Crossing the Symbolic Rubicon in the Southeast. In *Signs of Power: The Rise of Cultural Complexity in the Southeast,* edited by J. L. Gibson and P. J. Carr, pp. 214–233. University of Alabama Press, Tuscaloosa.
Saunders, Joe
1992 A Study of Procurement Sites in the Lower Pecos Region. *Journal of Field Archaeology* 19(3):335–349.
1993 *Annual Report for Management Unit 2: Regional Archaeology Program, Department of Geosciences, Northeast Louisiana University.* Report submitted to Division of Archaeology, Louisiana Department of Culture, Recreation and Tourism, Baton Rouge.
1994 *Annual Report for Management Unit 2: Regional Archaeology Program, Department of Geosciences, Northeast Louisiana University.* Report submitted to Division of Archaeology, Louisiana Department of Culture, Recreation and Tourism, Baton Rouge.
Saunders, Joe W.
2010 Late Archaic? What the Hell Happened to the Middle Archaic? In *Trend, Tradition, and Turmoil: What Happened to the Southeastern Archaic?: Proceedings of the Third Caldwell Conference, St. Catherines Island, Georgia, May 9–11, 2008,*

edited by David Hurst Thomas, Matthew C. Singer, and David G. Anderson, pp. 237–243. American Museum of Natural History, New York.

Saunders, Joe W., and Thurman Allen
1994 Hedgepeth Mounds: An Archaic Mound Complex in North-Central Louisiana. *American Antiquity* 59(3):471–489.
1998 The Archaic Period. *Louisiana Archaeology* 22:1–30.

Saunders, Joe W., Thurman Allen, Dennis LaBatt, Reca Jones, and David Griffing
2001 An Assessment of the Antiquity of the Lower Jackson Mound South of Poverty Point. *Southeastern Archaeology* 20(1):67–77.

Saunders, Joe, Thurman Allen, and Roger T. Saucier
1994 Four Archaic? Mound Complexes in Northeast Louisiana. *Southeastern Archaeology* 13:134–153.

Saunders, Joe W., Thurman Allen, Reca Jones, and Gloria Swoveland
2000 Caney Mounds (16CT5). *Louisiana Archaeological Society Newsletter* 27:14–21.

Saunders, Joe, and Reca Bamburg Jones
2002 Annual Report for Management Unit 2: *Regional Archaeology Program, Department of Geosciences, Northeast Louisiana University*. Report submitted to Division of Archaeology, Louisiana Department of Culture, Recreation and Tourism, Baton Rouge.

Saunders, Joe, Reca Bamburg Jones, and Thurman Allen
2006 *Annual Report for Management Unit 2: Regional Archaeology Program, Department of Geosciences, Northeast Louisiana University*. Report submitted to Division of Archaeology, Louisiana Department of Culture, Recreation and Tourism, Baton Rouge.
2007 *Annual Report for Management Unit 2: Regional Archaeology Program, Department of Geosciences, Northeast Louisiana University*. College of Arts and Sciences, Department of Geosciences, University of Louisiana at Monroe. Report submitted to Division of Archaeology, Louisiana Department of Culture, Recreation and Tourism, Baton Rouge.

Saunders, Joe W., Reca Bamburg Jones, Jim Delahoussaye, Malcolm Vidrine, and Thurman Allen
2009 *Annual Report for Management Unit 2: Regional Archaeology Program, Department of Geosciences, Northeast Louisiana University*. College of Arts and Sciences, Department of Geosciences, University of Louisiana at Monroe. Report submitted to the Division of Archaeology, Louisiana Department of Culture, Recreation and Tourism, Baton Rouge

Saunders, Joe, Reca Jones, Kathryn Moorhead, and Brian Davis
1998 An Unusual Artifact Type from Northeast Louisiana. *Southeastern Archaeology* 17:72–79.

Saunders, Joe W., Rolfe D. Mandel, C. Garth Sampson, Charles M. Allen, E. Thurman Allen, Daniel A. Bush, James K. Feathers, Kristen J. Gremillion, C. T. Hallmark, H. Edwin Jackson, Jay K. Johnson, Reca Jones, Roger T. Saucier, Gary L. Stringer, and Malcolm Vidrine
2005 Watson Brake, A Middle Archaic Mound Complex in Northeast Louisiana. *American Antiquity* 70(4):630–667.

Saunders, Joe W., Rolfe D. Mandel, Roger T. Saucier, E. Thurman Allen, C. T. Hallmark, Jay K. Johnson, Edwin H. Jackson, Charles M. Allen, Gary L. Stringer, Douglas S. Frink, James K. Feathers, Stephen Williams, Kristen J. Gremillion, Malcolm F. Vidrine, and Reca Jones
1997   A Mound Complex in Louisiana at 5400–5000 Years B.P. *Science* 277 (5333):1796–1799.

Saunders, Rebecca
1994   The Case for Archaic Mound Sites in Southeastern Louisiana. *Southeastern Archaeology* 13(2):118–134.

Scott, Susan L., and H. Edwin Jackson
2000   Analysis of Vertebrate Fauna. In *Regional Archaeology Program, Management Unit 1: Eleventh Annual Report*, edited by J. S. Girard, pp. 50–57. Report on file at the Louisiana Division of Archaeology, Baton Rouge.

Sheffield, Mason West
2003   Archaic Faunal Exploitation In the Lower Mississippi Valley: Analysis of Faunal Remains from Plum Creek Archaic (16OU89). MA thesis, Anthropology, University of Southern Mississippi.

Silberbauer, George B.
1981   *Hunter and Habitat in the Central Kalahari Desert*. Cambridge University Press, Cambridge.

Taylor, Walter
1964   Tethered Nomadism and Water Territoriality: An Hypothesis. *Actas y Memorias del XXXV Congreso Internacionale Americanistas, 1962*, pp. 197–203. Mexico City.

Thoms, Alston
2008   The Fire Stones Carry: Ethnographic Records and Archaeological Expectations for Hot Rock Cookery in Western North America. *Journal of Anthropological Archaeology* 27:443–460.

Vasbinder, Fiona Helena
2005   The King George Island Mound Site (16LV22): A Late Archaic Mound Complex along the Lower Amite River. MA thesis, Department of Anthropology, Louisiana State University, Baton Rouge.

Yellen, J. E.
1977   *Archaeological Approaches to the Present*. Academic Press, New York.

3

Shell Mounds of the Middle St. Johns Basin, Northeast Florida

KENNETH E. SASSAMAN AND ASA R. RANDALL

Monumentality has many origins across the globe, and multiple causes and conditions surround its various origins. In the southeastern United States, the oldest monuments were constructed at least four millennia before agriculture became important and by populations that were neither large nor sedentary (see Saunders this volume). That foragers in this region of North America built monuments in the absence of food production, permanent settlement, and the institutional leadership usually associated with these other two traits encourages us to consider monumentality on its own terms and not simply as one of several emergent properties of increasing cultural complexity (Bradley 1998; see also Roosevelt this volume). For instance, monumentality can be explained not as a consequence of enabling conditions but rather as a medium of discursive practice that structured the trajectory and pace of culture change.

This is the approach we take in explaining the origins of monument construction in northeast Florida. Our ongoing work in the middle St. Johns Basin offers an opportunity to explore how monumentality originated in the context of major structural changes through which relationships between distinct communities and "traditional lands" were creatively reworked. In reconstituting communities under changing environmental and demographic circumstances, monuments were a medium of commemorative practice that enabled people to make reference to the past and to past places of dwelling as they constructed new identities from disparate parts. We preface our exposition with consideration of the conceptual impediments to viewing shell mounds of the St. Johns Basin as anything other than refuse heaps and provide an alternative framework based on the notion of shell mound construction as historical practice.

Changing Perspectives on St. Johns Shell Mounds

Shell mounds in the St. Johns River valley numbered in the hundreds before the twentieth century, when most were mined for road fill or fertilizer (Figure 3.1). The few that remain unmolested today are but a faint vestige of the anthropogenic deposits that brought an otherwise flat, wet terrain into sharp relief. Those investigated in the nineteenth century became the chief frame of reference for modern interpretations of their age, function, and structure. Because so many of these early digs uncovered pottery, shell mounds were often registered in modern site files as late-period constructions. But some investigated by C. B. Moore (1999) and Jeffries Wyman (1875) were without pottery, which in the pre-^{14}C world was suggestive (but not definitive) evidence of more ancient origins.

We now know that many, perhaps most, of the hundreds of shell mounds in northeast Florida began to take form more than 5,000 years ago, during the Archaic Period, at least 1,000 years before pottery and at least 4,000 years before agriculture. Earthen mounds this old are now widely recognized across the greater Southeast (Saunders this volume), and archaeologists are grappling with the conceptual challenges they pose to deeply entrenched, orthodox thinking (Russo 1994). Some of the oldest mounds in the St. Johns Basin were also constructed from earth (Endonino 2008; Piatek 1994; Sears 1960), evidently for human interment. Other mounds contained dedicated mortuaries constructed of both shell and earth (Aten 1999). In countless other cases, mounds consisted primarily of shell and lack evidence for human burials.

Irrespective of inferred functions, because mounds consist of shell from species known to have been consumed by humans and typically contain the inedible remains of other food resources (notably fish bone), investigators since the days of Wyman (1875, 11; see also Moore 1892, 913–914) have generally assumed that shell mounds were the accumulated results of routine, residential practice. Having accepted that shell mounds were composed of primarily subsistence remains, investigators of the modern era turned to ecological factors to explain the origin, duration, and cessation of shell deposition. The development of wetland habitat in the early mid-Holocene has long been considered an enabling factor for intensive settlement of the middle St. Johns region, while the presumed continuity

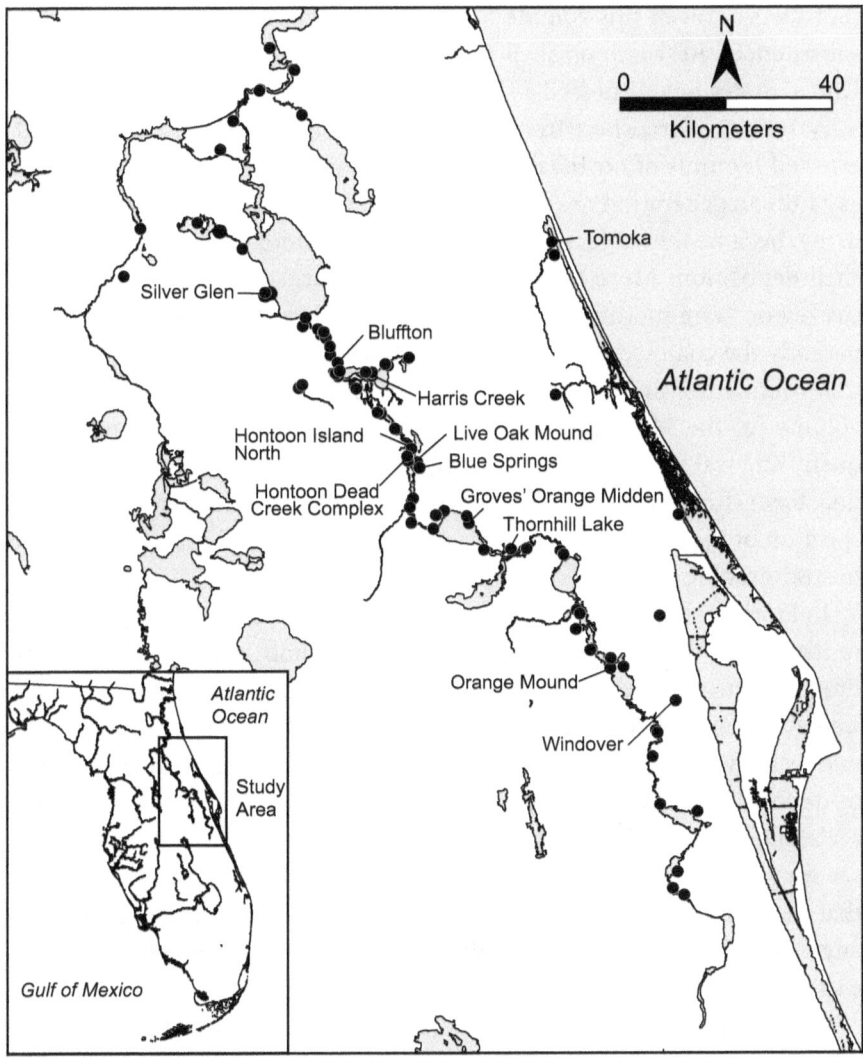

Figure 3.1. Map of the middle St. Johns Basin, showing locations of recorded Mount Taylor period sites, and place names for those mentioned in the text.

of this lifestyle served testimony to the stability and productivity of wetland biomes over millennia (Goggin 1952; Milanich 1994, 86–87; Miller 1992, 1998). Similar subsistence-centric perspectives have long structured the interpretation of shell mounds in the lower Midwest and Midsouth of the United States (Marquardt and Watson 2005), the San Francisco Bay area of California (Luby, Drescher, and Lightfoot 2006), southwest Mexico (Voorhies 2004), south coastal Brazil (Gaspar 1998), and the lower Amazon (but see Roosevelt this volume for patterning that invokes factors beyond subsistence). Research on shell rings of the Atlantic and Gulf coasts of the United States has witnessed a similar interpretive bias (Russo 2004).

As we summarize here from our recent field investigations, the very oldest shell mounds of northeast Florida took form rather quickly, in as little as a human generation or two, and then, after being abandoned as places of living, became the subject of routinized commemorative practice involving shell deposition. More than a millennium later, certain shell mounds of the region were modified to accommodate new social circumstances, apparently the coalescence of formerly distinct communities (see Rosenswig this volume for similar circumstances in Chiapas; and Estrada-Belli this volume for the Maya Lowlands). Acts of initial construction and subsequent renewal or modification of mounds cannot be inferred from their final form (Rosenswig and Burger this volume) but instead require close inspection of the context and organization of depositional practices revealed in stratigraphic profiles.

In Florida, shell mounds indeed encapsulate the residue of what appears to have been domestic living, but they also contain evidence for depositional events that are hard to explain in quotidian terms alone. In no case we have seen to date were entire shell mounds constructed instantly or in merely a few major stages. But over time, through the enactment of scores of depositional events and occasional transformations in the mode and scale of deposition, shell mounds achieved monumental scale. Despite the seemingly unintended nature of St. Johns shell mounds, we do not think that the small-scale cyclical acts of deposition evident in layered strata are any less discursive or purposeful than the large-scale public acts of building earthen mounds.

Our logic here follows from a definition of monumentality as historical practice. History in this sense is what people make of the past, and its purpose has far less to do with the past than it does with the future. Depositional acts, then, are instruments of intervention or interference (sensu Wobst 2000). Inasmuch as such acts draw on metaphors of the "past," they may be considered commemorative. But in the social construction of memory, depositional acts are far more than nostalgic. Rather, such acts are mobilized, or politicized, to chart a course of action. We suggest that this is as true among small-scale mobile foragers as it is among state-level societies (see Haas and Creamer this volume). In fact, one might argue that the monumentality of small-scale societies is more complex than that of states because in the latter, only dominant (state) discourse is evident in its deployment, but in the former, nothing prevents the participation of multiple diverse constituencies.

What sorts of "triggering" events or processes may have necessitated collective statements involving mound deposition? To be sure, St. Johns communities encountered changes in the inhabitability or subsistence potential of locations that repeatedly challenged "traditional" living. Likewise, the response of humans to acute environmental change involved both small- and large-scale displacements that disarticulated and then rearticulated communities in new structures of co-residency and alliance. In terms of human perception of change, responses to demographic or ecological events, no matter how unfamiliar, are likely to make reference to the material and symbolic resources of past experience. During times of rapid change, particularly where regional populations reorganize around novel scenarios, preexisting associations with places can be drawn on as historical resources to make new encounters or ecologies meaningful. We would argue that it is in these moments that discursive monumental acts are deployed.

The shell mounds of the St. Johns Basin offer some of the best evidence for interpreting mounds as historical practice because they span centuries, if not millennia, and thus register, in stratified fashion, many depositional acts. Our challenge in interpreting these complex sequences is to differentiate depositional acts aimed at renewing the world as it had come to be known from those that were enacted to "re-write" history and thus set a different course for the future. In the following section we briefly detail our current understanding of the variation and history of shell mounds along the St. Johns based on our own recent fieldwork. In particular, we focus on variations in the content, scale, location, and temporality of depositional events documented within stratigraphic sequences. We then place our findings within the broader regional picture of environmental and social change to discuss how monumentality as historical practice figured within the broader geopolitics of Archaic community building.

St. Johns Shell Mound Variations

Field schools directed by the senior author since 2000 have targeted shell mounds and related sites in a locale of the middle St. Johns that is now occupied by two state parks, Hontoon Island and Blue Spring, and a third locale along the western shore of Lake George (Figure 3.1). Technical reports are available for all work to date (Randall 2007; Randall and Sassaman 2005; Sassaman 2003a; Sassaman et al. 2011), and these form the basis for the summaries that follow. Shell mounds we have investigated take one of two basic forms. The earliest examples are represented by linear or crescent-shaped ridges with dimensions up to 200 meters long and 5 meters high and incorporate up to 10,000 cubic meters of materials. U-shaped mound complexes, 300 meters on a side, 8 meters high and more than 75,000 cubic meters in volume, represent a later and fundamental transformation of earlier constructions.

Mount Taylor Shell Ridges

The oldest shell mounds in northeast Florida are the linear or crescent-shaped ridges attributed to the Mount Taylor period of ca. 6000–4200 radiocarbon years before present (RCYBP). We have investigated three such ridges, the Hontoon Dead Creek Mound (8VO214), Live Oak Mound (8VO41), and the Silver Glen Run West Mound (8LA1W). Mounds in this configuration typically lack significant later deposition and likely reflect the form at the time of their abandonment toward the end of the fifth millennium BP.

The Hontoon Dead Creek Mound is one of the few remaining intact shell mounds in the region. It is a 140-meter-long arcuate construction with an offset summit of about 5 meters high (Figure 3.2). It sits at the edge of a cypress swamp fronting Hontoon Dead Creek, a partially in-filled relict channel of the St. Johns River. The mound slope to the west, toward the swamp, is steeper than the landward slope to the east. The lengthwise slope falls sharply to the south from the apex and gently to the north. After dropping some 2 meters in elevation over a 40 meters distance from the summit, the ramp-like contours to the north flatten over a stretch of some 20 m, giving it the appearance of a small platform or plateau.

We excavated a trench nine meters long into the west slope of the mound, near the summit. Although the trench did not penetrate to the core of the mound, it exposed a long stepped profile of the outer stages of construction, and the west end of the trench reached to the top of the basal component just above the water table (Figure 3.3). Augering in the base of the trench and across the adjacent swamp revealed the presence of a buried midden below as much as one meter of aggraded floodplain sediment.

The stratigraphy of Hontoon Dead Creek Mound registers some marked variations in the content, scale, and rhythm of depositional events. Like all the shell-bearing deposits we discuss in this chapter, the mound consists primarily of the shells of freshwater snails, most notably *Viviparus*

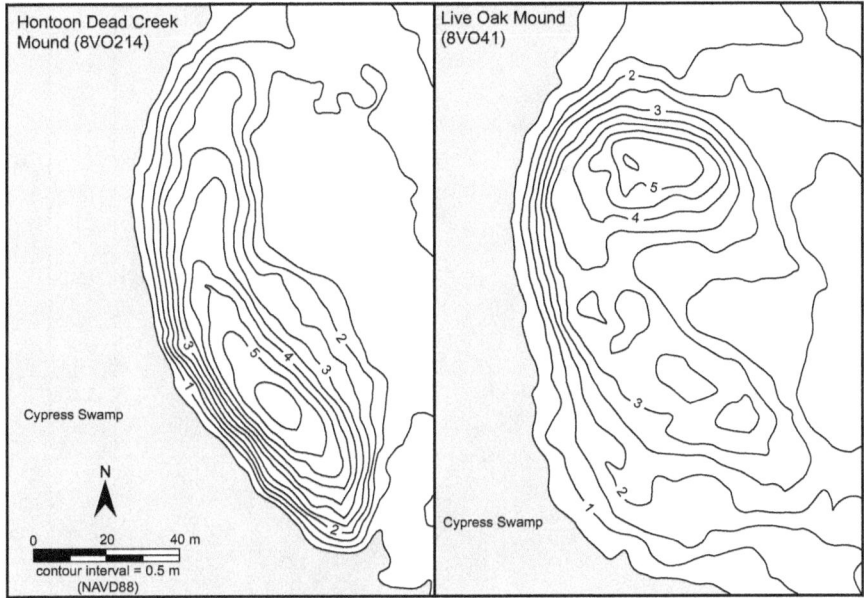

Figure 3.2. Topographic map of Hontoon Dead Creek Mound (8VO214) (left), and Live Oak Mound (8VO41) (right).

georgianus, the banded mystery snail. Apple snails (*Pomacea paludosa*) and freshwater bivalves (Unionids) comprise minority species that occasionally dominate individual depositional units. Shell deposits vary across units in species diversity; degree of crushing, compaction, and concretion; and evidence for burning. Depositional units, or strata, vary in extent, thickness, inorganic matrix, and amount of associated vertebrate fauna, other organic matter (e.g., paleofeces), and artifacts. Crushed and/or burned shell strata that express continuity across profiles are good evidence for buried surfaces, while evidence for soil development and large tree roots provide some basis for inferring the relative longevity of such surfaces. Facies of mound fill register differences in the volume, temporality, and placement of deposition.

Apparently only the basal episodes of shell deposition at Hontoon Dead Creek Mound involved routine domestic activities. Our trench was insufficient to fully explore this basal midden, but a core placed in the floor of the trench produced charcoal with an AMS age estimate of 6460 ±50 conventional RCYPB. Models for the scale and composition of this initial deposit are found just to the south of the mound. Along the terrace edge overlooking the floodplain is a series of five small mounds spaced some

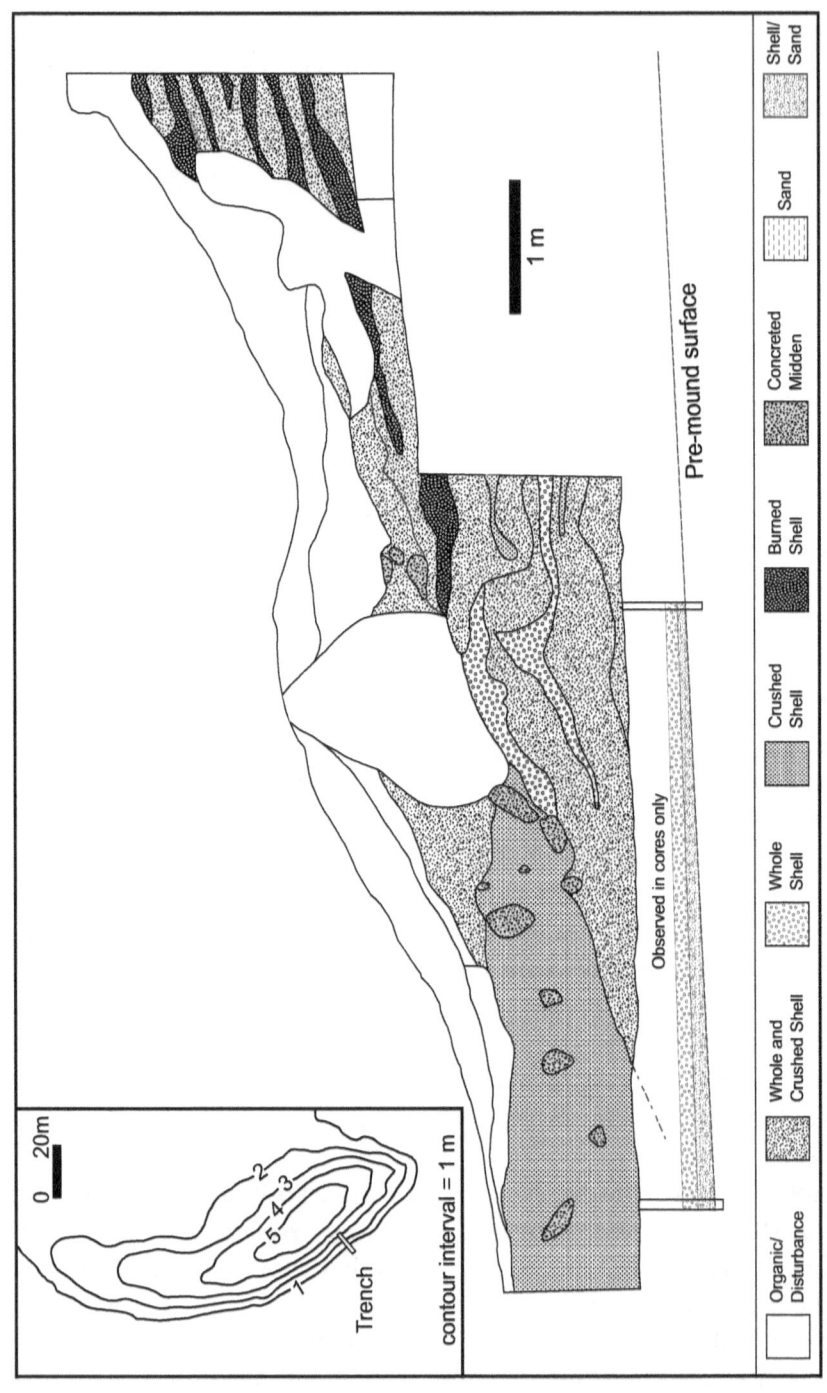

Figure 3.3. Stratigraphic profile of trench in western slope of Hontoon Dead Creek Mound (8VO214).

30–40 meters apart (Randall 2007, 2010). Recorded as 8VO215 (Hontoon Dead Creek Village), these apparent house mounds contain stacked surfaces of varying age (not unlike the Olmec islotes described by Cyphers and Zurita-Noguera this volume). The two closest to Hontoon Dead Creek Mound lack any traces of pottery and returned AMS assays of 6280 ±40 RCYBP and 5950 ±60 RCYBP; the remaining three yielded pottery that was progressively younger (<4000 RCYBP) with increasing distance from the large mound. These small mounds (<20 meters long, usually less than 1 meter high) have all the hallmarks of relatively intensive riverside dwelling, with abundant food remains, ash, charcoal, shell tools, closely stacked crushed surfaces, and areas of primary and secondary deposition.

The upper depositional units of Hontoon Dead Creek Mound are altogether different. Overlying the buried premound midden is a deposit ca. two meters thick of largely clean and whole shell. The upper 0.75 meter of this unit consists entirely of shell lacking any inorganic matrix and limited vertebrate fauna and artifacts. Diffuse lenses of burned shell in the lower half of this unit suggest it may not have been emplaced all at once, but nothing in the profile indicates prolonged exposure or the accumulation of domestic refuse through the entire depth of two meters. A sample of charred hickory shell from the very top of this unit returned an AMS assay of 6110 ±40 RCYBP. We interpret this two-meter-thick shell unit as a "capping" event. It was massive in scope and seemingly rapidly emplaced. The deposition of large quantities of shell above debris that was demonstrably associated with habitation implies that the existing anthropogenic surface was reconfigured into a large ridge with an expansive and level summit.

Overlying this shell cap is a series of thin depositional units of alternating burned and unburned shell. These appear to occur in depositional couplets, possibly separated by relatively short periods of abandonment. AMS assays on depositional couplets roughly 0.5 meter and 1 meter above the capped surface yielded dates of 6140 ±50 and 5910 ±50 RCYBP, respectively. Although we have yet to establish the precise temporality of deposition, the radiocarbon assays indicate that mound surface renewal events occurred at a regular and rapid pace. What is more, none contained the sorts of associated fauna and artifacts we have documented in similar strata elsewhere (see Silver Glen Run West below). There is a regularity and rhythm to these events that suggests some manner of cyclical practice.

A second intact shell ridge in the vicinity corroborates the timing and sequence of depositional events at Hontoon Dead Creek Mound. Live Oak (8VO41) is a shell ridge 120 meters long and 5 meters tall fronting an in-filled swamp on the east bank of the St. Johns River (Figure 3.2). Despite a spate of looting in the 1960s, this ridge expresses its more-or-less original form. Our testing at Live Oak Mound was limited to two excavation units sited on partially backfilled looters' pits. One test unit near the conical apex of the mound penetrated nearly 3 meters of shell strata, mostly light and dark couplets, and a bucket auger at the base of the unit penetrated clean, whole shell to reach a submound midden at a depth of 4.26 m. A second unit at the south end of the ridge provided good exposure of the basal strata, and charcoal from the submound midden returned an AMS assay of 6260 ±50 RCYBP.

A clean shell cap 1.5 meters thick overlying the basal midden contained charcoal that returned an age estimate of 6210 ±50 RCYBP, the exact same estimate obtained on charcoal from the first of sequential shell couplets some 2.5 meters deep. A third assay on charcoal from a couplet 0.8 meter above the first couplet was 6110 ±50 RCYBP. Collectively, AMS assays suggest that the cap and at least half of the couplets of Live Oak Mound were deposited in relatively rapid order, possibly over less than a single human generation.

In sum, both Hontoon Dead Creek Mound and Live Oak consist of three distinct macrounits: a submound midden indicative of domestic activity, a cap 1.5–2 meters thick of whole, clean shell that effectively sealed off places of dwelling, and a series of thin couplets of burned and unburned shell that were emplaced in seemingly cyclical fashion as the ridge grew taller and wider. These macrounits, despite their differences, actually represent a relatively short time span given the size of the mounds and the cumulative volume of shell. We do not know when communities discontinued significant deposition on the mound surface. The presence of an aggraded floodplain as well as smaller community middens to the south of the mound would suggest that area shellfish beds suffered from decreased productivity.

Hontoon Dead Creek and Live Oak mounds are but two of the scores of shell ridges that were erected during Mount Taylor times. While many are now removed from main channels and sources of water, others are situated in areas less susceptible to floodplain degradation. In the two ridges we have tested in such locations (8LA1W and 8VO202), depositional histories are indicative of intensive living. For example, Locus A at 8LA1-West is the remnant of a Preceramic ridge 200 meters long that contains about 4 meters of stratified anthropogenic deposition dating from ca. 5500 to at least 5000 RCYBP. The ridge is part of the larger Silver Glen Run complex which

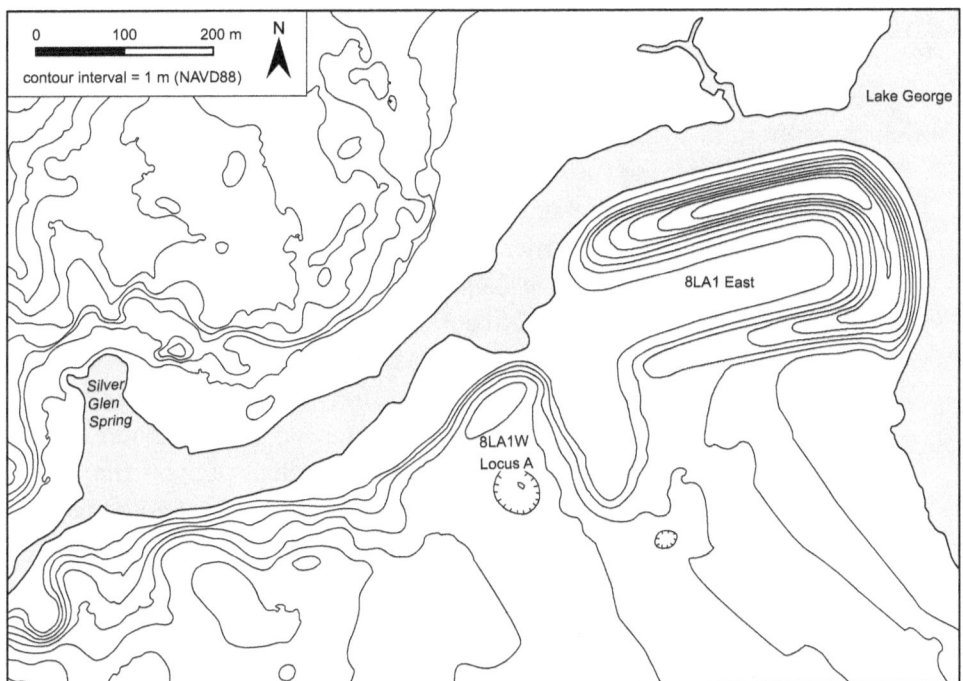

Figure 3.4. Topographic map of sites along Silver Glen Run, showing reconstructed plans for Mount Taylor shell ridge (Locus A) at 8LA1-West, and the U-shaped, Orange period shell mound at 8LA1-East.

fronts a first-order-magnitude spring that discharges into Lake George, Florida's second largest body of water (Figure 3.4). Extensive mining, which removed much of the Silver Glen Run complex in 1923, left perimeter segments with escarpments 2.5 meters high and up to 1.5 meters of intact midden below the graded interior surface.

Although too complex to detail here, we would note that the 12 meters we have exposed in profiles across the ridge have revealed three macrounits representing a submound midden, a capping event consisting of 30–40 centimeters of fine brown sand, and stacked sequences of shell and earth containing relatively dense assemblages of vertebrate fauna and assorted domestic refuse. These last depositional units resemble the upper alternating strata of Live Oak and Hontoon Dead Creek mounds. Sequences consistent with these strata have been detailed in our excavations at the Hontoon Island North site (8VO202) as well. Despite the lack of a clean shell cap, the sand that sealed off the basal midden from the overlying living surfaces appears to have been an equivalent unit. This sand unit is unequivocally anthropogenic and provides a link to decidedly nondomestic mortuary mounds (see below).

Locus A at 8LA1W was without question a locus of intensive, repeated habitation from ca. 5500 to at least 5000 RCYBP. Again, the relative stability of its first-magnitude spring helps explain the ecological potential of this locale for sustaining human settlement. It also provides a benchmark for comparison with what we infer to be purposefully mounded deposits at Hontoon Dead Creek and Live Oak, locations vulnerable to hydrologic change. In this respect, two sets of contrasts are worth noting. First, the density of vertebrate faunal remains at Locus A, Hontoon Island North, and other locations of demonstrable habitation is as at least three times and as much as six times the density of vertebrate fauna at the two mounded ridges. Second, the average size of *Viviparus* shell at sites of habitation is about 30 percent greater than counterparts in mounded contexts. Although these differences may be explicable in ecological terms alone, they clearly covary with the placement, structure, and scale of shell deposition, specifically in that large-scale rapid deposition in a fixed location (i.e., ridges) involved the smallest snails and the least amount of vertebrate fauna.

Orange Period Monuments

Orange is the name given to the early pottery horizon in Florida (Bullen 1972), dating regionally from 4200 to 3500 RCYBP. Best known from coastal sites that include massive rings of shell (Russo and Heide 2001), the Orange tradition has long been regarded as an outgrowth Mount Taylor culture, especially in the middle St. Johns region, where sequences such as the those documented at Groves Orange Midden (8VO2601) (Russo et al. 1992) and Blue Spring (8VO43; Sassaman 2003a) register continuity in settlement. That the Orange period witnessed major cultural change in the middle St. Johns is evidenced by the construction of massive U-shaped monuments of shell. None of these has survived mining efforts, but we have Wyman's descriptions of their unmolested condition as well as analogs (if not homologs) in the roughly contemporaneous shell rings of the Atlantic and Gulf coasts. Unlike Mount Taylor ridges, which were numerous and widespread in the middle St. Johns, U-shaped monuments are known from only a handful of locations.

The best evidence to date for such places is provided from excavations at the Silver Glen Run complex, where shell mining has removed all surface traces of the mound (8LA1-East). In 1871, Jeffries Wyman recorded a U-shaped mound at the mouth of the spring run. His published description of the mound is relatively thin, but additional information has been gleaned from Wyman's field journal (curated at Harvard University's Francis A. Countway Library of Medicine), including a simple plan sketch (Randall 2010). Figure 3.4 shows a reconstruction of the mound based on Wyman's description and our own subsurface testing. The plan includes a ridge 300 meters long fronting the spring run, a ridge 200 meters long fronting the lake, and a landward ridge 300 meters long running parallel to the first ridge. AMS assays on sooted Orange vessel sherds indicate that the mound was erected between roughly 4100 and 3600 RCYBP.

Excavation units have targeted the basal component of the south and north ridges, where upward of two meters of deposits are still present just above and below the water table. South ridge test units exposed the basal stratum of anthropogenic deposits overlying the natural sandy substrate. Radiometric dates for this basal stratum indicate that portions of the south ridge underwent construction around 3600 RCYBP. Tests units yielded plain Orange pottery, limited amounts of vertebrate fauna, traces of chipped stone, and broad shallow pit features with evidence of burning. Whole clean *Viviparus* shell appears to have been emplaced over the original ground surface, with pits dug into this stratum and penetrating subsoil. Because both units were truncated by mining, we have no basis for inferring anything about depositional units overlying this clean shell stratum. However, the clean shell and low density of associated debris is suggestive of rapid and likely planned construction.

The north ridge that fronts the spring run and its adjoining lakefront segment have proved to be difficult to characterize due to advanced disturbance of remaining subsurface deposits. Eroding from the bank of the run and the lakeshore to the east are deposits of freshwater shell that contain Orange period pottery. Particularly noteworthy is the juncture between the north and lake-facing ridges. Cutbank remnants of the mound and the small islands at the mouth of the run have yielded large assemblages of highly ornate Orange Incised pottery. We have been successful in dating soot from the exterior surfaces of three of these sherds, with two assays exceeding 4000 RCYBP and the third a few centuries younger. We have been less successful in locating intact basal strata of this component due to mining-related disturbance and erosion. However, we suspect that people making and using Orange pottery were responsible for much (if not all) of the mounded shell along the run and lakefront that marks the conjunction of these ridges and the highest point of the entire mound (ca. 8 meters high).

As our efforts to locate intact portions of the run and lakefront ridges continue, we expect to find solid evidence for a Mount Taylor component along the spring run. Circumstantial evidence to date is compelling. At the western end of the ridge fronting the spring run, mining exposed a dome of concreted shell similar to those observed at other Mount Taylor ridges. Human skeletal remains are exposed in one location at the surface, paralleling evidence for a Mount Taylor mortuary facility elsewhere. The point here is that Orange monuments were not constructed sui generis but incorporated preexisting monuments into their design.

St. Johns Shell Mounds in Context

Shell mounds and other shell-bearing deposits we have investigated to date demonstrate considerable variation in age, size, form, and internal structure. Other sites in the region add more variation to the mix, including dedicated mortuary facilities. No matter the form or scale of mounded deposits across the region, every profile evinces a history of repeated or staged deposition. At the risk of reducing this variability, we have inferred three kinds of depositional events that vary in content, scale, and temporality: (1) massive strata of whole shell, what we have referred to as "capping" events; (2) small-scale, redundant, or cyclical events; and (3) depositional acts that reconfigured the structure and organization of shell mounds. In the balance of this chapter we consider how each of these distinct modes of deposition figured as historical practices that were enacted during periods of regional community reorganization and reproduction.

Mount Taylor Capping Events

The two oldest examples of major capping events involving shell (Hontoon Dead Creek and Live Oak mounds) did not necessarily entail human interment, but they may have. Lacking any exposure of the cores of these mounds, we simply do not know if shell caps were emplaced over burials at these particular locations. Fortunately, another Mount Taylor mound complex in the region provides an unambiguous example of capping, using both shell and sand, over human interments.

The Harris Creek site (8VO24) on Tick Island in the middle St. Johns Basin was the locus of one of the region's largest shell mound complexes, reaching 10 meters high and extending over five acres (Moore 1999). It may have been arranged in a U-shaped fashion, but that has yet to be substantiated. In the early 1960s, Bullen salvaged 175 Mount Taylor burials from a basal shell ridge that was being mined for road fill (Jahn and Bullen 1978). The inhumations were mostly flexed and placed on two successive platforms, the first capped with white sand, the second with shell midden. Most interments within the mortuary layers were single, but they were occasionally multiple, and at least one large grave was dug to hold 11 individuals early in the use of the mound. A deposit of black earth, postholes, and other features on the platforms suggested to Aten (1999, 147) that the constructions of Harris Creek were not burial mounds per se but were repeatedly enlarged platforms on which burials were placed in discrete sections off the summit of the mound. Shell midden apparently continued to accumulate over the basal mortuaries through the Mount Taylor period.

Determining the age of mortuary construction is somewhat problematic. Initial determinations in the 1960s were acquired on burial fill charcoal, and yielded intercepts clustered between 5500–5300 RCYBP, but individual standard deviations ranged from 184 to 303 years. However, a recent program of bioarchaeological analysis by Tucker (2009) and others (Quinn, Tucker, and Krigbaum 2008) has provided four AMS assays on human teeth that were among samples that were analyzed for stable isotopes. Ranging from 6125 ±83 to 5825 ±62 RCYBP, these new assays place mortuary practices at Harris Creek in the time frame of capping events at Hontoon Dead Creek and Live Oak mounds. Parenthetically, the results of stable isotopes shows that people interred at Harris Creek included both locals and nonlocals, some from as far afield as Tennessee or Virginia (Tucker 2009).

If its new age estimates accurately date the interment and capping of burials more than 6,000 years ago, then Harris Creek stands as the oldest mortuary mound in Florida. It is not, however, the oldest cemetery in the state, because starting as much as 2,000 years earlier, humans were interred in mortuary ponds. The most thoroughly investigated and documented is Windover (8BR246), on the Atlantic coast near Cape Canveral, where over 168 individuals were recovered from peat deposits (Doran 2002). Most interments were deposited in the pond from ca. 7350–7100 RCYBP (ibid., 72). Other mortuary ponds in Florida include Bay West (Beriault et al.

1981), Little Salt Spring (Clausen et al. 1979), and Republic Groves (Wharton, Ballo, and Hope 1981), all dating between ca. 6650–5200 RCYBP. Like Windover, these Middle Archaic cemeteries do not appear to be associated with habitation, although survey in the vicinity of these sites is limited. None of the known mortuary ponds postdates 5000 RCYBP.

Pond burials began to give way to mounds at the time when postglacial rise in sea level was transforming interior Florida from a landscape that was sparse in surface water to one that was literally drowned over vast areas. What was once at a premium (i.e., surface water) had become pervasive, and what was once pervasive (i.e., dry land) had become a premium. It is tempting to infer that the emergent tradition of mounding shell was the symbolic inversion of subaqueous contexts. That is, mounds had become inverted ponds, with freshwater shell and occasional muck (see below) the material link to the underwater world. We could take this even further with ethnohistoric analogs to suggest that shell itself and perhaps its contrast with dark substances (burned shell, muck, midden, murky depths of water) symbolizes cycles of life and death (see for example Claassen 2008).

It is in this symbolic context that the capping events at Hontoon Dead Creek and Live Oak mounds may signal the "death" of a location as a place of (mortal) dwelling. Whether or not they involved human interments, these locations were subject to major ecological change as the once-flowing channels adjacent to settlements were abandoned and in-filled. Beyond the local challenges at these two sites was the pervasive pattern of sites becoming inundated, including those along drowning coastlines. The overall trend of abandonment, displacement, and resettlement across the greater region implicates realignments of communities in locations that were relatively stable, such as landforms in proximity to first-magnitude springs. Harris Creek was one such place (near the outflow of Alexander and DeLeon springs). The diversity of interments evident in the stable isotope patterns noted above may be one indication that relocations resulted in convergences or coalescence of formally separate communities.

How the deposition of sand factors into these emergent new social formations takes us even farther afield in the greater Southeast. Dating after ca. 5000 RCYBP, certain Mount Taylor mortuary mounds were constructed largely of sand, sometimes in addition to shell and other materials, such as muck. The first sand cap at Harris Creek anticipates a growing tradition of earth moving that was manifested later at Orange Mound (8OR1), where Moore (1999, 98–104) describes an earthen mortuary encased in shell; Bluffton (8VO23) (ibid., 166–170; Sears 1960), where an isolated interment was covered with distinctive layers of sand, shell, and muck; and the Thornhill Lake complex (8VO58–60) (Moore 1999, 277–283), where recent work by Endonino (2008, 2010) provides good perspective on the emplacement of sand burial mounds over a Mount Taylor shell ridge at ca. 5000 RCYBP. The coastal mound complex at Tomoka (8VO81) includes an earthen mortuary mound roughly coeval with Thornhill.

Aten (1999, 177) suggests that mounds made from earth or sand, such as Tomoka and Thornhill Lake, were the late form of Mount Taylor mortuary construction. Thus, the Mount Taylor mortuary tradition underwent two major transformations over time: first a transition from pond burials to shell mound burials and then from shell to earthen mound burials. The material culture of these various phases is similar enough to suggest cultural continuity (Wheeler, Newman, and McGee 2000, 153), but items of extraregional origin show that the contours of cultural affiliation were expanding outward with the emergence of an earthen mound tradition. Mortuary contexts dating from ca. 5000–4500 RCYBP include items such as bannerstones and stone beads that originated from locations as distant as South Carolina and Mississippi. That these items were interred in caches and graves of mounds—sometimes in elaborate fashion (Endonino 2008, 2010)—suggests that symbolic acts at mounds were altered to include referents to faraway places, and, one could argue, nonlocal histories (Randall and Sassaman 2010).

The use of sand and other earthen materials substantiates not only the claim that Mount Taylor mounds were purposeful but also the claim that their construction sequence was highly structured. Nothing demonstrates this more than the use of building materials of contrastive color. Layers of black muck over either white sand or clean shell are a consummate dichotomy that likely symbolized the cycle of life and death, especially in mortuary contexts. If this basic contrast was pervasive in Mount Taylor worldview, it stands to reason that the contrastive layers of unburned and burned shell in Mount Taylor ridges held similar symbolic import, even outside of mortuary contexts (Randall 2010, 2011).

Mount Taylor Cyclical Deposition

Our review of Mount Taylor shell ridges shows that relatively thin couplets of light (unburned) and dark (burned) shell strata overlie capping events (of sand or shell) at locations of abandoned settlement. They also occur at locations of sustained or repeated settlement, where shell strata are rife in vertebrate fauna, paleofeces, and other indications of daily living. Because our exposures at all sites investigated to date are limited, we admit that these contrastive patterns may one day be documented as coeval facies at single sites (e.g., facies of primary and secondary midden). However, based on current radiometric age estimates, clean shell couplets occurred as early as 6,000 years ago, while those characterized by habitation debris are later in age. Regardless, both types of deposits followed a cyclical or recurrent pattern, irrespective of particular context. Given the possible symbolic significance of light-dark couplets, we suspect that these depositional practices were purposeful and meaningful. Moreover, the recurrent structured deposition of materials in post-abandonment capping appears to represent attempts to reproduce the same meaning and associations with a place once it had been transformed.

Ultimately, we need to determine the precise temporality of these couplets. Microsampling of archaeological shell for isotopic analysis is under way (Blessing 2009) and will provide good data on the seasonal variation of shell collecting. We are inclined to believe that the deposition of couplets was actually more "eventful" than it was routine, stimulated by the need to confront change that was not tied to seasonal or annual cycles familiar to all. In this sense, renewal of mound surfaces may have mediated against change (be it relocation prompted by changing hydrology or the remaking of a community promoted by realignments of people). Thus, mounding was a "traditional" practice that invoked past places and actions to make claims of identity (i.e., ancestry, real or stipulated) (Randall 2010, 2011).

New World Order

Modern skepticism about the purposefulness of Archaic mounds is hardest to uphold when mound complexes assume regular form and orientation. The elaborate Poverty Point mound complex of northeast Louisiana is the strongest case in point (Gibson 2000), followed closely by the Middle Archaic mound complexes of the same region (Saunders this volume), whose geometry was replicated across several sites and was likely integrated at the regional scale (Sassaman and Heckenberger 2004). We can add to this list the shell rings and arcuate mounds of the Archaic of Florida (Russo and Heide 2001), where regularity in form evokes dualistic social structure and variations in the size of mounded shell evokes inequality among factions.

Recent work on coastal sites by Michael Russo (2004) provides a strong basis for inferring a sociological grammar for the construction and use of shell rings. Without repeating the entire argument here, we can summarize it by noting that rings and U-shaped constructions (i.e., open rings) show spatial regularities to suggest they were built and occupied by societies that were divided into two factions, perhaps something akin to moieties. And if patterned accumulation of shell at rings reflects directly the outputs of large-scale feasting, as Saunders (2004) argues, then factions at each ring site had differential capacities to mobilize labor and material resources for social and political purposes.

Although Russo and Saunders have not addressed the conditions under which dual social organization arose at Orange period coastal ring sites, our work at Silver Glen Run provides one possible explanation for the middle St. Johns region. That Orange pottery marked the incursion of a "foreign" element on the Florida landscape—specifically from the Caribbean or South America—has not been seriously entertained since the 1960s, when James Ford (1969) made the case (but see Clark and Knoll 2005). Regardless of the source of this innovation, Orange pottery at some locales accompanied changes in cultural dispositions that for at least the middle St. Johns region are hard to trace in local ancestry alone. We hypothesize that U-shaped shellworks embody dual social organization whose genesis derived from the coalescence of two formerly distinct people, one indigenous (Mount Taylor), the other foreign (coastal Orange). Preexisting alliances between communities of the middle St. Johns and the coast are apparent in the pervasive use of marine shell by Mount Taylor communities along the river. It is hardly coincidental that the supply of marine shell waned at the same time that pottery was first used and large U-shaped mounds began to take form at Silver Glen and elsewhere in the region.

The spatiality of the U-shaped mound at Silver Glen Run (as well as the others in the region) is patently dualistic, with each of the parallel ridges corresponding to each faction and the unifying ridge linking them in ritual practice. As indicated earlier, elaborate Orange Incised pottery is concentrated at the northeast corner of the outer ridge, while the inner ridge, at least at its base, is dominated by Orange Plain pottery. The distinction between these types goes well beyond surface treatment to include marked contrast in vessel form, size, wall thickness, and use. Orange Incised pottery is large, thick, and used directly over fire. Orange Plain is thin, small, and apparently rarely (if ever) used directly over fire.

Sampling biases in the spatial segregation of pottery types at Silver Glen Run may be at play here, but given other recent findings, we suspect that this pattern is sound. Since the early days of ^{14}C dating, Orange Plain was believed to be the original ware in a series that eventually gave way to Orange Incised and then to spiculate paste wares of the early St. Johns series (Bullen 1972; Milanich 1994, 94). Recent dating shows that incised and plain wares were actually contemporaneous (Sassaman 2003b; Saunders 2004), both appearing at ca. 4200 RCYBP but typically spatially segregated. On the coast, segregation is between rings (incised pottery) and nonring shell sites (plain pottery), while at Silver Glen it appears to be between opposite ridges of the U-shaped structure. Ongoing work on St. Catherine's Island in Georgia suggests that some coastal rings also embody this spatial dichotomy (Sanger 2008).

We will continue to investigate the hypothesis that U-shaped mounds in the middle St. Johns were the historical consequence of coalescent dualistic societies and here observe that the process was not likely to have been uncontested. Had coastal groups moved into the St. Johns at the invitation of indigenous Mount Taylor communities, with whom they had existing alliances, and simply assimilated into local life without imposing new order or new structure, we might expect the long-standing Mount Taylor tradition of linear or crescent ridges to continue unchanged. Alternatively, if we assume that the process of coalescence entailed some manner of differentiation between "original" and "foreign" people, we might expect the outer ridge of Silver Glen Run to show continuity of practice and the inner ridge to provide evidence of new practices added by the interlopers. Neither of these expectations, however, stands up to observations to date. Rather, there may have been no direct relationship between stipulated ancestry in this case and the actual genealogy of resident peoples. We have no means at this point to determine the patterns of intermarriage and related norms for determining social obligations and responsibilities. No doubt proscriptive practices were complex and at times contested, and it is precisely under these sorts of circumstances that we find rationale for the depositional practices people used to stipulate ancestry through mound ritual.

Conclusion

Shell mounds of the middle St. Johns Basin began as locations of intensive habitation during the sixth and fifth millennia BP. Many such locations were capped by shell at or shortly after abandonment. Shell capping was sometimes done in conjunction with human interment, but whether or not mounds were literally transformed into cemeteries, capping likely symbolized the end of one process or stage and the beginning of another. In this sense, the depositional acts were acts of historicism that drew on a process of differentiated time to direct the course of history (i.e., the future). We have observed in several contexts that the "triggering" event for mounding shell (and/or sand or muck) was apparently the abandonment of settlements at locations undergoing marked ecological change. At others, however, the convergence of diverse communities likely precipitated the reconfiguration of mound structure. The U-shaped constructions coincident with the adoption of pottery provide the best example of this process in the middle St. Johns.

In the centuries before Europeans arrived, shell mounds of the ancients were reused for ritual purposes. Over the millennia between the onset of mound building and late prehistoric mortuary use, mounds were repeatedly occupied, sometimes as residential loci, at other times as nonresidential loci. Continued investigations may someday show how mounds were functionally differentiated at times, but given the protracted histories involved, it seems unlikely that any given structural arrangement persisted over long stretches of time or could be construed as the work of a "single" people, no matter how that is conceived. This suggests that any deep understanding of St. Johns mounds will benefit from theory that regards monuments as the codification of oral tradition and memory (Bradley 2002, 222; Connerton 1989) and that takes into account how the siting, orientation, and use of mounds evoke larger scales of time and place (e.g., Edmonds 1999). The details and meaning of these symbolic acts will not likely be known to us, but enough is known to defend the position that St. Johns mounds are much more than accumulations of garbage.

References Cited

Aten, Lawrence E.
1999   Middle Archaic Ceremonialism at Tick Island, Florida: Ripley P. Bullen's 1961 Excavations at the Harris Creek Site. *The Florida Anthropologist* 52(3):131–200.
Beriault, John, Robert Carr, Jerry Stipp, Richard Johnson, and Jack Meeder
1981   The Archaeological Salvage of the Bay West Site, Collier County, Florida. *The Florida Anthropologist* 34:39–58.
Blessing, Meggan E.
2009   The Snails' Tale: The Isotopic Record of Freshwater Gastropods in Archaic Shell Deposits of Northeast Florida. Paper presented at the 66th Annual Meeting of the Southeastern Archaeological Conference, Mobile, Alabama.

Bradley, Richard
1998   *The Significance of Monuments*. Routledge, London.
2002   *The Past in Prehistoric Societies*. Routledge, London.
Bullen, Ripley P.
1972   The Orange Period of Peninsular Florida. *The Florida Anthropologist* 25(2), part 2:9–33.
Claassen, Cheryl
2008   Shell Symbolism in Pre-Columbian North America. In *Early Human Impact on Megamolluscs*, edited by A. Antczak and R. Cipriana, pp. 37–43. Archaeopress, Oxford.
Clark, John E., and Michelle Knoll
2005   The American Formative Revisited. In *Gulf Coast Archaeology: The Southeastern United States and Mexico*, edited by N. M. White, pp. 281–303. University Press of Florida, Gainesville.
Clausen, Carl J., A. D. Cohen, Cesare Emiliani, J. A. Holman, and J. J. Stipp
1979   Little Salt Springs, Florida: A Unique Underwater Site. *Science* 203:609–614.
Connerton, Paul
1989   *How Societies Remember*. Cambridge University Press, Cambridge.
Doran, Glen H.
2002   *Windover: Multidisciplinary Investigations of an Early Archaic Florida Cemetery*. University Press of Florida, Gainesville.
Edmonds, Mark R.
1999   *Ancestral Geographies of the Neolithic: Landscape, Monuments and Memory*. Routledge, New York.
Endonino, Jon C.
2008   The Thornhill Lake Archaeological Research Project: 2005–2008. *The Florida Anthropologist* 61(3–4):121–137.
2010   Thornhill Lake: Hunter-Gatherers, Monuments, and Memory. Ph.D. dissertation, Department of Anthropology, University of Florida, Gainesville.
Ford, James A.
1969   *A Comparison of the Formative Cultures in the Americas: Diffusion or the Psychic Unity of Man*. Smithsonian Contributions to Anthropology 11. Smithsonian Institution, Washington, D.C.
Gaspar, Maria Dulce
1998   Considerations of Sambaquis on the Brazilian Coast. *Antiquity* 72:592–615.
Gibson, Jon L.
2000   *The Ancient Mounds of Poverty Point: Place of the Rings*. University Press of Florida, Gainesville.
Goggin, John M.
1952   *Space and Time Perspectives in Northern St. Johns Archaeology, Florida*. Yale University Publications in Anthropology 47. Yale University, New Haven, Connecticut.
Jahn, Otto, and Ripley P. Bullen
1978   *The Tick Island Site, St. Johns River, Florida*. Florida Anthropological Society Publications 10. Florida Anthropological Society, Gainesville.

Luby, Edward M., Clayton D. Drescher, and K. G. Lightfoot
2006   Shell Mounds and Mounded Landscapes in the San Francisco Bay Area: An Integrated Approach. *Journal of Island and Coastal Archaeology* 1:191–214.

Marquardt, William H., and Patty Jo Watson (editors)
2005   *Archaeology of the Middle Green River Region, Kentucky.* Institute of Archaeology and Palaeoenvironmental Studies Monograph 5. University Press of Florida, Gainesville.

Milanich, Jerald T.
1994   *Archaeology of Precolumbian Florida.* University Press of Florida, Gainesville.

Miller, James J.
1992   Effects of Environmental Change on Late Archaic People of Northeast Florida. *The Florida Anthropologist* 45:100–106.
1998   *An Environmental History of Northeast Florida.* University Press of Florida, Gainesville.

Moore, Clarence B.
1892   Certain Shell Heaps of the St. John's River, Florida, Hitherto Unexplored. (First Paper). *The American Naturalist* 26:912–922.
1999   *The East Florida Expeditions of Clarence Bloomfield Moore.* Edited by Jeffrey M. Mitchum. Classics in Southeastern Archaeology. University of Alabama Press, Tuscaloosa.

Piatek, Bruce J.
1994   The Tomoka Mound Complex in Northeast Florida. *Southeastern Archaeology* 13:109–118.

Quinn, Rhonda L., Bryan D. Tucker, and John Krigbaum
2008   Diet and Mobility in Middle Archaic Florida: Stable Isotopic and Faunal Data from the Harris Creek Archaeological Site (8vo24), Tick Island. *Journal of Archaeological Science* 35(8):2346–2356.

Randall, Asa R.
2007   *St. Johns Archaeological Field School 2005: Hontoon Island State Park.* Technical Report 7. Laboratory of Southeastern Archaeology, Department of Anthropology, University of Florida, Gainesville.
2010   Remapping Histories: Archaic Period Community Construction along the St. Johns River, Florida. Ph.D. dissertation, Department of Anthropology, University of Florida, Gainesville.
2011   Remapping Archaic Social Histories along the St. Johns River, Florida. In *Hunter Gatherer Archaeology as Historical Process,* edited by K. E. Sassaman and D. H. Holly Jr., pp. 120–142. University of Arizona Press, Tucson.

Randall, Asa R., and Kenneth E. Sassaman
2005   *St. Johns Archaeological Field School 2003–2004: Hontoon Island State Park.* Technical Report 6. Laboratory of Southeastern Archaeology, Department of Anthropology, University of Florida, Gainesville.
2010   (E)mergent Complexities during the Archaic in Northeast Florida. In *Ancient Complexities: New Perspectives in Pre-Columbian North America,* edited by Susan M. Alt, pp. 8–31 University of Utah Press, Salt Lake City.

Russo, Michael
1994   Why We Don't Believe in Archaic Ceremonial Mounds and Why We Should: The Case from Florida. *Southeastern Archaeology* 13:93–109.
2004   Measuring Shell Rings for Social Inequality. In *Signs of Power: The Rise of Cultural Complexity in the Southeast,* edited by L. Gibson and P. Carr, pp. 26–70. University of Alabama Press, Tuscaloosa.

Russo, Michael, and Greg Heide
2001   Shell Rings of the Southeast USA. *Antiquity* 75:491–492.

Russo, Michael, Barbara Purdy, Lee A. Newsom, and Ray M. McGee
1992   A Reinterpretation of Late Archaic Adaptations in Central-East Florida: Grove's Orange Midden (8VO2601). *Southeastern Archaeology* 11:95–108.

Sanger, Matthew C.
2008   Paired Rings—Shared and Divergent Histories amongst Late Archaic Shell Rings. Paper presented at the 65th Annual Southeastern Archaeological Conference, Charlotte, North Carolina.

Sassaman, Kenneth E.
2003a   *St. Johns Archaeological Field School 2000–2001: Blue Spring and Hontoon Island State Parks.* Technical Report 4. Laboratory of Southeastern Archaeology, Department of Anthropology, University of Florida, Gainesville.
2003b   New AMS Dates on Orange Fiber-Tempered Pottery from the Middle St. Johns Valley and Their Implications for Culture History in Northeast Florida. *The Florida Anthropologist* 56(1):5–14.

Sassaman, Kenneth E., and Michael J. Heckenberger
2004   Crossing the Symbolic Rubicon in the Southeast. In *Signs of Power: The Rise of Cultural Complexity in the Southeast,* edited by L. Gibson and P. Carr, pp. 214–233. University of Alabama Press, Tuscaloosa.

Sassaman, Kenneth E., Zackary I. Gilmore, and Asa R. Randall
2011   *St. Johns Archaeological Field School 2007–10: Silver Glen Run.* Technical Report 12. Laboratory of Southeastern Archaeology, Department of Anthropology, University of Florida, Gainesville.

Saunders, Rebecca
2004   Spatial Variation in Orange Culture Pottery: Interaction and Function. In *Early Pottery: Technology, Function, Style and Interaction in the Lower Southeast,* edited by R. Saunders and C. T. Hays, pp. 40–62. University of Alabama Press, Tuscaloosa.

Sears, William H.
1960   The Bluffton Burial Mound. *Florida Anthropologist* 13(2–3):55–60.

Tucker, Bryan
2009   Isotopic Investigations of Archaic Period Subsistence and Settlement in the St. Johns River Drainage, Florida. Ph.D. dissertation, Department of Anthropology, University of Florida, Gainesville.

Voorhies, Barbara
2004   *Coastal Collectors in the Holocene: The Chantuto People of Southwest Mexico.* University Press of Florida, Gainesville.

Wharton, Barry, George Ballo, and Mitchell Hope
1981   The Republic Groves Site, Hardee County, Florida. *The Florida Anthropologist* 34:59–80.

Wheeler, Ryan J., Christine L. Newman, and Ray M. McGee
2000   A New Look at the Mount Taylor and Bluffton Sites, Volusia County, with an Outline of the Mount Taylor Culture. *Florida Anthropologist* 53(2–3):133–157.

Wobst, H. Martin
2000   Agency in (Spite of) Material Culture. In *Agency in Archaeology*, edited by M. A. Bobres and J. Robb, pp. 40–50. Routledge, London.

Wyman, Jeffries
1875   *Fresh-Water Shell Mounds of the St. John's River, Florida*. Peabody Academy of Science Memoir 4. Peabody Academy of Science, Salem, Massachusetts.

4

Monumentality in Eastern North America during the Mississippian Period

DAVID G. ANDERSON

The Mississippian period in eastern North America is dated to between ca. 1000 and 400 cal. BP in most sequences, encompassing the last few centuries before sustained European contact across much of the region. Exactly what Mississippian is as a cultural entity has been the subject of as much debate as its beginning and end points, and indeed, the two subjects are intertwined. Over the past century, Mississippian societies have been defined based on the presence of attributes taken individually or collectively that have included such things as the presence of intensive maize agriculture, the widespread use of shell-tempered pottery, the appearance of wall-trench architecture, aspects of iconography and religion, or adaptations to specific environments such as riverine floodplains or oxbow lakes (e.g., Griffin 1967, 189; 1985, 63; Knight 1986; Pauketat 2007, 82–87; Smith 1986, 486, 488). Most scholars would agree that monumental construction—specifically the building of mounds, earthworks, and enclosures and their placement adjacent to or around plazas, with sturdy fortifications at larger centers—is a particularly characteristic feature of Mississippian culture. While not all Mississippian sites are characterized by the construction of monuments, or monumentality, and indeed it is rare or nonexistent in hamlets or smaller communities, it does appear to have been an integral part of life in larger communities. In this chapter what is meant by monumentality during the Mississippian period is explored, with a particular emphasis on its origins and on the ways the subject is currently being examined by local archaeologists.

Origins of Mississippian Culture and Monumentality

Mound and plaza arrangements have great time depth in eastern North America. The existence of an architectural grammar, or an appropriate way to design communities, has long been assumed to exist within Mississippian culture. To one group of scholars, its "main architectural elements include plazas, platform mounds and other earthworks, entryways, various

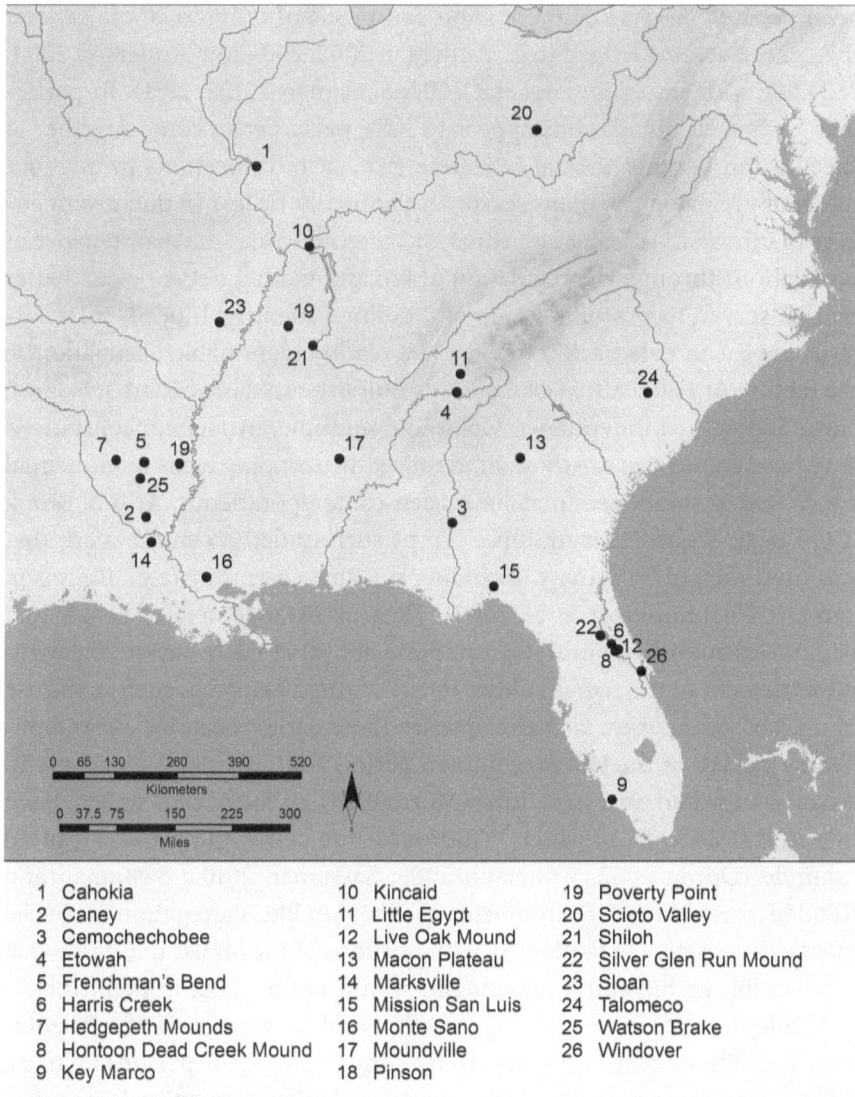

1 Cahokia	10 Kincaid	19 Poverty Point
2 Caney	11 Little Egypt	20 Scioto Valley
3 Cemochechobee	12 Live Oak Mound	21 Shiloh
4 Etowah	13 Macon Plateau	22 Silver Glen Run Mound
5 Frenchman's Bend	14 Marksville	23 Sloan
6 Harris Creek	15 Mission San Luis	24 Talomeco
7 Hedgepeth Mounds	16 Monte Sano	25 Watson Brake
8 Hontoon Dead Creek Mound	17 Moundville	26 Windover
9 Key Marco	18 Pinson	

Figure 4.1 Location of Archaic, Woodland, and Mississippian sites mentioned in the text.

means of segregating space and activities, defensive works, and natural terrain features" (Lewis, Stout, and Wesson 1998, 5). Indeed, some have argued that such a grammar was cosmologically grounded, ritually proscribed, and precisely determined and had great time depth in the region and perhaps across the Americas (Clark 2004; Lewis, Stout, and Wesson 1998; Sassaman 2010a, 2011, 203–206). Whether such consistency existed even during the Mississippian period, much less across the almost twelve millennia of human occupation across the region that came before it, has been debated, and while there is no consensus of opinion, some general themes are acknowledged (e.g., Anderson 2002, 268–269; Anderson 2004, 282–293; Milner 2004a; Pauketat 2007; Sassaman 2010a, 2011). In particular, dispersed populations appear to have periodically come together at specific and perhaps special (resource-rich, sacred) locations throughout much of prehistory, perhaps seasonally, annually, or less frequently, to engage in information exchange, ritual and ceremony, and the maintenance of populations through the regulation of kin and mating networks, activities that all served to promote group and cultural identity. Indeed, such patterns appear to date back to the earliest readily identifiable occupation of the region. At Paleoindian sites such as Bull Brook, Massachusetts; Debert, Nova Scotia; or Lindenmeier, Colorado, multiple artifact concentrations have been found that are thought to reflect the camping areas of individual bands and in some cases may have been contemporaneous. At Bull Brook it has been argued that multiple camps surrounded a central space that was used for public activity, including possible ceremony (e.g., Robinson and Ort 2011; Robinson et al. 2009). Thus, an arrangement of people and structures around a central space or plaza appears to date back to the earliest settlement of the region. Other forms of ritual behavior, such as the use of marked cemeteries, also characterize these earlier periods, as exemplified by burials at the late Paleoindian period Dalton culture Sloan site in Arkansas, located on a sand dune (Morse 1997), or the burials staked down in ponds in Florida, of which Windover is the best-known and -reported example (Doran 2002; Anderson 2009; Sassaman 2010a; Sassaman and Randall, this volume). Such mortuary behavior, like aggregation at special places, caused people to identify with portions of the landscape, a role that more visible architectural monuments would assume later in prehistory.

While the nature of group aggregation and interaction in the Paleoindian/Late Pleistocene and Early Archaic/initial Holocene periods up to ca. 8900 cal. BP remains only poorly understood at present, there is no question that true monumentality appears in a number of parts of eastern North

America during the latter part of the ensuing Mid-Holocene era, from ca. 8900 to 5700 cal. BP (Anderson and Sassaman 2004; Kidder and Sassaman 2009; Sassaman 2010a, 2011; Sassaman and Anderson 1996, 2004). Isolated earthen mounds and groups of mounds are present in the lower Mississippi Valley from ca. 6500 to 4700 cal. BP, at places such as Caney, Frenchman's Bend, Hedgepeth Mounds, Monte Sano, and Watson Brake (Russo 1994, 1996a; Saunders et al. 1997, 2005; Saunders 2010, this volume), while mounds of earth and shell appear about the same time or slightly earlier in coastal areas and along the St. Johns River in Florida at locations such as Harris Creek, Hontoon Dead Creek Mound, Live Oak Mound, and the Silver Glen Run Mound (Randall 2011; Russo 1996b, 2006; Sassaman 2010a; Sassaman and Randall this volume). The actual number of sites characterized by mounded deposits is far greater in these areas than these few examples, and accumulations of shell and earth have also been found along many interior waterways of the region, particularly in the Midsouth and along the Savannah and Ogeechee rivers of Georgia, with the earliest dating back to ca. 8000 cal. BP (e.g., Anderson, Russo, and Sassaman 2007; Claassen 1996, 2010; Dye 1996; Marquardt and Watson 2005; Sassaman 2005a, 2010a, 2010b, 2011; Thompson 2010).

As many of the essays in this volume make clear, monumentality and particularly mound building is often if not ubiquitously cosmologically grounded, tied with ideas of lower and upper worlds, and is frequently associated with mortuary behavior (Rosenswig and Burger this volume; Sassaman and Randall this volume) in some (but not all) cases (Saunders this volume). The monumental architecture that appears during the Mid-Holocene has links to earlier practices of group aggregation and dispersal, as seen in earlier Paleoindian sites, and to concepts of a watery or lower world, as seen in Florida with its submerged cemeteries and in later mounds built in or near wet areas, in some cases composed of materials from watery environments such as shellfish or back-swamp clays. Of course, appreciable debate attends whether accumulations of shell of whatever size or shape can be considered monuments (cf. Anderson 2010, 287–289, Claassen 2010, Russo 2010, Sanger 2010a; Sassaman 2005a, 2010a; Vento and Sanger 2010; Marquardt 2010a, 2010b; Milner 2004a; and Saunders 2004). Curiously, while no one argues the point when these accumulations are of earth or stone, when subsistence remains are involved (i.e., shellfish) the matter becomes much more contentious. Some investigators have even questioned whether very complex societies were present at all in the region during the Mid-Holocene, noting that evidence for status differentiation among clearly identifiable social segments is fairly minimal at present, beyond that provided by the architecture itself (Milner 2004a, 2004b; Saunders 2004). These alternative "minimalist" and "exaggerationalist," or perhaps more accurately, "downsizing" and "upsizing," perspectives will likely be the focus of research and debate for some time to come.

Appreciable variability is evident in the location and scale of monumental architecture in the Mid-Holocene in eastern North America, a pattern that continues throughout the Late Holocene. After ca. 3200 cal. BP, during the Woodland and Mississippian periods locally, what are assumed to have been tribal and chiefdom-level societies were present in a number of areas. Monumental architecture occurred in many parts of the region, in the form of causeways, ditches and embankments, enclosures, fortifications, mounds, and plazas, with surviving evidence indicating that earth, earth and shell, and occasionally stone were commonly used (e.g., Mainfort and Sullivan 1998; Anderson and Mainfort 2002; Sassaman and Anderson 2004). Wood, of course, is known to have been used in the Mississippian and early historic periods to create massive structures such as earth lodges, council houses, marker posts, wood henges, and, during earlier times, log tombs and charnel houses/temples, although the full extent of its use in creating monumental architecture prehistorically is unknown (e.g., Knight 2010; Rodning 2010; Pauketat 2004, 2007, 2009). Perhaps the best descriptions of the potential of perishables such as wood, aside from discoveries at submerged sites such as Key Marco (Cushing 1897), are those of historic council houses like the one at Mission San Luis (Shapiro and McEwan 1992) or the description of the Temple of Talomeco encountered by DeSoto in AD 1540 in the province of Cofitachequi (Garcilaso de la Vega in Clayton, Knight, and Moore 1993, II:298–306). This temple, atop an earthen mound, was described as being large with a high and steeply pitched roof of reed and cane and covered with shells, giving it a striking appearance. Inside were carved human figures, numerous chests of human/ancestral bones, river pearls, and other valued objects. Around the main temple building were eight smaller structures filled with weapons, "apparently for its embellishment and service" (Clayton, Knight, and Moore 1993, II:303). While the description may be somewhat fanciful and overdrawn, it indicates that great care and crafting likely went into the perishable structures and other objects that were associated with the more imperishable monuments that survive.

During the Woodland and Mississippian periods, shell accumulations or middens continued to be created in coastal and riverine settings, and while sometimes occurring in shapes suggesting monumental intent, these were typically nowhere near the size and complexity of sites of the preceding Archaic period (e.g., Anderson and Mainfort 2002; Claassen 2010; Peacock 2002; Stephenson, Bense, and Snow 2002). At the end of the Archaic, in the centuries around 3000 cal. BP, centers such as Poverty Point—one of the largest mound and earthwork complexes ever built in the Americas—were abandoned, as were large ring- and U-shaped shell middens in coastal areas, for reasons as of yet incompletely understood, although climate change and sociopolitical upheaval have both been suggested (Anderson 2001, 2010; Gibson 1996, 2000, 2004, 2010; Kidder 2006, 2010, 2011; Kidder and Sassaman 2009, 681–682; Sassaman 2005a, 2010a; Sanger 2010b). During the subsequent Woodland period, comparatively small earthen burial mounds and associated mortuary facilities began to be built in many areas, and collective mortuary ritual rather than public feasting and large-scale monumental construction may have come to serve better to bind people together (Anderson and Mainfort 2002; Clay 1998; Russo 2010, 171–172). From ca. 2200 to 1600 cal. BP, when Middle Woodland Hopewell culture was at its peak, massive mound and earthwork complexes were built in many parts of the Midwest and Southeast (Anderson and Mainfort 2002; Brose and Greber 1979; Smith 1986). Circular, square, and octagonal enclosures and linear causeways and in some cases elaborate variants and combinations thereof were built in several parts of the region, and the largest centers—at places such as Pinson, Tennessee, Marksville, Louisiana, and the Scioto Valley of Ohio—encompassed dozens and in some cases hundreds of acres (DeBoer 1997). Large-scale public ceremony is inferred, and in some cases this was likely associated with elaborate mortuary rituals, with individual or collective burials placed in log-lined tombs or structures within or under mounds (Brose and Greber 1979, Carr and Case 2005; Charles and Buikstra 2006). While the monumentality that occurred has been traditionally subsumed under an umbrella-like construct of Hopewellian interaction and ritual and has been assumed to be similar over large areas, appreciable local variation is evident, as was the case during earlier periods.

Individual status during the Woodland period appears to have been achieved and, as during the Archaic, linked to successful participation in warfare, long-distance exchange, or collective ceremony, including the building of monuments. How monuments were erected, however, has received far less attention than the contents of the structures or burials associated with them, although recent research at sites such as Shiloh and Poverty Point and at Cahokia indicates that their construction was often, from an engineering perspective, a highly sophisticated endeavor, and at least on occasion a ritually highly charged activity (e.g., Kidder 2011; Kidder, Ortmann, and Arco 2008; Kidder et al. 2009; Pauketat 2007, 98–99; Pursell 2004; Sherwood 2006; Sherwood and Kidder 2011). Construction of monuments in all periods likely required appreciable technical as well as leadership skills, and how this was manifest is not well understood, especially in Archaic and Woodland societies where coercive authority was weak or absent. While at some sites and in some areas evidence for hereditary inequality is suggested during the Woodland period in eastern North America and is clearly present in the ensuing Mississippian period, social integration and organization in many areas was much like it was in the preceding Archaic period: fluid and uncomplicated much of the time and becoming more structured only when people came together in larger numbers, such as when they engaged in monumentality.

The centuries prior to the emergence of Mississippian culture, the Late Woodland period from ca. 1600 to 1000 cal. BP, were characterized by a marked decline in monumental construction in most parts of the east save in the Gulf Coast region and the central and lower Mississippi River Valley, where impressive monumentality was ongoing in the Weeden Island and Coles Creek cultures (Anderson 2008; I. Brown 2004; Kidder 2004a; Pauketat 2007, 70–77; Pluckhahn 2003; Rolingson 2002). The construction included platform mounds, which had appeared earlier at a number of Middle Woodland period sites (Anderson 1998; Dickens 1975; Knight 1991, 2001; Lindauer and Blitz 1997), rendering moot assumptions that these mound types were unique to Mississippian culture and monumentality. During the later Woodland the bow and arrow spread rapidly over the region and, concurrently, evidence for fortifications, a form of monumental architecture, increases dramatically. Intensive maize agriculture appears after ca. 1100 cal. BP, and becomes increasingly important in some areas and appears to contribute to an observed growth in regional population (Milner 2004b). About the same time, chiefdoms characterized by hereditary inequality emerged in portions of the central and lower Mississippi valley and spread rapidly over the region, albeit with appreciable local variation and within a span of three to four centuries were found across much of the southeast and lower Midwest (Anderson 1999, 225–227; J. Brown 2004; Pauketat 2007; Smith 1990). The origin and spread of *chiefdom organization* is not, however, the same thing as that of *Mississippian culture*, especially Mississippian ideology, iconography, and religion, including aspects of monumentality such as the construction of sub-pyramidal mounds as platforms for temples and elite residences. There is some evidence that Mississippian culture did not exist until after the emergence of Cahokia as a regional center around AD 1050 (Anderson 1997, 1999; J. Brown 2004; Pauketat and Emerson 1997; Pauketat 2004, 2007). The fact that the most impressive Mississippian society in terms of size and complexity, Cahokia, was also the earliest, meant it would have had a tremendous influence through example (if not outright force) on the behavior of contemporaneous societies. Once formed, the ideas represented and made form at Cahokia would have spread, probably through competitive emulation but also possibly through warfare or the threat if not the actual use of force (i.e., Carneiro 1970, 1981). While the emergence of Cahokia has been called the "Big Bang" by Pauketat for its seemingly sudden and dramatic emergence, in recent years it has been recognized that early Cahokia resulted from a coalescence of peoples from across the surrounding region, with the resulting Mississippian culture and society that emerged different from its constituent parts (Alt 2002, 2006; Pauketat 2004, 2007, 2009).

Approaches to the Study of Mississippian Monumentality

Mounds in Eastern North America have captured the attention of investigators both professional and otherwise for generations, and thousands have been examined over the past two centuries, since Jefferson's day. Indeed, the occurrence of truncated pyramidal or platform mounds about plazas is perhaps the most visible symbol of Mississippian culture to many archaeologists, even though we now know that such platforms appeared far earlier in prehistory in the region. A first step at any site with monumental architecture, accordingly, should be dating the individual features (i.e., mounds, plazas, earthworks, fortifications) and their constituent stages or major construction episodes. This is especially critical in areas in the lower Southeast, where monumental construction dates back thousands of years. Just because a site or mound looks to be later Archaic, Woodland, or Mississippian in age and has artifacts on top of or around it dating to this period doesn't mean that it dates to that time or that earlier components aren't present, buried by subsequent construction or alluvial or other depositional activity (e.g., Arco et al. 2006; Arco and Ortmann 2010; Morse 1986).

Likewise, wherever possible, centers need to be studied as complexes and not in a piecemeal fashion. This is easier said than done, of course, given the high costs of survey and excavation. Nonetheless, any work should consider how the area examined fits into the totality of occupation and use. One way to do this is to conduct careful and comprehensive mapping and remote sensing of as much of a site's extent as possible as a first step in a long-term investigation, as has been done recently at sites such as Etowah, Kincaid, Poverty Point, and Shiloh (e.g., Anderson, Cornelison, and Sherwood 2012; Kidder 2002; Kidder, Ortmann, and Arco 2008; Kidder et al. 2009; King et al. 2011; Lydick 2008). Such information can guide subsequent excavation and interpretation. The arrangement of monuments at large centers, for example, are thought to have represented sociograms, depictions of the social order, spatial representations of kin groups or other subsets of society. Knight has argued that at Moundville, for example, the arrangement of paired mounds about the central plaza represented the residence and mortuary/burial areas of ranked clans (Knight 1998, 2010, 360–364; Steponaitis and Knight 2004, 168). The size and position of specific mounds or other monuments at prehistoric sites, furthermore, may reflect the status or power of the groups building and using them, according to arguments based on social space and space syntax theory (e.g., Grøn 1991; Hillier and Hanson 1984; Hillier 1999; Russo 2004). Such linkages between the built environment—specifically the size and spacing of structures, monuments, and settlements—and social organization may well reflect cultural practices dating back to the earliest mound building in the region during the Mid-Holocene (e.g., Anderson 2002, 2004; Randall 2011; Russo 2004, 2010; Saunders, Allen, and Saucier 1994; Saunders et al. 1997, 2005; Saunders 2004, 2010, this volume; Saunders 1994; Sassaman 2005b, 2010a, 2010b, 2011; Sassaman and Randall this volume).

Focused geoarchaeological research on how site features were constructed is a third direction recent research has taken. The effort that went into the construction of Mississippian site complexes was far greater than the constraints of excavating and moving earth (Pauketat 2007, 98–99; Sherwood 2006; Sherwood and Kidder 2011). As Sherwood and Kidder (2011) have documented, based on careful geoarchaeological analyses at settings such as Shiloh's Mound A, Monks Mound at Cahokia, and the main or "bird" mound at Poverty Point, the labor required to build mounds was often appreciable, involving the careful selection, processing, and placement of special sediments. As such, traditional estimates of the labor required to build such monuments are likely understated in some and perhaps many cases (e.g., Blitz and Livingood 2004; Milner 1998, 144–150; Muller 1997, 273–275; Steponaitis 1978, 446–449). Statements such as "the most important factor influencing the costs of digging and moving earth was the distance over which soil was carried" (Milner 1998, 15) or that "even given differences in tools and enthusiasm, the costs of construction . . . were probably close to 1 person-day per 1.25 m^3" (Muller 1997, 273–274) must be reconsidered, and construction estimates must be derived on a case-by-case or stage-by-stage or even fill-by-fill basis. That is, while ethnohistoric research has shown that the amount of fill that can be excavated using hand labor may be impressive (e.g., Erasmus 1965; Kaplin 1963; Rosenswig and Masson 2002, 224–229; Trigger 1990), these estimates can be considered viable only in certain cases. Where monumentality involved more than simply digging and moving fill—that is, if the processing, mixing, or careful placement of fill was involved—then much more time, effort, and ceremony may have been involved. In the construction of earthen monuments, particularly in the Mississippian period where the use of colored fills is widely documented (e.g., Pursell 2004), sometimes all of these circumstances may have applied. As Tim Pauketat (2007, 98) has observed, "Building an earthen pyramid was about much more than digging, carrying, and dumping dirt" (see also Sherwood and Kidder 2011). Actualistic experiments—that is, time-task studies of the effort involved to acquire fill or construct a segment of a ditch or palisade—may help yield more accurate estimates for construction (e.g., Blitz 1993, 121–123; Coles 1973).

But the effort involved in the construction of earthen mounds from one site to the next cannot be assumed to be a fixed relationship between time and manpower in the absence of excavations to document construction practices. At Shiloh, for example, as Sherwood's (2006) careful and exquisitely documented geoarchaeological research at Mound A has demonstrated, while great care went into the selection of fills used in some of the mound stages, in other stages it is clear that general midden from nearby areas was used (Sherwood 2006; Sherwood and Kidder 2011; the excavations at Mound A are fully documented in Anderson, Cornelison, and Sherwood 2012). A small mound elaborately constructed, such as the Stage III mound at Shiloh with its carefully selected, processed, and layered colored fills, likely took far more labor to erect than a much larger mound of nearby midden such as large portions of the upper two stages of Mound A Shiloh (Anderson, Cornelison, and Sherwood 2011; Sherwood 2006). Focused geoarchaeological research can also reveal details of fill preparation and construction, such as the removal of organic matter or the mixing of differing sediments, the use of sod blocks or embankments to contain fills, or how thin colored fills or veneers were laid down (Sherwood 2006; Sherwood and Kidder 2012). Examinations of the weathering or lack thereof of mound fill, particularly exposed surface sediments, can, furthermore,

Figure 4.2. Traditional interpretation of mounds as green and covered with cropped grass, as seen at Cahokia. (Painting by L. K. Townsend, courtesy Cahokia Mounds State Historic Site.)

give an idea of how long the construction process may have taken. At Poverty Point, for example, such evidence has been used to argue for a rapid construction of portions of the primary mound (Kidder 2011; Kidder, Ortmann, and Arco 2008; Kidder et al. 2009). The maintenance of mounds, particularly to deal with weathering and erosion, were likely as major a concern and perhaps required as much effort as the initial construction (Pauketat 2007, 98–99; Sherwood and Kidder 2011).

This is particularly likely given recent indications that our traditional perspective on the appearance of Mississippian mounds, and indeed of many earthen monuments, at least those that were used regularly, is likely incorrect. As John Cornelison and I noted in our 2002 report on the fieldwork on the main mound at Shiloh:

> Perhaps the most important finding from our fieldwork is that Mound A was dramatically different in appearance when it was in use than it looks at present, and that even when in use its appearance changed somewhat from stage to stage. During the Mississippian era, a series of large buildings were located at the base of the mound, that probably represent associated ceremonial structures, storage areas, temples,

and possibly the residences of lesser elites. The mound itself was colored with red, gray, white, and yellowish orange surfaces and possibly bands, and interior filling episodes made use of similar bright colors. Large and elaborate structures were apparently built on the summit, and a raised platform with a bright red surface was present atop one stage, like a smaller mound atop a larger one. There is some evidence to suggest large areas of the summit were fired, perhaps to help stabilize the surface or accentuate the firing colors. Structures atop the mound were likely elaborately decorated, based on descriptions of what they looked like from early historic accounts (e.g., Garcilaso de la Vega in Clayton, Knight, and Moore 1993, 298–304). The mound would have been a dramatic feature when viewed by visitors, or from a distance, as from the river below.

The traditional way Mound A at Shiloh, and indeed perhaps many Mississippian mounds are interpreted in park exhibits, paintings, and archaeological writings, as green, cropped grass covered earthen masses, with simple thatched buildings on top, and few if any structures near the base is probably dead wrong. Mississippian ceremonial centers were instead, we believe, appreciably more dramatic and impressive cultural landscapes than we have given them credit for and portrayed to date. While we shouldn't accept such a perspective uncritically, we need to think about it, and test its possibility at the sites we explore (Anderson and Cornelison 2002, 51–52).

When I read essentially these same paragraphs at the 2002 meeting of the Southeastern Archaeological Conference, they were accompanied by two images, the first showing L. K. Townsend's classic painting of the Cahokia mounds as green and covered with cropped grass (Figure 4.2), and the second showing the same painting with the caption "The way the mounds may have actually looked" showing them colored either all red or banded red, gray, and white (see http://anderson.pidba.org/figures.html). I will never forget the audible gasp throughout the hall when the second image went up. Paul Welch (2006), who at the time had worked for several years synthesizing earlier work at the site with my assistant Emily Yates, helped produce versions of the images depicting the colored mounds, and he and I helped guide interpretive paintings subsequently produced for the site. We know that pyramids in Mesoamerica were often elaborately colored, so that the same should be true in the Southeast, at least on occasion, is not altogether surprising. Likewise, while stone sickles could have kept vegetation down on the sides and tops of mounds, clay surfaces would have likely been equally if not more resistant to both vegetation and erosion. Besides being more colorful if carefully maintained, they would have been difficult to climb, especially when wet, when they were slippery and treacherous, as anyone working at Shiloh from 2001 to 2004 can attest from personal experience. Since weed whackers and lawnmowers, the tools park personnel across the region use to maintain these sites, were unknown to Mississippian and earlier peoples, most traditional depictions of them as covered in short green grass are in need of rethinking (Pauketat 2007, 98–99). Recent paintings of life at Shiloh correct this deficiency, it should be noted, although how accurate they are will require far more fieldwork.

Cosmological considerations as well as the perhaps more mundane aspects of life, such as the maintenance of cultural identity, can also be considered when examining monuments. Knight (1986, 678) has argued that southeastern Mississippian mounds were receptacles of the sacred that had

> deeply rooted and expressive symbolic significance, related to the ubiquity of multi-stage episodes of destruction and construction. ... Periodic rebuilding of the mound surfaces by the addition of a new blanket mantle of earth, the special characteristic of these mounds, demands to be seen as a purely expressive act . . . arguably an act of

burial, a mortuary rite for the mound itself rather than for any individual, sometimes complete with funereal furnishings placed upon the old surface (Schnell, Knight, and Schnell 1981, 133–134). . . . The symbolism of the earthen platform is that of an icon representative of earth, manipulated by periodic burial as a temporary means of achieving purification in the context of a communal rite of intensification.

Knight (1986, 678–679) further argued that linguistic and ethnohistoric evidence, specifically terminology used among Muskogean and Choctaw peoples to describe mounds as well the rituals associated with their construction and use, indicated that their symbolic importance was tied as much to their building and maintenance as to their finished appearance. The truncated pyramid shape of platform mounds in particular, Knight suggested, was related to the quartering of the cosmos, reflected in some cases by mound orientations aligned to cardinal directions (Knight 1986, 679). A similar pattern is widespread in Mississippian art and iconography (e.g., Lankford 2004). The regular gathering together of people in the collective ceremony and ritual associated with mound construction was thus, at least to some southeastern peoples, deeply important activity, as much about reinforcing belief systems and the creation and maintenance of cosmological principles and individual and group identity as it was about the production of a final monument. Likewise, the fact that monumentality occurred so widely and in societies of such varying levels complexity suggests that it was not primarily or exclusively about maintaining power relationships, although these may well have been a consideration in labor mobilization, given evidence for the suppression of monumentality at outlying sites in some cases (i.e., Steponaitis 1978; Blitz 1993, 50, 58). Given that monumentalization continued at many Mississippian sites, no "final" product was likely envisioned. Because of this, greater effort should be directed to how monuments were built than to the objects found in or on them.

When considering the process of monumentalization, it is as important to emphasize open and empty areas within sites, particularly plazas, as well as the features that demarcate them and the community as a whole, such as embankments or ditch and palisade lines. At many sites in eastern North America, as exemplified by fieldwork at Cahokia, Poverty Point, and Shiloh, great labor apparently went into construction of the plazas, with appreciable cutting and filling to create the surface appearance and characteristics desired, sometimes covering over substantial features created by earlier occupants (Anderson, Cornelison, and Sherwood 2012; Holley, Dalan, and

Smith 1993; Kidder 2001, 2004b; Pauketat et al. 2002; Pauketat 2007, 93–96; Stout and Lewis 1998, 235). As Pauketat (2007, 93) has argued, "The central plazas, not the encircling mounds, were the anchoring features of these central built landscapes" (Dalan et al. 2003; Holley 1999, 24). Likewise, palisades at such sites, while not traditionally thought of in this fashion, required great labor investment, comparable to that put into mounds and plazas themselves. In addition to serving as defensive works, they served to delimit monumental compounds (e.g., Milner 1998, 147–148; Pauketat 2007, 99–101). Within Mississippian centers there may be features related to monumentality, such as borrow pits, whose extent and contents should be determined. Sometimes the exploration of these features can yield unexpected results. At Shiloh, for example, a roughly 9,000-year pollen record, with particularly fine-grained temporal resolution during the period the center was occupied, was found in a pond just off the plaza a few meters from a small mound (Meeks 2006). Assumed to be a water-filled borrow pit, it instead turned out to have been a permanent water source within the palisaded center. Its sediments provided a record of climax forest clearance and reemergence, signaling the initial occupation, use, and abandonment of the center over the interval from ca. AD 900 to 1350.

It is likely that both cultural and environmental factors shaped the extent of Mississippian monumentality, and consideration of the latter is important, especially for societies dependent upon the production of agricultural surpluses for their continued well-being. The emergence of Mississippian culture occurs during the Medieval Warm Period from ca. AD 800 to 1300, a period thought to have been highly favorable to agricultural food production in the southeast (Anderson 2001, 166; Broecker 2001; Crowley 2000; DeMenocal et al. 2000; Hughes and Diaz 1994). When the climate was favorable for surplus mobilization or redistribution, monumentality was likely more feasible; indeed, the very existence of social complexity, including among Mississippian societies, was apparently tied, at least in part, to climatic conditions, as demonstrated in several areas in the Southeast and lower Midwest, such as at Cahokia and along the Chattahoochee, Tennessee, and Savannah Rivers (e.g., Anderson 1994, 274–289, 2001, 165–166; Anderson, Stahle, and Cleaveland 1995; Benson, Pauketat, and Cook 2009; Blitz and Lorenz 2006, 131–135; Nolan and Cook 2010). Indeed, during the first three centuries of the Mississippian era, from AD 1000 to 1300, far more monumental architecture appears to have been created across the region than during the centuries that followed (e.g., Anderson 1994, 136–137; Payne 1994), although the effects of contact after 1500 likely played a major role, through disease-related depopulation. After AD 1100 and particularly a century or two later, following the onset of the Little Ice Age, there is evidence for increased warfare and fortification, particularly in the northern part of the region, together with greater settlement nucleation in some areas or dispersal away from major transportation arteries in others and a decrease in long-distance exchange and monumental construction (Anderson 1994, 136–137; Fagan 2000; Griffin 1961, 711–713; Milner 1999, 123–126). While fortifications appear to occur with roughly similar incidence throughout the Mississippian area (Milner 1999, 123), they increase in the northern part of eastern North America after ca. AD 1300, when agriculture would have been more difficult.

Finally, it is critical to examine how often or regular the practices of monumentality were that occurred at centers. Just as mound-building traditions varied over time and over space in eastern North America (e.g., Sassaman 2010b), so too did the tempo of mound building and use change, with "very different timing or rhythms of creation" in differing areas (Thompson 2010, 219). Examination of the number and duration of stages in Mississippian mounds has received appreciable attention in recent years (e.g., Anderson 1994, 126–129; Blitz and Livingood 2004; Hally 1993, 145; Hally 1995). Major episodes of stage construction appear to have occurred about every 25 to 50 years (e.g., Blitz and Livingood 2004, 296–297; Hally 1995, 112), and while variously inferred to reflect instances of chiefly succession or alternatively or concurrently purification and earth fertility/renewal ceremonies (e.g., Anderson 1994, 126–129; Knight 1986), they clearly were not common events. Instead, their infrequency meant that when they occurred, they were likely the focus of appreciable societal energy. These same studies, furthermore, indicate that most Mississippian societies characterized by mound building lasted from less than a century to perhaps twice this duration (Hally 1995, 124; Blitz and Livingood 2004, 296) and that "rules" about mound construction, inferred from relationships between mound volume, duration, and number of construction stages, while similar for most sites, were decidedly different at the largest centers. At the largest centers these relationship were much less direct, in part because mound volumes were so much larger and the number of stages was typically greater (Blitz and Livingood 2004, 298–299).

Monumentality thus played out somewhat differently in individual Mississippian societies, and while some commonalities may have existed, each case must be examined separately. Inspection of Mississippian site plans indicate that no ideal size or layout existed, however often certain elements appeared (e.g., Holley 1999; Lewis, Stout, and Wesson 1998; Pauketat 2007, 87–106). In areas where there has been more fieldwork, estimates of site hierarchies and polity duration based on the number and size or volume of mounds or other monuments are likely to be much more accurate than such estimates in areas where less work has occurred. Political geography, the location of centers on the landscape, and the relationship of centers to each other, accordingly, must also be considered. Some major polities appear to have deliberately suppressed the construction efforts and hence presumably the religious and political behavior of their smaller neighbors. At the centers around Moundville, mounds were reduced in size and number, and fortifications may not have been tolerated, although mound size does appear to have increased with distance from the center (Blitz 1993; Steponaitis 1978, 444–449). Even when abandoned or depopulated, as for example when centers of power moved elsewhere, some sites likely maintained an "aura of grandeur and power long after they ceased to function as administrative centers" (Hally 1995, 119). The site of Moundville, for example, went from a densely populated center around ca. AD 1200 to 1300 to a nearly deserted "vacant" ceremonial center/necropolis during the period ca. 1300 to AD 1400 (Knight and Steponaitis 1998; Knight 2010, 361–363). The site of Etowah was still occupied centuries after mound building ceased and political power had moved north to the Little Egypt site, the presumed capital of the Coosa paramountcy (Smith 2000, 32) The later population at Etowah was only a fraction of that formerly present, living literally in the shadow of and not atop the massive mounds (King 2003, 81–83). Macon Plateau and Shiloh were vibrant centers that were abandoned after ca. AD 1150 and 1300, respectively, and were not used again for centuries in the case of the former or ever again in the case of Shiloh, save perhaps for occasional visits by historic Indian war or hunting parties in the latter case (Hally 1995, 119–120; Welch 2006, 263). The decline or abandonment history of Mississippian centers, as numerous examples from across the region indicate, was highly varied. The fact that centers once abandoned were not inevitably or invariably reoccupied suggests that the production of the monuments was closely tied to the people who made them and that once the people left, such locations no longer held their former importance and were perhaps considered places as much to be avoided as reused. The lack of evidence for the regular or routine co-optation of former places of power by subsequent elites, in fact, suggests that group identify was closely linked to home communities and that finished architecture by itself did not symbolize that identity. The process of monumentalization, and not just the finished monument, was what was important.

Conclusions

While common themes are evident, particularly an arrangement of people, dwellings, or monuments around open areas or plazas, it is clear that variation characterizes the long tradition of monumentality in eastern North America. While no constant and exacting architectural grammar existed over the course of prehistory that dictated precisely the forms that were created, there is also no doubt that later inhabitants were well aware of the constructions of those who came before them, which occurred widely and obviously upon the landscape. Mississippian monumentality is not, I would thus argue, "clearly distinguishable from that of societies in other times and places" (Lewis, Stout, and Wesson 1998, 5). It is neither unique nor appreciably different in scale from much of what came before it, even if the peoples engaged in it used differently designed or tempered pottery or favored earth instead of shell, used different iconography, or were ranked instead of more egalitarian in nature. Instead, peoples in many areas continued to follow a pattern established thousands of years previously during the Archaic, if not earlier: the periodic and typically brief aggregation of people who in many cases were dispersed over the landscape much of the time in small household or village groupings (Anderson 2002, 268–269; Blitz 1993, 123–125). When they came together, these peoples engaged in a range of activities that varied from society to society but likely included such things as communal ceremony, ritual, and monumental construction; elaborate mortuary behavior; promotion or differentiation of group identities; buffering of subsistence or other resource uncertainties; and aggrandizing behavior on the part of certain individuals or groups. In their monumentality these people were writing their history on the landscape and continually creating and reaffirming their identity, and while the monuments that remain may be the most archaeologically visible aspect of their existence, it was only a part of a much larger picture.

Acknowledgments

The preparation of this essay came about through the invitation (and subsequent patience) of Robert M. Rosenswig (Rob). Watching this volume come to fruition from its original 2006 Society for American Archaeology session, where as a member of the audience and as then editor of the SAA Press I asked him to consider publishing it, has been very satisfying. Of course, at the time I had no idea I might be a part of the endeavor. I thank Rob and his co-editor Richard L. Burger for advice and assistance in the preparation of this chapter. Other scholars whose work or ideas inspired or contributed to the thinking herein include Thaddeus G. Bissett, John E. Clark, T. R. Kidder, Timothy R. Pauketat, Kenneth E. Sassaman, and Gerald Schroedl. Above all, I wish to thank my colleagues John E. Cornelison Jr. and Sarah C. Sherwood, co-directors of the excavations at Shiloh Mound A, for their help in thinking about Mississippian monumentality. Sarah's geoarchaeological investigations at the site did much to help us understand the remarkable deposits we were encountering, and her work on the subject should be required reading for anyone exploring earthen architecture. I thank William R. Iseminger and Mark Esarey at Cahokia Mounds State Historic Site for permission to use the painting of Cahokia mounds depicted in Figure 4.2. Finally, Erik Johanson at the University of Tennessee and Emily Yates, my assistant at the National Park Service's Southeast Archeological Center at the time of the Shiloh project, are to be thanked for help with the graphics. Emily, in fact, produced the original version of the colored mounds at Cahokia originally presented at the 2002 Southeastern Archaeological Conference meetings, which can be seen at my faculty website at http://anderson.pidba.org/figures.html.

References Cited

Alt, Susan
2002 Identities, Traditions and Diversity in Cahokia's Uplands. *Midcontinental Journal of Archaeology* 27:217–236.
2006 The Power of Diversity: The Roles of Migration and Hybridity in Culture Change. In *Leadership and Polity in Mississippian Society*, edited by Brian M. Butler and Paul D. Welch, pp. 289–308. Center for Archaeological Investigations Occasional Paper No. 33, Southern Illinois University Carbondale.

Anderson, David G.
1994 *The Savannah River Chiefdoms: Political Change in the Late Prehistoric Southeast.* University of Alabama Press, Tuscaloosa.
1997 The Role of Cahokia in the Evolution of Mississippian Society. In *Cahokia: Domination and Ideology in the Mississippian World*, edited by Timothy R. Pauketat and Thomas E. Emerson, pp. 248–268. University of Nebraska Press, Lincoln.
1998 Swift Creek in a Regional Perspective. In *A World Engraved: Archaeology of the*

Swift Creek Culture, edited by J. Mark Williams and Daniel T. Elliott, pp. 274–300. University of Alabama Press, Tuscaloosa.

1999 Examining Chiefdoms in the Southeast: An Application of Multiscalar Analysis. In *Great Towns and Regional Polities in the Prehistoric American Southwest and Southeast,* edited by Jill E. Neitzel, pp. 215–241. Amerind Foundation New World Study Series 3. University of New Mexico Press, Albuquerque.

2001 Climate and Culture Change in Prehistoric and Early Historic Eastern North America. *Archaeology of Eastern North America* 29:143–186.

2002 Evolution of Tribal Social Organization in the Southeast. In *The Archaeology of Tribal Societies,* edited by William A. Parkinson, pp. 246–277. International Monographs in Prehistory, Ann Arbor.

2004 Archaic Mounds and the Archaeology of Southeastern Tribal Societies. In *Signs of Power: The Rise of Cultural Complexity in the Southeast,* edited by Jon L. Gibson and Philip J. Carr, pp. 270–299. University of Alabama Press, Tuscaloosa.

2008 The Toltec Mounds Site in Southeastern Prehistory: Inferences from Early Collections. *The Arkansas Archeologist* 47:9–30.

2009 Caminos hacia el poder en el Sureste prehistórico de Norteamérica [Pathways to power in Southeastern North America]. In *Procesos y expresiones de poder, identidad y orden tempranos en Sudamérica,* segunda parte, edited by Peter Kaulicke and Tom D. Dillehay, *Boletín de Arqueología PUCP* 11: 205–232. ,

2010 The End of the Southeastern Archaic: Regional Interaction and Archaeological Interpretation. In *Trend, Tradition, and Turmoil: What Happened to the Southeastern Archaic? Proceedings of the Third Caldwell Conference, St. Catherines Island, Georgia, May 9–11, 2008,* edited by David Hurst Thomas and Matthew C. Sanger, pp. 273–302. Anthropological Papers of the American Museum of Natural History, New York.

Anderson, David G., and John E. Cornelison Jr.
2002 Excavations at Mound A, Shiloh: The 2002 Season. Paper presented at the 59th Annual Meeting of the Southeastern Archaeological Conference, Biloxi, Mississippi. Manuscript on file, Southeast Archeological Center, National Park Service, Tallahassee, Florida.

Anderson, David G., and Robert C. Mainfort Jr. (editors)
2002 *Woodland Archaeology in the Southeast.* University of Alabama Press, Tuscaloosa.

Anderson, David G., and Kenneth E. Sassaman
2004 Early and Middle Holocene Periods, 9500–3750 B.C. In *Southeast,* vol. 14 of *Smithsonian Handbook of North American Indians,* edited by Raymond D. Fogelson, pp. 87–100. Smithsonian Institution, Washington, D.C.

Anderson, David G., David W. Stahle, and Malcolm R. Cleaveland
1995 Paleoclimate and the Potential Food Reserves of Mississippian Societies: A Case Study from the Savannah River Valley. *American Antiquity* 60:258–286.

Anderson, David G., Michael Russo, and Kenneth Sassaman
2007 Mid-Holocene Cultural Dynamics in Southeastern North America. In *Climate Change and Cultural Dynamics: A Global Perspective on Mid-Holocene Transitions,* edited by David G. Anderson, Kirk A. Maasch, and Daniel H. Sandweiss, pp. 457–489. Academic Press, Amsterdam.

Anderson, David G., John E. Cornelison, and Sarah C. Sherwood
2012 Archeological Investigations at Shiloh Indian Mounds National Historic Landmark (40HR7) 1999–2004. Manuscript on file, Southeast Archeological Center, National Park Service, Tallahassee, Florida.

Arco, Lee J., and Anthony L. Ortmann
2010 Jaketown's Buried Landscape: Recent Research at a Poverty Point Settlement in the Yazoo Basin, Mississippi. Paper presented at the 75th Annual Meeting of the Society for American Archaeology, St. Louis, Missouri.

Arco, Lee J., Katie A. Adelsberger, Ling-yu Hung, and Tristram R. Kidder
2006 Alluvial Geoarchaeology of a Middle Archaic Mound Complex in the Lower Mississippi Valley, U.S.A. *Geoarchaeology* 21(6):591–614.

Benson, Larry V., Timothy R. Pauketat, and Edward R. Cook
2009 Cahokia's Boom and Bust in the Context of Climate Change. *American Antiquity* 74:467–483.

Blitz, John H.
1993 *Ancient Chiefdoms of the Tombigbee*. University of Alabama Press, Tuscaloosa.
1999 Mississippian Chiefdoms and the Fission: Fusion Process. *American Antiquity* 64:577–592.

Blitz, John H., and Patrick Livingood
2004 Sociopolitical Implications of Mississippian Mound Volume. *American Antiquity* 69(2):291–301.

Blitz, John H., and Karl G. Lorenz
2006 *The Chattahoochee Chiefdoms*. University of Alabama Press, Tuscaloosa.

Broecker, Wallace S.
2001 Was the Medieval Warm Period Global? *Science* 291:1497–1499.

Brose, David S., and N'omi Greber (editors)
1979 *Hopewell Archaeology: The Chillicothe Conference*. Kent State University Press, Kent, Ohio.

Brown, Ian W.
2004 Prehistory of the Gulf Coastal Plain after 500 B.C. In *Southeast*, vol. 14 of *Smithsonian Handbook of North American Indians*, edited by Raymond D. Fogelson, pp. 574–585. Smithsonian Institution, Washington, D.C.

Brown, James A.
2004 The Cahokia Expansion: Creating Court and Cult. In *The Hero, Hawk, and the Open Hand: American Indian Art of the Ancient Midwest and South*, edited by R. Townsend and R. Sharp, pp. 108–127. Art Institute of Chicago, Chicago, Illinois.

Carneiro, Robert L.
1970 A Theory of the Origin of the State. *Science* 169:733–739.
1981 The Chiefdom: Precursor of the State. In *The Transition to Statehood in the New World*, edited by Grant D. Jones and Robert R. Kautz, pp. 37–79. Cambridge University Press, Cambridge.

Carr, Christopher, and D. Troy Case (editors)
2005 *Gathering Hopewell Society, Ritual, and Ritual Interaction*. Kluwer Academic/Plenum Publishers, New York.

Charles, Douglas K., and Jane E. Buikstra
2006   *Recreating Hopewell.* University Press of Florida, Gainesville.
Claassen, Cheryl P.
1996   A Consideration of the Social Organization of the Shell Mound Archaic. In *Archaeology of the Mid-Holocene Southeast,* edited by Kenneth E. Sassaman and David G. Anderson, pp. 235–258. University Press of Florida, Gainesville.
2010   *Feasting with Shellfish in the Southern Ohio Valley.* University of Tennessee Press, Knoxville.
Clark, John E.
2004   Surrounding the Sacred: Geometry and Design of Early Mound Groups as Meaning and Function. In *Signs of Power: The Rise of Cultural Complexity in the Southeast,* edited by Jon L. Gibson and Philip J. Carr, pp. 162–213. University of Alabama Press, Tuscaloosa.
Clay, R. Berle
1998   The Essential Features of Adena Ritual and Their Implications. *Southeastern Archaeology* 17:1–21.
Clayton, Lawrence A., Vernon James Knight Jr., and Edward C. Moore (editors)
1993   *The De Soto Chronicles: The Expedition of Hernando de Soto to North America in 1539–1543.* 2 vols. University of Alabama Press, Tuscaloosa.
Coles, John
1973   *Archaeology by Experiment.* Charles Scribner's Sons, New York.
Crowley, Thomas J.
2000   Causes of Climate Change over the Past 1000 Years. *Science* 289:270–277.
Cushing, Frank Hamilton
1897   Exploration of Ancient Key-Dweller Remains on the Gulf Coast of Florida. *Proceedings of the American Philosophical Society* 25(153):329–448.
Dalan, Rinita A., George R. Holley, William I. Woods, Harold W. Watters Jr., and John A. Koepke
2003   *Envisioning Cahokia: A Landscape Perspective.* Northern Illinois Press, DeKalb.
DeBoer, Warren R.
1997   Ceremonial Centers from Cayapas (Esmeraldas, Ecuador), to Chillicothe (Ohio, USA). *Cambridge Archaeological Journal* 7:225–253.
DeMenocal, Peter, Joseph Ortiz, Tom Guilderson, and Michael Sarnthein
2000   Coherent High- and Low-Latitude Climate Variability During the Holocene Warm Period. *Science* 288:2198–2202.
Dickens, Roy S.
1975   A Processual Approach to Mississippian Origins on the Georgia Piedmont. *Southeastern Archaeological Conference Bulletin* 18:31–42.
Doran, Glen H. (editor)
2002   *Windover: Multidisciplinary Investigations of an Early Archaic Florida Cemetery.* University Press of Florida, Gainesville.
Dye, David H.
1996   Initial Riverine Adaptation in the Midsouth: An Examination of Three Middle Holocene Shell Middens. In *Of Caves and Shell Mounds,* edited by Kenneth C.

Carstens and Patty Jo Watson, pp. 140–158. University of Alabama Press, Tuscaloosa.

Erasmus, Charles J.
1965   Monument Building: Some Field Experiments. *Southwestern Journal of Anthropology* 21:277–301.

Fagan, Brian
2000   *The Little Ice Age: How Climate Made History 1300–1850*. Basic Books, New York.

Gibson, Jon L.
1996   Poverty Point and Greater Southeastern Prehistory: The Culture that Did Not Fit. In *Archaeology of the Mid-Holocene Southeast*, edited by Kenneth E. Sassaman and David G. Anderson, pp. 288–305. University Press of Florida, Gainesville.
2000   *The Ancient Mounds of Poverty Point Place of Rings*. University Press of Florida, Gainesville, Florida.
2004   The Power of Beneficent Obligation in First Mound-Building Societies. In *Signs of Power: The Rise of Cultural Complexity in the Southeast*, edited by Jon L. Gibson and Philip J. Carr, pp. 254–269. University of Alabama Press, Tuscaloosa.
2010   "Nothing But the River's Flood": Late Archaic Diaspora or Disengagement in the Lower Mississippi Valley and Southeastern North America. In *Trend, Tradition, and Turmoil: What Happened to the Southeastern Archaic? Proceedings of the Third Caldwell Conference, St. Catherines Island, Georgia, May 9–11, 2008*, edited by David Hurst Thomas and Matthew C. Sanger, pp. 33–42. Anthropological Papers of the American Museum of Natural History, New York.

Griffin, James B.
1961   Some Correlations of Climatic and Cultural Change in Eastern North American Prehistory. *Annals of the New York Academy of Sciences* 95:710–717.
1967   Eastern North American Archaeology: A Summary. *Science* 156:175–191.
1985   Changing Concepts of the Prehistoric Mississippian Cultures of the Eastern United States. In *Alabama and the Borderlands: From Prehistory to Statehood*, edited by R. Reid Badger and Lawrence A. Clayton, pp. 40–63. University of Alabama Press, Tuscaloosa.

Grøn, Ole
1991   A Method for Reconstruction of Social Organization in Prehistoric Societies and Examples of Practical Application. In *Social Space Human Spatial Behavior in Dwellings and Settlements*, edited by Ole Grøn, Ericka Engelsted, and Inge Lindblom, pp. 100–117. Odense University Press, Odense, Denmark.

Hally, David J.
1993   The Territorial Size of Mississippian Chiefdoms. In *Archaeology of Eastern North America, Papers in Honor of Stephen Williams*, edited by James B. Stoltman, pp. 143–168. Archaeological Report No. 25. Mississippi Department of Archives and History, Jackson.
1995   199 Platform Mound Construction and the Political Stability of Mississippian Chiefdoms. In *Political Structure and Change in the Prehistoric Southeastern United States*, edited by John F. Scarry, pp. 92–127. University Press of Florida, Gainesville.

Hillier, Bill
1999   *Space Is the Machine: A Configurational Theory of Architecture.* Cambridge University Press, Cambridge.
Hillier, Bill, and Julienne Hanson
1984   *The Social Logic of Space.* Cambridge University Press, Cambridge.
Holley, George R.
1999   Late Prehistoric Towns in the Southeast. In *Great Towns and Regional Polities in the Prehistoric American Southwest and Southeast,* edited by Jill E. Neitzel, pp. 22–38. Amerind Foundation New World Study Series 3. University of New Mexico Press, Albuquerque, New Mexico.
Holley, George R., Rinita A. Dalan, and Phillip A. Smith
1993   Investigations in the Cahokia Site Grand Plaza. *American Antiquity* 58:306–319.
Hughes, M. K., and H. F. Diaz
1994   Was There a "Medieval Warm Period" and If So, When and Where? *Climatic Change* 26:109–142.
Kaplin, David
1963   Men, Monuments, and Political Systems. *Southwestern Journal of Anthropology* 19:397–410.
Kidder, Tristram R.
2001   Mapping Poverty Point. *American Antiquity* 67:89–101.
2002   Woodland Period Archaeology of the Lower Mississippi Valley. In *The Woodland Southeast,* edited by David G. Anderson and Robert C. Mainfort Jr., pp. 66–90. University of Alabama Press, Tuscaloosa.
2004a Prehistory of the Lower Mississippi Valley after 500 B.C. In *Southeast,* vol. 14 of *Smithsonian Handbook of North American Indians,* edited by Raymond D. Fogelson, pp. 545–559. Smithsonian Institution, Washington, D.C.
2004b Plazas as Architecture: An Example from the Raffman Site, Northeast Louisiana. *American Antiquity* 69:514–532.
2006   Climate Change and the Archaic to Woodland Transition (3000–2500 cal B.P.) in the Mississippi River Basin. *American Antiquity* 71:195–231.
2010   Trend and Tradition at the End of the Late Archaic. In *Trend, Tradition, and Turmoil: What Happened to the Southeastern Archaic? Proceedings of the Third Caldwell Conference, St. Catherines Island, Georgia, May 9–11, 2008,* edited by David Hurst Thomas and Matthew C. Sanger, pp. 23–32. Anthropological Papers of the American Museum of Natural History, New York.
2011   Transforming Hunter-Gatherer History at Poverty Point. In *Hunter-Gatherer Archaeology as Historical Process,* edited by Kenneth E. Sassaman and Donald H. Holley Jr., pp. 95–119. University of Arizona Press, Tucson.
Kidder, Tristram R., and Kenneth E. Sassaman
2009   The View from the Southeast. In *Archaic Societies: Diversity and Complexity Across the Midcontinent,* edited by Thomas E. Emerson, Dale L. McElrath, and Andrew C. Fortier, pp. 667–694. University of Nebraska Press, Lincoln.
Kidder, Tristram R., Anthony L. Ortmann, and Lee J. Arco
2008   Poverty Point and the Archaeology of Singularity. *The SAA Archaeological Record* 8(5):9–12.

Kidder, Tristram R., Lee J. Arco, Anthony L. Ortmann, Timothy M. Schilling, C. Boeke, R. Bielitz, and Katie A. Adelsberger,
2009   *Poverty Point Mound A: Final Report of the 2005 and 2006 Field Seasons*. Louisiana Division of Archaeology and the Louisiana Archaeological Survey and Antiquities Commission, Baton Rouge.

King, Adam
2003   *Etowah: The Political History of a Chiefdom Capital*. University of Alabama Press, Tuscaloosa.

King, Adam, Chester P. Walker, F. Kent Reilly III, Robert V. Sharp, and Duncan P. McKinnon
2011   Remote Sensing from Etowah's Mound A: Architecture and the Re-Creation of Mississippian Tradition. *American Antiquity* 76:355–371.

Knight, Vernon James, Jr.
1986   The Institutional Organization of Mississippian Religion. *American Antiquity* 51(4):675–687.
1991   *Excavation of the Truncated Mound at the Walling Site: Middle Woodland Culture and Copena in the Tennessee Valley*. Alabama State Museum of Natural History Report of Investigations 56. University of Alabama, Tuscaloosa.
1998   Moundville as a Diagrammatic Ceremonial Center. In *Archaeology of the Moundville Chiefdom*, edited by Vernon J. Knight and Vincas P. Steponaitis, pp. 44–62. Smithsonian Institution Press, Washington, D.C.
2001   Feasting and the Emergence of Platform Mound Ceremonialism in Eastern North America. In *Feasts: Archaeological and Ethnographic Perspectives on Food, Politics, and Power*, edited by Michael Dietler and Brian Hayden, pp. 311–333. Smithsonian Institution Press, Washington, D.C.2010 *Mound Excavations at Moundville Architecture, Elites and Social Order*. University of Alabama Press, Tuscaloosa.
2010   *Mound Excavations at Moundville: Architecture, Elites and Social Order*. University of Alabama Press, Tuscaloosa.

Knight, Vernon James, Jr., and Vincas P. Steponaitis
1998   A New History of Moundville. In *Archaeology of the Moundville Chiefdom*, edited by Vernon J. Knight and Vincas P. Steponaitis, pp. 1–25. Smithsonian Institution Press, Washington, D.C.

Lankford, George E.
2004   World on a String: Some Cosmological Components of the Southeastern Ceremonial Complex. In *Hero, Hawk, and Open Hand: American Indian Art of the Ancient Midwest and South*, edited by Richard F. Townsend and Robert V. Sharp, pp. 207–217. The Art Institute of Chicago and Yale University Press, New Haven, Connecticut.

Lewis, R. Berry, Charles Stout, and Cameron B. Wesson
1998   The Design of Mississippian Towns. In *Mississippian Towns and Sacred Spaces: Searching for an Architectural Grammar*, edited by Berry R. Lewis and Charles Stout, pp. 1–21. University of Alabama Press, Tuscaloosa.

Lindauer, Owen, and John H. Blitz
1997   Higher Ground: The Archaeology of North American Platform Mounds. *Journal of Archaeological Research* 5:169–207.

Lydick, Christopher M.
2008   Sensor Fusion: Integrated Remote Sensing Surveys at Shiloh Mounds National Historic Landmark, Shiloh, Tennessee. Master's thesis, Department of Anthropology, Florida State University, Tallahassee.

Mainfort, Robert C., Jr., and Lynne P. Sullivan (editors)
1998   *Ancient Earthen Enclosures of the Eastern Woodlands.* University Press of Florida, Gainesville.

Marquardt, William H.
2010a Shell Mounds in the Southeast: Middens, Monuments, Temple Mounds, Rings, or Works? *American Antiquity* 75(3):551–570.
2010b Mounds, Middens, and Rapid Climate Change during the Archaic-Woodland Transition in the Southeastern United States. In *Trend, Tradition, and Turmoil: What Happened to the Southeastern Archaic? Proceedings of the Third Caldwell Conference, St. Catherines Island, Georgia, May 9–11, 2008,* edited by David Hurst Thomas and Matthew C. Sanger, pp. 253–271. Anthropological Papers of the American Museum of Natural History, New York.

Marquardt, William H., and Patty Jo Watson (editors)
2005   *Archaeology of the Middle Green River Region, Kentucky.* Institute of Archaeology and Paleoenvironmental Studies Monograph 5. University Press of Florida, Gainesville.

Meeks, Scott C.
2006   Paleoecological Analysis of Sediments from Mound G Pond, Shiloh Indian Mounds, Tennessee. Manuscript on file, Southeast Archeological Center, National Park Service, Tallahassee, Florida.

Milner, George R.
1998   *The Cahokia Chiefdom: The Archaeology of a Mississippian Society.* Smithsonian Institution Press, Washington, D.C.
1999   Warfare in Prehistoric and Early Historic North America. *Journal of Archaeological Research* 7:105–151.
2004a Old Mounds, Ancient Hunter-Gatherers, and Modern Archaeologists. In *Signs of Power: The Rise of Cultural Complexity in the Southeast,* edited by Jon L. Gibson and Philip J. Carr, pp. 300–316. University of Alabama Press, Tuscaloosa.
2004b *The Mound Builders: Ancient Peoples of Eastern North America.* Thames and Hudson, London.

Morse, Dan F.
1986   Preliminary Investigation of the Pinson Mounds Site: 1963 Field Season. In *Pinson Mounds, A Middle Woodland Ceremonial Center,* edited by Robert C. Mainfort Jr., pp. 96–119. Division of Archaeology Research Series 7. Tennessee Department of Conservation, Nashville.
1997   *Sloan: A Paleoindian Dalton Cemetery in Arkansas.* Smithsonian Institution Press, Washington, D.C.

Muller, Jon
1997   *Mississippian Political Economy.* Plenum Press, New York.

Nolan, Kevin C., and Robert A. Cook
2010   Volatile Climate Conditions Cahokia: Comment on Benson, Pauketat and Cook 2009. *American Antiquity* 75:975–983.

Pauketat, Timothy R.
2004 *Ancient Cahokia and the Mississippians*. Cambridge University Press, Cambridge.
2007 *Chiefdoms and Other Archaeological Delusions*. Altamira Press, Lanham, Maryland.
2009 *Cahokia: Ancient America's Great City on the Mississippi*. Penguin Press, New York.

Pauketat, Timothy R., and Thomas E. Emerson
1997 *Cahokia: Domination and Ideology in the Mississippian World*. University of Nebraska Press, Lincoln.

Pauketat, Timothy R., Lucretia S. Kelly, Gayle J. Fritz, Neal H. Lopinot, Scott Elias, and Eve Hargrave
2002 The Residues of Feasting and Public Ritual at Cahokia. *American Antiquity* 67(2):257–279.

Payne, Claudine
1994 Mississippian Capitals: An Archaeological Investigation of Precolumbian Political Structure. Ph.D. dissertation, University of Florida.

Peacock, Evan
2002 Shellfish Use during the Woodland Period in the Middle South. In *The Woodland Southeast*, edited by David G. Anderson and Robert C. Mainfort Jr., pp. 444–460. University of Alabama Press, Tuscaloosa.

Pluckhahn, Thomas J.
2003 *Kolomoki: Settlement, Ceremony, and Status in the Deep South, c. 350 to 750 AD*. University of Alabama Press, Tuscaloosa

Pursell, Corin
2004 Geographic Distribution and Symbolism of Colored Mound Architecture in the Mississippian Southeast. Master's thesis, Department of Anthropology, Southern Illinois University, Carbondale, Illinois.

Randall, Asa R.
2011 Remapping Archaic Social Histories along the St. John's River in Florida. In *Hunter-Gatherer Archaeology as Historical Process*, edited by Kenneth E. Sassaman and Donald H. Holley Jr., pp. 120–142. University of Arizona Press, Tucson.

Robinson, Brian S., and Jennifer C. Ort
2011 Paleoindian and Archaic Period Traditions: Particular Explanations from New England. In *Hunter-Gatherer Archaeology as Historical Process*, edited by Kenneth E. Sassaman and Donald H. Holley Jr., pp. 209–226. University of Arizona Press, Tucson.

Robinson, Brian S., Jennifer C. Ort, William E. Eldridge, Adrian L. Burke, and Bertrand G. Pelletier
2009 Paleoindian Aggregation and Social Context at Bull Brook. *American Antiquity* 74(3):423–447.

Rodning, Christopher B.
2010 Architectural Symbolism and Cherokee Townhouses. *Southeastern Archaeology* 29:59–79.

Rolingson, Martha A.
2002 Plum Bayou Culture of the Arkansas-White River Basin. In *The Woodland South-*

east, edited by David G. Anderson and Robert C. Mainfort Jr., pp. 44–65. University of Alabama Press, Tuscaloosa.

Rosenswig, Robert M., and Marilyn A. Masson
2002   Transformation of the Terminal Classic to Postclassic Architectural Landscape at Caye Coco, Belize. *Ancient Mesoamerica* 13:213–235.

Russo, Michael
1994   Why We Don't Believe in Archaic Ceremonial Mounds and Why We Should: The Case from Florida. *Southeastern Archaeology* 13:93–109.
1996a Southeastern Preceramic Archaic Ceremonial Mounds. In *Archaeology of the Mid-Holocene Southeast*, edited by Kenneth E. Sassaman and David G. Anderson, pp. 259–287. University Press of Florida, Gainesville.
1996b Southeastern Mid-Holocene Coastal Settlements. In *Archaeology of the Mid-Holocene Southeast*, edited by Kenneth E. Sassaman and David G. Anderson, pp. 177–199. University Press of Florida, Gainesville.
2004   Measuring Shell Rings for Social Inequality. In *Signs of Power: The Rise of Cultural Complexity in the Southeast*, edited by Jon L. Gibson and Philip J. Carr, pp. 26–70. University of Alabama Press, Tuscaloosa.
2006   *Archaic Shell Rings of the Southeast*. U.S. National Historic Landmark Theme Study submitted to the National Park Service, Washington D.C.
2010   Shell Rings and Other Settlement Features as Indictors of Cultural Continuity between the Late Archaic and Woodland Periods of Coastal Florida. In *Trend, Tradition, and Turmoil: What Happened to the Southeastern Archaic? Proceedings of the Third Caldwell Conference, St. Catherines Island, Georgia, May 9–11, 2008*, edited by David Hurst Thomas and Matthew C. Sanger, pp. 149–172. Anthropological Papers of the American Museum of Natural History, New York.

Sanger, Matthew
2010a Monument Creation in "Simple" Societies: Theoretical Impact of Southeastern Archaic Mounds. Paper presented at the 67th Annual meeting of the Southeastern Archaeological Conference, Lexington, Kentucky.
2010b Leaving the Rings; Shell Ring Abandonment and the End of the Late Archaic. In *Trend, Tradition, and Turmoil: What Happened to the Southeastern Archaic? Proceedings of the Third Caldwell Conference, St. Catherines Island, Georgia, May 9–11, 2008*, edited by David Hurst Thomas and Matthew C. Sanger, pp. 201–215. Anthropological Papers of the American Museum of Natural History, New York.

Sassaman, Kenneth E.
2005a Structure and Practice in the Archaic Southeast. In *North American Archaeology*, edited by Timothy R. Pauketat and Diana DiPaolo Loren, pp. 79–107. Blackwell Publishing, Malden, Massachusetts.
2005b Poverty Point as Structure, Event, Process. *Journal of Archaeological Method and Theory* 12:335–364.
2010a *The Eastern Archaic, Historicized*. Altamira Press, Lanham, Maryland.
2010b Getting from the Late Archaic to Early Woodland in Three Middle Valleys (Those Being the Savannah, St. Johns, and Tennessee). In *Trend, Tradition, and Turmoil: What Happened to the Southeastern Archaic? Proceedings of the Third Caldwell Conference, St. Catherines Island, Georgia, May 9–11, 2008*, edited by David Hurst

Thomas and Matthew C. Sanger, pp. 229–235. Anthropological Papers of the American Museum of Natural History, New York.

2011   History and Alterity in the Eastern Archaic. In *Hunter-Gatherer Archaeology as Historical Process*, edited by Kenneth E. Sassaman and Donald H. Holley Jr., pp. 187–208. University of Arizona Press, Tucson.

Sassaman, Kenneth E., and David G. Anderson (editors)

1996   *Archaeology of the Mid-Holocene Southeast*. University Press of Florida, Gainesville.

Sassaman, Kenneth E., and David G. Anderson

2004   Late Holocene Period, 3750 to 650 B.C. In *Southeast*, vol. 14 of *Smithsonian Handbook of North American Indians*, edited by Raymond D. Fogelson, pp. 101–114. Smithsonian Institution, Washington, D.C.

Saunders, Joe W.

2004   Are We Fixing to Make the Same Mistake Again? In *Signs of Power: The Rise of Cultural Complexity in the Southeast*, edited by Jon L. Gibson and Philip J. Carr, pp. 146–161. University of Alabama Press, Tuscaloosa.

2010   Late Archaic? What the Hell Happened to the Middle Archaic? In *Trend, Tradition, and Turmoil: What Happened to the Southeastern Archaic? Proceedings of the Third Caldwell Conference, St. Catherines Island, Georgia, May 9–11, 2008*, edited by David Hurst Thomas and Matthew C. Sanger, pp. 237–243. Anthropological Papers of the American Museum of Natural History, New York.

Saunders, Joe W., Thurman Allen, and Roger T. Saucier

1994   Four Archaic? Mound Complexes in Northeast Louisiana. *Southeastern Archaeology* 13:134–153.

Saunders, Joe W., Rolfe D. Mandel, C. Garth Sampson, Charles M. Allen, E. Thurman Allen, Daniel A. Bush, James K. Feathers, Kristen J. Gremillion, C. T. Hallmark, H. Edwin Jackson, Jay K. Johnson, Reca Jones, Roger T. Saucier, Gary L. Stringer, and Malcolm F. Vidrine

2005   Watson Brake: A Middle Archaic Mound Complex in Northeast Louisiana. *American Antiquity* 70:631–668.

Saunders, Joe W., Rolfe D. Mandel, Roger T. Saucier, E. Thurman Allen, C. T. Hallmark, Jay K. Johnson, Edwin H. Jackson, Charles M. Allen, Gary L. Stringer, Douglas S. Frink, James K. Feathers, Stephen Williams, Kristen J. Gremillion, Malcolm F. Vidrine, and Reca Jones

1997   A Mound Complex in Louisiana at 5400–5000 Years Before the Present. *Science* 277:1796–1799.

Saunders, Rebecca

1994   The Case for Archaic Mound Sites in Southeastern Louisiana. *Southeastern Archaeology* 13(2):118–134.

Schnell, Frank T., Vernon J. Knight Jr., and Gail S. Schnell

1981   *Cemochechobee: Archaeology of a Mississippian Ceremonial Center on the Chattahoochee River*. University Presses of Florida, Gainesville.

Shapiro, Gary, and Bonnie G. McEwan

1992   *Archaeology at San Luis. Part One: The Apalachee Council House*. Florida Archaeology, no. 6. Florida Bureau of Archaeological Research, Tallahassee.

Sherwood, Sarah C.
2006 Geoarchaeological Study of the Mound A Stratigraphy, Shiloh National Military Park, Hardin County, Tennessee. Manuscript on file, Southeast Archeological Center, National Park Service, Tallahassee, Florida.

Sherwood, Sarah C., and Tristram R. Kidder
2011 The DaVincis of Dirt: Geoarchaeological Perspectives on Native American Mound Building in the Mississippi River Basin. *Journal of Anthropological Archaeology* 30:69–87.

Smith, Bruce D.
1984 Mississippian Expansion: Tracing the Historical Development of an Explanatory Model. *Southeastern Archaeology* 3(1):13–32.
1986 The Archaeology of the Southeastern United States: From Dalton to De Soto, 10,500–500 B.P. *Advances in World Archaeology* 5:1–92.
1990 *The Mississippian Emergence*. Smithsonian Institution Press, Washington, DC.

Smith, Marvin T.
2000 *Coosa: The Rise and Fall of a Southeastern Mississippian Chiefdom*. University Press of Florida, Gainesville.

Stephenson, Keith L., Judith A. Bense, and Frankie Snow
2002 Some Aspects of Deptford and Swift Creek of the South Atlantic and Gulf Coastal Plains. In *The Woodland Southeast*, edited by David G. Anderson and Robert C. Mainfort Jr., pp. 318–351. University of Alabama Press, Tuscaloosa.

Steponaitis, Vincas P.
1978 Location Theory and Complex Chiefdoms: A Mississippian Example. In *Mississippian Settlement Patterns*, edited by Bruce D. Smith, pp. 417–453. Academic Press, New York.

Steponaitis, Vincas P., and Vernon J. Knight Jr.
2004 Moundville Art in Historical and Social Context. In *Hero, Hawk, and Open Hand American Indian Art of the Ancient Midwest and South*, edited by Richard F. Townsend and Robert V. Sharp, pp. 167–181. The Art Institute of Chicago and Yale University Press, New Haven, Connecticut.

Stout, Charles, and R. Barry Lewis
1998 The Town as Metaphor. In *Mississippian Towns and Sacred Spaces: Searching for an Architectural Grammar*, edited by Berry R. Lewis and Charles Stout, pp. 227–241. University of Alabama Press, Tuscaloosa

Thompson, Victor D.
2010 The Rhythms of Space-Time and the Making of Monuments and Places during the Archaic. In *Trend, Tradition, and Turmoil: What Happened to the Southeastern Archaic? Proceedings of the Third Caldwell Conference, St. Catherines Island, Georgia, May 9–11, 2008*, edited by David Hurst Thomas and Matthew C. Sanger, pp. 217–228. Anthropological Papers of the American Museum of Natural History, New York.

Trigger, Bruce G.
1990 Monumental Architecture: A Thermodynamic Explanation of Symbolic Behaviour. *World Archaeology* 22:119–132.

Vento, Frank, and Matthew Sanger
2010   Dam Theory—Why Adaptationist Models Hold No Water in Explaining Monuments. Paper presented at the 67th Annual meeting of the Southeastern Archaeological Conference, Lexington, Kentucky.

Welch, Paul D.
2006   *Archaeology at Shiloh Indian Mounds, 1899–1999*. University of Alabama Press, Tuscaloosa.

III

MESOAMERICA

5

Agriculture and Monumentality in the Soconusco Region of Chiapas, Mexico

ROBERT M. ROSENSWIG

In many early civilizations, low platforms, used to raise the floors of buildings above damp ground or the danger of flooding, developed into truncated, solid "pyramids" that rendered the structures built on top of them visible from afar and affirmed their social importance (Trigger 2004, 239).

At Los Naranjos, Yarumela and many other early sites, initial monumental platforms are juxtaposed in later construction stages to additional platforms framing plaza spaces. The centering effect of monumental platforms, a function of their heightened visibility, appears to have been reacted to and elaborated on, not necessarily intended, planned for, and produced from the beginning. Once Formative monumental platforms existed, the idea of building to last at the monumental scale was irrevocably a part of the traditional knowledge of later Mesoamerican peoples (Joyce 2004, 23).

As outlined in Chapter 1, monumental construction projects can be explored at two temporal scales: the initial organization of labor and the creation of locations in the local landscape that are imbued with meaning for the centuries that follow (Rosenswig and Burger this volume). In his thermodynamic explanation, Bruce Trigger (1990, 2004) lays out why construction at a monumental scale violates the principle of least effort and so is encountered cross-culturally to symbolize the control of labor, and thus power itself. A universal symbolic meaning of monumentality may explain why archaeologists are themselves drawn to study large buildings, mounds, and monuments from the past. In fact, large Prehispanic construction projects may well induce awe in twenty-first-century peoples much as they would have for the peoples that built and used them (see also Dietler 1998).

After its initial construction, architecture determines how people move through towns, villages, and cities (Rapoport 1982, 1988, 1990; and see Fletcher 1995; Love 1999; Smith 2000, 2003). While this may be true of all societies, the structure and norms of hierarchical societies are incorporated into the constructions of monumental architecture. Hierarchical relations can thus be naturalized during the initial labor projects—as those dominant social positions likely organized the labor required to build them. Hierarchical social structures may further be routinized by architecture when elite residences are centrally located and spatially associated with religious and/or administrative buildings. The study of monumental construction projects can thus provide a productive analytical vantage point from which to explore the development of social stratification and political hierarchy. The thermodynamic explanation is most productively used as a theoretically coherent hypothesis to be evaluated in relation to archaeological patterns.

In South America and the southeastern United States, large earthen mounds are documented very early relative to such developments as increased social stratification or intensified food production. Interpretation of the social meaning of early monumentality in these parts of the New World can thus be controversial. Trigger's thermodynamic explanation (which equates monumentality with social and/or political power) may therefore not clearly account for the earliest large construction projects in these regions (e.g., Burger and Salazar-Burger this volume; Roosevelt this volume; Saunders this volume). In contrast, monumental architecture (and in particular the large conical mounds that permanently alter the built environment) was a relatively late development in Mesoamerica. Approximately half a millennium after the first ceramic-using peoples are documented in Mesoamerica, unprecedented amounts of labor were expended at San Lorenzo to remodel the plateau on which the site is found as well as to construct and transport the stone sculpture distributed across the site during the second part of the Early Formative period (Cyphers 2004; Cyphers and Zurita-Noguera this volume). However, it was not until the Middle Formative period—that is, after approximately 1000 cal. BCE—that pyramid mounds were built at San Lorenzo or other Gulf Coast centers (Diehl 1981). The pattern of large mounds defining the center of important political centers is documented across Mesoamerica at this time and was a characteristic of all subsequent centers of power (e.g., Estrata-Belli this volume; Grove 1999; Joyce 2004, 23; Love 1999; Paradis this volume). So how were the Middle Formative Mesoamerican peoples who built large mounds different from their predecessors who did not? What was it that began to occur at approximately 1000 cal. BCE?

In this chapter, I present the cultural context in which a polity-wide system of conical pyramid mounds was first used in the Soconusco region of southern Mexico (see Figure 1.1). Because of a refined chronology (Figure 5.1), the Soconusco patterns allow for a detailed exploration of the political and adaptive context in which early developments occurred. Monumental construction can thus be explored relative to the timing of increased social stratification and intensified food production during the early Middle Formative Conchas phase (1000–850 cal. BCE). I begin by reviewing what has been published about early monumental architecture in the Soconusco. Then I discuss evidence of the origins of monumentality, increased stratification and greater reliance on food production from the site of Cuauhtémoc. Evidence from Cuauhtémoc is useful for exploring these developments because the site was occupied for just over a millennium from 1900–850 cal. BCE—the final 150-year ceramic phase during which conical mounds were built at this site, which had already been occupied for centuries without them.

The Early and Middle Formative Soconusco

The southeastern half of the Soconusco is approximately 60 km long and 20 to 30 km wide and is defined on all sides by geographic features (Voorhies 2004, 6–13, 20–21). To the southwest is the Pacific Ocean, to the northeast are the Sierra Madres, and to both the northwest and the southeast are the Cantileña and Guamuchal swamps (Figure 5.1). This relatively small area has the greatest concentration of fertile land on the Pacific coast of Mexico and Guatemala, so it is not surprising that many significant early developments on the Pacific coast of Mesoamerica transpired between these two large swamp systems (Rosenswig 2010, 2011). The land between these swamp systems is cut by four major rivers: from north to south, they are the Coatán, the Cahuacán, the Suchiate, and the Naranjo (Figure 5.1). A number of smaller streams originate on the coastal plain and form a series of mangrove swamp systems parallel to the ocean (see Coe and Flannery 1967; Lowe, Lee, and Espinoza 1982). These rivers create a dynamic set of microenvironments where some of the earliest ceramics in Mesoamerica are documented by 1900 cal. BCE (Clark and Gosser 1995).

Barbara Voorhies (2004) has documented numerous shell mounds in the Cantileña swamp dating to the Middle and Late Archaic periods (5000–2000 BC). These mounds were seasonally occupied to exploit estuary

Figure 5.1. Map of the Soconusco and the land between swamps and a chronology chart for the Early and Middle Formative phases. Triangles represent known Conchas phase centers; their size depicts their relative importance in the La Blanca polity.

resources, and some are quite large; Tlacuachero is 7 meters high (Voorhies 2004, 31). John Hodgson (personal communication 2006) has encountered other Archaic period mounds in the Mazatán estuary. As the result of accretional formations from shell processing, these mounds are not monumental in the sense that Trigger (1990) describes (see also Sassaman and Randall this volume).

John Clark and Michael Blake (1994; Blake and Clark 1999) have documented a number of centers in the Mazatán zone southeast of the Cantileña swamp during the early part of the Early Formative period. By 1700 cal. BCE, Paso de la Amada was the largest of these centers and contained a series of elite residences built on low platforms (Lesure 1997) as well as the earliest ballcourt yet reported from Mesoamerica (Hill, Blake, and Clark 1998). The best documented structure at Paso de La Amada is Mound 6 (Blake 1991; Blake et al. 2006). This elite residence was occupied during the Locona and Ocós phases and was rebuilt in at least six different construction episodes. Mound 6 is currently 2.7 meters high and may have measured 4.2 meters before being plowed during the past 50 years (Blake et al. 2006, Table 7.1). I have previously estimated that Mound 6 contained a total of approximately 2500 m^3 of fill (Rosenswig 2000, Table 3; and see Blake et al. 2006, 196–198). Clark (2004a, 2004b) proposes that the mounds at Paso de la Amada were arranged to form a number of courtyards. This would make it one of the earliest examples of site planning in Mesoamerica. While likely impressive when they were first built and occupied, the relative size of the mounds at Paso de la Amada is modest by later standards. Further, mounds were relatively low and would not have transformed the local landscape once the pole-and-thatch structures that sat atop the platforms had deteriorated. This point is emphasized by visiting the site today; the remains of the mounds are evident only to the trained eye of the professional archaeologist. In contrast, later mounds are obvious to any casual observer. So while they did require labor to build, the platforms at Paso de la Amada (and other early Early Formative sites in the Mazatán zone) did not permanently transform the local landscape.

Little is known of Soconusco architectural practices during the second part of the Early Formative period. Paso de la Amada and Cantón Corralito were two of half a dozen competing centers in the Mazatán zone during the Cherla phase (Clark 1997; Clark and Blake 1989; Blake and Clark 1999). Cantón Corralito, located on the shore of the Coatán River, then emerged as the largest site in the area during the subsequent Cuadros phase (1300– 1200 cal. BCE), when Paso de la Amada was abandoned (Cheetham 2006; Pérez 2002). The Cantón Corralito elite may have taken over the Mazatán area after outcompeting neighboring rivals, as Clark (1997; Clark and Blake 1989) has long argued. However, despite multiple years of excavation, no Cuadros-phase architecture (monumental or otherwise) has been documented at Cantón Corralito. At the end of the Cuadros phase, Cantón Corralito was abandoned after being covered with 1–2 meters of sediment. In 2005, because of flooding in the aftermath of Hurricane Stan, a similarly massive discharge of sediment was documented in the area of the meandering Coatán River (Gutierrez 2011). It is likely that a similar prehistoric disaster resulted in the destruction of Cantón Corralito at approximately 1200 cal. BCE.

Relatively more is known of architectural construction in the Soconusco during the final Early Formative Jocotal phase (1200–1000 cal. BCE). Jocotal phase mounds are known from the Soconusco estuary, including Salinas la Blanca (Coe and Flannery 1967), El Varal (Lesure 2009) and El Mesak (Pye and Demarest 1991). I have also recently encountered a mound six meters high at Estero el Ponce in the estuary north of the Cahuacán River (Figure 5.1; and see Rosenswig 2010, 227–258). Although larger than anything previously built in the estuary, these Jocotal phase mounds were likely used for the extraction of local resources that may have included salt (Lesure

2009; Pye, Hodgson, and Clark 2011). The political center in the Mazatán zone was rebuilt at this time on the other side of the Coatán River from Cantón Corralito at a site known today as Ojo de Agua (Clark and Pye 2000). Ojo de Agua is located on the bank of the Coatán River that is safe from its episodic overflow. The extent of Ojo de Agua has just recently been understood (Pye, Hodgson, and Clark 2011). The site center is defined by a platform one meter high and 100 meters long and three conical mounds seven meters high (Pinkowski 2006). The Jocotal phase mounds at Ojo de Agua were the first conical mounds built in the Soconusco that served neither residential nor resource extraction functions. The timing of the Jocotal phase mounds at the very end of the Early Formative period is consistent with other early mounds in Mesoamerica such as those reported from Honduras (e.g., Joyce 2004). However, the Ojo de Agua polity was short lived and by 1000 cal. BCE, the entire Mazatán zone was abandoned, as was the Rio Jesus zone around the site of El Mesak on the southeast side of the Guamuchal swamp (Blake and Clark 1999; Pye and Demarest 1991; Pye, Hodgson, and Clark 2011).

During the early Middle Formative Conchas phase (1000–850 cal. BCE), a new political system with conical mounds built at primary, secondary, and tertiary centers was established at the southeast end of the Soconusco. The paramount center of this new polity was the site of La Blanca, which covered at least 200 hectares (and as much as 300 hectares) and had a mound 25 meters high (Mound 1) at its center (Love 2002a, 2002b; Love and Guernsey 2011). I have previously estimated that Mound 1 consisted of 140 000 m^3 of fill and would have taken over 50,000 person-days to build (Rosenswig 2000, Table 3). In terms of labor expenditure, it is therefore larger than the mounds at Paso de la Amada by well over an order of magnitude and more than three times as high as any known Jocotal phase mound. Because of its scale and the permanent mark left on the landscape, the central mound at La Blanca represents a very different use of monumentality than anything that had preceded it in the region (Love 1999).

La Blanca was part of a system of Conchas phase centers that each had a large central mound. Secondary centers are known from the La Blanca polity: La Zarca, which had a 20-meter-high mound and El Infierno, which had a 18-meter-high mound (Love 2002a). Cuauhtémoc, with its central mound five meters high, was a tertiary center in the La Blanca polity (Rosenswig 2007, 2010, 105–131). There are other likely tertiary centers in the La Blanca polity, such as the Don Hermelindo site, that have modest conical mounds, but no excavations have yet been undertaken (Figure 5.1). Each center in the La Blanca polity had a single large mound that defined the site as an important location on the flat coastal plain and could have been seen for great distances.

The La Blanca polity persisted for approximately 15 decades, and then in turn it collapsed. The largest center in the Soconusco during the second part of the Middle Formative period was Izapa, located on the edge of the nearby piedmont (Lowe, Lee, and Espinoza 1982). Izapa may have begun as a secondary center in the La Blanca polity (Love 1999, 137), but unlike other Conchas phase centers such as La Blanca, La Zarca, El Infierno, and Cuauhtémoc, it grew throughout the Middle Formative and reached its greatest extents in the Late Formative when nearly 200 stelae were erected in and around a dozen plazas. It is noteworthy that of all the Early or Middle Formative political centers, La Blanca was the only one that did not emerge as a secondary center that grew to replace an established primary center. Cantón Corralito and Izapa were lesser centers that surpassed Paso de la Amada and La Blanca, respectively, at the same time that the latter two were abandoned. In contrast, La Blanca was created without any direct link in settlement to Ojo de Agua, the most elaborate center that had preceded it. Rather than a political evolution we seem to be dealing with a political revolution.

Cuauhtémoc Zone Settlement

I now shift to the developments documented at the site of Cuauhtémoc and the surrounding area between the Cahuacán and Suchiate rivers (see Figure 5.1). Cuauhtémoc was the center of a small polity during the Locona and Ocós phases when Paso de la Amada dominated the Mazatán zone. The site expanded through the late Early Formative as the Mazatán capital shifted to the banks of the Coatán River. However, unlike the sites in the Mazatán zone, Cuauhtémoc flourished after the transition that occurred at 1000 cal. BCE and was incorporated into the La Blanca polity during the Conchas phase (Rosenswig 2007, 2010).

A full-coverage survey was undertaken around the site of Cuauhtémoc that covered 28 sq km and documented 42 new Early and Middle Formative period sites (Rosenswig 2008). There are many methodological problems associated with interpreting the results of surface survey, but such data provide the only reliable source of information on regional organization. As the Cuauhtémoc survey zone does not encompass a complete political system, I simply report how relative population levels (measured

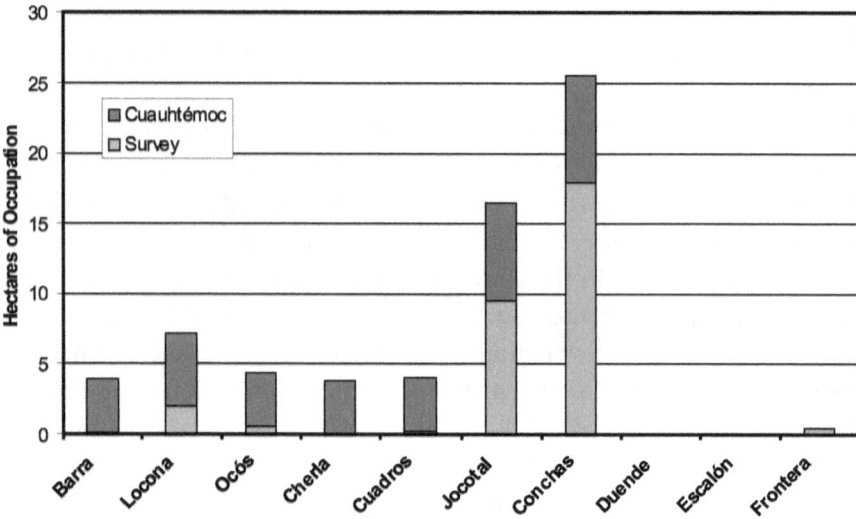

Figure 5.2. Graph of total hectares of occupation in the Cuauhtémoc survey zone for the ten Early and Middle Formative phases.

as the number of hectares covered by ceramics attributable to each phase) changed over time (Figure 5.2).

During the Early Formative period, the Cuauhtémoc site formed the greatest part of the occupation in the area, making it the demographic center within the 28 sq km survey zone. The Locona phase increase in hectares of occupation is significant at both the Cuauhtémoc site and surrounding area (Figure 5.2). This suggests that the site, as a local center, attracted increasing numbers of people to its political orbit by the Locona phase (1700–1500 cal. BCE). Excavation data from the Cuauhtémoc site support the interpretation that this was a political center based on a concentration of prestige and specialized craft objects (Rosenswig 2010). During the late Early Formative, there was a slight decrease in population during Cherla and Cuadros times followed by a more significant increase during the Jocotal phase. These fluctuations are similar to patterns observed in the Mazatán survey zone when the center of political activity shifted to the sites of Cantón Corralito and Ojo de Agua on the Coatán River (Clark and Pye 2000). Similarities in demography and material culture within the area defined by the Cantileña and Guamuchal swamps and the differences from the surrounding area are reasons why I interpret this as an Early Formative island of cultural complexity (Rosenswig 2010, 13–46; 2011).

Middle Formative settlement patterns are even more volatile than Early Formative changes. In the Cuauhtémoc survey zone, Conchas phase population increased beyond that of the Jocotal phase (Figure 5.2). The La Blanca polity dominated the Soconusco at this time, and Cuauhtémoc appears to have benefited from the new configuration of political organization (Rosenswig 2007). As discussed in the previous section, the Cahuacán/Suchiate/Naranjo zone pattern contrasts with that in the Mazatán zone as well as that in the area around El Mesak, where no Conchas phase sites have been documented despite intensive survey. Clark and Blake (1989; Blake and Clark 1999) interpret this as representing a time when virtually all of the inhabitants of the Soconusco were drawn to the political phenomenon at La Blanca (and see Love 1991, 1999, 2002a). The preceding Jocotal phase settlement system was replaced by a more centralized (and hierarchical) system that focused population in the southeast half of the land between the two large swamp systems (Figure 5.1). As previously noted, La Blanca and Cuauhtémoc were then both abruptly abandoned after the Conchas phase—a pattern documented quantitatively by the Cuauhtémoc zone survey (Figure 5.2).

Cuauhtémoc Architectural Development

Excavations undertaken at the site of Cuauhtémoc complement the demographic patterns presented in the previous section. At its maximum extent during the Conchas phase, the Cuauhtémoc site covered 10 hectares and contained three mounds (Figure 5.3). The mounds were recently flattened by heavy machinery when the area was prepared for banana production. When drainage canals were cut for the banana plantation, the site was exposed by trenches that are three meters deep and several kilometers long and are spaced 100 meters apart. These trenches expose cultural deposits down to sterile clay layers and allow this early village to be documented in cross-section. Although the damage to the site is unfortunate, it provides a remarkably extensive subsurface view of a millennium of cultural deposits at one community (Rosenswig 2009, 2010). These profiles document how the site formed on top of a river levee made of sand. The initial inhabitants of the site were attracted to this naturally occurring high ground in an area prone to seasonal flooding.

Two Locona phase structures were documented from posthole patterns and associated features. These structures measured approximately 11.5 × 5 meters and 8.5 × 4 meters, respectively (Rosenswig 2006, Figure 7). One of the most significant facts about the two structures is their orientation. The long axes of both structures align northwest-southeast, which is the same

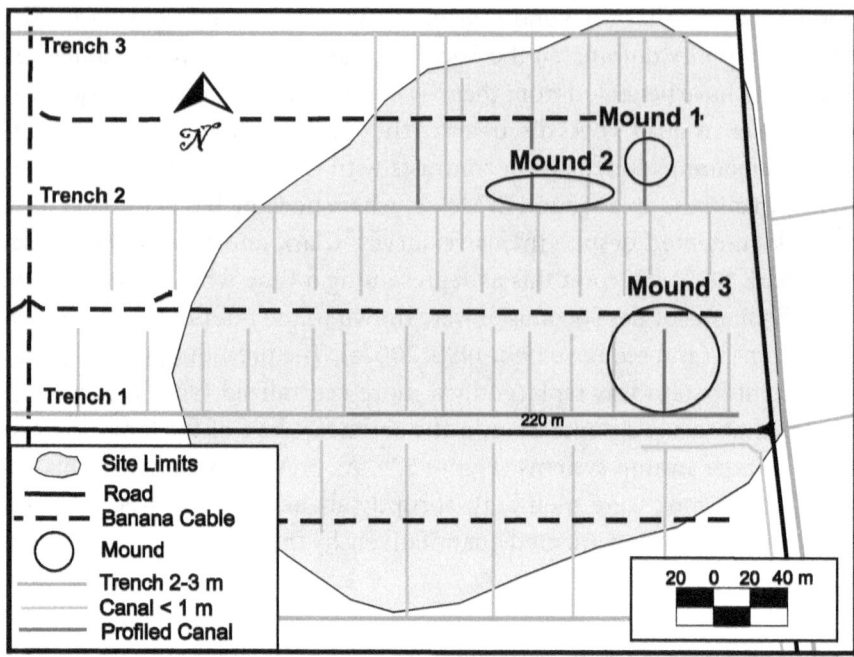

Figure 5.3. Map of Cuauhtémoc showing location of mounds.

as the long axis of Mound 6 at Paso de la Amada (Clark 2004a, 2004b). The orientations of residential structures, from these sites at either end of the land between the Soconusco swamps, suggests a coherent regional pattern (Rosenswig 2010, 105–131). The glimpse of Locona phase architecture at Cuauhtémoc does not provide a sufficiently large view to determine if structures were laid out around plazas, as Clark (2004b) proposes for Paso de la Amada.

The next glimpse of architecture at Cuauhtémoc dates to the end of the Early Formative period. During the Jocotal phase (1200–1000 cal. BCE), Mound 2, a platform 100 meters long, 20 meters wide, and 1 meter high, was built through the center of Cuauhtémoc (Figure 5.3). This long, low platform mound—similar to the one at Ojo de Agua (Pye, Hodgson, and Clark 2011) as well as others in the Soconusco estuary (e.g., Coe and Flannery 1967; Lesure 2009)—was comprised of approximately 2000 m³ of fill (Table 5.1). The initial construction and use of Mound 2 at Cuauhtémoc during the Jocotal phase likely represented a reorganization of the community (Rosenswig 2010, 105–131). By creating a raised platform, a limited segment of the inhabitants of Cuauhtémoc could have had their residences segregated from the rest of the community (Rosenswig 2007, 2009). During

Table 5.1. Conchas phase architecture in the Soconusco

Site	Structure	Height (m)	Dimensions (m)	Volume $(m^3)^a$	Source
La Blanca	Mound 1	25	120 × 140	140,000	Rosenswig 2000, Table 3
La Zarca	Central Mound	20	70 diameter	10,667	
El Infierno	Central Mound	18	80 diameter	14,400	
Cuauhtémoc	Mound 1	3	30 diameter	707	Rosenswig 2010 and this chapter, Figure 5.3
	Mound 2	1	20 × 100	2000	
	Mound 3	5	50 diameter	3271	
	East side of site	2.5	30 × 180	13,500	
Total				19,478	

Note: a. Volume of mounds calculated as the volume of a pyramid, i.e., 1/3 n r^2 h, or 1/3 (area of base) × (height).

the subsequent Conchas phase, Mound 2 continued to be occupied, and there is evidence that it was an elite habitation area because this is the only area of the site where the fancy Ramirez Ware ceramics are documented (Rosenswig 2006). Furthermore, unique features and distinctive patterns of ceramic, ground stone, and faunal debris suggests that the residents of this mound regularly sponsored feasts (Rosenswig 2007).

Two conical mounds were built at Cuauhtémoc during the Conchas phase. Mound 1 (3 meters high) and Mound 3 (5 meters high) were constructed north and south of each other at the east side of the site (Figures 5.3). Therefore, at Cuauhtémoc, as at La Zarca, El Infierno, and La Blanca (and likely other sites yet to be tested), a single conical mound defined the center of each site. I argue that this was a coordinated political strategy that linked the elite at each tier in the La Blanca polity. No excavations have been undertaken at the secondary centers of La Zarca or El Infierno, and the dating of their central mounds is based on surface reconnaissance (Love 2002a). Excavations at Izapa only suggest that one mound was built during the Conchas phase (Ekholm 1969). As a result, La Blanca and Cuauhtémoc provide the only excavation evidence of Conchas phase mound construction and its relationship to other activities. The only other site where excavations have been carried out is La Victoria, where Michael Coe (1961) originally defined the Conchas phase.

The construction of Mounds 1 and 3 required more labor input than anything previously built at Cuauhtémoc and contained 707 m^3 and 3270 m^3 of fill, respectively (Table 5.1). Together, these Conchas phase mounds required twice as much effort to construct as Mound 2. The labor required to build Mounds 1 and 3 at Cuauhtémoc is actually greater than it first appears because the east side of the levee on which the site was initially built was extended by approximately 30 meters before mound construction began. Raising a section of the site's east side by 2.5 meters in an area that was 180 meters long and 30 meters wide would have required approximately 13,500 m^3 of fill. This extension of Cuauhtémoc's east side contained over twice as much fill as all three of the mounds at the site combined (i.e., 5,978 m^3). Further, the 13,500 m^3 of fill contained in the expansion of Cuauhtémoc was comparable in volume to the largest mounds at the secondary sites of La Zarca and El Infierno (Table 5.1).

The construction of this extension to the Cuauhtémoc site means that very little area of Jocotal phase occupation was covered to erect this new ceremonial structure. In the finite area of raised ground, space would itself have been a valuable resource. An extension of Cuauhtémoc to build the two conical mounds suggests continuity in the political order as the Conchas phase mound builders did not need to disturb the houses of established residents who occupied the site prior to the emergence of the La Blanca polity. In fact, more elevated space was created than was needed to build Mounds 1 and 3. Further, the residential continuity at Mound 2 (based on superimposed middens and features from both phases) indicates that the abandonment of the Mazatán zone (and the polity that had been centered at Cantón Corralito and then Ojo de Agua) did not adversely affect the Cuauhtémoc elite. Instead, it may have helped them by supplying a new source of labor as people from surrounding areas moved into the La Blanca polity (see Rosenswig 2010, 259–290).

The Conchas phase construction of large central mounds marks the first time that such impressive endeavors were undertaken in a coordinated manner at all political centers. Although the 25-meter-high mound at La Blanca was substantially larger than the 5-meter-high mound at Cuauhtémoc, the former site was inhabited by at least 20 times as many people (based on the number of hectares of occupation at each site; i.e., 10 hectares versus 200 to 300 hectares). If we also include the labor required to extend the east side of Cuauhtémoc, then the smaller population at this site would have worked for at least the same length of time as those at La Blanca to build their more modest central mound. This means that the initial construction project was at least as laborious and labor demands at least as heavy, even though the final product was considerably less impressive. Perhaps as a third-tier center, it was not permitted to build a mound more than five meters high. Or perhaps the most important purpose of the initial construction was to give residents (and new immigrants from surrounding areas) a communal project to work on together.

Conchas Phase Political and Social Stratification

There was increased political and social stratification in the La Blanca polity compared to any previous society in the Soconusco. Evidence for this is based on six material patterns (Table 5.2). First, as previously mentioned, this was when the Mazatán and Rio Jesus zones were abandoned and when population nucleated in the area around the Cahuacán, Suchiate and Naranjo rivers. Second, as also mentioned previously, for the first time in the Soconusco there was a four-tiered settlement system with La Blanca at the head; La Zarca and El Infierno (and perhaps Izapa) as second-tier sites; Cuauhtémoc and Don Hermelindo as third-tier sites and scores of smaller villages with no mounded architecture. More people lived in closer proximity to each other within the La Blanca polity and the internal organization of this territory was more formally integrated than any of the previous Early Formative Mazatán polities.

The next three patterns that indicate the presence of social stratification are based on the restricted distribution of imported artifacts and those that required specialized knowledge to produce (Love 1991, 2002a; Love and Guernsey 2011; Rosenswig 2007). The third pattern was an increased use of greenstone at the time and much greater quantities of these prestige objects at La Blanca than at Cuauhtémoc. Fourth, thin, intricately incised Ramirez Ware ceramics were recovered in much higher proportions at La Blanca than at Cuauhtémoc. Further, at Cuauhtémoc, Ramirez Wares are documented only in elite contexts (Rosenswig 2007). Fifth, large, ornate earspools have been documented only at La Blanca, whereas at Cuauhtémoc only a smaller, simpler variety has been recovered—even in elite contexts. Earspools are depicted on all anthropomorphic figurines made at the time and appear to represent an important aspect of human identity. Sixth, the Conchas phase elite living on Mound 2 built residences that resulted in greater quantities of daub debris (Rosenswig 2009). So either their houses were more substantially built or they were refinished more often and were thus kept in better repair than those of the community's residents who did not live on this central platform.

Table 5.2. Conchas phase developments, material correlates, and references

	Material Correlate	Reference	Documented here
MONUMENTAL CONSTRUCTION			
	Conical mounds built at political centers	Love 2002a; Rosenswig 2000, Table 3	Fig. 5.1, 5.3
POLITICAL AND SOCIAL STRATIFICATION			
	1) Population nucleation	Blake and Clark 1999; Love 2002a; Rosenswig 2008	Fig. 5.1, 5.2
	2) Four-tier settlement hierarchy	Rosenswig 2007, 2010, Chapter 4	Fig. 5.1
	3) Increased use of greenstone	Love 1999, 2002a; Love and Guernsey 2011; Rosenswig 2006	
	4) Restricted use of elite ceramics	Love 1991, 2002a; Love and Guernsey n.d.; Rosenswig 2007	
	5) Restricted use of large earspools	Love 1991, 2002a; Love and Guernsey n.d.; Rosenswig 2007	
	6) More substantial elite residences built on Mound 2 at Cuauhtémoc	Rosenswig 2009; Love and Guernsey n.d.	
INCREASED RELIANCE ON FOOD PRODUCTION			
	1) Increased level of C4 to C3 isotopes	Blake et al. 1992	
	2) Increased density of macrobotanical maize remains	Rosenswig 2010: Chapter 5, Rosenswig, VanDerwarker, and Kennett n.d.	
	3) Increased overall quantity of ground stone	Love 2002a; Rosenswig 2006	Fig. 5.4

Material Correlate	Reference	Documented here
4) More manos and metates relative to mortars and pestles	Rosenswig 2006	Fig. 5.4
5) Iconography with maize imagery and cleft motifs	Taube 2000; Blake 2006; Rosenswig 2010, Chapter 6	Fig. 5.5

Conchas Phase Food Production

A significant increase in the reliance on food production in the Soconusco appears to also date to the Conchas phase. In this section, five lines of evidence are marshaled that indicate an increased importance of maize use at this time (Table 5.2). Macrobotanical maize remains have been documented from most Early Formative period contexts (Blake 2006; Feddema 1993), and they have also been documented from pollen analysis at an even earlier date (Neff et al. 2006). However, based on isotope results produced by Blake et al. (1992; and see Chisholm and Blake 2006), C4 plants were consumed at higher levels by Soconusco residents during the Conchas phase compared to Early Formative period peoples. This increase in C4 consumption persists through all later periods that were sampled, but originated when the La Blanca polity was established. Recent work at Cuauhtémoc documents a clear increase in the density of maize remains from contexts dating to the Conchas phase compared to maize densities from all earlier contexts (Rosenswig 2010, 132–174; Rosenswig, VanDerwarker, and Kennett n.d.).

While botanicals and isotopes provide direct evidence of maize use, changing patterns of ground stone tools also reflect the processing of these grains (Rosenswig 2006). At Cuauhtémoc, the overall quantity of ground stone increased significantly during the Conchas phase (Figure 5.4A). This is to be expected if more grinding tools were used to process maize. In addition, the type of ground stone tools also changed during the Conchas phase, and the number of manos and metates increased relative to the number of mortars and pestles at Cuauhtémoc (Figure 5.4B). This ratio provides a proxy measure for increased grinding surface because the entire edge of a mano is used, whereas pestles are used only on one end. Figure 5.4B thus

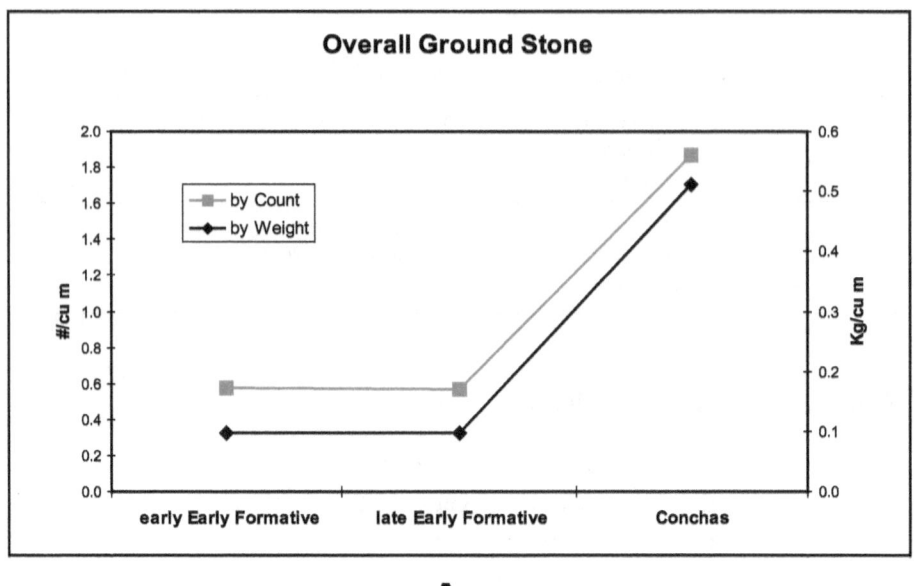

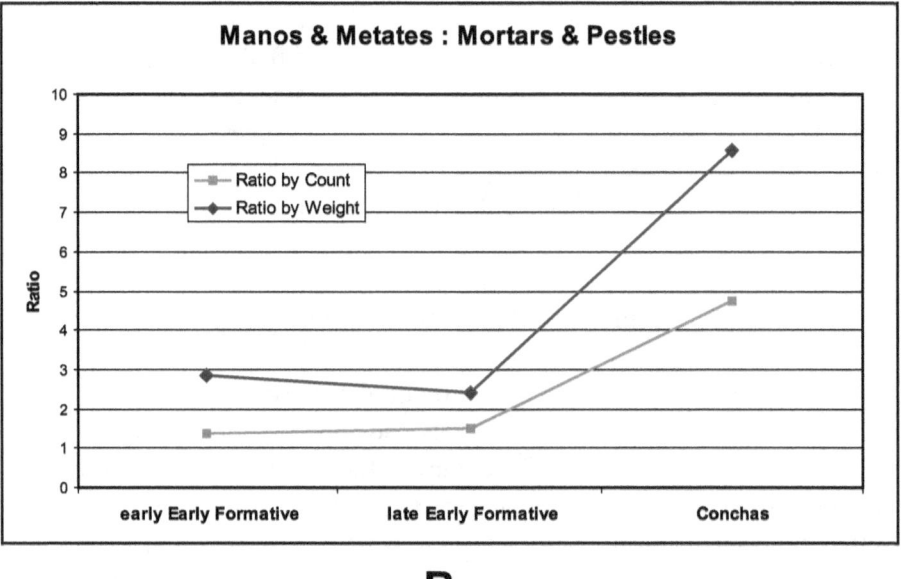

Figure 5.4. Ground stone patterns from Cuauhtémoc: overall quantity (A) and proportion of manos and metates to mortars and pestles (B).

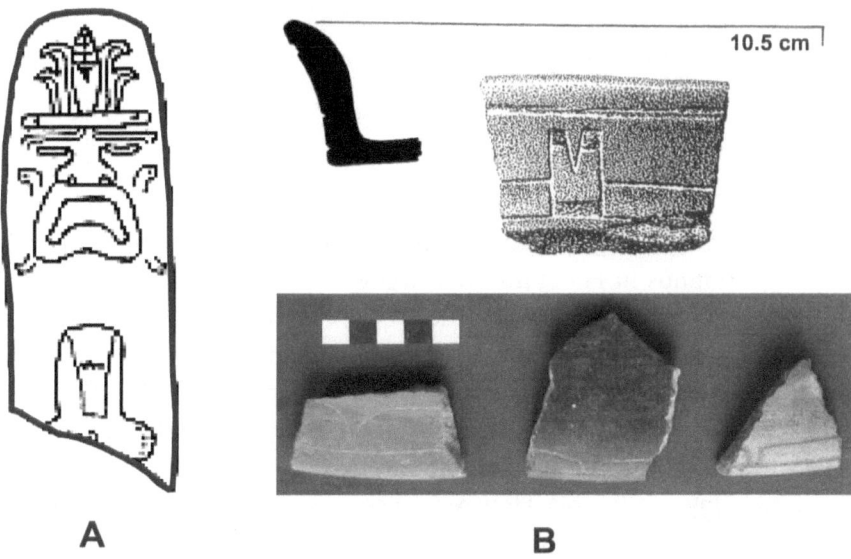

Figure 5.5. El Sitio Axe (A) as well as cleft and double line-break iconography from Cuauhtémoc (B). The three ceramic sherds are purposefully presented upside down to emphasize the similarity between double line-break and cleft motifs.

documents the technological result of intensified maize processing during the Conchas phase.

Finally, the timing of the artistic representations of maize and the related cleft motif is consistent with isotope and ground stone data. Karl Taube (2000), among others, observes that maize imagery first appears during the Middle Formative period, generally as a maize cob or axe emerging from a cleft in the head of a ruler. The El Sitio Axe, purportedly found on the Guatemalan side of the Soconusco, is one of the most literal examples of such imagery (Figure 5.5A). This axe depicts an Olmec-style face, with downturned mouth and closed eyes, holding an axe in its hand similar to the one on which it is carved. The axe would have been an increasingly important agricultural tool during the Middle Formative period, used to turn the soil and plant maize. This literal representation of maize helps explain the more abstract forms of cleft imagery and is explored more fully elsewhere (Rosenswig 2010, 175–226). At Cuauhtémoc, the cleft and the double-line-break motifs became very common during Conchas times (Figure 5.5B). Viewed from the exterior of the vessel rim looking in, the double-line-break is the most abstracted version of the cleft head. Changes in artistic representations and decorative motifs that represent maize thus change in tandem with isotope, macrobotanical and ground stone patterns and all point to the Conchas phase as a time of major change in the intensity of maize production.

Summary and Discussion

Recently, Joyce (2004) has addressed the effects of the novelty of building large mounds in Honduras. She argues that low broad mounds were initially built to raise certain activities above that of everyday occurrences. Achieving greater visibility, these platforms could incorporate larger numbers of people in "feasts, dances and games . . . [and] the builders of early monumental platforms can be understood as acting within traditional structures of technical, ritual, and domestic productive and reproductive practices" (Joyce 2004, 24). However, once these modest structures turned out to be durable, it was only a small step to building larger mounds and raising certain activities even higher above the level of the mundane. Large mounds—the hallmark of all later Mesoamerican civilizations—mark sites on the regional landscape and establish focal points (see Love 1999, 144; Love 2002b, 231–232; Smith 2003). Kent Reilly (1999) suggests that the large conical earthen Mound C-1 at La Venta may have represented the mountain of creation and served as a ritual stage for political performances (see also Grove 1999). La Venta's 30-meter-high central mound commands a view of the entire site, which also means that it would have been visible from everywhere in the site. As with La Blanca's Mound 1, La Venta's central mound would have been a constant reminder of the building event(s) and the founding of the site. Therefore, after 1000 cal. BCE in both these areas (and in other parts of Mesoamerica as well), large conical mounds marked political centers for the first time and created long-lasting reminders to all of the inhabitants of the sites of the labor required to build and maintain these mounds.

One of the earliest systems of monumental mound construction in Mesoamerica is documented in the Soconusco during the early Middle Formative Conchas phase (1000–850 cal. BCE). I argue that a significant aspect of building these Conchas phase mounds is how communal labor projects were coordinated across the entire polity and how the resulting mounds permanently altered the built environment. The 25-meter-high mound at La Blanca and the 5-meter-high mound at Cuauhtémoc (as well as those at other centers) may have been built with reference to the three conical mounds built at Ojo de Agua during the preceding Jocotal phase. Whether this was the case or not, the Conchas phase mounds established a new spatial syntax. As Love notes, the La Blanca architecture "warp(s) social space much more than earlier constructions; they modify daily routines." Further, these large mounds "become reference points for regionalization and the social categorization of space" (Love 1999, 144). The Conchas phase elite outdid their Mazatán predecessors in terms of both the scale of the mounds built at political centers and the degree of political organization.

Mounds measuring up to 7 meters high were built in the Soconusco at Ojo de Agua during the Jocotal phase as well as low platform mounds at this site and at Cuauhtémoc (and at various other sites in the estuary). However, during the Conchas phase, when populations from the Mazatán and Rio Jesus zones resettled in the area surrounding La Blanca, the scale of such mounds increased dramatically. Mound construction also became a more integrative act as conical mounds were built at each newly formed political center in the La Blanca polity. The act of building large mounds and the social unity produced by such coordinated labor projects may have been as important as the ultimate function that such newly erected structures were put. One way to integrate people at newly congregating centers would have been through the coordinated labor projects that transformed the built environment and left a permanent reminder of these founding events in the form of mounds that literally raised subsequent rituals above the level of everyday events. In fact, people may have initially come to the La Blanca polity to participate in the construction of mounds built at various political centers. This is consistent with arguments I have made elsewhere that Conchas phase elites sponsored integrative feasts (Rosenswig 2007) and took advantage of their greater control of maize production to allow greater population concentration and increasingly hierarchical society (Rosenswig 2006; and see Blake and Clark 1999; Love 2002a). At Cuauhtémoc, a stretch of the high ground 180 meters long that the site rested on was extended 30 meters and a mound five meters high was built on top of this newly created space. Such construction projects could have helped unite the site's inhabitants by engaging them in a communal endeavor that was perceived to benefit everyone.

The Conchas phase polity lasted only a century and a half, from approximately 1000 to 850 cal. BCE. Most of the communities that built and used the Conchas phase mounds were then abandoned when the focus of settlement in the immediate area moved to the region around Izapa on the edge of the Sierra Madre piedmont. In fact, one reason why the early Middle Formative La Blanca polity is relatively well known is that many of its centers were not covered by centuries of subsequent construction projects. The size of Conchas phase mounds reflects the position of these polities' rulers in the local political hierarchy, but the site's abandonment also tells us of the symbolic power of the mounds themselves. When a new regime was founded at Izapa during the second part of the Middle Formative, the coastal plain was largely abandoned (Rosenswig 2008). However, the early occupation of Izapa is too poorly known to say much for certain (Lowe, Lee, and Espinoza 1982).

Joyce's description of Los Naranjos and Yarumela in the epigraph that begins this chapter describes how the earliest mounds "centered" the communities in which they were built. Trigger's epigraph describes a similar process, observed from his comparison of societies around the world. This suggests that the Mesoamerican pattern has general anthropological relevance. However, in the Soconusco the three conical mounds built at Ojo de Agua did not "center" subsequent Conchas phase society. In fact, the founders of the La Blanca polity chose the other end of the land between the large swamp systems to establish their new polity. Not only was a new location selected (on land that had not been previously occupied) but the nature of monumentality was consolidated and amplified into a single huge mound at the site's center that was many times higher than anything built before. Furthermore, the use of mounds was no longer confined to the political capitals but was used to integrate the top three levels of political centers and create a more hierarchical (and demographically concentrated) society. The power and memory of the mounds at Ojo de Agua were rejected by the newly established regime at La Blanca, whose rulers both literally and figuratively distanced themselves from what had come before.

Mounds and other forms of monumental building projects can be powerful symbols that, when augmented, incorporate the power of those that had gone before. This pattern is clearly exemplified in the Maya area, where mounds were sometimes expanded and rebuilt dozens of times. However, a related logic was followed in the Spanish conquest of the Americas. Cortez built his palace on top of Moctezuma's and the Catholic cathedral next to the Templo Mayor (Matos Moctezuma 1989). Not only was the cathedral built next to the Templo Mayor but the Spanish used the stones from its final enlargement episode to construct the Christian temple that maintained spatially their religious and political authority (Low 1995, 757). This spatial syncretism was reinforced by staging open-air masses to convert the Aztecs in a manner reminiscent of their own religious ceremonies and through the use of pre-Columbian art forms to relay Christian biblical stories (Matos Moctezuma 1989, 16). The Mexico City example follows similar logic to the Maya case in that both maintain the location of past rulers as significant locations on the landscape. Maya kings augmented what their predecessors had built and so were linked to them. Cortez, in contrast, used stones from the Aztec architecture to build the new Spanish structures—symbolically incorporating the Aztec power but replacing it with the civic-ceremonial architecture of the Spanish empire.

The Formative period peoples of the Soconusco were clearly not organized like the Spanish empire, nor did successive regimes co-opt the political center of their predecessors. In the Mazatán zone, Cantón Corralito began as a competing polity that surpassed Paso de la Amada and replaced it as the dominant center during the Cuadros phase. When Cantón Corralito was wiped out by a natural disaster, the elite seem to have made the very practical decision to rebuild on the other side of the Coatán River and avoid risking future flood damage. In contrast, there is no known "practical" reason to have abandoned the Mazatán zone at 1000 cal. BCE and to have moved down the coast to the Cahuacán, Suchiate, and Naranjo rivers. The La Blanca polity either represents a new group of people immigrating into the Soconusco after the previous inhabitants disappeared (which is unlikely) or a new regime that was purposefully distancing itself and its authority from what had come before. Either way, a break from the past was inherent in the building of La Blanca where it was, next to the Guamuchal swamp.

The rejection of the previous Mazatán regime was achieved spatially. This move was not as extreme as that described by Adam T. Smith of the Urartian Empire's practice of "obliterating the built environments of prior political communities by demolishing Late Bronze Age and early Iron Age fortresses," which reflected "a desire to empty conquered regions of the physical vestiges of prior polities" (Smith 2004, 16). In the Soconusco case, the new Conchas phase regime used distance to disengage from the Mazatán polities, whereas the "Urartian kings attempted . . . a brutal reordering of the cartography of memory achieved in both the destruction of place and the production of forgetting" (ibid., 18). All of these cases highlight the importance of controlling the built environment for political ends. The centers of earlier regimes were powerful places that could either be co-opted (as in the Spanish rebuilding of Tenochtitlan; or augmented, as in the case of Maya states) or erased, as with the Urartian destruction or Conchas phase recentering of the population in the southeast part of the Soconusco.

Conclusion

The early Middle Formative Conchas phase witnessed a dramatic reorganization of Soconusco society at approximately 1000 cal. BCE. Population nucleated in the southeast part of the Soconusco when surrounding areas (such as the Mazatán zone, which had contained a series of Early Formative centers) were abandoned. This nucleated polity was organized with four tiers of settlement—at least one more tier than anything previously seen in the Soconusco. At the top three tiers, political centers were each built around a central conical mound. Only two of these sites are documented by excavation: the paramount center of La Blanca with its 25-meter-high central mound (Love 2002a; Love and Guernsey 2011) and the third-tier center of Cuauhtémoc with its 5-meter-high central mound (Rosenswig 2010). Clear social stratification is also evident at this time; more prestige items have been recovered from La Blanca than from Cuauhtémoc, and the use of such items was restricted to elite contexts within each site (Love 2002a; Rosenswig 2007). The Conchas phase was also when food production became markedly more important than at any time during the Early Formative period, and inhabitants of the Soconusco relied on maize to a much greater extent than before. However, the correspondence of these developments does not indicate which phenomenon was causative. What is clear is that in the Soconusco the first regional program of "non-functional" (sensu Trigger 1990) monumental architecture was part of a cultural reorganization that also included increased stratification and a greater reliance of food production.

In contrast, in the southeastern United States and in South America the first monumental architecture predates ceramic use, agricultural intensification, and political and social stratification by centuries. Early mounds may have served a very different purpose in Mesoamerica compared to these other regions of the New World. Labor projects were organized that transformed the local landscape in all cases, but the underlying political and social mechanism could have differed. In the Soconusco, the construction of a system of conical mounds at the beginning of the Middle Formative period was part of a new adaptation that also established more hierarchical sociopolitical relations and increasingly relied on maize production (see Table 5.2). This chapter summarizes independent lines of evidence for each of these processes, and it does not use the mere presence of monumentality as a proxy for either hierarchy or food production. An additional indication of the political role that Conchas phase mounds served in the Soconusco was their avoidance by subsequent regimes—which is strongly suggestive of their lasting symbolic power. In sum, I have argued that conical mounds were a central component of the creation of the La Blanca polity in terms of both the labor for their initial construction as well as the long-term symbolic meaning of their subsequent use and that Trigger's (1990, 2004) thermodynamic explanation accurately describes early monumentality in the Soconusco.

References Cited

Blake, Michael
1991   An Emerging Early Formative Chiefdom at Paso de la Amada, Chiapas, Mexico. In *The Formation of Complex Society in Southeastern Mesoamerica*, edited by William R. Fowler Jr., pp. 27–45. CRC Press, Boca Raton.
2006   Dating the Initial Spread of *Zea mays*. In *Histories of Maize*, edited by John E. Staller, Robert Tykot, and Bruce Benz, pp. 55–72. Academic Press, New York.
Blake, Michael and John E. Clark
1999   The Emergence of Hereditary Inequality: The Case of Pacific Coastal Chiapas. In *Pacific Latin America in Prehistory*, edited by Michael Blake, pp. 55–73. Washington State University Press, Seattle.
Blake, Michael, B. S. Chisholm, John E. Clark, Barbara Voorhies, and Michael W. Love
1992   Prehistoric Subsistence in the Soconusco Region. *Current Anthropology* 33:83–94.
Blake, Michael, Richard G. Lesure, Warren D. Hill, Luis Barba and John E. Clark
2006   The Residence of Power at Paso de la Amada, Mexico. In *Palaces and Power in the Americas: From Peru to the Northwest Coast*, edited by Jessica Joyce Christie and Patricia Joan Sarro, pp. 191–210. University of Texas Press, Austin.
Cheetham, David
2006   America's First Colony? A Possible Olmec Outpost in Southern Mexico *Archaeology* 59(1):42–46.
Chisholm, Brian and Michael Blake
2006   Diet in Prehistoric Soconusco. In *Histories of Maize*, edited by John E. Staller, Robert Tykot, and Bruce Benz, pp. 161–172. Academic Press, New York.
Clark, John E.
1997   The Arts of Government in Early Mesoamerica. *Annual Review of Anthropology* 26: 211–234.
2004a Mesoamerica Goes Public: Early Ceremonial Centers, Leaders and Communities. In *Mesoamerican Archaeology: Theory and Practice*, edited by Julia A. Hendon and Rosemary A. Joyce, pp. 43–72. Blackwell, Oxford.
2004b Surrounding the Sacred: Geometry and Design of Early Mound Groups as Meaning and Function. In *Signs of Power: The Rise of Cultural Complexity in the Southeast*, edited by Jon L. Gibson and Philip J. Carr, pp. 162–213. University of Alabama Press, Tuscaloosa.

Clark, John E., and Michael Blake
1989   El Origen de la Civilización en Mesoamerica: Los Olmecas y Mokaya del Soconusco de Chiapas, México. In *El Preclásico o Formativo: Avances y Perspectivas*, edited by M. Carmona Macias, pp. 385–403. Museo Nacional de Antropología, Mexico City.
1994   The Power of Prestige: Competitive Generosity and the Emergence of Rank Societies in Lowland Mesoamerica. In *Factional Competition and Political Development in the New World*, edited by E. M. Brumfiel and J. W. Fox, pp. 17–30. Cambridge University Press, Cambridge.

Clark, John E., and Dennis Gosser
1995   Reinventing Mesoamerica's First Pottery. In *The Emergence of Pottery: Technology and Innovation in Ancient Societies*, edited by William K. Barnett and John W. Hoopes, pp. 209–921. Smithsonian Institution Press, Washington, D.C.

Clark, John E., and Mary E. Pye
2000   The Pacific Coast and the Olmec Question. In *Olmec Art and Archaeology in Mesoamerica*, edited by John E. Clark and Mary E. Pye, pp. 217–251. National Gallery of Art, Washington, D.C.

Coe, Michael D.
1961   *La Victoria: An Early Site on the Pacific Coast of Guatemala*. Papers of the Peabody Museum of Archaeology and Ethnology, Vol. 53. Peabody Museum, Cambridge, Massachusetts.

Coe, Michael D., and Kent V. Flannery
1967   *Early Cultures and Human Ecology in South Coastal Guatemala*. Smithsonian Contributions to Anthropology Vol. 3. Smithsonian Institute, Washington, D.C.

Cyphers, Ann
2004   *Escultura Olmec de San Lorenzo Tenochtitlán*. Universidad Nacional Autonomo de Mexico, Mexico, DF.

Diehl, Richard A.
1981   Olmec Architecture: A Comparison of San Lorenzo and La Venta. In *The Olmec and Their Neighbors: Essays in Memory of Mathew W. Sterling*, edited by E. P. Benson, pp. 69–82. Dumbarton Oaks, Washington, D.C.

Dietler, Michael
1998   A Tale of Three Sites: The Monumentalization of Celtic Oppida and the Politics of Collective Memory and Identity. *World Archaeology* 30:72–89.

Ekholm, Susanna M.
1969   *Mound 30a and the Preclassic Ceramic Sequence of Izapa, Chiapas, Mexico*. Papers, New World Archaeological Foundation 25. Brigham Young University, Provo.

Feddema, Vicki
1993   Early Formative Subsistence and Agriculture in Southeastern Mesoamerica. Master's thesis, Department of Anthropology and Sociology, University of British Columbia, Vancouver.

Fletcher, Roland
1995   *The Limits of Settlement Growth: A Theoretical Outline*. Cambridge University Press, New York.

Grove, David C.
1999   Public Monuments and Sacred Mountains: Observations on Three Formative Period Sacred Landscapes. In *Social Patterns in Preclassic Mesoamerica*, edited by D. C. Grove and R. Joyce, pp. 255–299. Dunbarton Oaks, Washington, D.C.

Gutiérrez, Gerardo
2011   A History of Disaster and Cultural Change in the Coatan River Drainage of the Soconusco, Chiapas, Mexico. In *Sociopolitical Transformation in Early Mesoamerica: Archaic to Formative in the Soconusco Region,* edited by Richard Lesure, pp. 146–169. University of California Press, Berkeley.

Hill, Warren D., Michael Blake and John E. Clark
1998   Ball Court Design Date Back 3,400 years. *Nature* 392:878–879.

Joyce, Rosemary A.
2004   Unintended Consequences? Monumentality As a Novel Experience in Formative Mesoamerica. *Journal of Anthropological Method and Theory* 11:5–29.

Lesure, Richard G.
1997   Early Formative Platforms at Paso de la Amada, Chiapas, Mexico. *Latin American Antiquity* 8:217–235.
2009   *Settlement and Subsistence in Early Formative Soconusco: El Varal and the Problem of Inter-Site Assemblage Variation*. Cotsen Institute of Archaeology Press, Los Angeles.

Love, Michael W.
1991   Style and Social Complexity in Formative Mesoamerica. In *The Formation of Complex Society in Southeastern Mesoamerica*, edited by William R. Fowler Jr., pp. 47–76. CRC Press, Boca Raton.
1999   Ideology, Material Culture and Daily Practice in Pre-Classic Mesoamerica: A Pacific Coast Perspective. In *Social Patterns in Pre-Classic Mesoamerica*, edited by D. G. Grove and R. A. Joyce, pp. 127–154. Dunbarton Oaks, Washington, D.C.
2002a   *Early Complex Society in Pacific Guatemala: Settlements and Chronology of the Rio Naranjo, Guatemala*. Papers of the New World Archaeological Foundation 66. Brigham Young University, Provo.
2002b   Domination, Resistance, and Political Cycling in Formative Period Pacific Guatemala. In *The Dynamics of Power,* edited by Maria O'Donovan, pp. 214–237. Center for Archaeological Investigations Occasional Paper No. 30. Southern Illinois University, Carbondale.

Love, Michael, and Julia Guernsey
2011   La Blanca and the Soconusco Middle Formative Period. In *Sociopolitical Transformation in Early Mesoamerica: Archaic to Formative in the Soconusco Region,* edited by Richard Lesure, 170–188. University of California Press, Berkeley.

Low, Setha M.
1995   Indigenous Architecture and the Spanish American Plaza in Mesoamerica and the Caribbean. *American Anthropologist* 97:748–762.

Lowe, Gareth W., Thomas A. Lee Jr., and E. M. Espinoza
1982   *Izapa: An Introduction to the Ruins and Monuments*. Papers of the New World Archaeological Foundation, No. 31. Brigham Young University, Provo, Utah.

Matos Moctezuma, Eduardo
1989 The Templo Major of Tenochtitlan. In *The Great Temple of Tenochtitlan*, edited by J. Broda, D. Carrasco, and E. Matos Moctezuma, pp. 15–60. University of California Press, Berkeley.
Neff, Hector, Deborah M. Pearsall, John G. Jones, Bárbara Arroyo, Shawn K. Collins, and Dorothy E. Freidel
2006 Early Maya Adaptive Patterns: Mid-Late Holocene Paleoenvironmental Evidence from Pacific Guatemala. *Latin American Antiquity* 17:287–315.
Pérez Suárez, Tomás
2002 Cantón Corralito: un sitio Olmeca en el litoral chiapaneco. In *Arqueología mexicana, historia y esencia*, vol. 20, *En reconocimiento al Dr. Román Piña Chán*, edited by J. Nava Rivero, pp. 71–92. Instituto Nacional de Antropología e Historia, Mexico City.
Pinkowski, Jennifer
2006 A City by the Sea: Early Urban Planning on Mexico's Pacific Coast. *Archaeology* 59 (1):46–49.
Pye, Mary E., and Arthur A. Demarest
1991 The Evolution of Complex Societies in Southeastern Mesoamerica: New Evidence from El Mesak, Guatemala. In *The Formation of Complex Societies in Southeastern Mesoamerica*, edited by William R. Fowler Jr., pp. 77–100. CRC Press, Boca Raton.
Pye, Mary, John Hodgson, and John Clark
2011 Jocotal Settlement Patterns, Salt Production and Pacific Coast Interaction. In *Sociopolitical Transformation in Early Mesoamerica: Archaic to Formative in the Soconusco Region*, edited by Richard Lesure, pp. 217–241. University of California Press, Berkeley.
Rapoport, Amos
1982 *The Meaning of the Built Environment: A Nonverbal Communication Approach.* Sage Press, Beverly Hills, California.
1988 Levels of Meaning in the Built Environment. In *Cross-Cultural Perspectives in Nonverbal Communication*, edited by Fernando Poyatos, pp. 317–336. Hogrefe, Toronto.
1990 Systems of Activities and Systems of Settings. In *Domestic Architecture and the Use of Space: An Interdisciplinary Cross-Cultural Study*, edited by Susan Kent, pp. 9–20. Cambridge University Press, Cambridge.
Reilly, F. Kent
Mountains of Creation and Underworld Portals: The Ritual Function of Olmec Architecture at La Venta, Tabasco. In *Mesoamerican Architecture as a Cultural Symbol* edited by Jeff K. Kowalski, pp. 14–39. Oxford University Press, Oxford, England.
Rosenswig, Robert M.
2000 Some Political Processes of Ranked Societies. *Journal of Anthropological Archaeology* 19:413–460.
2006 Sedentism and Food Production in Early Complex Societies of the Soconusco, Mexico. *World Archaeology* 38:329–354.
2007 Beyond Identifying Elites: Feasting as a Means to Understand Early Middle Formative Society on the Pacific Coast of Mexico. *Journal of Anthropological Archaeology* 26:1–27.

2008   Prehispanic Settlement in the Cuauhtémoc Zone of the Soconusco, Chiapas, Mexico. *Journal of Field Archaeology* 33:389–411.
2009   Early Mesoamerican Garbage: Ceramic and Daub Discard Patterns from Cuauhtémoc, Soconusco, Mexico. *Journal of Archaeological Method and Theory* 16:1–32.
2010   *The Beginnings of Mesoamerican Civilization: Inter-Regional Interaction and the Olmec.* Cambridge University Press, New York.
2011   An Early Mesoamerican Archipelago of Complexity: As Seen from Changing Population and Human Depictions at Cuauhtémoc. In *Sociopolitical Transformation in Early Mesoamerica: Archaic to Formative in the Soconusco Region,* edited by Richard Lesure, pp. 242–271. University of California Press, Berkeley.

Rosenswig, Robert M., Amber M. VanDerwarker, and Douglas J. Kennett
n.d.   The Origins of Maize Agriculture in Mesoamerica. Unpublished manuscript.

Smith, Adam T.
2000   Rendering the Political Aesthetic: Political Legitimacy in Urartian Representations of the Built Environment. *Journal of Anthropological Archaeology* 19:131–163.
2003   *The Political Landscape: Constellations of Authority in Early Complex Polities.* University of California Press, Berkeley.
2004   The End of the Essential Archaeological Subject. *Archaeological Dialogues* 11:1–20.

Taube, Karl
2000   Lightning Celts and Corn Fetishes: The formative Olmec and the Development of Maize Symbolism in Mesoamerica and the American Southwest. In *Olmec Art and Archaeology in Mesoamerica,* edited by J. E. Clark and M. E. Pye, pp. 297–337. National Gallery of Art, Washington.

Trigger, Bruce G.
1990   Monumental Architecture: A Thermodynamic Explanation of Symbolic Behaviour. *World Archaeology* 22:119–132.
2004   Settlement Patterns in the Postmodern World: A Study of Monumental Architecture in Early Civilizations. In *The Archaeologist: Detective and Thinker,* edited by L. Vishnyatsky, A. Kovalev, and O. Scheglova, pp. 237–248. St. Petersburg University Press, St. Petersburg, Russia.

Voorhies, Barbara
2004   *Coastal Collectors in the Holocene: The Chantuto People of Southwest Mexico.* University Press of Florida, Gainesville.

6

Early Olmec Wetland Mounds

Investing Energy to Produce Energy

ANN CYPHERS AND JUDITH ZURITA-NOGUERA

By the time monumentality was explicitly manifested in the massive stone sculptures and earthen edifices created by the Olmec of Mexico's southern Gulf Coast, its elusive origins were cloaked in the cultural foundations that made their creation possible. The colossal heads of monolithic stone cannot tell us how the rulers they portray came to power since these celebrated examples of Olmec high-energy investments are merely the final result of centuries of sorting out and rearranging complicated social, political, and economic relations in order to mobilize work forces.

The same is true of the well-known artificial plateau of the early Olmec capital of San Lorenzo, Veracruz, Mexico (Figure 6.1). The episodic construction of its stacked habitation terraces and relatively flat summit through the placement of six to eight million m^3 of artificial earthen fill occurred during its florescence, between 1400 and 1000 BCE, and involved work efforts involving a total of 14–18 million person-hours of labor (Cyphers et al. 2007–2008). The design and dynamic construction of the plateau provided tangible but changing parameters for continually modeling and remodeling a pattern of population distribution in which social and political status declined with diminishing elevation and distance from the center of the site. This roughly concentric pattern appears to replicate the cosmic map of the sacred mountain, a model that governed quotidian life and reinforced the principles of sociopolitical differentiation. The origins of plateau building, however, are far less spectacular. During several centuries prior to 1400 cal. BCE, the 125-hectare natural promontory was gradually leveled with 1,300,000 m^3 of earthen fill, a long-term effort well within work capacity of the early population and thus a task that did not require centralized coordination. Yet these early expenditures of energy to shape the landform laid the groundwork for raising the great plateau.

Another important but less impressive example of early construction consists of relatively small artificial mounds built in the wetlands (Symonds, Cyphers, and Lunagómez 2002), which are the focus of this chapter. These dry base camps are a previously unrecognized component of San Lorenzo's settlement pattern (Figure 6.1), but they figured prominently in the wetland-focused lifeways of the founding groups and their descendants. Our data indicate that the initial construction of the majority of these mounds in the broad wetland just north of San Lorenzo likely predates the initial stage of plateau building, making them one of the earliest and perhaps the first manifestations of artificial mound construction by the inhabitants of San Lorenzo. (From now on we will use the accepted Mexican archaeological term *islotes* instead of the cumbersome but synonymous English phrase "artificial wetland mound.")

As we shall demonstrate, the *islotes*, taken individually or collectively, do not represent a conspicuous consumption of energy, one of Trigger's criteria of monumentality (1990). Yet they represent noteworthy labor investments over a long period of time for the people who built and maintained them (see Rosenswig and Burger this volume). These important economic assets constitute technological infrastructure and were built to minimize risk by facilitating a diversified set of subsistence strategies in the surrounding wetlands. Although they have little apparent fit with concepts of monumentality because of the low amount of energy invested in building them, their relevance to the theme of the present volume lies in the returns on that investment. Each *islote* represented a trade-off, a capital investment of human energy in an earthen structure in order to obtain more dependable and greater returns in food energy; in other words, energy was used to produce more energy (see Price 1971, 1982). Ultimately, as Trigger points out (1990, 125), the production of surplus food is key in controlling labor, which is involved in the creation of power and prestige symbols.

In this sense, *islote* construction and use were relevant to the emergent social and political relations that laid the foundations for Olmec monumentality. In the following sections, we explore the functions of *islotes*, the nature and source of the labor mobilized to construct them, the identity of their builders and their implications for food production and social development that contributed, at least in part, to subsequent Olmec apogee developments characterized by incontrovertible monumentality—the large-scale earthen and stone monuments imbued with power, artistic

Figure 6.1. Photograph of a large *islote* in San Lorenzo's northern plain.

beauty, and symbolism. In short, our findings indicate that the *islotes* may be included in an array of early Olmec strategies for managing subsistence security in a high-risk situation and were implicated in the development of hierarchical relations (see O'Shea 1990).

We have organized the subsequent discussion by topics such as *islote* characteristics and brief comparisons with other similar structures in Mesoamerica and the world, followed by an evaluation of the construction effort involved in the San Lorenzo *islotes*. Then the high frequency of *islotes* in the northern plain is linked to resource concentration in this key zone, followed by discussions of construction and occupation trends and their functions. The chapter concludes with an overview of early Olmec subsistence, particularly with regard to the wetlands; possible ideological associations of the *islotes*; and a diachronic synopsis.

Islote Characteristics

Today water-logged areas are often considered "marginal," but it is clear that the Olmec preferred the soggy coastal plains where most of the major sites are located. In addition, *islote* distribution suggests that contemporary views of the wetlands were not shared by ancient peoples.

The *islotes* around San Lorenzo are artificial earthen mounds averaging 1.3 m high and 50 m in basal diameter and containing 170 m^3 of fill (Figure 6.1). The fact that they are present only in the wetlands of yesteryear (Symonds, Cyphers, and Lunagómez 2002, 42–43) signals that they were useful for activities particular to this setting. They are not spaces for cultivation but furnish dry areas for erecting superstructures. Nor do they appear as planned layouts similar to mound and plaza architecture, although linear distribution and clusters are discernable. Even though their practical function is different from those of raised fields and *chinampa*s, they are comparable to them in a broad sense as artificial land fashioned in watery spaces for carrying out subsistence activities.

Surveys conducted in an area 400 km² around San Lorenzo identified 81 Early Formative period *islotes*. The highest frequency (n=47) was found in the 2,100-hectare alluvial plain (3–10 MASL) occupying the northern end of the San Lorenzo island, here designated as the "northern plain." It is important to note that *islote* frequency in the northern plain is underrepresented because of the dense surface cover that existed when survey was conducted, Mexican crowngrass (*Paspalum fasciculatum* Willd.) that was nearly two meters high (Symonds, Cyphers, and Lunagómez 2002, 53). Poor visibility did not favor the detection of smaller *islotes*. A detailed topographic map of a portion of the northern plain (which was made after crowngrass removal) reveals almost twice as many *islotes* as the number detected in survey (Figure 6.2; see also Symonds Cyphers, and Lunagómez 2002, fig. 4.2), so the surveyed *islotes* may be considered a 50 percent sample.

The characteristics of the annual hydrological cycle suggest that *islote* use was seasonal or intermittent (Symonds, Cyphers, and Lunagómez 2002, 42–43). The highest floods, which take place between September and December, create the greatest risks for wetland habitation. Permanent occupation of the wetland is hazardous for human life during flood stages, as has been noted in analogous situations (see Denevan 1996; Meggers 1984). Modern-day high floods attain depths of 1.5–2 m in the northern plain, and ancient levels may have been similar or greater, judging from the flood-battered *islote* superstructures that have been excavated. This damage is strong evidence for their periodic use (contra Clark 2007, 25, 44, 46).

Artificial wetland mounds are found across Mesoamerica and throughout the world and were used for a variety of activities. They have been reported around the Middle Formative Olmec capital of La Venta (González Lauck 1988, 137) and are known from other parts of Mesoamerica in later times (e.g., Serra Puche 1988; Sugiura 1998). Some Aztec *tlateles* of Lake Texcoco may have been used for seasonal salt production in Lake Texcoco (Charlton 1969, 1971; Noguera 1975), and others scattered throughout the Basin of Mexico were foundations for permanent residential and

142 · Ann Cyphers and Judith Zurita-Noguera

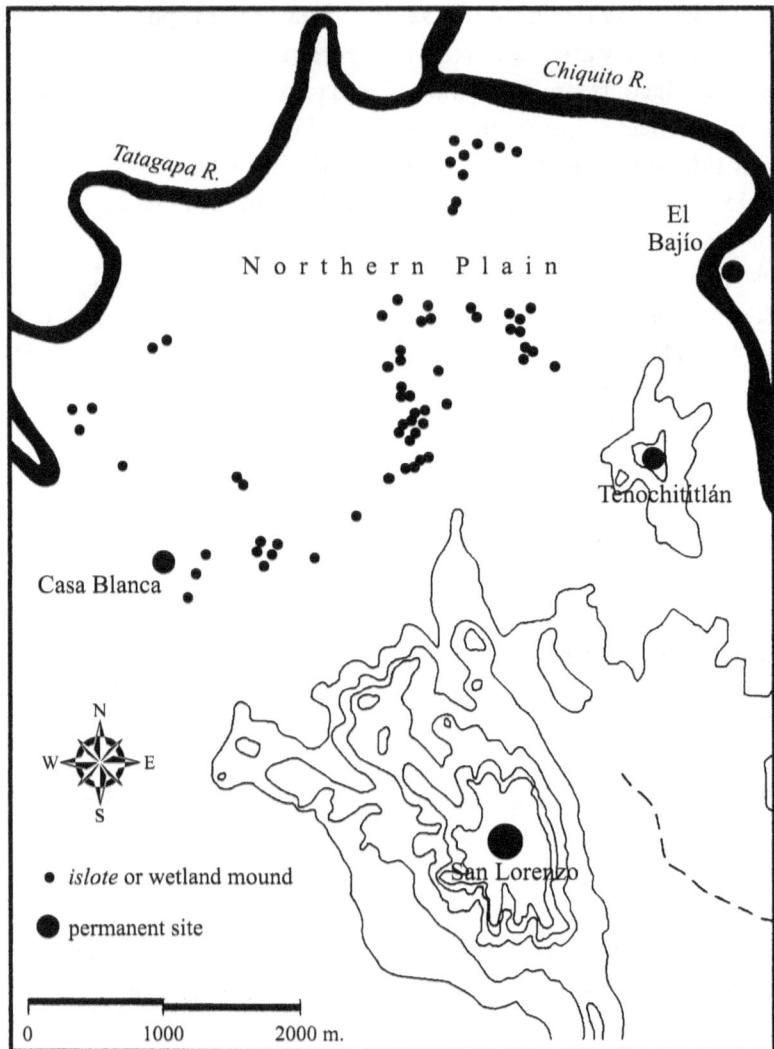

Figure 6.2. Map of the San Lorenzo region showing the principal permanent sites and the *islotes* identified through survey and detailed mapping in the northern plain (after Symonds et al. 2002, Figs. 4.2 and 4.6).

civic-ceremonial occupation (Arciniega-Ceballos et al. 2009; Parsons 1971). Structures facilitating wetland occupation occur in other world areas and surely there are many more examples than the ones briefly surveyed here. Analogous archaeological constructions are found on Marajó Island in Brazil, which Schaan aptly describes as "moving earth to control water" (Schaan 2008, 341). They are also reported for the Hertenrits culture of the Arauquinoid Tradition of Suriname and the Guyanas (Rothstain 2008;

Versteeg 2008) and Llano de Moxos, Bolivia (Erickson 2000). Further afield, the Marsh Arabs, for example, lived on earthen tumuli in the lower Tigris-Euphrates floodplains and were involved in the dried fish trade (Dougherty 1927, 11–12; Thesiger 1964).

Comparable basal platforms for houses are still built in the coastal wetlands of the southern Gulf of Mexico. In several contemporary settlements in southeastern Mexico, *islotes* are occupied and owned by households that are strongly oriented to aquatic resource procurement and wetland agriculture. This is the case of some Chontal groups of Tabasco, who occupy such earthen platforms in the swamps but move to safer places in flood times (Inchaustegi 1987).

Islote Construction

The scale of *islote* construction at San Lorenzo—as an investment in energy framed in person-hours—may help reveal the identity of their creators. A central issue is whether *islotes* were the product of a central organization or were constructed by households. Information on earth-moving activities specific to the modern San Lorenzo region provides useful parameters for evaluating the overall scale of *islote* construction efforts.

How were the *islotes* built? Soil was taken from near each *islote*, as confirmed by the presence of freshwater sponge spicules in their earthen fill (Zurita n.d.; see also Schwandes and Collins 1994), and earth transport probably did not cover a distance greater than 25 m. Given the sogginess of the floodplain and the timing of precipitation, the window of opportunity for construction may have been restricted to about 30 days during the hottest and driest months of the year (late April to early June). In this period each structure had to be completed quickly to avoid ruin during the impending rainy season. The following calculations refer exclusively to this short annual period. It is important to mention that this period is traditionally the period for cleaning upland fields and preparing them for cultivation, a time of high labor expenditure.

Based on our decades of supervising labor in the region, during which we have observed human resistance to the climate, we consider Erasmus' proposal of a five-hour work day (1965, 285) a reasonable labor figure for the hottest month of the year, when maximum temperatures hover around 40–45° C. During the field seasons of the San Lorenzo Tenochtitlán Archaeological Project, we have had the opportunity to calculate and verify the workers' capacity for digging and carrying silty sandy soil. We consistently observed that the speed of extraction and transport of sediments occurred at a rate of 0.43 m³ per person-hour, a figure only slightly lower than Erasmus' estimate of 2.6 m³ per five-hour day (1965).

Our attempt to examine the capacity for *islote* construction was also hindered by lack of knowledge of the size and composition of households and of residential patterns, so we use the figures presented by Arco and Abrams (2006) in their energy-use study of Postclassic *chinampa* construction, in which they estimate the labor of two individuals per family of five. In addition, taking a cue from Webster and Kirker (1995), we chose to use the pre–San Lorenzo phase mean population estimate of 444 inhabitants of San Lorenzo's inner hinterland (following Symonds, Cyphers, and Lunagómez 2002, 57) as the limit for a statistical model of annual population increase. Paleodemographer Allan Ortega kindly provided a mathematical model of continuous composite growth that allowed us to make a crude estimate of household frequency and the available annual labor.

The estimation of *islote* volume based on their visible size indicates the relatively small scale of construction as compared to later monumental efforts in the region during the apogee phase. The total volume of all the 47 surveyed *islotes* concentrated in the plain north of San Lorenzo did not exceed 20,000 m³ of earth, which represents about 46,500 person-hours of labor. Comparatively speaking, about 15–20 percent of the *islotes* represent an individual construction effort (15–90 person-hours) similar to or less than the effort required to construct a single central Mexican *chinampa*, which has been calculated as involving 10 person-days, or 50 person-hours (Arco and Abrams 2006). However, the labor investment in the remaining *islotes* is higher, ranging from 100 to 1,350 person-hours. The preliminary nature of this exercise in calculation energy use may be refined with time, but in very general terms, it shows that the 46,500 person-hours required for all *islote* construction represents little overall effort.

The available labor supply of the average household (300 person-hours for the 30-day period in a given year) was sufficient to erect any of the *islotes*, which range in size from 24 to 145 m³ and required 56 to 337 person-hours to build. Of course, as is well known in ethnographic situations, household construction efforts often entail the voluntary participation of kin and non-kin, which would further ease the process. Thus, *islote* construction was well within the work capacity of the average household, known ethnographically as *islote* builders and users.

Islote Location and Temporal Trends

The high concentration of *islotes* in the northern plain is linked to this area's high potential for subsistence resource exploitation and to its exceptional natural characteristics, which favor the implementation of a variety of risk-reducing subsistence strategies in tandem with seasonal variations in the hydrological and climatic cycle.[1] The northern plain's potential for efficient resource exploitation and control (see Carneiro 1988) enhanced the importance of these resources in risk minimization, making it a key resource zone.

The northern plain was once a perennial freshwater, or *popal*, wetland (see Bozarth 2001; Zurita 1997, n.d.) subject to fluctuating seasonal and long-term hydrology and with periodic low salinity because of tidal influence. It was, in essence, the wettest portion of the terrain surrounding San Lorenzo. The uneven distribution of its morphological features, such as branching and migrating waterways, abandoned meanders, point bar formations, back-swamps, floodplain bottoms, decantation basins or floodplain pools, and abundant active and extinct levees (see Ortiz and Cyphers 1997), conditioned differences in resource availability. Its subsistence potential differed from that of southern floodplains, since its great width (7 km), deep water, and slow post-floodwater reduction fostered the concentration of high-biomass aquatic resources (e.g., invertebrates, birds and fish) (see Power et al. 1979).

As Limp and Reidhead (1979, 71) point out, resource abundance is only one critical subsistence factor; the cost of procurement is equally important. The northern plain has particular features, such oxbow lakes, floodplain pools, and side channels, that facilitate cost-efficient techniques for harvesting aquatic resources (see Coe and Diehl 1980; Limp and Reidhead 1979; Ortiz and Cyphers 1997). Post-flood reduction in water levels confines fish in floodplain lakes and pools, making mass capture feasible; such places are also attractive for migratory fowl. Side channels also provide opportunities for harvesting; water backs up into them during low floods, which temporarily introduces fish that can be easily captured when the water level descends.

The spatial distribution of *islotes* corresponds to locations favorable for the mass harvesting of aquatic fauna in side channels, lakes, and other spots in the wetlands. The distribution shows a minor preference for slightly higher elevations (such as levee tops) and proximity to water-filled depressions and lakes. *Islotes* would be particularly useful as shelters at night, when channel fishing is done (see Coe and Diehl 1980, II:117). In addition, they may have been used as campsites from November to January, when recession agriculture may have been initiated in the higher and drier portions of the floodplain (see Symonds, Cyphers, and Lunagómez 2002, 43). Potentially exploitable floristic resources include cultivable trees for fruit and seed production and Marantaceae and Cyperaceae (such as *tule*) that are useful in producing basketry (Zurita 1997).

Islote occupation shows important temporal trends. The dating provided by Symonds, Cyphers, and Lunagómez (2002) was based on surface collections and was quite coarse because several phases had to be combined on account of the poor sample of ceramic types and vessel forms reported in the chronological sequences then available (i.e., Coe and Diehl 1980; Symonds, Cyphers, and Lunagómez 2002, Appendix II). We proceeded to remediate this situation by re-dating the survey material based on a more representative sequence (i.e., Cyphers n.d.) in order to obtain a finer-grained phase-by-phase view of *islote* use.

We were able to assign 44 *islotes* to the Early Formative. It should be noted that nine of these *islotes* cannot be dated to specific phases. Nonetheless, an interesting picture emerges from these data. We found that 90 percent of the datable *islotes* were founded in the Ojochi phase (1800–1600 BCE) and only 8 percent were created in the subsequent Bajío phase (1600–1500 BCE). None were founded in the Chicharras and San Lorenzo A phases (1500–1200 BCE), and only one may have been built in the San Lorenzo B phase (1200–1000 BCE). At least 71 percent of the *islotes* continued to be used in the Chicharras and San Lorenzo A and B phases.

The erection of the majority of *islotes* during the Ojochi phase coincides with low regional population densities (see Symonds, Cyphers, and Lunagóme 2002), and thus the wide availability of high ground excludes land scarcity as a factor that influenced their construction. Rather than population pressure, risk management was likely involved in their creation by founder groups.

The continuous use and maintenance of *islotes* from Ojochi to the San Lorenzo B phase points to the recognition of their ownership, the formalization of property rights, and the transfer of those rights from generation to generation. It appears that labor investments in the creation, continued use, maintenance, and rebuilding of enduring construction such as *islotes* begot property rights whose continuation was insured by inheritance rules (e.g., Adler 1996; Bayman and Sullivan 2008; Earle 2000; Smith 2004; Park

1992). The existence of inheritable rights is also supported by the apparent absence of further *islote* building in this zone and points to exclusive ownership by founding groups and their descendants.

Thus, *islotes* not only facilitated access to aquatic resources during harvest times, but their construction and maintenance also suggest that they were involved in the establishment of property rights in the northern plain (see Parsons 2010, 130, 132, regarding similar observations for the Basin of Mexico). The focus in the Ojochi phase on building *islotes* in this zone and the continued use of these structures was a means to establish and conserve rights to a specific area of the floodplains, a key resource zone that is particularly appropriate for strategic resource harvesting.

Concepts of tenure are most frequently applied to landed situations, but watery spaces and their resources also may be owned and alienated (e.g., Parsons 2006; Vennum 1988; contra Coe and Diehl 1980, II:146). Studies of fisheries increasingly show that territoriality and rights can be established in watery spaces (see Cordell 1978; Durrenburger and Pálsson 1987; Joly 1981), leading to the rejection of the idea that they invariably have unrestricted access. Open or de facto use may develop into a system of de jure rights or the coexistence of both systems insofar as temporary territorial claims are brought to bear on certain areas in order to control water space and its resources (Acheson 1981; Cordell 1978; Levieil and Orlove 1990; Nietschmann 1974; Pollnac and Littlefield 1983; Schlager and Ostrom 1992). Territoriality and property regimes are means of guaranteeing access to resources disputed by individuals and groups (Begossi 1995, 2). This outcome may be predictable in some cases, such as in places conducive to fish harvesting in which there is a greater return on energy per labor investment compared to the energy required for agricultural activities (Limp and Reidhead 1979), as is the case in the northern plain.

Islote Functions

Excavations in 16 *islotes* provide evidence of special functions. Archaeological work was largely restricted to centrally located test units, although several held more extensive operations. Most *islotes* show evidence of prepared floors that correspond to the interior of structures. The remains of earthen walls indicate that the superstructures rested directly on the ground surfaces; it is unknown if portions of them were elevated on stilts over the water. Floors and wall remains show evidence of water damage and destruction. The recovery of floral and faunal remains is poor, which could be result of the environmental conditions unfavorable to their preservation and water-edge garbage disposal practices.

A common element consists of an unusual burned pit feature. Its central location in the superstructures strongly suggests that it is related to the principal function of these buildings. Five superimposed burned pit features in one test unit illustrate the temporal continuity of the related activities, as well as their periodic destruction from flooding during the apogee phase. These apsidal-to-rectangular pits vary from 50 to 190 cm long but their width is fairly standard at around 30–60 cm. Interior depth averages about 30 cm, and their 3–8 cm thick walls are made of plastered clay that was fire-hardened by frequent use. Phytolith analysis of the ashy soil in their interior shows an inordinate frequency of palm (Arecaceae or Palmaceae), which is far higher than the microscopic remnants of palm roof thatch resting on the adjacent floors (Zurita n.d.). This evidence strongly suggests the use of palm as fuel, which is readily at hand in the wetlands. The thick leaf base of the *palma real* (*Scheelea liebmannii*) is still used as fuel by Tenochtitlán potters to fire their oxidized wares (see Krotser 1980, 135).

These features suggest that the central and safest part of the superstructures was used for preparing and preserving food, including drying and smoking (Figure 6.3). We propose that one of the products that may have been dried and smoked in these structures is fish and are currently testing this idea with chemical evidence.

Small fish are particularly desirable because the thinness of their flesh allows them to be dried or smoked whole. Once preserved, they may be stored for up to five months under optimum conditions. Dressed, salted, dried, and smoked individuals of large peripheral marine species have a shorter shelf life of about one month. Archaeological evidence for dried fish is expectedly meager, but the presence of a marine snapper in the Chicharras phase is interpreted by Coe and Diehl as a dried product (1980, I:390; see also Wing 1980, 376, 381). Another possible resource prepared in these hearths is the *chopontil* turtle, which is abundant in archaeological contexts (Wing 1980; Zúñiga n.d.), and the shell often shows evidence of heat alteration, probably from roasting. It is also possible that turtle meat was dried. We find no ethnographic reference for dried turtle meat in Mesoamerica, but it is reported for northeastern South America (Lathrap 1973).

Faunal studies, although hindered by poor preservation conditions, show that the Olmec relied heavily on aquatic species, including freshwater and peripheral forms (Wing 1980; Zúñiga n.d.). Wing's study of the quantity of usable meat shows that land sources contributed more than half,

Figure 6.3. Reconstruction of an *islote* showing the smoking of fish on a slatted stand placed above a sunken fire pit within a semi-enclosed structure (courtesy Fernando Botas).

and in the aquatic portion, peripheral forms predominate over freshwater species. However, these data may be affected by differential preservation, particularly of larger terrestrial and aquatic species, and by archaeological recovery techniques that cause an underemphasis on small aquatic individuals. Studies of the bias against the archaeological retrieval of small fish remains indicate that loss rates range from 50 percent (Limp and Reidhead 1979) to almost 100 percent (Garson 1980). Since small fish are generally recognized as important foods in riverine areas (Limp and Reidhead 1979), it is important to consider that the contribution of usable meat from small freshwater fish in the Olmec diet likely was more significant than is apparent in the data. The improved recovery of such remains also might provide insights on the difficult problem of the carrying capacity and depletion of fish.

Across the southern Gulf Coast, from the Chontalpa to the Tuxtlas to San Lorenzo, small whole fish are traditionally dried and smoked for prolonged storage and then used for household consumption and for distribution and sale. Foods are processed with slow heat and smoke. Whole small fish and other protein resources are placed on slatted stands (called *tapexte* or *tapesco*) that are elevated above an oxidizing fire, generally in semi-closed spaces. Brief soaking in salt water prior to drying inhibits bacterial growth and aids in extending preservation time. This activity does not leave significant remains of the foods that were processed.

The past and present importance of dried and smoked foods in the Gulf Coast tropical lowlands is related to the annual crisis time. Short-term food storage is critical for mitigating subsistence insecurity during the midsummer drought (July to September) and subsequent high flood.[2] The midsummer drought—a time of high water in the rivers, diminished rainfall, and high temperatures—occurs after the onset of the rainy season (see Roosevelt 1980 regarding the Amazonian case). For modern peasant farmers this is a time of maize scarcity, since in the month of June, upland crops have just been planted and stored reserves from the last harvest are depleted. Fish and turtle disperse in the high volume of water and are difficult to obtain at this time, as they are during the largest annual flood in late September to October. Hardship and food shortfalls are prevalent from July to October.

Survival in this long critical period requires the planned procurement and preparation of storable foods. Aquatic foods may be mass harvested in the northern plain following the retreat of the waters during the period of low floods in late June to mid-July. The waters do not flood over banks there at this time, and the water that backs up into side channels and accumulates in the deepest parts of the plain facilitates harvesting. Small fish are captured in traps set at stream confluences, and *chopontil* turtles (*Claudius angustatus*) are hunted in the shallow waters as they emerge from their aestivation period to feed and reproduce (Aguirre, Cázares, and Sánchez 2002). The harvested fish are dried and smoked during this season, and other foods are prepared, such as storable flour made from sun-dried root crops. The overall high humidity of the Gulf Coast lowlands is not conducive to long-term storage, but the hot dry conditions at the onset of the midsummer drought makes food drying and short-term storage possible. During the crisis time, the foods prepared in June and July are complemented by seasonally available freshwater shrimp and carbohydrate foods such as palm fruits.

The *islotes* were key elements that facilitated wetland subsistence procurement and must have been particularly important before the crisis period, when they would have been essential for the harvesting and production of storable aquatic provisions. When food availability dropped significantly during the midsummer drought and large annual flood, such foods were critical to the survival of the residents of permanent settlements.

Differences in the sizes of *islotes* suggest possible status differences among the households that built and owned them. By the apogee phase, a few *islotes* had become significantly larger and taller during their final construction stage. At the same time two permanent large sites were established in the northern plain (see Figure 6.2). First, the El Remolino site, situated on slightly elevated terrain at the northeastern end of the plain, figured prominently in the fluvial transportation network and in the organization of settlement in the region. It also had specialized functions as a locus for processing bitumen (Symonds, Cyphers, and Lunagómez 2002, 70; Wendt 2003; contra Clark 2007). And second, the Casa Blanca site, an extensive artificial island, is located at the southern entrance to the key resource zone. The coincident appearance of these permanent sites and the notable size increment in a few *islotes* suggest that social differences were becoming evident in the wetlands.

Olmec Energy Production

The investment of energy in buildings of any kind, whether ostentatious or modest, is linked to food production and consumption. Interestingly, the acclaimed icon of Mesoamerican subsistence, maize, does not figure prominently in early Olmec development despite the common view that the tropical southern Gulf Coast plains provided generally homogeneous conditions of abundant water, predictable hydrology and fertile soils that made it the "maize basket" that sustained the rise of Olmec civilization (e.g., Bernal 1969; Caso 1965; Clark 2007; Coe 1974; Coe and Diehl 1980; Heizer 1960). This view assumes that the production of a maize surplus was necessary for sociopolitical evolution, but despite the early presence of maize in Tabasco at 5100 cal. BCE (Goman and Byrne 1998; Pope et al. 2001; Pohl et al. 2007; see also Blake 2006; Sluyter and Domínguez 2006; Von Nagy 2003), it has not been shown to have been the centerpiece of Olmec subsistence at San Lorenzo at the onset of the Early Formative period (see Borstein 2001; Symonds, Cyphers, and Lunagómez 2002; Zurita 1997).

The common assumption that the Olmec were dependent on maize rides the wave of interest in the close correlation of grain cultivation (e.g., wheat, barley, rice, and maize) with the rise of complex societies in the Old and New Worlds, which underscores the importance of increased food production as a fundamental dimension of their development. In addition, the well-known advantages of maize include its genetic plasticity, which can result in increasing yields in the long run, and its storability, especially in environments of relatively low humidity. Studies have often focused on the role of agricultural intensification strategies aimed at increasing the amount of food produced and consumed by early complex societies (Boserup 1965; Morrison 1994; O'Shea 1989). A dimension of some (but not all) agricultural intensification strategies was to specialize on the most productive crops or those that had the greatest genetic potential for achieving increased yields through selective modification (Abruzzi 1987). However, maize agriculture, like all intensification strategies, carries with it an increased level of risk, especially in regions where favorable conditions fluctuate either as a result of variable environmental conditions or where crop productivity is inherently low or more varied because of incomplete or ongoing adaptation of cultigens to the environments.

For the Ojochi, Bajío, and Chicharras phases at San Lorenzo, there is negligible evidence for maize in the hundreds of samples so far analyzed during the ongoing studies of pollen, phytoliths and macroremains. Based on the distribution of settlement types by geomorphic unit, Symonds, Cyphers, and Lunagómez (2002) accord maize a lesser importance in the overall diet, arguing instead that aquatic protein and root crops may possibly have figured prominently. Root crops (*Manihot* sp.) identified in pre-1400 BCE phytolith samples (Zurita n.d.) may have been the early carbohydrate mainstay.

Although maize was known to the earliest Olmec of San Lorenzo, it was probably a very low productivity crop (see Kirkby 1973; Logan and Sanders 1976; López Corral 2006; Sanders and Nichols 1988; Sanders et al. 1979). It was gradually incorporated into the Olmec's broad mixed subsistence economy that combined fishing, hunting, and collecting with the cultivation of root crops and arboriculture. The appearance of cross-shaped and maize-cob phytoliths and carbonized kernels in San Lorenzo A and B phase contexts (Bozarth 2001; Zurita 1997, n.d.; Zurita-Noguera and Lane Rodríguez 2004) coincides with the appearance of seasonal camps positioned around permanent upland settlements, which is a pattern typically resulting from transitory agricultural activities associated with the swidden cycle (Symonds, Cyphers, and Lunagómez 2002; contra Clark 2007, 25). Site displacement away from permanent fluvial courses in the Tuxtlas piedmont at this time also may indicate a shift in patterns of food production, such as an increase in rain-fed maize agriculture. Site relocations also may have been influenced by sociopolitical factors (Borstein 2001).

River levees often figure prominently in discussions of early agriculture in the San Lorenzo region because of theories that they were highly fertile (and thus produced high levels of maize) and that they played a role in the emergence of elite power (e.g., Coe and Diehl 1980). This model, often taken as an accepted truth, is flawed in several ways. First, it assumes that river levees are a homogeneous category of landforms with a specific uniform soil type, which is a gross oversimplification of their variability and ignores the changeable impacts of the hydrological cycle and biome degradation from deforestation (see Latrubesse et al. 2009). Second, the high and potentially renewable fertility of the Coatzacoalcos series soils is considered to be the overarching factor that enabled extraordinary agricultural yields, which has been shown to be a faulty assumption (see Lane Rodríguez, Aguirre, and González 1997). And third, the supposition that the pre-planting preparation of the levee ground was less labor intensive than similar work in the uplands fails to appreciate the high labor investment required for weeding (see Shorr 2000).

Coe and Diehl (1980) did not take into account the fact that wetland agricultural production was quite a gamble for the modern local farmers upon whom they based their model, no matter how rich the soil. If the timing of maize planting is misjudged, late floods bring total or partial crop loss, and yields plummet if there is insufficient precipitation in El Niño years (see Lane Rodríguez, Aguirre, and González 1997; Cyphers 2009, 2010). The farmers in question took this risk so they could export products to downriver markets to obtain cash income during the dry season when food prices are high, reserving the more reliable upland maize harvest for their personal use. They also planted crops with shorter maturation periods such as watermelon and sweet corn on the levees in order to hedge their risk and obtain cash. In fact, the levee lands acquired by these contemporary peasant agriculturalists were not the basis of their emergence as local *caciques*, since they had acquired power, wealth, and influence long before buying them.

Nonetheless, archaeological fixation on the levees around San Lorenzo continues (e.g., Arnold 2009; Pool 2006, 2007) without a full appreciation of how humans can adapt agricultural practices in response to the constraints of the tropical riverine environment. The "myth of the river levees" around San Lorenzo may be attributable to the prevalence of optimization models for the last 30 years. Pool (2006, 202) promotes the idea of higher *average* productivity on the levee in the long run as compared to productivity in the uplands but misses the point that high levee productivity cannot be considered a constant over time because of variable climatic factors and erratic floods. An emphasis on high average yields, which is typical of the optimization models, may seem attractive from the armchair, but in practice, average yields are intangible and cannot be eaten (and long-term storage is not an option, as mentioned above). All it takes is one lost harvest to spawn a crisis, and the unpredictability inherent in levee cultivation in a given cycle can result in critical food shortages with serious repercussions that ripple through the social system.

The river levees and adjacent wetlands would not have been favorable for Olmec maize cultivation if mature seeds were the desired product, since the planting-to-harvest interval, a restricted window of opportunity, overlaps the period of flood hazards. However, these lands would have been of interest if sweet immature grains and stalks were sought (see Smalley and Blake 2003). While the risk of failure in upland cultivation increases with unforeseen fluctuations in rainfall and temperature, wetland crop growing is even riskier since it is constrained by the "time-above-water" principle (Denevan 1984; Shorr 2000) and is negatively affected by unexpected floods. As long as sufficient upland terrain was available, wetland cultivation likely was minimal. As the population approached its maximum size and diversity, the spread of upland habitation reduced the amount of cultivable high ground, which likely coincided with soil infertility and diminishing yields. Symonds, Cyphers, and Lunagómez (2002) propose that such displacement and insufficient food production gave rise to food importation from upriver zones, a proposal that closely follows studies of bulk transport in fluvial systems (e.g., Algaze 2001; Burghardt 1959; Castle 1992; Fulton and Hoch 1959; Gardiner 1941; Hassan 1997; Hu 1955; Mayer 1955; Patton 1956; Taaffe and Gauthier 1973; Wanklyn 1996; Weber 1909; Weigend 1958; Wenke 1989; contra Clark 2007, 36–37).

We agree with Symonds, Cyphers, and Lunagómez on the probability of apogee-phase food imports and in addition propose that subsistence stress and the reduction in cultivable upland terrain presaged the regular practice of highly risky recessional agriculture during the apogee period. Regardless of whether the Olmec sought high yields, low labor investment, minimal subsistence production, or all of the above, they had to deal with uncertain water levels and recognize potential losses from early or high flooding when cultivating the wetlands. They could not guarantee yields because of the high risk factors inherent in an unpredictable environment and had to rely on alternatives. Perhaps a complex economic spiral was set in motion, analogous to the Tikuna Campo Alegre case of Upper Amazonia (Shorr 2000), where the local overexploitation of fish and turtle prompted the exchange of maize with downriver communities in order to obtain these aquatic resources with the aim of alleviating hunger during the yearly drought period.

The rise of the San Lorenzo Olmec thus appears to have been unrelated to a maize subsistence base. Early on, they developed an alternative and less risky adaptive strategy that involved diversifying in a broad spectrum of subsistence resources (see Bird et al. 2002) rather than specializing in relatively low-yield crop such as maize. The variable success of Olmec subsistence activities was affected at all times by water levels and had to be conducted within constraints set by the ancient environment. These constraints were characterized by extremes rather than by average conditions (see Dunlap 1980). Optimization models (e.g., Arnold 2009; Coe and Diehl 1980, 1:389–390) assume good-year economics and take little notice of the role of resource fluctuations and risk in sociopolitical evolution. Food shortages are just as important, or more so, than food abundance. Unpredictable fluctuations in the food supply or bad-year economics play a causal role in development, along with population pressure, conflict, competition, and technological improvement (Halstead and O'Shea 1989).

It is significant that the earliest evidence of built infrastructure used for resource exploitation within the San Lorenzo region, the *islotes*, has to do with a particularly rich but highly risky portion of the wetland ecotone where protein resources may be mass harvested and a wide range of collectigens may be procured. We consider that exploiting and managing these resources was significant for the growth of emerging elite households at San Lorenzo and that the *islotes* were built as part of risk management strategies (see Colson 1979; Halstead and O'Shea 1989; O'Shea 1989) in order to produce foods with high and low returns, the former playing an important role in wealth and debt accumulation.

A Missing Link

In addressing the theme of the present volume, we deliberately chose to focus on an example of early Olmec artificial construction that does not strictly qualify as "monumental" in order to seek a partial understanding of the antecedents of subsequent labor mobilizations that were involved in the truly monumental projects that have made the Olmec famous. Although the *islotes* lack the accepted size and elaborateness that are considered characteristic of monumentality, they may have ideological associations that we have ignored until now because of the absence of evidence that was not circumstantial. We now entertain the possibility that these early buildings played a role in the crystallization of cosmological concepts implicated in later sociopolitical asymmetry.

It is generally accepted that Olmec ruling lineages calculated their descent from divine ancestors (Coe 1968), usually the legendary founders of the social group (see McAnany 1995). Ancestors provided the cosmological charter for authority and privilege and were associated with cave and mountain origins, which in turn were linked to the Earth deity (Grove 1970, 1973). This monster-like deity was the emblem of the rulers and of their capitals throughout Mesoamerican time, and it is often described as floating on the primordial waters or emerging from them (Bassie-Sweet 1996; Gillespie 1993). The Maya association of the Witz Monster with "mountains of water" and the *altepetl* among Nahua peoples both illustrate the inseparability of cosmology and sociopolitical hierarchy in ancient thought.

It is this symbolic connection between founding ancestors and the Earth deity that is intriguing with regard to the *islotes*. Their construction and ownership by founding groups and their descendants, when added to their physical configuration as tiny artificial islands surrounded by water, seems to replicate later associations of ancestors, origins, and the Earth deity, who was synonymous with the concept of the "sacred mountain surrounded by water."

We see this symbolic association replicated on various scales in the San Lorenzo region, ranging from its maximum expression, the San Lorenzo island, to architectural precincts and stone monuments. The great center of La Venta is the only other example of an Olmec "island" capital (see Elzey 1991) that has architecture imbued with related symbolism (see Heizer 1968; Grove 1999; Reilly 1994). In fact, the island locations of both capitals require further consideration since the Olmec could have founded them at any number of equally or more advantageous places but did not choose to do so. Instead, they opted for two of the narrowest islands that exist in the waterlogged southern plains of the Gulf coast. This arouses the suspicion that the Olmec built landscape was knowingly tiered with nested material replicas of a guiding cosmological notion that was essential to reinforcing their beliefs, behaviors, and values—clearly akin to Houston's "layers of reciprocal metaphors" (1998).

The ostensible pervasiveness of layered reciprocal metaphors is one reason why we do not discard the idea that the *islotes* were imbued with cosmological meanings. An additional reason is that they were constructed by founder-groups that instilled the identity of the first settlers, the "living ancestors" (Helms 1998), in these buildings. The shared identity of the founder groups who owned the *islotes* rapidly became a basis for asymmetrical relationships, as we have seen, and laid the foundations for later striking patterns of sociopolitical differentiation and monumental declarations of power.

Final Observations

In the previous sections we outlined the characteristics, functions, and distribution of *islotes* in relation to seasonal and spatial factors as a prelude to the present interpretation of diachronic change. Now we place the *islotes* in a broader picture of San Lorenzo's development. We include preliminary observations on long-term climatic fluctuations because of the possible impact of meteorological changes on cultural development, particularly in reference to the influence of heightened risk on shifting subsistence patterns.[3]

Unfortunately, paleoclimate studies in the Olmec region generally do not have sufficient temporal depth to enable us to reconstruct Early Formative conditions (e.g., Byrne and Horn 1989; Ortega et al. 2006). More information is available for the Classic period trends, which tend to match those from nearby areas, such as the Maya lowlands (e.g., Hodell, Brenner, and Curtis 2005; Polk, Van Beynen, and Reeder 2007). It is significant that proxy support (particularly Neff et al. 2006; as well as Curtis, Hodell, and Brenner 1996; Mayewski et al. 2004; Rosenmeier et al. 2002; Webster et al. 2007, among others) of the long interval climatic trends seen in the Cariaco core data (Haug et al. 2001) that correspond to the Formative period indicates the latter's broad applicability to the Olmec region. The climate trends that we mention in the following discussion are based on the Cariaco study. We do not assume the causality of climate for all social phenomena, although we agree that abrupt climate events may have triggered change (Duroy and Gowdy 2004).

The low population density at the onset of the Ojochi phase precluded severe competition for resources, and the early settlers had generalized open access to the uplands, levees, and wetlands, which formed a *terra nullius* with a wide range of subsistence choices. The first settlers who moved between the safe high ground of the uplands to the wetlands on a seasonal basis to obtain food were the founder groups. Olmec subsistence in the earliest phases largely involved mixed strategies that included high-yield, low-labor wetland aquatic resource withdrawal and the low-risk labor-intensive upland cultivation of nutritionally complementary root crops. Risky conditions appear to have been the norm rather than the exception in their way of life.

Following an initial period of de facto wetland use, the first *islotes* were established in the key resource zone with a minimal labor investment by founder groups for the purpose of self-sustaining procurement for household subsistence. They initially functioned as auxiliary features in subsistence exploitation and later became the basis for resource claims by these groups. The creation of land in the wetlands denotes a significant shift from a simple portable extractive technology to a conspicuous and exclusive landscape modification for the mass harvesting of concentrated resources in accord with the seasonality of the wetland mosaic, which imposed controls on the opportunity structure of resource exploitation. *Islotes* built by self-sufficient households provided strategic stations that facilitated the capture of channel resources and the use of harvesting strategies as waters receded (e.g., traps, weirs, seines, and poisons) to obtain high-protein yields with a low labor investment.

The seeds of social stratification are to be found in the kinship structure of the Ojochi lineages. It is expected that production differentials and the demographic cycle of the household created transitory asymmetries of labor and wealth in these groups that were made permanent under specific conditions (see O'Shea 1990, 353). Not all households were capable of achieving the same degree of annual subsistence success because of variable luck at fishing, hunting, and cultivation and the place of a household in the domestic cycle (see Yanagisako 1979). Immediate solutions to this dilemma include several alternatives such as the forcible appropriation of the resources of others, reduction in household size by emigration or other mechanisms, or having subsistence deficits covered by more successful households. The latter option was ostensibly the easiest way out for the early Olmec and would have generated debts in patron-client relationships.

Competition for aquatic resources increased as the number of households multiplied, and extraction also increased to fulfill needs. Resource claims became more and more important as population grew, and the *islotes* were recognized as the property of the founder groups. Permanent rights of access to mass-harvesting locales provided by the extra-residential *islote* infrastructure underwrote high returns of storable foods in the hands of a few. Consequently, the subsistence security of genealogically related and distant households experiencing stress during annual and longer-term crises was in their hands. These higher-surplus yields were important in the expansion and fission of advantaged households that had differential access to aquatic resources. Household specialization in resource harvesting during specific times of the year allowed *islote* owners to supply other upland households with stored foods during a crisis or a famine. Crisis food flows to disadvantaged households, both kin and non-kin, formed social debts and underwrote vertical dyadic relationships (see Hirth 1993; Santley 1993). The composition of these patron and client dyads would have varied from year to year, with concomitant fluctuating allegiances, and such relations may have extended to numerous households across the region. Debts could be paid with political support and labor, the latter perhaps invested in intensifying surplus production, but they did not ensure client allegiance, which constantly shifted, depending on the patron of the moment. Household management of subsistence security and client debts dispersed, rather than concentrated, labor obligations.

The continued but reduced amount of *islote* construction in the Bajío phase indicates a sustained response to the fissioning of founder groups and to seasonal fluctuations in water levels, since the population remained low. *Islote* subsistence production played a key role in survival during the midsummer drought, and property rights both deterred migration and made preexisting inequalities permanent. From the end of the Ojochi phase, have-nots outnumbered the founder-group *islote* owners. The latter group had exclusive access to prime harvesting spots that helped alleviate their subsistence needs and made possible the production of surplus food. Exclusive access to strategic protein resources and consequent regular production permitted *islote* owners to allocate food to buffer risk, such as through gifts or feasts (see Hayden 2003). This continued to create social debts that enhanced the status of founder-group households above others. Competition for technology to extract resources, particularly watercraft, large nets, and traps, also must have increased, as is frequently mentioned in fisheries studies.

During the subsequent phases, founder groups continued to monopolize resource harvesting and the production of protein surpluses for distribution to a wider consumer audience. The San Lorenzo A phase began with the gradual turnaround of drought conditions but had relatively short-interval periods of dryness that affected resource availability. Population increased significantly, and social differentiation increased as well. Root crops and aquatic protein continued to form the subsistence core.

A gradual but dramatic drop in precipitation occurred during the San Lorenzo B zenith phase, a time when population drew to its maximum size and diversity and the final massive construction stage of the great plateau drew to completion. Severe drought conditions combined with higher subsistence demands and the reduction of uplands for cultivation to produce greater subsistence stress in people's lives. The aquatic assets of the northern plain resource zone became increasingly important for surviving the critical midsummer drought and high flood time. As a result, new *islote* construction extended to more distant floodplains. The relevance of the intensified production of storable foods on the *islotes* was heightened and firmly maintained in the hands of the elite, who used these products to create debts with the population.

The permanent sites established in the northern plain may have acted as vertical linkage nodes for the elite management of the production and outward flow of wetland products, and their presence also suggests a significant reorganization of activities that includes the delimitation, protection, and monitoring of territory that is consistent with the increasing attempts of one or more founding groups to control critical resources. Competition or conflicts among founder groups as well as subsistence insecurity may have influenced the reorganization of the production of high-yield aquatic food, which would have fomented the hierarchization of related patron-client relationships and the concentration of labor debts in the hands of these groups.

One way for the elite lineages of San Lorenzo to obtain increasing amounts of labor for monumental work such as terrace construction and stone transport during the San Lorenzo A and B phases was to cash in social debts created through the unbalanced reciprocal exchanges of vital subsistence resources with genealogically distant groups. Through their ownership of subsistence infrastructure, they were able to reorganize the means of production of essential crisis resources, control disbursement of such resources, and automatically gain the future labor and allegiance of clients participating in the same social hierarchy (see Gilman 1981 and Hirth 1993).

The long-term trend of spreading habitation across the uplands, which negatively affected the availability of wild game, reached a critical mass. These protein sources were replaced, in part, by domestic animals such as dogs. The reduction in cultivable upland terrain forced the inhabitants of the San Lorenzo island to seek solutions such as importing food, cultivating vegetables and condiments in domestic gardens, producing domestic crafted goods for exchange, and engaging in highly risky food production ventures. More and more, the risks involved in wetland cultivation were outweighed by need, making it an increasingly attractive alternative. The wetland cultivation of immature maize for brewing beverages would have produced a coveted product for local use and external trade.

At this time, there are indications that San Lorenzo became increasingly important in regional transportation systems that helped expand its supply hinterland. Upstream-downstream transportation networks linked to terrestrial corridors were a means of mobilizing food, raw materials, products, and people while promoting physical interconnectivity and regional sociopolitical integration (Symonds, Cyphers, and Lunagómez 2002). This system was in no way related to the long-distance exchange of essential tools and products for ritual paraphernalia, as misconstrued by Clark (2007) and Arnold (2009). Rather, these trade corridors contributed to heightened regional interdependence and resource flows, which fomented the development of economic interaction spheres, regional specialization and administration, and importantly, were crucial for buffering risk (see, e.g., Batten 1998; Fleming and Hayuth 1994; Halstead and O'Shea 1989; Hassig 1985; Harris and Ullman 1945; Sanders and Santley 1983).

A number of factors contributed to the gradual decline of San Lorenzo. These included increasing local stress; growing competition; environmental changes such as outward river channel shifts, which negatively affected its role as a transport hub (Ortiz and Cyphers 1997); and the worst protracted drought of the Early Formative period. Mounting pressure on commoners to work in monumental construction activities and inefficiencies in the food network caused suffering. Other factors include conflicts over the political succession, fractures in the social and economic system, and ideological shifts that undermined traditional ceremonies and economic exchanges. Famine and migration are the expected results of such a scenario, but at the present time there is archaeological evidence to support only the latter (see Symonds, Cyphers, and Lunagómez 2002, 94).

To conclude, the present exploration of the roots of Olmec monumentality at San Lorenzo has not dealt with its first material manifestations but rather has focused on the significance and implications of one type of small-scale construction that preceded later grand-scale elaborate works. Early artificial wetland mounds formed an integral part of a dynamic setting of human interactions, nascent cosmic meanings, emerging privilege, and latent power that were constantly restructured and transformed along the tangled pathways to Olmec monumentality. Investing energy to create and maintain these structures was critical to food production, a necessary prerequisite to the "conspicuous consumption of energy" in later monumental displays.

Acknowledgments

We have benefited from discussions with Irene Domínguez, Juan Domínguez, Perfecto Domínguez, Ignacio González, Ranulfo González, Esteban Hernández, Ken Hirth, Gerardo Jiménez, Allan Ortega, Laura O'Rourke, Barbara Price and Belem Zúñiga, even as we accept our joint responsibility for the content. The San Lorenzo Tenochtitlán Archaeological Project has received generous and greatly appreciated support from the following agencies: the Instituto de Investigaciones Antropológicas and the Dirección General de Asuntos del Personal Académico de la Universidad Nacional Autónoma de México, the American Philosophical Society, the Consejo Nacional de Ciencia y Tecnología, the National Endowment for the Humanities, the National Science Foundation, the National Geographic Society, and the Foundation for the Advancement of Mesoamerican Studies, Inc. Fieldwork was authorized by the Consejo de Arqueología del Instituto Nacional de Antropología e Historia.

Notes

1. Even with chronological refinements, the length of the temporal phases does not permit a full appreciation of the intricate complexity of the potential human response to myriad temporal-spatial combinations and short- and long-term environmental trends. Consequently, it is not possible to answer many important questions regarding themes such as possible *islote* use in tandem with water recession and the relation of *islote* location per geomorphic unit to variable water levels associated with long-term climatic fluctuations, among others.

2. The annual crisis time, including the midsummer drought and the major flood, have year-to-year and long-term variations. For example, the midsummer drought nearly disappears in warm El Niño years (see Pereyra, Cordoba, and Grayeb 1994; Pereyra-Díaz, Bandon Murrieta, and Natividad Baizabal 2004) but brings earlier rains and disastrous flooding. It appears to be accentuated and of longer duration (and to begin earlier) in wet La Niña years (Galindo 1995; Pereyra-Díaz, Bandon Murrieta, and Natividad Baizabal 2004), as does the highest rainy season flood. Despite such variations, these months are predictable moments of stress.

3. To what degree subsistence producers are and were able to predict climatic changes

is unknown. Dillehay, Kolata, and Mosely (2004, 4326) suggest that El Niño-Southern Oscillation events were "experienced, monitored, and responded to by human populations through cumulative generational response mechanisms" and that acute observation allowed them to identify precursors to the phenomenon.

References Cited

Abruzzi, William S.
1987   Ecological Stability and Community Diversity during Mormon Colonization of the Little Colorado River Basin. *Human Ecology* 15(3):317–338.
Acheson, James M.
1981   Anthropology of Fishing. *Annual Review of Anthropology* 10:275–216.
Adler, Michael A.
1996   Land Tenure, Archaeology, and the Ancestral Pueblo Social Landscape. *Journal of Anthropological Archaeology* 15:337–371.
Aguirre, Gustavo, Erasmo Cázares, and Basilio Sánchez
2002   *Conservación y aprovechamiento del chopontil (Claudius angustatus)*. Instituto de Ecología, A.C., Veracruz.
Algaze, Guillermo
2001   Initial Social Complexity in Southwestern Asia: The Mesopotamian Advantage. *Current Anthropology* 42(2):199–233.
Arciniega-Ceballos, A., E. Hernandez-Quintero, E. Cabral-Cano, L. Morett-Alatorre, O. Diaz-Molina, A. Soler-Arechalde, and R. Chavez-Segura
2009   Shallow Geophysical Survey at the Archaeological Site of San Miguel Tocuela, Basin of Mexico. *Journal of Archaeological Science* 36:1199–1205.
Arco, Lee J., and Elliot M. Abrams
2006   An Essay on Energetics: The Construction of the Aztec Chinampa System. *Antiquity* 80(310):906–918.
Arnold, Philip J., III
2009   Settlement and Subsistence among the Early Formative Gulf Olmec. *Journal of Anthropological Archaeology* 28:397–411.
Batten, David C.
1998   Transport and Urban Growth in Preindustrial Europe: Implications for Archaeology. *Human Ecology* 26(3):489–516.
Bassie-Sweet, Karen
1996   *At the Edge of the World*. University of Oklahoma Press, Norman.
Bayman, James M., and Alan P. Sullivan III
2008   Property, Identity, and Macroeconomy in the Prehispanic Southwest. *American Anthropologist* 110 (1):6–20.
Begossi, Alpina
1995   Fishing Spots and Sea Tenure: Incipient Forms of Local Management in Atlantic Forest Coastal Communities. *Human Ecology* 23 (3):387–406.
Bernal, Ignacio
1969   *The Olmec World*. Berkeley: University of California Press.

Bird, Rebecca Bliege, Douglas W. Bird, Eric Alden Smith, and Geoffrey C. Kushnick
2002   Risk and Reciprocity in Meriam Food Sharing. *Evolution and Human Behavior* 23:297–321.

Blake, Michael
2006   Dating the Initial Spread of Zea mays. In *Histories of Maize: Multidisciplinary Approaches to the Prehistory, Biogeography, Domestication, and Evolution of Maize*, edited by J. E. Staller, R. H. Tykot, B. F. Benz, pp. 55–72. Elsevier, New York.

Borstein, Joshua A.
2001   Tripping over Colossal Heads: Settlement Patterns and Population Development in the Upland Olmec Heartland. Ph.D. dissertation, Department of Anthropology, Pennsylvania State University, State College.

Boserup, Ester
1965   *The Conditions of Agricultural Growth*. Aldine, Chicago.

Bozarth, Steven
2001   Phytolith Investigations at El Bajío, Veracruz. Report submitted to Carl J. Wendt, PAEB, Department of Anthropology, Pennsylvania State University, State College.

Buol, Stanley W., Randal J. Southard, Robert C. Graham, and Paul A. McDaniel
2003   *Soil Genesis and Classification*. Iowa States Press, Ames.

Burghardt, Andrew F.
1959   The Location of River Towns in the Central Lowland of the United States. *Annals of the Association of American Geographers* 49(3):305–323.

Byrne, Roger, and Sally P. Horn
1989   Prehistoric Agriculture and Forest Clearance in the Sierra de Los Tuxtlas, Veracruz, Mexico. *Palynology* 13:181–193.

Carneiro, Robert
1988   Reflexiones adicionales sobre la concentración de recursos y su papel en el surgimento del Estado. In *Coloquio V. Gordon Childe, Estudios sobre la Revolución Neolítica y la Revolución Urbana*, edited by L. Manzanilla, pp. 265–282. Instituto de Investigaciones Antropológicas, Universidad Nacional Autónoma de México, Mexico City.

Caso, Alfonso
1965   ¿Existió un imperio olmeca? *Memorias de El Colegio Nacional* 5(3):11–60.

Castle, Edward W.
1992   Shipping and Trade in Ramesside Egypt. *Journal of the Economic and Social History of the Orient* 35(3):239–77.

Charlton, Thomas H.
1969   Texcoco Fabric-Marked Pottery, Tlateles, and Salt-Making. *American Antiquity* 34(1):73–76.
1971   Texcoco Fabric-Marked Pottery and Salt-Making: A Further Note. *American Antiquity* 36(2):217–218.

Clark, John E.
2007   Mesoamerica's First State. In *The Political Economy of Ancient Mesoamerica: Transformations during the Formative and Classic Periods*, edited by V. L. Scarborough and J. E. Clark, pp. 11–46. University of New Mexico Press, Albuquerque.

Coe, Michael D.
1968 *America's First Civilization, Discovering the Olmec*. American Heritage Publishing, New York.
1974 Photogrammetry and the Ecology of Olmec Civilization. In *Aerial Photography in Anthropological Field Research*, edited by E. Z. Vogt, pp. 1–13. Harvard University Press, Cambridge, Massachusetts.

Coe, Michael D., and Richard A. Diehl
1980 *In the Land of the Olmec*. University of Texas Press, Austin.

Colson, Elizabeth
1979 In Good Years and in Bad: Food Strategies of Self-Reliant Societies. *Journal of Anthropological Research* 35(1):18–29.

Cordell, John
1978 Carrying Capacity Analysis of Fixed-Territorial Fishing. *Ethnology* 17(1):1–24.

Curtis, Jason H., David A. Hodell, and Mark Brenner
1996 Climate Variability on the Yucatan Peninsula (Mexico) during the Past 3500 Years, and Implications for Maya Cultural Evolution. *Quaternary Research* 46:37–47.

Cyphers, Ann
2009 Bad-Year Economics and the San Lorenzo Olmec. Public lecture delivered at Dumbarton Oaks, Washington, D.C., November 5.
2010 Subsistence Strategies at San Lorenzo. Paper presented at the annual meeting of the Society for American Archaeology, St. Louis, Missouri.
n.d. La cerámica de San Lorenzo Tenochtitlán. Manuscript on file, archives of the San Lorenzo Tenochtitlán Archaeological Project

Cyphers, A., T. Murtha, J. Borstein, J. Zurita-Noguera, R. Lunagómez, S. Symonds, G. Jiménez, M. A. Ortiz, and J. M. Figueroa
2007–2008 Arqueología digital en la primera capital olmeca, San Lorenzo. *Thule* 22–25: 121–144.

Denevan, William M.
1984 Ecological Heterogeneity and Horizontal Zonation of Agriculture in the Amazon Floodplain. In *Frontier Expansion in Amazonia*, edited by M. Schmink and C. Wood, pp. 311–336. University Presses of Florida, Gainesville.
1996 A Bluff Model of Riverine Settlement in Prehistoric Amazonia. *Annals of the Association of American Geographers* 86:654–681.

Dillehay, Tom D., Alan L. Kolata, and Michael E. Mosely
2004 Long-Term Human Response to Uncertain Environmental Conditions in the Andes. *Proceedings of the National Academy of Sciences of the United States of America* 101(12):4325–4330.

Duroy, Quentin, and John Gowdy
2004 Evolutionary Economics and Energy. *Encyclopedia of Energy* 2:569–576.

Dougherty, Raymond P.
1927 An Archaeological Survey in Southern Babylonia (Continued). *Bulletin of the American Schools of Oriental Research* 25:5–13.

Dunlap, Riley R.
1980 Paradigmatic Change in Social Science: "From Human Exemptions to an Ecological Paradigm." *American Behavioral Scientist* 24(1):5–14.

Durrenberger, E. Paul, and Gísli Pálsson
1987   Ownership at Sea: Fishing Territories and Access to Sea Resources. *American Anthropologist* 14(3):508–522.
Earle, Timothy
2000   Archaeology, Property, and Prehistory. *Annual Review of Anthropology* 29:39–60.
Elzey, Wayne
1991   A Hill on a Land Surrounded by Water: An Aztec Story of Origin and Destiny. *History of Religions* 31(2):105–149.
Erasmus, Charles J.
1965   Monument Building: Some Field Experiments. *Southwestern Journal of Anthropology* 21(4):277–301.
Erickson, Clark L.
2000   Lomas de ocupación en los Llanos de Moxos. In *Arqueología de las tierras bajas*, edited by A. Durán and R. Bracco, pp. 207–226. Comisión Nacional de Arqueología, Ministerio de Educación y Cultura, Montevideo, Uruguay.
Fleming, Douglas K., and Yehuda Hayuth
1994   Spatial Characteristics of Transportation Hubs: Centrality and Intermediacy. *Journal of Transport Geography* 2(1):3–18.
Fulton, Maurice, and L. Clinton Hoch
1959   Transportation Factors Affecting Locational Decisions. *Economic Geography* 35 (1):51–59.
Galindo, I.
1995   La oscilación del sur, El Niño: El caso de México. In *Breve Historia de la Sequía en México*, edited by E. Florescano and S. Swan, pp. 135–158. Universidad Veracruzana, Xalapa.
Gardiner, Alan H.
1941   Ramesside Texts Relating to the Taxation and Transport of Corn. *Journal of Egyptian Archaeology* 27:19–73.
Garson, Adam G.
1980   Comment on the Economic Potential of Fish Utilization in Riverine Environments and Potential Archaeological Biases. *American Antiquity* 45 (3):562–567.
Gillespie, Susan D.
1993   Power, Pathways, and Appropriations in Mesoamerican art. In *Imagery and Creativity: Ethnoaesthetics and Art Worlds in the Americas*, edited by D. Whitten and N. Whitten, pp. 67–107. University of Arizona Press, Tucson.
Gilman, Antonio
1981   The Development of Social Stratification in Bronze Age Europe. *Current Anthropology* 22(1):1–23.
Goman, Michelle, and Roger Byrne
1998   A 5000-Year Record of Agriculture and Tropical Forest Clearance in the Tuxtlas, Veracruz, Mexico. *The Holocene* 8(1):83–89.
González Lauck, Rebecca
1988   Recientes trabajos en la zona arqueológica de La Venta, Tabasco, 1984–1988. *Arqueología* 4:121–165.

Grove, David C.
1970   *The Olmec Paintings of Oxtotitlán Cave, Guerrero, México*. Studies in Pre-Columbian Art and Archaeology 6. Dumbarton Oaks, Washington, D.C.
1973   Olmec Altars and Myths. *Archaeology* 26:128–135.
1999   Public Monuments and Sacred Mountains: Observations on Three Formative Period Sacred Landscapes. In *Social Patterns in Preclassic Mesoamerica*, edited by D. C. Grove and R. Joyce, pp. 255–299. Dumbarton Oaks, Washington, D.C.

Halstead, Paul, and John O'Shea
1989   Introduction: Cultural Responses to Risk and Uncertainty. In *Bad Year Economics: Cultural Responses to Risk and Uncertainty*, edited by P. Halstead and J. O'Shea, pp. 1–10. Cambridge University Press, New York.

Harris, Chauncy D., and Edward L. Ullman
1945   The Nature of Cities. *Annals of the American Academy of Political and Social Science* 242:7–17.

Hassan, Fekri A.
1997   The Dynamics of a Riverine Civilization: A Geoarchaeological Perspective on the Nile Valley, Egypt. *World Archaeology* 29(1):51–74.

Hassig, Ross
1985   *Trade, Tribute, and Transportation: The Sixteenth-Century Political Economy of the Valley of Mexico*. University of Oklahoma Press, Norman.

Haug, Gerald, Konrad A. Hughen, Daniel M. Sigman, Larry C. Peterson, and Ursula Röhl
2001   Southward Migration of the Intertropical Convergence Zone through the Holocene. *Science* 293(5533):1304–1308.

Hayden, Brian
2003   Were Luxury Foods the First Domesticates? Ethnoarchaeological Perspectives from Southeast Asia. *World Archaeology* 34(3):458–469.

Heizer, Robert F.
1960   Agriculture and the Theocratic State in Lowland Southeastern Mexico. *American Antiquity* 26(2):215–222.
1968   New Observations on La Venta. In *Dumbarton Oaks Conference on the Olmec*, edited by E. Benson, pp. 9–36. Dumbarton Oaks, Washington D.C.

Helms, Mary
1998   *Access to Origins: Affines, Ancestors, and Aristocrats*. University of Texas Press, Austin.

Hirth, Kenneth G.
1993   The Household as an Analytical Unit: Problems in Method and Theory. In *Prehispanic Domestic Units in Western Mesoamerica*, edited by R. S. Santley and K. G. Hirth, pp. 21–36. CRC, Boca Raton, Florida.

Hodell, D. A., M. Brenner, and J. H. Curtis
2005   Terminal Classic Drought in the Northern Maya Lowlands Inferred from Multiple Sediment Core in Lake Chichancanab (Mexico). *Quaternary Science Reviews* 24:1413–1427.

Houston, Stephen D.
1998   Finding Function and Meaning in Classic Maya Architecture. In *Function and*

Meaning in Classic Maya Architecture, edited by S. D. Houston, pp. 519–538. Dumbarton Oaks, Washington, D.C.

Hu, Ch'ang-Tu
1955 The Yellow River Administration in the Ch'ing Dynasty. *Far Eastern Quarterly* 14(4):505–513.

Inchaustegui, Carlos
1987 *Los márgenes del Tabasco Chontal*. Gobierno del Estado de Tabasco, Instituto de Cultura, Villahermosa.

Joly, Luz Graciela
1981 Feeding and Trapping Fish with *Piper auritum*. *Economic Botany* 35 (4):383–390.

Kirkby, A. V. T.
1973 *The Use of Land and Water Resources in the Past and Present Valley of Oaxaca, Mexico*. Vol. 1 of *Prehistory and Human Ecology of the Valley of Oaxaca*. University of Michigan, Ann Arbor.

Krotser, Paula
1980 Potters in the Land of the Olmec. In *In the Land of the Olmec*, edited by M. D. Coe and R. A. Diehl, vol. 2, pp. 125–138. University of Texas Press, Austin.

Lane Rodríguez, Marci, Rogelio Aguirre, and Javier González
1997 Producción campesina del maíz en San Lorenzo Tenochtitlán. In *Población, subsistencia y medio ambiente en San Lorenzo Tenochtitlán*, edited by A. Cyphers, pp. 55–73. Instituto de Investigaciones Antropológicas, Universidad Nacional Autónoma de México, Mexico City.

Lathrap, Donald W.
1973 The Antiquity and Importance of Long-Distance Trade Relationships in the Moist Tropics of Pre-Columbian South America. *World Archaeology* 5(2):170–186.

Latrubesse, E. M., M. L. Amsler, R. P. de Morais, and S. Aquino
2009 The Geomorphologic Response of a Large Pristine Alluvial River to Tremendous Deforestation in the South American Tropics: The Case of the Araguaia River. *Geomorphology* 113:239–252.

Levieil, Dominique P., and Benjamin Orlove
1990 Local Control of Aquatic Resources: Community and Ecology in Lake Titicaca, Peru. *American Anthropologist* 92(2):362–382.

Limp, W. Frederick, and Van A. Reidhead
1979 An Economic Evaluation of Fish Utilization in Riverine Environments. *American Antiquity* 44(1):70–78.

Logan, Michael H., and William T. Sanders
1976 The Model. In *The Valley of Mexico: Studies in Pre-Hispanic Ecology and Society*, edited by Eric R. Wolf, pp. 31–58. University of New Mexico Press, Albuquerque.

López Corral, Aurelio
2006 Productividad agrícola y explotación de recursos naturales durante el Formativo en Tetimpa, Pueba. Master's thesis, Departamento de Antropología, Universidad de las Américas, Cholula.

Mayer, Harold M.
1955 Prospects and Problems of the Port of Chicago. *Economic Geography* 31(2):95–125.

Mayewski, Paul A., Eelco E. Rohling, J. Curt Stager, Wibjörn Karlén, Kirk A. Maasch, L. David Meeker, Eric A. Meyerson, Francoise Gasse, Shirley van Kreveld, Karin Homlgren, Julia Lee-Thorp, Gunhild Rosqvist, Frank Rack, Michael Staubwasser, Ralph R. Schneider, and Eric J. Steig
2004 Holocene Climate Variability. *Quaternary Research* 62:243–255.

McAnany, Patricia
1995 *Living with the Ancestors: Kinship and Kingship in Ancient Maya Society*. University of Texas Press, Austin.

Meggers, Betty J.
1984 The Indigenous Peoples of Amazonia, Their Cultures, Land Use Patterns and Effects on the Landscape and Biota. In *The Amazon: Limnology and Landscape Ecology of a Mighty Tropical River and Its Basin*, edited by H. Sioli, pp. 627–648. W. Junk, Dordrecht.

Morrison, Kathleen D.
1994 The Intensification of Production: Archaeological Approaches. *Journal of Archaeological Method and Theory* 1(2):111–159.

Neff, Hector, Deborah M. Pearsall, John G. Jones, Bárbara Arroyo de Pieters, and Dorothy E. Freidel
2006 Climate Change and Population History in the Pacific Lowlands of Southern Mesoamerica. *Quaternary Research* 65:390–400.

Nietschmann, B. O.
1974 When the Turtle Collapses, the World Ends. *Natural History* 83:34–43.

Noguera, Eduardo
1975 Identificación de una saladera. *Anales de Antropología* 12:117–151.

O'Shea, John M.
1989 The Role of Wild Resources in Small-Scale Agricultural Systems: Tales from the Lakes and the Plains. In *Bad Year Economics: Cultural Responses to Risk and Uncertainty*, edited by P. Halstead and J. O'Shea, pp. 57–67. Cambridge University Press, New York.
1990 Comment. *Current Anthropology* 31(4):353–354.

Ortega, Beatriz, Margarita Caballero, Socorro Lozano, Gloria Vilaclara, and Alejandro Rodríguez
2006 Rock Magnetic and Geochemical Proxies for Iron Mineral Diagenesis in a Tropical Lake: Lago Verde, Los Tuxtlas, East-Central Mexico. *Earth and Planetary Science Letters* 250:444–458.

Ortiz, Mario Arturo, and Ann Cyphers
1997 La geomorfología y las evidencias arqueológicas en la región de San Lorenzo Tenochtitlán, Veracruz. In *Población, subsistencia y medio ambiente en San Lorenzo Tenochtitlán*, edited by A. Cyphers, pp. 31–54. Instituto de Investigaciones Antropológicas, Universidad Nacional Autónoma de México, Mexico City.

Park, Thomas K.
1992 Early Trends toward Class Stratification: Chaos, Common Property, and Flood Recession Agriculture. *American Anthropologist* 94(1):90–117.

Parsons, Jeffrey R.
1971 Prehistoric Settlement Patterns in the Texcoco Region, Mexico. Memoirs of the Museum of Anthropology 3. University of Michigan, Ann Arbor.
2006 *The Last Pescadores of Chimalhuacán, Mexico: An Archaeological Ethnography.* Anthropological Papers of the Museum of Anthropology 96. University of Michigan, Ann Arbor.
2010 The Pastoral Niche in Pre-Hispanic Mesoamerica. In *Pre-Columbian Foodways: Interdisciplinary Approaches to Food, Culture, and Markets in Ancient Mesoamerica*, edited by J. Staller and M. Carrasco, pp. 109–136. Springer, New York.

Patton, Donald
1956 The Traffic Pattern on American Inland Waterways. *Economic Geography* 32(1):29–37.

Pereyra-Díaz, D., U. Bandon Murrieta, and M. A. Natividad Baizabal
2004 Influencia de La Niña y El Niño sobre la precipitación de la Ciudad de Villahermosa, Tabasco, Mexico. *Universidad y Ciencia* 20(39):33–38.

Pereyra, Domitilo, Quintiliano Angulo Cordoba, and Beatriz Elena Palma Grayeb
1994 Effect of ENSO on the Mid-Summer Drought in Veracruz State, Mexico. *Atmósfera* 7:111–219.

Pohl, Mary E. D., Dolores R. Piperno, Kevin O. Pope, and John G. Jones
2007 Microfossil Evidence for Pre-Columbian Maize Dispersals in the Neotropics from San Andrés, Tabasco, Mexico. *Proceedings of the National Academy of Science* 104(16):6870–6875.

Polk, Jason S., Philip E. van Beynen, and Philip P. Reeder
2007 Late Holocene Environmental Reconstruction Using Cave Sediments from Belize. *Quaternary Research* 68(1):53–63.

Pollnac, R. B., and S. J. Littlefield
1983 Sociocultural Aspects of Fisheries Management. *Ocean Development and International Law Journal* 12(3–4):209–246.

Pool, Christopher A.
2006 Current Research on the Gulf Coast of Mexico. *Journal of Archaeological Research* 14:189–241.
2007 *Olmec Archaeology and Early Mesoamerica.* Cambridge University Press, Cambridge.

Pope, Kevin O., Mary D. Pohl, John G. Jones, David L. Lentz, Christopher L. von Nagy, Francisco J. Vega, and Irvy R. Quitmyer
2001 Origin and Environmental Setting of Ancient Agriculture in the Lowlands of Mesoamerica. *Science* 292:1370–1373.

Power, Mary E., Gary Parker, William E. Dietrich, and Adrian Sun
1979 How Does Floodplain Width Affect Floodplain River Ecology? *Geomorphology* 13:301–317.

Price, Barbara J.
1971 Prehispanic Irrigation Agriculture in Nuclear America. *Latin American Research Review* 6(3):3–60.
1982 Cultural Materialism: A Theoretical Review. *American Antiquity* 47 (4):709–741.

Reilly, F. Kent, III
1994 Enclosed Ritual Spaces and the Watery Underworld in Formative Period Architecture: New Observations on the Function of La Venta Complex A. In *Seventh Palenque Round Table*, edited by M. G. Robertson and V. M. Fields, pp. 125–135. Pre-Columbian Art Research Institute, San Francisco.

Roosevelt, Anna C.
1980 *Parmana: Prehistoric Maize and Manioc Subsistence along the Amazon and Orinoco*. Academic Press, New York.

Rosenmeier, Michael F., David A. Hodell, Mark Brenner, Jason H. Curtis, and Thomas P. Guilderson
2002 A 4000-Year Lacustrine Record of Environmental Change in the Southern Maya Lowlands, Petén, Guatemala. *Quaternary Research* 57:183–190.

Rothstain, Stéphen
2008 The Archaeology of the Guianas: An Overview. In *Handbook of South American Archaeology*, edited by H. Silverman and W. H. Isbell, 279–302. Springer, New York.

Sanders, William T., and Deborah L. Nichols
1988 Ecological Theory and Cultural Evolution in the Valley of Oaxaca. *Current Anthropology* 29(1):33–88.

Sanders, William T., and Robert S. Santley
1983 A Tale of Three Cities: Energetics and Urbanization in Pre-Hispanic Central Mexico. In *Prehistoric Settlement Patterns*, edited by E. Vogt and R. Leventhal, pp. 243–291. University of New Mexico Press, Albuquerque.

Sanders, William T., Jeffrey R. Parsons, and Robert S. Santley
1979 *The Basin of Mexico: Ecological Processes in the Evolution of a Civilization*. Academic Press, New York.

Santley, Robert S.
1993 Late Formative Period Society at Loma Torremote: A Consideration of the Redistribution vs. Great Provider Models as a Basis for the Emergence of Complexity in the Basin of Mexico. In *Prehispanic Domestic Units in Western Mesoamerica*, edited by R. S. Stanley and K. G. Hirth, p. 67–86. CRC, Boca Raton.

Schaan, Denise P.
2008 The Non-Agricultural Chiefdoms of Marajó Island. In *Handbook of South American Archaeology*, edited by H. Silverman and W. H. Isbell, 339–357. Springer, New York.

Schlager, Edella, and Elinor Ostrom
1992 Property-Rights Regimes and Natural Resources: A Conceptual Analysis. *Land Economics* 68(3):249–262.

Schwandes, L. P., and M. E. Collins
1994 Distribution and Significance of Freshwater Sponge Spicules in Selected Florida Soils. *Transactions of the American Microscopical Society* 113(3):242–257.

Serra Puche, Mari Carmen
1988 *Los recursos lacustres de la cuenca de México durante el Formativo*. Universidad Nacional Autónoma de México, Mexico City.

Shorr, Nicholas
2000   Early Utilization of Flood-Recession Soils as a Response to the Intensification of Fishing and Upland Agriculture: Resource-Use Dynamics in a Large Tikuna Community. *Human Ecology* 28(1):73–107.

Sluyter, Andrew, and Gabriela Domínguez
2006   Early Maize (*Zea mays* L.) Cultivation in Mexico: Dating Sedimentary Pollen Records and Its Implications. *Proceedings of the National Academy of Science* 103(4):1147–1151.

Smalley, John, and Michael Blake
2003   Sweet Beginning: Stalk Sugar and the Domestication of Maize. *Current Anthropology* 44(5):675–689.

Smith, Michael E.
2004   The Archaeology of Ancient State Economies. *Annual Review of Anthropology* 33:73–102.

Sugiura, Yoko
1998   *La caza, la pesca y la recolección: Etnoarqueología del modo de subsistencia lacustre en las ciénagas del Alto Lerma*. Universidad Nacional Autónoma de México, México.

Symonds, Stacey, Ann Cyphers, and Roberto Lunagómez
2002   *Asentamiento prehispánico en San Lorenzo Tenochtitlán*. Instituto de Investigaciones Antropológicas, Universidad Nacional Autónoma de México, Mexico City.

Taaffe, E. J., and H. L. Gauthier
1973   *Geography of Transportation*. Prentice-Hall, Englewood Cliffs, New Jersey.

Thesiger, Wilfred
1964   *The Marsh Arabs*. Longmans, Green and Co., London.

Trigger, Bruce G.
1990   Monumental Architecture: A Thermodynamic Explanation of Symbolic Behaviour. *World Archaeology* 22(2):119–132.

Vennum, Thomas, Jr.
1988   *Wild Rice and the Ojibway People*. Minnesota Historical Society Press, St. Paul.

Versteeg, Aad H.
2008   Barrancoid and Arauquinoid Mound Builders in Coastal Suriname. In *Handbook of South American Archaeology*, edited by H. Silverman and W. H. Isbell, 303–318. Springer, New York.

Von Nagy, Christopher L.
2003   Of Meandering Rivers and Shifting Towns: Landscape Evolution and Community within the Grijalva Delta. Ph.D. dissertation, Tulane University, New Orleans.

Wanklyn, Malcolm
1996   The Impact of Water Transport Facilities on the Economies of English River Ports, c. 1660–c. 1760. *Economic History Review* 49(1):20–34.

Weber, A.
1909   *The Theory of the Location of Industries*. University of Chicago Press, Chicago.

Webster, David, and Jennifer Kirker
1995   Too Many Maya, Too Few Buildings: Investigating Construction Potential at Copan, Honduras. *Journal of Anthropological Research* 51(4):363–387.

Webster, James W., George A. Brook, L. Bruce Railsback, Hai Cheng, R. Lawrence Edwards, Clark Alexander, and Philip P. Reeder
2007 Stalagmite Evidence from Belize Indicating Significant Droughts at the Time of Preclassic Abandonment, the Maya Hiatus, and the Classic Maya Collapse. *Palaeogeography, Palaeoclimatology, Palaeoecology* 250:1–17.

Weigend, G.
1958 Some Elements in the Study of Port Geography. *Geographical Review* 48:185–200.

Wendt, Carl J.
2003 Early Formative Domestic Organization and Community Patterning in the San Lorenzo Tenochtitlán Region, Veracruz, Mexico. Ph.D. dissertation, Pennsylvania State University.

Wenke, Robert J.
1989 Egypt: Origins of Complex Societies. *Annual Review of Anthropology* 18:129–155.

Wing, Elizabeth
1980 Faunal Remains from San Lorenzo. In *In the Land of the Olmec*, edited by M. D. Coe and R. A. Diehl, vol. 1, pp. 375–386. University of Texas Press, Austin.

Yanagisako, Sylvia Junko
1979 Family and Household: The Analysis of Domestic Groups. *Annual Review of Anthropology* 8:161–205.

Zúñiga, Belem
n.d. Informe del análisis de los restos faunísticos del Proyecto Arqueológico San Lorenzo Tenochtitlán. Manuscript on file, archives of the San Lorenzo Tenochtitlán Archaeological Project.

Zurita-Noguera, Judith
1997 Los fitolitos: Indicaciones sobre dieta y vivienda en San Lorenzo. In *Población, subsistencia y medio ambiente en San Lorenzo Tenochtitlán*, edited by A. Cyphers, pp. 75–87. Instituto de Investigaciones Antropológicas, Universidad Nacional Autónoma de México, Mexico City.
n.d. Informe del análisis de fitolitos del Proyecto Arqueológico San Lorenzo Tenochtitlán. Manuscript on file, archives of the San Lorenzo Tenochtitlán Archaeological Project.

Zurita-Noguera, Judith, and Marci Lane Rodríguez
2004 Considerations of the Importance of Maize in Olmec Subsistence. Paper presented at the annual meeting of the Society for American Archaeology, Montreal, Canada.

7

The Origins of Monumentality in Ancient Guerrero, Mexico

LOUISE I. PARADIS

Monumentality is a cultural expression of social creativity and complexity. It has been considered one of numerous criteria in the characterization of ancient civilizations. Like many of the authors in this book, I drew guidance from an article by Bruce Trigger in defining monumentality and the forms and meanings they could assume (Trigger 1992). Trigger discusses two types of monuments or monumental works: non-utilitarian and utilitarian. The first category had a social, political, or ideological function; such monuments defined a sacred space, but they are neither practical nor utilitarian. In this category, one can mention ceremonial or public architecture—representational forms such as the sculptures or the paintings that adorn sacred spaces. Less visible works, such as tombs or crypts that show elaborate architecture or decor, are included in this group. The second category of monuments implies sophisticated technology and complex planning in their elaboration and administration. They also imply a utilitarian function. The archaeological examples that come to mind are hydraulic works such as irrigation systems, channels, and dams.

The objective of this chapter is to explore the earliest evidence for monumentality in Ancient Guerrero, Mexico. I suggest that in Mesoamerica, monumentality developed with the first Mesoamerican civilization; that is, the cultural regions of Mesoamerica that used and shared the Olmec symbolic system as their code of communication. It developed there in association with social complexity, itself a consequence of the adoption of agriculture and village life. The earliest forms of monumentality appear in San Lorenzo around 1250 BCE. They are not temple mounds but are rather monumental sculptures and stelae set in a natural plateau that was transformed to imitate a mountain (Coe and Diehl 1980; Cyphers 2008). The first temple mounds developed after 1000 BCE in La Venta and other sites of the first Mesoamerican civilization (González Lauck 1996; Heizer, Drucker, and Graham 1968). As expressed in the introductory chapter, such is not the case in all the examples of the New World examined in this book. The dates and the contexts vary; there are much earlier dates for monumental works in North and South America (Donnan 1985; Gibson 2000; Hass and Creamer 2006; Sassaman 2005; Saunders this volume). And these sometimes appear in societies that do not depend on food production and show little signs of social complexity (Gibson 2000; Hass and Creamer 2006). This should be kept in mind in the review and analysis of the evidence from Guerrero. What meaning can be attributed to these earliest traces of monumentality in Ancient Guerrero? To answer this question, the specific contexts in which it developed should be considered, in Guerrero as well as in the other cultural entities that are part of the first Mesoamerican civilization. What are the types of monumentality? When and in what natural and social contexts did they appear and develop? What were their economic, social, political, and ideological meanings?

The first evidence for monumental works shows up in Guerrero in the Early and Middle Formative Period or the Early Horizon, between 1200 and 700 BCE. The Early Horizon has been divided in two phases based on stylistic changes in ceramics (Henderson 1979; Niederberger 1987; Paradis 1974, 1990; Tolstoy 1989): Olmec Horizon I (1200–1000/900 BCE) and Olmec Horizon II (1000/900–700 BCE). At that time, village life and agriculture were the economic bases of Mesoamerica. Exchange networks, which allowed the circulation of goods, persons, and ideas between its regional entities, of which Guerrero was one, had been in use for a long time (Paradis 2001). As to its sociopolitical organization, there is archaeological evidence that illustrates the development of social complexity in parts of the territory. This degree of social complexity may be defined in part (but not exclusively) by the presence of monumental works.

It is in the center and the south of Ancient Guerrero that we see the first monumental works: Teopantecuanitlán with its monumental architecture and sculpture as well as its hydraulic works; Amuco de la Reforma with its stele in domestic context; Coovisur with its elaborate burials and tombs. Last, a series of caves exists, such as Oxtotitlan and Juxtlahuaca, that are adorned with mural paintings (Figure 7.1). The two categories of monumentality are represented with both utilitarian and non-utilitarian works. Nevertheless, all of them have a point in common: they are related to the

Figure 7.1. Map of Ancient Guerrero in the Early and Middle Formative Period

symbolic code used for the first time by the members of the first Mesoamerican civilization.

To elucidate why monumentality emerged when and where it does in Guerrero, we first have to address the question of who was responsible for the construction of the monumental works. In other words, can it be shown that monumentality was associated with the development of ranked society, with an elite who would have ordered the construction of monumental works? Second, the association between monumentality and the Olmec symbolic code has to be considered. We have to envision various scenarios here: Did local elites adopt the symbolic system and if they did, for what purpose? Was it introduced in the region by others? If the latter, did those people bring with them concepts of monumentality? There is no evidence for a conquest or a colonization of Guerrero at that time, however, and we have to look for more nuanced processes to understand how and why the Olmec code was developed and used by most cultural entities in Mesoamerica, including Guerrero. Kirchhoff defined Mesoamerica as a "cultural area of related Civilizations" (Kirchhoff 1943). These regions developed a mechanism of integration through the interaction and exchange of goods, people, and ideas. The size, extent, and nature of these spheres of interaction varied through time. During the Olmec Horizon it included all cultural and political entities of inhabited Mesoamerica. It is in that context that I will consider the development of monumentality in Guerrero. I will try to show that both monumentality and the Olmec symbolic system developed as a response to the political relationships between elites using the Olmec symbolic system as their language of power.

Teopantecuanitlán: The Place of the Temple of the Jaguar

The site of Teopantecuanitlán is located at the junction of the Balsas and Amacuzac rivers in northeastern Guerrero. Guadalupe Martínez Donjuán (1986) salvaged it from looters in the early 1980s. With the collaboration of Christine Niederberger and Rosa Reyna Robles, Martínez Donjuán revealed the existence of an urban site containing a civic-religious center associated with residential areas and a complex hydraulic system (Martínez Donjuán 1994). Its cultural content relates it to the first Mesoamerican civilization.

The dating of Teopantecuanitlán is based on noncalibrated radiocarbon dates (Martínez Donjuán 1986). Though as yet still uncertain, the earliest dates for the Phase I occupations are between 1400 and 1000 BCE (see Table 7.1 for radiocarbon dates). Phase II, from 1000 to 800 BCE, dates the construction of monumental stone architecture and the development of residential areas. These processes continued during Phase III, from 800 to 700 BCE. During Phase IV, from 700 to 500 BCE (623 ± 69 and 610 ± 12), the capital declined and the area returned to regionalism. At its height, during Phases II and III, the site occupied 160 hectares (Martínez Donjuán personal communication). Teopantecuanitlán lost its urban status after

Table 7.1. Noncalibrated radiocarbon dates for Teopantecuanitlán, Amuco, and Xochipala

---
1530 BCE ± 230 (Amuco Abelino, residence) = 1760–1300 BCE
1423 BCE ± 112 (Teopan, ceremonial precinct) = 1535–1311 BCE
1393 BCE ± 126 (Teopan, ceremonial precinct) = 1519–1267 BCE
1220 BCE ± 110 (Amuco Abelino, residence) = 1330–1110 BCE
844 BCE ± 58 (Teopan, ceremonial precinct) = 902–786 BCE
822 BCE ± 117 (Teopan, ceremonial precinct) = 939–705 BCE
790 BCE ± 42 (Teopan, ceremonial precinct) = 832–748 BCE
623 BCE ± 69 (Teopan, ceremonial precinct) = 692–554 BCE
610 BCE ± 12 (Teopan, ceremonial precinct) = 622–598 BCE
585 BCE ± 379 (Xochipala?) = 964–206 BCE

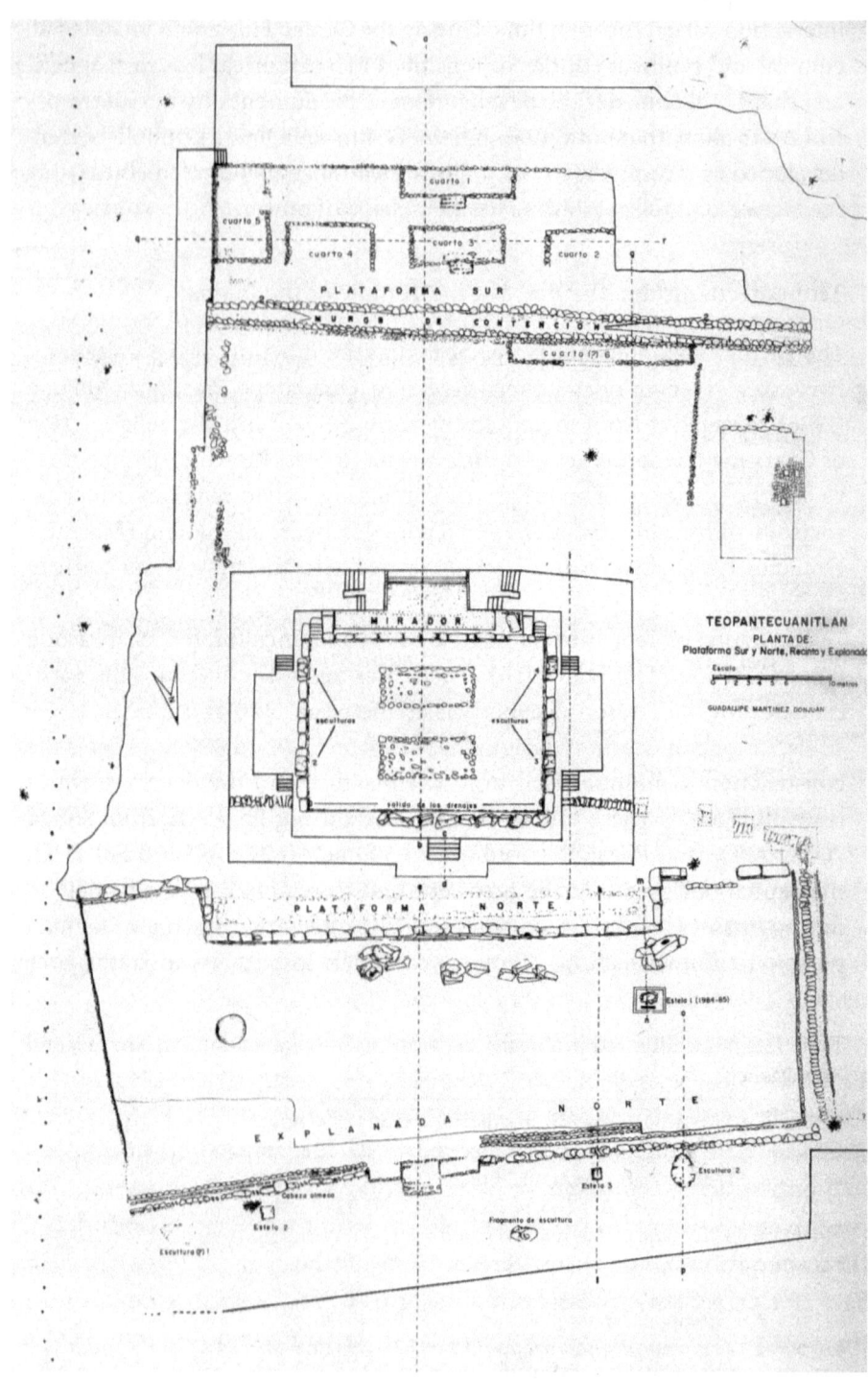

Figure 7.2. Ceremonial zone and precinct for Teopantecuanitlán.

500 BCE; only a few scattered occupations are observed between AD 200 and 400 and around 1200.

The religious and political center of Teopantecuanitlán shows a series of monumental structures built along a north-south axis, with a deviation of 13° 39' east of magnetic north. The southern platform, a natural remodeled elevation located at the base of a hill, dominates a series of platform and esplanades. In this area, which serves as the entrance to the ceremonial center, were excavated several sculptures, including a blank stela, a reptilian creature, a triangular block resembling a throne with a human head in a cartouche, and a monolith showing a mutilated human figure. This ascending series of platforms and esplanades is interrupted by a sunken patio, one of the most striking features of the city (Figure 7.2). The patio includes a precinct of 18.6 × 14.2 meters, surrounded by a corridor with stairways. In Phase I, it was made of yellowish clay and compacted earth. The two double stairways, located in the southern corridor, have a divided ramp, which ends with a pillar in the very stylized shape of a feline with flaming eyebrows characteristic of Olmec style.

During Phase II, the interior walls of the precinct are covered with large travertine stones (Figure 7.3). Inside the wall stand four monumental sculptures in the shape of an inverted T, each weighing around three tons (Figure 7.4). The stone was transported from the nearby mountains and probably carved in situ. Each monolith represents an anthropomorphic feline with almond-shaped eyes, an inverted U-shaped mouth, and a frontal band with the motifs of the St. Andrew's cross and the cleft in the head (in the posterior part and not in the front, which is more common) (Martínez Donjuán 1982, 124–125). They hold in their paws an object that could be a plant or a torch. The four monoliths are associated with the cardinal directions and, according to Martínez Donjuán (1994), with the movements of the celestial bodies. This sacred space has been interpreted in different ways. The patio could be seen as a metaphor for the portal leading to the underworld. The monolith would then symbolize the sacred mountains and the four corners of the universe (Reilly 1994). Or the patio could symbolize a ball-game court in which the solar movements were recreated under the protection of the four deified felines (Angulo 1994). Whatever the interpretation, one clearly recognizes here the themes and motifs of Olmec symbolism.

Two types of hydraulic works are present in Teopantecuanitlán and fall primarily within the definition of utilitarian monumentality. According to Martínez Donjuán, they were built during Phase II, between 1000 and 700 BCE. The first type, which is also found in San Lorenzo and La Venta, is

Figure 7.3. Ceremonial zone and two of the four monoliths at Teopantecuanitlán.

Figure 7.4. One of the four monoliths at Teopantecuanitlán.

Figure 7.5. Hydraulic work at Teopantecuanitlán.

a system of channels made of U-shaped stones covered with flat stones that was used to drain the ceremonial area. The second type (Figure 7.5), a hydraulic work of megalithic proportions that could provide irrigation to agricultural lands around the city, implied a much more elaborate organization of the waters and lands. A megalithic conduit/channel 0.7 to 0.9 meters wide made of two parallel rows of thick paving stones 1.2 to 1.9 meters high covered with flat stones is connected to a reservoir. Only a section of a hundred meters has been explored so far, representing a very small portion of the entire network of channels making up the hydraulic work. More investigation is still needed to evaluate its size. Martínez Donjuán suggests that it is the oldest example of such a sophisticated irrigation technology in Mesoamerica (Martínez Donjuán 1994). However, confirmation of such a statement requires more secure dating. For the time being, no radiocarbon dates have been obtained and the dating rests on the relative age of the artifacts found in or near the portion of hydraulic work that has been investigated.

Outside the ceremonial section of Teopantecuanitlán, a substantial residential area was built during Phase II. Niederberger Betton has explored one of its residential units, Lomeríos, located near the Mezcala-Balsas River (Niederberger Betton 1986). It consists of several houses around a central court. The structures include a rectangular house made of perishable materials on a stone foundation and a residence of adobe built on a platform made of stone fill. The neighboring domestic space consists of work areas, hearths, and storage pits that were at times used as burial pits. At Lomeríos one may find many remains of activity related to subsistence and to craft production. Ceramic production was essentially local but also includes pan-Mesoamerican motifs related to Olmec II Horizon, such as the hybrid motif human-reptile-feline, hollow "baby-face" figurines, and the double line break.

The inhabitants of Lomeríos wore personal ornaments made of exotic materials, which seems to indicate their high status. Their participation in the interregional exchange system could account for this high status. Indeed, fragments of iron ore mirrors, plaques of mica, earrings made of onyx, and ornaments made of serpentine or green stone were found (Niederberger Betton 1986). Finally, Teopantecuanitlán seems to have been a center for seashell exchange (Niederberger Betton 1986, 2002). A shell workshop was found in Lomeríos that was dedicated to the transformation of the pearl oyster (*Pinctada matlazinca*). These shells are also found in San Pablo Nexpa in Morelos and in Tlatilco y Tlapacoya in the Basin of Mexico. Actually, Niederberger Betton has proposed the existence of a fluvial axis of the Amacuzac, Omitlán, and Papagayo rivers linking the Basin of Mexico and the Pacific coast. Teopantecuanitlán was the center of this axis (Niederberger Betton 2002).

Teopantecuanitlán was the capital of an extensive territory and of a ranked society (Martínez Donjuán 1994; Paradis 2008a, 2008b). The city, which was composed of an impressive civic and religious center, a substantial residential area, and an elaborate hydraulic system, testifies to an unquestionable social complexity that cannot be dissociated from its participation in the first Mesoamerican civilization. It is certainly the first and earliest to show this degree of complexity in Ancient Guerrero, although, as I will show, other sites show signs of monumentality and complexity in Guerrero. What should be evaluated are the relations of these sites to Teopantecuanitlán. Its localization at the crossing of east-west (to be defined later in this chapter) and south-north axes of communication and its access and control of resources such as seashells and possibly serpentine and other green stones and cacao could explain its active role as an actor in the first Mesoamerican civilization and its association with the pan-Mesoamerican interaction sphere.

Oxtotitlán: Place of Caves

So far, Ancient Guerrero is the only region to have produced Olmec-style mural paintings. I have included them in my discussion of monumentality because of their location in caves and their narratives. In Mesoamerica, caves have been (and are to this day) sacred places. Archaeological examples come to mind: the engraving of the "Rey" in Chalcatzingo, showing a dignitary sitting inside a cave (Grove 1987), and the cave at the origin of the Pyramid of the Sun in Teotihuacan (Heyden 2000). In Maya and Aztec mythology, the mouth of the cave often represents the entry to the underworld or the residence of the gods (Duverger 1983; Tedlock 1996; Miller and Taube 1993; Schele and Mathews 1998; Soustelle 1979). Obviously, the sacredness of these caves does not by itself warrant monumentality. It is the mural paintings and more specifically their narratives that display monumentality in the caves of Guerrero. The use of the Olmec code to express the symbols of rulership such as dignitaries, a throne, ceremonial clothes, and headdresses suggest a hierarchical society and the respect with which their rulers were held. I have chosen the Oxtotitlán caves as the best known and best documented to illustrate this point (Grove 1969, 1970, 1987, 1994, 1996, 1999).

Two caves in Oxtotitlán are among some five sites to show such paintings. The site is located a few kilometers east of the village of Acatlán, next to the town of Chilapa, in the mountainous region of southeast Guerrero. So far, there has not been any systematic archaeological investigation in the region of Acatlán or in Oxtotitlán (but the current investigations of Paul Schmidt should change this). What we know about these caves is the result of David Grove's observations and analysis, which started nearly forty years ago (Grove 1969, 1970). There are three groups of paintings: those of the Central Group and of the North Cave are Olmec-style, whereas those of the South Cave are more recent.

Central Group

The most spectacular and most studied painting in the Central Group is certainly Painting C-1 (Figure 7.6). The polychrome painting is 4.0 meters wide and 2.3 meters high. It shows an important personage with the head of were-jaguar sitting on a throne. He wears a bird headdress-mask, probably representing an owl. His left arm stands up whereas his right is extended toward his leg, which rests on a jaguar throne. The polychrome paint creates a contrast between the dignitary's clothes and ornaments, which are red

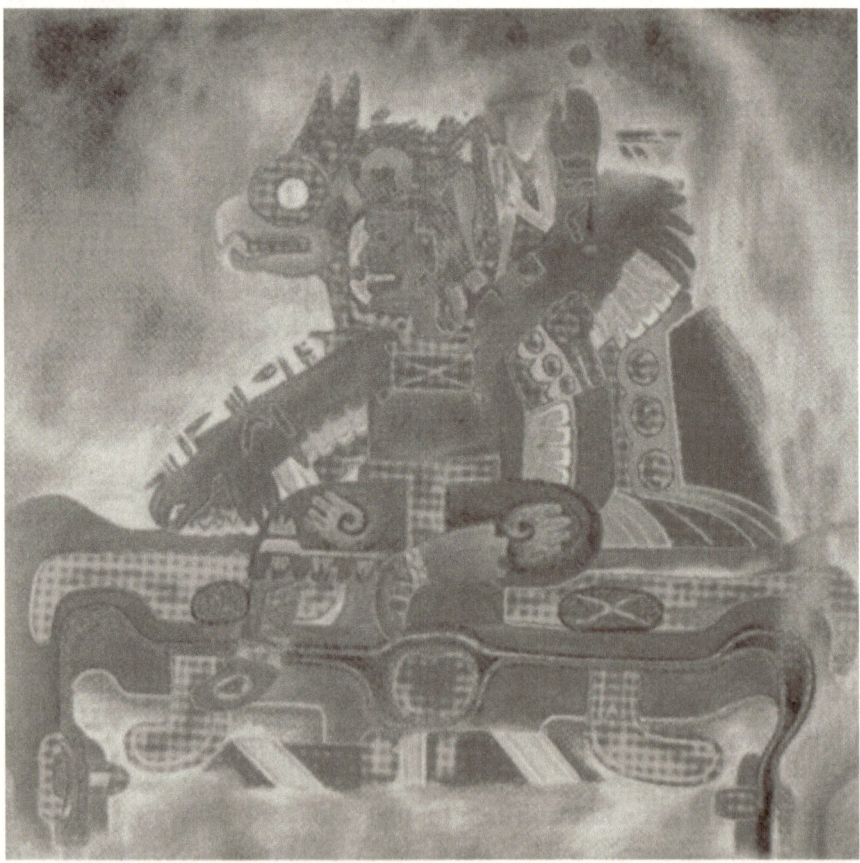

Figure 7.6. Oxtotitlán, Painting C-1, showing an important personage sitting on a throne.

and blue, and his body, which has the color of human skin. The headdress-mask transforms into a cape made of red, ocher, and blue-green feathers. On top of the headdress are white and blue circular and geometric motifs. The latter are often found in the large jaguar pavements buried at La Venta. The dignitary wears a pectoral with the motif of the St. Andrew's cross, a blue belt, a white loincloth, and a red-fringed skirt decorated with human hands and volutes. While the left leg is flexed, the right crosses the right eye of the were-jaguar. Although shoes are not frequent in Olmec art, we do find them here and at La Venta (monument 13 and possibly Stela 3) (Grove 1970). The head of the were-jaguar, upon which the dignitary is sitting, serves as a throne. We actually find the same representation on the "altars" of San Lorenzo and La Venta, which we now know were used as thrones. The eyes look like those of the were-jaguars of Altar 1 at La Venta Monument 41 at San Lorenzo (Grove 1970). The pupils are decorated with the St. Andrew's cross as in Relief 1 at Chalcatzingo and in Juxtlahuaca. Based on these stylistic resemblances with Olmec art, Grove (1970) suggests that the iconography as well as the localization of C-1 painting is related to rain, water, and vegetation. The dignitary seated on the throne refers without doubt to the power of the leaders and to its association with cosmic forces. There could also be a relation between the cave and the were-jaguar, on the one hand, and the entry to the underworld, on the other. I follow here Michael D. Coe, who has made a case for the relationship between the Olmec were-jaguar and the Aztec god Tepeyolotl ("Heart of the Mountain"), who resides inside the mountain (Coe 1971).

North Cave

The majority of the paintings are black monochrome in the Olmec style. The only exceptions are Paintings 8 and 9.

Painting 1 presents scenes that seem to be related. Among them are a human face in profile set in a flower of four petals (1a) and an animal(?), perhaps a *cipactli* (crocodile; 1c). The most important of the north group is a man standing near a jaguar on its hind legs; this has been interpreted as suggesting a sexual relation (1a–1d)(Figure 7.7).

Painting 2 shows two impressions of right hands painted in red. This kind of motif is found through the ancient history of Mesoamerica and has no particular stylistic or chronological meaning. Painting 3, which is particularly interesting, is on the roof of the north cave. It shows another variety of lizard or perhaps a mixture of a lizard and a bird. Underneath the

Figure 7.7. Oxtotitlán, Painting 1-D, showing a man standing near a jaguar.

jawless head are painted three circles. Grove sees in this combination of a symbolic element and possibly numerals an example, one of the most ancient, of a date in the 260-day calendar (Grove 1970). Painting 4 could represent a glyph, the meaning of which is unknown. Painting 5, which is not more than 10 centimeters long, is one of the "purest" examples of Olmec style; it shows a black drawing of a head. It could prefigure the magnificent Painting 7, which illustrates, but in a more elaborate way, a head in profile with a simple headdress and a serpent mask over the mouth (Figure 7.8). Painting 6 is another ideographic example of the Olmec style. The superior part of the face is very stylized, with large eyes and a mouth with its canines showing. The central part of the drawing looks like a bat.

This presentation of the mural paintings of Oxtotitlán reveals various elements of the Olmec representational system such as the depiction of

Figure 7.8. Oxtotitlán, Painting 7, showing a head in profile with a serpent mask over the mouth.

human beings, sometimes alone, but more often related to vegetation and to animals such as jaguars, lizards, birds, and hybrid beings. Ancient Guerrero is the only region that chose mural painting to express its ideology during the Olmec Horizon II. We now know that other sites, generally caves, show the same pattern: in Juxtlahuaca, in Cahuaziziqui near Tlapa (Villela 1989), in Texayac, and in Tepila, east of Tierra Colorada (Niederberger Betton 1996, 96). The mural paintings' impressive aspect, their iconographic complexity, and their placement in Oxtotitlan cave warrant the attribute of monumentality, as do other in mural paintings in Ancient Guerrero. The importance of caves as sacred space is very well documented in both ancient and contemporary Mesoamerican cultures (Stone 1995; Taube 1986; Tedlock 1996). They are used as ritual sites, places of reunion to worship or present offerings to deities or their human representatives. The caves at Oxtotitlan and the other caves with mural paintings of that time period (1000–700 BCE) are the first known examples of the use of caves as sacred space. Their association with the symbolic code of the Olmec civilization is well established. But what about their relationships with other sites from

Ancient Guerrero where monumental works with the same symbolic affiliations are found? Until we have more details about the cultural context of the locality and the region around Oxtotitlán, we can only offer directions in which to search for meaning. One of them is that Oxtotitlán, Juxtlahuaca, Cahuaziziqui, Tepila, and Texayac lie in the terrestrial and fluvial axis that links Teopantecuanitlán and the Pacific coast. We can imagine that goods, people and ideas exchanged among these localities. I would also suggest that these sites were part of the territory controlled by the capital Teopantecuanitlán, from which they were politically dependent. One should not forget that nowhere else in Guerrero during this time period has a city that large (160 hectares) and that complex been found.

Amuco de la Reforma

In 1969, I was in Guerrero looking for a place to do my doctoral work. At the time, I was interested in the presence of Olmec style in Guerrero and I wanted to find an archaeological context that would date and help us understand this presence. I first visited Oxtotitlán, and afterward, upon the suggestion of David Grove, I went to Arcelia, where I was shown a stela that was definitely in the Olmec style (Figure 7.9). The owner told me he had found it in the Tierra Caliente of Guerrero, more specifically from the village of Amuco de la Reforma (Grove and Paradis 1971). After three attempts to reach Amuco (it was during the rainy season and I could not get through the roads because of overflowing waters or fallen bridges), I reached the village and decided that was where I would do my doctoral investigation. My work in the approximate place where the stela had been found, the site of Amuco Abelino, allowed me to document the presence of a residential area that was occupied during the Early, Middle and Late Formative and the beginnings of the Classic Period (1200 BCE to AD 200). The domestic structure that was excavated produced a local ceramic tradition as well as elements related to the Olmec style, such as two figurines and double line-break vessels. As such, it can be compared to Lomeríos, the residential unit excavated by Niederberger Betton in Teopantecuanitlán (Niederberger Betton 1986). Both were occupied during the Olmec Horizon II, between 1000 and 700 BCE.

The Amuco stela that was found approximately 200 meters from Amuco Abelino is stylistically related to the Olmec style of La Venta y Chalcatzingo, which is based on a greater use of bas-relief sculpture and a more cursive style (Grove and Paradis 1971). The glyphic elements found on the

Figure 7.9.
Amuco Stele.

stela, a foot and possibly a *cipactli*, could have been added later. That is why we date it in the Middle or perhaps the Late Formative. There is no doubt that the Amuco stela is a monument, the material expression of a symbolic code shared by the inhabitants of Amuco, Teopantecuanitlán, and Oxtotitlán, among others, and possibly with the other regions that were part of the Olmec civilization. Nevertheless, it was found in a residential and domestic context. How can one explain this? In the region of Amuco at this time, the political structure was egalitarian or (most likely) slightly ranked, suggesting a lineage structure (Paradis 1974). Most settlements were hamlets and villages that practiced agriculture. These show a certain amount of variation, which could indicate incipient inequality of status between these settlements, even though no regional center was found. As is the case with Oxtotitlán and other cave sites with mural paintings, Amuco is related to Teopantecuanitlán because of its stele and its cultural production. Why and how? For the moment, we can only suggest that Amuco was aligned with the west-east axis of communication, the high and middle Balsas River. In economic terms, obsidian from Michoacan and serpentine and other green stone could circulate from west to east, from Amuco to Teopantecuanitlán and eastern Mesoamerica. That is why I suggest that Amuco was part of (if not subject to) the Teopantecuanitlán realm.

Coovisur (Chilpancingo)

Complex burials, some of which are in a corbeled-vault tomb, and Olmec-style offerings were found in Coovisur (Figure 7.10). They are part of a series of burials that Reyna Robles and Quintero attribute to a cemetery (18 individuals in an area of 35 square meters). Two groups of burials were dated during the Middle (1000 to 700 BCE) and Late (700 to 400 BCE) Formative Period. The corbel arch tomb belongs to the first of these epochs (Reyna Robles and Quintero 1998).

The investigation of Reyna Robles and Quintero was a salvage project, and nothing more is known of the sociocultural context of the site. Nevertheless, the nature and content of the cemetery suggest a ranked society. I consider the complex funerary practices documented in Coovisur to be early signs of monumentality. And, once more, they are related to the Olmec style and Olmec civilization. In reference to Ancient Guerrero, Coovisur could have been part, even subject, of the realm of Teopantecuanitlán. The cultural similarities as well as the location of Coovisur near the

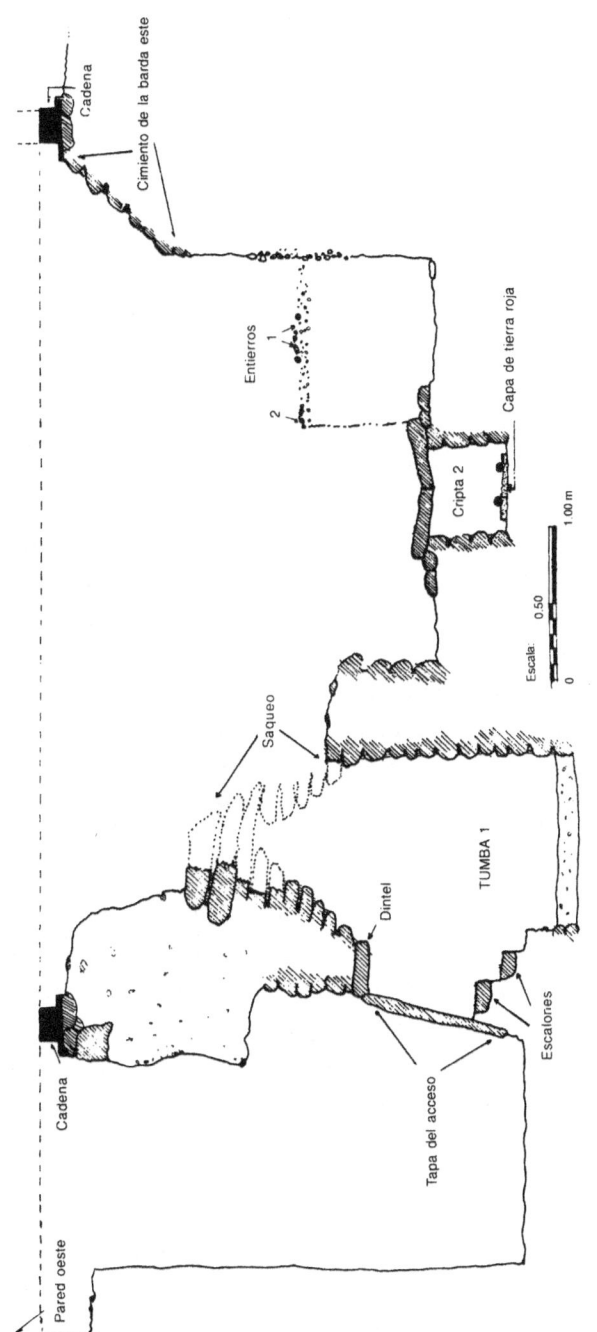

Figure 7.10. Burials and Tomb 1 with corbelled arch at Coovisur.

southern exchange roads that linked Teopantecuanitlán to the Pacific are significant facts that suggest this argument.

Discussion

Whereas the Olmec art style is present in all of the occupied portions of Ancient Guerrero, the distribution of the first monumental works are concentrated in the Upper and Middle Balsas River drainage. One site, Teopantecuanitlán, acted as the capital of a complex society; its area of influence would have included other sites in the region that included expressions of monumentality. These site are located on at least two of the trade roads to resources that were part of the pan-Mesoamerican sphere of exchange: seashell and cacao from the Pacific Coast (Papagayo, Omitlán, and upper Balsas rivers) and serpentine, green stone, and obsidian from Michoacan (upper and middle Balsas River).

Central to the understanding of the meaning of the earliest monumentality in Ancient Guerrero is proper dating. I have demonstrated elsewhere (Paradis 2008a) that despite the early and noncalibrated radiocarbon dates for the monumental architecture of Teopantecuanitlán and for the Olmec-style figurines of Amuco Abelino (Table 7.1), I would date Teopantecuanitlán's ceremonial architecture, the Amuco stele, Coovisur, Oxtotitlán, and the other caves with mural paintings, in the Middle Formative Period or Olmec II Horizon, between 1000 and 700 BCE, because of both the style and context of these sites and monuments.

At this time, there were four known capitals in the Olmec archipelago (the term is borrowed from Rosenswig 2010): La Venta, Chalcatzingo, Teopantecuanitlán, and San José Mogote. I am quite certain there were more such sites, for example in the Basin of Mexico, but in that case at least urban growth has erased all traces of them. By capitals, I mean complex human agglomerations (cities) with monumental architecture and residential and specialized areas. I also mean heads of complex political structures (complex chiefdoms or archaic states). As such, capitals represent the generalization and the development of a pattern of social complexity that first appeared in San Lorenzo in the Olmec I Horizon. The first Mesoamerican symbolic system had been codified for at least 200 years by that point and was shared by all its cultural regions. It was in the context of long-term interactions in and between the inhabitants of these regions that this symbolic system was elaborated, transmitted, and transformed. Such a complex symbolic system must have been codified first in one place, even though the ideas may have come from many places through travel and oral transmission. And because of the precedence of San Lorenzo in monumentality and social complexity, I would select the area as the one that first codified this symbolic system. At that time, around 1200 BCE, there is evidence for the presence of the symbolic code in the Gulf Coast, in Soconusco, in Morelos, in Oaxaca, in Ancient Guerrero, in Highland Mexico, and in most inhabited regions of Mesoamerica. But in the Olmec I Period, only San Lorenzo and its territory provide definite traces of monumentality associated with the rise of sociopolitical complexity.

Thus, it is during the second part of the First Horizon, starting around 1000 BCE, that monumental works and social complexity are associated with five regions of Mesoamerica: Veracuz-Tabasco with La Venta, Morelos with Chalcatzingo, Guerrero with Teopantecuanitlán, Oaxaca with San José Mogote, and Soconusco with La Blanca (Rosenswig, this volume). How does one account for this pattern? Among the possibilities, I would reject any form of conquest, colonization, or political domination of La Venta over these regions and the rest of inhabited Mesoamerica because of the lack of archaeological evidence to support these inferences. I would instead expand, on the basis of new archeological evidence, on what I proposed in my doctoral thesis (Paradis 1974, 1982). The cultural regions of Mesoamerica, born from the adoption of agriculture and village life, were communicating and exchanging goods, ideas, and persons in a complex interaction system. Each region developed independently, but never in isolation. The picture one gets is that of differential rhythms in the development of social complexity. In all five regions where it first appears, non-utilitarian monumentality expresses itself with the Olmec symbolic code. On the one hand, this code was already known and was not imposed. Yet on the other hand, each case is unique: its cultural production reflects continuity with its own regional history. The Olmec code was the language of the political and ideological power of the leaders of the capitals of La Venta, Chalcatzingo, Teopantecuanitlán, San José Mogote, and La Blanca and probably others as well.

In this review of the earliest evidence of monumentality in Ancient Guerrero, we find some answers but are left with more questions. I have described the earliest and various expressions of monumentality (monumental architecture and sculpture; mural paintings; elaborate tombs; hydraulic works). I located them in time (1000 to 700 BCE) and in space (upper and middle Balsas, upper Balsas, Omitlán, and Papagayo rivers). I proposed that the sites showing monumentality were related to (if not subject to) Teopantecuanitlán, the first capital of Ancient Guerrero. Economic incentives, such as the circulation and control of resources that were part of the pan-Mesoamerican sphere of exchange, may explain the distribution of the sites with monumental works. Finally, I related the earliest monumentality to the development of the first Mesoamerican civilization and the earliest symbolic code that was used as the language of political power between its known capitals.

But I was not able to determine the energy expenditure implied in the construction of the monumental works. The nature of the evidence and the lack of context, except for the sunken court and the drainage system of Teopantecuanitlán, which could provide that kind of data, account for this lack of information. For the most part, the origin of monumentality in Ancient Guerrero remains unexplained. Even though it was clearly associated with the development of the first Mesoamerican civilization, and even if we reject the conquest or colonization explanation, we will have to look further to answer this question.

References Cited

Angulo, Jorge V.
1994   Observación sobre su pensamiento cosmogónico y la organización sociopolítica. In *Los Olmecas en Mesoamérica*, edited by John Clark, pp. 223–238. Equilibrista, México y Turner Libros, Madrid.
Coe, Michael D.
1971   Olmec Jaguars and Olmec Kings. In *The Cult of the Feline,* edited by Elizabeth P. Benson, pp. 1–18. Dumbarton Oaks Research Library and Collections, Washington, D.C.
Coe, Michael D., and R. Diehl
1980   *In the Land of the Olmec*. University of Texas Press, Austin.
Cyphers, Ann
2008   Los tronos y la configuración del poder Olmeca. In *Ideología, política y sociedad en el Período Formativo: Ensayos en homenaje al doctor David C. Grove,* edited by Kenneth Hirth, and Ann Cyphers, pp. 311–341. Instituto de Investigaciones Antropológicas, and Instituto Nacional de Antropología e Historia, Mexica.
Donnan, Christopher (editor)
1985   *Early Ceremonial Architecture in the Andes*. Dumbarton Oaks Research Library and Collections, Washington, D.C.
Duverger, Christian
1983   *L'origine des Aztèques*. Seuil, Paris.

Gibson, Jon L.
2000   *The Ancient Mounds of Poverty Point: Place of Rings.* University Press of Florida, Gainesville.

González Lauck, Rebecca
1996   La Venta: An Olmec Capital. In *Olmec Art of Ancient Mexico,* edited by E. Benson, and B. de la Fuente, 73–81. National Gallery of Art, Washington, D.C.

Grove, David C.
1969   Olmec Cave Paintings: Discovery from Guerrero, Mexico. *Science* 164 (3878) 421–423.
1970   *The Olmec Paintings of Oxtotitlan Cave, Guerrero, Mexico.* Studies in Precolumbian Art and Archaeology 6, Dumbarton Oaks Study and Collections, Washington, D.C.
1987   *Ancient Chalcatzingo.* University of Texas Press, Austin.
1994   Chalcatzingo. In *Los Olmecas en Mesoamérica,* edited by John Clark, pp. 164–173. El Equilibrista, México, and Turner Libros, Madrid.
1996   Archaeological Contexts of Olmec Art Outside of the Gulf Coast." In *Olmec Art of Ancient Mexico,* edited by E. P. Benson, and B. de la Fuente, pp. 105–118. National Gallery of Art, Washington, D.C.
1999   Public Monuments and Sacred Mountains: Observations on Three Formative Period Sacred Landscapes. In *Social Patterns in Preclassic Mesoamerica,* edited by D. C. Grove and R. Joyce, pp. 255–299. Dumbarton Oaks, Washington, D.C.

Grove, David C., and Louise I. Paradis
1971   An Olmec Stela from San Miguel Amuco, Guerrero. *American Antiquity* 36:95–102.

Hass, Jonathan, and W. Creamer
2006   Crucible of Andean Civilization: The Peruvian COSAT from 3000 to 1800 BC. *Current Anthropology* 47(5): 745–775.

Heizer R. F., E. P. Drucker, and J. A. Graham
1968   Investigations at La Venta, 1967. In *Papers on Mesoamerican Archaeology,* pp. 1–34. Archaeology Research Facility, Berkeley, California.

Henderson, John H.
1979   *Atopula, Guerrero and Olmec Horizons in Mesoamerica.* Yale University Press, New Haven, Connecticut.

Heyden, Doris
2000   From Teotihuacan to Tenochtitlan. City Planning, Caves, and Streams of Red and Blue Waters. In *Mesoamerican Classic Heritage,* edited by David Carrasco, Lindsay Jones, and Scott Sessions, pp. 165–184. University Press of Colorado, Boulder.

Kirchhoff, Paul
1943   Mesoamerica. *Acta Americana* 1: 92–107

Martínez Donjuán, Guadalupe
1986   Teopantecuanitlán. In *Arqueología y Etnohistoria del Estado de Guerrero,* 55–80. INAH and Gobierno del Estado de Guerrero, México D.F.
1994   Los Olmecas en el Estado de Guerrero. In *Los Olmecas en Mesoamérica,* edited by John Clark, pp. 143–164. Equilibrista, México y Turner Libros, Madrid.

Miller, Mary, and Karl Taube
1993   *The Gods and Symbols of Ancient Mexico and the Maya.* Thames and Hudson, London.

Niederberger Betton, Christine
1986   Excavación de un área de habitación doméstica en la capital "olmeca" de Tlacozotitlán. In *Arqueología y Etnohistoria del Estado de Guerrero,* pp. 83–103. INAH and Gobierno del Estado de Guerrero, México D.F.
1996   Olmec Horizon, Guerrero. In *Olmec Art of Ancient Mexico,* edited by Elizabeth P. Benson, and Beatriz de la Fuente, pp. 95–104. National Gallery of Art, Washington, D.C.
2002   Nacar, "jade" y cinabrio: Guerrero y las redes de intercambio en la Mesoamérica antigua (1000–600 a.C.). In *El pasado arqueológico de Guerrero,* edited by Christine Niederberger and Rosa Reyna, pp. 175–223. CEMCA, Gobierno del Estado de Guerrero e INAH, México.

Paradis, Louise I.
1974   The Tierra Caliente of Guerrero, Mexico: An Archaeological and Ecological Study. Ph.D. dissertation, Anthropology Department, Yale University, New Haven, Connecticut.
1982   Les échanges en Mésoamérique: un train peut en cacher un autre. *Recherches Amérindiennes au Québec* 12(3):163–177.
1990   El fenómeno olmeca revisitado. *Arqueología* n.s. 3: 33–40.
2001   Guerrero Region. In *The Archaeology of Ancient Mexico and Central America: An Encyclopedia,* edited by S. T. Evans and D. L. Webster, pp. 311–321. Garland Publishing, New York.
2008a Contribución del Guerrero antiguo a la civilización olmeca. In *Olmeca, Balance y perspectivas. Memorias de la Primera Mesa Redonda,* vol. 2, edited by M. T. Uriarte and R. González Lauck, pp. 533–546. UNAM and INAH, Mexico.
2008b Guerrero y la primera civilización mesoamericana. In *Tributo a Jaime Litvak,* edited by P. Schmidt, E. Ortiz Diaz, and J. Santos Ramírez, pp. 233–248. UNAM, Mexico.

Reilly, Kent F., III
1994   Cosmología, soberanismo y espacio ritual en la Mesoamerica del Formativo. In *Los Olmecas en Mesoamérica,* edited by John Clark, pp. 239–260. Equilibrista, México y Turner Libros, Madrid.

Reyna Robles, Rosa, and Lauro Gonzáles Quintero
1998   *Rescate Arqueológico de un espacio funerario de época olmeca en Chilpancingo.* Instituto Nacional de Antropología e Historia, México D.F.

Rosenswig, Robert M.
2010   *The Beginnings of Mesoamerican Civilization: Inter-Regional Interaction and the Olmec.* Cambridge University Press, New York.

Sassaman, Kenneth E.
2005   Poverty Point as Structure, Event, Process. *Journal of Archaeological Method and Theory* 12:335–364.

Schele, Linda, and Peter Mathews
1998   *The Code of Kings: The Language of Seven Sacred Maya Temples and Tombs.* Scribner, New York.

Soustelle, Jacques
1979   *L'univers des Aztèques.* Collection Savoir, Hermann, Paris.

Stone, Andrea J.
1995   *Images from the Underworld, Naj Tunich and the Tradition of Maya Cave Painting.* University of Texas Press, Austin.

Taube, Karl A.
1986   The Teotihuacan Cave of Origin. *Res* 12:51–82.

Tedlock, Dennis
1996   *Popol Vuh: The Definitive Edition of the Mayan Book of the Dawn of Life and the Glories of Gods and Kings.* Simon and Schuster, New York.

Tolstoy, Paul
1989   Western Mesoamerica and the Olmec. In *Regional Perspectives on the Olmec*, edited by R. J. Sharer, and D. C. Grove, pp. 275–302. Cambridge University Press, New York.

Trigger, Bruce G.
1992   Monumental Architecture: A Thermodynamic Explanation of Symbolic Behavior. *World Archaeology* 22:119–132.

Villela, Samuel
1989   Nuevo testimonio rupestre olmeca en el oriente de Guerrero. *Arqueología* época 2a: 37–48.

8

Early Civilization in the Maya Lowlands, Monumentality, and Place Making

A View from the Holmul Region

FRANCISCO ESTRADA-BELLI

The appearance of monumental architecture in the Maya Lowlands is closely related to a new level of community integration across the region and to the appearance of many cultural manifestations that we recognize as part of Maya civilization. It likely marked a new generative phase of power and ritual relations within Maya communities that led to the creation of regional polities. Following the consensus view that monumentality is a correlation of well-formed political institutions (kingships and/or states), the apparent precocity of early Lowland Maya architecture at sites such as Nakbe and Tikal has been typically dealt with as an anomaly of cultural evolution and therefore explained by an array of migration and diffusion theories (e.g. Clark et al. 2000; Coe 1977; Hansen 2005; Lowe 1977, 1989). In this chapter, I propose that early Lowland Maya monumental architecture should not be viewed as the reflection of complex social organizations already in place. Doing so may lead one to accept the view that the complex forms of power, economic relations, ritual relations—that is, the institutions we associate with civilization—developed elsewhere and were imported into the Lowlands. Instead, the erection of the earliest formal ritual complexes may be related to the building of ceremonial centers by communities within bounded regions. Such newly established centers likely served as spaces of social interaction and integration that generated new political orders and complexity. When monumental architecture is seen as part of a generative process it is not surprising that the earliest construction projects were carried out so close in time to the "appearance" of Lowland farming

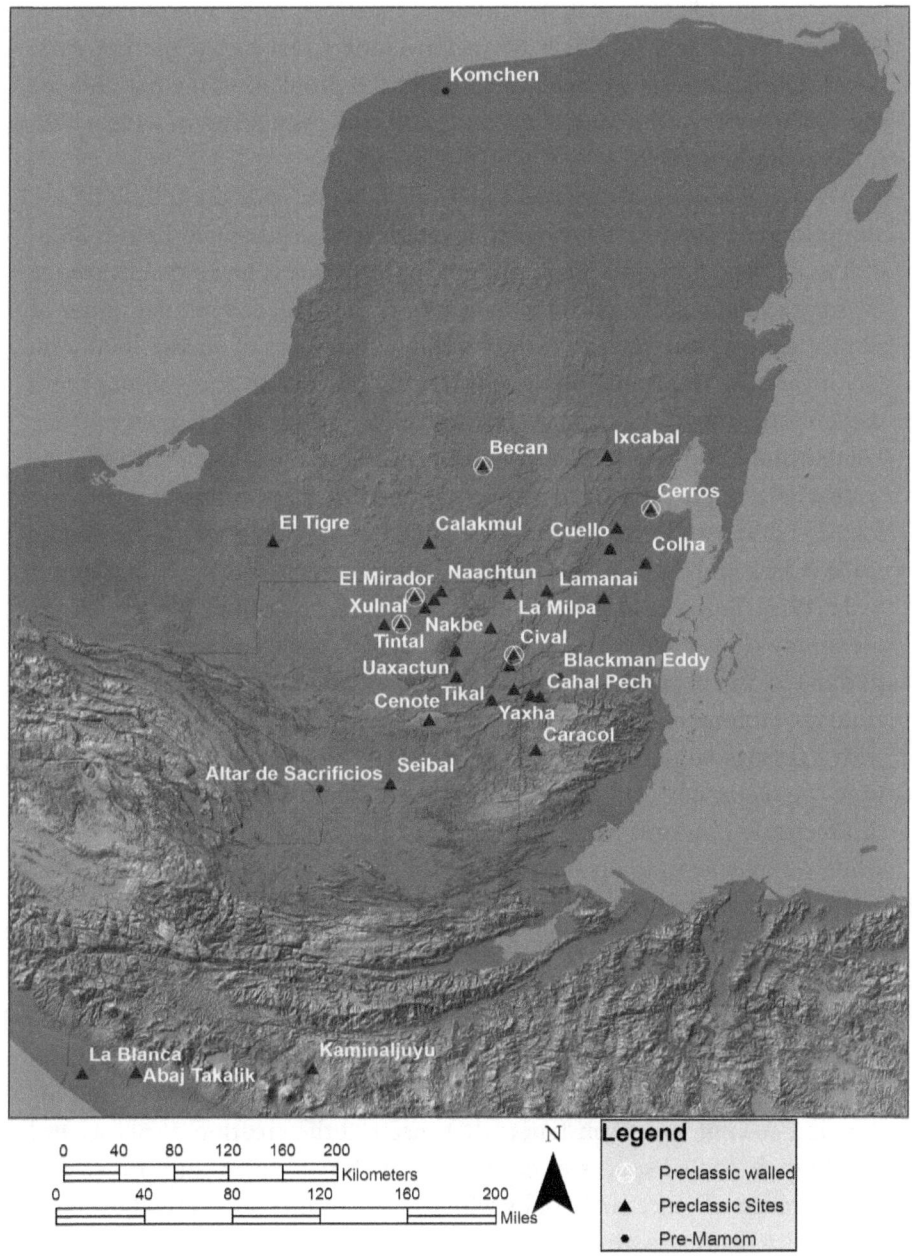

Figure 8.1. Map of the Maya Lowlands showing sites with Pre-Mamom ceramics and early architecture.

communities in the archaeological record. This took place within a century—too quickly for a state to develop. Therefore, to be able to correctly evaluate the context in which Maya Lowlanders first began monumental construction projects we need to consider the problem of the peopling of the vast interior of the Maya Lowlands and reassess a series of widely held notions on the subject.

Most discussions of the Preclassic Maya begin with the following assumptions: 1) The Maya Lowlands were largely uninhabited before 800–600 BC. 2) The Lowland Maya did not make progress beyond subsistence farming and village life until the founding of the great ceremonial center of El Mirador ca. 300 BC. The earlier architectural mass of Nakbe (600–400 BC) invariably stands out as extraordinarily precocious (i.e., unique) and is therefore difficult to explain (Hansen 2005; Hansen and Guenter 2005). Furthermore, 3) the rise of El Mirador and Lowland Maya civilization is widely believed to have occurred on the heels of great influences from the former La Venta Olmec neighbors and/or Izapan culture from the Pacific slope (Clark and Blake 1989; Coe 1966, 2005; Covarrubias 1957; Sharer and Sedat 1973; Taube et al. 2004; Valdés 1999). These notions have been increasingly challenged by recent archaeological data from several sites, especially by the data on early ceramics and architecture recently recovered from the Holmul region. Another set of related issues that can be addressed with existing data are questions about the socioeconomic processes behind the seemingly unprecedented and conspicuous architectural projects of Preclassic Lowland Maya sites such as El Mirador and Nakbe. Finally, while we may be in the position of establishing the construction dates for many Preclassic buildings, in most cases we are still far from understanding their function. When we can identify the function of architecture, we can gain insight about the social processes that caused it to be constructed. The simple forms and plain facades of the earliest architecture provide little clues to function. However, astronomical sightlines and foundation offerings of ceramics, jade, and other symbolic materials reveal the underlying cosmological constructs that inspired the creation of plazas and buildings as sacred spaces in connection with particular landforms. This was a process of place-making by which communities across the Lowlands and within regions instituted an inclusive collective memory that may have replaced the ethnic (lineage) diversity of quasi-autonomous communities of earlier periods.

Early Farmers and Early Ritual

A long-held and now-problematic notion about the earliest Lowland Maya is that they were groups of migrant farmers who penetrated the vast and uninhabited Lowland interior by way of the eastern and western river systems sometime between 900 and 800 BC (Puleston and Puleston 1971). Many scholars have looked at the Highland regions of Chiapas, Guatemala, and El Salvador and the Gulf of Mexico as the most likely regions of origin of the "first" Lowland Maya farmers (Adams 1971; Clark and Pye 2000; Coe 1966; Lowe 1977; Parsons 1986; Borhegyi 1965; Jiménez Moreno 1966; Ball and Taschek 2003; Sabloff 1975). By extension, the origins of the accoutrements of Maya civilization, foremost among them monumental architecture, have been sought outside the Lowland region. The primary data by which early Lowlanders are recognized typically do not include architecture but are limited to ceramic vessels prior to 800 BC. Sculpture, which is abundant in the Olmec region in the Middle Preclassic (1000–400 BC), is nonexistent in the Maya Lowlands during the same period. On the other hand, there are rare but significant examples of monumental architecture in the Middle Preclassic period. Most notable are broad platform constructions at Nakbe beginning at 600 BC. As noted above, these should not be regarded as unique since large Middle Preclassic public structures and platforms have been documented at a few other sites, such as at Tikal's Mundo Perdido complex, at 800 BC (Figure 8.1; Laporte and Fialko 1993).

The notion that early Lowland ceramics represent the actual peopling of the Lowlands from nearby regions is at odds with the available evidence. The earliest Lowland Maya ceramics are found in a small number of locations, at Tikal, at Uaxactun (Culbert 1977; Laporte and Valdes 1993), at Seibal (Sabloff 1975) and at Altar de Sacrificios (Adams 1971); at Belize River Valley sites (Awe 1992); and at Holmul and Komchen in the northern Lowlands (Andrews et al. 2008). Because these ceramics were first found in some cases near the margins of the southern Lowlands, they were regarded as evidence of the first migration of "advanced" farmers into a difficult wilderness region (Adams 1971; Kidder et al. 1946; Tozzer 1957). These ceramics are generally described as regionally diverse. According to John Clark and David Cheetam (2002), they represent at least four subtly distinct groups characterized by common forms, surface finish, and incised decorative motifs. These regional groups consist of the Tikal early Eb complex in central Peten (Culbert 1977), possibly including the ceramics from Uaxactun and Yaxha/Sacnab (Ax Pam complex; Rice 1979); the Pasion region complex, including the Xe and Real Xe ceramics of Altar de Sacrificios and Seibal (Adams 1971; Sabloff 1975); and the Cunil complex found at Xunantunich, Cahal Pech, Pacbitun, and Blackman Eddy in the Belize River Valley (Awe 1992; Garber et al. 2004; Healy, Hohmann, and Powis 2004; Strelow and LeCount 2001). In addition to these is the newly discovered Holmul K'awiil complex (Callaghan 2006, 2008). Ongoing analysis suggests that this complex might not be subsumed under the Tikal or Belizean groups and may therefore represent a fifth regional group. Finally, the Swasey/Bladen complex of northern Belize appears to be closely related and therefore subsumed to the Belize River Valley Cunil group. All these regional ceramic groups are chronologically and stylistically antecedent to the Lowlands' first homogeneous ceramic complex, the Mamom complex, and have been placed by ^{14}C dates to between 1100 and 850 BC. Certain stylistic features of form, color, and incised decoration seem to link early Lowland ceramics to the nearby highland regions and to the Gulf of Mexico but also to a much wider network of Early and Middle Preclassic sites across Mesoamerica from Central Mexico to Honduras and El Salvador. Perhaps even more significant, the greatest amount of overlap in the form and decoration can be found *among* the regional Lowland Maya complexes rather than *between* any of them and complexes of outside regions. The most consistent similarities among Pre-Mamom ceramic complexes are found in the incised motifs. These motifs more than any other ceramic attribute can be found on contemporary ceramics of other regions across Mesoamerica and are therefore likely to represent a pan-Mesoamerican sphere of interaction at this time rather than migrations into the Maya Lowlands or anywhere else.

The suggestion that the motifs found on Pre-Mamom ceramics originated as an iconographic set in the Olmec heartland has found fewer supporters over the last two decades and with it the notion that the first Maya farmers came from the Gulf of Mexico or the nearby Highland regions of Chiapas and Guatemala (Clark and Cheetam 2002). Increasingly, lithic and paleoenvironmental data from across the Lowlands are reaffirming a pattern that was long known but seldom emphasized: the Maya Lowlands were occupied by slash-and-burn farmers for 1,500 years prior to the first appearance of ceramics and villages in the archaeological record. Hunters and gatherers and human-induced forest disturbances appear in the Maya Lowlands as early as in the fourth millennium BC (Deevey et al. 1979; Lohse et al. 2006; Wahl et al. 2006; Iceland 2005; Jacob 1995; Pohl et al. 1996; Rosenswig and Masson 2001).

Figure 8.2. Artist's reconstruction of vessels from the Holmul Pre-Mamom ceramic complex.

The discovery of Pre-Mamom ceramics in the lowest stratigraphic levels of ritual plazas at Holmul and Cival has led to a reconsideration of their function and meaning because these may relate to the monumental architecture they lie directly under (Figure 8.2; Neivens de Estrada 2006). While Pre-Mamom ceramics are found below Middle Preclassic and Late Preclassic strata, they are typically mixed with Middle Preclassic Mamom phase ceramics. The repertoire of forms includes plates with broad everted rims, dishes with vertical or outflaring sides, *tecomate* jars, jars with strap handles, and short-sided and round-sided bowls (Callaghan 2006). They are often finished by deep red and cream or white slips or they can be a burnished or an unslipped buff color. The decorations include incision as well as some filleting on the shoulder. The incisions are done post-slip and include motifs such as the flamed eyebrow, music brackets, woven designs, the bloodletter, cleft heads, step-frets, and k'an crosses. As noted earlier, stylistically these incised ceramics most closely resemble the Early Eb and Cunil early Middle Preclassic material from Tikal and Cahal Pech, Belize, respectively.

The overall quality of the Holmul Pre-Mamom ceramics is as striking as their finely executed incised decoration. Direct comparisons with ceramics of the subsequent early Mamom phase clearly shows a relative decrease in slip and paste quality and the disappearance of complex incised motifs in the Mamom phase, but overall direct continuity is apparent. Serving ware makes up the larger proportion of these early ceramics. The incisions appear only on a small subset of the serving ware (typically 5 percent).

Extensive testing has shown that in the Holmul region, the contexts of early ceramics appear to have been spatially restricted to a few central locations. These are the Cival main plaza and Holmul's Group II platform. The latter location has produced by far the largest amount and greatest variety of decorated Pre-Mamom ceramics in the region. Interestingly, both locations were loci of continuous ritual activity for a millennium following the initial occupation.

It is possible that early ceramics such as these may have been used primarily in feasting events and that the symbols they carried have ritual significance in such social gatherings. The earliest ceramics in neighboring coastal Guatemala, which are similarly decorated, have been interpreted as serving ware for public feasts (Clark 1991; Clark and Blake 1994). In the Valley of Oaxaca, similar abstract symbols were incised on contemporary San Jose phase ceramics and are believe to reflect both a pan-Mesoamerican belief system and local feasting rituals. Other Central Mexican ceramic assemblages dating to between 1150 and 900 BC bear similar decorations (Flannery and Marcus 1994), as do those from the Soconusco (Love 2002; Rosenswig 2010).

Furthermore, the set of symbols appearing on Pre-Mamom Lowland ceramics denotes supernatural concepts familiar to Maya cosmology of later periods, as comparison with later iconography carved on Middle and Late Preclassic monuments has shown. Most of the incised symbols appear to be abstract versions of later iconographic symbols such as those found in the Late Preclassic period architectural "mask" sculptures. Many, if not all, can be linked to the main deities and places associated with the Maya creation story and Classic Maya dynastic iconography, such as reptilian or avian composites (the storm god), cleft heads (earth, maize), bloodletting (ancestor veneration), and the Maize God (Fields 2005). The most complex elaboration of these iconographic themes in a Preclassic Lowland Maya context is found in the San Bartolo murals almost eight centuries after the Pre-Mamom ceramics (Saturno et al. 2005). In summary, several lines of evidence should be considered in interpreting the appearance of surprisingly sophisticated ceramics in the Maya Lowlands at around 1100 BC vis-à-vis the type of social context that produced them. The form and decorative motifs as well as their limited quantities suggest a restricted circulation. The location as well as their decoration suggest a primarily ritual function for all Pre-Mamom ceramics. Remarkably, specific links are evident between symbols found on ceramics and those found in association with public buildings of later eras. Most notable among these are the references to storm and earth (maize) gods of Maya creation (see below). These same symbols constitute the core of the iconographic motifs associated with some of the earliest monumental sculpture on Late Preclassic platforms and pyramids. But in a less explicit and nevertheless tangible way this set of motifs constitutes the ideological charter that appears to form the basis for the erection of the first truly monumental buildings in the Maya Lowlands. As we have seen from paleoenvironmental and lithic data, the Lowlands were populated by groups of semi-sedentary farmers for 1,500 years prior to the adoption of ceramics. This also corresponds with the settling of permanent villages, less ephemeral forms of domestic architecture, and the concomitant use of clay figurines (Awe 1992; Garber et al. 2004). Therefore, the introduction of ceramics should no longer be seen as signaling the arrival of "peasant migrants" from the highlands or other nearby regions of greater cultural complexity. It may in fact signal the development of public or semi-public ritual feasting events in central places that served a number of communities within a large region. The extent of each ceramic style likely reflects the region of interaction served by each central place, similar to the "tribal groups" hypothesized by Clark and Cheetam (2002). These early foci of ritual gatherings would eventually require formal monumental architecture to be erected to accommodate more formal ritual events.

Cival and the Lowland's Earliest Monumental Architecture

The most climactic moment in the history of the Preclassic ceremonial center of Cival occurs at the very beginning of its occupation history. Surprisingly, this significant moment was not in the Late Preclassic period but in the Middle Preclassic period, in spite of the impressive mass of buildings and platforms erected in that later phase (Figure 8.3). In the ninth century BC, the Cival ceremonial center was created by the occupants of what must have been a sparsely populated cluster of hilltop settlements within a wide area. Several villages lay around a large sinkhole (the "cival") and the Holmul River on one side and near a vast wetland on the other side. The birth of Cival as a ceremonial center was marked by the laborious leveling and infilling of a broad (0.5 sq km) hilltop, which raised the surface by as much as seven meters (in the south) and an average of four meters in the north and west margins (Figure 8.4). At that time, in the center of this newly created space, the first version of an E-Group architectural complex was built (Estrada-Belli 2006). A small radial platform one to two meters high faced

Figure 8.3. Perspective view of three phases of construction in the ceremonial center at Cival. Relief based on GIS field map and excavation data. A) unmodified hill; B) leveled hill and first E-Group (Middle Preclassic); C) Pyramids and platforms of Late Preclassic period.

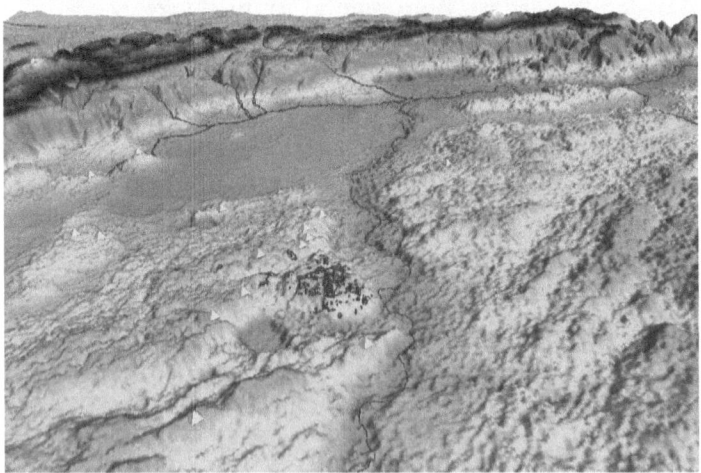

Figure 8.4. View of the landforms of the Cival area. GIS topography based on AIRSAR interferometry data (Star3i 1999 take) courtesy of NASA. Pyramid symbols indicate Middle Preclassic hilltop settlements around the Cival main hill. Late Preclassic architecture of the ceremonial center also shown as lines. Scale varies in this view.

a low long platform (also one to two meters high) to the east. The latter was not built in masonry but carved out of a natural rise in the soft limestone bedrock.

Stratigraphy recorded in six deep soundings on this hilltop has shown that the leveling of the hill and the construction of the low-profile E-Group complex were part of a single episode of construction that may have occurred within a 50-year period. The date of this construction episode centers on the year 800 BC. It is bracketed by an 840–800 BC AMS date from a skeleton (Burial 33[1]) in a *chultun* that predates the paving of the plaza under the North Pyramid and a piece of charcoal from the plaster capping of the jade cache (Cache 4) that marks the dedication of the E-Group complex; its most probable 1-Sigma range is 790–760 BC.[2]

The volume of material brought in to fill the sides of the hill and thus create a flat open space half a kilometer wide was estimated by comparing the shape of the underlying bedrock surface and fill thicknesses recorded on plaza excavations.[3] The total volume for the Middle Preclassic plaza-leveling project, which includes the volume of the E-Group eastern platform (carved in bedrock) and the small (two meters tall) western radial pyramid is 1,304,026 m^3. Figure 8.5 shows the areas of the hill where greater amounts of fill were deposited and their relative depths expressed by midtone gray shading; darker and lighter tones indicate little or no fill. As stated earlier, the maximum depth of the fill was near seven meters in the south and 4.5 meters in the north. The type of material used was unlike that used in later construction projects at Cival, as it was composed mostly of boulders larger than what one person would be able to lift. Little marl was added to the fill. The Middle Preclassic plaza floor was 5–10 cm thick and of great quality and hardness. It was laid out throughout the hilltop forming a squared plaza of 0.5 km, including the E-Group plaza in its center. Our limited soundings of the lowest levels of the plaza do not permit us to determine whether other structures previously existed on the hilltop.

The Middle Preclassic construction of the E-Group and associated plaza-leveling project was greater than all other subsequent construction projects combined. Beginning in the Late Preclassic period, by roughly 350 BC, a number of small pyramid complexes were erected at the four cardinal points of the hilltop plaza. These are the Triadic Group I on the east; the North Pyramid, oriented N-S perpendicular to the E-Group plaza's axis; the South Pyramid on the south end of the plaza and exactly 305 m from the North Pyramid along its main axis; and finally, Str.20, the westernmost pyramid, on the far end of the main plaza and on axis with the E-Group

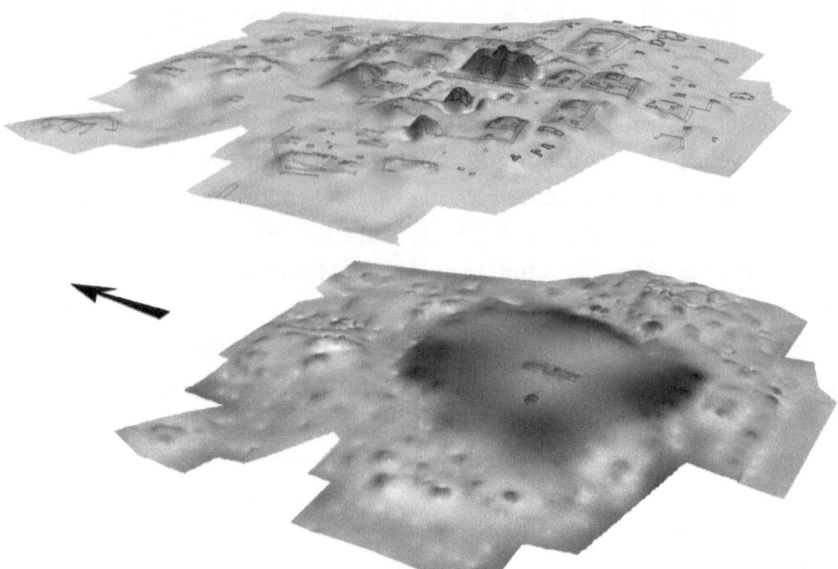

Figure 8.5. Views from the west of the A) Middle Preclassic and B) Late Preclassic hilltop at Cival. Tones indicate areas of greater infilling. Relief based on field map and excavation data.

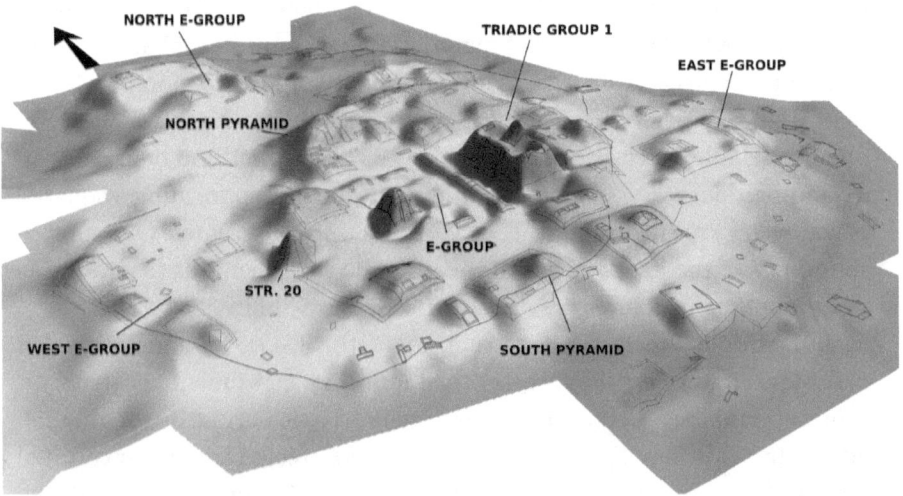

Figure 8.6. Map of the ceremonial center at Cival showing all Late Preclassic architecture and the defensive wall.

radial pyramid and with the Triadic Group I and located some 305 m from it (Figure 8.6). The current form of these axially laid out pyramidal complexes dates to the end of the Late Preclassic period, which we estimate to be AD 100 based on ceramic and architectural cross-ties. It is certainly no later than AD 250, a time when the site was largely abandoned and construction in the center had ceased. The current volume of each of these complexes is the result of multiple incremental construction episodes that took place throughout the Late Preclassic period. So far, our excavations have been able to document five construction episodes for the Triadic Group I and three for the North Pyramid and Str. 20 (Figure 8.7).

The first version of the Triadic Group I, dating to ca. 350 BC, rose to no more than three meters from the plaza. Its width is unknown but it likely included all the architectural components of the latest version—that is, a main platform supporting three temples on the east, north, and south, with the eastern temple slightly larger than the other two. In addition, there were two small stepped platforms on the west end of the complex flanking the group's inset stairway. These small platforms had stairways on their east side and were accessible only to someone already on the main platform. This architectural pattern, which includes more than three and up to five structures, is typical of some of the earliest monumental complexes at Lowland sites such as Nakbe, Wakna, El Mirador (Danta Pyramid), and Uaxactun (Group H) (Hansen 1998; Laporte and Valdes 1993).

The North Pyramid, which rose to 23 m in its last version, was a large two-stage pyramidal structure; its upper section was set back from the lower one to form an intermediate terrace. Above it stood the final pyramidal platform and its temple building (now destroyed). A broad inset stairway led to the first terrace from the plaza and a narrower one from the terrace to the pyramid's top. The volume of the first of its five construction episodes is not known but was likely much smaller and shorter than the last two. Because our excavations did not penetrate to the center of this structure, it can only be supposed that the North Pyramid was the result of five major episodes of remodeling and enlargement, as most other deeply sampled groups in the center are (i.e., Group XIII next to the North Pyramid).

In sum, the currently visible mass of Late Preclassic architecture is the cumulative result of several construction episodes, three to five in most cases, that took place between 350 BC AND 100 AD (Figure 8.8). The combined volume of all Late Preclassic buildings and platforms on the Cival main hill, not including the first Middle Preclassic version of the E-Group,

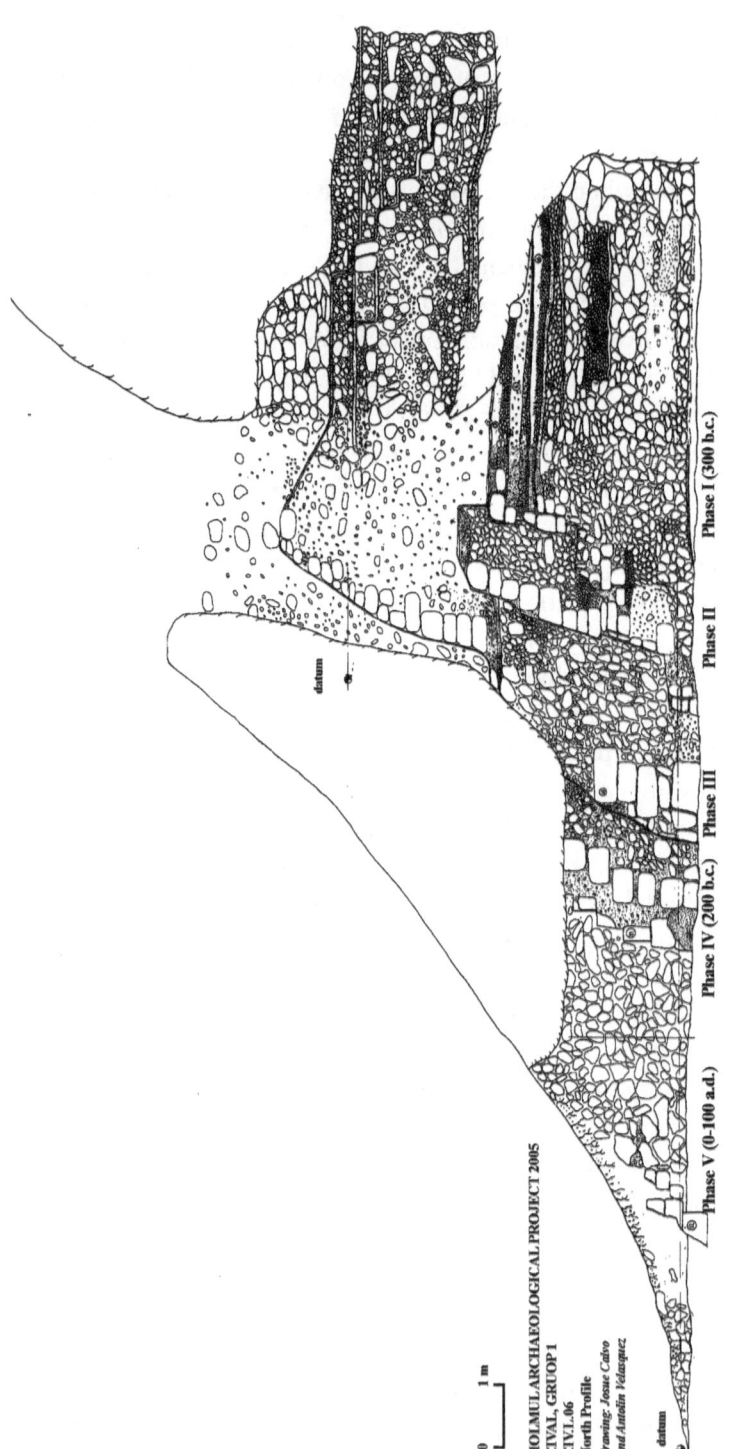

Figure 8.7. Profile of looters' trench in Triadic Group I at Cival, which cut through five construction stages of the platform dating to the Late Preclassic period.

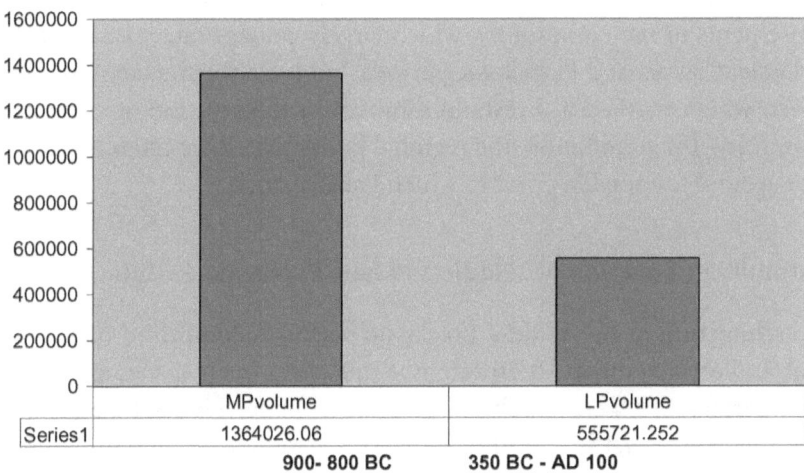

Figure 8.8. Comparison of combined volume of construction between the Middle and Late Preclassic periods at Cival.

is 555,721.3 m³. The volume of the Middle Preclassic single construction event is 2.45 times greater than the volume of all subsequent architectural projects combined.

The frequent remodeling of pyramids and platforms during the Late Preclassic would have required the movement of 61,726 m³ of earth per 50-year period, or a mere 1,234 m³ per decade. The population of Cival in the Middle and Late Preclassic period is difficult to estimate. The survey of the greater area surrounding Cival found 191 residential groups that ranged from very large multihousehold platforms (patio hilltop groups) to small isolated structures, dating to the Late Preclassic (Estrada-Belli 2009). A preliminary population estimate would range anywhere from a minimum of 2,000 to 5,000 people to a maximum of 10,000 people for the greater supporting area of Cival in a three-kilometer radius. In our mapping and excavation sample, only about one-fifth of all residential groups revealed Middle Preclassic occupation. These simple figures emphasize even further the extraordinary investment in material and labor of the initial, much smaller Cival community in establishing a ceremonial center. The longevity of the first plaza layout and E-Group is also remarkable; we estimate that it lasted for 400 years, during which only one remodeling of the E-Groups platforms likely took place. All of these facts may reflect a fundamental difference between the first and all subsequent construction projects at Cival, one of kind as well as scale. The difference in scale is obvious; the difference in kind is less so. It may have derived not as much from the ritual requirements of the community, which largely presage later rituals of the Preclassic, Classic, and Postclassic periods, but from the first construction project, which marked a threshold moment in the creation of a broader community. The foundation of a regional polity that, once established was never again refounded, a point to which I shall return.

Continuity in Function of Middle and Late Preclassic Architecture

The architecture of the Middle Preclassic period is comprised of specific forms and arrangements. It especially emphasizes open spaces and vistas on the horizon that were largely superseded or changed in the Late Preclassic period. However, the underlying ideological foundation and function of the architecture as a setting for certain rituals may have continued largely unchanged through the Preclassic eras.

As noted earlier, in the Cival E-Group plaza a small radial platform faced a long structure on the east. A small substructure stood in the center of the eastern platform flanked by two additional smaller ones at the far ends. Three major alignments with points on the horizon were possible from the western platform through the eastern structures. The main axial line corresponded with the sunrise on the day of the equinox as viewed from the western pyramid (90–92°). The northern edge of the long platform connected the viewer with the sunrise of the first and second passage of the sun through its zenith. At the Cival latitude, this happens on May 10 and August 6. The southern edge of the structure pointed the viewer to the sunrise on the day of its geometric opposite, the anti-zenith. The dates for the passage of the sun through the zenith in the southern Lowlands are associated with the arrival of the first and second wave of monsoons and therefore mark the beginning of the growing season of the first and second maize crops. Cival's axial orientation and the size of the eastern platform, which dictated these particular sightlines, are found at a few other sites with E-Groups dating to the Middle Preclassic period (Aveni et al. 2003). Far from being places of abstract celestial observations, Preclassic E-Group plazas and the rituals enacted within them were tied to the solar calendar, to the agricultural cycle of maize, and to Maya cosmology as a whole.

At the time of construction of the Cival E-Group, an offering was placed in bedrock along the main axial line, in front of the central steps of the eastern platform. Here was a pit one meter deep shaped as a large k'an cross

Figure 8.9. Artist's reconstruction of Cache 4 at Cival. (Artist: Joel Zovar.)

(Estrada-Belli 2006; Estrada-Belli and Bauer et al. 2003). This offering was a complex multilayered feature that included an unlikely amount of jade (wealth) for a small farming community. The pit was a multilevel k'an cross containing five jars (one in each arm of the cross plus one in the center) and 109 polished pebbles of jade in a lower recess below the central jar (Figure 8.9). In plan view, this pit forms a k'an cross with a dot inside a square in the center, similar to numerous iconographic and epigraphic elements associated with the concept of k'an as yellow, precious, the place of creation, and the *axis mundi*. Five axes rose from the base of the center pit at each cardinal position. We imagine that the ritual involved the smashing of the jars and the spilling of their liquid content onto the jade pebbles. The pebbles were placed at the bottom of the central pit to represent the pool of water from which the earth emerged and is the watery interface with the underworld. Each standing jade ax represented one of the four maize plants of the cardinal directions plus the central one, which turned into world-trees to raise the sky from the water at the time of creation. The final act of this ritual was to erect a post in the center of this pit once it had been filled in. The decay of this post left a gap in the floor that capped the offering. As we have seen in countless Classic Period representations of the Maya cosmos in stone monuments and portable objects, this central post represents the materialization of the central jade as the Maize God, a world tree, and the *axis mundi* of the Maya (Freidel et al. 1993; Schele and Freidel 1990).

The cosmological metaphors expressed in this complex offering are not unique to the Maya, of course. The k'an cross, the maize cycle, the Maize God, the *axis mundi*, the directional jades, and the rain gods are documented in Maya as well as Mesoamerican iconography of all periods from the Middle Preclassic onward (see Rosenswig this volume; Paradis this volume). Direct comparisons can be made with examples of the dedication offerings to the Aztec Templo Mayor of Tenochtitlan, which reflects Mesoamerican cosmology (López Luján 2005). These caches, associated with each construction project of the temple, invoked the forces of the cosmos for the reestablishment of world order. The cosmological significance of axes and directionality in creation myths and rituals of fertility/founding are similarly expressed in the pages of the Mexican codices Borgia and Vaticanus B, in which stone celts and bowls evoke the rain gods and the birth of the maize plant/Maize God (Estrada-Belli 2006). Directional jade offerings are also quite common in Mesoamerica during the Middle Preclassic, especially in the Gulf and Chiapas regions of Mexico, and may likewise reflect dedication/founding rituals.

Charcoal preserved in the floor cap of this offering provided an AMS date range of between 790 and 550 BC.[4] This date accords with the preliminary dating derived from the ceramic analysis, which identified the jars as diagnostic of the Pre-Mamom intermediate phase, or Early Mamom phase, from 850 to 700 BC (Smith 1950). Even in the face of such an early date, this offering cannot be described as the result of a ritual sponsored by a community of subsistence farmers. It shows advanced craft specialization and long-distance trade connections in prestige items that were unimaginable for this time period prior to this find. Furthermore, the offering is situated in monumental space, such as the E-Group plaza, and by association may represent a ritual performed in front of a large audience. Public ceremonies and the attendant disposal of material wealth and labor on a grand scale may have coexisted in this early architectural complex. Finally, it should be noted that the sophisticated interlacing of cosmic symbols, esoteric knowledge, and material wealth in this offering is most commonly associated with dynastic accession rituals of the Classic period, which scholars often cite as the most emblematic manifestations of Maya civilization. It is also interesting to note that the suggested early date of this offering, about 800–700 BC, places the observed and inferred developments at Cival in the same time frame as when impressive cultural developments were beginning at La Venta on the Gulf Coast, at La Blanca on the Pacific Coast of Guatemala (Rosenswig this volume), and at Chalcatzingo and Teopantecuanitlan in Highland Mexico (Paradis this volume). Thus, it is one of the earliest instances of monumentality, and of iconography associated with centralized authority in Mesoamerica.

The next important phase in the history of Cival was inaugurated when a stela was erected in its main E-Group plaza sometime between 300 and 200 BC. Stela 2 was placed on top of a broad one-step-high platform in front of the E-Group eastern range structure, inches above the k'an cross offering (Estrada-Belli and Grube et al. 2003).

On this broken monument is the low-relief portrait of a striding human figure. Unfortunately the section above the torso, which would have presented the face and headdress of this individual, is missing and probably has been since ancient times. The body posture suggests movement, possibly a dance performance, if Classic period royal painted and carved scenes can be used as examples to aid in its interpretation. On the chest is the only identifying attribute, a pectoral in the shape of long-beaked bird from which three jade plaques hang. The rulers of the Guatemalan highlands, the Pacific coast, and the Gulf Coast wore this ornament in the Terminal Preclassic period (see La Mojarra Stela 1, Kaminaljuyu Stela 11; Parsons 1986; Winfield Capitaine 1987). This personage was probably a ruler of Cival and wearing the avian costume often worn by the Maize God as many other Preclassic rulers did, likely performed a dance in celebration of the victory over his avian rival, the so-called Principal Bird Deity.

Roughly at the same time as this monument was erected, the first version of the Triadic Group I was built, behind the stela and the E-Group plaza. The fourth construction phase was explored by way of tunneling and presents a triadic arrangement, as does the last (fifth) one. Two monumental carved masks decorated the façade of the eastern temple pyramid. Their iconography suggests they represent a celestial deity (Estrada-Belli 2006). A piece of charcoal from the mask's stucco lining provided an AMS calibrated date of between 220 and 170 BC for this phase of the temple.[5]

As noted earlier, the construction sequence of Cival's Triadic Group I reveals that the increase in the volume of the platforms was remarkably gradual and steady, rather than taking place by leaps and bounds. It is important to note the relative synchronicity of major temple building projects at Cival and Holmul (i.e., Building B of Group II). Other site sequences show a similar gradual increase over the Late Preclassic period. Among them are, the construction of buildings 5C-54 and 5D-84–88 of the Mundo Perdido, at Tikal; the construction stages of Groups E and H at Uaxactun (Laporte and Valdes 1993); the six to eight remodeling projects of the Pinturas and Ventanas complexes at San Bartolo (Saturno et al. 2006; Saturno and Urquizú 2005); and Calakmul Structure 2 (Carrasco and Colon 2005). At El Mirador, the El Tigre triadic group appears to be the result of several construction stages, and the La Danta complex may well be the Maya's most impressive structure. Ongoing excavations will determine whether it is the result of the Maya's single most impressive construction episode (Hansen 1990; Hansen and Guenter 2005).

The existing data show a pattern of gradual increase in architectural scale at the site of El Mirador as at the sites of Cival and Holmul. The scale of the architecture at El Mirador is considerably greater than that of any other contemporary Lowland site. Nevertheless, the differences are confined to matters of scale. El Mirador was certainly the site of the most grandiose architectural projects in the Late Preclassic period. Sites such as Cival show a development that is smaller in scale but qualitatively equal to that of El Mirador. Unlike El Mirador, Tikal, Cival, and Nakbe were sites where monumental construction had greater antiquity. More to the point, I speculate that the pattern of Late Preclassic incremental construction projects noted above may have been synchronous, a possibility that is not at odds with the available evidence. There appears to be a single architectural style across the Lowlands in the Late Preclassic period. In addition, in this period more than in any other period in Maya history, the inhabitants of settlements large and small across the Lowlands produced ceramics in a remarkably homogeneous style (Chicanel sphere). Any synchronicity in construction would point to El Mirador (in the likelihood that El Mirador had great influence over the rest of the Lowlands) or Maya calendar cycles as the inspiration for renewal projects at specific intervals during the Late Preclassic period at other centers across the Maya Lowlands.

Conclusions

The data on monumentality from Cival and Holmul allow us to identify important junctures in the long-term history of Maya social development in the Lowlands and reject some previous assumptions. Perhaps most prominent among these is the notion that the Middle Preclassic Lowland Maya were recent immigrants from nearby regions and lived a subsistence farming way of life without much progress toward "civilization" until 350 BC. At that time, the ceremonial center of El Mirador was founded and monumental pyramid architecture appeared throughout the Lowlands. This is said to correspond with the emergence of the first Lowland Maya state (El Mirador and Hansen 2005). By contrast, I am proposing that the first important juncture in the Lowland's long-term history should be identified with the first appearance of decorated ceramics at the beginning of the first millennium BC. This corresponds with 1) a change in subsistence strategies and social relations from semi-nomadic to permanent, interacting hilltop communities; 2) intensified social networking and regional groups (communities or provinces) whose interactions are manifested in the distribution of ceramic styles across the Lowlands; 3) the existence of social inequality in the region at this time, which we infer from burial and artifact evidence (crafted and traded jade and obsidian objects). We may interpret the regional units of ceramic interaction as "tribal groups," following John Clark and David Cheetam (2002), or as distinct ethnic groups descending from the antecedent Archaic and Early Preclassic period semi-sedentary farmers that roamed those same lands. What is apparent is that the distinct ceramic styles have limited spatial distribution and form small regional units.

The greater abundance of Pre-Mamom decorated ceramics in locations that later saw great architectural growth is also significant. It is possible that those locations and those ceramics may have been used for ritual performances during the sites' early occupation. I have argued above that these ceramics (as others have argued for early ceramics elsewhere in Mesoamerica; Clark and Blake 1994) were used as vehicles for ritual feasting. Cival and Holmul may have been two important centers of such ritual interaction among farming hamlets along the middle course of the Holmul River. The communities in the territory that was one day's walking distance from Cival and Holmul apparently differentiated themselves from the communities centered at Yaxha (Ah Pam ceramic complex), which was 28.5 km linear distance to the south; at Tikal, 35 km to the west; and at Xunantunich and Cahal Pech, Belize, 40 km to the south. The similarity of the iconography on these ceramics with the ceramic assemblages of the Gulf Coast and Highland Mexico suggest the inclusion of these early regional groupings of interacting communities in the Maya Lowlands into a broader network of less frequent ritual political interactions throughout Mesoamerica.

The second and perhaps most important juncture in the long-term cultural history of the Lowland Maya occurred when several villages convened to modify the Cival hilltop and created a large plaza for ritual performances. I see this type of major construction project and its associated architecture and offerings as a unique founding episode in the history of the lowlands, which heralded the beginning of Maya regional ceremonial centers. Other sites were probably founded at this time in similar ways, for example the Mundo Perdido E-Group plaza of Tikal. Cival is just one well-documented early example.

The earliest form of ritual architecture in the Maya Lowlands is the E-Group plaza complex, which evokes the agricultural and ritual life cycle of maize and its centrality in Maya religion with its astronomical orientation and cosmological symbolism. Through a number of agricultural and cosmological metaphors expressed in the E-Group's layout and offerings (the jade caches), the Maize God was elevated to the status of the supreme god in the Maya pantheon. In later periods he became identified with royal powers, as illustrated by the San Bartolo murals (Saturno et al. 2005). In the conceptual associations of the materials, shapes, and spaces of Middle Preclassic ritual performances, such as in Cival Cache 4, we see the iconographic metaphors later associated with Classic Maya kings. It is important to note, however, that these do not appear to be simpler or less elaborate versions of Classic icons but fully developed palimpsests. Can we infer the existence of kings for this time? Perhaps. The manufacture of jade axes of such perfect shape and polished finish required skilled craftsmanship and long-distance trade. These are traits often associated with elites, but there is little evidence otherwise that tells us about the social hierarchy, if any, of that time at Cival. Similarly, there are caches at Seibal and other sites in the Lowlands that may be used to infer the presence of economic specialization, but there is little else to document social hierarchy at this time. What the evidence allows us to say is that at this juncture within the long-term history of the Maya Lowlands, between 900 and 700 BC, several lines of evidence suggest the emergence of public architecture and ceremonialism and also a number of other important elements of what we call civilization, including craft specialization, long-distance trade in exotic materials, disposal of wealth, and an ideology that was later consistent with divine rule. What is missing is large-scale nonpublic architecture (palaces and tombs), large concentrated populations, intensified agriculture (which we have not found in spite of extensive surveys at Cival), and (with the exception of organization of labor) any other sign of centralized control of resources and production. Surprisingly, the scale of the public works appears to be greater by several degrees of magnitude in this initial juncture than that of later construction projects associated with temple pyramids at times when we are confident about the existence of kings and social hierarchies. How can we reconcile these contrasting elements?

The early construction projects of Cival and other early sites laid out a grandiose initial design that was later built upon and populated by many pyramids but not enlarged. Instead, the initial grand plaza space was increasingly segmented into smaller plazas as buildings were added. It appears that the limits of the ceremonial area laid out with the initial foundation could not be expanded by later projects for reasons unknown to us. Instead, labor was devoted to raising ritual spaces atop pyramid platforms and to restricting access by enclosing spaces among buildings. In addition, the volume of construction of all Late Preclassic period structures combined was much more modest than the initial construction project and was the result of a gradual process of accretion on the investments of earlier generations. In light of this, we could infer that a similarly gradual process may have been in operation in the social and political sectors of Cival's society in the centuries that followed.

In sum, we should not rush to equate the scale of construction and complexity of offerings with complex social organization or with an already formed new political order similar to that of Classic Maya states. The paradigmatic line of reasoning of cultural evolutionists is that sociopolitical institutions come first while their correlates (monumentality) appear obviously later, at least archaeologically (Yoffe 2005; see also Pauketat 2007). This modus operandi has forced us to race increasingly far back in time to find "signs" of institutions before their actual correlates (a futile quest, some may say). We should probably also consider that this way of thinking has often forced us to assume complexity in the face of monumentality rather than to demonstrate it with direct (or indirect) evidence. On the other hand, monumentality in the absence of kings and complex social hierarchies is certainly possible. The realities of early monumentality in many parts of the New World are cases in point (see Saunders this volume; Roosevelt et al. this volume; and Sassaman and Randall this volume). It is just possible that monumentality, in some cases, may have served as the catalyst for the development of more formalized political institutions rather than being its correlate or by-product.

At Cival, the residential areas around the ceremonial hill were dotted by sparse hilltop farming hamlets during the Middle Preclassic period and did not reach semi-urban population density until the Late Preclassic period. Thus, the construction of the Cival plaza could not be the result of any sort of population increase or a need for administrative centralization. Instead, it may be seen as the beginning of a new ritual and political *process* by which hamlets and communities came together to form a new more encompassing sense of community around ceremonial spaces. Population density and centralized administration came later. The communities within regions that had formerly been identified with the distribution of the highly decorated Pre-Mamom ceramics were simply integrated into a new cultural system with fixed sacred places. The emergence of similarly arranged architectural spaces (E-Groups) at Cival, Tikal, and other places in the Lowlands suggests that this is a pan-Lowland process. The integration of people from different "neighborhoods" or "provinces" was facilitated by a common language and common architectural, ceramic, and iconographic symbols that mitigated prior differences in favor of a narrative that created a more inclusive collective memory, a mythological past that gave community members an identity and a stronger sense of belonging. This narrative was tied to specific places, the ceremonial centers where the narrative was retold and enacted. The elements of this narrative—its sacred spaces, forms, and symbolism—form the core elements of what we associate with Maya civilization (and its elite ideology). The process of integration that had begun by 900 BC gradually came to completion with the homogeneous Chicanel ceramic style in the Late Preclassic period (300 BC). One of the remarkable aspects of this juncture is that the inception of monumental architecture of E-Group complexes at Cival, Tikal, and a few other sites scattered throughout the Lowlands coincided with the replacing of the great regionalism of Pre-Mamom by a much more homogeneous ceramic style (Mamom) across the Lowlands. Thus, for the inhabitants of each region, the 900–800 BC[6] period marked the beginning of a new era of cultural conformity, of belonging to a nearby ceremonial center. This was the beginning of a political process within the larger regional polities that would lead to the rule of divine kings. On the other hand, from this point onward each region was firmly integrated into a Lowland-wide network of ritual (and perhaps political) interactions, producing homogeneous cultural manifestations that we, for the first time, recognize as Maya civilization.

The time when E-Group plazas gave way to new forms of architecture, when the first temple pyramids rose from plazas atop pyramid platforms such as triadic groups, beginning at 350 BC, appears to coincide with a period of consolidation of Preclassic Maya regional polities. The persona of the king manifests itself clearly at this time, such as those depicted on the

Cival stela and the San Bartolo mural in the first and second centuries BC. The primordial metaphors of world order were then carved on the façades of buildings, materializing them as sacred landscapes. Through the myth of rebirth, the Maize God became the ancestral avatar of Preclassic and Classic Maya kings. The forces evoked in founding ceremonies of the past continued to be evoked in royal accession ceremonies through architecture, imagery, and performance. In this third important juncture we see an increase in the exclusionary nature of public rituals in architecture. In the iconography, we see a greater emphasis on the esoteric source of ritual and centralized authority (the divine king). At the same time, we do not see a marked increase in the labor expenditure for public construction throughout this time compared to that of earlier periods. From the point of view of sociocultural organization, there appears to be a consolidation of central authority within Lowland Maya society in the Late Preclassic period rather than a brand new political order.

This sequence of punctuated developments throughout the long-term trajectory of early Lowland Maya states is consistent with the cross-cultural patterns of monumental constructions in pre-state societies illustrated in this volume. The first landscape-modifying construction projects on a grandiose scale in the Maya Lowlands coincide with the founding of centers of interaction of region-wide communities in the Middle Preclassic period. This pattern is consistent with large-scale earthworks occurring in Mesoamerica in the period between 1100 and 800 BC. I have proposed that these construction projects represent the founding of new systems of political interaction (political order) that led to the emergence of what we recognize as Maya kingdoms (states), which then became more evident by 350 BC.

In sum, the earliest Lowland Maya monumental construction projects were the beginning of a political and cultural process that integrated previously separate regional communities. By 900 BC, the Maya were founding their own civilization with ceremonial centers. In my view, these centers were not the consequence of state formation but were rather their incubators. With the evidence we have (craft specialization, long-distance trade, labor management), one could argue that kings were responsible for the foundation of Cival, Tikal, and other early Maya monumental centers. Certainly there are signs of relative social complexity. But the presence or absence of kings seems to be beside the point in the face of the evidence pointing to the formulation of nothing less than a new civilization at this time. For all we know, the monumental spaces of Cival at 900 BC were more similar to the earthworks of much greater antiquity in non- and semi-sedentary societies in North and South America illustrated in this volume than to the comparatively small-scale building projects of state societies.

Notes

1. Beta-234440, conventional radiocarbon age 2670±40 BP, 2-sigma calibrated result (95% probability) cal. BC 900 to 790 (cal. BP 2850 to 2740); 1-sigma calibrated result (68% probability) Cal BC 840 to 800.

2. Beta-213528, conventional radiocarbon age 2520±40 BP, 2-sigma calibrated result(95% probability) cal. BC 800 to 520; 1-sigma calibrated results (68% probability) cal. BC 790 to 760 and cal. BC 680 to 550.

3. Comparison of volumetric maps in 3D GIS analytical environment using open-source software (http://www.osgeo.org).

4. Beta-213528; 2529±40 BP uncalibrated 790–760 and 680–550 BC, 1-sigma calibrated.

5. Beta-199570; 2170_/_40 BP uncalibrated; 220–170 BC, 1-sigma calibrated.

6. In calibrated years.

References Cited

Adams, Richard E. W.
1971   *The Ceramics of Altar de Sacrificios.* Papers of the Peabody Museum of Archaeology and Ethnology 2. Harvard University Press, Cambridge, Massachusetts.

Andrews, E. Wyllys, George J. Bey, and Christopher Gunn
2008   Rethinking the Early Ceramic History of the Northern Maya Lowlands: New Evidence and Interpretations. Paper presented at the 74th Annual Meeting of the Society for American Archaeology, Vancouver, B.C.

Aveni, Anthony F., Anne S. Dowd, and Benjamin Vining
2003   Maya Calendar Reform? Evidence from Orientations of Specialized Architectural Assemblages. *Latin American Antiquity* 14(2):159–178.

Awe, Jaime
1992   Dawn in the Land between the Rivers: Formative Occupation at Cahal Pech, Belize and Its Implications for Preclassic Development in the Maya Lowlands. Ph.D. Dissertation, University College London.

Ball, Joseph W., and Jennifer T. Taschek
2003   Reconsidering the Belize Valley Preclassic: A Case for Multiethnic Interactions in the Development of a Regional Culture Tradition. *Ancient Mesoamerica* 2(2003):179–217.

Borhegyi, Stephan Francis de
1965   *Archaeological synthesis of the Guatemalan Highlands.* Handbook of Middle American Indians 2. University of Texas Press, Austin.

Callaghan, Michael G.
2006   Cerámica del Proyecto Arqueológico Holmul, muestras de 2004 y 2005. In *Investigaciones arqueológicas en la region de Holmul, Petén, Guatemala. Informe*

preliminar de la temporada 2005, edited by F. Estrada-Belli, pp. 225–228. Boston University. Electronic document, http://www.bu.edu/holmul/reports/, accessed on December 1, 2006.

2008   "Technologies of Power: Ritual Economy and Ceramic Production in the Terminal Preclassic Period Holmul Region, Guatemala." Ph.D. diss., Vanderbilt University, Nashville, Tennessee.

Carrasco, Ramon, and Marines Colon

2005   El Reino de Kaan y la antigua ciudad maya de Calakmul. *Arqueología Mexicana* 13(75):40–47.

Clark, J. E., Richard D. Hansen, and T. Perez Suarez

2000   La Zona Maya en el Preclasico. In *Historia antigua de México*. Vol. 1, *El México antiguo, sus áreas culturales, los origenes, y el horizonte Preclásico*, edited by L. Manzanilla and L. Lopez Lujan, pp. 437–510. Mexico, D.F.

Clark, John E.

1991   Beginnings of Mesoamerica: Apologia for the Soconusco Early Formative. In *Formation of Complex Society in Southeastern Mesoamerica*, edited by W. R. Fowler, pp. 13–26. CRC Press, Boca Raton, Florida.

Clark, John E., and Michael Blake

1989   El origen de la civilizacion en Mesoamerica: Los Olmecas y Mokaya de Soconusco de Chiapas, Mexico. In *El Preclasico o Formativo: Avances y Perspectivas*, edited by M. Carmona, pp. 385–403. Instituto Nacional de Antropologia, Mexico, D.F.

1994   Power of Prestige: Competitive Generosity and the Emergence of Rank in Lowland Mesoamerica. In *Factional Competition and Political Development in the New World*, edited by E. M. Brufiel and J. W. Fox, pp. 17–30. Cambridge University Press, New York.

Clark, John E., and David Cheetam

2002   Mesoamerica's Tribal Foundations. In *The Archaeology of Tribal Societies*, edited by W. A. Parkinson, pp. 278–339. Archaeological Series. International Monographs in Prehistory, Ann Arbor.

Clark, John E., and Mary E. Pye

2000   *Olmec Art and Archaeology in Mesoamerica*. Studies in the History of Art, 58. National Gallery of Art, Washington, D.C.; and Yale University Press, New Haven.

Coe, M. D.

1977   Olmec and Maya: A Study in Relationships. In *The Origins of Maya Civilization*, edited by R. E. W. Adams, pp. 183–196. University of New Mexico Press, Albuquerque.

Coe, Michael D.

1966   *The Maya*. Thames and Hudson, London.

2005   *The Maya*. 7th fully rev. and expanded ed. Thames and Hudson, New York.

Covarrubias, Miguel A.

1957   *Indian Art of Mexico and Central America*. Alfred A. Knopf, New York.

Culbert, T. Patrick

1977   Early Maya Development at Tikal, Guatemala. In *The Origins of Maya Civilization*, edited by R. E. W. Adams, pp. 27–43. University of New Mexico Press, Albuquerque.

Deevey, E. S., D. S. Rice, P. M. Rice, H. H. Vaughan, M. Brenner, and M. S. Flannery
1979   Mayan Urbanism: Impact on a Tropical Karst Environment. *Science* 206:298–306.
Estrada-Belli, Francisco
2006   Lightning Sky, Rain and the Maize God: The Ideology of Preclassic Maya Rulers at Cival, Peten, Guatemala. *Ancient Mesoamerica* 17(1):57–78.
Estrada-Belli, Francisco (editor)
2009   *Investigaciones arqueológicas en la region de Holmul, Petén, Guatemala. Informe preliminar de la temporada 2008: Cival y K'o.* Boston University Archaeology Department, Boston. Electronic document, www.bu.edu/holmul/reports, accessed May 8, 2011.
Estrada-Belli, Francisco, Jeremy Bauer, Molly Morgan, and Angel Chavez
2003   Symbols of Early Maya Kingship at Cival, Petén, Guatemala. *Antiquity* 77(298). Electronic document, http://www.antiquity.ac.uk/projgall/estrada_belli298/, accessed May 8, 2011.
Estrada-Belli, Francisco, Nikolai Grube, Marc Wolf, Kristen Gardella, and Claudio Guerra-Librero
2003   Preclassic Maya Monuments and Temples at Cival, Petén, Guatemala. *Antiquity* 77(296). Electronic document, http://antiquity.ac.uk/projgall/belli296/, accessed 23 September 2011.
Flannery, Kent V., and Joyce Marcus
1994   *Early Formative Pottery of the Valley of Oaxaca.* Memoirs of the Museum of Anthropology, University of Michigan No. 27. Museum of Anthropology, University of Michigan, Ann Arbor.
Freidel, David A., Linda Schele, and Joy Parker
1993   *Maya Cosmos: Three Thousand Years on the Shaman's Path.* Morrow and Co., New York.
Garber, James F., Kathryn M. Brown, Jaime Awe, and Christopher Hartman
2004   Middle Formative Prehistory of the Central Belize Valley: An Examination of Architecture, Material Culture, and Sociopolitical Change at Blackman Eddy. In *The Ancient Maya of the Belize Valley: Half a Century of Archaeological Research,* edited by J. F. Garber, pp. 25–47. University Press of Florida, Gainesville.
Hansen, Richard
1990   *Excavations in the Tigre Complex, El Mirador, Petén, Guatemala.* Papers of the New World Archaeological Foundation 62. New World Archaeological Foundation, Brigham Young University, Provo, Utah.
1998   Continuity and Disjunction: The Preclassic Antecedents of Pre-Classic Maya Architecture. In *Function and Meaning in Classic Maya Architecture,* edited by S. D. Houston, pp. 49–122. Dumbarton Oaks, Washington, D.C.
2005   Perspectives on Olmec-Maya Interaction in the Middle Formative Period. In *New Perspectives on Formative Mesoamerican Cultures,* edited by T. Powis, pp. 51–72. British Archaeological Reports International Series 1377. Archaeopress, Oxford.
Hansen, Richard, and Stanley P. Guenter
2005   Early Social Complexity and Kingship in the Mirador Basin. In *Lords of Creation: The Origins of Sacred Maya Kinship,* edited by V. M. Fields and D. Reents-Budet, pp. 60–61. Los Angeles County Museum of Art, Los Angeles.

Healy, Paul F., Bobbi Hohmann, and Terry Powis
2004   The Ancient Maya Center of Pacbitun. In *The Ancient Maya of the Belize River Valley. Half a Century of Archaeological Research*, edited by J. F. Garber, pp. 207–228. University Press of Florida, Gainesville.

Iceland, Harry B.
2005   The Preceramic to Early Middle Formative Transition in Northern Belize: Evidence for the Ethnic Identity of the Preceramic Inhabitants. In *New Perspectives on Formative Mesoamerican Cultures*, edited by T. G. Powis, pp. 15–26. International Series vol. 1377. British Archaeological Reports, Oxford.

Jacob, John S.
1995   Ancient Maya Wetland Agricultural Fields in Cobweb Swamp, Belize: Construction, Chronology, and Function. *Journal of Field Archaeology* 22(2):175–190.

Jiménez Moreno, Wigberto
1966   Mesoamerica Before the Toltecs. In *Ancient Oaxaca: Discoveries in Mexican Archaeology and History*, edited by J. Paddock, pp. 1–82. Stanford University Press, Stanford, Calif.

Kidder, Alfred Vincent, Jesse David Jennings, and Edwin M. Shook
1946   *Excavations at Kaminaljuyu, Guatemala*. Carnegie Institution of Washington, Washington, D.C.

Laporte, Juan Pedro, and Vilma Fialko
1993   El Preclásico de Mundo Perdido: Algunos Aportes sobre los orígenes de Tikal. In *Tikal y Uaxactun en el Preclásico*, edited by J. P. Laporte and J. A. Valdés, pp. 9–47. Universidad Nacional Autonoma de Mexico, Mexico, D.F.

Laporte, Juan Pedro, and Juan Antonio Valdes
1993   *Tikal y Uaxactun en el Preclasico*. Universidad Nacional Autonoma de Mexico, Mexico, D.F.

Lohse, Jon C., Jaime Awe, Cameron Griffith, Robert M. Rosenswig, and Fred Valdez Jr.
2006   Preceramic Occupations in Belize: Updating the Paleoindian and Archaic Record. *Latin American Antiquity* 17(2):209–226.

López Luján, Leonardo
2005   *The Offerings of the Templo Mayor of Tenochtitlan*. Rev. ed. University of New Mexico Press, Albuquerque.

Love, Michael W.
2002   *Early Complex Society in Pacific Guatemala: Settlements and Chronology of the Rio Naranjo, Guatemala*. Papers of the New World Archaeological Foundation No. 66. Brigham Young University, Provo.

Lowe, Gareth W.
1977   The Mixe-Zoque as Competing Neighbors of the Early Lowland Maya. In *Origins of Maya Civilization*, pp. 197–248. Albuquerque: University of New Mexico Press.
1989   Algunas aclaraciones sobre la presencia olmeca y maya en el Preclásico de Chiapas. In *Preclásico o Formativo: Avances y Perspectivas*, edited by Martha Carmona Macías, pp. 363–383. Museo Nacional de Antropología, Instituto Nacional de Antroplogía e Historia, México, D.F.

Neivens de Estrada, Nina
2006   Edificio B, Grupo II, Holmul, 2005. In *Investigaciones Arqueológicas en la región*

de Holmul, Petén, Guatemala. Informe preliminar de la temporada 2005, edited by F. Estrada-Belli, pp. 22–27. Boston University, Boston. Electronic document, http://www.bu.edu/holmul/reports/, accessed December 1, 2006.

Parsons, Lee A.
1986 *The Origins of Maya Art: Monumental Sculpture of Kaminaljuyú, Guatemala and the Southern Pacific Coast.* Studies in Pre-Columbian Art and Archaeology No. 22. Dumbarton Oaks Research Library and Collections, Washington, D.C.

Pauketat, T. R.
2007 *Chiefdoms and Other Archaeological Delusions.* AltaMira Press, Lanham, Maryland.

Pohl, Mary D, Kevin O. Pope, John G. Jones, John S. Jacob, Dolores R. Piperno, Susan D. deFrance, David Lentz, John A. Gifford, Mary E. Denforth, and Kathryn J. Josserand
1996 Early Agriculture in the Maya Lowlands. *Latin American Antiquity* 7:355–372.

Puleston, Olga Staurakis, and Dennis Edward Puleston
1971 A Processual Model for the Rise of Classic Maya Civilization in the Southern Lowlands. In *Atti del XL Congresso Internazionale degli Americanisti,* pp. 119–124. Tilgher, Genoa

Rice, Prudence M.
1979 Ceramic and Non-Ceramic Artifacts of Lakes Yaxha and Sacnab, El Petén, Guatemala, The Ceramics, Section B: Postclassic Pottery from Topoxte. *Cerámica de Cultura Maya* 11:1–86.

Rosenswig, Robert M.
2010 *Early Mesoamerican Civilization: Inter-Regional Interaction and the Olmec.* Cambridge University Press, New York.

Rosenswig, Robert M., and Marilyn A. Masson
2001 Seven New Preceramic Sites Documented in Northern Belize. *Mexicon* 23:138–140.

Sabloff, Jeremy
1975 Ceramics. In *Excavations at Seibal, Department of Peten, Guatemala,* edited by G. R. Willey, L. A. Smith, and J. Sabloff, pp. 1–261. Memoir of the Peabody Museum of Archaeology and Ethnology No. 2., vol. 13. Harvard University, Cambridge, Massachusetts.

Saturno, William A., David Stuart, and Boris Beltran
2006 Early Maya Writing at San Bartolo, Guatemala. *Science* 311(5795):1281–1283.

Saturno, William A., Karl Taube, and David Stuart
2005 The Murals of San Bartolo, El Petén, Guatemala. Part 1: The North Wall. *Ancient America* 7:1–56.

Saturno, William A., and Mónica Urquizú
2005 Proyecto Arqueológico Regional San Bartolo, Petén: Resultados de la tercera temporada de campo 2004. In *XVIII Simposio de Investigaciones Arqueológicas en Guatemala, 2004,* edited by J. P. Laporte, Barbara Arroyo, and Héctor Mejía, pp. 276–283. Museo Nacional de Arqueología y Etnología, Guatemala.

Schele, L., and D. A. Freidel
1990 *A Forest of Kings.* William Morrow and Co., New York.

Sharer, Robert J., and D. Sedat
1973   Monument 1, El Porton, Guatemala and the Development of Maya Calendrical and Writing Systems. In *Studies in Ancient Mesoamerica,* edited by John A. Graham, pp. 177–194. Contributions of the University of California Archaeological Research Facility No. 18. University of California, Berkeley.

Smith, Robert E.
1950   *Ceramic Sequence at Uaxactun, Guatemala.* 2 vols. Middle American Research Institute, Tulane University, New Orleans, Louisiana.

Strelow, David, and Lisa LeCount
2001   Regional Interaction in the Formative Southern Maya Lowlands: Evidence of Olmecoid Stylistic Motifs in a Cunil Ceramic Assemblage from Xunantunich, Belize. Paper presented at the 66th Annual Meeting of the Society for American Archaeology, New Orleans, Louisiana.

Taube, Karl A., William A. Saturno, and David Stuart
2004   Identificación mitológica de los personajes en el muro norte de la piramide de Las Pinturas sub-1, San Bartolo, Petén. In *XVII Simposio de Investigaciones Arqueologicas en Guatemala,* edited by J. P. Laporte, B. Arroyo, H. Escobedo, and H. E. Mejía, pp. 871–880. Museo Nacional de Arqueología y Etnología, Ministerio de Cultura y Deportes, Asociación Tikal, Guatemala.

Tozzer, Alfred M.
1957   *Chichen Itza and Its Cenote of Sacrifice: A Comparative Study of Contemporaneous Maya and Toltec.* Peabody Museum, Cambridge, Massachusetts.

Valdés, Juan Antonio
1999   Desarrollo cultural y señales de alarma entre los mayas: el Preclásico Tardío y la transición hacia el Clásico Temprano. In *The Emergence of Lowland Maya Civilization: The Transition from the Preclassic to the Early Classic,* edited by N. Grube, pp. 71–85. Acta Mesoamericana, vol. 8. Anton Saurwein, Möckmühl, Germany.

Wahl, David, R. Byrne, T. Schreiner, and Richard Hansen
2006   Holocene Vegetation Change in the Northern Peten and Its Implications for Maya Prehistory. *Quaternary Research* 65(3):380–389.

Winfield Capitaine, Fernando
1987   *La Estela 1 de La Mojarra.* Universidad Nacional Autonoma de Mexico, Mexico D.F.

Yoffee, N.
2005   *Myths of the Archaic State: Evolution of the Earliest Cities, States and Civilizations.* Cambridge University Press, Cambridge.

IV

INTERMEDIATE AREA

9

Monumental Architecture and Social Complexity in the Intermediate Area

R. JEFFREY FROST AND JEFFREY QUILTER

The region from eastern El Salvador and Honduras through Nicaragua, Costa Rica, Panama, and Colombia is well known for its goldwork and as a center of highly developed chiefdom societies. But it should be equally renowned for its extensive and impressive large-scale constructions. For those not familiar with the region this may come as surprise. But throughout the Intermediate Area, pre-Hispanic peoples erected impressive structures and extensively modified landscapes, creating extensive built environments of monumental proportions. Considerable variability is present in these constructions, but there are many similarities, an internal consistency in patterns, and commonalities with other New World architectural traditions.

In this chapter we offer a review of the salient features of monumental architecture and social complexity in the Intermediate Area. We will begin by briefly reviewing the natural and cultural landscape of the region and the pre-Hispanic chronology. This will be followed by some general remarks on the issue of monumental architecture.

The Intermediate Area

The "Intermediate Area" lies between the two "high" culture areas of Mesoamerica to the north and the Central Andes to the south. There now are a number of publications (Sheets 1992; Hoopes and Fonseca Z. 2003) that review the intellectual pathways followed to categorize the area as a secondary one compared to these two "nuclear" regions. One criterion for such a judgment is the supposed absence of large-scale corporate architecture of comparable scale to the architecture of the Maya or Inca, for example.

To this negative criterion can be added the lack of state-level political systems. These broad generalizations overlook the presence of remarkable and impressive endeavors in sociocultural diversity, political complexity, and engineering feats. Indeed, in almost any sense in which the term is used, monumental architecture is present in the region.

The high Andean sierras and tablelands and their extensive river systems in Colombia; the flat, torrid, coastal wetlands of the isthmian region; and the relatively dry grasslands of northwestern Costa Rica, among many other microregions, are all in the Intermediate Area. At the time of first European contact, along the "rich coast" Columbus traveled on his last voyage (1502–1504), there was considerable variability in sociopolitical systems there, from nomadic peoples to complexly ranked chiefdom societies. These people shared a common value system in prizing gold jewelry, although there were distinct preferences for more or less copper in alloys produced in different regions. Gold objects were exchanged over large regions, as far as Mesoamerica, with both people and objects moving through the landscape (Cooke et al. 2003), and their possession was linked to esoteric knowledge (Helms 1979). Indeed, the widespread use of gold objects and their association with religious concepts and social ranking may been seen as marking a cultural horizon for the Intermediate Area as a whole (Quilter 2003), from about AD 700 to contact.

In addition to fairly detailed accounts of Intermediate Area cultures at the time of first European contact, strong evidence exists for cultural continuities from prehistory into the historic era. In many regions, Europeans barely penetrated or made only minor inroads into dense forests and remote valleys, and native people retreated but survived. The Tairona of Colombia are an example of this; strong evidence suggests that they represent a continuum from prehistoric times (Bray 2003; Reichel-Dolmatoff 1951). As we move from the ethnological present or the ethnohistoric past deeper into prehistory, however, views of the past quickly become obscured. A combination of dense vegetation in much of the region, poor preservation of organic remains, and relatively little research compared to that done in other areas has resulted in relatively poor knowledge of ancient peoples of the region beyond a few hundred years at most prior to the European encounter.

Chronologies in the Intermediate Area vary considerably, often consisting of long periods, sometimes stretching over a millennium, such as for La Montaña (ca. 1500–100 BC) in Costa Rica and Early Quimbaya (ca. 600 BC–900 AD) in Colombia, with little discernable change within them. At the same time, however, recent advances in both genetic (Barrantes 1993, 1998) and linguistic studies (Constenla Umaña 1995) indicate great antiquity for the human occupation of the region, including the isthmus, with Paleo-Indian occupations in many places (Bird and Cooke 1978; Snarskis 1978) and the earliest evidence for ceramics in the New World in Colombia, circa 6000 BC (Oyuela-Caycedo 1995). Although some early eras are fairly well chronicled for some places, most patterning tends to involve changes in lithics, the introduction of ceramics, and subsequent and inferred social changes based on these two materials.

There was considerable heterogeneity in cultural patterns in the Intermediate Area, and many subregional systems are in evidence, especially in the contact era. For prehistory, divisions are made by scholars on the basis of distinct suites of archaeological evidence, including styles of goldwork, ceramic traditions, and patterns of stoneworking, including the carving and erection of statues or monoliths often associated with funerary centers. On a macro scale, a salient consideration is the differences present on either side of a diagonal line roughly following the trend of the Talamanca Mountain Range, running from northwest to southeast in Costa Rica. North of this line people were influenced by and participated in Mesoamerican patterns, while south of it cultures were within the orbit of general Andean patterns. This statement ignores distinctive local patterns at the same time that it presents a general truth, and it does not account for change through time. These different north-south orientations were most distinct in late prehistory; at earlier times, patterning was different with more homogeneity in Archaic or Formative cultures, for example.

The Intermediate Area and the "Monumental Dilemma"

The degree to which Intermediate Area large-scale constructions should be considered in the category of "monumental" architecture is a potentially debatable issue. While ancient constructions of the Intermediate Area generally lack the vertical impressiveness of the stone-on-stone constructions of Maya or Inca temples, extensive modifications of the landscape that included expansive horizontal constructions of plazas and patios, fountains and pools, temples and tombs, and similar features attest to considerable sophistication in planning and prodigious efforts in constructing works of great scale that are impressive achievements.

While archaeology as anthropology demands that we take cross-cultural views of human endeavors, we strongly believe that such exercises should be done with caution and within appropriate contexts. Comparative statements, such as in issues of large-scale architecture, often fail to inform well because the architecture is extracted from the larger cultural context in which it was built and used. Considering the term "monumental" in its more recent use to refer to constructions of large scale and within specific social-cultural formations, our definition is close to that proposed by Trigger (1990). We define monumental constructions as works made by humans at a scale that is exponentially larger than those used for quotidian purposes and often of a form or pattern that is unique or rare and made of rare materials or ones that have had great amounts of energy invested in them such as polishing, carving, and similar activities.

While we believe that this definition may be of use elsewhere, it is particularly valuable for considering impressive works in the Intermediate Area. However, this definition focuses only on unusual and exceptional architecture and other constructions. Such a definition can ignore cases in which many large constructions were made but none stand out as exceptional in comparison to others. In other words, in societies in which very large construction projects occurred, perhaps large palisaded villages, if the site sizes were plotted on a graph and all the sites were clustered relatively close together with no outliers at the large end of the graph, under our definition, that society would be said to have no monumental architecture.

If our definition of monumentality is valid, then we need to clarify two aspects of the subject in relation to considerations of the Intermediate Area. The first is that because of the relatively little amount of research conducted in the region and the tropical forest growth that inhibits easy detection of sites, we have less than an ideal understanding of the range of variability of sites and constructions in the region in general and for any one period of time. Thus, sites that currently are considered as candidates for monumental architecture may in the long run be less exceptional than they presently seem or at least might rank lower on any hierarchy of monumental sites that might be eventually developed.

The second consideration is that while we have selected the following case studies as examples of monumental architecture, we wish to emphasize that there were impressive constructions throughout the region at the time of the first contact with Europeans, many of which were not particularly exceptional within the Intermediate Area. We make this statement partly because we believe that many of our colleagues and the general public may not fully appreciate the degree to which communities in northern South

America and the isthmus were able to marshal labor for constructions even of the quotidian kind.

Origins of Intermediate Area Monumental Constructions

The earliest identifiable constructions in the Intermediate Area correspond with the late Formative period (AD 300–600), a time of rapid social and technological change throughout Costa Rica and Panama (Hoopes 2005, 11, 18). The most clear developments are changes in settlement patterns, the appearance of large architectural constructions, and the development of formal artistic industries, which included carved stone columns, elaborate metates, life-size stone sculptures, and jade pendants.

It is during this period that a priestly elite might have developed that presided over ritual centers or mortuary complexes (Hoopes 2005, 17–25). Evidence for this development is particularly strong in southern Costa Rica and western Panama, where archaeologists have identified dozens of ceremonial mound sites. Barriles, located in western Panama, is the best known and most intensively investigated late Formative site in and is unique for it size and for its architectural elaboration and artifact assemblage. The site covers an area of approximately 30 hectares (Linares, Sheets, and Rosenthal 1975; Palumbo 2009; Rosenthal 1980). Matthew Stirling's 1949 excavations of the central zone revealed a large platform mound 30 meters by 50 meters with a series of life-size stone sculptures along its perimeter (Stirling 1950). These sculptures are in human form and appear to portray hierarchical relations.

The various and impressive efforts of early peoples in the northern Intermediate Area in the Formative Period were the foundations for later developments. Such developments appear to have accelerated beginning some time circa AD 700 when a suite of new ideas and practices developed. These were stimulated, in part, by influences from northern South America and were associated with the introduction of goldworking technology.

Scholars generally agree that goldworking diffused from northern South America into the isthmus region; its presence is clearly indicated in the northern Intermediate Area around AD 700 (Snarskis 2003). Although the construction of mounds and the working of large stone objects was practiced before this time, there seems to have been a dramatic increase in such activities and a reorientation of styles with the appearance of gold working. It may be significant that these changes occurred within a general time period when major cultural transformations were taking place in the Early Intermediate–Early Horizon transitions in the Central Andes and the Late Classic Period in Mesoamerica, though explanations for such patterns are currently somewhat elusive.

The post-700 AD suite of cultural traits emanating from South America was most strongly adopted south of the Costa Rican division mentioned above, although there was no hard and fast frontier. Goldworking was adopted with gusto in the northern Intermediate Area, and the value of polished green and other semiprecious stones declined significantly as prestige goods. In apparent association with the adoption of gold, there were significant changes in site organization, social organization, material culture, and mortuary practices. In particular, the nature of monumental construction changed dramatically during this period. This change along with the adoption of the suite of traits discussed above quite likely was tied to new socioeconomic relations.

Below, we turn to two examples of monumental architecture that are distinctive not only for their scale and unique qualities but also for the thoroughness with which they have been archaeologically investigated in order to look more closely at the issue of monumental constructions in the Intermediate Area. The Guayabo de Turrialba and the Rivas–Panteón de la Reina complexes are both well-understood large-scale constructions in the Intermediate Area and are both emblematic of the unique features of southern Central American monumental architecture that have only recently started to be delineated.

Guayabo de Turrialba

The site of Guayabo de Turrialba, hereafter called Guayabo, is located at an altitude of 1100 meters, approximately nine kilometers northeast of the modern town of Turrialba, on the Atlantic Watershed of Costa Rica. While it technically falls on the north side of the Mesoamerica–South America dividing line, its cultural patterns were distinctly Costa Rican. While it shared some traits in late prehistory with southern Costa Rican communities, it exhibits relatively few clear Mesoamerican influences.

A central site area of approximately two hectares has been cleared of tropical forest vegetation, exposing more than 50 architectural features, including mounds, plazas, house foundations, a central causeway, and other constructions (Figure 9.1). Exploration of areas still under the forest canopy suggest that the site is many times larger than the area currently exposed,

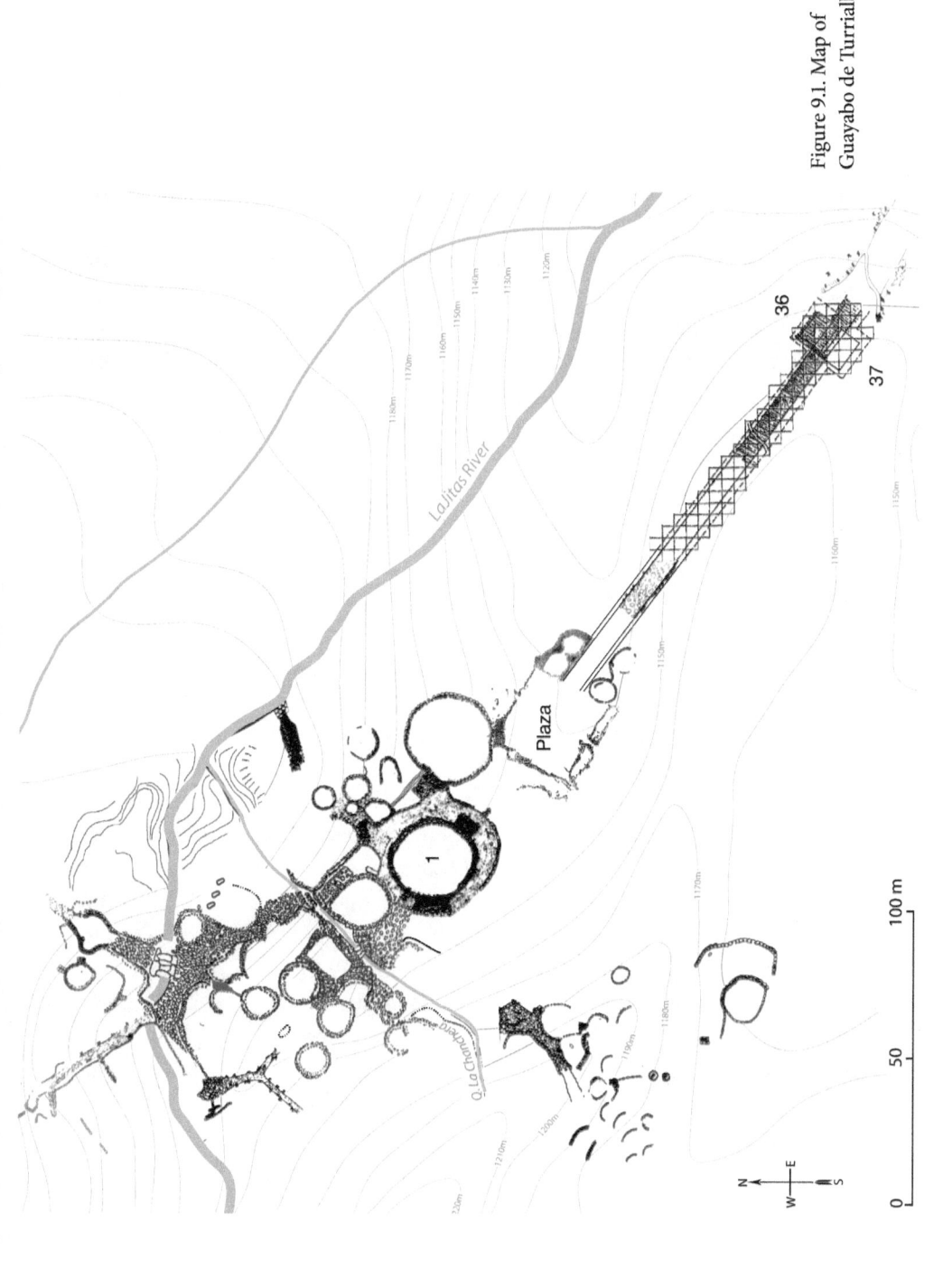

Figure 9.1. Map of Guayabo de Turrialba.

although the most impressive architectural features appear to be in the core zone. Outside of this zone, while some significant constructions may be present, such as canals, large houses, and patios, there appears to be a gradual diminution in the size of constructions located farther away from the center. It is likely that these areas consist of residences, perhaps with small local ceremonial precincts that are widely spaced in a suburban-to-rural sequence in which the terminus of the Guayabo complex is not clearly defined.

Circular house foundations between 10 and 30 meters in diameter are located throughout the site's core and on the slopes of surrounding hills. The largest foundations, located at the center of the site, were constructed on mounds up to three meters tall (Fonseca Zamora 1979, 1980; Hurtado de Mendoza 2004; Troyo 2002). In addition, various paved patios, paths, steps, and other features are located in the heart of the complex.

One of the most impressive features at the site is a cobblestone causeway eight meters wide and 150 meters long, running from the southeast edge of the site toward the central mound complex. This was apparently the principal access to the site, and it was made to impress. Its orientation created a central axis aligning the entry, the causeway, the core site area, and the smoking cone of the Turrialba Volcano, which was located in the distance behind the complex (Figure 9.2). To further accentuate the importance of this route, the easternmost boundary of the causeway is flanked by a pair of rectangular stone-faced mounds, each 2.5 meters high (Structures 36 and 37). These mounds may have served as sentry posts or as a formal entrance to the site, but they may also have imparted a special aura to Guayabo, as rectangular structures are extremely rare throughout the Intermediate Area. Archaeologists have traced the causeway one kilometer farther southeast, however, where it ends in another pair of mounds, each seven meters in diameter. From there, several smaller paths extend outward to link Guayabo to distant sites (Fonseca Zamora 1980, 106). The northwest end of the causeway terminates within Guayabo at a central rectangular plaza 30 meters by 50 meters. Excavation within the plaza produced a wide variety of artifacts, including stone tools, fragments of ceramics, stone sculpture, and petroglyphs (Troyo and Garnier 2002).

Located at the west end of the axis and west of the plaza is Mound 1. At 28 meters in diameter and 2.76 meters tall it is largest mound at the site and consists of an earthen core faced with stone cobbles (Figure 9.3). Evidence has been found of the presence of a circular structure on top of Mound 1 (Fonseca Zamora 1979). If it followed widespread conventions for

Figure 9.2. Causeway at Guayabo. Mound 1 in the background and Turrialba Volcano in the distance. (Photo by J. Quilter.)

Figure 9.3. Mound 1 and plaza/pool at Guayabo de Turrialba. (Photo by J. Quilter.)

the region, this pole-and-thatch structure would have either been conical in shape or had a conical roof and thus would have mimicked the conical form of the Turrialba Volcano, making a clear micro-macro cosmic relationship between the two. The house on the Mound 1 feature is commonly interpreted as having been the residence of a paramount chief who controlled Guayabo and surrounding communities (Fonseca Zamora 1980; Snarskis 2003).

Another striking feature at the site is a series of exposed and subterranean aqueducts that diverted fresh water from nearby steams into pools located throughout the site core. Other underground aqueducts drained water away from the site. Bridges made from single slabs of rock, weighing several tons each, serve to connect different sectors of the site that were separated by canals and pools. In a land where water was abundant almost year round, this water system was apparently constructed to impress rather than for practical reasons. Michael Snarskis believes that many low paved areas of the central core of Guayabo that are generally interpreted as patios were instead pools that were perhaps only intermittently filled for ritual purposes. If an oval plaza on the west side of Mound 1 was filled with water diverted from Guayabo's hydraulic system, the conical shape of the structure on Mound 1 would have created the illusion of a two three-dimensional cones meeting at their bases when reflected by the water in the pool. They would thus mimic the form of the universe as envisioned by Talamancan people, according to ethnographic accounts (Snarskis, personal communication 2004).

To the northwest of Mound 1 and the adjacent oval patio/pool are a series of circular cobble formations that are likely the bases of conical structures made of perishable materials. No clear patterning is in evidence in the arrangement of these structures, which could likely have been dwellings of high-status families, perhaps families related to the chief who resided on Mound 1.

Guayabo is not the result of a single construction event but was produced by gradual growth over a period of approximately 1,000 years, beginning during the El Bosque–La Selva phase (200 BC–AD 800) and continuing into the La Cabaña phase (AD 800–1500). Guayabo was abandoned for unknown reasons at around AD 1300 (Troyo and Garnier 2002; Hurtado de Mendoza 2004). Although Guayabo is the largest known site of its kind, other sites exhibit similar general patterns at smaller scales, such as Anita Grande and Costa Rica Farm (Skinner 1926; Stone 1977). Las Mercedes was a major site and was the first to receive extensive archaeological study by

Carl V. Hartman (1901) in the late nineteenth century, but unfortunately it is now destroyed. The only other contemporary site in the region similar to Guayabo that has been extensively horizontally excavated to reveal the pattern of architecture is La Cabaña (Snarskis 1978, 1992). The core site area there consists of two adjacent circular mounds, each 10 meters in diameter and less than two meters high, a roughly 17-meter cobble-formed square plaza in front of the mounds, a nonmound house circle, and a paved causeway leading to the plaza.

From the relatively sparse information available it appears that large-scale site complexes in Atlantic Costa Rica between circa AD 500 to 1300 were built and occupied by chiefly families and their followers. The roads that connect Guayabo with other sites (many of which are unknown) suggest that alliances including perhaps ritual ties linked some sites together. Whether Guayabo was an exceptionally large example of this kind of chiefly center, as currently appears to be the case, cannot be fully known until more work is done on such architectural complexes.

Rivas and the Panteón de la Reina

The Rivas–Panteón de la Reina site complex is in the northeast sector of the General Valley between 840 and 880 meters above sea level in the foothills of the Talamanca Mountains, where the Río Chirripó Pacífico and the Río Buenavista meet to form the Río General. The compound name is the result of two separate site designations, for Rivas, a residential and ceremonial complex on river terraces, and the Panteón de la Reina mortuary complex on an adjacent ridge top. These are part of a single site complex, however.

The Rivas–Panteón de la Reina complex is located in what is commonly referred to as the Southern Zone of Costa Rica, separated from the Central Valley and the Atlantic Watershed by the Talamanca Mountains. The Río General flows southward, and in ancient times its people had close ties with communities in Panama; the pottery styles and residential and ceremonial architecture of the two groups were similar, although there were subregional variations.

The Panteón de la Reina was first identified in the late 1800s by local *huaqueros* (looters) looking for gold, and it suffered severe damage as it gained a reputation as one of the richest gold-bearing cemeteries in southern Central America (Bozzoli de Wille 1966; Lothrop 1926; Pérez-Zeledón 1907–1908; Pittier 1892).

In the period between AD 900 and 1300, Rivas–Panteón de la Reina was

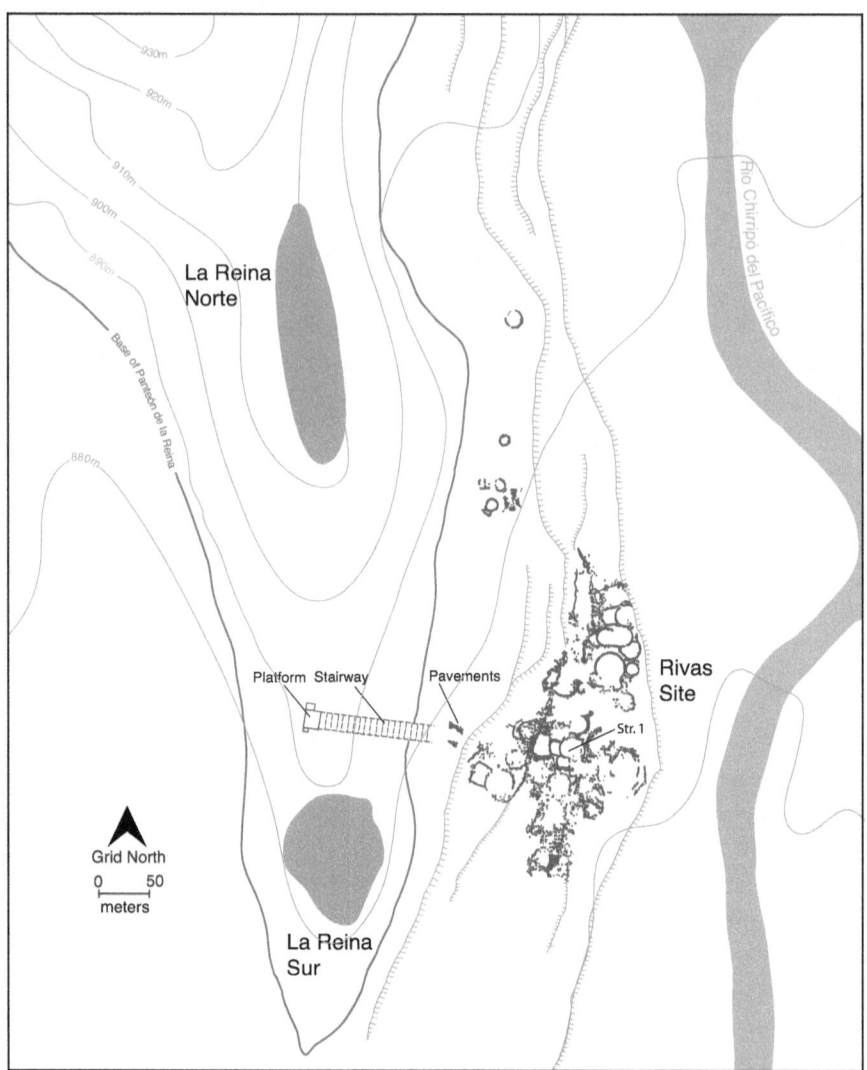

Figure 9.4. Rivas–Panteón de la Reina site.

a single ceremonial-mortuary complex of regional significance (Quilter 2004) (Figure 9.4). Rivas includes densely built areas of architecture covering 30,000 square meters and includes dwellings, ramps, stairs, plazas, drains, walls, and other architectural features dispersed along the third and fourth terraces above the west bank of the Río Chirripó Pacífico (Figure 9.5). Rivas abuts the base of the 60-meter-high ridge of the Panteón de la Reina, on which are located numerous tombs, funerary architecture, and other features that cover an area of 20,000 square meters.

Figure 9.5. Complex II in Operation D at the Rivas Site. A cobble ring that served as a foundation for a perishable structure. It abuts a stairway from a lower terrace seen to the right of the human figure. (Photo by J. Quilter.)

At Rivas, andesite cobbles and boulders were used to construct a variety of features. The most prominent are large circular "house rings," similar to those described above at Guayabo. One line of cobbles was usually arranged in a circle (but more commonly two lines or more); these served as the foundations in which poles could be placed to build thatched structures, today referred to as *ranchos*. This was a pan-regional building technique.

Throughout the Rivas site, multiple circular foundations between 10 and 30 meters in diameter intersected to form a single contiguous expanse of architecture that does not follow a clear organizational plan at first view. It includes structures and other architectural features of varying sizes, shapes, and construction techniques. Each structure connects with neighboring structures that are often joined by walls, steps, drains, or other features, making it difficult to clearly define the precise boundaries of any individual structure.

Some of the larger circular structures exhibit upright stones set at regular intervals around their perimeter, perhaps foundations for wooden posts that supported roofs. Most circles had massive quadrangular additions on one side. At Rivas, these porches invariably face west, toward the Panteón de la Reina.

Generally similar patterns of construction and of distribution of refuse made it difficult to differentiate activities in site sectors, which were in evidence by the arrangement of architectural features. The interiors of the structures, both large and small, yielded few features or artifacts. Dense accumulations of sherds with fewer remains of chipped and ground stone tools were found on top of and immediately adjacent to buried cobble rings, and soils in the same areas were dark and organically rich, suggesting that substantial midden had been deposited there.

Not all *ranchos* likely were residences nor were all cobble circles roofed. Some spaces appear to have been unroofed and may have served as courtyards or plazas shared by multiple structures. Within some of the structures was a layer of bright reddish-orange soil, one of the few clearly defined occupation surfaces at the site. This prepared surface suggests that the structure may have been a public space for dances, ceremonies, or other public performances, with the bright soil used to help create a colorful and visually pleasing platform on which to perform.

In comparison to Guayabo, there was little vertical construction at Rivas, where the highest standing walls were less than two meters high. The builders utilized and modified natural features such as rock outcroppings, alluvial terraces, and changes in topography to give their constructions a vertical dimension. Further vertical differentiation was provided by long narrow ridges of Pleistocene gravel, known as *ballenas,* which mostly run parallel to the general direction of the terraces. In many places natural rises were combined with human-made constructions to produce causeway-like features and stairways.

Excavation identified evidence of two construction phases. A lower construction phase associated with numerous ceramic artifacts and organically rich soils was overlaid with a sterile layer of reddish-orange laterite approximately 30 centimeters thick (Quilter 2004, 53, 70). The local name for this is *piedra muerta* (dead rock), named for the small fragments of heavily weathered rock it contains. *Piedra muerta* is not found on the river terraces where the Rivas site is located, but it is the predominant soil type in the surrounding hills, including the area of the Panteón de la Reina. It seems that *piedra muerta* was brought in to bury earlier architecture and fill low areas in order to construct a level base for the second phase of architecture. It is difficult to characterize how the later phase differs from the earlier phase because we were able to expose only small sections of the lower levels. It does seem that the upper architecture was constructed on a larger scale than the lower and that it corresponds with the porch-like additions oriented toward the Panteón de la Reina. Elsewhere at the site, some structures appeared to have been partially disassembled, perhaps to obtain building materials for newer construction. Radiocarbon dates indicate near-contemporaneity for the two building phases, suggesting that the fill and second building phase occurred during a relatively short period of time.

A set of linked architectural features was the center of important activities at Rivas. On the west side of the site are large circular structures with patios located immediately below the highest terrace at the site, which rises sharply to a height of three meters. On this terrace, close to its edge, we identified two spatially discrete sets of pavement. Although the features did not cover graves, the shape and size of the pavement presented strong parallels to cemetery pavement. Furthermore, the presence of several stone columns, common elements in Chiriquí cemeteries, and the placement of these features in relation to the larger site plan further suggested that this area served mortuary functions.

The pavement is positioned directly between the Rivas site and the base of a large cobble stairway 18 meters wide and more than 100 meters long that rises to the top of the Panteón de la Reina ridge. The stairway links the Rivas ceremonial sector to an earth and stone platform mound positioned between two ridge-top cemeteries: La Reina Norte and La Reina Sur.

The center of the stairway also forms a principal east-west axis to the site.[1] The axis passes between the two sets of pavements on the uppermost terrace, interpreted as a preparation area for mortuary rites, and continues eastward to bisect several paired sets of architectural features within the residential-ceremonial sector of Rivas. Some of the architecture along the axis is unique for the Rivas site and includes a rectangular plaza, paired causeways, and a set of steps. The east end of the axis appears to originate or end within Structure 1, which is 28 meters in diameter and is the second largest structure at Rivas. The primary access of the structure is oriented with a direct line of sight down the central axis of the site to the platform at the summit of the stairway.

The privileged location of Structure 1 strongly suggests that it served important mortuary functions; funeral activities likely originated within this structure and progressed westward through several sets of specialized architectural features, up the stairway to the platform, and eventually to the two cemeteries. The importance of the Rivas site as a locale for funeral rites is further emphasized by the fact that not only are the large structures discussed above oriented to the axis of the stairs but more distant structures also are oriented toward it, as evidenced by the sight lines from the center of circular structures running through quadrangular patios that point to the stairs.

Beyond the platform at the summit of the stairway, to the north and south, lie two spatially distinct interment areas: La Reina Norte and La Reina Sur, each approximately 5,300 square meters. Walls of stacked stone up to 50 centimeters tall define their boundaries and discrete burial areas within them. Looting has been extremely severe throughout the cemetery areas, and the internal organization of each cemetery area was difficult to discern. Based on a number of lines of evidence, however, we concluded that each cemetery was subdivided into smaller units that may have represented family or other corporate group units. These divisions are demarcated by several spatial and architectural features that include lines of stones, stone walls, changes in elevation, vacant spaces, and rows of stone columns (Frost 2009). The overall pattern in the cemeteries and at the site in general, however, emphasizes duality.

The Rivas–Panteón de la Reina complex was established around AD 900 and was occupied continuously until sometime after AD 1300, when it was abandoned or population levels dropped so low that they are not archaeologically visible (Quilter and Frost 2007, 29–30). Native peoples in the region were left relatively undisturbed compared to others in Latin America and continued to gather at regional centers to conduct mortuary rituals. A report of one such festival (Gabb 1875) describes activities that were used as a general interpretive model for activities at Rivas–Panteón de la Reina.

Summary and Conclusions

Like so many other world regions, the first signs of monumental constructions in the Intermediate Area are the erection of tumuli for the burial and memorialization of high-ranking individuals. The fact that so many sites consist of clusters of mounds suggests that these were regional centers. The degree to which such regional leaders exercised authority through religious practices rather than through more direct political control is hard to assess. We might suggest that such roles combined religious authority that was intimately associated with access to prestige goods, such as jade from Mesoamerica, and with a large group of kin-based followers. Such issues, however, await further study, especially in regard to earlier sites such as Barriles. How labor was recruited to make and install large stone monuments at such centers is another issue that we cannot fully evaluate at present. We can state, however, that continuing research indicates that sociopolitical systems were complexly organized throughout the Intermediate Area from (at least) AD 700 onward, whether they are called "complex chiefdoms" or are recognized as more elaborately constituted social systems.

Enough work has been carried out at Guayabo and Rivas–Panteón de la Reina that they can be compared with regard to their plans and construction. In addition, some suggestions can be made as to how labor may have been recruited to build them and how populations were mobilized in their use.

Guayabo and Rivas–Panteón de la Reina were occupied at roughly the same time period and shared a basic architectural vocabulary—the use of cobbles and flagstones, circular house rings, patios, rectangular plazas, and causeway-like structures. Nevertheless, there are notable differences in architecture at the two sites, such as the high number of mounds at Guayabo and the comparatively low number at Rivas–Panteón de la Reina. However, despite these differences, a basic architectural pattern is present at both sites: long cobbled walkways—a causeway at Guayabo and stairs on the Panteón de la Reina—flanked by mounds and leading from an area relatively low in sacrality to the most important and symbolically charged site centers. At Guayabo the causeway went from the edge of the area of monumental constructions to the main mound, which may have been both a chief's residence and a funerary tumulus, while at Rivas–Panteón de la Reina the stairway connected an area that may have contained residences and mortuary preparation areas to the cemetery on the ridge top.

Whereas the architectural patterning and other evidence at Guayabo suggests chiefly authority, Rivas–Panteón de la Reina appears to have been organized as a regional center for the gathering of relatively equal social groups that were likely organized on segmentary principles using concepts of duality. These different social systems appear to correlate with the great divide in late prehistoric Costa Rica noted earlier in this chapter. The Rivas–Panteón de la Reina pattern likely represents the "new wave" that came from the south that consisted of a bundle of practices and beliefs that included goldworking, new ceramic styles, new architectural forms, and new social relations manifest in the site complex and its mortuary practices.

While the Guayabo pattern includes a mortuary component, it appears to have been more heavily weighted toward the authority of a living chief and his (or her) claim to authority through claims of access to spiritual power in a sacred landscape (the Turrialba Volcano and the cosmic "cone"), through ancestors (the Mound 1 tumulus), and through links to other power centers in the region (causeways and paths connected to other sites). This pattern was apparently widespread in the Atlantic Watershed region of Costa Rica. The extent of this system, south and north, remains a topic to be explored, as does its degree of originality.

Many more issues about the monumental constructions and works and social complexity in the Intermediate Area could be addressed than the brief discussion presented above; Rivas–Panteón de la Reina and Guayabo are the best known of scores of similar sites that originated earlier or later or were contemporary with these two sites. Even within Costa Rica, a full discussion of monumentality should include the great ceremonial complex of the sites at Palmar Sur in the Diquís Delta (Lothrop 1963). Farther afield, the El Caño site in Central Panama represents a completely different pattern of late prehistoric monumental construction (Verrill 1927, 1929), while the well-known Sitio Conte Cemetery Complex (Lothrop 1937, 1942; Mason 1941, 1942), five kilometers distant from and likely related to El Caño, offers a great amount of information on social complexity. While the monumental architecture of southern Central America does not have the "verticality" of many New World structures, these sites abundantly demonstrate that both their extent and the societies that produced them were impressive. We hope that this discussion of two sites has helped point out the richness and diversity of the archaeological record and their social correlates in the Intermediate Area.

Notes

1. The Rivas terraces and the Panteón de la Reina are oriented approximately northeast-southwest. For purposes of this discussion, however, we will refer to the northeast direction as north, the southeast direction as east, the southeast-northwest direction as east-west, and so forth.

References Cited

Barrantes, Ramiro
1993 *Evolución en el Trópico: Los Amerindios de Costa Rica y Panamá.* Editorial de la Universidad de Costa Rica, San José, Costa Rica.
1998 Orígen y relaciones entre los amerindios chibcha de Costa Rica: Una perspectiva genética y evolutiva. In *Congreso Científico Sobre Pueblos Indígenas de Costa Rica y sus Fronteras,* edited by M. E. Bozzoli, R. Barrantes, D. Obando, and M. Rojas, pp. 3–14. EUNED, San José, Costa Rica.

Bird, Junius, and Richard G. Cooke
1978 The Occurrence in Panama of Two Types of Paleo-Indian Projectile Points. In *Early Man in America from a Circum-Pacific Perspective,* edited by Alan Lyle Bryan, pp. 263–272. Department of Anthropology Occasional Papers. University of Alberta, Edmonton.

Bozzoli de Wille, María Eugenia
1966 Observaciones arqueológicas en los valles del Parrita y del General. *Boletín de la Asociacion de Amigos del Museo* 19. Museo Nacional de Costa Rica, San José.

Bray, Warwick
2003 Gold, Stone, and Ideology: Symbols of Power in the Tairona Tradition of Northern Colombia. In *Gold and Power in Ancient Costa Rica, Panama, and Colombia,* edited by J. Quilter and J. W. Hoopes, pp. 301–344. Dumbarton Oaks, Washington, D.C.

Constenla Umaña, Adolfo
1995 Sobre el estudio diacrónico de la lenguas chichenses y su contribución al concocimiento del pasado de sus hablantes. *Boletín del Museo del Oro* (Bogotá) 38–39:13–56.

Cooke, Richard, Ilean Isaza, John Griggs, Benoit Desjardins, and Luís Alberto Sánchez
2003 Who Crafted, Exchanged, and Displayed Gold in Pre-Columbian Panama? In *Gold and Power in Ancient Costa Rica, Panama, and Colombia,* edited by Jeffrey Quilter and John W. Hoopes, pp. 91–158. Dumbarton Oaks, Washington, D.C.

Fonseca Zamora, Oscar Manuel
1979 Informe de la primera temporada de reexcavación de Guayabo de Turrialba. *Vínculos* 5(1–2):35–52.
1980 Guayabo de Turrialba and its Significance. In *Between Continents/Between Seas: Precolombian Art of Costa Rica,* edited by Elizabeth P. Benson, pp. 104–111. Harry N. Abrams, New York

Frost, R. Jeffrey
2009 *The Ancestors Above, the People Below: Cemeteries, Landscape, and Dual Organization in Late Pre-Columbian Costa Rica.* Ph.D. dissertation, University of Wisconsin at Madison. University Microfilms, Ann Arbor.

Gabb, William M.
1875 On the Indian Tribes and Languages of Costa Rica. *American Philosophical Society* 14:483–602.

Garnier Zamora, José Enrique, and Elena Troyo Vargas
2002   El uso del espacio y la arquitectura del Sitio. In *Guayabo de Turrialba: Una Aldea Prehispanica Compleja,* edited by Elena Troyo Vargas, pp. 59-70. Centro Investigación y Conservación del Patrimonio Cultural. Ministerio de Cultura, Juventud y Desportes, San José, Costa Rica.

Hartman, Carl V.
1901   *Archaeological Researches in Costa Rica.* Royal Ethnographical Museum, Stockholm.

Helms, Mary
1979   *Ancient Panama: Chiefs in Search of Power.* University of Texas Press, Austin.

Hoopes, John
2005   The Emergence of Social Complexity in the Chibchan World of Southern Central America and Northern Columbia, AD 300-600. *Journal of Archaeological Research* 13(1): 1-47.

Hoopes, John, and Oscar M. Fonseca Z.
2003   Goldwork and Chibchan Identity: Endogenous Change and Diffuse Unity in the Isthmo-Colombian Area. In *Gold and Power in Ancient Costa Rica, Panama, and Colombia,* edited by Jeffrey Quilter and John W. Hoopes, pp. 49-89. Dumbarton Oaks, Washington, D.C.

Hurtado de Mendoza, Luis
2004   *Guayabo. Historia Antigua de Turrialba.* Litigrafía e Imprenta LIL, San Jose.

Linares, Olga F., Payson D. Sheets, and E. Jane Rosenthal
1975   Prehistoric Agriculture in Tropical Highlands. *Science* 187(4172):137-145.

Lothrop, Samuel K.
1926   *Pottery of Nicaragua and Costa Rica.* 2 vols. Contribution 8. Museum of the American Indian, Heye Foundation, New York.
1937   *Coclé: An archaeological Study of Central Panama: Part 1.* Memoirs of the Peabody Museum of Archaeology and Ethnology 7. Harvard University, Cambridge, Massachusetts.
1942   *Coclé: An Archaeological Study of Central Panama: Part 2.* Memoirs of the Peabody Museum of Archaeology and Ethnology 8. Harvard University, Cambridge, Massachusetts.
1963   *Archaeology of the Diquís Delta, Costa Rica.* Papers of the Peabody Museum of Archaeology and Ethnology, vol. 51. Harvard University, Cambridge, Massachusetts.

Mason, J. Alden
1941   Gold from the Grave. *Scientific American* 165(5):261-263.
1942   New Excavations at the Sitio Conte, Coclé, Panama. In *Native American Cultures: Proceedings of the Eighth American Scientific Congress Held in Washington, May 8-18, 1940,* vol. 2, pp.103-107. Department of State, Washington, D.C.

Oyuela-Caycedo, Augusto
1995   Rock versus Clay: The Evolution of Potter Technology in the Case of San Jacinto 1, Colombia. In *The Emergence of Pottery: Technology and Innovation in Ancient Societies,* edited by William K. Barnett and John W. Hoopes, pp. 133-144. Smithsonian Institution Press, Washington, D.C.

Palumbo, Scott D.
2009   *The development of complex society in the Volcán Barú region of Western Panama.* Ph.D. dissertation, University of Pittsburgh. University Microfilms, Ann Arbor.

Pérez-Zeledón, Pedro
1907–1908   Las Ilurnas de Pirrís y Valle del Río General ó Grande de Térraba. *Informes presentados a La Secretaría de Fomento.* Tipografía Nacional, San José, Costa Rica.

Pittier, Henri
1892   Viaje de exploración al Río Grande de Térraba. Estudios Científicos X. In *Annales del Instituto Físico-Geográfico y del Museo Nacional de Costa Rica.* Tomo III, 1890. Tipografia Nacional, San José.

Quilter, Jeffrey
2003   Introduction: The Golden Bridge of Darién. In *Gold and Power in Ancient Costa Rica, Panama, and Colombia,* edited by Jeffrey Quilter and John W. Hoopes, pp. 1–14. Dumbarton Oaks Research Library and Collection, Washington, D.C.
2004   *Cobble Circles and Standing Stones: Archaeology at the Rivas Site, Costa Rica.* University of Iowa Press, Iowa City.

Quilter, Jeffrey, and R. Jeffrey Frost
2007   Investigaciones en el Complejo Arqueológico Rivas-Panteón de la Reina en el Suroeste de Costa Rica. *Vínculos* 30(1–2): 23–56.

Reichel-Dolmatoff, Gerardo
1951   *Datos histórico-culturales sobre las tribus d la Antigua Gobernación de Santa Marta.* Instituto Etnológico de Magdalena, Santa Marta.

Rosenthal, E. Jane
1980   Excavations at Barriles (BU-24): A Small Testing Program. In *Adaptive Radiations in Prehistoric Panama,* edited by Olga F. Linares and Anthony J. Ranere, pp. 288–292. Peabody Museum of Archaeology and Ethnology, Cambridge, Massachusetts.

Sheets, Payson
1992   The Pervasive Pejorative in Intermediate Area Studies. In *Wealth and Hierarchy in the Intermediate Area,* edited by Frederick. W. Lange, pp. 14–42. Dumbarton Oaks Research Library and Collections, Washington, D.C.

Skinner, Alanson
1926   Notes on Las Mercedes, Costa Rica Farm, and Anita Grande. In *Pottery of Costa Rica and Nicaragua.* Contributions from the Museum of the American Indian, Heye Foundation, No. 8, vol. 2, pp. 451–567. Museum of the American Indian, Heye Foundation, New York.

Snarskis, Michael J.
1978   *The Archaeology of the Central Atlantic Watershed of Costa Rica.* Ph.D. dissertation, Columbia University, New York. University Microfilms, Ann Arbor.
1992   Wealth and Hierarchy in the Archaeology of Easter and Central Costa Rica. In *Wealth and Hierarchy in the Intermediate Area,* edited by Frederick. W. Lange, pp. 141–164. Dumbarton Oaks Research Library and Collections, Washington, D.C.
2003   From Jade to gold in Costa Rica: How, why, and when. In *Gold and Power in Ancient Costa Rica, Panama, and Colombia,* edited by Jeffrey Quilter and John W.

Hoopes, pp. 159–204. Dumbarton Oaks Research Library and Collections, Washington, D.C.

Stirling, Matthew
1950   Exploring Ancient Panama by Helicopter. *National Geographic* 97(2):227–246.

Stone, Doris
1977   *Pre-Columbian Man in Costa Rica.* Peabody Museum Press, Cambridge, Massachusetts.

Trigger, Bruce G.
1990   Monumental Architecture: A Thermodynamic Explanation of Symbolic Behaviour. World *Archaeology* 22:119–132.

Troyo V., Elena (editor)
2002   *Guayabo de Turrialba: Una Aldea Prehispánica Compleja.* Centro Investigación y Conservación del Patrimonio Cultural, Ministerio de Cultura, Juventud y Desportes, San José.

Troyo V., Elena, and José Enrique Garnier Z.
2002   Acciones para la preservación del sitio Guayabo: Consolidación y restauración. In *Guayabo de Turrialba: Una Aldea Prehispanica Compleja,* edited by Elena Troyo Vargas, pp. 71–135. Centro Investigación y Conservación del Patrimonio Cultural. Ministerio de Cultura, Juventud y Desportes. San José.

Verrill, Hyatt
1927   Excavations in Coclé Province, Panama. *Museum of the American Indian, Heye Foundation, Indian Notes* 4(1):47–61.
1929   *Old Civilizations of the New World.* Tudor Publishing, New York.

V

SOUTH AMERICA

10

Early Mounds and Monumental Art in Ancient Amazonia

History, Scale, Function, and Social Ecology

ANNA C. ROOSEVELT, J. DOUGLAS, B. BEVAN,
MAURA IMAZIO DA SILVEIRA, AND L. BROWN

In twentieth-century schemes of early human cultural evolution, large-scale public works were interpreted as characteristic of preindustrial state societies but not of small-scale or egalitarian societies. The idea was that only complex, centralized, stratified, agricultural societies have what it takes to build, maintain, and use monumental architecture and art. We archaeologists have even considered the presence of such works in ancient sites to be sufficient proof of such a society. But evidence is mounting that social organization, subsistence, architecture, and art often have not interacted as described in twentieth-century theory. A new paradigm of social political causality has emerged recently. Called heterarchy, it explores the role of nonstate organizations in monumental public works projects and other complex cultural achievements. In this chapter, we evaluate both these theories with the information available about the history, function, and socioeconomic context of early monumental architecture and art in ancient Amazonia.

Two recent Society for American Archaeology sessions on the theory and evidence of monumental constructions in the New World encouraged a review of these issues. In 2006, Dan Sandweiss and Maria Dulce Gaspar organized a session on shell mounds, and Robert Rosenswig and Richard Burger organized a session on monumentality in Latin America. In this second symposium, the organizers began with twentieth-century theory about the social context of monumental constructions and asked participants to

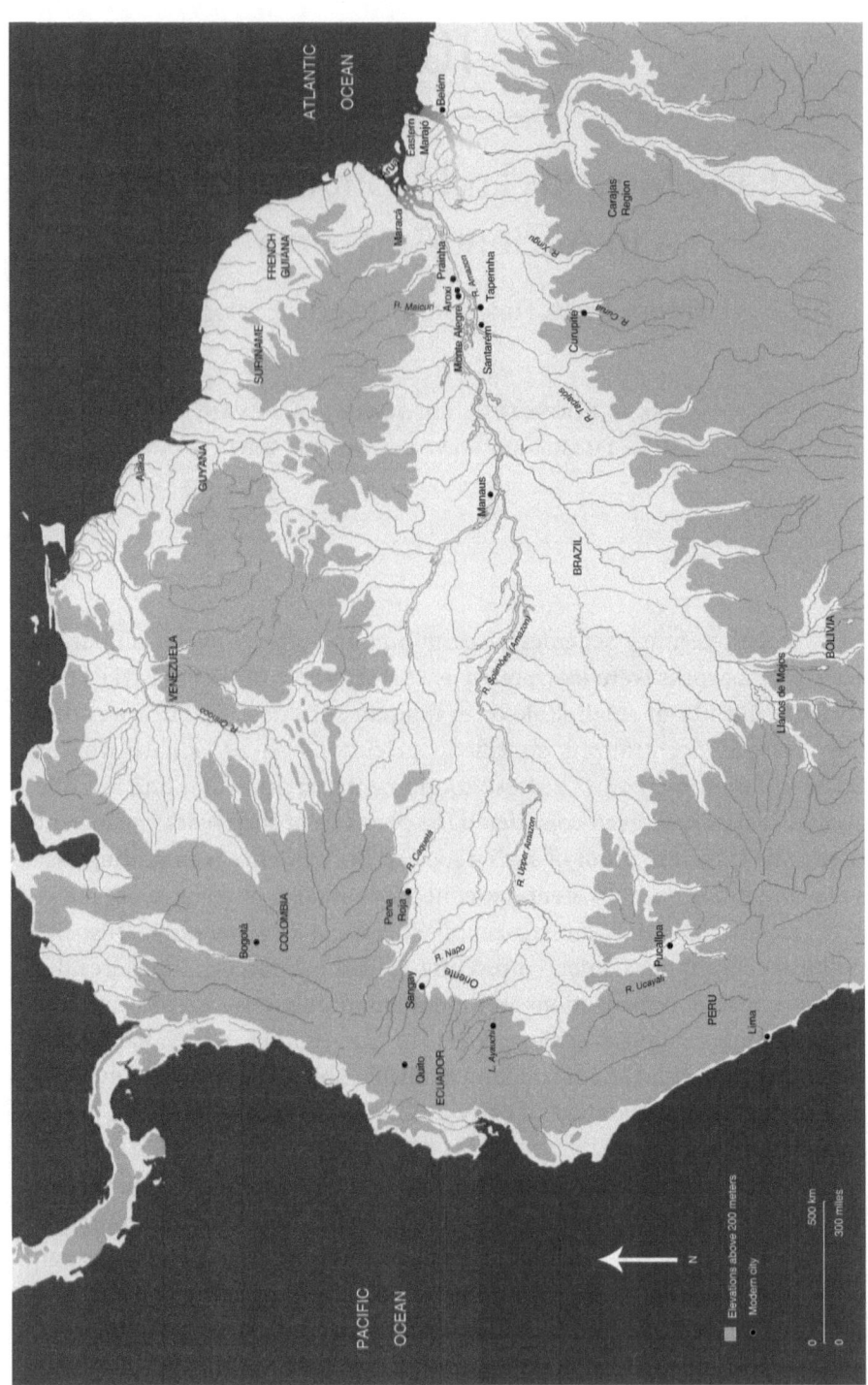

Figure 10.1. Map of the Amazon.

trace independently the emergence of the elements assumed to be linked causally: large constructions; monumental art; intensive agriculture; large, dense, sedentary settlements; social and economic differentiation; and central rule.

Inspired by both these conferences, we will try to characterize the available evidence on early monumental works complexes in Amazonia in light of theory. After briefly reviewing theories about cultural evolution, we will analyze cultures that we have some experience with—Paleoindian rock-painting cultures, the coastal and riverine shell mounds of the Pottery Archaic and Formative in the Lower Amazon, and Formative earth mounds of the Upper Amazon (Figure 10.1)—as well as cultures that we know only from the literature and/or museum collections; for example, the early Llanos de Mojos region cultures of Bolivia and the mound complex of the Faldas de Sangay site in Ecuador. Given the thrust of this book on early prehistoric periods, we will leave out consideration of the Polychrome Horizon earth mounds on Marajo Island at the mouth of the Amazon, Incised and Punctate Horizon mounds at the Tapajos mouth in the Lower Amazon, and the raised field and mound complexes of the Llanos de Mojos and Guianas coasts. We will try to be attentive to evidence of societies' environmental relations and subsistence, settlement patterns, human health status, demography, degrees of sociocultural and economic differentiation, patterning of arts and crafts, ritual systems and organizational strategies, and the construction, magnitude, and apparent uses of mounds.

Theoretical Background

Both cultural anthropologists and archaeologists have been very interested in explaining the origin and functioning of early state societies (e.g., Carneiro 1970; Earle 1987; Johnson and Earle 1987; Fried 1967; Meggers 1954; Roosevelt 1980, 1989; Sanders and Price 1968; Service 1975). And whether from the point of view of evolutionary theory or of human organization, the preindustrial state has been a popular focus of this research. Many of us once believed or still believe that only state societies are able to make the great cultural achievements associated with ancient civilization: high art and architecture, writing, intensive agriculture, urban settlements, and, above all, monumental constructions. The belief has been that only large-scale, centralized, and hierarchical societies have the administrative means to carry out such achievements and to organize the large settled populations whose labor is required. Such means range from armed coercion by state-controlled police forces, effective taxation and tribute collection, and central control of technology and production to centralized redistribution of artifacts, raw materials, and food. Grassroots community-based organizations in small-scale societies that can rely only on such means as family relations, persuasion and manipulation of group opinion, gift exchange, and ritual sanctions are thought to be unable to organize and run such large-scale and complex social, ritual, and economic systems. Most researchers have also thought that only under state authority can social classes and specialized occupations be maintained.

The rise of agriculture is thought to be important in state systems because it furnishes the material needs for the dense settled populations that societies need to provision and organize to do necessary communal work. Hunting and gathering are assumed to be insufficiently productive to provision such populations and underwrite their specialized activities. Following from this reasoning is the conclusion that where intensive agriculture is not possible, nonindustrial states could not arise. State organization could be introduced temporarily to such areas, but it would fail without economic support from the outside. And without the help of state administrative methods and resources, complex social organizations would be unstable and short lived.

The relatively new theoretical school of heterarchy suggests that there also are many nonhierarchical, noncentralized ways that local communities have organized to do "great works" (Arnold 1996; Bacus and Lucero 1999; Burger 1992; Ehrenreich, Crumley, and Levy 1995; Higham and Thosarat 1998; Potter and King 1995; Roosevelt 1999b, 1999d; Schildkraut and Keim 1990; Stein 2005). People can organize as horizontal or ranked segmentary groups such as kin groups, cults, clubs, craft or trade specialties, artists, performers, or even sports teams. Effective leaders can be elected, can rule by reason of seniority or kinship, or can gain leadership through charisma or personal efficacy in activities such as raiding, ritual, curing, arts or crafts, subsistence, or games. They can arise as spokespeople from committees of elders or gender groups; as excellent hunters, warriors, or successful shamans; or for some other notable skill or attributed characteristic. The general population can contribute resources to the community for great works through traditional labor or gift obligations, as members of the kin group or a production cooperative, or through ad hoc tithes for a project or fees for a sodality, cult, or residence group. Heterarchy theorists (cited above) point out that many examples of such ways to organize are known from the ethnographic and ethnohistoric records.

Although earlier theories of state origins stated that only centralized organizations can effectively run large communities and projects in the long term, heterarchy theory predicts that locally based leadership may be more balanced, effective, and stable than outside control from above. Local leaders could be more knowledgeable than higher-ups or outsiders about the community and its interests, local technologies and crafts, and ecology, and "knowledge is power," after all. The local leaders would know the resource potentials and risks better than outsiders and so could better avoid ill-conceived projects that were likely to fail. They also would know enough about the community and its interests to know better how to persuade people to join in public works and could more accurately evaluate people's skills to deploy them better in the work. Like state leaders, they could use religious influence to help persuade people, and they also would know enough about individuals to better negotiate their positions. Being closer spatially, they also would be easier for the community to observe and influence, and they would have to be more responsive to community interests because it would be harder for them to evade the consequences of unpopular actions than it would be for outsiders.

They would usually lack the coercive tools and outside means of economic support that help administrations of high-ranking outsiders avoid the immediate unfavorable social or ecological consequences of their actions. Also, there would be less for them to gain from the job, given the need for them to keep giving back to the community. They would gain some prosperity, wealth, prestige, and respect and a lot of influence but would probably not get riches, leisure, privacy, and impunity. Coups and succession battles therefore would not be as much of a problem because the job would require a lot of effort and generosity, and leaders might feel relief at the end of their reigns. Finally, if local leaders' degree of power and freedom of action were more constrained than those of outsiders, there would be a better balance of power among the parties of the community and thus a more equitable and stable social system. In all, then, such organizations would be expected to be longer lived than top-heavy, self-serving, uninformed, and uninfluential organizations imposed from the outside.

If grand cultural achievements usually attributed to state societies can indeed be made by societies organized in such nonstate ways, then evidence of the achievements should not be used as proxy evidence for prehistoric state organizations. One could not class a society as a state just because one found it to have monumental constructions, high art and conspicuous wealth, or substantial habitations. Rather, archaeologists interested in the trajectories of rulership would have to develop more direct ways to detect specific organizational modes and particular forms of internal differentiation of societies. One would need to trace independently the history of the relevant elements of the past societies: monumental constructions, arts and crafts, subsistence, settlement patterns, and sociopolitical and economic differentiation and how these were organized over time and space. Such kinds of inquiries have produced useful insights in several parts of the world (e.g., Blake et al. 1992; Coe and Diehl 1980; Hasdorf 1993; Grieder et al. 1988; Marquardt 1988; Price and Brown 1985; Quilter et al. 1991; Salazar 1998; Stein 2005).

Methodologies for Tracing the History of Mound-Building Societies

For investigating rulership or administration modes, we need to map and sample the contents of structures and facilities in settlements to look for special residences, administrative buildings, fortifications, meeting places, and religious facilities. We also need to look for ceremonial, iconographic, and funerary patterns that could be related to concepts and rituals of rulership, administration, organization, and ritual power. Such work requires not only detailed topographic mapping and geophysical surveys but also extensive excavations to sample features for datable or functionally illuminating objects and analyze them for sociotechnic characteristics (Roosevelt 1991, 1999c, 2007). Some archaeologists in Amazonia have made a good start, but detailed mapping needs to become a routine aspect of the relevant projects. Without making detailed contour and locational maps of sites and carrying out controlled sampling of them, how could one find out the scale of the mounds and their function, and relation to other structures, to the economic system, and to the organization of the community?

If we are to understand the subsistence economies that provisioned the societies, we need to collect and identify plants and fauna from sites and look at related aspects of craft objects, facilities, and human skeletons where possible. It is clear by now that in Amazonia there was not just one prehistoric tropical forest culture based on manioc, fish, and game but a wide range of ecological orientations and subsistence solutions at different times and places in Amazonia (Roosevelt 1994, 2000). That being so, we simply cannot rely on guesswork to say what a given community's food economy could have been. Empirical work on Amazonian human ecology and subsistence at particular sites has revealed counterintuitive patterns, such as early foraging societies that did not rely on big game hunting, early pottery cultures that relied on foraging rather than on agriculture, and late prehistoric societies that used maize more than manioc. Stable isotopes can refine interpretations based on biological macro- or microspecimens with quantitative data (e.g., Roosevelt 1984, 1997, 2000a; van der Merwe, Roosevelt, and Vogel 1981). (Although some archaeologists feel constrained from investigating indigenous skeletons, some indigenous communities do not oppose cemetery studies because they, too, are interested in the lifestyles of their ancestors.) If theoretical considerations of economy are important, then problem-oriented research ought to include such sampling.

To understand the nature of social organization, we need to compare the health status, food patterns, work effects, housing, and wealth of the members of populations. We also need to know about their access to special or rare goods and the patterns of feasting. Such evidence can help us decide whether we are dealing with hierarchical social classes, ranking, or more egalitarian or family-level organization systems. Funerary facilities, which are common in certain types of Amazonian sites, can be an important source of information, but such research takes time, since the facilities are often large and in use over a long period of time.

The Relevance of Amazonia

Amazonia can be a useful test case for theories about mound building in ancient societies. It has often been assumed that agricultural states could not develop and persist in the tropical rainforest and that therefore the region would never have populous permanent settlements, intensive agriculture, monumental constructions and art, and the complex organization to rule them. Indeed, Roosevelt came to work there initially because of its value for investigating such anthropological issues. Could intensive agriculture be done there if tropical forest soils are poor? Without agriculture, could there be urban or even sedentary settlement? Without economies and populations typical of states, could complex societies exist, and, without state organization, could the societies create monumental constructions and high art styles?

By now most anthropologists would agree that in Amazonia monumental constructions and elaborate art styles abound. Both have been known for more than a hundred years. The answers to the above questions, then, could be various. The soils in some areas might not be that bad, so people could have achieved intensive agriculture; could therefore have supported dense, sedentary populations; and accordingly could have organized into class societies with central rulers who could have commissioned fine art and monuments. Alternatively, if the soils were so bad as to make intensive agriculture impossible, maybe people developed stratified state societies with other types of economies. As a further alternative, perhaps people were able to organize their economies and populations in nonstate ways to achieve the cultural heights usually attributed to state organization, including monumental works.

In order to try to sort out the picture for the Amazon, we will give a brief assessment of early monument building and the associated cultural achievements, ritual and symbolic patterns, settlement patterns, and ecological adaptations in several parts the Brazilian Amazon and its environs. In the last two decades, archaeologists in Amazonia have made a concerted effort to investigate several different mound-building societies in the field. Fanning out into different areas of the region, they have made finds that illuminate the nature, history, and contexts of archaeological mounds there. As in other regions of the world, the results from their field research reveals an unexpectedly wide range of mound-building patterns and contexts. This surprising variation inspires a rethinking of assumptions about two related theoretical issues. The first is the nature of the organization, use, and conceptual meaning of mounds in early human complex societies through time (as in Sassaman and Randall this volume). The second is the nature of Amazonia as an ecological setting for the development of human societies that built monuments.

Monumental Works in Prehistoric Amazonian Societies

Paleoindian Rock Art

The recently discovered Paleoindian and Early Archaic foraging cultures of the Amazon date to the last 4,000 years of the Ice Age, between ca. 11,000 and 7,000 years ago (uncalibrated). It is generally assumed that nomadic hunter-gatherers would not have created monumental constructions or high art. Their few excavated sites are smallish camps or scattered transient activity areas without built facilities, but Holocene hydrological changes have covered up the floodplains of the time, where larger and more sedentary settlements might have been. Despite their likely nomadism, the Paleoindian cultures of Eastern Brazilian America are notable for their abundant large-scale rock art, which is found on numerous outcrops and in caves they occupied (Pereira 2003; Prous 1991, 1999; Roosevelt 1999; Roosevelt,

Figure 10.2. Rock painting panel, Serra da Lua, Monte Alegre, Brazil. The panel shows a diving or falling personage with a single eye, a head with rays emanating from it, and wispy arms, possibly an interpretation of a comet. Nearby is a concentric circle image that could depict an eclipse of some kind.

Douglas, and Brown 2002). The culture area of the early rock-painting horizon styles is large, extending from southeastern Brazil to northern Brazil. Not only are some rock art sites large, but individual panels and art motifs can be huge. For example, a panel series at Serra da Lua, Monte Alegre, in the Lower Amazon, extends several hundreds of meters along a hillside, and several archaeoastronomical images are more than a meter across. At another series, Pedra Pintada do Painel do Pilao, paintings are tens of meters above the ground and would have required scaffolds for access. The sky symbols at Serra da Lua faces a long series of range peaks suitable for sighting astronomical changes. In view of the setting and the frequency of images shaped like suns, moons, ecliptics, stars, planets, or comets (Figure 10.2), it is likely that the people actively used the rock art in conjunction with a system of heavenly observations and interpretation (Davis 2009). The large corpus of rock art seems to have been produced over a relatively short period early in the period. The pigment and paint remains related to the art are concentrated in the earliest Paleoindian cave layers, dating between ca. 11,000 and 10,500 BP (Roosevelt et al. 1996; Michab et al. 1998), and isolated lithics comparable to the cave lithics are found below the open-air panels. If these Paleoindian cultures represent new arrivals to the area, the art could have been an attempt to create cultural landscapes to help people comprehend and deal with unfamiliar natural ones.

Paleoindians may have left large shell mounds, as did the people of the Archaic in the area. We know from their food remains that they harvested aquatic fauna intensively for food, including shellfish, and regarded them highly enough to carry them to sites well away from and above the shore. Eurasian "Mesolithic" societies, such as the early Jomon, living in sometimes comparable ways at about the same time as the Amazonian Paleoindians and Archaics, sometimes created large mound structures; facilities for food processing, burials, and rituals; and elaborate sociotechnic art (Roosevelt 1999a). Like other early foragers, the Amazonians may have congregated seasonally or for seasonal feasts and/or initiations where fishing was productive. Up to now, no one has found shoreline sites of the period in the Amazon, but the ancient shorelines probably lie under water or deep sediment because ocean and river levels rose rapidly after 10,000 BP, covering their former shores. In any case, Paleoindians assuredly did not have an intensive agricultural economy, although they may have planted and cultivated some plants in certain regions (Gnecco and Mora 1997). Most of their diverse food remains are nutritious oily nuts, fatty or sugary fruits, proteinaceous legumes, abundant aquatic faunas such as fish and turtles, some shellfish, and small terrestrial animals. Thus, their monumental rock art is a massive intellectual and aesthetic achievement made without the help of intensive agriculture, settled populations, or complex organization.

Archaic Stage Shell Mounds

The earliest mounds known in the Amazon are shell mounds of the Pottery Archaic, dated between about 7,500 to 5,000 BP (uncalibrated) during a period of elevated sea levels in the early Holocene period. Three main cultures have been defined from excavations: Taperinha in the Lower Amazon and Alaka and Mina along the seacoasts north and south of the Amazon mouth. These cultures now have more than 34 radiometric dates in the Archaic range, run directly on pottery, fauna, and carbonized plants excavated from a total of nine shell mounds (Gaspar and Imazio da Silveira 1999; Evans and Meggers 1960; Imazio da Silveira and Schaan 2005; Roosevelt 1995, 1998b, 2007; Roosevelt et al. 1991; Roosevelt et al. 1996). A few archaeologists have suggested that some of the excavated shell mounds have pre-ceramic layers (Simoes 1981; Williams 1981, 1982), but no pre-ceramic layers have been demonstrated yet in Amazonian shell mounds (Imazio da Silveira and Schaan 2005; Roosevelt 1995).

Ever since early geologists figured out from the combination of sherds, broken lithics, burials, shells, and other foods that the Amazonian shell mounds were human, not paleontological, the mounds have been classified as middens of fishing villages. Nonetheless, some archaeologists now reject that Brazilian shell mounds are necessarily just middens. They base their conclusions on the results from excavations in some large Archaic shell mounds in south coastal Brazil (Gaspar 1999). They argue that some of the southern mounds were special constructions built of shellfish collected for that purpose, not for food refuse. On top of such mounds, the archaeologists have uncovered floors and structures with ritual features. Such special-purpose shell mounds have inspired a reinterpretation of the functions of shell mounds in the Amazon region.

Definitive conclusions about Amazonian shell mounds await systematic mapping and more extensive testing, but some research results suggest that some of these mounds could have been built for special purposes other than simple garbage disposal. Although few have been mapped topographically, the Amazonian shell mounds seem to vary from one to as many as 20 hectares in size. All those published so far do seem to be composed of archaeological refuse, in contrast to the purely architectural mounds of clean shells documented in southern Brazil. Nevertheless, some Amazonian mounds seem to be secondary constructions built of refuse moved from its initial primary disposal area. Other remains suggest that the sites were more than undifferentiated refuse heaps. Postholes, possible floors, hearths, human burials, and feasting areas with special food remains reflect multiple functions, including residences and ceremonial activity areas. So far, no annular shell mound arrangements, such as have been found in the Caribbean Colombia and Florida (Sassaman and Randall this volume), have been discovered, though late prehistoric and modern Amazonians frequently lived in ring, or round, moiety villages (see below on the Upper Xingu).

Preliminary mapping, geophysical survey, and test excavation at Taperinha near the mouth of the Tapajos River in the Lower Amazon have revealed some complexity in plan and stratigraphy (Figure 10.3; Roosevelt 1995, 2007; Roosevelt et al. 1991). The shell mound is not the whole of the settlement, which incorporates both a mound and other types of deposit. Although partly bulldozed for lime mining, the ca. one-hectare shell

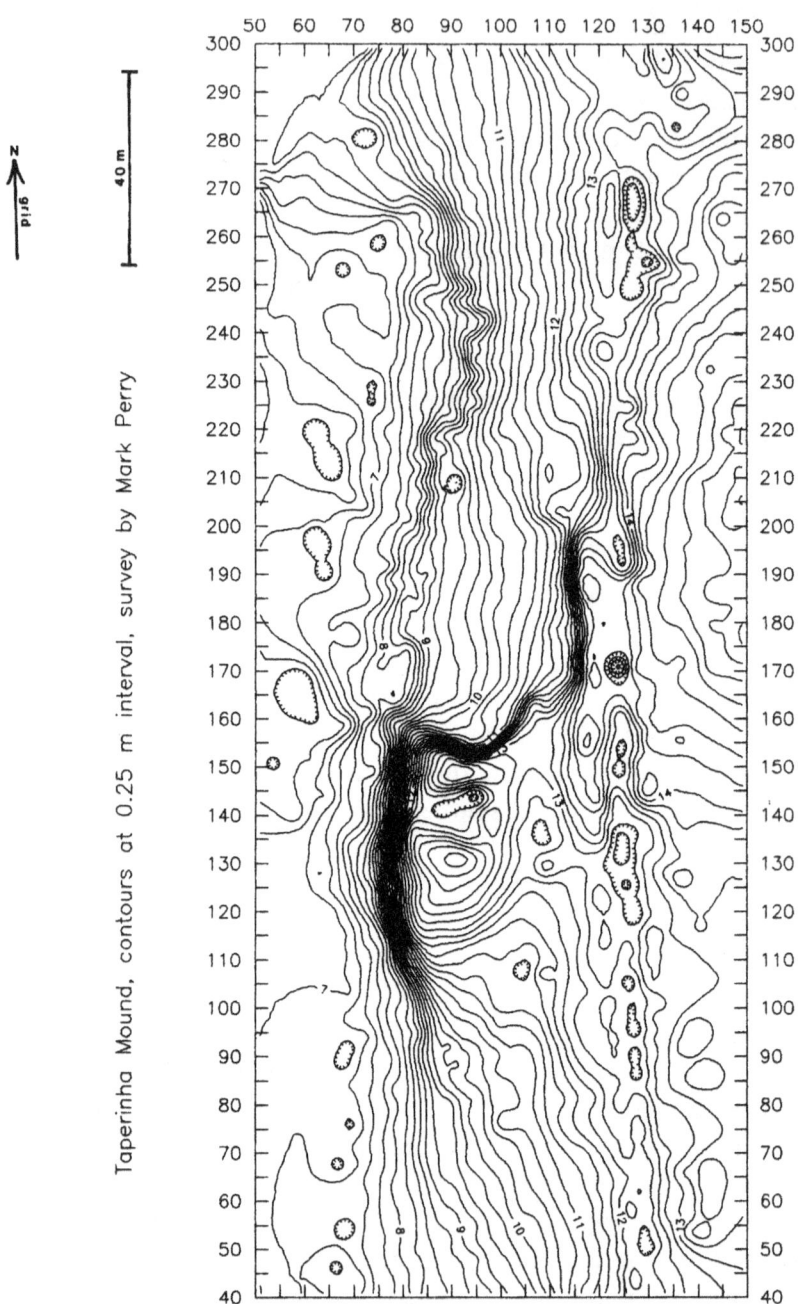

Figure 10.3. Taperinha shell mound and surrounding site area. (The long linear feature in the figure is a late nineteenth-century aqueduct, and the carved out area in the shell mound is a bulldozer pit from Ludwig Jari Plantation's lime mining at the site.)

mound is still more than six meters tall and left a chemical signature of over five hectares in area. Within the mound, geophysical surveys reveal enigmatic features several meters across that have not yet been excavated. The mound projects high above a wide, flattish sandy area containing remains of structures and ceremonies. These sandy deposits are much thinner than the mound layers, less than 60 centimeters thick instead of more than six meters thick. There, special food animals such as turtles were prepared and eaten, ornaments were made or used, a burial was placed, and posts were erected.

Taperinha and other Amazonian shell mound sites look like the remains of relatively long-term villages, to judge from their size, layout, stratigraphy, and dating. Taperinha shell mound was occupied at least between 7100 and 5700 BP, and people of other cultures lived on and around the mound until the arrival of Europeans. The use of the Archaic pottery is consistent with (although not proof of) a relatively sedentary settlement pattern during the early occupation. Heavy and breakable ceramic pots are more commonly used in larger, more permanent communities in Amazonia today. Modern groups that move camp every few weeks prefer less breakable containers, such as baskets, gourds, plastic, or aluminum kettles (e.g., Politis 1996). Amazonian shell mound pottery often was used for cooking and bears abundant carbon powder on the outside. But pot diameters were small, either due to technical limitations or to the small size of eating groups.

The ecological orientation was to rivers, coasts, estuaries, and swamps. This particular Amazonian culture has not yet been found away from those biomes. Its resource base clearly was aquatic fauna, freshwater or brackish for the most part: primarily fish, supplemented heavily with different shellfish and turtles. Rare other fauna such as crocodilians and amphibians also have been found in the sites. Plant remains are much rarer, in contrast to their great abundance in Paleoindian sites and in later prehistoric sites. There must have been some cultigens by the time of the Pottery Archaic since there were some even in Paleoindian times, but comparatively few plant remains or even plant organic matter are preserved in the shell mound deposits. Pollen cores from sampling sites near mounds do not have pollen that is identified as from cultivated plants, though there are general indicators of human disturbance of vegetation.

In choosing aquatic fauna as a staple, the Pottery Archaic villagers focused on abundant local resources whose exploitation could be intensified any time of the year (Roosevelt 1999e, 2000a). Fish are very abundant in Amazon water bodies even under modern exploitation, but abundance and distribution change seasonally. Shellfish also are abundant, are available year-round, and are densely distributed locally. Some mollusks grow relatively large—as large as a woman's hand. Because of their abundance and their appreciable mineral, protein, and carbohydrate content, they are a good food for large, sedentary, nonagricultural groups. Among ethnographically known foragers (Roosevelt 1999a), women in particular specialize in shellfishing when it is important in the food supply. In the Formative period, when cultivated plants apparently become staple carbohydrate sources, shellfishing drops off markedly, presumably because cultivated plants have taken over the function that shellfish had in the diet. In contrast, fish remain important throughout prehistory, although after the Archaic they seem to become a supplement to plant food rather than a staple food. No modern Amazonian Indians use shellfish and fish for staple foods; all use plant foods of some kind for the majority of their calories.

Art, in the form of incised patterning or colored washes on pottery and the figurative shaping of bone and shell ornaments, is known from shell mound sites, but not apparently monumental art. Given the difficulty of preservation, however, one cannot exclude the possibility that there were large artworks made of straw, mud, and wood, such as have been discovered at some Archaic sites in the Andes region (Burger and Salazar-Burger 1985; Grieder et al. 1988). If gender roles in crafts in Amazonia have any continuity, then women made the pottery. Pottery decoration in the Amazon Archaic cultures is very rare, so motifs really cannot be usefully analyzed. However, some sherds from the Lower Amazon bear incised geometric motifs on rims and shoulders that continue in different forms in the zoomorphic art of the following Formative period and later on. Although pottery is varied in shape and treatment among the Archaic cultures, the manufacturing method—joining patches of clay together—seems to be shared throughout the pottery-making regions at the time (Roosevelt 1995). Why pottery-making is characteristic of Amazonian shell mounds and not of southern Brazilian early shell mounds is a mystery. But early Amazonian pottery seems linked somehow to the intensification of aquatic resources there, for Archaic broad-spectrum foraging people in the interfluvial terra firme of Amazonia did not make pottery. Pottery-making does not appear there until the Formative period, which is generally assumed to have a horticultural economy. Perhaps large sedentary settlements were difficult to maintain in the interfluves before staple horticulture.

Be that as it may, the configuration of some Amazonian shell mounds as massive integral constructions of secondary refuse within sites may reflect a sociotechnic function for the mounds rather a purely sanitary disposal function. The evidence for nondomestic activities—burials, jewelry, special as well as domestic foods, and largish structural features—are consistent with a community ceremonial function for at least some mounds. It seems possible that people raised up the large shell mounds in the middle of their settlements to use as platforms for special activities or structures, in contrast to modern Amazonian villages, where garbage middens are usually placed behind house groups, not in the central open area, which is kept relatively clear of refuse for meetings and ceremonies (Siegel and Roe 1986). But much more detailed work at sites is needed before we can really define their layouts and compare them to settlements at other times and places.

There is as yet no way to reconstruct Archaic social organization, given that we have so little evidence of site plans, structures, activity areas, and patterns of ceremonialism, but so far there is little evidence that social classes and ruling hierarchies existed. However, fishing and shellfishing cultures in other parts of the world, such as in California, on the Northwest Coast, and in Japan, did develop major art styles and elaborate ranking systems, ritual and political specialists, and important community and regional ceremonial cults. Their considerable cultural elaboration is only apparent when their perishable cultural remains are preserved in wet sites. Wide-area excavations at Amazonian sites are needed to uncover the patterning of structures, craftwork, food preparation, feasting, and funerary activities. Wet sites could be studied to search for wet-preserved perishable food remains, tools, art, and architecture that have been found beside early shell mounds in other regions (Sassaman and Randall this volume). More skeletal remains need to be excavated and analyzed. Bones sometimes are not well preserved, but teeth always are, and they allow very useful observations about health status during the lifetime. The scant but intriguing evidence and the host of unanswered questions are an incentive to more intensive site investigations in the future.

Formative Stage Mounds

The roots of the late prehistoric florescence of earth mound building in Amazonia lie in the Formative occupation, during the last 2,000 years or so before the Christian era, between about 4,000 to 2,000 years ago (uncalibrated). The term Formative originally was coined to refer to the first sedentary agricultural villages in Latin America; these were considered to be the necessary developmental precursor for the Pre-Hispanic urban civilizations. In Amazonia, however, most known sites of the Formative period appear to have been communities with mixed horticultural—not agricultural—economies. That is, although crops may have become important foods, fish and other foraged foods and possibly small game were important supplements. Shellfish is a much less common food in the Formative, perhaps because it was replaced as a carbohydrate source by crops. Such a subsistence pattern is still typical of indigenous Amazonians today.

Furthermore, as in other parts of Latin America, some Amazonian Formative societies were not simple independent village societies but were complex societies with elaborate ceremonial activities and sometimes links to supraregional cultural horizons. These societies were originally assumed to represent expansionist state societies (Roosevelt 1993, 1999c, 1999d, 2000a). The Formative in Amazonia was not, however, a uniform cultural horizon, and the cultural horizons have sloping distributions through time and space. The cultures in different areas differed a lot from each other in settlement pattern, subsistence, art, architecture, and crafts. It seems that this was a time of great experimentation in all areas of culture.

In terms of subsistence, it seems that many cultigens used as staples later on must have been cultivated by the Formative, but we do not yet have much specific evidence for them. Manioc presumably was cultivated by this time, but it has been more difficult to identify archaeologically to species. The bone chemistries of most Formative phase skeletons are consistent with manioc but are not specific to manioc. Unhelpfully, most South American cultigens other than maize share the same general stable carbon isotope pattern as manioc. We know that maize already was being cultivated in parts of Amazonia, but it does not seem to have reached the level of a staple.

Formative period lake cores in Ecuador contain evidence of maize, which some think indicates that it was the staple food there (Piperno and Pearsall 1998). The evidence for Formative maize there is the appreciable maize pollen and phytoliths retrieved from cores cut into the bottom of Lake Ayauchi (ibid.). The dates from the core levels with abundant maize microfossils fall about 3000 BP, but it is not known whether maize was a staple crop or simply one of several crops in the region. No skeletons there have been tested for stable isotope ratios, a necessary process for evaluating whether maize was a staple or not (Roosevelt 2000b; van der Merwe, Vogel, and Roosevelt 1981). Also, the role of faunal foods and collected plants is unknown for the region. In other regions, stable isotopes offer some evidence of the quantitative roles of some foods and the status of vegetation (Roosevelt 2000b).

In the Peruvian Amazon nearby, Formative human skeletons do not yet show the stable isotope pattern of staple maize consumption seen in late prehistoric skeletons there (Roosevelt 1989, 2000b). Instead, the Formative human bones show stable nitrogen and carbon isotope chemistry consistent with a reliance on foods such as manioc, fish, and game, but not maize (Roosevelt 1997). A manioc-like pattern is also found in Formative human bones from a cave site at Monte Alegre (Roosevelt 2000a). In the Orinoco, just north of the Amazon, maize does not become a staple food much before about AD 1000 during the Arauquinoid phase, according to human bone chemistry, although carbonized maize has been dated to the Late Formative at the beginning of the Common Era (Roosevelt 1997). Before then, the bone chemistry pattern is the generalized manioc pattern. Similarly, in the raised fields in the Guianas associated with mound sites, maize evidence (phytoliths) is confined to the Arauquinoid occupation (Iriarte et al. 2010). So presence of a crop is not the same thing as its use as a staple, and the bone chemistries so far show that maize was not yet a staple in the lowlands in Formative times.

Despite the evidence for cultivation, then, Formative period forests around the sites that have been studied seem quite intact, in contrast to the pattern of some large, late sites. Forest-stable carbon isotopes at sites in the Peruvian Amazon and at Santarem, Brazil, show a pattern of a very dense closed canopy forest, not one of wide-open fields (Roosevelt 1989; Roosevelt 2000b). Over all, instead of intensive agriculture, then, Formative subsistence patterns seem to resemble those of modern indigenous Amazonians, who rely on a variety of staples cultivated in comparatively small temporary forest clearings, heavily supplemented with fish, game, and gathered foods (Roosevelt 1994).

The use of plant staples may be the reason why deposits at Formative sites tend to be rich in carbonized plant remains, in contrast to some Archaic sites, where shell and fishbone predominate. Fish, though, remained an important protein supplement; fish bones continue to be common in Formative sites. Shellfish are often present but not as abundant as at Archaic sites. In the Formative levels of Santarem, for example, most bones are fish bones. There are also bones of land game in those levels, but they tend to be from small species, such as agouti. Even such small mammal bones are rare in large late prehistoric floodplain sites such as Santarem, though they are common in Santarem phase hamlets or camps dispersed in the interior, where the forest appears to have remained quite intact even then (Roosevelt 2000a). But in the Peruvian Amazon, in sites on smaller rivers, such as the Ucayali and its tributaries, bone assemblages still include a diversity of large and small game (Roosevelt 1989).

Long-distance cultural interaction in the form of supra-regional horizon styles is a strong pattern in Amazonia in the Formative, but its associations with mound building are not close. Some cultures taking part in horizon styles do not have mounds that we know of, and the most elaborate Formative mound complex known—in Ecuador—is not clearly linked to a horizon style. Some regions of Amazonia are more linked together stylistically in the Formative than they were in the Archaic, but other regions continue to have independent pottery styles. For example, although the Zoned Incised Hachure Horizon is found in much of the mainstream Amazon, Ananatuba, an eastern style of the horizon on Marajo island, is found in only a few artificial mounds, and a related Formative hachure style at Ponta do Jauari on the north bank of the Lower Amazon apparently lacks earth mounds. Much of this horizon's pottery art has geometricized biomorphic motifs that are hard to interpret when fragmented on sherds. However, some of the human and animal images and artifacts recognizable in middle Amazon styles of the horizon depict spirit animals, smoking pipes, and stamps, elements which may relate to shamanistic concepts (Figure 10.4). Animal images, smoking, and painting are closely related to the practice of shamanism in existing Amazonian indigenous cultures.

In other ways, the Amazonian Formative contrasts with the original concept. Settlement patterns were highly diverse. Most Amazonian Formative sites represent small, simple, dispersed villages—hamlets, as expected, but many were large and some had mounds. At least one site, in the Ecuadorian Amazon, was a huge site with a nucleated complex of mounds. Both at the mouth of the Amazon and in the Bolivian Amazon, radiocarbon dates on pottery from deep excavations show that Formative people built mounds almost 3,000 years ago, and some of those sites seem to have had more or less continuous occupation from the Formative until today. That continuing pattern of mound building along with the Formative stylistic features retained in later pottery horizons, such as the Polychrome Horizon, and the Incised and Punctate Horizon, indicates a very stable, long-term pattern of mound-building cultures in Amazonia. But we know very little about most Formative mounds, except that they existed and were made of earth. Because they often lie under later mounds, even less investigation of site plans has been done for these mounds than for the Archaic shell mounds.

One example of a Formative mound of the Zoned Incised Hachure Horizon is the Castanheira site on eastern Marajo Island at the mouth of the

Figure 10.4. Formative pottery artifacts of the Zoned Hachure Horizon, Ponta do Jauari, near Alenquer, Brazil. Left, smoking pipe. Right, stamp. (Source: De la Penha 1985, 121.)

Amazon, a freestanding Ananatuba phase mound that is just under 100 meters diameter, about 3,000 meters in area, and almost two meters tall (Figure 10.5) (Simoes 1969). It appears to be a nearly round conical platform for a small settlement and lacks any figurative sculpturing. The mound is connected to the small river by a narrow channel of water and is surrounded by a wider channel of water, apparently created by the excavation of earth to build the mound. Such mounds on Marajo, where there is extensive seasonal flooding, have been interpreted as platforms to maintain settlements above flood levels. As such, they indicate a permanent settlement pattern at the time, a conclusion also supported by the presence of superimposed occupation levels atop them.

The excavations started about a meter and a half below the top of the mound down and extended down 70 centimeters. Like later Marajoara platform earth mounds for settlements, the Formative levels of this site have abundant pottery and fragments of adobe-built cooking facilities. Almost 90 percent of the pottery recovered was of the Ananatuba phase, the end of which phase the researchers dated with a single assay at 2930 BP. Ananatuba pottery resembles the later prehistoric Marajoara pottery in the

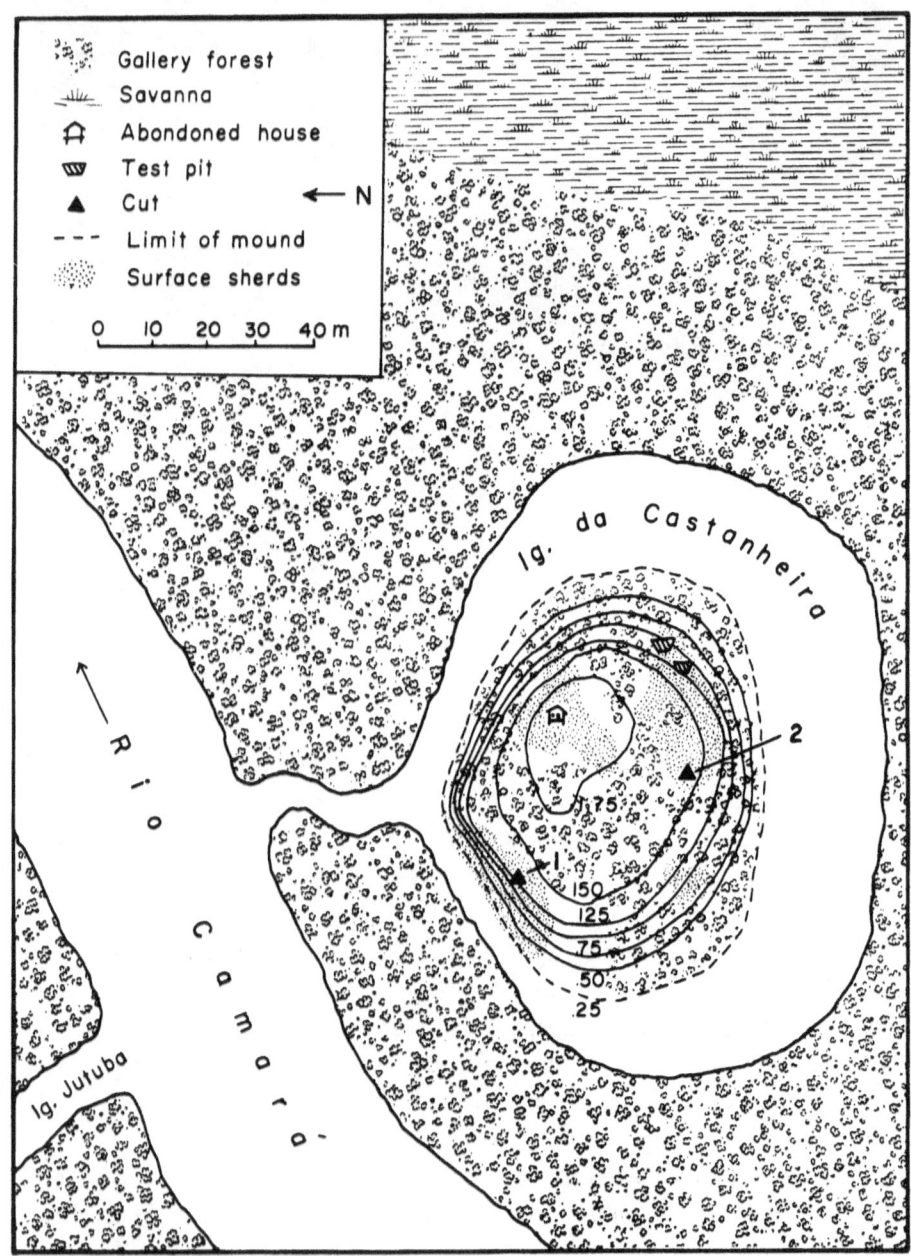

Figure 10.5. Castanheira Site, a Formative earth mound of the Incised-Hachure Horizon, Marajo Island. (Source: Simoes 1969.)

region in having abundant sherd temper, and its primary decorative motif of zoned incision also was carried over into Marajoara. The figurative iconography of Ananatuba culture, though, has not been analyzed, perhaps because the images on the sherds are so fragmented. Ananatuba sherds are commonly found in the vicinity of Marajoara phase mounds, so it seems likely that Ananatuba levels lie undiscovered below later mound-building levels at those sites, none of which have been probed with deep excavations. The cooking facilities at the Castalia site were built of coarse clay that became fired red and hard in the course of use. Such facilities, an important very common feature of the later Marajoara sites, suggest another strong continuity of the Formative culture into later prehistory. Their use by Amazonian Indians and peasants nowadays correlates with permanent settlement patterns. Work at six other Ananatuba sites on Marajo also found nearly circular or oval mounds with occupation layers of dense cultural remains from 60 centimeters to a meter of thickness.

At Santarem in the Lower Amazon, Formative dates in the period from ca. 2200 to 3200 years ago have been found in levels beneath the late prehistoric Santarem phase settlement (Roosevelt 2000a). The associated thin pottery sherds are occasionally decorated with fine parallel-line incision or punctation. The scant finds do not permit firm classification of the style yet, but comparable decoration has turned up in Formative levels of several sites in the adjacent lower Tapajós River area. At Santarem, the sherds are associated with prepared clay floors apparently supported by earth platforms. Food remains include bones of diverse fish and small forest game and carbonized fruits both cultivated and wild. The date's stable isotope ratios are more negative than later samples, and *terra mulata* (light brown soil) rather than black Indian soils is present; both of these facts indicate land use probably involving swiddens, not the wider clearing and more intense burning characteristic of the Santarem phase occupation.

At least one Formative site in the Lower Amazon, Castalia, has been characterized as a shell mound (Hilbert and Hilbert 1959). However, the artifacts, mostly from a mixed surface collection, suggest a multicomponent assemblage, so it may simply be an Archaic shell mound occupied by Formative and later groups, as is the case at Taperinha and many other Brazilian shell mounds (Imazio da Silveira and Schaan 2005).

In the Upper Amazon, Formative-age mounds also have been discovered in several areas: the Bolivian Amazon, the Colombian Amazon, and the Ecuadorian Amazon. In Bolivia, Formative deposits have been found to exist many meters down at the base of later prehistoric earth mounds.

At the Casarabe site (Dougherty and Calandra 1981–1982), Barrancoid pottery decorated with incision, modeling, and painting recovered eight or nine meters down was dated to the early first millennium before Christ. With so little area of the Formative deposits excavated, however, the culture remains basically undocumented. It does show, though, that earth mound building there began in the Formative. We cannot yet tell whether these early mound levels, like their later levels, were built to support settlements above the floodwaters, because the local history of river levels is not known.

The Ecuadorian Amazon seems to have the most elaborate development of mound building known for Amazonian societies of any period. Faldas de Sangay, a large mound center on the Huapula River, has been described, sketch mapped, partly surveyed, and extensively photographed (Porras 1987; Rostain 1991; Salazar 1998). It is the largest and most complex multi-mound site of any age yet found in the Amazon. It shows a pattern of nucleated settlement and ceremonialism involving mounds as well as complex residential mounds and terraces. It is characterized by large numbers of diversely shaped and constructed mounds disposed over an area of several square kilometers, indicating a high rate of building and population aggregation at the time. A possible problem with the evidence for such sites, however, is verifying the date of the many structures mapped and sampled. Most mounds have not yet been dated, though the dates run so far fall in the Formative between 3000 and 2000 BP.

The overall organization of the site is a highly nucleated pattern. There is a grouping of larger, more diverse mounds along the small river, surrounded by a wide area with numerous rectilinear mounds (Figure 10.6). Among the larger mounds, some may be shaped in human or animal form (Porras 1987; Rostain does not agree with Porras); these include a seated male-female pair and a feline. Male and female seated images, which also occur later as pottery effigy urns in several later Amazonian styles around Santarem in the Lower Amazon, have been interpreted as depictions of dead and possibly deified ancestors (Roosevelt 1991). The numerous rectangular mounds at Sangay seem to have been platforms for smaller earthworks and perishable structures. Postholes and bands of geometric patterns in different earth colors have been uncovered during excavations.

The material culture from the mounds at Faldas de Sangay is very diverse and elaborate (Figure 10.7). There is diverse pottery with geometric, zoomorphic, and anthropomorphic decoration in incision, painting, and modeling as well as human figurines. In addition, there are large and small stone carvings of monkeys, other animals, and many tools of ground stone.

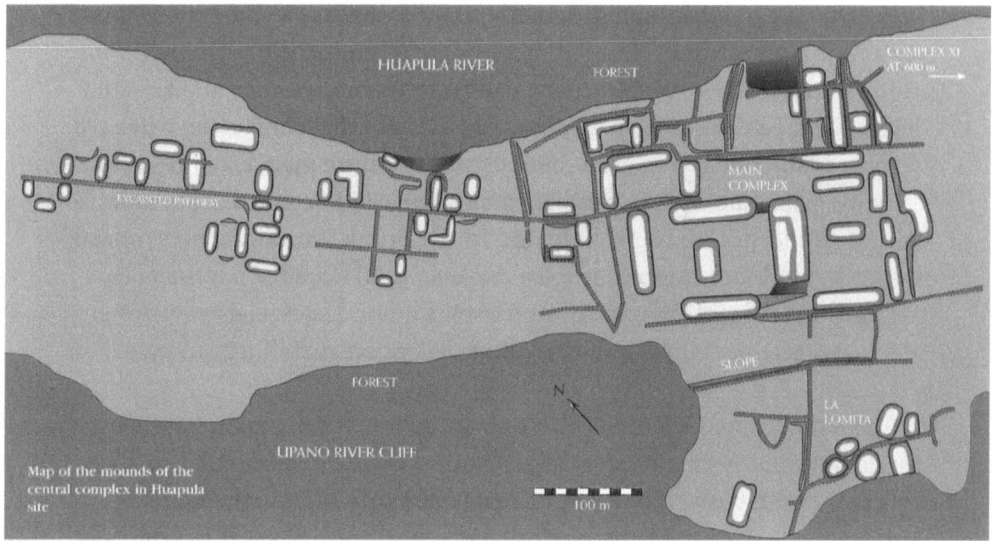

Figure 10.6. Faldas de Sangay mound site, Ecuadorian Amazon (Porras 1987). Although the map is not a fully controlled theodolite topographic map, it nonetheless correctly shows the large size of the mound group and the distinct nucleus of formally arranged decorated mounds.

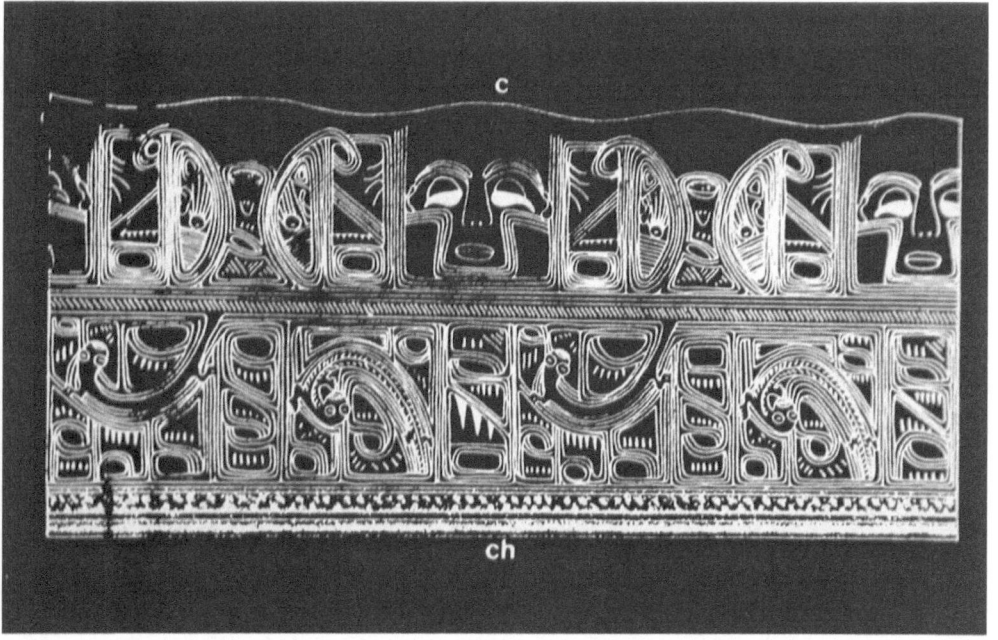

Figure 10.7. Incised and modeled jar, "Faldas de Sangay." The decoration focuses on a central human face with closed eyes and zoned geometric patterns combined with modeled lizards. (Source: Porras 1987.)

The clustering of larger and differently shaped mounds at the center of the site and the presence of midden material between the mounds makes the site look rather like one of the urbanized administrative central places that theorists expected early state societies to have. But that conclusion will have to await evaluation of the settlement plan with future map, excavation, and chronological data. If it is confirmed as primarily Formative, this mound culture would not be unprecedented in the South American neotropical lowlands. Northern lowland tropical forest coastal Ecuador has the Formative La Tolita culture, famous for its complex mound sites, elaborate pottery styles, and accomplished and innovative decorative metallurgy in gold and platinum.

The Ecuadorian Oriente is also one of the few Amazonian areas where the existence of Formative maize cultivation is well documented, as mentioned above. However, only the presence of maize then in the Ecuadorian Amazon region is established, not that it was a staple then. It has also not been established that it was important in the subsistence of people at Faldas de Sangay.

Based on the Formative evidence for the Amazon region, then, we see several different patterns of mound-building cultures. In a very few terra firme regions, state-like mound-building societies with agricultural economies may perhaps have existed. However, in other Amazonian regions, people seem to have built mounds along floodplains while subsisting on horticulture and practicing significant foraging, an economy less intensive than expected for states, according to twentieth-century theory. How these latter societies may have been organized is not documented for most areas yet, since neither regional settlement patterns nor within-site patterns have been recorded.

Summary

It seems apparent from this evidence that quite a few early Amazonian societies built and maintained very large structures. Several also created elaborate, large-scale art, but these societies varied greatly in time and space and in their characteristics. Along the lower Amazon floodplains, Paleoindians created monumental rock paintings but lived in transitory or seasonal camps for foraging. Pottery Archaic fishing villagers in the lower Amazon and mouth of the Amazon built up large mounds of shell-rich garbage in relatively permanent habitation sites that included feasting and burial areas either in or around these shell mounds. Formative period people built the first monumental earthworks that we know of in the region, and most of these seem to have supported habitations with some ceremonial features. Floodplain regions seem to have had more Formative sites with earthworks, but the largest, most complex earth mound site—Faldas de Sangay—is in the terra firme. This site, unlike the others, has what appear to be ceremonial mound complexes and possibly figurative mounds in a nucleated core at the center of fields of house mounds. Although subsistence at most Formative sites seems to have been mixed horticulture and foraging, it is possible that this large terra firme mound complex was supported by intensive maize subsistence, although this has not been confirmed.

Where known, habitats and subsistence patterns of the early mound-building societies appear to have been extraordinarily diverse. Patterns include broad-spectrum foraging, intensive aquatic foraging, horticulture supplemented with aquatic foraging, and, in a few cases, staple manioc or maize agriculture supplemented with other cultigens and collected foods, such as tree fruit and fish. In contrast to findings in more arid areas of Latin America, no known cultures in Amazonia relied exclusively on agriculture, and few even relied primarily on agriculture for macronutrients and raw materials. All relied in one way or another on foraged resources, such as fish, shellfish, turtles, fruits, and nuts, and of these, fish was by far the main resource.

But the great expansion of earth mound building in Amazonia took place in later prehistory, in the first thousand years of the Common Era during a proliferation of urn burial cemeteries with polychrome and/or plastic decorated pottery and statuary. Most of the earth mounds of this era at the mouth of the Amazon were large ones for entire villages. At the mouth of the Rio Negro there are villages with a circle of small house mounds placed on a circular platform. All these mound cultures appear to have subsisted on mixed horticulture and foraging. Some regional mound-building cultures—in the Bolivian Amazon and along the floodplains of the Guianas coasts—built mounded field systems and causeways that connected large habitation mounds (Erickson 1980; Nordenskiöld 1913). Those in the Guianas, which date to the last 500 years of prehistory, may have relied on maize cultivated in the raised fields (Iriarte et al. 2010). In that last period before the conquest, the Santarem culture, known for large sculptures of chief-shamans and elites, has large sites with neighborhoods of rows of smallish house mounds and large low ceremonial platforms. Another regional culture in the terra firme and floodplains of Acre and adjacent areas built large geometric earth mounds apparently without significant site populations, and another regional culture in the Upper Xingu had constructions that appear to have been limited to ditches, berms, and causeways (Heckenberger, Peterson, and Neves 1999). The specific subsistence of these last three cultures has yet to be determined.

Like ancient states in other parts of the world, some of these cultures became part of wide interregional cultural horizons marked by dramatic and large-scale fine art and long-distance exchange of valuables. Even the early prehistoric rock painters were part of a supraregional horizon of styles: the Eastern South American rock art sphere.

Mounds and art served several different purposes, where a purpose can be discerned. Rock painting is found both near and away from habitations, and its imagery seems definitely linked to astronomy, to some everyday activities, and perhaps also to mythology and animism. Many earth mounds were platforms for houses and even for whole villages. Only in a few societies do mounds seem to have been reserved for elite residences or ritual buildings. But the newly discovered type of geometric earthworks might have had primarily ceremonial uses. They seem to be separate from habitations. In a few regions, mounds served to create causeways or raised ceremonial roads between residential mounds, and in at least two floodplain regions, mounds were used to elevate and drain planting surfaces and/or create fishponds and waterways over large areas.

However, none of these cultures exhibit what could as yet be interpreted as state-like political organization and control, though several may have had high priest–chiefs and/or social ranking or differentiation between commoners and elites. Most do not seem to have had buildings that could have served as palaces, administrative buildings, or temples. Ritual and meeting facilities are usually part of habitation sites and seem limited to areas with feasting remains, special craft production, ritual caches, and sometimes funerary features.

These patterns beg to be interpreted theoretically, but interpretations remain highly preliminary because of a general lack of systematic relevant data to evaluate them.

Conclusions

The first problem for drawing conclusions about prehistoric Amazonian mounds is that most mound-building cultures probably have not yet been discovered because archaeologists have systematically examined only a small fraction of the land surface in Amazonia. Each decade of research brings the discovery or definition of new cultures, by accident or because development has exposed the monuments. The succession of finds of terra firme mound cultures—first in the Ecuadorian Oriente, then in upper Xingu, and most recently in Acre—suggests that surveys elsewhere in the Amazonian interfluves will likely uncover other cultures. If the unknown cultures are anywhere as diverse as the known ones, then their characteristics will probably differ from the known ones in ways that will require new interpretive schemes and revised explanations.

But even the small fraction of mound cultures that have been discovered and defined already tell us interesting and counterintuitive things about the evolution of human cultures in Amazonia. What insights for a general theory of early monumentality are possible? Keeping in mind that certain evidence still is lacking, we can say that the interaction of different factors in Amazonian mound-building societies does not follow the patterns expected by twentieth-century theorists.

In both floodplain and terra firme habitats, early Amazonian societies built mound complexes of significant magnitude, ceremonial facilities, large artworks, and/or regional field systems as well as domestic structures and facilities. Sometimes they joined supraregional style networks and made long-distance exchanges of valuables. Concepts of ranking, chiefship, and shamanism appear in the arts and crafts of several of the societies, but administrative buildings or obvious palaces or images that could be kings have not been found. The arts and crafts suggest the possibility of wealth and tribute or formalized gift-giving, trading, and exchange. But there are no known storehouses and no evidence that food was transported over long distances. In only a few of these societies could intensive agriculture have been the sole means of support. Most relied on quite a diversity of economies: some on intensive foraging and some on horticulture and foraging.

Amazonia adds to the growing evidence that societies not organized as states or even as chiefdoms in the anthropological sense managed to attain a wide range of cultural achievements that were once considered to be unique to states. In Amazonia, societies created mounds of significant magnitude and formal, monumental art and had organized ritual activities. Some developed considerable social complexity on an intensive foraging economic base, others relied on staple agriculture. Many had large dense populations, but some did not.

Naturally, then, we cannot use such achievements as proxies for evidence of their social and political organization. Instead, we must look for more direct evidence in the patterning of residences, meeting places, administrative and storage structures, ceremonial precincts, and craft and subsistence work areas.

Archaeology in Amazonia and elsewhere gives good reason to think that in organizing for such achievements, "there's more than one way to skin a cat." Evolutionary theories were created by Western scholars when diachronic and regional information about the development of particular societies was very scarce. In addition, much ethnographic organizational behavior and the rationale for such behavior can seem counterintuitive to us from our theoretical perspective as members of modern industrial, postcolonial, or neocolonial states. Accordingly, our interpretation and methodology may need to be refreshed with more knowledge of the diverse emic and etic patterns manifested by a range of nonindustrial societies observed while still in existence.

Acknowledgments

We would like to thank R. L. Burger and R. M. Rosenswig, who organized the 2006 SAA session "Understanding the Origins of Monumentality in Latin America," in which we presented parts of this article. We presented other parts of this article for the 2006 SAA session "New World Shellmounds and Shellmiddens: A Bicoastal Comparison," organized by Maria Dulce Gaspar and Daniel Sandwiess. Thanks to both sets of organizers for inviting us to reconsider this material. Also deserving acknowledgment are the archaeologists, students, and others who helped collect and analyze data from the Lower Amazon Project included in this article. Especially important were the research collaborations of Maura Imazio da Silveira, John Douglas, Bruce Bevan, Linda Brown, Megan Val Baker, Katie Watkins, Ellen Quinn, Mauro Barreto, Christiane Machado, Judith Gama, Lee Newsom, and Anderson Marcio Amaral Lima. The project has received funding from the National Science Foundation, the National Endowment for the Humanities, the National Endowment for the Arts, and the Fulbright Commission and research permits from the National Research Council of Brazil and the National Institute of the Historic and Artistic Patrimony of Brazil, thanks to Maria Teresa de Lima in Belem and Rogerio Dias in Brazilia. Affiliated institutions that have assisted the research logistically include the Museu Paraense Emilio Goeldi, the Federal University of Para, and the Federal University of Campinas, through the efforts of our counterparts, Jose Seixas Lourenco, Guilherme de la Penha, Adelia Oliveira de Rodrigues, Maura Imazio da Silveira, and Denise Schaan.

References Cited

Arnold, Jeanne E. (editor)
1996   *Emergent complexity: The evolution of intermediate societies.* International Monographs in Prehistory, Ann Arbor, Michigan.
Bacus, E. A., and L. Lucero (editors)
1999   *Complex polities in the ancient tropical world.* Archaeological Papers of the American Anthropological Association No. 9. American Anthropological Association, Arlington, Virginia.
Blake, M., B. S. Chisholm, J. E. Clark, B. Voorhies, and M. W. Love
1992   Prehistoric subsistence in the Soconusco region. *Current Anthropology* 33(1):83–94.
Burger, R. L.
1992   *Chavin and the Origins of Andean Civilization.* Thames and Hudson, London.
Burger, R. L., and L. Salazar-Burger
1985   The Early Ceremonial Center of Huaricoto. In *Early Ceremonial Architecture in the Andes,* edited by C. Donnan, pp. 111–139. Dumbarton Oaks, Washington, D.C.
Carneiro, R. L.
1970   A Theory of the Origin of the State. *Science* 169:733–738.
Coe, M. D., and R. A. Diehl
1980   *In the land of the Olmecs.* 2 vols. University of Texas Press, Austin, Texas.
Davis, Christopher
2009   Archaeoastronomy at Monte Alegre, Para: A research problem and research strategy. *Amazonica* 1(2):536–547.
Dougherty, B., and H. A. Calandra
1981–1982 Excavaciones arqueologicas en La Loma Alta de Casarabe, Llanos de Moxos, Departemento del Beni, Bolivia. *Relaciones de La Sociedad Argentina de Antropologia [N.S.]* 14(2):9–48.
Earle, T. K.
1987   Chiefdoms in Archaeological and Ethnohistorical Perspective. *Annual Review of Anthropology* 16:279–308.
Ehrenreich, R., C. Crumley, and J. E. Levy (editors)
1995   *Heterarchy and the Analysis of Complex Societies.* Archaeological Papers of the American Anthropological Association No. 6. American Anthropological Association, Arlington, Virginia.
Erickson, Clark
1980   Sistemas agrícolas prehispánicos en los Llanos de Mojos. *America Indígena* 40(4):731–755.
Evans, C., and B. J. Meggers
1960   Archaeological Investigations in British Guiana. *Bulletin of the Bureau of American Ethnology* 177.

Fried, M. H.
1967   *The Evolution of Political Society: An Essay in Political Anthropology.* Random House, New York.

Gaspar, M. D.
1999   Os ocupantes pre-historicos do litoral Brasileiro. In *Pre-historia da Terra Brasilis*, edited by C. M. Tenorio, pp. 159–170. Universidade Federal Rio de Janeiro, Rio de Janeiro.

Gaspar, M. D., and M. Imazio da Silveira
1999   Os pescadores-coletores-cacadores do litoral norte Brasileiro. In *Pre-historia da Terra Brasilis*, edited by C. M. Tenorio, 247–256. Universidade Federal Rio de Janeiro, Rio de Janeiro.

Gnecco, C., and S. Mora
1997   Late Pleistocene early Holocene tropical forest occupations at San Isidro and Pena Roja, Colombia. *Antiquity* 71:683–690.

Greider, T., A. Bueno, C. E. Smith, and R. Malina
1988   *La Galgada, Peru: A Preceramic Culture in Transition.* University of Texas, Austin.

Hastorf, C. A.
1993   *Agriculture and the Onset of Political Inequality before the Inka.* Cambridge University Press, Cambridge, Massachusetts.

Heckenberger, M. J., J. B. Peterson, and E. G. Neves
1999   Village Size and Permanence in Amazonia: Two Archaeological Examples in Brazil. *Latin American Antiquity* 10(4):353–376.

Higham, C., and R. Thosarat
1998   *Prehistoric Thailand, from First Settlement to Sokhothai.* Thames and Hudson, London.

Hilbert, P. P., and K. Hilbert
1959   Resultados preliminares da pesquisa arqueological nos rios Nhamunda e Trombetas, Baixo Amazonas. *Boletim do Museu Paraense Emilio Goeldi*, n.s. 75.

Imazio da Silveira, M., and D. P. Schaan
2005   Onde a Amazonia encontra o mar: Estudando os sambaquis do Para. *Revista de Arqueologia* 18:67–80.

Iriarte, J., B. Glaser, J. Watling, A. Wainwright, J. Birk, D. Renard, S. Rostain, and D. McKey
2010   Late Holocene Neotropical Agricultural Landscapes: Phytolith and Stable Carbon Isotope Analysis of Raised Fields from French Guiana Savannah. *Journal of Archaeological Science* 37:2984–2994.

Johnson, A. W., and T. Earle
1987   *The Evolution of Human Societies: From Foraging Group to Agrarian State.* Stanford University Press, Stanford, California.

Marquardt, W. H.
1988   Politics and Production among the Calusa of South Florida. In *Hunters and gatherers.* Vol. 1, *History, Evolution, and Social Change,* edited by T. Ingold, D. Riches, and J. Woodburn, pp. 161–188. Berg, Oxford.

Meggers, Betty J.
1954   Environmental Limitation on the Evolution of Culture. *American Anthropologist* 56:801–824.

Michab, M., J. K. Feathers, J.-L. Joron, N. Mercier, M. Selos, H. Valladas, J.-L. Reyss, and A. C. Roosevelt
1998 Luminescence Dates for the Paleoindian Site of Pedra Pintada, Brazil. *Quaternary Geochronology* 17(11):1041–1046.

Nordenskiöld, E.
1913 Urnengraber und mounds im Bolivianischen flachland. *Baessler Archiv* 3:205–255.

Penha, Guilherme de la
1986 *O Museu Paraense Emilio Goeldi*. Banco Safra, Sao Paulo.

Pereira, E.
2003 *Arte Rupestre na Amazonia—Para*. Museu Paraense Emilio Goeldi, Belem; and UNESP, Sao Paulo.

Piperno, D., and D. Pearsall
1998 *The Origins of Agriculture in the Lowland Tropics*. Academic Press, San Diego, California.

Politis, G.
1996 *Nukak*. Instituto Amazonico de Investigaciones Cientificas, Bogota.

Porras, A.
1987 *Investigaciones arqueologicas a las faldas del Sangay, Provincia Morona Santaiago, Tradicion Upano*. Artes Graficas Senal, Impresenal Cia. Ltda., Quito.

Potter, D. R., and E. R. King
1995 A Heterarchical Approach to Lowland Maya Socioeconomies. In *Heterarchy and the Analysis of Complex Societies*, edited by R. Ehrenreich, C. Crumley, and J. E. Levy, pp. 12–32. Archaeological Papers of the American Anthropological Association No. 6. American Anthropological Association, Arlington, Virginia.

Price, T. D., and J. A. Brown (editors)
1985 *Prehistoric Hunter-Gatherers*. Academic Press, Orlando, Florida.

Prous, A.
1991 Fouilles de l'Abri de Boquete, Minas Gerais, Bresil. *Journal de la Societe des Americanistes* 77:77–109.
1999 As premeiras populacoes do estado de Minas Gerais. In *Pre-historia da Terra Brasilis*, edited by C. M. Tenorio, pp. 101–114. Universidade Federal Rio de Janeiro, Rio de Janeiro.

Quilter, J., B. Ojeda, D. Pearsall, J. G. Jones, and E. Wing
1991 Subsistence Economy of El Paraiso, Peru. *Science* 251:277–283.

Roosevelt, A. C.
1980 *Parmana: Prehistoric Maize and Manioc Subsistence along the Amazon and Orinoco*. Academic Press, New York.
1984 Problems Interpreting the Spread of Cultivated Plants in the New World. In *Pre-Columbian Plant Migration*, edited by D. Stone, pp. 1–18. Papers of the Peabody Museum of Archaeology and Ethnology no. 76. Harvard University Press, Cambridge, Massachusetts.
1989 Resource Management in the Amazon Basin before the European Conquest: Beyond Ethnographic Projection. In *Natural Resource Management by Indigenous and Folk Societies in Amazonia*, edited by D. Posey and W. Balee, pp. 30–61. Advances in Economic Botany No. 7. New York Botanical Garden, Bronx, New York.

1991   *Moundbuilders of the Amazon: Geophysical Archaeology on Marajo Island, Brazil.* Academic Press, San Diego.
1993   The Rise and Fall of the Amazon Chiefdoms. *L'Homme* 33(126–128) 255–184. Special Issue. *Le Remontee de l'Amazone: Anthropologie et Histoire des Societes Amazoniennes,* edited by A.-C. Taylor and P. Descola.
1995   Early Pottery in the Amazon: Twenty Years of Scholarly Obscurity. In *The Emergence of Pottery: Technology and Innovation in Ancient Societies,* edited by W. Barnett and J. Hoopes, pp. 115–131. Smithsonian Institution Press, Washington, D.C.
1997   *The Excavations at Corozal, Venezuela: Stratigraphy and Ceramic Seriation.* Yale University Publications in Anthropology 83. Yale University Press, New Haven, Connecticut.
1998a Ancient and Modern Hunter-Gatherers of Lowland South America: An Evolutionary Problem. In *Advances in Historical Ecology,* edited by W. Balee, pp. 190–212. Columbia University Press, New York.
1998b Paleoindian and Archaic Occupations in the Lower Amazon, Brazil: A Summary and Comparison. In *Festschrift Honoring Wesley Hurt,* edited by Mark Plew, pp. 165–192. University Press of America, Lanham, Maryland.
1999a Archaeology. In *Cambridge University Encyclopedia of Hunter-Gatherers,* edited by R. Lee and R. Daly, pp. 86–92. Cambridge University Press, Cambridge, Massachusetts.
1999b Dating the Rock Art at Monte Alegre, Brazil. In *Dating and the Earliest Rock Art,* edited by M. A. Strecker and Paul Bahn, pp. 35–40. Oxbow Books, Oxford.
1999c The Development of Prehistoric Complex Societies: Amazonia, a Tropical Forest. In *Complex polities in the ancient tropical world,* edited by E. A. Bacus and L. Lucero, pp. 13–34. Archaeological Papers of the American Anthropological Association No. 9. American Anthropological Association, Arlington, Virginia.
1999d The Maritime-Highland-Forest Dynamic and the Origins of Complex Society. In *History of the Native Peoples of the Americas. South America, Part 1,* edited by F. Salomon and S. Schwartz, pp. 264–349. Cambridge University Press, New York.
1999e Twelve Thousand Years of Human-Environment Interaction in the Amazon Floodplain. In *Diversity, Development, and Conservation in Amazonia's Whitewater Floodplains,* edited by C. Padoch, J. M. Ayres, M. Pinedo-Vasquez, and A. Henderson, pp. 371–392. Advances in Economic Botany, Vol. 13. New York Botanical Garden, Bronx, New York.
2000a The Lower Amazon: A Dynamic Human Habitat. In *Imperfect Balance: Landscape Transformations in the Precolumbian Americas,* edited by D. L. Lentz, pp. 455–491. Columbia University Press, New York.
2000b Mound-Building Societies of the Amazon and Orinoco. In *Archaeologia de las Tierras Bajas,* edited by A. Duran Coirolo and Roberto Bracco Boksar. Comision Nacional de Arqueologia, Ministerio de Educacion y Cultura, Montevideo.
2005   Ecology in Human Evolution: Origins of the Species and of Complex Societies. In *A Catalyst for Ideas: Anthropological Archaeology and the Legacy of Douglas Schwartz,* edited by V. Scarborough, pp. 169–208. School of American Research, Santa Fe, New Mexico.
2007   Geophysical Archaeology in the Lower Amazon: A Research Strategy. In *Remote*

Sensing in Archaeology, edited by Farouk El Baz and James R. Wiseman, pp. 435–467. Springer, New York.

Roosevelt, A. C., editor
1994 *Amazonian Indians from Prehistory to the Present: Anthropological Perspectives.* University of Arizona Press, Tucson, Arizona.

Roosevelt, A. C., J. E. Douglas, and L. J. Brown
2002 Migrations and Adaptations of the First Americans: Clovis and Pre-Clovis Viewed from South America. In *The First Americans: The Pleistocene Colonization of the New World,* edited by Nina Jablonski, pp. 159–236. Memoirs of the California Academy of Sciences No. 27. University of California Press and the California Academy of Sciences, Berkeley.

Roosevelt, A. C., R. Housley, I. Imazio da Silveira, S. Maranca, and R. Johnson
1991 Eighth Millennium Pottery from a Prehistoric Shell Midden in the Brazilian Amazon. *Science* 254(5038):1621–1624.

Roosevelt, A. C., M. Lima Costa, C. Lopes Machado, M. Michab, N. Mercier, H. Valladas, J. Feathers, W. Barnett, M. Imazio da Silveira, A. Henderson, J. Sliva, B. Chernoff, D. Reese, J. A. Holman, N. Toth, and K. Schick
1996 Paleoindian Cave Dwellers in the Amazon: The Peopling of the Americas. *Science* 272(5260):373–384.

Rostain, S.
1991 *Les Champs Sureleves Amerindiens de la Guyane.* ORSTOM, Paris.

Salazar, E.
1998 De vuelta a Sangay: Investigaciones arqueologicas en el alto Upano, Amazonia Ecuatoriana. *Bulletin de l'Institut Francais des Etudes Andines* 27:213–240.

Sanders, W. T., and B. J. Price
1968 *Mesoamerica: The Evolution of a Civilization.* Random House, New York.

Schildkraut, E., and C. Keim (editors)
1990 *African Reflections: Art from Northeastern Zaire.* American Museum of Natural History, New York; and University of Washington Press, Seattle.

Service, E. R.
1975 *Origins of the State and Civilization: The Process of Cultural Evolution.* Random House, New York.

Siegel, P., and P. Roe
1986 Shipibo Archaeo-Ethnology: Site Formation Processes and Archaeological Interpretation. *World Archaeology* 18(1):96–115.

Simoes, M. F.
1969 The Castanheira Site: New Evidence on the Antiquity and History of the Ananatuba Phase (Marajo Island, Brazil). *American Antiquity* 34(4):402–410.
1981 Coletores-pescadores-ceramistas do litoral do Salgado (para). *Boletim do Museu Paraense Emilio Goeldi* (n.s.) 78:1–26.

Stein, G.
2005 "Invisible" Social Sectors in Early Mesopotamian State Societies. In *A Catalyst for Ideas: Anthropological Archaeology and the Legacy of Douglas Schwartz,* edited by V. Scarborough, pp. 121–148. School of American Research, Santa Fe, New Mexico.

van der Merwe, A., C. Roosevelt, and J. C. Vogel
1981   Isotopic Evidence for Prehistoric Subsistence Change at Parmana, Venezuela. *Nature* 292(5823):536–538.

Walker, J. H.
2004   *Agricultural Change in the Bolivian Amazon. Ambio Agricola en la Amazonia Boliviana.* University of Pittsburgh Memoirs in Latin American Archaeology No. 13. Department of Anthropology, University of Pittsburgh, Pittsburgh, Pennsylvania; and Fundacion Kenneth Lee, Trinidad, Bolivia.

Williams, Denis
1981   Excavation of the Barambina Shell Mound Northwest District: An Interim Report. *Archaeology and Anthropology* 4:13–38.
1982   Some Subsistence Implications of Holocene Climate Change in Northwestern Guyana. *Archaeology and Anthropology* 5:83–93.

11

Why Do People Build Monuments?

Late Archaic Platform Mounds in the Norte Chico

JONATHAN HAAS AND WINIFRED CREAMER

This chapter diverges from others in this volume by proposing that all monumental architecture requires leadership and centralized decision making. The construction of monumental architecture is relatively rare in a global and historical context. The vast majority of people over the past 200,000 years of human history did not build monuments on any scale. True monumental architecture first appears around 5,000–6,000 years ago, and it appears only in a tiny minority of the world's cultures. It then becomes a reasonable and anthropologically interesting question to ask why people build monuments at all and why they were not built earlier in human history. The answer, we would argue, is always the same: People build monuments because someone tells them to. Although this may seem an overtly simplistic response, it places focus on critical issues in trying to understand why monumental architecture appears only at certain times comparatively very late in human history and in only a small number of places. This breaks into two questions of agency: Why do some people (societal leaders) have other people (their followers) put their energy into constructing monuments? Further, why do those followers go along with the requests or demands of their leaders? The motivations of people who direct the constructions are quite distinct from the motivations of the people who actually do the construction. Both sides of this equation need to be addressed to understand why people build monuments.

If we look at the construction of monumental architecture from a broad evolutionary perspective, it marks a major transformation in the structure of social relations. It is generally although not always connected to and/or correlated with a number of other significant changes in human history,

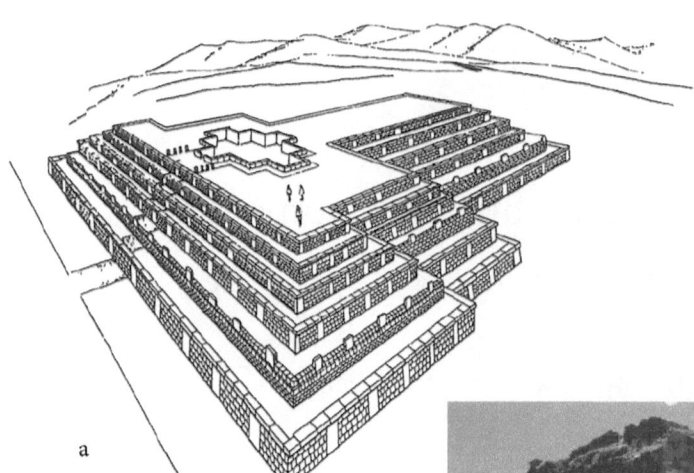

Figure 11.1. Examples of Andean monumental architecture: a. Kuntur Wasi, Cajamarca; b. Chavín de Huantar, Huari; c. Huaca del Sol, Moche; d. Huaca Pucllana, Lima; e. Sacsaywaman, Cuzco; f. Huaca Grande, Lambayeque.

e

f

including the subsistence transition from hunting and gathering to agriculture, emergence of centralized religion, political centralization and social hierarchies. Monument construction is also not something that develops gradually over long periods of time, starting out small and building up to larger and larger structures over the centuries or millennia. In Egypt, for example the first pyramid at Saqqara was built at around 2600 BC and measured 120 × 110 × 60 meters. Although this stepped pyramid was constructed in six phases, its final form was planned from the start. There was no gradual development of monumentality.

In the specific case of South America, monumental platform mounds have been a ubiquitous phenomenon on the Andean landscape for 5,000 years (Figure 11.1). While they are most common on the Pacific coastal plain of present-day Peru, they also occur prominently in the highlands at early sites such as Chavín de Huántar at 1000 BC and late sites such as Tiwanaku at AD 1000. The first appearance of distinctive monumental terraced platform mounds in the Andes is in the Norte Chico region of the

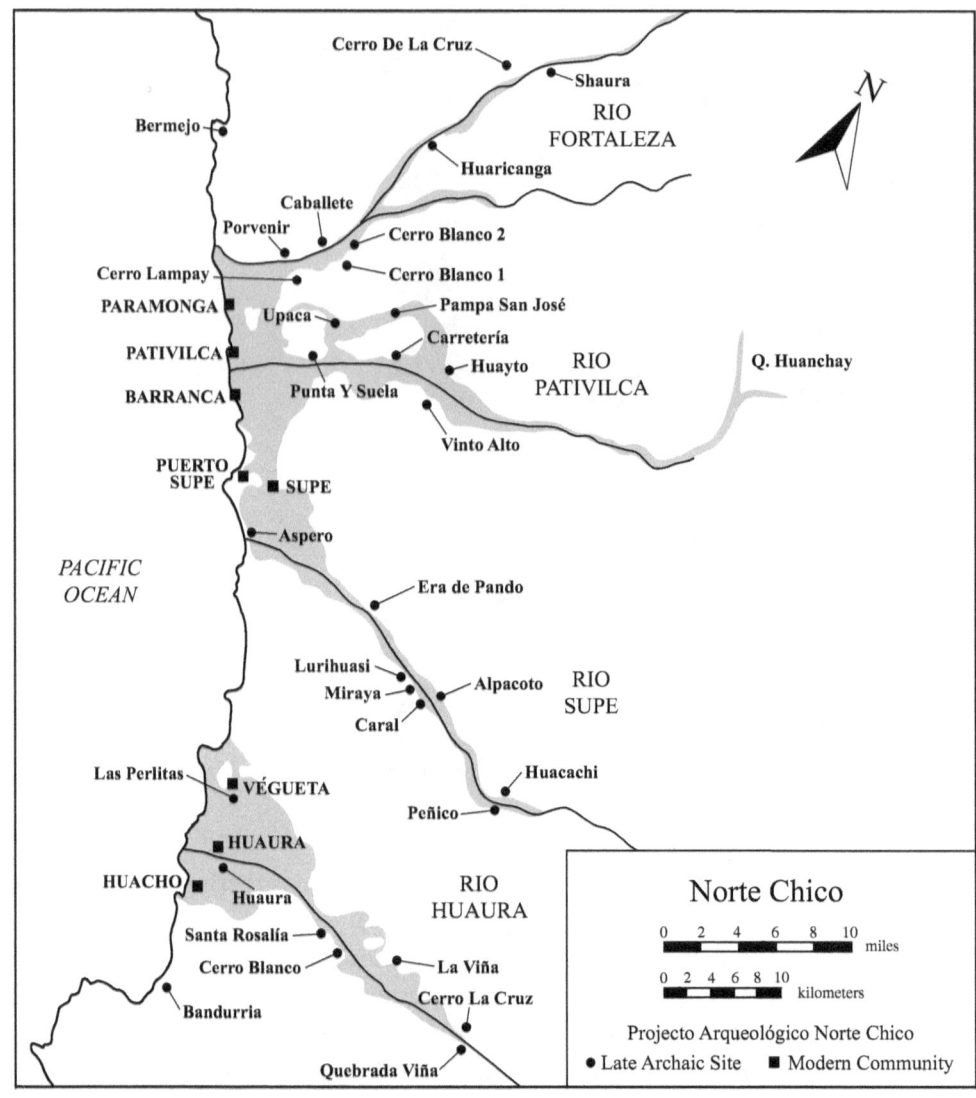

Figure 11.2. Map of Late Archaic sites with monumental architecture in the Norte Chico region.

Peruvian coast at the beginning of the third millennium BC. The Norte Chico consists of four adjoining valleys, Huaura, Supe, Pativilca and Fortaleza, which run south to north, respectively (Figure 11.2). Within this area of approximately 1,800 square kilometers, there are more than 30 sites with monumental architecture dating to the Late Archaic period from 3000 to 1800 BC.

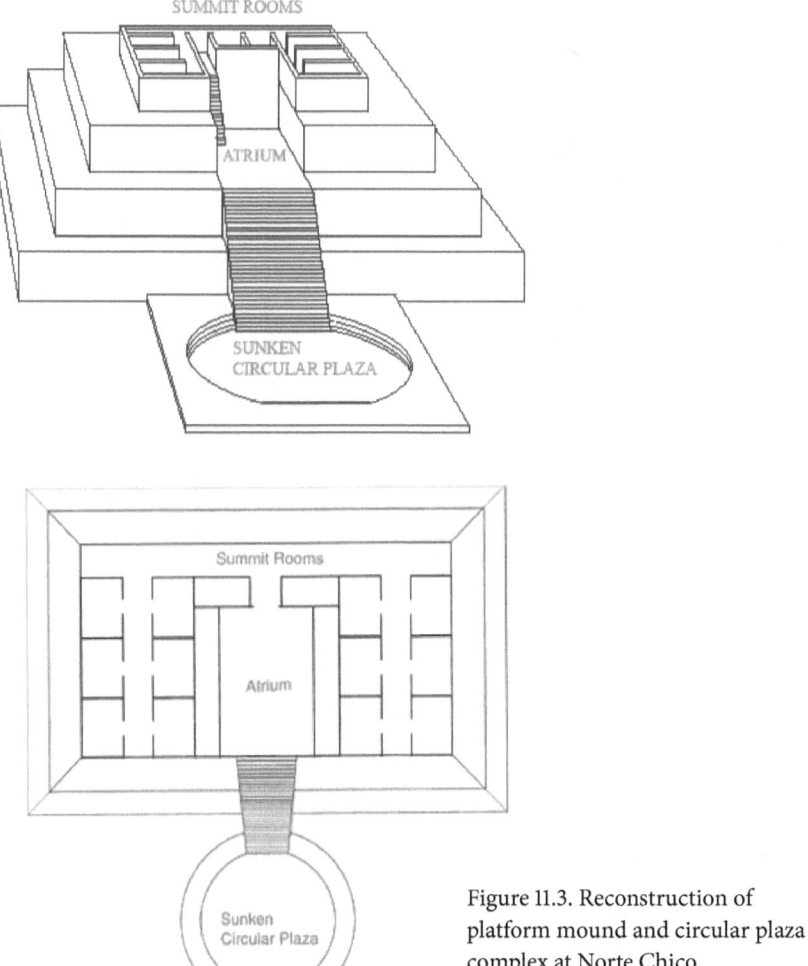

Figure 11.3. Reconstruction of platform mound and circular plaza complex at Norte Chico.

There are two kinds of monumental architecture in the Norte Chico: terraced platform mounds and sunken circular plazas (Figure 11.3). While the circular plazas are almost always associated with a mound, mounds are not always associated with a plaza. Circular plazas show considerable variability, ranging from shallow depressions of only a meter or so up to structures that are almost three meters deep. They range from 15 to 45 meters in diameter. There is also considerable variability both in the size of platform mounds at different sites and the size of mounds at any given site. Some sites, such as Cerro Blanco 2 (Figure 11.4) in the Fortaleza Valley, have only

Figure 11.4. Cerro Blanco 2, Fortaleza Valley.

Figure 11.5. Caballete, Fortaleza Valley.

Figure 11.6. Huaricanga, Fortaleza Valley.

one relatively small platform mound, while others such as Porvenir, Caballete, and Vinto Alto (Figures 11.5 and 11.7) have multiple, distinct large mounds and smaller mounds. Some sites such as Huayto in the Pativilca Valley or Huaricanga in the Fortaleza Valley (Figure 11.6) have large agglutinated masses of monumental construction that cannot be separated into distinct structures based on surface evidence.

The large number of Late Archaic sites in the Norte Chico raises questions with regard to why people build monuments. The pattern of mound building does not have clear precedents in the area or the larger Andean region. Single small platforms of approximately 200 cubic meters were built at Nan Choc in the Zaña Valley in the fifth millennium BC (Dillehay, Netherly, and Rossen 1989) and at Real Alto (approximately 400 cu m) in Ecuador at 3500 BC (Lathrap, Marcos, and Zeidler 1977). However, there are spatial and chronological gaps between these very early examples of small scale

Figure 11.7. Vinto Alto, Pativilca Valley, profile of upper portion of Mound C, showing multiple construction phases.

communal architecture and the much larger and much more numerous monumental structures throughout the Norte Chico. Thus, monuments in the Norte Chico appear to be an endogenous development. The question of why people built these monuments is brought into sharper focus because it cannot be argued that they were imitating an existing exogenous pattern.

Another aspect of the Norte Chico monuments related to the motivation for construction is the sheer number of monuments and number of sites with monuments. With more than 30 sites in an area of only 1200 square kilometers, and each of these sites having from one to seven large-scale constructed mounds, the Norte Chico stands out as an exception in the Americas and the world in general. (Although there are a number of early sites in the Soconusco area with some kind of communal architecture, as described by Rosenswig in this volume; Clark [2004]; and others, a relatively small number of these have monumental architecture greater than 2000–5000 cubic meters.) The Norte Chico monuments also different from the tamped-earth mounds from Mesoamerica discussed by Rosenswig (this volume) and the shell-mound structures in the southeastern United States discussed by Sassaman and Randall (this volume), in that they are constructed of quarried stone or cobbles and are built with carefully faced retaining walls as distinct terraced platforms. While there is a wide range of radiocarbon dates for the Norte Chico mounds, over 150 dates that are currently available indicate considerable chronological overlap among sites and mounds. These radiocarbon data also confirm that mound construction was continuous over a period of at least 1,300 years. The significance of this millennial occupation lies in the transcendence of the political/economic/ ideological organization across many generations. An emergent cultural pattern arose at the beginning of the third millennium BC and continued as a distinct monumental assemblage and centralized organization system that lasted far beyond the lives of any individuals or families.

Coupled with this long period of mound construction are very standardized methods of construction. Although site layout and the details of mound construction varied considerably, there were definite patterns in site plan, construction techniques, and types of structures. Monumental architecture consisted of the platform mound and the sunken circular plaza, both of which were quite standardized from one site and one valley to another. The large majority of sites in all four valleys have a common pattern of a single, centrally located main mound with an associated circular plaza. These main mounds tend to share a rectangular plan of terraced structures. Large mounds all have a central atrium at the top that is accessed by a stairway leading up from the sunken circular plaza. On either side of the atrium are smaller rooms accessed by narrow stairways and hallways. The mounds also all share a common construction technique using a distinctive form of stone-filled fiber bags, known as shicra (Shady Solís 2004; Quilter 1985). Shicra bags are known from such sites as El Paraíso, outside the Norte Chico, and consistently date to the Late Archaic Period. The outside walls of the mounds were built with carefully crafted faced stone and covered with fine beige, yellow, red, or white plaster. The basic form of sunken plazas is also consistent across sites and valleys. Although the plazas vary in diameter and depth, they are characterized by their distinctive circular (as opposed to square or rectangular) form, with a bench around the inside of the surrounding wall and keyhole-shaped staircases leading up toward the main mound and out the other side. There is no evidence the plazas were roofed, and they would have been open for a seated audience around the inner margin of the plaza and a standing audience around the outside. Several sites, including Caballete, Porvenir in the Fortaleza Valley, and Pampa San Jose and Huayto in the Pativilca Valley, were carefully laid out in a U-shaped arrangement with the main mound and associated sunken circular plaza at the closed end of the U. Although the U-shaped arrangement of mounds was not used at all Late Archaic sites in the Norte Chico, the pattern is very widespread throughout Peru in subsequent time periods (Moore 1992, 1996; Donnan 1985).

Both the great longevity and internal consistency of the Norte Chico pattern of monumental construction distinguishes it quite clearly from all other early episodes of monument construction in the Americas. At the remarkable site of Watson Brake in Louisiana, a series of monumental constructions including a main mound and auxiliary mounds and ridges were created (Saunders et al. 2005; Saunders this volume). However, so far this is the only site found in the southeastern United States with this large-scale architecture, and the period of construction lasted at most 350 years, from 3350 to 3000 BC. Similarly, Poverty Point has a single main mound and associated auxiliary mounds and ridges. Although the site was occupied from approximately 1650 to 700 BC, excavation shows that the monumental construction took place only during the last 100 years of occupation and that the main mound itself was apparently built in a single short burst of activity (Gibson 2000; Kidder, Ortmann, and Arco 2008). As with Watson Brake, Poverty Point is a unique construction on the landscape at the time. A somewhat similar pattern of mound construction developed in parts of Mesoamerica in a comparable manner. The only real exception is in the Maya area, where developments were later than elsewhere.

San Jose Mogote in the Oaxaca Valley in Mexico is a well-known example. The site itself was occupied for over a millennium and had public architecture for most of that period. The one monumental platform mound at the site, however, was constructed only during the final period of occupation at the site (Flannery 1976; Blanton et al. 1993; Flannery and Marcus 2005). San Jose Mogote is also different from the Louisiana sites in that it was immediately succeeded by the founding of the much larger site of Monte Alban less than 20 kilometers away. The partially contemporaneous

Olmec in the Mexican state of Veracruz offer yet another pattern of individual sites with distinct monumental architecture. Coe and Diehl (1980) have argued that the Olmec center of San Lorenzo Tenochtitlan, built in the second millennium BC, was a single gigantic monumental construction of up to 3,000,000 cubic meters, possibly in the shape of a bird (on large-scale construction at San Lorenzo, see also Cyphers 2004 and Cyphers and Zurita-Noguera this volume). The later Olmec site of La Venta, in contrast, had a monumental conical pyramid structure and associated auxiliary mounds (Heizer and Drucker 1968; Diehl 1981). At the same time, although the monumental architecture at these two important Olmec centers was very different, both were characterized by highly distinctive Classical Olmec iconography and sculptural art. The sequence of mound construction in the Soconusco area of Mexico (described by Rosenswig in the present volume) and in other parts of Mesoamerica represents a pattern of more gradual, incremental, and widespread development of monumental architecture.

Both the Norte Chico cultural pattern of long-term occupation and monument construction and the intersite and intervalley similarities differ markedly from these other cases of early monumental construction in the Americas. The significance of these differences between the Norte Chico and other areas is threefold: 1) Cultural development in the Late Archaic Norte Chico represents an emergent phenomenon with a long period of endogenous development characterized by extensive interaction between sites. 2) There was extensive interaction between contemporaneous sites within the Norte Chico region, and within this network of communication there were accepted standards for both the form and construction technology of monumental ceremonial architecture. 3) The architectural and associated ceremonial patterns established in the Norte Chico in the third millennium BC served as ancestral prototypes for descendant cultural development in the Andean region to the north and south on the coast and in the adjacent central highlands. At the same time, although some have proposed that the Late Archaic site of Caral in the Supe Valley was somehow the capital of a pan-regional state polity (Shady Solís 2004; Shady and Leiva 2003), there is no evidence that the different valleys or sites were under the control or hegemony of Caral or any other site. There is no rank-ordered site-size hierarchy in the Norte Chico, no evidence of centralized production or storage, and no evidence of distinct or qualitatively larger monuments or other types of ceremonial structures at any of the sites, Caral included.

It is therefore reasonable to infer that within the Norte Chico region, different groups of people were working under the direction of different leaders to build mounds that shared common norms of construction and standards of basic form and layout at multiple sites over a long period of time. Again, this seemingly simple inference means that similar motivations of leaders and followers at multiple sites applied to many discrete social relations over many generations. It also means that mound construction at any given community was taking place within a social context of a wider regional pattern of mound construction. The challenge, then, is to try to figure out why the Norte Chico leaders wanted so many mounds built and why their followers so consistently went along with their directions. Overall, the Norte Chico Late Archaic offers an excellent laboratory for looking at the development of a stable relationship between power-holding elites and their respective respondent populations

In terms of power relations, it is necessary to consider what benefits each leader and/or follower gains from the construction of mounds. A first step is to ask what was happening on the mounds themselves. Here we need to rely on relatively limited excavations at Aspero (Feldman 1980, 1985) and Caral (Shady and Leiva 2003) in the Supe Valley, Cerro Lampay (Vega-Centeno 2005, 2006) in the Fortaleza Valley, and our own work at multiple sites in the Pativilca and Fortaleza valleys (Creamer, Ruiz, and Haas 2007; Haas, Creamer, and Ruiz 2004). Some additional insights can be gained by looking outside the Norte Chico at the Late Archaic site of La Galgada and at physically similar but later Initial Period mound constructions at sites such as Pampa de las Llamas–Moxeke, Sechín Alto (Pozorski and Pozorski 1990, 1992, this volume) in the Casma Valley, Garagay (Ravines and Isbell 1976) in the Rimac Valley, or Cardal and other sites in the Lurín Valley (Burger and Salazar-Burger 1991; Burger and Salazar this volume). In all cases where there is data available on the structures on tops of mounds, it appears that they had ceremonial or economic rather than residential functions. Typical features and material remains associated with residential living, such as hearths, sleeping areas, and everyday trash and residue associated with residence, are absent from these structures. Luxury goods such as food, jewelry, or crafts are also absent. Excavated mounds are largely devoid of artifactual material. The implication of this pattern is that motivation of the leaders was not to have grand palaces built for their personal use.

If the mounds were not being built for personal use by the leaders, then some kind of community function, whether religious or economic or both, can be inferred. So what were the community functions of the Norte Chico platform mounds? A specific answer to this question may never be known, but certain aspects of their communal function can be examined. In almost all cases, the mounds are located next to large open areas where large numbers of people could assemble. The presence of a stairway leading to the atrium and upper surfaces of the mounds points to activities that could be observed by people assembled in the facing open areas at the foot of the mound. On many of the largest mounds, the stairway leads to the sunken circular plaza; such stairways were ideal for public viewing of related activities. At least some of these plazas have benches around the circumference, and none appear to have been protected or screened with roofing or side walls of any kind.

In contrast to the publicly visible plazas, in the mound complexes, stairs and atria are much more inaccessible and closed to public view. Tom Pozorski was one of the first to comment on the decreasing accessibility of rooms and courtyards in the mound complex at the Initial Period site of Caballo Muerto in the Moche Valley (1980). The further one moves from the "front," or public face, of the platform mound, the narrower are the stairs, entries, and passageways. This pattern noted by Pozorski extends back to the Late Archaic constructions as well, where rooms higher up on the mounds and those farthest from the center of the mound are not visible from the public spaces below and are accessed by narrow entries and hallways. Altogether, the evidence strongly suggests that the mound/plaza complexes of the Norte Chico were designed to hide some activities and overtly display others to the public.

But there is more to the mounds than just public visibility and controlled access. The mounds themselves are huge and demanded great amounts of labor. They were very obvious, even ostentatious features on the landscape. Indeed, the Late Archaic mounds remain the most dominant prehistoric features on the modern landscape of the Norte Chico region. In this regard, the mounds are overt signaling devices that display a measure of the strength, power, and grandeur of the people who built the platforms and the leaders who had them built. The importance of this external signaling of mound size can be seen in several ways. First, in a number of cases, residents of Norte Chico sites used natural hills to augment the apparent size of the mound. Second, on the main mounds found at the sites, the side of the mound facing toward the valley appears higher than the side facing the valley margins. The leaders who were directing the construction of the mounds were thus making a deliberate effort to artificially enhance their signals to anyone approaching the site from up or down the valley. Creamer has argued (2006) that the Late Archaic mounds in the Norte Chico are an overt manifestation of a kind of peer polity interaction between the leaders at different sites (see also Vega-Centeno 2005). The motivation of the leaders in having the mounds built was then two-sided: Construction of mounds served to demonstrate the power of leaders in competition with their rivals at other sites, and the size and grandeur of architecture at a site served to attract and maintain followers.

If the motivation of the leaders for building monumental architecture was to amass power and prestige, what was the motivation of the followers who actually built these structures? Here it is helpful to look at the balance between the compliance costs to the respondent population—that is, the cost to go along with the demands of the leaders. There are also refusal costs to that population—what it costs them if they refuse to go along—and potential gains—what they stand to get out of the construction (Haas 1982)?

The compliance costs can be directly measured in terms of how much labor/energy was involved in the construction of the mounds and plazas. While this sounds simple, it is in fact difficult to measure. The labor involved in public construction has to be measured in terms of the size of the population doing the labor and the amount of labor conducted at any given time. Thus, what it would take one person 1,000 years to accomplish could conceivably be accomplished by 1,000 people in one year. On a more realistic level, Burger and Burger-Salazar have argued that the construction of Initial Period monuments in the Lurín Valley could be done by relatively small groups of people working in episodic bursts over a relatively long period of time (Burger and Salazar-Burger 1991). When the mounds of the Norte Chico are examined in terms of construction, there seems to be a similar pattern of multiple smaller-scale construction events rather than one grand episode of monument building. While there are a small number of much larger construction episodes, these seem to be the exception rather than the rule. There is also evidence of periodic maintenance, specifically plastering and replastering of platform mounds that involved considerable labor, but not on a grand scale.

While it is possible to estimate the kilocalories involved in the construction of a given phase of construction, the difficulty comes in estimating the population involved in that construction. At this point, there are no scientifically based estimates of how many people may have occupied any specific site in the Norte Chico. To develop such specific estimates will entail extensive excavation of all types of residential units with accompanying absolute dates using radiocarbon or other methods. At the same time, excavations at Caral by Shady (Shady and Leiva 2003) and extensive testing and surface observations at other Late Archaic sites do not indicate large permanent residential populations numbering in the thousands (cf. Shady Solís 2004). There is residential architecture at Norte Chico sites that helps identify social status differences. At Caral specifically, Shady Solís (2004) has recorded high-status formal residential architecture associated with each of the six main platform mounds. These are large multiroom complexes with faced and plastered stone walls and carefully constructed floors. At Huaricanga, the Proyecto Arqueológico Norte Chico (PANC) has recorded a large complex of much more informal aggregated middle-status architecture (Ruiz and Haas 2007). This residential complex included small rooms with walls made of cane or *yapana* (blocks of dried alluvial mud) and use floors. The rooms are surrounded by use surfaces, residential trash, hearths, and activity areas. At Caballete, PANC also recorded both formal and informal residential architecture. However, none of the sites have the extensive remains of residential architecture that are found in many later sites in the Andes, where the available data do indicate residential populations in the thousands. Within the valleys, comprehensive surveys have also demonstrated that no significant Late Archaic residential sites lack large-scale public architecture.

At the same time, however, there are growing indications that significant numbers of people were coming in to Norte Chico sites on a seasonal or temporary basis. For the sites that have not been extensively disturbed in historic times, there are large expanses of land (up to 100 hectares or more) that are dotted with tiny shell and lithic fragments. Testing the site of Caballete in the Fortaleza Valley shows that these shell and lithic scatters mark the presence of stratified remains of use surfaces, hearths, cooking pits, residential trash, and temporary cane shelters (Haas and Creamer 2006; Wulffen 2009). How many people may have been in temporary residence at any given site at one time is even harder to estimate than the number of people living in more permanent structures. In the absence of even approximate population estimates we cannot make direct observations on the exact compliance costs in terms of how much work any particular group of people may have put into any specific construction episode. All we can conclude for certain is that the mounds were built in multiple stages and remodeled often. Based on limited evidence, we can make an order-of-magnitude estimate that the labor force likely numbered in the hundreds rather than the tens or thousands.

Whatever the exact labor input or compliance costs by any given individual, we can infer that a group of people came together on a regular basis and contributed significant labor to building mounds and plazas. We can also make inferences about the potential gains to this laboring group. As it was possible to infer that the mounds were not built for the immediate use of the leaders, it is equally evident that the mounds did not serve an immediate economic or defensive role for the population. An economic feature of this scale would be an irrigation canal or large-scale storage facilities. A defensive role would be demonstrated by community fortifications. There was thus no immediate material gain to be made in contributing one's labor to constructions that provided neither direct economic nor defensive advantage to the community.

Without a functional advantage to monument construction, there are at least two other potential positive benefits to be gained by the responding population: the blessings or goodwill of the gods and priests and increased access to material resources through feasting or some other kind of redistribution. Based on historic and ethnographic analogies, it is difficult to make a substantive case for people contributing significant labor to construction projects just for the perceived benefits of religious redemption. Throughout the world, people have lived with the promise of redemption yet have contributed little if any labor to large-scale religious architecture with highly restricted access. Although people in villages around the world do build and maintain local churches, these are relatively small-scale constructions and they are deliberately designed for open access to the population doing the building. Although some have argued that the Gothic cathedrals of Europe were built with volunteer labor, any quick review of historical records shows that the Catholic Church was a major economic powerhouse during this time and used its economic resources—land and lucre—quite liberally in ensuring the construction of churches. Likewise, one only has to look at the construction of Gaudi's Sagrada Familia cathedral in Barcelona, which stalled at Gaudi's death in 1926, to see the critical importance of economic resources in the completion of church construction.

Religious redemption or reward may be one of the proffered benefits of participating in monument construction, but it has never been sufficient to serve as the sole motivation of respondent populations. This is not to say that people don't "believe" in their religions or follow the guidance of religious leaders. However, the strictly ideological power of religious leaders, which lacks concrete immediate consequences, is relatively weak. This is especially true when compared to the relative strength of leaders who exercise some combination of economic or physical power. In the Norte Chico, the leaders who had the monuments constructed did not have to rely strictly on ideological power but could offer the material benefit of access to the agricultural resources grown and consumed at all the monument-bearing sites. Excavation at a number of sites in the Norte Chico have uncovered a rich mix of domesticated food and nonfood plants, including *achira* (*Canna edulis*), amaranth (*Amaranthus sp.*), beans (*Phaseolus lunatus* and *vulgaris*), jicama (*Pachyrrhizus tuberosus*), squash (*Curcubita* sp.), avocado (*Persea americana*), lúcuma (*Pouteria lucuma*), *pacae* (a long bean pod–type fruit with large seeds encased in a juicy edible pulp—only the pulp is eaten) (*Inga feuillei*), guava (*Psidium guajava*), chilies (*aji*; *Capsicum* sp.), and other members of the Solanaceae family (*Physalis* and *Solanum*), maize (*Zea mays*), peanuts (*Arachis hypogaea*), cotton (*Gossypium barbadense*) used for nets and cloth, and gourds (*Lagenaria siceraria*) used in fishing and for containers (Feldman 1985; Zechenter 1988; Shady and Leiva 2003; Alarcon 2005; Huaman et al. 2005; Creamer, Ruiz, and Haas 2007). Vega-Centeno has argued for feasting activities at the Late Archaic site of Cerro Lampay (2006), and there are material indications of communal feasting at sites tested by the Proyecto Arqueológico Norte Chico (Haas and Creamer 2006). The practice of hosting feasts and supplying laborers with food and cotton is widespread in later stages of the archaeological and historical records of the Andes (see Moore 1996), and its presence associated with monument building in the Norte Chico pushes its origins back into the Late Archaic. The agricultural crops produced at the numerous inland sites coupled with initial indications of feasting provides a positive material incentive or at least potential gains for the respondent populations responsible in exchange for building the monumental platform mounds and circular plazas.

The other side of the coin is refusal costs, material and religious, to the responding population. Religious refusal costs are somewhat similar to the potential gains, but instead of redemption (or its Late Archaic equivalent) there is condemnation. The noncompliant person may be threatened with damnation, disease, bad luck, and so forth. Noncompliant individuals may also be "excommunicated" or prevented from participating in religious ceremonies. While there is little question that the threat of negative ideological sanctions can influence peoples' behaviors, there is little evidence that such sanctions can induce people to freely contribute large amounts of labor to community projects with no material payoff. As with positive ideological sanctions, negative ideological sanctions, alone and without economic or physical reinforcement, are relatively weak.

A much more potent threat is that of excluding noncompliant individuals from the economic activities that accompany the ceremonial activities and large-scale constructions. Thus, such individuals not only risk the wrath of the gods and/or priests but they are also denied access to the agricultural resources the leaders provide. In a desert environment where natural plant resources are extremely scarce and exploitation of a majority of marine resources depends on cotton for nets, denial of access to agricultural resources represents a strong negative sanction. Access to domesticated plant products, the primary source of calories on the coast, provided a strong incentive for people to comply with the demands of leaders. Participation in the economic system provides both a push and pull for the responding population to cooperate in the construction of monumental architecture.

With both ideological and economic bases of power available to the leaders in the Norte Chico, a final question is whether or not the leaders also had the physical power base provided by a police or army. One persistent question that can be asked about the centrality of the Norte Chico in the Late Archaic is why people did not just move into one of the other valleys up or down the coast to produce their own crops and escape the labor demands of the Norte Chico leaders. This is an important question when considered in light of the fact that monument construction during most of the Late Archaic was heavily concentrated in the four valleys of the Norte Chico. Other Late Archaic sites include La Galgada and Salinas de Chao to the north and El Paraíso to the south, all of which have at least some communal architecture and Late Archaic dates. But with more than 30 sites in the Norte Chico, the outsiders are the exception rather than the rule. Why then did the Norte Chico leaders maintain a near-monopoly on the exercise of power and construction of monumental architecture by respondent populations for over 1,200 years? One possibility is that the leaders of Norte Chico polities may have used strategically targeted physical violence to enforce cooperation and compliance by the responding population.

Within the Norte Chico itself, there are absolutely no archaeological signs of warfare. Sites are not located in defensible positions, defensive architecture (e.g. walls or moats) are absent, no identifiable weapons have been found (aside from the occasional projectile point), and there are no signs of burning or violence associated with site abandonment or rebuilding. There are, however, hints of violence and warfare outside the Norte Chico at small contemporaneous fishing villages. Two Late Archaic sites, Unit 1 in the Asia Valley (Engel 1963) and Ostra Site (Topic and Topic 1987; Topic 1989) at the mouth of the Santa Valley, show possible signs of violence and defense. At Asia, there are signs of violence in skeletal remains, including headless individuals and one individual whose face had been peeled off. At Ostra, the interpretation of warfare is inferred from the presence of two lines of possible sling stones on either side of the site occupation area. The presence of indicators of warfare at these two sites is weak and may be coincidental, but it suggests at least the possibility of armed aggression and some kind of military force during the Late Archaic on the coast. Given the marked disparity in size between the Norte Chico communities with monumental architecture and the fishing communities up and down the coast, it is not surprising that the violence is manifested in the latter and not the former. While the Norte Chico polities were large enough to threaten the much smaller fishing communities, the reverse was not true. We have argued recently that the labor force for Norte Chico monument building was drawn from a pan-coastal population of fishing communities (Haas and Creamer 2006), and the pattern of warfare fits this broad regional interaction sphere. Armed conflict also would have given the Norte Chico leaders a way to apply—or threaten to apply—physical sanctions to create concrete refusal costs to ensure cooperation and compliance by a responding population and successfully recruit participation in the economic/religious/construction complex. However, we do acknowledge that the evidence of warfare and violence is not convincing at this time.

With a foundation of power dominated by economic and ideological bases and possibly supplemented by some degree of physical force, the leaders in the Norte Chico were able to get their followers to build numerous monumental structures over a span of more than 1,000 years. In this regard, the Norte Chico is quite distinct from the episodic cases of early monument building in North America and Mesoamerica. The significance of distinction is that the Norte Chico leaders had a stable power base that spanned many generations. Furthermore, the elements of this power base were consistent from one large site to the next. All of the leaders were relying on a combination of control over agricultural resources and ceremonialism and religious ideology to gain the obedience of their respondent populations. Although it is possible that some of the smaller sites with monumental architecture were the "offspring" or subsidiaries of larger sites (Rutherford 2008), at least 20 of the Norte Chico centers were economically and politically independent of each other. At the same time, all the leaders at all of the sites shared a common ideology and all had similar patterns of economic organization, engineering technology, and cultural assemblages. It seems clear that interaction between leaders at the different sites—a kind of peer-polity interaction (Creamer 2006; Vega-Centeno 2005)—was an inherent part of the emergence and maintenance of the regional pattern of monument construction in the Norte Chico. The nature of this interaction between leaders and sites, however, has yet to be elucidated.

When broken into component parts, the question of why people build monuments can only be understood from the perspective of the motivations of leaders directing the building and the people actually doing the building. In the case of the Late Archaic occupation of the Norte Chico region of Peru, we have the opportunity to see the first appearance of monumental architecture on the Andean landscape. From the perspective of agency and the nature of power relationships, the building of monuments comes from a combination of economic and ideological factors. For the leaders who are commanding the labor and directing the work, the monuments themselves serve as a statement of strength, grandeur, and potency in the eyes of their own respondent, potentially respondent populations, and leaders in contemporaneous sites in the region. For the respondents, the people actually building the monuments, the motives were more immediate and visceral. They received a supply of domestic plant products critical to both a balanced diet and the technology of production (such as cotton for nets) and at the same time got to participate in cyclical ceremonialism and feasting. There is minimal evidence (and none in the Norte Chico itself) that respondents were being physically forced to contribute labor in this system. But it is possible that physical violence was strategically applied to "encourage" recalcitrant outside communities to participate. There were also the negative aspects of not participating in the system; noncompliant people or communities would have been denied access to agricultural products, feasting, and ceremonialism. Clearly, however, for a system that thrived for over 1,000 years with modest monuments built in relatively small stages, coercive force was not the dominant reason behind the people's continuing compliance with the demands of their leaders. There is also no evidence that the leaders in this system were "pushing the envelope" in trying to exploit their bases of power for great accumulations of wealth or self-aggrandizement. Leaders and respondents in the

Late Archaic Norte Chico reached a long-lived stable balance between the scope of demands made by the rulers and the costs and benefits realized by the respondent population.

References Cited

Alarcon, Carmela
2005 Evidencias Botánicas Durante el Preceramico Tardio en el Norte Chico de Perú, Botanical Evidence from the Late Preceramic Period in the Norte Chico, Peru. Paper presented at the 70th annual meeting of the Society for American Archaeology, Salt Lake City.

Blanton, Richard, Stanley Kowalewski, Gary Feinman, and L. M. Finster
1993 *Ancient Mesoamerica*. Cambridge University Press, New York.

Burger, Richard, and Lucy Salazar-Burger
1991 The Second Season of Investigation at the Initial Period Center of Cardal, Peru. *Journal of Field Archaeology* 18:275–296.

Clark, John
2004 Mesoamerica Goes Public: Early Ceremonial Centers, Leaders, and Communities. In *Mesoamerican Archaeology*, edited by Julia A. Hendon and Rosemary A. Joyce, pp. 43–72. Blackwell Publishing, Malden, Massachusetts.

Coe, Michael, and Richard Diehl
1980 *In the Land of the Olmec*. University of Texas Press, Austin.

Creamer, Winifred
2006 A Peer-Polity Model of Late Preceramic Regional Organization in the Norte Chico, Peru. Paper presented at the 71st annual meeting of the Society for American Archaeology. San Juan, Puerto Rico.

Creamer, Winifred, Alvaro Ruiz, and Jonathan Haas
2007 *Archaeological Investigation of Late Archaic Sites (3000–1800 B.C.) in the Pativilca Valley, Peru*. Fieldiana, New Series, No. 40. Field Museum of Natural History, Chicago.

Cyphers, Ann
2004 *Escultura Olmec de San Lorenzo Tenochtitlán*. UNAM, Mexico, D.F.

Diehl, Richard A.
1981 Olmec Architecture: A Comparison of San Lorenzo and La Venta. In *The Olmec and Their Neighbors: Essays in Honor of Matthew W. Stirling*, edited by Elizabeth P. Benson, pp. 69–82. Dumbarton Oaks Research Library and Collections, Washington, D.C.

Dillehay, P., J. Netherly, and J. Rossen
1989 Middle Preceramic Public and Residential Sites on the Forested Slope of the Western Andes, Northern Peru. *American Antiquity* 54(4):733–759.

Donnan, Christopher (editor)
1985 *Early Ceremonial Architecture in the Andes*. Dumbarton Oaks Research Library and Collections, Washington, D.C.

Engel, Frederic
1963   A Preceramic Settlement on the Central Coast of Peru: Asia, Unit 1. *Transactions of the American Philosophical Society,* n.s. 53, part 3:a–139.

Feldman, Robert
1980   Aspero, Peru: Architecture, Subsistence Economy and Other Artifacts of a Preceramic Maritime Chiefdom. Ph.D. dissertation, Harvard University, Cambridge, Massachusetts.
1985   Preceramic Corporate Architecture: Evidence for the Development of Non-Egalitarian Social Systems in Peru. In *Early Ceremonial Architecture in the Andes,* edited by C. Donnan, pp. 71–92. Dumbarton Oaks, Washington, D. C.

Flannery, Kent V. (editor)
1976   *The Early Mesoamerican Village.* Academic Press, New York.

Flannery, Kent V., and Joyce Marcus
2005   *Excavations at San Jose Mogote: The Household Archaeology.* Memoirs of the Museum of Anthropology, University of Michigan, vol. 40. Museum of Anthropology, University of Michigan, Ann Arbor.

Gibson, Jon L.
2000   *The Ancient Mounds of Poverty Point: Place of Rings.* University Press of Florida, Gainesville.

Haas, Jonathan
1982   *The Evolution of the Prehistoric State.* Columbia University Press, New York.

Haas, Jonathan, and Winifred Creamer
2006   Crucible of Andean Civilization: The Peruvian Coast from 3000 to 1800 B.C. *Current Anthropology* 47(5):745–775.

Haas, Jonathan, Winifred Creamer, and Alvaro Ruiz
2004   Dating the Late Archaic Occupation of the Norte Chico Region in Peru. *Nature* 432:1020–1023.

Heizer, Robert, and Philip Drucker
1968   The Fluted Pyramid of the La Venta Site. *Antiquity* 42:52–56.

Huaman, Luis, Karen Ventura, Erika Paulino, and Liliana Zegarra
2005   Palynological and Botanical Studies from the Proyecto Arqueológico Norte Chico, Peru. Paper presented at the 70th Annual Meeting of the Society for American Archaeologists, Salt Lake City.

Kidder, Tristram R., Anthony Ortmann, and Lee Arco
2008   Poverty Point and the Archaeology of Singularity. *Archaeological Record* 8(5):9–12.

Lathrap, D. W., J. G. Marcos, and J. Z. Zeidler
1977   Real Alto: An Ancient Ceremonial Center. *Archaeology* 30:3–13.

Moore, Jerry D.
1992   Pattern and Meaning in Prehistoric Peruvian Architecture: The Architecture of Social Control in the Chimu State. *Latin American Antiquity* 3:95–113.
1996   *Architecture and Power in the Ancient Andes.* Cambridge University Press, New York.

Pozorski, S. G., and T. Pozorski
1990 Reexamining the Critical Preceramic/Ceramic Period Transition: New Data from Coastal Peru. *American Anthropologist* 92(2):481–491.
1992 Early Civilization in the Casma Valley, Peru. *Antiquity* 66:845–870.

Pozorski, T.
1980 The Early Horizon Site of Huaca de los Reyes: Societal Implications. *American Antiquity* 45(1):100–110.

Quilter, Jeffery
1985 Architecture and Chronology at El Paraíso. *Journal of Field Anthropology* 12:279–297.

Ravines, Rogger, and William Isbell
1976 Garagay: Sitio Temprano en el Valle de Lima. *Revista del Museo Nacional* 41(1975):253–272.

Ruiz, Alvaro, and Jonathan Haas
2007 *Proyecto de Investigación Arqueológica: Excavacions en Huaricanga, Valle de Fortaleza, Peru*. Final report submitted to the Instituto Nacional de Cultura, Lima, Peru.

Rutherford, Allen
2008 Space and Landscape in the Norte Chico Region, Peru: An Analysis of Socio-Political Organization through Monumental Architecture. Master's thesis, Northern Illinois University, DeKalb.

Saunders, Joe W., Rolfe D. Mandel, Garth Sampson, Charles Allen, Allen Thurman, Daniel Bush, James Feathers, Kristen Gremillion, C. T. Hallmark, Edwin Jackson, Jay Johnson, Reca Jones, Roger Saucier, Gary Stringer, and Malcome Vidrine.
2005 Watson Brake, a Middle Archaic Mound Complex in Northeast Louisiana. *American Antiquity* 70(4):631–668.

Shady, Ruth, and Carlos Leiva (editors)
2003 *La Ciudad Sagrada de Caral-Supe Los Orígenes de la Civilización Andina y la Formación del Estado Prístino en el Antiguo Perú*. Instituto Nacional de Cultura, Lima.

Shady Solís, Ruth
2004 *Caral: La Ciudad del Fuego Sagrado, The City of the Sacred Fire*. Translated by M. Dalton. Interbank, Lima.

Topic, John
1989 The Ostra Site: The Earliest Fortified Site in the New World. In *Cultures in Conflict: Current Archaeological Perspectives*, edited by Diana C. Tkaczuk and Brian C. Vivian, pp. 215–228. Archaeological Association of the University of Calgary, Calgary.

Topic, John, and Theresa Topic
1987 The Archaeological Investigation of Andean Militarism: Some Cautionary Observations. In *The Origins and Development of the Andean State*, edited by Jonathan Haas, Shelia Pozorski, and Thomas Pozorski, pp. 47–55. Cambridge University Press, Cambridge, England.

Vega-Centeno, Rafael
2005   Ritual and Architecture in a Context of Emergent Complexity: A Perspective from Cerro Lampay, a Late Archaic Site in the Central Andes. Ph.D. dissertation, University of Arizona, Tucson.
2006   Construction, Labor Organization, and Feasting during the Late Archaic Period in the Central Andes. *Journal of Anthropological Archaeology* 26(2):150–171.

Wulffen, Jennifer
2009   *Two Test Excavations at Caballete, Norte Chico, Peru.* Master's thesis, Northern Illinois University, DeKalb.

Zechenter, Elzbieta
1988   Subsistence Strategies in the Supe Valley of the Peruvian Central Coast during the Complex Preceramic and Initial Periods. Ph.D. dissertation, Department of Anthropology, University of California, Los Angeles, California.

12

Monumental Architecture Arising from an Early Astronomical-Religious Complex in Perú, 2200–1750 BC

ROBERT A. BENFER JR.

This chapter advances the hypothesis that astronomer-priests directed the construction and adornment of the first monumental architecture in the Americas, the Late Preceramic stepped platform mounds in coastal Peruvian valleys. These astronomer-priests managed installation of the earliest public art at the Late Preceramic site of Buena Vista, Chillón Valley, Perú. The art is an essential part of the astronomical complex. Constructions included walls, monuments, and special astronomical instruments aligned to sky events. Art included three-dimensional and low-relief sculptures, paintings, and incised figures. Media ranged from stone to paint to mud plaster. Offerings were directed to the earth in special adorned semi-subterranean structures placed on the top of mounds. Unlike early accumulations in North America discussed in this volume, these mounds were purposeful constructions built over relatively short periods of time. I argue that their construction and maintenance was directed by astronomer-priests who managed offerings to the earth and fit those ceremonies to an astronomical calendar that functioned to mark agricultural and fishing times of economic importance. This hypothesis differs from others presented in this volume, although it is not inconsistent with them. It is directly testable. Preliminary fieldwork finds evidence for this hypothesis in early monumental constructions in Peruvian coastal valleys that date from 3500 BC to 1750 BC.

Investigations at the very early Neolithic site of Göbekli Tepe from Turkey have defined only ritual activities (Schmidt 2000). A hole drilled through the top of one of the megaliths (Figure 7, Enclosure D-P30 in

Peters and Schmidt 2004) could suggest an astronomical function that has not yet been studied. The finding in Turkey that the earliest megalithic architecture was associated with a religious site rather than a domestic settlement parallels our findings in Perú, where the earliest monumental architecture appears to have been associated with ritual centers, probably pilgrimage sites, with astronomical orientations and alignments and offering chambers (Benfer et al. 2010). I will argue below that the ritual function was a practical one.

Special structures placed on top of the coastal platform pyramids in Perú served simultaneously as observatories for sky events and chambers for offerings to the earth. Such structures are referred to as *ushnus* in Andean archaeology, a topic to be discussed in more detail below. The oldest Peruvian monumental sites with secure astronomical alignments are Sechín Bajo (Fuchs and Lorenz 2009) and Salinas de Chao (Benfer et al. 2010), which was excavated by Alva (1986). These sites date to 3500 BC (Alva 1986; Fuchs and Lorenz 2011). Here I will focus on the Late Preceramic site of Buena Vista (Figure 12.1), which dates from 2200 BC to 1750 BC (Table 12.1). Elsewhere I have defined the Late Preceramic association of offerings to the earth with management of sky events by naked-eye astronomical instruments as the Buena Vista Astronomical/Religious Tradition (Benfer et al. 2010). This coastal valley tradition relates to the more Andean Kotosh Religious Tradition (Moseley 1992a) through a Kotosh-style Mito offering chamber (Bonnier 1997) found in the coastal site of Buena Vista. The Buena Vista tradition continued throughout prehistory in Perú (Benfer and Adkins 2009; Benfer et al. 2010).

The stairway to the top of M-I, the principle mound at the Buena Vista site, appears to face the river valley in a general sort of way. However, I will show below that the main stairway is also aligned with a major lunar standstill—the most southerly moonrise and the time of increased probability of multiple lunar eclipses and rare solar eclipses (Adkins and Benfer 2009). Special structures, observational instruments, were built on and in the platforms asymmetrically in order to be correctly oriented toward sky events such as the rising and setting of the sun, the moon, and constellations. Entrances to temples served as observational positions. At Buena Vista, there are multiple reference points (up to six) for the three observing points in the temple. As many as three astronomical events may be seen from a single viewing point over different reference points (Benfer et al. 2010). What function did these observatories serve?

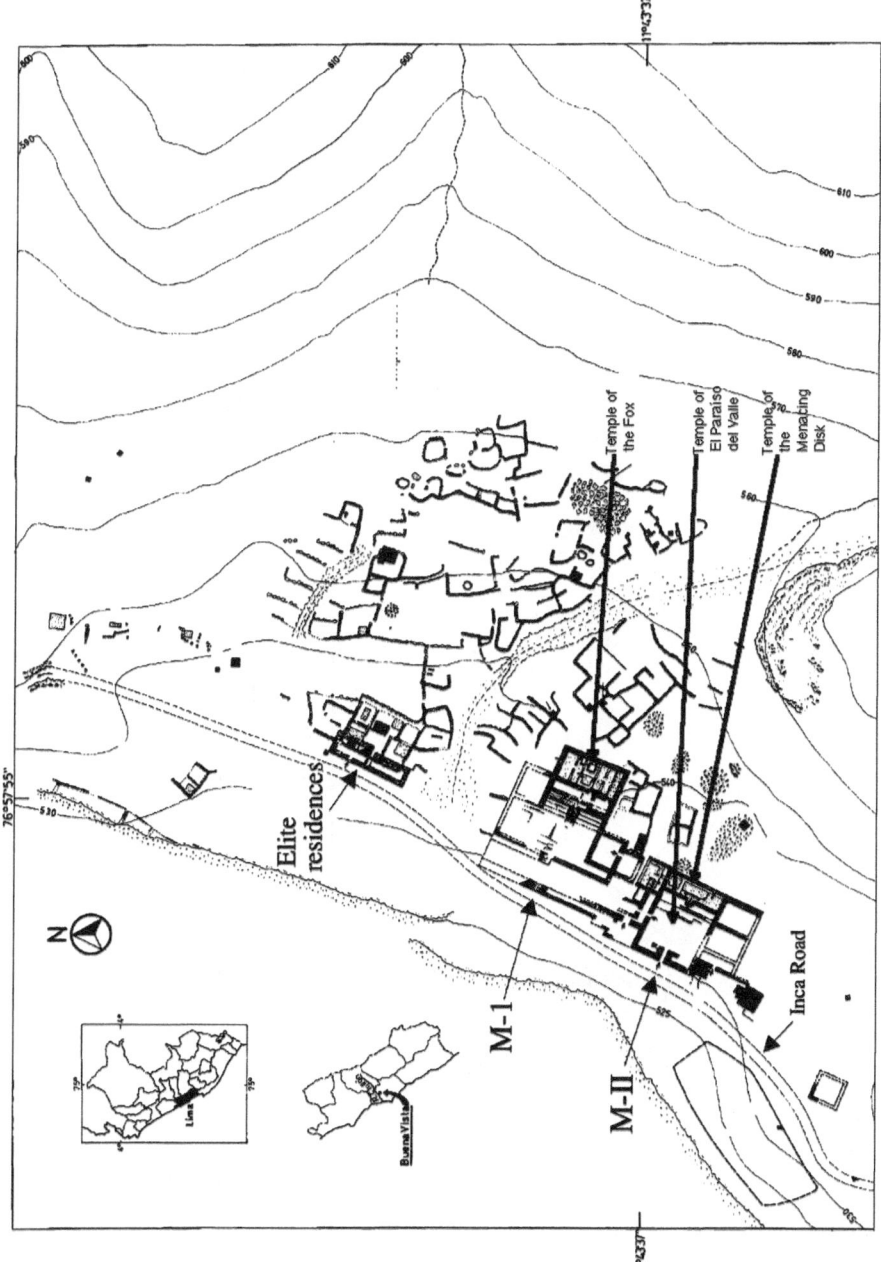

Figure 12.1. Late Preceramic monumental architecture at Buena Vista. Arrows show azimuths.

Table 12.1. Radiocarbon dates from Late Preceramic component at Buena Vista

Sample #/Citation	Lab #	Provenience	Radiocarbon years BP	2-sigma calibrated age range	Precision date[a]
BXI-073	GX-31276	M-I: Offering chamber, Temple of the Fox, #300, charcoalized twigs in plant offerings, below round stones	3770 ± 80	2460–1980 BC	2220 BC
BXI-099	GX-32177	M-I: Offering chamber, Temple of the Fox, #425, charcoalized twigs in plant offerings, below round stones	3790 ± 80	2470–2020 BC	2220 BC
SB-UXII-300	GX-31920	M-II: Temple of the Menacing Disk, grass from mud plaster, base of sculpture	3660 ± 90	2,290–1,850 BC	2030 BC
13.12725	UGAMS 02685	M-II: Solstice Light Chamber, grass from mud plaster, ceiling	3600 ± 30	2030–1890 BC	2000 BC
13.11457	GX-30695	Elite residences, Sec. C, U, VI #250	3660 ± 50	2060–1870 BC	2000 BC
13.11437	GX 30684	Sec. B, U X, #300, stairwell	3570 ± 70	2060–1740 BC	1900 BC
Dolfus (1960)	not available	Base main plaza	3202 ± 114	1748–2292 BC	1610 BC
Engel (1974)	PI-1845	M-I: Sec. B, U, X viga, lower niched wall	3390 ± 70	1880–1520 BC	1680 BC

2.10874	GX-29935	M-1: Sec. B, U. X, wood viga, upper niched wall, Mound I	3290 ± 80	1750–1410 BC	1540 BC
13.13047	UGAMS 3126	M-II: Templo Paraíso del Valle, #200, carbonized twigs on floor	3490 ± 25	1886–1746 BC	1780 BC
13.1305	UGAMS 3128	M-II: Templo Paraíso del Valle, #400, carbonized twigs, central pit	3520 ± 25	1920–1690 BC	1850 BC
12.13049	UGAMS 3127	M-II: Templo Paraíso del Valle, #300, carbonized twigs, central pit	3450 ± 25	1784–1690 BC	1750 BC
13.13053	UGAMS 3129	M-II: Templo Paraíso del Valle, #300, charcoalized twigs, between the two floors	3420 ± 25	1774–1659 BC	1730 BC
13.10825	GX-29938	M-2: Sec. B, U. 10, #300, F104, hearth	3410 ± 70	1730–1659 BC	1730 BC

Note: a. Interpolated by linear regression of five nearest bristlecone pine dates on each side of the radiocarbon year date, then rounded to the decade.

I do not find the distinction between practical and ceremonial constructions (Trigger 1990) useful in describing the monumental architecture from Buena Vista or the many other sites with astronomical orientations and alignments. From an anthropological perspective, structures that permitted astronomer-priests to manage rituals for improving the fertility of the land while warning against adverse sky events such as floods and droughts or lunar eclipses, the possible harbingers of such events, were of the utmost practicality. At the same time the structures described here served as important ritual calendars that were also of practical importance in maintaining stable social relations.

In Andean cosmology, offerings to the earth and control of astronomical events were both important. The Inca used special structures, *ushnus*, from which they reckoned sky events. They also used them to organize time and space as calendars for ceremonies (Zuidema 1990; Zeidler 1998; Pino Matos 2005). Further, the special offering chambers may be distinguished by the presence of smooth river pebbles as suggested from ethnography (Pino Matos 2005), ethnohistory (Pino Matos 2010), and archaeology (Duncan, Pearsall, and Benfer 2009; Benfer, Furbee, and Ludeña R. 2011).

Archaeologically, *ushnus* have usually been thought to be manifest by platforms on mounds with stairs leading to them (Staller 2008, 285). Although some investigators ignore astronomical alignments (e.g., Moore 1996, 760), most incorporate them into their definition of the term *ushnu* (Zuidema 1981; Isbell 1997; Urton 1981; Bauer and Dearborn 1995; and Pino Matos 2005). My colleagues and I have extended Inca cosmology back to the Preceramic periods (Benfer and Adkins 2008; Benfer et al. 2010; Benfer, Furbee, and Ludeña R. 2011). Here I will summarize some of the evidence developed from the study of the monumental architecture at Buena Vista. I begin with the economic basis of the society that built these early complexes.

Economic Factors Influencing the Construction of Monuments as Astronomical Observatories

What was nature of the political economy of the first settlements with monumental architecture in Peruvian coastal valleys? This was the main question that drove our original investigations. Moseley (1992a, 1992b) suggests that the economic foundation for these early sites was a dual economy with inland resources that supplemented maritime ones. The data from our recent excavations agree with earlier hypotheses (Lanning 1963; Patterson

1999) that marine resources continued to be important in early monumental sites because the chief plant cultivated was an economic one—cotton. Our studies of coprolites from the pre-cotton Middle Preceramic fishing village of Paloma showed that even with an overwhelming predominance of marine products, at least one plant, often cultivated, was consumed with each meal (Deborah Pearsall, personal communication). Although marine remains were also ubiquitous at the Late Preceramic site of Buena Vista, we found substantially more agricultural produce—in one case, in a feasting context (Duncan, Pearsall, and Benfer 2009). Béarez and Muñoz (2000) report similar findings for the middle valley site of Chupacigarro/Caral. Quilter and his team confirmed the overwhelming importance of maritime resources at the large near-coastal Late Preceramic site of El Paraíso in the lower Chillón Valley (1991).

My colleagues and I also found evidence for the continued importance of marine resources in the periods that followed the Late Preceramic in the central western Andes (Weir, Benfer, and Jones 1988). Burger and van der Merwe (1990) noted the importance of marine animal protein into the Initial Period. For recent reviews of this question, see Haas and Creamer (2008), Sandweiss (2008), and Meador and Benfer (2009). Both agriculture in coastal valleys and fishing on the Peruvian coast are affected by ocean current activity.

Sandweiss and his associates (2001) propose that sporadic El Niños (or ENSO, El Niño–Southern Oscillation) were established by 5800 BP and that modern, more frequent frequencies not present before 3000 BP (1996). I have argued elsewhere that evidence from a variety of worldwide sources suggests another important date for climate change in the Late Preceramic, about 2300 BC (Benfer and Pechenkina 2001). The data from the Quelccaya ice cores in the Andes (Thompson, Moseley-Thompson, and Thompson 1995) shows a sharp increase in aridity around 3800 BC. It shows an almost equally steep drop at 2200 BC (Figure 12.2), the date of the earliest Buena Vista astronomical structure and the time of a second peak in population (Rick 1987).

Demographic and economic stress at the end of the Global Climatic Optimum may have caused greater intensification of field management in the Chillón Valley and possibly other valleys as a response to the greater variability caused by El Niño years (Sandweiss 1996). The central coastal valleys perhaps had characteristics that made them the most successful location for this development (Sandweiss et al. 1996). The runoff from the Chillón River is much less than that from the neighboring Rímac, perhaps

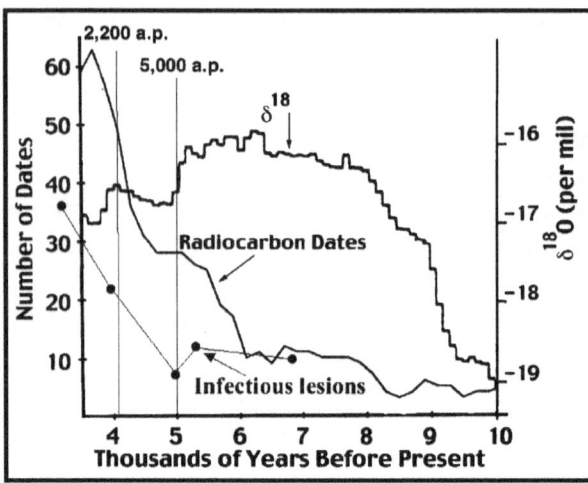

Figure 12.2. Moisture as measured from oxygen isotope concentration in ice cores (Thompson et al. 1995), population density as registered in the number of radiocarbon dates per time period (Rick 1987), and health registered as average number of bone elements with infectious lesions (see Pechenkina et al. 2007).

making it more manageable for canal irrigation (Bernardino Ojeda, personal communication). The earlier and larger centers in the Norte Chico may have collapsed (Haas and Creamer 2004), with more successful adjustments emerging to the north and south (Shady Solís et al. 2000; Benfer 2007). The pattern of inundations or droughts in ENSO years is registered in early twentieth-century records for the Chillón River (Servicio de Agrometerolía e Hidrología 1963). The variance of runoff is five times greater in ENSO years than in other years ($f = 4.8$ with 4 and 33 df, $p < 0.01$), and it is likely that inundations or droughts occurred in ENSO years. These data are from a time period before extensive canalization and reservoir development greatly changed the runoff behavior of the river.

Reitz (1988) studied faunal remains at the largest Middle Preceramic village, Paloma (Benfer and Gehlert 1980; Benfer 1990, 1999, 2007), and reported evidence of increased use of schooling fish after 2700 BC. The extreme aridity of the central coast distinguishes it from the north (Richardson and Sandweiss 2008). The ice core data suggest that greater aridity and variability occurred at the end of the third millennium BC. For the purposes of this discussion, I assume that El Niños were common on the central coast by 2200 BC.

Management of marine resources and canal irrigation is more efficient with a useful calendar. This is because the end of December, the Austral summer solstice, is a critical date for both endeavors, the date when it will be known whether an ENSO year has arrived. Local vegetation and animal indicators are useful, but the flooding of the river from glacial runoff and highland rain is determined by a different climatic system than the florescence of the coastal hills from fog. Thus, an astronomical calendar could be more consistently reliable than any other. Offerings made in advance would be presumed to reduce the occurrence of an ENSO year. When an El Niño year did not occur by the astronomical calendric date, fishers would know that normal marine resources would be plentiful and farmers would know that floods or drought would be avoided. For both fishers and farmers, even if they were joined in a dual and mutually supportive economy, an ENSO year would have required different subsistence strategies that in general would have proved stressful for the people of the coastal valleys.

From human skeletal indicators of stress (Dickinson 1995), my colleagues and I have shown that there is evidence that stress did increase in the Late Preceramic (Pechenkina et al. 2007), as predicted by Sandweiss (1996). Our work at the Middle Preceramic fishing village of Paloma showed that a large village of 400 persons could be supported by fishing (Vradenburg, Benfer, and Sattinspiel 1997). This number was estimated from paleodemography and house floor area, both of which gave corresponding figures. The health of both adult and child villagers steadily improved over the time period 4500 to 3000 BC (Benfer 1990, 1999, 2007). However, adult health declined sharply in the Late Preceramic (Pechenkina et al. 2007), possibly a density effect of the larger groups (Figure 12.2) (Rick 1987). The seemingly paradoxical increase in population associated with declining health can be explained by differential investment in children (Benfer and Pechenkina 1998). The need to store food in the context of increasingly common El Niños would have encouraged greater intensification of crops and taking of small fish; this would have increased the economic value of children (Benfer and Pechenkina 2001). As is well known, population increase arises primarily from increased fertility, not increased life expectancy (e.g., Vradenburg, Benfer, and Sattinspiel 1997). Health improved gradually after the Initial Period, especially for children (Benfer and Pechenkina 2001). However, adult stature never returned to the height achieved before the beginning of monumental architecture on the Andean coast (Pechenkina et al. 2007), presumably due to stress on adolescents who were still growing but were acting as adults in subsistence activities. It is possible that the change in the value of children began to occur at the end of the Middle Preceramic, where greater elaboration was found in children's burials in the last period at Paloma (Quilter 1989; Benfer 1990). If there was increasing fertility, this might explain abandonment of the Paloma site, which was located near the Chilca River valley where more crops could be planted and above prime fishing beaches (Benfer 2008). However, the extremely arid Chilca has too modest a carrying capacity to accommodate a rapidly growing population (Joe Gunn, personal communication), which could have accounted for the shift to the Chillón Valley. This was the most productive nearby valley that had a large carrying capacity through agriculture and did not have flooding that was too strong for simple canal irrigation (Bernardino Ojeda, personal communication). In any case, the hypothesis is that parental investment in children increased at the expense of adults in the Late Preceramic Andean coast (Benfer and Pechenkina 1998).

The Andean Coast

The western flanks of the Andes provide a full archaeological record for study of the development of the pristine complex societies that arose there. It is a novel feature of the record that Late Preceramic sites have been associated with a religious tradition, the Kotosh tradition, the existence of which suggests social and political ranking (Donnan 1985) and priestly elites before 2200 BC (Moseley 1992a). Religious traditions, monumental architecture, and distinctive public art styles developed earlier in the central western Andes than they did elsewhere in the Western Hemisphere (Haas and Creamer 2004, this volume). These developments were preceded on the coast by large early sedentary coastal fishing villages (Malpass and Stothert 1992, 150; Benfer 2007). A maritime economy supported the villages with limited wild and cultivated supplemental foods (Weir, Benfer, and Jones 1988; Reitz 2001). Public architecture appeared much earlier on the coast than in the Andes. It occurred with the abandonment of large fishing villages in coastal valleys. The radiocarbon dates provided by Haas and Creamer (Shady Solís et al. 2000) confirmed Engel's identification of the large monumental sites in the north central coastal valleys as Preceramic and earlier than similar sites in the highlands (e.g., Burger and Salazar-Burger 1986). The long debate over whether coastal or Andean centers came first (Tello 1943; Larco Hoyle 1948) is for now settled in favor of the coast.

These large monumental Late Preceramic sites in middle valleys to the north of Buena Vista in the Norte Chico region securely date from before 3000 BC (Alva 1986; Haas and Creamer 2008, 767; Fuchs and Lorenz 2009). My colleagues and I have proposed Buena Vista as the nexus of the subsequent events that occurred to the south of the area (Benfer et al. 2010) after the decline and ultimate collapse of the Norte Chico polities, which had happened by 1800 BC (Haas and Creamer 2008).

The early Late Preceramic sites with plazas surrounded by mounds in the Norte Chico area have long been known for their importance (Engel 1987; Williams 1978–1980). These complexes are the oldest purposefully constructed monumental architecture in the Americas (Haas and Creamer 2008, this volume). Even more ancient are middens, large concentrations of cooking materials, known from coastal Perú sites such as Curayacu (Engel 1987) and Huaca Prieta (Bird, Hyslop, and Skinner 1985). The site of Paloma has domestic architecture in low shell mounds that dates to 5700 cal. BC (Benfer 1990). Scattered midden remains are found elsewhere from the immediate post-Pleistocene, and domestic architecture dating from more than 7000 cal BC is known from the central coastal site of Quipa (Engel 1987; Duncan et al. 2009). Accumulations of debris from food processing have long been known to have been established in coastal and estuary environments around the world in the Early Archaic/Neolithic periods (Binford 1968) and coastal Perú is no exception, except in the exceptional richness of the marine resources available. Exchange between coastal and middle valley Late Preceramic sites was intense. As shown here, the members of the two cooperating economic systems also shared a common cosmology. This cosmology was pan-Andean, and in some mythologies, it was pan–South American (Benfer, Furbee, and Ludeña R. 2011). It has been studied most intensively at the monumental site of Buena Vista in the Chillón Valley.

Late Preceramic Monumental Architecture in the Chillón Valley

In order to support the principle hypothesis that astronomer-priests controlled stepped mounds as *ushnus* in the late third millennium BC, it will be necessary to first describe the monumental architecture and the temples on them. For the hypothesis to be viable and general in application, the following must be true:

Temples for offerings were associated with astronomical instruments or were viewing points.
Astronomical alignments are much older than were previously thought, and if this is correct, radiocarbon dating of materials must document this antiquity.

For the pattern to be widespread, most Late Preceramic sites should have astronomical alignments associated with offering chambers.

Suspected viewing sites must have *multiple* reference points or alignments that cast light or shadows.

Constructions that capture sunlight in a dark chamber or in mines (with an additional reference point) may be oriented to solstices. These constructions will be reported on in detail elsewhere.

Early Astronomical Alignments

I will use the following abbreviations throughout, which correspond to the azimuths as if they were viewed on a flat horizon at a latitude of about 12° S. Adjustments for altitude are usually necessary in Andean valleys, where in general a few degrees must be added for sunsets or subtracted for sunrises for every 10° of elevation of a ridge or mountain:

(Austral) Summer Solstice Sunset, December 21—SSSS (246°)
(Austral) Winter Solstice Sunset, June 21—WSSS (294°)
(Austral) Summer Solstice Sunrise, December 21—SSSR (114°)
(Austral) Winter Solstice Sunrise, June 21—WSSR (66°)
Maximum Southern Lunar Standstill (rising of the moon at its most southerly point)—MLSS (approximately 5° greater than the December solstice sunrises).

Zeidler (1998) reported an example of astronomical alignments of structures with declination-corrected astronomical alignments of simple Valdivian structures at Real Alto (2700–2400 BC). A summer solstice sunrise (SSSR) alignment can be seen at Loma Alta, another Valdivia site (Benfer et al. 2010), through the entrance from the center of a structure (Damp 1984, Fig. 5). These structures are more elaborate than the domestic architecture of the final occupation of Paloma in the central coast, where entryways faced the azimuth of the SSSR of about 114° at 3000 BC (Benfer 2007). They are less monumental than the Peruvian sites from about the same time period, all of which also appear to have astronomical orientations.

Azimuths of astronomical events are calculated in the remainder of this chapter with Starry Night Pro (V. 5), which corrects for refraction (-0.49°), precession, obliquity for date of construction by latitude, and altitude of reference points. Comparisons of calculations made with Starry Night to those made with published formulae never reveal a difference of more than a few minutes.

Following Mackie (1977), I will make a distinction between *orientation* as a direction for major walls and precise *alignments* of observational instruments. An alignment is defined by its ability to mark an astronomical event to within a few days. For example, many streets of Boulder, Colorado, are oriented toward the equinox, but the Rocky Mountains establish the western horizon of the city. This means that the true equinoctial sunset is seen at greater than an azimuth of 270°; streets would not define a specific azimuth to more than plus or minus 5°, in any case. Azimuths of pre-Hispanic walls or plazas that have an astronomical importance indicate a concern with the orientation of the built environment and surrounding landscape. The structures demonstrate a respect for celestial axes. Most of the studies from maps and from Google Earth that I discuss next must be limited to orientations, although in some cases, sight lines are sufficiently long to speak of alignments.

Cardenas (1979, Fig. 38) reported a Late Preceramic circular structure from the north coastal site of Salinas de Chao that she thought had an astronomical function, although her suggested alignments could not be confirmed. However, the edges of the entryway and the exit of a circular structure are oriented to a lunar event, the MLSS, when her map is corrected for declination. The map of the entire site published by Alva (1986, Fig. 35) shows that the line from the two entryways of a large circular structure extend to the center of a stepped platform to the south with an azimuth of 114° (Benfer and Adkins 2009). At that latitude in 2000 BC, the SSSR would have been observed at 114° 20'. I could make no correction for azimuths that would have been affected by the elevation of surrounding hills, since these elevations are not available in published sources. Another orientation between mounds (Benfer et al. 2009) traces the MLSS in Alva's map when it is corrected for declination (1987).

An additional example of a circular structure associated with an astronomical alignment is known, this one from the early Initial Period site of Cardal, in the central coastal valley of the Lurín (12° 11' 10.67" S and 76° 50' 57.41" W). One circular structure at the site is located asymmetrically to the east of the main plaza. That alignment has an azimuth of 114° in the site map provided by Burger and Salazar-Burger (1991) but was not visible in my investigation there due to vegetation. Fieldwork done by my team also confirmed an alignment seen in Google Earth from the top of the main mound to a large rectangular rock on a ridge to the west (Pan de Azucar), a precise alignment with the equinoctial sunset (Benfer 2010b). Burger and Salazar-Burger (1986) had previously reported equinoctial alignments of Initial Period Andean sites.

At the late Late Preceramic site of Sechín Bajo, in the Casma Valley to the north, Fuchs and his colleagues (2006, 13) have reported a temple in which a line passes from five entryways, the first four of which are narrow, to produce an azimuth of 66°, the WSSR. Sechín Alto, the largest site in the world for its time, lies just 2,500 meters up the valley from Sechín Bajo. Sechín Alto too has one site whose axis was oriented to 66° (Benfer and Adkins 2009). Pozorski and Pozorski present plans of two temples in the Casma Valley (in this volume, their Figures 13.3 and 13.4) from the site of Sechín Alta, which shows declination-corrected openings to an azimuth of 66°, the June 21 winter solstice (WSSR). It should be noted that neither Sechín Alto nor Sechín Bajo is oriented to face the nearby river valley. Instead, they lie precisely along an east-west solstice line that links the main entry stairs of both mounds. A cut in the top of an intervening ridge further establishes the line (Benfer et al. 2009). Thus the two sites make clear that knowledge of how to precisely determine the equinox to within a degree of accuracy predates known cases in the Initial Period. Another site in the north coast, Huaynuná (Pozorski and Pozorski 1990b, Fig. 3), shows a similar SSSR alignment.

At the large early coastal Late Preceramic site of Aspero (Feldman 1985), the entryway to the Huaca de los Idolos chamber faces east through the middle of an entryway at 66°, toward the WSSR. Later sites with this orientation to the June solstice sunrise can be found on the central coast, for example at Huaral and Huando in the Chancay Valley (Williams 1978–1980, Fig. 5).

Chupacigarro/Caral has achieved worldwide notice following Ruth Shady Solís's extensive excavations there (Shady Solís 1997, 2000; Shady Solís et al. 2000; Shady Solís, Haas, and Creamer 2001). Her work builds on the investigations of Kosak (1965) and Engel (1980, 1987) and the findings of the Peruvian architect Carlos Williams (1978–1980), which remain to be cited in her published work. The history of investigations of this important site must be found elsewhere (Benfer 2005; Fung Pineda 2006; Haas and Creamer 2004). Briefly, Engel and Williams, not Shady Solís, were the first to publish the Preceramic nature of this site. In fact, Engel furnished a map of the site for Shady for her first investigations.

While visiting the site in July of 2007 with my field school, I encountered a surveying team of an astronomer and an archaeologist in the center of a circular structure, the *anfiteatro,* working with an astronomical theodolite. They asked me for an azimuth to investigate, so I suggested 114° 36', the average value I obtained from the offering chamber alignment from the Temple of the Fox at Buena Vista and approximately the same as the value obtained from the site of El Paraíso, both to be discussed below. They were astonished to see a small stone structure at that azimuth on a nearby hill, not represented on any map but visible in the telescope and, later I was to find, visible in Google Earth. At the latitude of Chupacigarro/Caral, the actual summer solstice sunrise would have been seen from the *anfiteatro* to the structures at 114° 50' at 2000 BC given the 2° 50' elevation of the hill. This is just a 14 ' deviation from the theoretical expectation. The distance from the *anfiteatro* to the stone structures, 390 meters, permits this azimuth to be taken as an astronomical *alignment.* Google Earth also suggests a lunar alignment of 119° between two mounds at the site (Benfer 2006).

Pampa Chica, a late Early Horizon central coastal valley site, demonstrates a 114° solstice line in the wall that separates the principle structure into two closed spaces (Dulanto 2008, 103). Space does not permit discussion of the astronomical orientations of the numerous other sites form the Late Preceramic and later periods visible in maps and through Google Earth. I turn now to the Late Preceramic Chillón Valley, where our team has made an intensive excavation of one site and studied several others to a lesser degree.

Late Preceramic Chillón Valley Sites with Astronomical Alignments

There are two large Late Preceramic sites, both with monumental architecture, in the Chillón Valley proper. These are El Paraíso and Buena Vista. A third monumental Late Preceramic site, La Pacifica (Silva Sifuentes and Tello 2005; Traslaviña Arias, Carrasio, and Bautista Cornejo 2007), lies just within the drainage of the Rímac River to the south, whose flood plain interlaces with that of the Chillón.

Canto Grande, another Late Preceramic site in the Chillón Valley, has small structures and very large geoglyphs. Before being destroyed by urbanization, it was the second largest field of Peruvian geoglyphs, after Nazca. One circular structure at Canto Grande is divided by an equinoctial axis (Roselló 1978, 50), and a SSSS ray extends from it. A radiocarbon date of cal. 2545±70 BC has been made available for the structure by Kelley and Milone (2005, 439, citing Roselló, Manco, and Mazzotti 1985 and Roselló 1997, unavailable). This date would presumably correspond to the date of initial construction at Buena Vista or later, since the penultimate occupation of the principle mounds was dated to 2200 BC (Table 12.1). The geoglyphs from Canto Grande, like the similar rays extending from structures that Pitluga focused on at Nazca (Pitluga 2003, 2005), were involved in marking sky events. However, since the focus of this book is monumentality, I will not treat them further but turn now to the monumental Late Preceramic sites in the Chillón and Rímac valleys.

El Paraíso is one of the largest Late Preceramic sites in Perú. It was first discussed by Patterson and Lanning (1964), who used the name of the hacienda, Chuquitanta; the site was renamed for the district, El Paraíso, when hacienda names were no longer politically useful (Engel 1966). In 2006, I briefly investigated the site and found two reference points for astronomical alignments, one of which was the SSSR viewed from the center of the offering chamber in the main temple (Unit I) over a small platform that was itself oriented to the equinoxes (Benfer et al. 2010). Another reference point, to approximately the SSSS, was a D-shaped cluster of circular stone pits that resemble a similar reference point reported by Bauer and Dearborn (1995) at Cuzco. A line defining their axis is close to an orientation to the WSSS (Benfer et al. 2010). A small unexcavated rectangular structure to the northeast of the restored temple is oriented toward the equinox and the highest level of the ridge to the southeast and is visible in Google Earth (Benfer 2010a). Further, it establishes one end of the SSSS line to the stone semi-subterranean circles on the ridge to the southwest. The small structure, which was visible in the September 30, 2007, Google Earth image (11° 57' 7.2" S and 77° 06' 56.16" W), was unfortunately removed in an expansion of a parking lot in 2009. The equinoctial structure appears to lack depth below courses of stones laid directly on the surface, and wall collapse is also not present. In these features, it resembles an astronomical structure near Huánuco Pampa that Pino Matos (2009) labels a geoglyph.

La Pacifica (Traslaviña Arias, Carrasio, and Bautista Cornejo 2007), a few kilometers south of El Paraíso, is probably a Late Preceramic site. It shows that astronomical alignments were used to organize the construction of the complex. However, unlike El Paraíso and Buena Vista, the major orientation of the structure is to an azimuth of 66°, the WSSR (Traslaviña Arias, Carrasio, and Bautista Cornejo 2007, Figure 12.1). This site resembles the Late Preceramic sites to the north discussed above with similar temple alignments. Pampa de Cueva (Williams 1978–1980, Fig. 3), a small site in the Rímac, is either Late Preceramic or more likely Initial Period. Its U-shaped walls extending from the principle monument face 66°, also the WSSR. A ray extends from the central structure, which was the pattern visible for other lower valley, Initial Period sites before urban destruction (Roselló 1978, 522).

The Late Preceramic monumental site of Buena Vista, Chillón Valley, exhibits numerous orientations and alignments, perhaps because it has been studied most intensively.

The Buena Vista Astronomical-Religious Complex

A possibly important point that cannot be developed here is that the "Late" Preceramic designation of Buena Vista may be incorrect; its actual state is aceramic. The nearby Initial Period Rímac site of La Florída has radiocarbon dates with good context (Patterson 1985) that completely overlap those of Buena Vista (Table 12.1) and those of El Paraíso (Quilter et al. 1991). It should also be noted that the Late Preceramic Canto Grande site is separated by just a stone wall from a similar site associated with La Florída (Roselló 1978). A pattern of overlap of occupations during the late Late Preceramic and early Initial Period has been suggested for the north coast (Pozorski and Pozorski 1990a, although see Bischof 2000). For the purposes of this explication, I will continue using the traditional periodization, reserving the right of later revision.

The site of Buena Vista is found in area 11b_IX of the Carta Nacional 1:100,000 map of the Instituto Geográfico Nacional. The site is located at the mouth of a ravine that is usually dry, a location typical of Late Preceramic sites (e.g., Lanning 1963; Shady Solís 2000). Although the site extends to at least six hectares, the Late Preceramic monumental component is much smaller. The coordinates of the center of the Late Preceramic principle mounds, M-I and M-II, are 11° 43' 51" S and 76° 58' 5" W at 460 meters AMSL. It is about 45 kilometers from the coast and about 30 kilometers from El Paraíso, which is located on the bank of the Chillón River. Canto Grande lies about 25 kilometers toward the coast. The Chillón is one of a handful of coastal valleys that has water, at least in some parts, throughout the year. Buena Vista is situated in the middle valley, facing two side canyons that bring subsurface water to the Chillón floodplain, which creates a year-round swampy area.

Coca was intensively cultivated in the zone immediately above the site.

Today, plants such as corn, sweet potatoes, chili peppers, and diverse legumes are grown in the river valley in front of the site. Cotton is also still cultivated; it was ubiquitous at Buena Vista. Fruit orchards provide avocados, *lúcuma*, *guanábana*, *pacae*, prickly pear fruit, and loquats. Goats are herded. The climate is very mild: the temperature varies only between 17° C and 24° C and rain rarely falls, although fog is common. The site is protected from the rivers of coastal fog by encircling hills.

The desirability of the location is signaled by an Early Preceramic midden with a calibrated radiocarbon date of 5800 cal. BC (Benfer et al. 2010), perhaps not coincidentally the approximate time when the Middle Preceramic site of Paloma was first occupied (Benfer 1990), since this was a time of population increase on the coast (Rick 1987). Dates for later occupations from our testing show multiple occupations (Benfer et al. 2010). The Late Preceramic component dates from 2200 to 1750 cal. BC (Table 12.1). An Inca road was brought down to run directly in front the Late Preceramic structures (Figure 12.1). There are vestiges of an older road visible above the Inca road in the valley. A Chavín reoccupation of the site made some relatively slight additions to the Late Preceramic architecture. Buena Vista lacks the U-shaped configuration with circular sunken platforms characteristic of Initial Period ceramic-bearing sites such as La Florída, even though such architecture was present early in the Chillón Valley (Williams 1985). Circular structures (but not sunken ones) are found in Late Preceramic sites such as Chupacigarro/Caral (Williams 1978–1980, 1985) and are known in Late Preceramic sites such as Salinas de Chao (Cardenas 1979) and in the central coast at Canto Grande (Roselló 1978), among other sites. They are not present at Buena Vista, but sunken circular structures do exist at El Paraíso (Benfer 2011).

Buena Vista Late Preceramic Non-Monumental Architecture

The presence of rectangular stone domestic architecture at Buena Vista is interesting. Structures such as these were presumably the residences of elites. It is reasonable to assume, as Malpass and Stothert (1992, 150) have suggested, that the appearance of quadrangular house forms signals a shift toward accumulation of resources, which could have provisioned an elite. Pozorski and Pozorski (this volume) discuss square rooms in structures as characterizing Late Preceramic monumental architecture. At Buena Vista, astronomer-priests may have occupied these square structures, one of which has a ventilated hearth. A ventilated hearth is found in a domestic structure in the elite residences at Buena Vista as well as in the offering chamber of the Temple of the Fox in M-I (Benfer et al. 2010). The elite domestic structures were all heavily looted, although my colleagues and I did learn that each had a reoccupation; the earlier level appeared to have had different wall orientations, but we were not able to determine them accurately. It is possible that the lower level of structures was associated with M-I. These are the only examples of domestic architecture that we found in the Late Preceramic component at Buena Vista.

Dillehay (1992) has noted that the absence of domestic architecture at monumental Late Preceramic sites was common (see also Haas in this volume). Quilter did find substantial refuse in front of the temple at El Paraíso (Quilter et al. 1991). One might expect pilgrims to have lived there for a short period of time. His limited test pitting was not sufficient for the purpose of establishing if there was a large resident population, although there is little evidence against such a proposal (ibid., 281). If there was such a population, El Paraíso stands as an exception to Dillehay's generalization. At recent excavations at Chupacigarro/Caral by Shady Solís, considerable refuse and domestic architecture has been exposed, although upon examination, I found it not proportionate to the size of the site if it functioned as an urban center, as Shady Solís proposes (Shady Solís 1997; Shady Solís et al. 2000, Shady Solís, Haas, and Creamer 2001). Engel (1987) has noted that the carrying capacity of the nearby Supe River valley alone would not have been adequate to support a large residential population at Chupacigarro.

The Late Preceramic occupation at Buena Vista is of a much smaller scale than the occupation at Chupacigarro/Caral. Here too the numbers of domestic structures found seem too few for the magnitude of the monumental architecture, even at the smaller scale of the site. It better fits the pattern of a religious center, one with *ushnus* to which pilgrims might come and participate in ceremonies during which offerings were made. Hyslop (1990) suggests that open platforms for *ushnus* defined the center of Inca public ceremonies, although as we will see, the earliest ceremonies at Buena Vista were in structures with very restricted access. In sum, while there is abundant evidence of ritual activities, there is no secure evidence for domestic architecture near monumental architecture in the Late Preceramic to provide for more than a skeleton population, although the population was perhaps augmented for special ceremonies or to serve pilgrims (see Makowski 2006).

Buena Vista Late Preceramic Monumental Architecture

Visitors walking up the Chillón Valley toward Buena Vista in the Late Preceramic would have first seen a side of the hill that projects into the valley from south end of the site as a prominent architectural feature. Today, it is still covered with adobe bricks on some surfaces. If it was plastered and painted, it would have been visible for kilometers up and down the valley. Passing that monument, two stepped mounds, M-I (Figure 12.3) and M-II (Figure 12.4), with structures connecting them would have been visible. Each mound would have had a platform on top. Across the dry canal

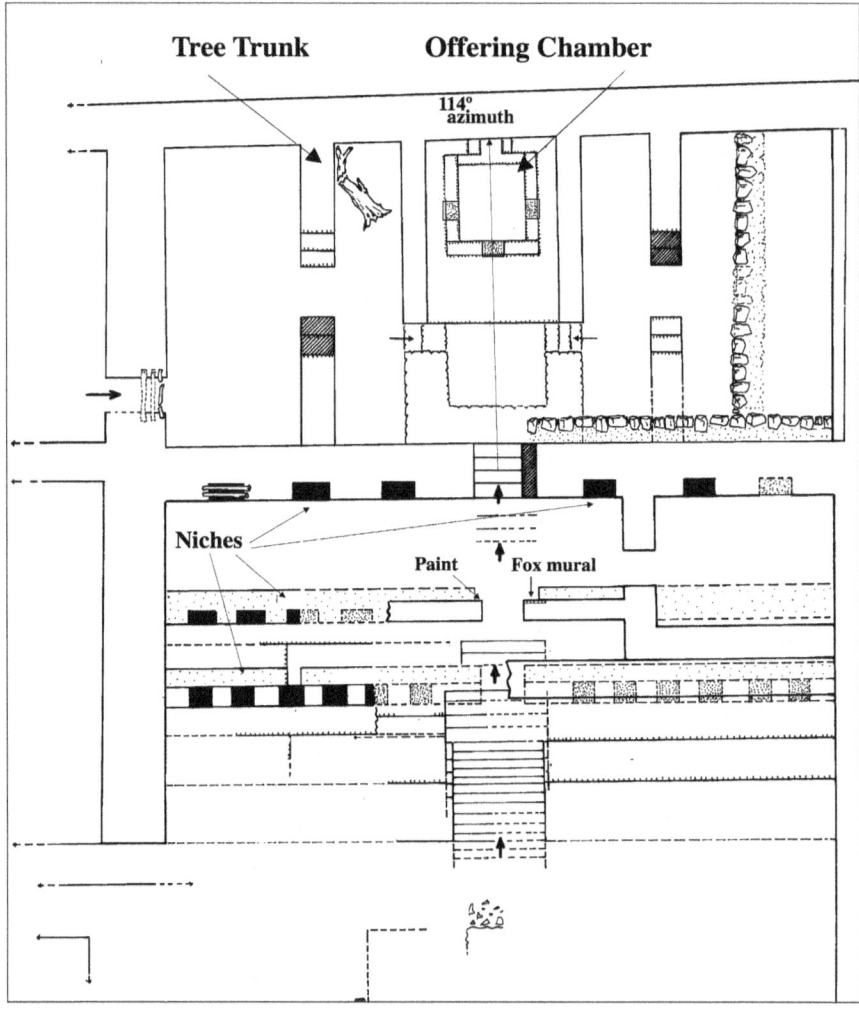

Figure 12.3. Plan view of upper section of Mound 1 showing the Temple of the Fox and niched walls.

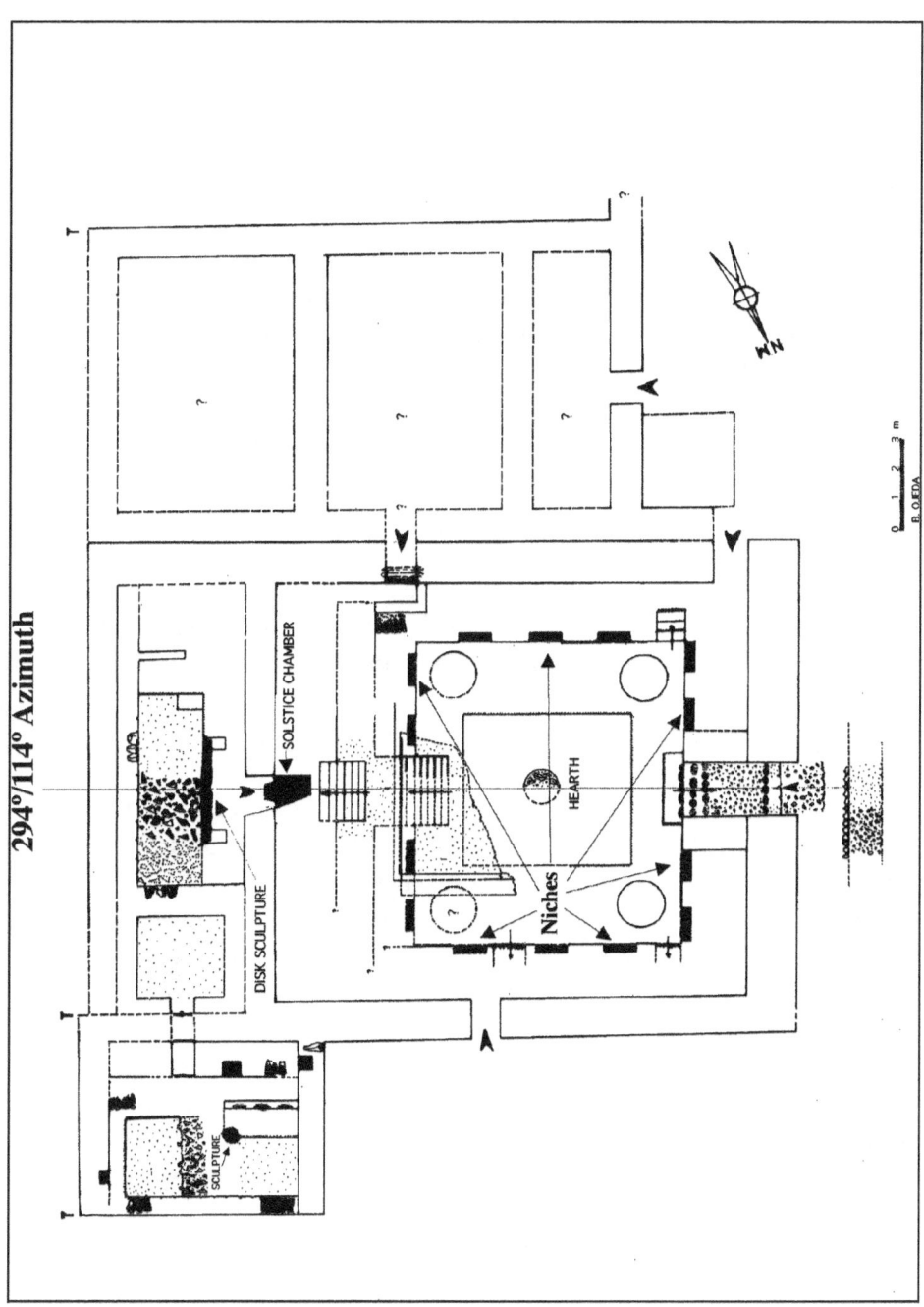

Figure 12.4. Plan view of Mound II showing Temple of El Paraiso del Valle with hearth in the lower section and Temple of the Menacing Disk in the upper section.

that drains the ravine, six stone domestic structures for elite use would have been visible (Figure 12.1). Looking to the east, three prominent stone spheres on the ridge would have attracted the eye—each appeared as the profile of a human head from below.

In the valley in front of the site are over 30 mounds that may be animal effigy mounds associated with the site (Benfer 2011). They are quite visible in Google Earth. They were incorrectly identified as late structures in a survey of the valley (Silva Sifuentes 1996). Although our team has mapped them, investigation is in the beginning stages for these structures, which range from 15 to 150 meters in length and from 1 meter to 5 meters in height. Pairs of giant effigy mounds, each with an astronomical orientation, are found at El Paraíso and in other coastal valleys (Benfer 2011). El Paraíso also has smaller mounds like the ones in front of Buena Vista. The mounds appear to be associated with Late Preceramic or Early Initial sites, but much work remains to be done to delimit these connections. Although the effigy mounds rise to the level of monumental architecture, they have only recently been identified and a fuller account will be given in another venue. Here I note that the few studied in detail are associated with Late Preceramic and/or Initial Period sites with astronomical complexes. The mounds in front of Buena Vista are clearly visible from the temples there.

Buena Vista Late Preceramic Temples

These temples have been described in detail elsewhere (Duncan, Pearsall, and Benfer 2009; Benfer et al. 2010; Benfer and Adkins in press). Three temples, one at M-I and two at M-II, were excavated.

The Temple of the Fox, a Mito temple located atop M-I (Bonnier 1997), was named for a fox incised in an entryway. In addition, an alignment of 114° 36' from the entryway to a rock placed on a ridge to the east defines the helical rise of the head of the Andean Fox constellation on December 21, shortly before the SSSR and the anticipated flood of the Chillón River. The Fox is fully risen after sunset on the March 21 equinox, when the river begins to subside. The temple's offering chamber contains two levels of benches, a lower level with niches, and an excavated ventilated hearth (Duncan, Pearsall, and Benfer 2009).

The mounds in the valley required considerable construction. Here I discuss the effort required to construct monumental stepped platform mounds. If there was no large settled population, from where would the laborers for the job of constructing the monumental architecture at Buena Vista be drawn?

Construction Effort

Perhaps domestic architecture that would indicate a substantial resident population does exist and is buried in the river valley sediments. If it does not, could a small group of astronomer-priests have constructed the temples themselves, perhaps with just the help of members of the *ayllu* (the extended family)? Or were laborers recruited from the entire valley? How much labor was involved? We can make some crude estimates from our own labor.

Excavated rock fill in 2008 was removed and placed in a walled rock pile with a volume of 2,240 cubic meters. Four laborers and three archaeologists accomplished this in five days. With the same team, we excavated a major collapsed wall that was 5 meters × 1.2 meters × 16 meters and contained about 800 rocks, which gives a density of about 8–9 rocks per cubic meter of wall. In order to protect excavated structures, we made false walls of rock with rubble fill strong enough to withstand wheelbarrows loaded with rocks passing over them. In three days, we created about 60 linear meters of rubble-filled walls that withstood an earthquake that measured magnitude 6.9 on the Richter scale in Lima 50 kilometers to the south.

The volume of the larger monument, M-I, can be estimated as approximately 6,000 cubic meters from the plan and profiles, given the estimate of maximum height of the temple of 11 meters with half that volume for the ramp and stairs up to it. At 2,000 kilograms/cubic meter this would have produced about 12,000,000 kilograms of weight to be lifted and carried. Our small team moved rocks from the surface weighing about 180,000 kilograms in a few weeks. If the rocks were brought down from the nearest quarry, about 100 meters distant, the task of quarrying, transporting, and setting them into place would have taken some time. Quarrying the metamorphosed rock from the quarries above the site would have been simple and not labor intensive, according to our experimental results. The Pleistocene riverbank is about 100 meters below the site. From our work, we estimate that 180,000 kilograms of rocks could have been accumulated in a few weeks. A very large pile of very large stored rocks exists at the base of the hill at the eastern extent of the site, presumably cached after being brought down from the nearby quarries for constructions that never took place. Larger quarried rocks would have been brought down hill, and river pebbles had to be selected and brought up to the site. Creating the rubble-filled walls and entryways and plastering and painting floors and walls would have required still more time. Of course, we did not plaster or paint our walls; however, we did spend time layering screened earth over low-acid paper against original walls and floors, then covering this fine earth with black plastic to contain the screened earth, then adding dirt and twin rubble-filled courses of rock walls to create the retaining walls.

From the above information, it can be suggested that farmers who lived in sight of Buena Vista could have done the initial mound construction in a matter of months and that subsequent additions would have taken less time.

Large plazas stratified by fill are found to the northwest of the monumental architecture, directly below the elite residences. A bulldozer destroyed more than a meter of deposits from the final floors. The base of the lowest platform is five meters below the former surface of the upper platform, and its area is approximately 1,500 square meters. At much as 7,500 cubic meters of fill was brought to the area for the platform. A radiocarbon date is available from the very base of the lowest platform, from human bones eroding in the riverbank. These bones were dated by Dolfus (1960) at 1610 cal. BC. The elite residences above the plaza yielded a date from charcoal from a ventilated hearth (Feature 104) of 2000 BC. Two samples of carbonized wood from offerings in the Temple of the Fox on M-I produced the same date (rounded off to decade) of 2,200 cal. BC. The elite residences are more associated with M-II than with the initial plaza construction or M-I, unless the lower suite of undated rooms was built at the time M-I was being constructed (Table 12.1). Four sets of superimposed stairs suggest at least that many building episodes on M-I, while the three sets of niched walls on the eastern face (Figure 12.5) suggest at least three. In the upper wall in M-I, a wood viga has a calibrated date of 1540 cal. BC, which is slightly earlier than the base of the plaza's first construction (Table 12.1). The possibility that the viga was reused from another earlier context cannot be discounted. The later levels of the plazas may belong to a later occupation, although we have no dates for it. Early Horizon ceramics were superimposed on the Late Preceramic platform mounds after the two temples were filled with *shicra* (net bags filled with stone) and covered by a thin floor. Presumably the platform remained in use.

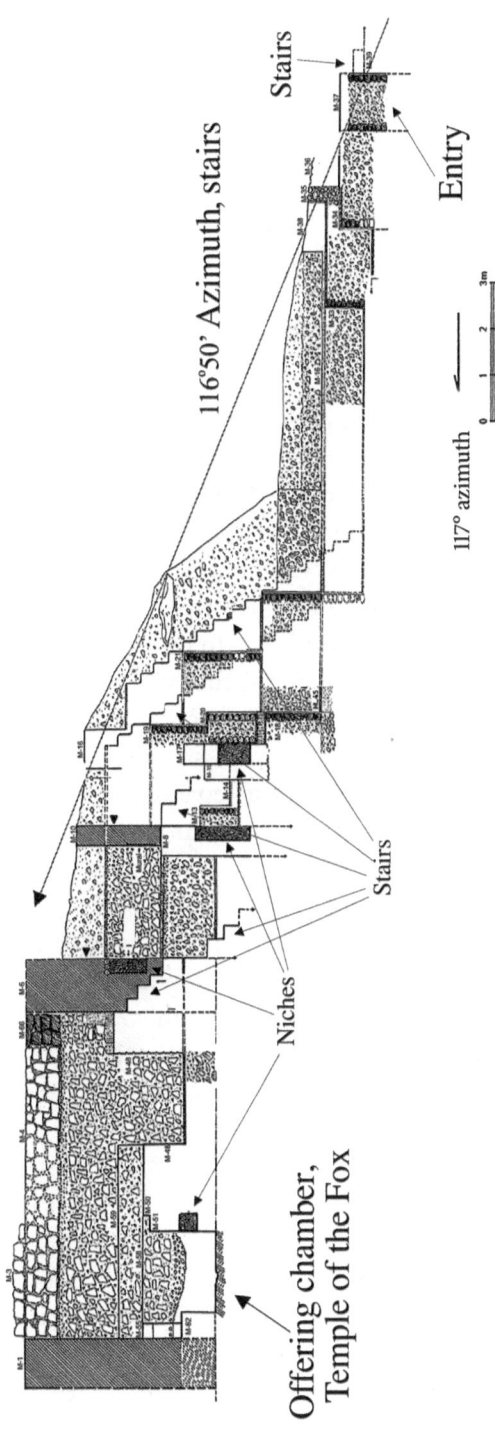

Figure 12.5. Profile of Mound I showing superimposed stairs and Temple of the Fox in the upper platform.

Two astronomical structures in M-II provide dates of 2000 BC and 2030 BC from fibers from mud plaster (Table 12.1). Their location at the top of M-II suggests that the mound was used for astronomical alignments after the temple on top of M-I was covered at 2200 BC in a final feast (Duncan, Pearsall, and Benfer 2009).

Sometimes a novel pattern appears in construction (Beck et al. 2007, 834). In the case of Buena Vista, observational instruments changed significantly over just a few centuries.

Construction Techniques

Space permits only a brief discussion of construction techniques. Dressed stones were used only in the outer courses of the western faces of M-I and M-II. Rubble-filled walls of stone were covered with mud plaster and were usually recovered, as many as 20 times in M-II. Traces of red, yellow, white, dark blue, and black paint have been found on the walls. *Shicra* were used to carefully inter temples before building a new floor over them, a common Late Preceramic practice (e.g., Bonnier 1997). In the earlier deposits, rocks were more commonly brought from the river than quarried from locations above the site, although in later fill, angular quarried rocks were mixed in with large river rocks. Small spheres of mud plaster were used as fill in the mud-plaster sculpture. An arch of river rocks separated by mud plaster preserved one low niche intact; it is still supporting three meters of overburden after 3,750 years. Other partially collapsed roofs made the construction of the arches visible. Since the dates from this temple are before 1700 BC (Table 12.1), we assume this to be one of the oldest reported uses of an arch—not a true arch, but an effective arch nonetheless. Wooden vigas in entryways suggest that temples were roofed, presumably with straw mats, as does a large tree trunk with a flattened base found in the Temple of the Fox in M-I. Floors were hard mud plaster, hard enough to survive 4,000 years. Offerings have continued in the deposits of M-II until the present.

Decorative Elements

A distinctive feature of Late Preceramic architecture is the horizontal lip, a bevel that divides the upper from the lower wall of rooms; it was ubiquitous at Buena Vista. Niches are another common feature. Inside the small sunken Mito offering chamber of the Temple of the Fox, niches were visible only to the few who could enter the temple or view them from above. Niched walls facing west from M-I would have been visible to large numbers of people (Figure 12.3). A sculpture in the form of a personified disk in M-I (but not its flanking mythical animals) would have been visible through the entryway. A variety of niche forms were noted. A hearth is located in the center of the Temple El Paraíso del Valle, to be discussed below. Low-relief panels are sculpted into a basket-weave motif on the inner wall, which covers an earlier wall of niches. Activities in the temple would have been visible to a larger group than could have been accommodated in either of the earlier temples (Figure 12.6).

Access to another possible offering chamber would have been limited. This one was found 5 meters below the surface to the north of the Temple of the Menacing Disk in M-II, to be discussed below. A life-size bust of a musician at the rear entry to the Temple of the Menacing Disk is described elsewhere (Benfer et al. 2010). Incised and painted murals adorn the site. A fox incised into a painted llama body wraps around the southern jamb of the western entryway of the Temple of the Fox in M-I. Fragments of paint on the more deteriorated northern jamb suggest that another mural was painted and incised there. Representations of all the mythical foxes depicted at Buena Vista are described elsewhere (Benfer, Furbee, and Ludeña R. 2011). A small painted mural was discovered in a later wall in the Temple Paraíso del Valle in M-II in 2008, but it has not been fully exposed or excavated.

Shiny black stones were placed in stairs at critical points, such as the step down and behind the Menacing Disk sculpture, and were also embedded in the center of the first entryway step of both M-I and M-II. The three stone heads on the eastern ridge attract the eye from any location at the site. The first (Rock A) was purposefully retouched in the form of a human head with a projection on top, a style that persists into the Initial Period, for example as stone talons at Chavín de Huántar. An as-yet-undescribed stone ax excavated from in front of the Menacing Disk appeared to have a Staff God painted in red on a pecked surface. The representation is known for Late Preceramic sites in an incised gourd reported by Haas, Creamer, and Ruiz (2003, 9), which dates to about the time of the Temple of the Fox at Buena Vista. The Staff God continued in later time periods (Isbell and Knobloch 2006). A stone pillar retouched to form a condor has recently been discovered at the point where the equinoctial sun would rise if viewed from the entryway to the Temple of the Fox (Benfer 2010a).

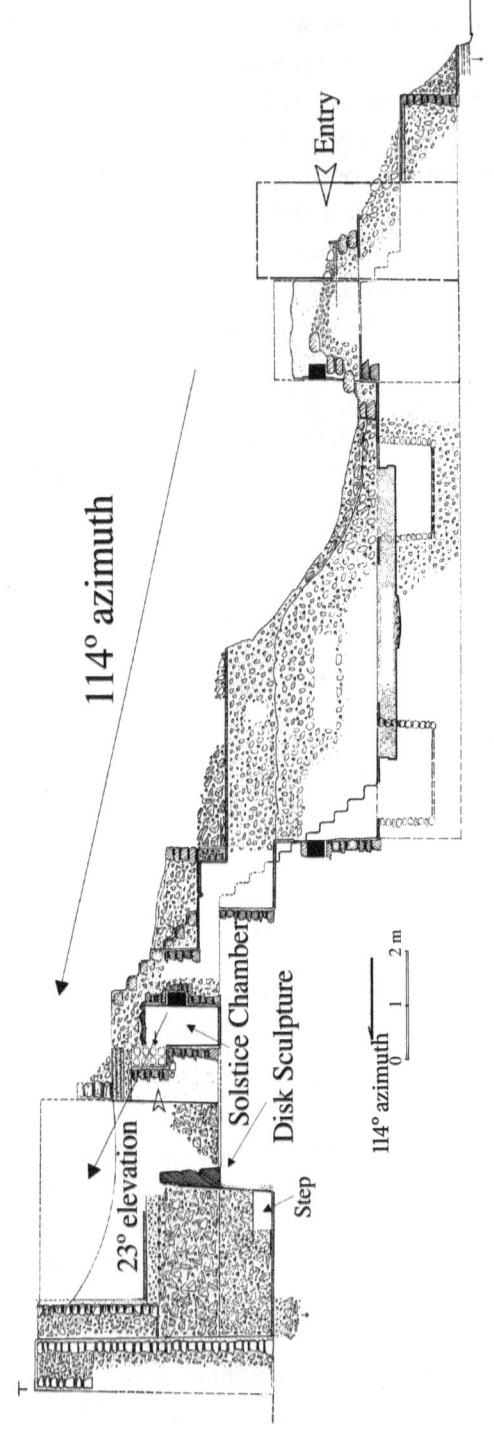

Figure 12.6. Profile of Mound II showing stairs to the platform of the Menacing Disk leading up from the Temple Paraíso del Valle with its central hearth and three (probably four) corner offering pits.

Special Structures as Alignments of Observational Instruments

Pilgrims and valley residents could have been drawn to the site for the ritual offerings to the earth and ceremonies that would take place on days determined by sky events. In order to keep track of the astronomical calendar, the astronomer-priests built special structures. These structures were systematically misaligned with the massive walls that surround them. This asymmetry, otherwise uncommon in Late Preceramic sites, could suggest competing systems of cosmology. The construction of the main mounds could have followed different prescriptions from the temples on their tops. As I will show below, features of the main construction, especially the stairs, can exhibit astronomical alignments independent of those from the temple on the platforms to which the stairs led.

Before I turn to astronomical alignments, I describe the architectural features that include astronomical orientations or alignments of the two principle mounds and the elite residences found just to the north of them.

Architectural Alignments and Orientations

A number of architectural features can themselves serve as means of making accurate astronomical observations through their alignment. These include long stairways, entryways to and exits from rooms, light and shadow casting from entryways to niches, and corridors, to suggest some likely candidates. In general, wall orientations will not serve this purpose. For example, at the central coast site of Pachacamac (Piñasco Carrella 2007), wall orientations from various time periods appear to point in the general direction toward astronomical events that we know were of interest. At Pachacamac, these include solar, lunar, and constellation risings and settings as well as the extreme orientation of the Milky Way.

Generally, the long axis of sites or the direction of U-shaped arms of Initial Period sites is around 25°–30°, the orientation of the Milky Way. The azimuth of the long axis of the Temple of the Fox at Buena Vista is 22° 24', the azimuth of the long axis of the Temple of the Menacing Disk is 25° 26', and the elite residences to the north of the Temple of the Fox have an orientation of 25° 32' (Figure 12.1), which suggests a clearer association of the elite residences with the Temple of the Menacing Disk than with the Fox (which corresponds well with the radiocarbon dates presented in Table 12.1). Quilter (1991) had earlier noted that the orientation of the principal mounds at El Paraíso, the other Late Preceramic site in the Chillón Valley, was 25°. However, I measure a slightly different orientation of about 34° (Benfer 2011). Other U-shaped Initial Period sites in the Chillón and Rímac tend toward this extreme axis of the Milky Way, as shown in the maps of Williams (1978–1980, Figures 3 and 4). Long axis orientations between 25° and 35° would accept astronomical instruments facing across the short axis to determine the solstices.

If the long axis parallels a river valley, as is the general case, then the ridges on each side provide a convenient place to establish reference points. Although the long axes of most Late Preceramic and Initial Period sites tend to be only those that permit an observatory to view astronomical events across their short axes, some sites are themselves oriented to a solstice along the long axis or by their major entry stairways. For example, when viewed from Google Earth, Sechín Bajo can be seen to be such an example. In general, however, we have found that it is the short axes of Late Preceramic sites that are oriented toward celestial events (Benfer and Adkins 2009). I turn next to astronomical alignments at Buena Vista that are directly associated with monumental architecture, recalling that in my definition of astronomical alignments, they must measure celestial events precisely to within a day or two.

Astronomical Alignments of Mound I

As discussed above, M-I faces the river valley, which at a glance appeared to be the organizing feature of the site. Alignment with a mountain peak has to be considered, since astronomical alignments of viewing points with mountain peaks (*apus*; animated mountain tops) have been reported (e.g., Meddens et al. 2008). As one looks from the center of the lower steps of M-I, which are still preserved, to the tallest mountain to the east, one obtains an azimuth of 119° 42' (Figures 12.1 and 12.5). This line does not parallel the stairs up the mound. The maximum distance south that a moon could ever rise, the major standstill, occurred every 18.6 years. Its alignment would have been at 119° 36' over a flat horizon. However, the altitude of the *apu* precluded seeing such a moonrise, which would have occurred about four degrees to the north, because the mountain would have blocked the horizon. There is another possibility that could connect M-I with an *apu*. The approximate center of the Andean dark-cloud Llama constellation would have risen over the *apu* at 24° elevation on December 21, 2200 BC, the SSSR, just before sunrise. It should also be noted that viewed from the entryway of the Temple of the Fox on top of M-I, a platform in living stone,

one of two, had an azimuth of 120° 30', further marking the event. This Fox constellation alignment must have been important both in the original construction of both the mounds and the temples on top.

Because of its length and narrowness, the orientation of the central stairway up M-I could be used as an alignment (Benfer and Adkins 2010). Instead of looking to the *apu*, we measured the alignment from the center of the lower and upper stairs. We observed an azimuth 116° 50'. A related alignment is also associated with the M-I stairs. Another platform pecked out in the living rock on the eastern ridge has an azimuth of 117° 30' when viewed from the center of the lower stairs up M-I. These two alignments are close to a major southern lunar standstill of the full moon at 2211 BC, which could have been seen by inhabitants of Buena Vista over the ridge from the stairways, with an elevation of 26° and an azimuth of 117° 30' (Adkins and Benfer 2010). How could this event, which took place only every 18.6 years, have been determined? A gnomon method could have done the job with simple materials (ibid.). Unfortunately, statements have been published suggesting the improbability of lunar alignments in coastal Perú (Ghezzi and Ruggles 2007). These claims are difficult to accept, since abundant evidence points to the prominence of the moon over the sun in coastal Perú. To mention just one example, coastal peoples celebrated the eclipse of the sun but lamented the eclipse of the moon (Itier 1997). A long-standing preexisting prejudice appears to have been brought from another continent by Clive Ruggles (e.g., Ruggles 1982; Ruggles 2011). Ruggles insists on interpreting a ridge at the site of Chankillo with 13 towers (the universal number of lunar months in a year) as solar (Ghezzi and Ruggles 2007). However, the major orientations of sites in the Casma differ from a random expectation, and the mode for lunar orientations is one of the principle modes (Benfer and Adkins 2011). The importance of the lunar and orientations of the site of Chankillo is well known to scholars (e.g., Pozorski and Pozorski 1987, 95–103; Adkins and Benfer 2010; Ianiszewski R. 2010, 162–163; Mallville 2011), and it would be impossible for most Peruvian scholars familiar with the archaeology, ethnohistory, and ethnography of coastal peoples to accept that the moon played no role in the cosmology represented in the architecture of these sites. In any case, I report examples of obvious lunar alignments in this chapter.

Since the river flows in a generally northern direction in this section of the valley, it was easy for astronomer-priests, indeed for farmers, to notice the extremes of the north-south rises and sets of the sun and moon over the valley ridges to the east and west. Reference points could easily be placed on a ridge a few hundred meters to the east at Buena Vista; the western horizon is much farther away. Three stone heads and the two stone platforms on the eastern ridge served as useful reference points. The chief feature on top of M-I, just beneath a later platform floor, is a Mito temple, the Temple of the Fox. Its entryway is a viewing point for a number of reference points.

The Temple of the Fox

The Temple of the Fox is located atop M-I. As noted above, it was named for a fox incised in an entryway. In addition, an alignment of 114° 36' from the entryway to a rock placed on a ridge to the east defines the helical rise of the head of the Andean Fox constellation on December 21, shortly before the anticipated rise of the Chillón River. The Fox is fully risen after the equinoctial sunset on March 21, when the river will soon subside. As was discussed above, the orientation of the entry to this temple is also to the rise of the Fox constellation.

When we encountered the western entryway of the Temple of the Fox, it was impossible to not see what looked like a "sighting device," a U-shaped niche in the eastern wall of the offering chamber. One's eye was attracted through it to the eastern ridge, where a round stone seemed to be aligned with the offering chamber. I set up a transit over the measured center of the original entryway and asked a workman to place a stadia rod as close to the center of the gunsight-shaped niche as possible. I recorded the azimuth as 114° 32 '. This, I found out later, is the azimuth of the Austral SSSR at the latitude of the site. Declination, the degree of change in magnetic north, happened to be 0' when the sight was taken in 2004. As I tipped the transit upward, the cross-hairs centered on the rock visible on the ridge, which we named Rock B.

Further reconnaissance showed that three stones had been placed on the ridge; the most northerly, Rock A, was the only one that had been certainly retouched to form a human head, and it had a projection on top. The other two rocks, although they have not been retouched, still present the profile of a human head when viewed from a distance. It was calculated later that the actual SSSR would have been observed in 2200 BC over Rock A, not Rock B, just before the SSSS. This is because although the flat horizon solstice is 114°, the ridges impede viewing of that event; the solstice sun actually rises over the ridge at 112° at 27° elevation, which is the azimuth of Rock A from the entry to the Temple of the Fox (Figure 12.7). The general *orientations* of the major walls of M-I are about 112°/292°. This SSSR wall

Figure 12.7. View of summer solstice sun rising over Rock A from the entryway of the Temple of the Fox on December 19, 2006. The sunrise from that viewing point on December 21, 2200 BC would have been almost one solar diameter to the north (left); the photograph accurately reproduces the view from the offering chamber of the Temple of the Fox on that date. The chamber lies in an azimuth of 114° from the point at which the photograph was taken, at the entry to the temple. The profiles of two of the three rocks are visible on the ridge to the east. Rock B provides the alignment for the flat-horizon sunrise on the solstice; it also marks the point that any moonrise at the right (or to the south) would signal an eminent lunar standstill. Finally, the Andean Fox constellation rose over Rock B shortly before sunrise on December 21, 2200 BC and was fully risen shortly after sunrise on March 21, 2200 BC.

orientation may be a widespread phenomenon. Fuchs and Lorenz (2009) found the same orientation for a newly discovered earlier component of the Sechín Alto site, which has structures that are oriented toward the SSSR, which is quite different from the WSSR described by the later component at the site.

Rock B at Buena Vista may be a reference point for the flat-horizon SSSS. More likely, it served to announce the rise of the Andean Fox constellation. Recall that the Fox constellation rises before the sun on the December solstice. Rock B is also the point beyond which a moonrise viewed from the Temple of the Fox signals an imminent major lunar standstill every 18.6 years (Adkins and Benfer 2009). Rock C serves the same purpose for the temple atop M-II (Benfer et al. 2010). The use of one astronomical event to mark another invisible one is well known in prehistory. Ancient Egyptians used the heliacal rise of Sirius to signal the solstice sunrise and oriented their temples to the solstices. Because of obscuring hills, the solstice sunrises were not visible. They used the heliacal rise of Sirius to signal that date. In the case of the Temple of Isis, the association of Isis with Sirius made the connection more evident (Kelley and Milone 2005, 268). This parallels the association of the fox image in its temple at Buena Vista with the rising of the Andean Fox constellation before the solstice sun.

In addition to the Fox mural in M-I, there is another fox image, this one in low relief, at the end of a small wall with an azimuth of 110° in M-II. This wall points toward Rock B and is quite asymmetrical to surrounding walls (Benfer et al. 2010). In M-II, two foxes frame the central disk sculpture. As mentioned, the Fox constellation alignments at Buena Vista are important. Urton (1981) has pointed out that this constellation is still important in Andean belief systems today.

The Andean Fox and Llama constellations are associated with the bringing of cultigens, canals for irrigation, and seasons as well as astronomical events in ethnographical (Urton 1981; Howard-Malverde 1984; Sullivan 1996), ethnohistorical (Salomon and Urioste 1991), and archaeological contexts at later sites (Bruhns 1976; Pinasco C. 2007; Sullivan 1996; Zeidler 1998; Pitluga 2003; Itier 1997; La Riva 2003).

One more alignment, this one associated with the fox and llama, is the equinox. It is defined at Buena Vista by viewing from the entryway of the Temple of the Fox to a rectangular rock placed on a ridge directly in front of one of two stone pillars, that one with the head heavily retouched into the shape of a condor head (Benfer and Adkins 2011).

Astronomical Alignments at Mound II

The Temple of the Menacing Disk

In 2005, we found an almost intact sculpture of *barro*, mud plaster, with grass temper that is covered with unbaked clay. The figure was found in a temple at the top of Mound II (Figures 12.8 and 12.9). Two psychologists with expertise in facial identification independently identified the countenance of the disk as menacing (Figure 12. 8). Therefore we refer to it as the

Monumental Architecture Arising from an Early Astronomical-Religious Complex in Perú · 347

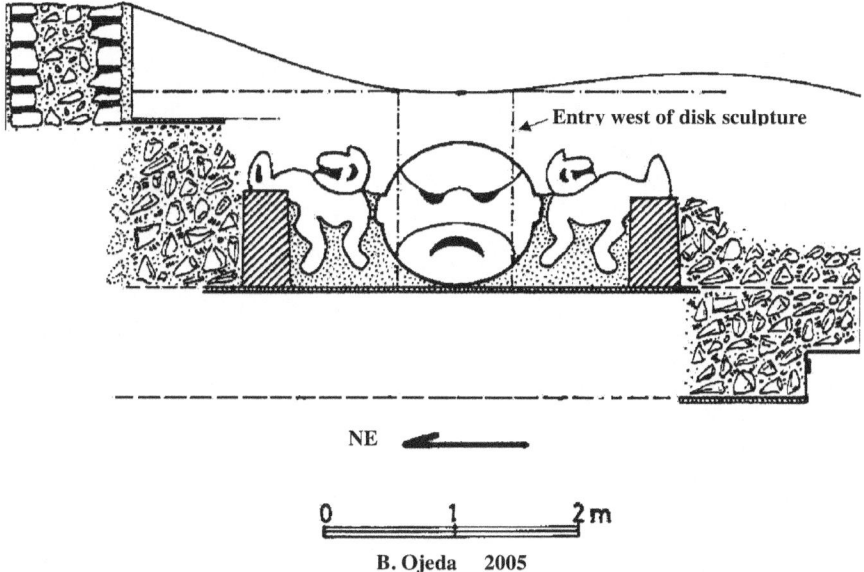

Figure 12.8. Drawing of Menacing Disk facing the WSSS. Note the crescent eyes on the two animals. Note that although the animal to the left has a larger tail, the one to the right has a much larger head. The patch in the tail corresponds to one found in the mural of the Fox on the left side of the entryway to the Temple of the Fox (Benfer and Adkins 2006).

Menacing Disk. The sculpture gazes through a narrow entryway (Figure 12.9) with an azimuth of 294° toward the SSSS. This is directly opposite the 114° azimuth defined by the Temple of the Fox. Mythical foxes, which flank the disk, look to the western SSSS through crescent-shaped lunar eyes. One round solar eye from the smaller fox sculpture stares at the actual SSSR over a rock placed there, Rock C, to the east (Figure 12.9). The orientation of the personified disk sculpture is not without precedent. Amenhotep had sculptures of two humans erected in the Theban necropolis in the second millennium BC. Their faces are oriented toward the solstice and (as at Buena Vista) announced the arrival of the annual floods that permitted agriculture (Lockyear 1894, 78).

The disk sculpture, like the offering chamber of the Temple of the Fox, is not constructed parallel to the large exterior walls. Like the Temple of the Fox, the Temple of the Menacing Disk marked both the summer solstice sunrise and the winter solstice sunset (with its solar and lunar eyes).

Figure 12.9. Gaze of Menacing Disk to WSSS, flanked by supernatural animals. The face of the disk (see Figure 12.8) is gazing through the subsequently filled entryway. Note the round eye on the animal to the left, which is the smaller; the animal to the right has a triangular patch in its tail like the mural of the Fox in the Temple of the Fox and like paired animals in later Moche times.

Human Sculpture

A sculpture partially excavated in the 2005 season is that of a life-sized bust of a seated human figure. Its legs are sculpted in high relief and hang over the edge of one of a series of platforms at the northern exit of the temple on top of M-II. It is looking toward an azimuth of approximately 35°. This is 180° from the average azimuth of the three rocks on the ridge, which is approximately the azimuth of the Milky Way. As noted, Late Preceramic sites such as Buena Vista and El Paraíso have a general long axis orientation of between 25° and 35°. The two giant effigy mounds we recently recognized at El Paraíso certainly also fall in this range (Benfer 2011). The largest Initial Period site in the Chillón valley, Huacoy, which has an Early Horizon component in its tallest mound, also has an azimuth of 35° looking from a temple on the mound through parallel arms (Silva Sifuentes and Tello 2000). The Buena Vista sculptures and murals show the control of public art exercised by astronomer-priests. Astronomical alignments are incorporated into the stone and into mud plaster heads and various representations of mythical foxes.

Solstice Light Chamber

A third instrument, a niched chamber with stone vigas that captures the solstice sunrise light, has been presented (Benfer and Adkins 2009) but will be published elsewhere (Benfer and Adkins in press). It obstructed the gaze of the disk and dates only shortly after the construction of the disk sculpture (Table 12.1).

The Temple of Paraíso del Valle

Below the temple of the Menacing Disk and solstice light chamber is another, slightly later one, the Temple of Paraíso del Valle (Figure 12.5), which dates to about 1750 to 1850 BC. This temple bears a very close resemblance to the temple at El Paraíso, which is near the coast of the same valley. It is an open structure. A central hearth provided two dates: 1850 BC for the lowest stratum, which is capped by hard baked earth and charcoal, and 1750 BC for the upper level (Table 12.1) Walls with niches were later covered and replastered with a basket-weave–faced pattern inside panels. Three cylindrical offering chambers were found (the probable location of the fourth was not excavated). A line crossing two of the circular pits is oriented to the WSSS. This line crosses the center of two stone pillars set on the hill to the east at 66°. The temple is quite similar to the one at El Paraíso (Engel 1966), in which the central area did not have an excavated hearth but was covered with ash. The cylindrical chambers at El Paraíso are above ground rather than below, as at Buena Vista.

An SSSR line with an azimuth of 114° runs from the center of the western entryway of the Temple Paraíso del Valle to the central hearth, then to the center of the stairs that go up to the disk sculpture, to a solstice chamber (briefly mentioned above), to the center of the disk, and on to the center of a platform pecked in the living rock on the ridge to the east. It finally crosses a prehistoric quartz mine (Benfer and Adkins in press). To the west, the disk face is gazing at a natural saddle on the mountains. We found early ceramics on the surface and ash deposits immediately beneath. This is a very large number of reference points, which demonstrates the importance of the summer solstice sunrise to the astronomer-priests who directed these constructions and possibly the rituals that took place on this natural saddle.

Even three reference points in a line are rare in reported archaeoastronomy investigations, possibly due to the lack of pedestrian searches. I conclude that the Temple Paraíso del Valle continued to mark the same events as the earlier temples did—the beginning and end of planting and harvesting festivals—even after the earlier temples were abandoned.

Conclusions

The Buena Vista site faces the river valley. However, the orientation of the principle stepped mound appears to be simultaneously associated with moonrises to the extreme south and the rise of the principle Andean water constellations, especially the Fox. The hypothesis that astronomer-priests placed special instruments for observing solstices and other sky events in the tops of the mounds is supported. These observational instruments are a few degrees off from being parallel with surrounding walls in otherwise symmetrical architecture. Each has multiple reference points. The solstice sunrises were marked by stones set on the ridge to the east along with other points that lay along the same line. These instruments provide clear evidence that the sky events associated with offerings to the earth, *ushnus,* are much older than previously known. That major walls show astronomical orientations makes their importance clear on an even larger scale than the instruments. Their orientations shows that the astronomer-priests played a role in the construction of these walls as well as in the construction of the observatories.

Within the Buena Vista Astronomer-Priest Tradition, the early centuries were a time of dramatic changes in ritual. For example, the Temple of the Fox was covered over to make a platform. Later, the Menacing Disk sculpture in M-II was covered to permit the solstice view of a chamber. It too was covered, and a new, larger, more open offering chamber was constructed to its west. In the end, the tops of both original mounds presented simple platforms after the arrival of the Chavín cult.

Early astronomer-priests exchanged their power to exclusively manage rituals in restricted locations for the power of public ritual. By the end of the Late Preceramic Period, the priests may have completely lost exclusive control of sky and terrestrial events (e.g., Hirth 1996). At Buena Vista, the last temple, Paraíso del Valle, was erected in the late Late Preceramic. It was much more open to the public. Unfortunately for those looking for evolutionary trends, this practice in fact harks back to much earlier, more public ceremonies that surely took place around the long rays from structures, as in Canto Grande.

Astronomer-priests continue to play important roles across much of indigenous South America. In Colombia, to give just a single example, the SSSR is still monitored by astronomer-priests (Reichel-Domatoff 1990) as the crossing of two hearths by the sun's rays (Krupp 2003). The ritual has returned to taking place in a location of restricted access. In Inca times, many rituals were public, and the role of the astronomer was merely that of an important specialist (Bauer and Dearborn 1995, 56). Astronomical/astrological knowledge can still be embedded in a culture, even without conscious knowledge of the culture's members. For example, we can align streets to equinoxes in modern cities, yet the role of the astrologer or astronomer is no longer one of great importance. We live in a built environment that reflects some aspects of ancient beliefs of organization. Many still look to astrology, the astronomy of the past, for daily guidance.

Did priests actually direct the building of monumental architecture, the hypothesis of this chapter? Since the major walls of most monumental architecture that we have examined in coastal valleys have astronomical orientations, it seems evident that they did. As Haas (this volume) notes, someone or some group was necessary to direct construction of monumental architecture. If the group consisted of astronomer-priests, how were they organized? Perhaps there was a heterarchy of power, as is known in European prehistory (Crumley 1995), a concept of possible utility in South American (Roosevelt this volume). However, it is known that almost 4,000 years later, Inca society was organized in an extreme hierarchy. We can ask, abductively (Benfer, Brent, and Furbee 1991), what evidence would support a different system in the third millennium BC? It seems possible that priests who directed the offerings to the earth could have controlled some aspects of ceremonies, and priests who managed the movements of celestial bodies in the sky could have controlled other aspects of ritual life, including the construction of pyramids and temples. There is some evidence that could support separation of ritual functions by cults.

The Temple of the Fox and the Temple of El Paraíso both have astronomical alignments and hearths for offerings to the earth. The Temple of the Menacing Disk lacks an offering chamber. It was covered up and the solstice chamber was constructed. Fill inside the solstice chamber contained many coca leaves, including some at a small hearth on the floor, so it qualifies as an *ushnu*, a structure that captured an astronomical event and provided a receptacle for offerings. If there was only one cult managed by a single group of astronomer-priests, it is surprising that a temple with such a dramatic sculpture looking at the solstice sunset would lack a place for offerings. It did have an axe buried in front of the disk, but there was no hearth. This is very slight evidence, but it does not support the idea that a single cult managed offerings to the sky and earth persistently over centuries.

By 1750 cal. BC, the Temple of the Menacing Disk and the later solstice chamber had been covered by platforms where more public ceremonies took place in the Temple of Paraíso del Valle. Astronomical orientations and a central hearth define it as an *ushnu*. Possibly the followers of Pachamama prevailed (Ludeña 2006) and established a new, more public cult. The reference points on the ridges continued to be available, but now the sightings would be from public *ushnus* that more nearly resemble the pattern later used by the Inca (Zuidema 1990; Staller 2008).

Perhaps the Late Preceramic occupation of Buena Vista was the time and the middle valley was the place where the solar cults began to challenge the older lunar cult of fishermen. Yet this is contradicted by the fact that in the Middle Preceramic village in Perú, Paloma, in the last occupation, at 3000 BC, there was an earlier summer solstice orientation to burials and entryways. The relation of solar and lunar cults remains to be established, but the preliminary evidence suggests there may have been changing fortunes for the sun and the moon in coastal Perú over a very long period of time. Nonetheless, the sun and moon played some role in the design of all mounds and structures studied to date.

More examples are necessary before we can treat the cases known so far as enough texts to attempt an interpretation. Or we might follow another methodology, mining the data of all possibilities using Monte Carlo simulation to exclude chance ones. More deductive tests of associations arrived at inductively are necessary to refine our understanding of the pattern of monumental architecture in coastal Perú. If there is a strong pattern, all methods should converge on the same explanation. The explanation I suggest is that astronomer-priests who managed the sky and the earth for the people directed the construction of mounds and temples.

If they were astronomer-priests, how were they organized? Perhaps there was a heterarchy of power, as known in European prehistory (Crumley 1995), a concept of possible utility in South American (Roosevelt et al. this volume). Knowledge of astronomical events was gained by those responsible for ensuring good harvests and good catches. Were these two cults that were organized in a hierarchical manner, just one cult, or two independent cults? Haas and Creamer (this volume) see hierarchy in the Late Preceramic mounds in Norte Chico. Pozorski and Pozorski (this volume) see a similarly early phenomenon in the Casma Valley in inland and coastal sites, which culminated in the hierarchical Sechín Alto polity during the Initial Period. In contrast, Burger and Salazar (this volume) do not see strong hierarchical relations among Initial Period sedentary food producers on Perú's south coast, where smaller mounds were erected.

Perhaps there was a heterarchy, with one group supervising construction of canals and agriculture and another managing the sky. An expression of heterarchy might have performed differently in the Andean world of dualities. As discussed above, the evidence is equivocal. The absence of an offering chamber hearth in the Temple of the Disk, which so clearly looks toward a solstice sunset, does suggest a possible divide between two cults of priests. If hierarchies characterized polities, might simple heterarchies have defined early priesthood?

Schmidt (2001, 46) has argued that temples preceded the oldest settlements in the Old World. Temples may have enjoyed the same precedence in the New World. In coastal Perú, early monumental architecture resembles pilgrimage centers more than towns (Silverman 1994; Makowski 2006; although see Shady Solís 1997). Thus, religious knowledge may have been more powerful than political power in early Peruvian prehistory at the time of the first erection of monumental architecture. The fact that hierarchies have not been detected in Middle Preceramic times makes this possibility more probable.

Further research is necessary to test the hypothesis that the very first purposefully constructed stepped pyramids, geoglyphs, and animal effigy mounds in the Americas were built under the supervision of astronomer-priests. Research in monumental architecture must include reconnaissance for reference points predicted by astronomical alignments. Preliminary results at El Paraíso and Sechín Bajo (Benfer and Adkins 2011) confirm viewing points with multiple alignments toward a reference point. Where such multiple points are found, excavation must be done below platform floors on truncated pyramids to search for associated offering chambers and layers of pebbles that once ritually purified libations. Radiocarbon assay of effigy mounds must be used to confirm the current date, their propinquity to Late Preceramic sites, and the absence of surface ceramics. The data presented so far are quite strong.

Any theory that purports to explain the development of monumental architecture in Perú, one of the pristine areas of development, must account for the role and organization of astronomer/priests who directed the construction of such structures.

Acknowledgments

I thank the National Geographic Society, the Curtiss and Mary G. Brennan Foundation, and the University of Missouri Research Board for financial support of the Buena Vista project. Hugo Ludeña R. has been the co-director of the project and Larry R. Adkins the essential astronomer. Gloria Villarreal directed the laboratory. Bernardino Ojeda and Neil A. Duncan have been field supervisors of the work at Buena Vista. The precision of their work can been seen in the fact that all radiocarbon dates are as expected in date and in order where samples stratified by either depth or architecture were taken. I also wish to thank the participants in the two field schools through the University of Missouri and the Universidad Nacional Federrico Villarreal of Perú. The Centro de Investigaciones de Zonas Áridas of the Universidad Nacional Agraria—La Molina continue to provide space and supporting staff, as they have for the last 35 years. I want to especially acknowledge the work of Peruvian volunteers for their exceptional contributions in the field and in the laboratory. Bernardino Ojeda made and drafted the maps. I thank the National Institute of Culture of Perú for permitting us to undertake this research. Finally, the University Press of Florida copy editor made many valuable critical suggestions, for which I am very grateful.

References Cited

Adkins, Larry R., and Robert A. Benfer
2009 Lunar Standstill Markers at Preceramic Temples at the Buena Vista Site in Peru. *Astronomical Society of the Pacific Conference Series* 409:267–278.
2010 Lunar Standstill Phenomena at the Preceramic Buena Vista Site in Perú. Paper presented at the 75th Annual Meeting of the Society for American Archaeology, St. Louis, Missouri.

Alva, Walter
1986 *Las Salinas de Chao: Asentamiento Temprano en el Norte del Perú*. Munich, C. H. Beck.

Bauer, Brian S., and David S. P. Dearborn
1995 *Astronomy and Empire in the Ancient Andes: The Cultural Origins of Inca Sky Watching*. University of Texas Press, Austin.

Béarez, L., and L. Miranda Muñoz
2000 Análisis Arqueoictiólogico del Sector Residencial del Sitio Arqueológico de Caral-Supe, Costa central del Perú. *Arqueología Sociedad* 13:67–78.

Beck, Robin A., Jr., D. J. Bolender, J. A. Browne, and T. K. Earle
2007   Eventful Archaeology: The Place of Space in Structural Transformation. *Current Anthropology* 48:833–860.
Benfer, Robert A.
1990   The Preceramic Period Site of Paloma, Peru: Bioindications of Improving Adaptation to Sedentism. *Latin American Antiquity* 1:284–318.
1999   Proyecto de Excavaciones en Paloma: El Valle de Chilca, Perú. *Boletín de Arqueologia PUCP* 3:213–237.
2005   Frederic-Andre Engel (1908–2002). *Andean Past* 7:1–14.
2006   Were Constellation Alignments Used to Orient Early Peruvian Monumental Architecture? Paper presented at the 75th annual meeting of the Society for American Archaeology, San Juan, Puerto Rico.
2007   Early Villages in South America. In *Encyclopedia of Archaeology*, edited by Deborah M. Pearsall, pp. 269–284. Orlando, Academic Press.
2008   Early Villages in South America. In *Encyclopedia of Archaeology*, edited by D. M. Pearsall, 368–380. Academic Press, Salt Lake City, Utah.
2010a   New Solar Alignments from Buena Vista, Perú. Paper presented at the 75th Annual Meeting of the Society for American Archaeology, St. Louis.
2010b   Report on the Equinoctial Alignment at Cardal to Richard Burger, Director, Cardal Project.
2011   Giant Preceramic animal effigy mounds in South America? *Antiquity Gallery* 85(329) http://antiquity.ac.uk/projgall/benfer329/.
Benfer, Robert A., and Larry R. Adkins
2008   The Americas' Oldest Observatory. *Astronomy Magazine* 35:40–43.
2009   Las Alineaciones Atonómicas y Orientaciónes Astronómicas en el Preceramico y en Periods Tardios de el Perú. Paper presented at the XVI Congreso Peruano del Hombre y la Cultura Andina y Amazónica, La Universidad Nacional Mayor de San Marcos, Lima.
2010   Preceramic Astronomical Alignments in Western Peru. Paper presented at the Society for American Archaeology Conference, St. Louis, April 15.
2011   Quartz Mines with Early Astronomical Orientations in the Valleys of Casma and Chillón, Perú. Paper presented at the 9th Oxford Symposium of Archaeoastronomy, AU, Lima, Perú.
Benfer, Robert A., Edward Brent, and Louanna Furbee
1991   *Expert Systems*. Sage Press, Newbury Park, California.
Benfer, Robert A., Louanna Furbee, and Hugo Ludeña R.
2011   Ancient South American Cosmology: Four Thousand Years of the Myth of the Fox in South American Cosmology. *Journal of Cosmology* 16. Electronic document, http://journalofcosmology.com/AncientAstronomy120.html, accessed July 3, 2011.
Benfer, R. A., and S. Gehlert
1980   Los Habitantes Precolombinos de La Paloma. In *El Hombre y La Cultural Andina*, edited by R. Matos M., 792–799. Editora Lasontay, Lima.
Benfer, Robert A., Bernardino Ojeda, Neil A. Duncan, Larry R. Adkins, Hugo Ludeña, Miriam Vallejos, Víctor Rojas, Andrés Ocas, Omar Ventocilla y Gloria Villarreal

2010 La Tradición Religioso-Astronómica en Buena Vista. *Boletín de Arqueología PUCP* 11:53–102.

Benfer, Robert A., Bernardino Ojeda E., Neil A. Duncan, Hugo Ludeña R., Miriam Vallejos A., Victor H. Rojas G., Andres Ocas Q., Omar Ventocilla V., Gloria Villarreal S.

2009 Buena Vista y Otros Templos Tempranos y Calendarios de Los Valles al Oeste del Perú. In *Procesos y Expresiones de Poder, Identidad y Orden Tempranos en Sudamérica*, vol. 2, edited by Peter Kaulicke and Tom D. Dillehay, pp. 53–102. Fondo Editorial de la Pontificia Universidad Católica del Perú, Lima

Benfer, R. A., and E. A. Pechenkina

1998 Biographical Stories: Parental Investment and the Health of Children in Prehistory. Paper presented at the 14th International Congress of Anthropological and Ethnological Sciences, Williamsburg, Virginia.

Benfer, Robert A., and Ekaterina A. Pechenkina

2001 Coastal Adjustments to the End of the Holocene Climatic Optimum. *American Journal of Physical Anthropology* 104(Suppl. 32):38.

Binford, Lewis R.

1968 Post-Pleistocene Adaptations. In *New Perspectives in Archaeology*, edited by Lewis R. Binford and Sally Binford, pp. 313–342. Aldine, Chicago.

Bird, Junius B., John Hyslop, and Milica D. Skinner

1985 The Preceramic Excavations at the Huaca Prieta, Chicama Valley, Peru. *Anthropological Papers of the American Museum of Natural History* 62, pt. 1:256–259.

Bischof, H.

2000 Cronología y Cultura en el Formativo Centroandino. *Estudios Latinoamericanos* 20:41–71.

Bonnier, Elizabeth

1997 Preceramic Architecture in the Andes: The Mito Tradition. In *Archaeological Peruana 2, Prehispanic Architecture and Civilization in the Andes*, edited by E. Bonnier and H. Bischof, pp. 120–144. Mueso de Mannheim, Mannheim.

Bruhns, Karen

1976 The Moon Animal in Northern Peruvian Art and Culture. *Ñawpa Pacha* 14:21–39.

Burger, Richard L., and Lucy Salazar-Burger

1986 Early Organizational Diversity in the Peruvian Highlands: Huaricoto and Kotosh. In *Andean Archaeology: Papers in Memory of Clifford Evans*, edited by R. Matos Mendieta, S. Turpin, and H. Eling, pp. 65–82, Institute of Archaeology, University of California, Los Angeles.

1991 The Second Season of Investigations at the Initial Period Center of Cardal, Peru. *Journal of Field Archaeology* 18:275–296.

Burger, R., and R. van der Merwe

1990 Maize and the Origin of Highland Chavin Civilization: An Isotopic Perspective. *American Anthropologist* 92:86–96.

Cardenas Mercedes, M.

1979 *A Chronology of the Use of Marine Resources in Ancient Perú*. Pontifica Universidad Catolica, Volkswagenwerk Stiffung, Lima.

Crumley, Carol
1995   Heterarchy and the Analysis of Complex Societies. In *Archeological Papers of the American Anthropological Association* 7:1-5
Damp, Jonathan
1984   Architecture of an Early Valdivia Village. *American Antiquity* 49:573-585.
Dickinson, William R.
1995   The Times Are Always Changing: The Holocene Saga. *Geological Society of America Bulletin* 107:1-7.
Dillehay, Tom D.
1992   Widening the Socio-Economic Foundations of Andean Civilization: Prototypes of Early Monumental Architecture. *Andean Past* 3:55-65.
Dolfus, Olivier
1960   Note sur une crise climatique récente dans le désert péruvien a partir de l'analyse d'ossements humains au C. 14. *Bulletin de l'Association de Giographes Fransais* 294-295:187-192.
Donnan, C., ed.
1985. *Early Ceremonial Architecture in the Andes.* Dumbarton Oaks, Washington, D.C.
Dulanto, J.
2008   Between Horizons: Diverse Configurations of Society and Power in the Late Pre-Hispanic Central Andes. In *Handbook of South American Archaeology*, edited by H. Silverman and W. H. Small, pp. 761-782. New York: Springer.
Duncan, Neil A., Robert A. Benfer, Hugo Ludeña, and Miriam Vallejos
2009   Investigaciones Arqueológicals en el Sitio de La Quipa, Chilca. In *Arqueología de la Costa Centro Sur Peruana,* edited by Omar Pinedo and Henry Tantaleán, pp. 63-74. Avqui Ediciones, Lima.
Duncan, Neil A., Deborah Pearsall, and Robert A. Benfer
2009   Gourd and Squash Artifacts Yield Starch Grains of Feasting Foods from Preceramic Perú. *Proceedings of the National Academy of Sciences* 196:13202-13206.
Engel, Frederic
1966   Le Complexe Précéramique d'El Pariso (Pérou). *Journal de la Société Américanistes* 55:43-95.
1980   Informe del Area Antropologica del CIZA: 15 Años de Actividad Antropológica. *Zonas Aridas* (Lima) 1:17-36.
1987   *De las Begonias al Maíz: Vida y Producción en el Perú Antiguo*. Centro de Investigaciones de Zonas Aridas de la Universidad Nacional Agraria, Lima.
Feldman, Larry A.
1985   Preceramic Corporate Architecture: Evidence for the Development of Non-Egalitarian Social Systems in Peru. In *Early Ceremonial Architecture in the Andes,* edited by C. B. Donnan, pp. 71-92. Dumbarton Oaks, Washington, D.C.
Fuchs, Peter R., R. Patzschke, C. Schmitz, and G. Yenque
2006   Im tal der kultanglagen. *Archäologie im Deutschland* 3:12-16.
Fuchs, Peter F., and Bernard Lorenz
2009   Sechín Bajo, the Origin of Ceremonial Circular Sunken Plazas in Costal Peru? Paper presented to the Northeastern Andean Conference, New York.
2011   New Findings of an Earlier December Solstice Alignment to the Sunrise in the

Earlier Occupation of Sechín Bajo, Whose Later Occupation Is Oriented Towards the June Solstice Sunrise. Paper presented at the 9th Oxford International Symposium on Archaeoastronomy, Lima.

Fung Pineda, R.
2006 Carlos Williams León y la Arqueología Peruana. *Waka* 4:70–76. Available at http://www.ifeanet.org/biblioteca/print-fiche.php?codigo=HUM00066135, accessed March 29, 2010.

Ghezzi, Iván and Clive Ruggles
2007 Chankillo: A 2300-Year-Old Solar Observatory in Coastal Peru. *Science* 316:1239–1243.

Haas, Jonathan, and Winifred Creamer
2004 Cultural Transformations in the Central Andean Late Archaic. In *Andean Archaeology*, edited by Helaine Silverman, pp. 3–50. Blackwell, Malden, Massachusetts.
2008 Crucible of Andean Civilization. *Current Anthropology* 47:745–775.

Haas, Jonathan, Winifred Creamer, and Alvario Ruiz
2003 Gourd Lord. *Archaeology* 56:7.

Hirth, K. G.
1996 Political Economy and Archaeology: Perspectives on Exchange and Production. *Journal of Archaeological Research* 4:203–239.

Howard-Malverde, R.
1984 *Achkay, una Tradición Quechua del Alto Marañón*. Chantiers Amérindia, Paris.

Hyslop, John
1990 *Inka Settlement Planning*. University of Texas Press, Austin.

Ianiszewski, Jorge R.
2010 *Guia a los Cielos Australes: Astronomía Básica para el Hemisferio Sur*. Salesianos Impresores, Santiago.

Isbell, William H.
1997 *Mummies and Mortuary Monuments: A Postprocessual Prehistory of Central Andean Social Organization*. University of Texas Press, Austin.

Isbell, William H., and Patricia J. Knobloch
2006 Missing Links, Imaginary Links: Staff God Imagery in the South Andean Past. In *Andean Archaeology III*, edited by William H. Isbell and Helaine Silverman, pp. 307–351. Springer, New York.

Itier, Cezár
1997 El Zorro del Cielo: Un mito sobre el Origin de las Plantas Cultivadas y los Intercambios con el Mundo Sobrenatural. *Bulletín Instituto Français études Andene* 26:307–346.

Kelley, David H., and E. F. Milone
2005 *Exploring Ancient Skies: An Encyclopedic Survey of Archaeoastronomy*. Springer, New York.

Kosak, Paul
1965 *Life, Land, and Water in Ancient Perú*. Long Island University Press, New York.

Krupp, Edward C.
2003 *Echoes of the Ancient Skies: The Astronomy of Lost Civilizations*. Oxford University Press, New York.

La Riva, P.
2003 Le Renard Mutilé, le Renard Éclaté: Répresentations de la Fertileté dans les Andes du Sud de Pérou. *Atelier* 25:17–39.

Lanning, Edward P.
1963 A Pre-Agricultural Occupation on the Central Coast of Peru. *American Antiquity* 28:336–371.

Larco Hoyle, R.
1948 *Cronología Arqueológica del Norte del Perú*. Hacienda Chiclín, Trujillo, Buenos Aires.

Lockyear, J. N.
1894 *The Dawn of Astronomy: A Study of the Temple Worship and Mythology of the Ancient Egyptians*. Cassell, London.

Ludeña, Hugo R.
2006 Ethnohistoric and Ethnographic Sources for the Sculptures at Buena Vista. Paper presented at the 71st Annual Meeting of the Society for America Archaeology, San Juan, Puerto Rico.

Mackie, E. W
1977 *Science and Society in Prehistoric Britain*. St. Martin's Press, New York.

Makowski, Krystoff
2006 La Arquitectura Pública del Periodo Precerámico Tardío y el Reto Conceptual del Urbanismo Andino. *Boletín de Arqueología PUCP* 10:167–199.

Mallville, J. Kimball
2011 Solar Axis, Lunar Ritual, and Shamanic Transformation. Paper presented at the 9th Oxford Symposium of Archaeoastronomy, IAU, Lima, Perú.

Malpass, Michael A., and Karen E. Stothert
1992 Evidence for Preceramic Houses and Household Organization in Western South America. *Andean Past* 3:137–163.

Meador, Sara, and Robert A. Benfer
2009 Adaptaciones de la Dieta Human a Nuevos Problemas y Oportunidades en la Costa Central del Perú (1,800–8000 a.C.). In *Arqueología del Periodo Formativo en la cuenca baja de Lurín: El Valle de Pachacamac,* edited by Richard Burger and Kryzstof Makowski, pp. 117–158. Pontifica Universedad Católica del Perú, Lima.

Meddens, F. N., N. P. Branch, C. Vivanco Pomacanchari, N. Ridiford, and R. Kemp
2008 High Altitude Ushnu Platforms in the Department of Ayacucho Peru: Structure, Ancestors and Animating Essence. In *Pre-Columbian Landscapes of Creation and Origin,* edited by J. R. Staller, pp. 315–355. Springer, New York.

Moore, Jerry
2005 *Cultural Landscapes in the Prehispanic Andes: Archaeologies of Place*. University Press of Florida, Gainesville.

Moseley, M. E.
1992a *The Incas and Their Ancestors*. Thames and Hudson Ltd., London.
1992b Maritime Foundations and Multilinear Evolution: Retrospect and Prospect. *Andean Past* 3:5–43.

Patterson, T. C.
1985   The Huaca La Florida, Rímac Valley, Peru. In *Early Ceremonial Architecture in the Andes,* edited by C. Donnan, pp. 59–70. Dumbarton Oaks, Washington, D.C.
1999   The Development of Agriculture and the Emergence of Formative Civilization in the Central Andes. In *Pacific Latin America in Prehistory: The Evolution of Archaic and Formative Cultures,* edited by Michael Blake, pp. 181–188. Washington State University Press, Pullman.

Patterson, Tom, and Edward B. Lanning
1964   Changing Settlement Pattern on the Central Peruvian Coast of Perú. *Ñawpa Pacha* 2:113–123.

Pechenkina, Ekaterina A., Joseph A. Vradenburg, Robert A. Benfer Jr., and Julie F. Farnum
2007   Skeletal Biology of the Central Peruvian Coast: Consequences of Changing Population Density and Progressive Dependence on Maize. In *Ancient Health,* edited by Mark N. Cohen and Gillian Crane-Kramer, pp. 92–112. Gainesville: University Press of Florida.

Pinasco C., Alfio
2007   *Con el Sol, la Luna y las Estrellas: Arqueoastronomía en Pachakamaq.* Lima, Instituto Peruano de Etnociencias.

Pino Matos, José L.
2005   El ushnu y la Organización Espacial Astronómica en la Sierra Central del Chinchaysuyu. *Estudios Atacameños* 29:143–161.
2009   Huánuco Pampa, Alineamientos Astronómicos Prehispanicos. Paper presented at the 16th Congreso Peruano del Hombre y la Cultura Andina y Amazónica, La Universidad Nacional Mayor de San Marcos, Lima.
2010   Yllapa Usno: Rituales de Libación, Culto a Ancestros y la Idea del Ushnu en los Andes Según los Documents Colonials de los Silos XVI–XVII. *Archaeologie y Sociedad* 21:77–108.

Pitluga, Phyllis B.
2003   Correlacion de Nuevas Mediciones de las Figuras/Lineas de Nasca con Figuras de la Via Lactea Andina. In *Etno y Arqueo-Astronomia en las Americas,* edited by Maxime Broccas, Johanna Broda, and Gonzola Pereira, pp. 21–37. Congresso Internacional de Americanistas, Santiago.
2005   Analysis of the Nazca Spirals. *Current Studies in Archaeoastronomy:* in: *Selected Papers from the Fifth Oxford International Conference, Santa Fe, 1996,* edited by J. W. Fountain and R. M. Sinclair, pp. 331–338. Carolina Academic Press, Durham, North Carolina

Pozorski, S., and T. Pozorski
1987   *Early Settlement Patterns in the Casma Valley, Peru.* University of Iowa Press, Iowa City.
1990a Reexamining the Critical Preceramic/Ceramic Period Transition New Data from Coastal Peru. *American Anthropologist* 92:481–491.
1990b Huaynuná, a Late Cotton Preceramic Site on the North Coast of Peru. *Journal of Field Archaeology* 17:17–26.

Quilter, Jeffrey
1989   *Life and Death at Paloma: Society and Mortuary Practices in a Preceramic Peruvian Village,* Iowa City: University of Iowa Press.

1991   Late Preceramic Peru. *Journal of World Prehistory* 5:387–438.

Quilter Jeffrey, E. Bernardino Ojeda, Deborah M. Pearsall, Daniel H. Sandweiss, John G. Jones, and Elizabeth S. Wing

1991   Subsistence Economy of El Paraíso, an Early Peruvian Site. *Science* 251(4991):277–293.

Reichel-Domatoff, Gerardo

1990   *The Sacred Mountain of Colombia's Kogi Indians*. E. J. Billing, Leiden.

Reitz, Elizabeth J.

1988   Faunal Remains from Paloma, an Archaic Site in Peru. *American Anthropologist*, n.s., 90(2):310–322.

2001   Fishing in Peru between 10 000 and 3750 BP. *International Journal of Osteoarchaeology* 11(1–2):163–171.

Richardson, J. B., III, and D. H. Sandweiss

2008   Climate Change, El Niño and the Rise of Complex Society on the Peruvian Coast during the Middle Holocene. In *El Niño, Catastrophism, and Climate Change in Ancient America*, edited by D. H. Sandweiss and J. Quilter, 59–75. Dumbarton Oaks, Washington, D.C.

Rick, John

1987   Dates as Data: An Examination of the Peruvian Archaeological Record. *American Antiquity* 52:55–73.

Roselló, Lorenzo T.

1978   Sistemas astromicos de campos de rays. *Actas y Trabajos del III Congreso Peruano El Hombre y la Cultura Peruana*, Tomo II:521–34. Lima.

1997   *Canto Grande y su Relación con los Centros Ceremoniales de Planta en U. Arqueología de la Costa Central*. Talleres de Mundo Gráfico S.A., Ind. Santa Rosa, Lima.

Roselló, Lorenzo T., Cirillo H. Manco, and Luis Mazzotti

1985   Rayas y figuras en la Pampa Canto Grande. *Boletín de Lima* 39:41–58.

Ruggles, C. L. N.

1982   A Reassessment of the High Precision Megalithic Lunar Sightlines 1: Backsights, Indicators and the Archaeological Status of the Sightlines. *Journal of History of Astronomy, Archaeoastronomy Supplement* 13:S21.

Ruggles, Clive L. N.

2011   Discussion Kim Malville's paper Chankillo: Solar Axis, Lunar Ritual, and Shamanic Transformation at the 9th Oxford Symposium of Archaeoastronomy, AU, Lima, Perú.

Salomon, F., and G. Urioste, translators

1991   *The Huarochirí Manuscript: A Testament of Ancient and Colonial Andean Religion*. University of Texas Press, Austin.

Sandweiss, Daniel H.

1996   The Development of Fishing Specialization on the Central Andean Coast. In *Prehistoric Hunter-Gatherer Fishing Strategies*, edited by Mark Plew, pp. 41–63. Boise State University Press, Boise, Idaho.

2008   Early Fishing Societies in Western South America. In *Handbook of South American Archaeology*, edited by Helaine Silverman and William H. Isbell, 145–156. Springer, New York.

Sandweiss, D. K., K. A. Maasch., R. L. Burger, J. B. Richardson III, H. B. Rollins, and A. Clement
2001   Variation in Holocene El Niño Frequencies: Climate Records and Cultural Consequences in Ancient Peru. *Geology* 7:603–606.

Sandweiss, D. H., J. B. Richardson III, E. J. Reitz, H. B. Rollins, and K. A. Maasch
1996   Geoarchaeological evidence from Peru for a 5000 years B.P. onset of El Niño. *Science* 273:1531–1533.

Schmidt, Klaus
2000   Göbekli Tepe, Southeastern Turkey. A Preliminary Report on the 1995–1999 Excavations. *Paléorient* 26:45–54.
2001   "Zuerst kam der Tempel, dann die Stadt": Vorläufiger Bericht zu den Grabungen am Göbekli Tepe und am Gürcütepe 1995–1999. *Istanbuler Mitteilungen* 50:5–41.

Servicio de Agrometerolía e Hidrología
1963   *Boletín de Estadistica Metorológica e Hidróligca*, no. 21. Lima.

Shady Solís, Ruth
1997   *La Ciudad Sagrada de Caral-Supe en los Albores de la Civilización en el Perú*. Universidad Nacional Mayor San Marcos, Lima.
2000   Sustento socioeconómico de la sociedad de Caral-Supe en los orignes de la civilización en el Perú. *Arqueología y Sociedad* 13:49–66.

Shady Solís, R., C. Dolier, F. Montesinos, and L. Casas
2000   Los Orígenes de la Civilización en el Perú en el área Norcentral y el Valle de Supe durane el Archaido Tardío. *Arqueologia y Sociedad* 13:13–48.

Shady Solís, Ruth, Jonathan Haas, and Winifred Creamer
2001   Dating Carál, a Preceramic Site in the Supé Valley on the Central Coast of Peru. *Science* 292:723–726.

Silva Sifuentes, Jorge
1996   Prehistoric Settlement Patterns in the Chillón River Valley, Peru. Ph.D. dissertation, Department of Anthropology, University of Michigan, Ann Arbor.

Silva Sifuentes, J., and C. J. Tello
2000   Investigation y Delimitación de Huacoy, Carabayllo: Notas Preliminares, Investigaciones Sociales. *Investigaciones Sociales* 4(6):55–70.
2005   Etnoarqueología del Bajo Rímac y el Callao Prehispánico. *Investigaciones Sociales* 9(15):29–42.

Silverman, H.
1994   The Archaeological Identification of an Ancient Peruvian Pilgrimage Center. *World Archaeology* 26:1–18.

Staller, J. E.
2008   Dimensions of Place: The Significance of Centers of the Development of Andean Civilization: An Exploration of the Ushnu Concept. In *Pre-Columbian Landscapes of Creation and Origin*, edited by John Staller, pp. 269–312. Springer, New York.

Sullivan, W. A.
1996   *The Secret of the Incas: Myth, Astronomy, and the War against Time*. Crown Publishers, New York.

Tello, Julio
1943   Discovery of the Chavín Culture in Perú. *American Antiquity* 9:135–160.

Thompson, L. G., E. Moseley-Thompson, and P. A. Thompson
1995 Reconstructing Interannual Climate Variability from Tropical and Subtropical Ice-Core Records. In *El Niño: Historical and Paleoclimatic Aspects of the Southern Oscillation*, edited by H. Diaz and V. Margraf, pp. 194–322. Cambridge University Press, New York.

Traslaviña Arias, T., N. L. Haro Carrasco, and E. D. Bautista Cornejo
2007 El Pacífico: Evidencias de un Probable Sitio del Arcaico Tardío en el Valle del Rímac. *Arqueología* (Lima) 1:31–54.

Trigger, B. G.
1990 Monumental Architecture: A Thermodynamic Explanation of Symbolic Behavior. *World Archaeology* 22:119–132.

Urton, Gary
1981 *At the Crossroads of the Earth and the Sky: An Andean Cosmology.* University of Texas Press, Austin.

Vradenburg, J. A., R. A. Benfer, and L. Sattinspiel
1997 Evaluating Archaeological Hypotheses of Population Growth and Decline on the Central Coast of Perú. In *Integrating Archaeological Demography: Multidisciplinary Approaches to Prehistoric Population*, edited by Richard R. Paine, pp. 150–174. Occasional Paper No. 24. Center for Archaeological Investigations, Southern Illinois University at Carbondale, Carbondale.

Weir, Glendon H., Robert A. Benfer, and John G. Jones
1988 Preceramic to Early Formative Subsistence on the Central Coast. In *Economic Prehistory of the Central Andes*, edited by Elizabeth S. Wing and Jane C. Wheeler, 56–94. BAR International Series 427. Centremead, Osney Mead, Oxford.

Williams, Carlos
1978–1980 Complejos de Pirámides con Planta en U.? Patrón Arquitectónico de la Costa Central. *Revista del Museo Nacional* 44:95–110.
1985 A Scheme for the Early Monumental Architecture of the Central Coast of Perú. In *Early Ceremonial Architecture in the Andes*, edited by C. Donnan, pp. 227–240. Dumbarton Oaks Research Library and Collection, Washington, D.C.

Zeidler, James A.
1998 Cosmology and Community Plan in Early Formative Ecuador: Some Lessons from Tropical Ethnoastronomy. *Journal of the Steward Anthropological Society* 16:37–68.

Zuidema, Reiner Tom
1981 Inca Observations of the Solar and Lunar Passages through Zenith and Anti-Zenith in Cuzco. In *Archaeoastronomy in the Americas*, comp. R. A. Williamson, 319–342. Ballena Press, Los Altos, California.
1990 *Inca Civilization in Perú.* Translated by Jean-Jacques Decoster. Austin: University of Texas Press, Austin.

13

Preceramic and Initial Period Monumentality within the Casma Valley of Peru

THOMAS POZORSKI AND SHELIA POZORSKI

Some 20 years ago, Trigger published his ideas about how monumental architecture and other examples of conspicuous consumption represented universally understood expressions of power (Trigger 1990). At that time, he was also expressing a universally assumed feature of the study of complex societies. In their introductory chapter, Rosenswig and Burger (this volume) discuss this more fully and point out that such assumptions can result in circular arguments if we assume a priori that big mounds necessarily reflect the presence of an elite individual or group. They call for independent evidence of the existence of a political hierarchy and its associated societal features. While we believe that due credit should be given to Trigger and Renfrew (1973) because they stimulated research and theoretical dialogue about complex societies, we also believe that a major potential theoretical contribution of this volume is its effort to better document the existence and nature of complex societies by questioning the assumption that monumental construction necessarily reflects political power and social hierarchy. The archaeology of the early sites in the Casma Valley on the north coast of Peru can contribute much to the debate concerning the nature of early complex societies.

The Casma Valley on the north coast of Peru saw its grandest development when the Sechín Alto polity existed there during the middle of the Initial Period (1800–1400 BC). At this time, both branches of the valley contained large planned cities composed of multiple mounds, substantial intermediate-sized architecture, and residential structures (Pozorski and Pozorski 1986, 1987, 1992, 2005, 2008). Paramount among this early architecture is the main mound at the Sechín Alto site, which was the largest structure in the entire New World at this time (Pozorski and Pozorski 2002a, 2005). While inland sites were predicated on irrigation agriculture, animal protein was largely supplied by coastal satellite sites with ready access to marine resources (Pozorski and Pozorski 1987).

This Initial Period florescence does not represent the first substantial prehistoric cultural development within the Casma Valley area. Sizeable Late Preceramic (3000–2100 BC) coastal settlements were documented there as early as the 1950s (Bischof 1995; Engel 1957a, 1957b; Fuchs 1997; Lanning 1967; Moseley 2001; Pozorski and Pozorski 2006), and there is tantalizing recent evidence of complementary inland Preceramic sites (Bischof 1995; Vallejos 2008; Fuchs 1997; Whalen 2008). This chapter is based on results of our archaeological fieldwork in the Casma Valley between 1980 and 2002 (Pozorski and Pozorski 1989, 1991, 1993, 1994a, 1994b, 1996, 1998, 1999a, 2000; T. Pozorski and S. Pozorski 1990). It traces the development of early monumentality within the Casma Valley by examining its Preceramic roots and by exploring the Initial Period florescence. Data on construction volume and techniques, labor estimates, site planning, and subsistence are critical to this reconstruction of early Casma Valley prehistory.

Preceramic Antecedents

Fieldwork since 1996 in the Supe Valley at the central coast site of Caral and more generally within the Huaura to Fortaleza valleys (an area known as the Norte Chico region) has revealed that coastal Peru is one of few areas of the world where civilization arose independently—with no evidence of outside influence (Haas and Creamer 2004, 2006; Haas, Creamer, and Ruiz 2004, 2005; Ruiz, Creamer, and Haas 2007; Shady 1997, 2001, 2003, 2004, 2006, 2007a, 2007b; Vega Centeno et al. 1998). By 3000 BC complex societies there were constructing sizeable planned sites characterized by clusters of mounds and supported by a subsistence exchange system involving both irrigation agriculture and marine resources. Excavation data available to date document important similarities among these early centers. Most notably, at inland sites individual mounds are internally symmetrical and are characterized by a central staircase, adjoining plazas that are also symmetrical, circular plazas that tend to be freestanding, principal mounds that exhibit multiple small construction phases; and some evidence of overall site planning but not precise site-level symmetry. Complementing the inland sites are complex sites such as Áspero (Shady and Cáceda 2008) and Bandurria (Chu 2008) that comprised the coastal components of the system.

Interpretations of the central coast data differ. Shady describes Caral as the center of an integrated statelike polity that governed the Norte Chico region (Shady 2000, 2006). Leading up to this complexity, relatively sedentary human occupation of the area started as isolated settlements of fishermen/shellfish collectors on the coast and inland farmers who soon developed trade networks to supply each other with essential products: cotton for nets and vital marine protein. Shady describes Supe Valley ecology as a critical variable because swamps and springs provided shallow underground water that could be readily harnessed for irrigation. She draws upon sixteenth-century ethnohistoric accounts to suggest that Supe was settled by clan groups governed by powerful *curacas* who embodied warrior, priestly, and managerial functions. The centrality of Caral within Shady's system is based on the site's size, construction volume, and planning relative to other Preceramic settlements within the overall system. However, Ruiz, Creamer, and Haas have pointed out that although Caral may be better preserved than other sites, it may not be the largest or most important (Ruiz, Creamer, and Haas 2007, 117).

Haas and Creamer interpret the Norte Chico data as representing numerous localized Preceramic polities that arose independently but quickly developed internal hierarchies that accompanied the advent of irrigation agriculture and public architecture (Haas and Creamer 2006, this volume). Based on their scenario, interaction with coastal communities intensified after about 1800 BC, resulting in political and religious systems that integrated coastal and inland communities through subsistence exchange, public construction projects, and public ceremonies. They view the result as a series of competing centers, and they suggest that ceremonial activities and especially construction projects may have intensified as part of this intraregional competition. The presence of so many mounds in close proximity and with their tallest faces facing the river valleys provides evidence that competition among centers may have been important (Ruiz, Creamer, and Haas 2007, 117–118). In another publication, Ruiz, Creamer, and Haas propose a third model for the sociopolitical organization of Preceramic complex society. They suggest that the late Preceramic sites of the Norte Chico region may have been part of a peaceful alliance or confederation (ibid., 117). Nevertheless, all these theoretical reconstructions are tentative because of the dearth of empirical evidence, especially with respect to relationships among sites and the time and duration of each center's occupation.

The sheer abundance of complex Preceramic sites in the Norte Chico region suggests that this zone might be the origin area for several key Andean developments: symmetrical monumental construction, irrigation agriculture, and a coastal-inland subsistence exchange system. However, unusually early dates from a buried Preceramic circular plaza at Sechín Bajo within the Casma Valley document the existence of a very early inland Preceramic site well north of the Caral–Norte Chico region (Vallejos 2008; Whalen 2008). Also within the Casma Valley, investigators at Cerro Sechín have suggested that interior constructions at this site may be Preceramic (Bischof 1995; Fuchs 1997, 159–160). Further north, Preceramic components are known from the inland site of Huaca El Gallo/La Gallina in the Viru Valley (Zoubek 2006). Such tantalizing data suggest that the Preceramic pattern of substantial inland settlements paired with coastal counterparts may be much more widespread. Nevertheless, the Norte Chico region appears to represent the apogee of this precocious development. Both the inland centers and their coastal counterparts there are the largest and most complex Preceramic settlements known.

The existence of these complex Preceramic antecedents and the complementary coastal-inland subsistence pattern of the central coast must be taken into account as efforts are made to assess and explain the phenomenal Initial Period developments within the Casma Valley. When we started our fieldwork in the Casma Valley in the 1980s, we viewed the coastal Preceramic components of Las Haldas, Bahía Seca, Tortugas, and Huaynuná as isolated coastal antecedents to the subsequent inland Initial Period florescence. As part of this scenario, the hillside mound at Huaynuná was interpreted as immediately antecedent to the inland mounds of the Sechín Alto polity because of its late date of about 1800 BC, its central staircase, and its balanced layout that seemed to anticipate the precise bilateral symmetry of early ceramic mounds (T. Pozorski and S. Pozorski 1990). These data and interpretations have been reexamined in light of the growing database from the Norte Chico region and especially the recent recognition of inland Preceramic sites within the Casma Valley system. Though less complete, the Casma Valley data seem to document a Preceramic coastal-inland exchange system of the type that is proposed for the Supe Valley (Haas and Creamer 2006; Shady 1997, 2001, 2006) and is well documented for the subsequent Initial Period (Pozorski and Pozorski 1979b, 1987, 2008). Preceramic coastal middens near Casma contain a variety of cultivated plants, including cotton, gourds, potatoes, sweet potatoes, *achira*, common beans, squash, avocadoes, and *lúcuma* (Pozorski and Pozorski 1987; Ugent, Pozorski, and Pozorski 1981, 1982, 1983, 1984), which were likely produced in irrigated fields near the inland sites and exchanged for the coastal fish and shellfish that provided vital protein. Thus, the agricultural subsistence base was well established by late Preceramic times.

The Huaynuná hillside mound also must be reexamined in light of new data for the Preceramic. Clearly, with its relatively late Preceramic date, it cannot be generally antecedent to the inland Initial Period mounds if substantial mound structures already existed well inland during early Preceramic times. Two interpretations are possible. The Huaynuná mound may be a late Preceramic, even aceramic construction overlapping slightly into early ceramic times and mimicking the large Initial Period mound constructions (Pozorski and Pozorski 1991; S. Pozorski and T. Pozorski 1990). Alternatively, because it was constructed in a single phase, the Huaynuná hillside mound may still be antecedent, not to Initial Period mound building in general but to the practice of constructing mounds in very few large phases that characterizes Initial Period mound building in valleys north of the Norte Chico region.

Well before the substantial inland Preceramic centers were recognized and excavated, coastal sites without ceramics were well known and well studied (Alva 1986; Bird and Hyslop 1985; Engel 1957a, 1957b, 1967; Feldman 1985; Lanning 1967; Moseley 1972, 1975; Pozorski and Pozorski 1979a, 1987; T. Pozorski and S. Pozorski 1990; Wendt 1964). Based on data from these studies, researchers proposed that major coastal sites were in contact and interacted with each other. This explains widespread similarities in artifact inventories such as shell fishhooks made from *Choromytilus chorus* shell and specific techniques for producing twined textiles. Though less complete, the growing database for inland sites suggests similar widespread patterns. Most notable is the freestanding circular plaza architectural element that is common in the Norte Chico region and also present at Sechín Bajo in the Casma Valley. Abundant remains of cultivated plants at the coastal sites also suggest that participation in subsistence exchange systems was widely practiced.

Initial Period Social Complexity in the Casma Valley

The phenomenal Initial Period development within the Casma Valley clearly has roots in the late Preceramic. By late Preceramic times, substantial sites were being built well inland at locations predicated on irrigation agriculture. In the absence of domesticated animals to provide protein, sizeable coastal sites supplied marine fish and shellfish to satisfy this need.

This arrangement created an economic symbiosis that endured for centuries. The best-preserved and best-known examples of this Preceramic settlement pattern and subsistence system come from the Norte Chico region, especially the Supe Valley. The situation there seems somewhat different from Casma, however, because the Norte Chico sites are much more complex and because the coastal-inland site relationship seems much more balanced. Both inland and coastal Preceramic sites contain multiple mounds, plazas, and residential architecture in arrangements that suggest planned construction (Chu 2008; Haas and Creamer 2006; Shady 2001, 2006; Shady and Cáceda 2008). In Casma, the limited data suggest that inland sites were less complex and were generally characterized by a single principal mound. Nevertheless, the inland sites appear larger and more complex than their coastal counterparts—a difference in magnitude that becomes extreme during the Initial Period.

These Preceramic developments set the stage for the subsequent Initial Period, but the transition within the Casma Valley was sudden, not gradual. Critical Preceramic elements were retained: mound building, site planning, symmetrical construction, the subsistence exchange system, and possibly large-phase mound construction. However, the inhabitants of the Casma Valley took these ideas to an extreme and added others, creating the Sechín Alto polity, which far surpassed other coastal valleys in its monumental construction and its underlying social, political, and economic organization (Pozorski and Pozorski 2002a, 2005, 2008). Given evidence of intervalley communication during the Preceramic, development of this polity may have been inspired by the social complexity within the Norte Chico region at that time. Within Casma, clear evidence of a developed social hierarchy appears early in the Initial Period, and the associated governing elite rapidly built an integrated system of settlements that both consolidated their power and ensured perpetuation of the polity.

At the peak of its development, the Sechín Alto polity was characterized by inland clusters of mounds within both the Sechín and Casma branches of the river (Figure 13.1). Coincident artifacts and radiocarbon dates confirm the contemporaneity of all these component sites. Polity control was centered in the Sechín River branch, where the site of Sechín Alto dominated the mound cluster known as the Sechín Alto Complex (Figure 13.2; Pozorski and Pozorski 2002a, 2005, 2008). The component sites of Sechín Alto, Taukachi-Konkán, Sechín Bajo, and Cerro Sechín are grouped into a single complex because of their spatial proximity and their coincident orientation as well as similarities in mound symmetry and site layout

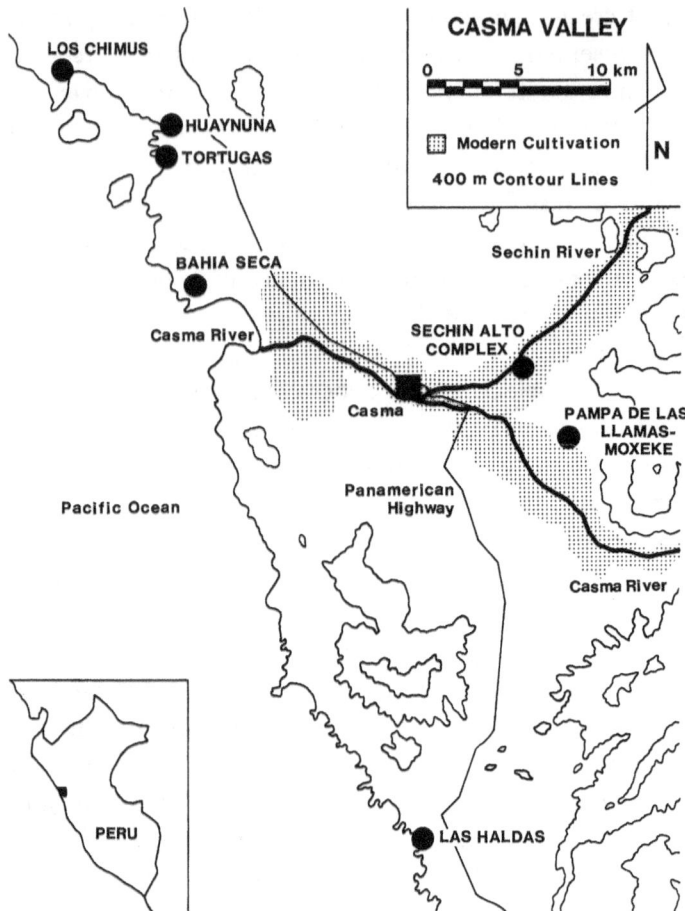

Figure 13.1. Map of the Casma Valley showing the location of early sites.

among the sites (Pozorski and Pozorski 1987, 82; Pozorski and Pozorski 1992, 860). The Sechín Alto site occupies arable land near the Sechín River; other Sechín Alto Complex sites lie just outside modern limits of cultivation. Most of the area between the various mounds of the Sechín Alto Complex is currently under modern cultivated fields. However, remnants of residential architecture and midden are preserved north of the mounds of Taukachi-Konkán and southeast of the main Sechín Alto mound complex. This evidence suggests that the intervening spaces within the complex contained substantial amounts of residential architecture and midden during Initial Period times.

Within the Sechín Alto Complex, different sites appear to have served distinct, complementary functions. The Sechín Alto site, the largest mound

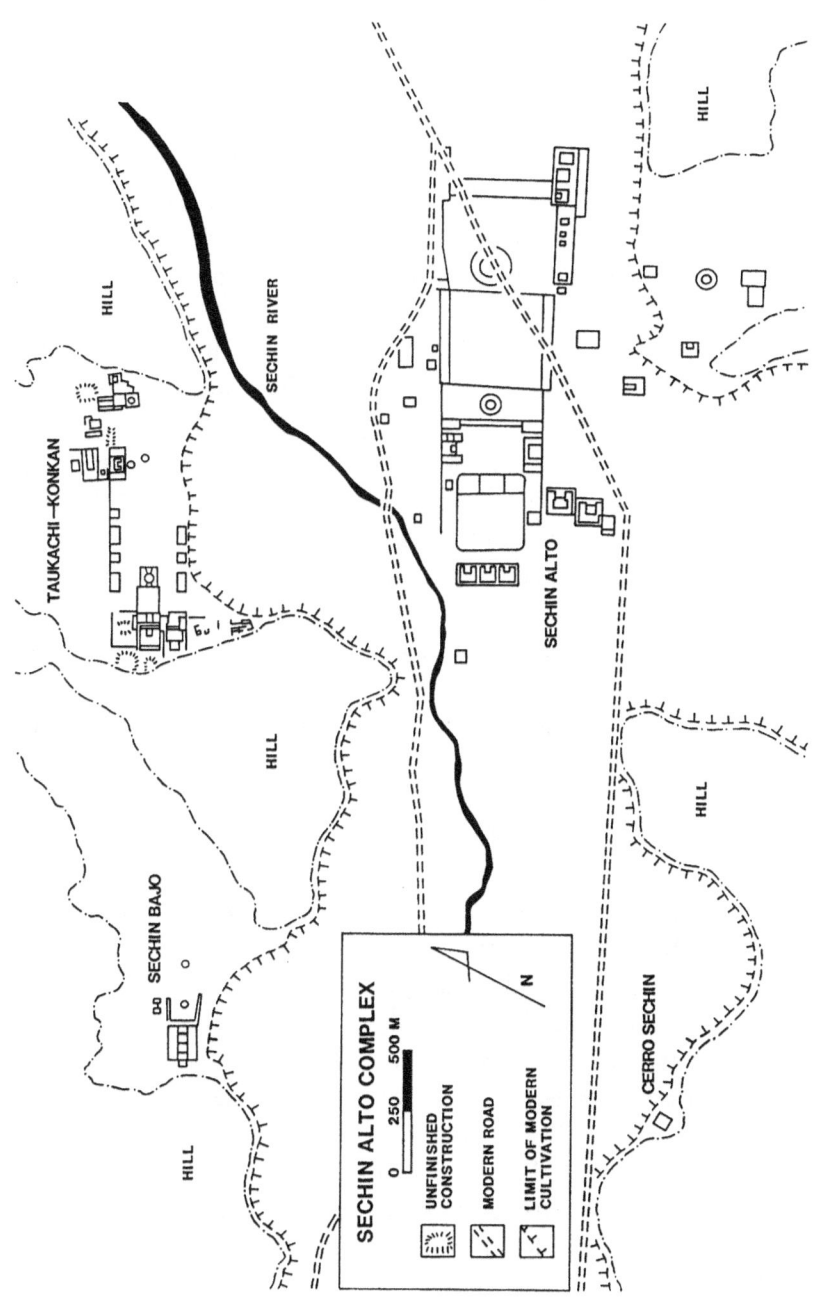

Figure 13.2. Plan of Sechín Alto Complex.

complex, likely served as the administrative center for the polity. The main Mound of the Columns at Taukachi-Konkán site establishes the orientation of that site and likely served as a royal residence (Figure 13.3, Pozorski and Pozorski 1999a, 101–106). Although Sechín Bajo, which is currently under excavation by Peter Fuchs, has not yet been reported upon in detail, surface evidence and images on the Internet (McGuinness 2010) reveal modular construction elements of the type used at Pampa de las Llamas-Moxeke (described below), suggesting a possible storage function for at least part of the mound. Cerro Sechín has been investigated by numerous researchers since Tello first worked there in 1937 (Collier 1962; Fuchs 1997; Maldonado 1992; Samaniego 1973; Samaniego and Cardenas 1995; Samaniego, Vergara, and Bischof 1985; Tello 1943). The central part of the site consists of a sequence of squarish, round-cornered rooms similar to the modular construction and intermediate-sized mounds explored more fully at Pampa de las Llamas-Moxeke. Successive inner modules are adorned with friezes of jaguars and fish. The outer stone facade is covered by stone carvings of human figures and body parts that we view as the commemoration of a conflict that occurred late in the Initial Period.

The Casma branch of the river system is dominated by the site of Pampa de las Llamas-Moxeke, which occupies a *quebrada* (ravine) north of the river (Figure 13.4). The southern part of the site now lies within modern cultivated fields, but the remainder of the site is relatively unaffected and is very well preserved. Moxeke and Huaca A, the main mounds at the site, face each other across a series of large plazas and establish the site's orientation. Huaca A also has an entrance toward the north which faces rectangular and circular plazas. Rows of at least 100 aligned intermediate-sized mounds facing the site center are present on either side of the site and residential architecture and midden occupy intervening areas (Pozorski and Pozorski 1986, 1987, 1994a).

Moxeke mound is interpreted as a public-oriented religious structure or temple because of the large, highly visible friezes that once adorned its front and extended slightly around to the sides of the mounds (Tello 1956, 60–64). In contrast to Moxeke, Huaca A is interpreted as a storage structure characterized by highly restricted access to the 38 round-cornered modular architectural forms with niches called square-room units (Pozorski and Pozorski 1991).

A key aspect of Casma Valley social organization that may help explain the phenomenal success of the Sechín Alto polity relates to the polity's structure. The political and economic system whereby distinct mounds

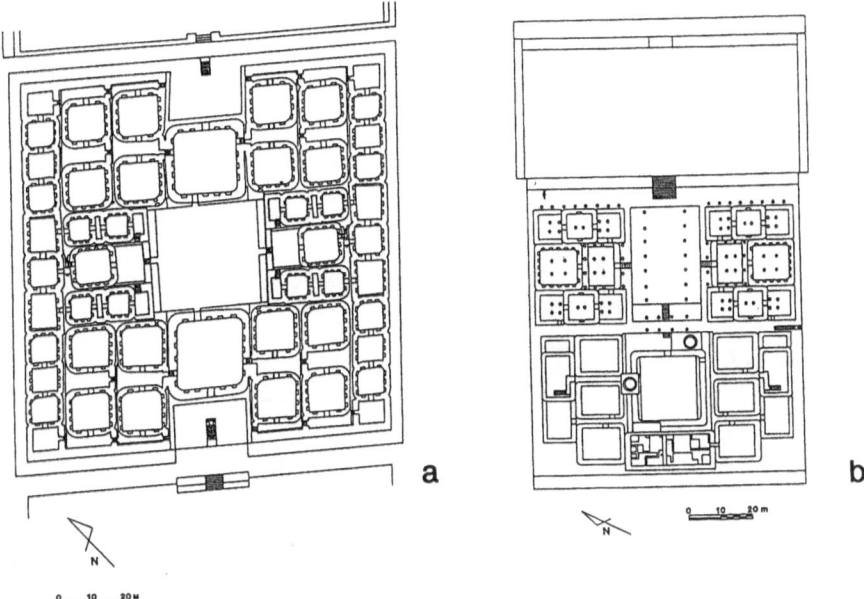

Figure 13.3. Plans of (A) Huaca A at Pampa de las Llamas-Moxeke; and (B) Mound of the Columns at Taukachi-Konkán.

had distinct functions transcended the limits of individual sites, creating a polity that was unified because of the diverse and vital functions of its component parts. The result was an integrated whole to which individual mounds and their associated sites and personnel made essential contributions (e.g., Huaca A for storage of comestibles, Mound of the Columns as a "palace," and Moxeke as a religious center) (Pozorski and Pozorski 1999a, 1999b). Remnants of road segments at Pampa de las Llamas-Moxeke and Taukachi-Konkán verify the importance of interconnections among sites (Pozorski and Pozorski 1991). The centripetal force that bonded societal elements based on their complementary vital functions was tangibly expressed and reinforced by the use of the square-room unit as a symbol of the elite's power and authority (described below). First identified at Pampa de las Llamas-Moxeke and more specifically on Huaca A, this modular architectural element occurs in administrative contexts at all inland Sechín Alto polity sites and at one coastal satellite (Pozorski and Pozorski 1992, 1994a). Ironically, the major strength and integrating force of the Sechín Alto polity was also a potential source of great weakness because the polity could be severely crippled if one or more vital elements stopped fulfilling vital roles.

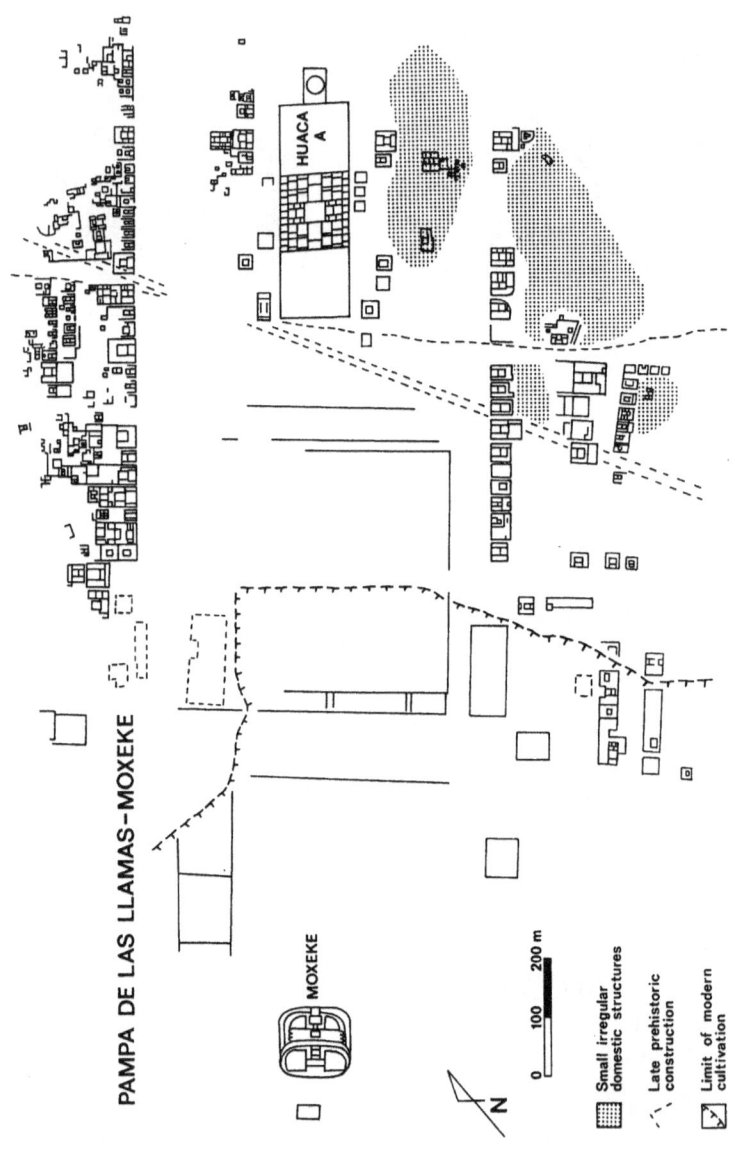

Figure 13.4. Plan of the site of Pampa de las Llamas-Moxeke.

Evidence of Social Hierarchy within the Sechín Alto Polity

Within the Sechín Alto Complex, there is ample evidence of a social hierarchy headed by an elite group that retained power over several generations. Political power exerted by this group took numerous tangible forms. Archaeological evidence for this social hierarchy, its associated political power, and its subsistence base includes relationships among sites; internal site planning; magnitude of mound construction; evidence of a "royal" residence; elements of the iconography; pervasive use of the square-room-unit architectural element; access restrictions, standardization of architecture, iconography, and artifacts; and physical remains of plants, animals, and subsistence-related artifacts.

Relationships among Sites

Existence of a site hierarchy with multiple levels has been cited as evidence of complex society with a centralized political organization (Flannery 1998, 16–21; Haas 1982, 103–106; Johnson 1973; Wilson 1988, 87; Wright and Johnson 1975). The Casma Valley data readily satisfy this criterion. Heading the site hierarchy is the Sechín Alto site with its immense principal mound and numerous subsidiary structures. Secondary to the Sechín Alto site are Pampa de las Llamas-Moxeke and Taukachi-Konkán, which are very similar to each other in layout. Among the sizeable inland sites, Sechín Bajo and Cerro Sechín are the smallest. Both are characterized by a sizeable central structure, and Cerro Sechín has lateral buildings as well. Among the coastal satellites, Initial Period Bahía Seca stands out because it contains an administrative structure, suggesting that marine resource procurement and exchange may have been coordinated from this site. Subsidiary to Bahía Seca are the Initial Period occupations of Tortugas and Huaynuná. Based on this analysis, the Sechín Alto polity may have been characterized by a site hierarchy of five or more levels because small inland sites such as field camps also likely existed (although such sites are difficult to locate).

As mentioned above, crosscutting the hierarchical relationships of the Casma Valley sites are the functional relationships among the sites. The Sechín Alto polity was organized such that individual sites and even individual mounds and associated structures had vital, distinct, complementary functions within the polity as a whole. We have discussed how this fostered cohesion among the inland sites, and this would also have been true of the coastal sites that functioned to provide essential marine protein.

Internal Site Planning

There is ample evidence of precise planning at all Sechín Alto polity inland sites. Principal mounds and associated plazas at these sites exhibit precise bilateral symmetry, and smaller structures are often arranged in rows and consistently follow site-level orientations established along the main mound central axis (Pozorski and Pozorski 1986, 1987). Within the Sechín Alto Complex, most component sites share an even more widely standardized E32°N orientation. The single exception to this is Cerro Sechín.

The clearest evidence of site-level planning comes from Pampa de las Llamas-Moxeke because structures on land that has not been cultivated are exceptionally well preserved. At this site, virtually all the intermediate architecture and the higher-status residences adhere to the orientation of N41°E established by the central axes of Moxeke and Huaca A (Pozorski and Pozorski 1986, 1987). Exceptions are intermediate-sized mounds oriented toward roads that lead into and out of the site, and these roadside mounds are precisely aligned relative to each other and to the roads (Pozorski and Pozorski 1991). This planning and its execution are so precise that the fronts of the longest row of mounds along the western side of the site diverge only 30 centimeters off a straight line across a distance of over 700 meters, even after 3,500 years of exposure to the elements. Furthermore, the preconceived site layout that this planning reflects was maintained through time and across generations of leaders. At Pampa de las Llamas-Moxeke there is clear evidence of intermediate-sized mounds under construction to fill spaces within incomplete rows of mounds. This new, often unfinished construction was carried out at the expense of residential architecture, which was razed to make space for new mounds (Pozorski and Pozorski 1994a).

Magnitude of Public Construction and Labor

Despite warnings from the editors of this volume to beware of equating massive construction with political power, the sheer magnitude of mound construction efforts in the Casma Valley makes this an appropriate topic for discussion. The main mound at the Sechín Alto site, which measures 300 × 250 meters in area, is 35 meters tall, and contains about 2,000,000 cubic meters of construction material (Table 13.1), was the largest structure in the New World when it was built. Materials used include stone, cone-shaped adobes, and mud mortar in the following proportions: 50 percent stone, 2 percent conical adobes, and 48 percent mud mortar and plaster.

Table 13.1. Construction volume and labor calculations for Casma Valley mound sites

Site/Mound	Construction volume in m³	Dates of use	Labor cost in person/ yrs (360 days/yr)	Duration (yrs) of construction— 500 workers	Duration (yrs) of construction— 1,000 workers	Numbers of workers/ yr for 20-yr completion
SECHIN ALTO						
Main mound: Phase 1	1,500,000	1800–1600 BC	66,259	132.52	66.26	3,313
Main mound: Phase 2	500,000	1600–1400 BC	21,853	43.70	21.85	1,093
Four plazas: Phase 2	203,000	1600–1400 BC	7,394	14.78	7.39	424
Additional mounds	592,000	1800–1400 BC	29,269	58.54	29.27	1,463
Total	2,795,000	1800–1400 BC	124,775	249.54	124.77	6,293
PAMPA LLAMAS-MOXEKE						
Moxeke	562,500	1800–1400 BC	22,024	44.04	22.02	1,101
Huaca A: Phase 1	85,000	1800–1500 BC	4,012	8.02	4.01	201
Huaca A: Phase 2	38,000	1500–1400 BC	1,793	3.58	1.79	90
Additional mounds & compounds	264,500	1800–1400 BC	10,947	21.90	10.95	547
Total	950,000	1800–1400 BC	38,776	77.54	38.77	1,939
TAUKACHI-KONKAN						
Mound of the Columns	81,000	1800–1400 BC	2,070	4.14	2.07	104
Additional mounds	73,000	1800–1400 BC	2,421	4.84	2.42	121
Total	154,000	1800–1400 BC	4,491	8.98	4.49	225

Silty clay for conical adobes, mud mortar, and plaster for the Sechín Alto main mound was available from Sechín River sediments about 1000 meters from the site where river water was slow moving, and the stone was quarried from a hillside at the south edge of the valley which was about 1,400 meters distant. Many stones used in the construction of the Sechín Alto main mound are massive, especially the shaped stones forming the outer facade. Stones measuring 150 × 120 × 100 centimeters and weighing over 4.5 tons would have involved a substantial, well-coordinated labor force as they were quarried, shaped, and moved into place. More significantly, the main Sechín Alto site mound was built in a very small number of immense construction phases. Our excavations there never reached sterile soil; however, we were able to identify two massive construction phases, and there may be a third phase within the 35-meter height of the mound.

Principal mounds at other Casma Valley sites range in size from 160 by 170 meters in area and 30 meters tall for Moxeke (construction volume: 562,500 cubic meters) to 90 by 80 meters in area by 10 meters tall for the Mound of the Columns (construction volume: 81,000 cubic meters). We conducted extensive excavations on both Huaca A of Pampa de las Llamas-Moxeke and the Mound of the Columns at Taukachi-Konkán, and we discovered that each mound was probably built in two massive construction phases. Few conical adobes were used at these mounds, resulting in a materials composition that was approximately 50 percent stone and 50 percent mud mortar and plaster.

Plaza size is also a factor to be considered in this evaluation of the magnitude of public construction. Even though less construction effort is involved in the creation of plazas, the area plazas occupied can serve as a measure of the importance of the ruling class and their associated public activities because they occupy space that could serve other functions. Plazas occupy central spaces at the three largest Sechín Alto polity sites—the main Sechín Alto mound, Taukachi-Konkán, and Pampa de las Llamas-Moxeke (Table 13.2), and most intermediate-sized mounds face the plazas at the sites' centers. At Taukachi-Konkán and Pampa de las Llamas-Moxeke, space occupied by plazas could theoretically have been used for administrative or residential structures. The vast plazas of Sechín Alto site also occupy substantial areas of arable land, thereby precluding both lesser constructions and agriculture. Thus, plazas can be viewed both as an additional example of conspicuous consumption by Sechín Alto polity elite and as evidence that public-oriented activities centered on the mounds were extremely important within Casma Valley society.

Table 13.2. Rectangular plaza sizes at Casma Valley sites

Site/Context	Plaza dimensions	Plaza area in m²
SECHÍN ALTO		
Plaza 1 (nearest main mound)	250 m N-S × 190 m E-W	47,500
Plaza 2	405 m N-S × 131 m E-W	53,055
Plaza 3	380 m N-S × 380 m E-W	144,400
Plaza 4	430 m N-S × 395 m E-W	169,850
Total		414,805
PAMPA LLAMAS-MOXEKE		
Moxeke: Plaza 1	495 m N-S × 375 m E-W	185,625
Moxeke: Plaza 2	415 m N-S × 360 m E-W	149,400
Huaca A: South Plaza	106 m N-S × 119 m E-W	12,614
Huaca A: North Plaza	119 m N-S × 119 m E-W	14,161
Total		361,800
TAUKACHI-KONKÁN		
Mound of Columns: Plaza 1	40 m N-S × 45 m E-W	1,800
Mound of Columns: Plaza 2	85 m N-S × 100 m E-W	8,500
Open plaza further east	220 m N-S × 420 m E-W	92,400
Total		102,700

When assessing the magnitude of construction at monumental sites, it is important to take into account all public works; and it is also informative to consider labor costs for such construction. We have made labor calculations using formulae and values developed by Abrams (1994, 45–52), Erasmus (1969), and Chang (1968, 205) for stone quarrying, earth digging, materials transport, and construction (Table 13.1). We also calculated the time required for each major construction unit based on both a 500-person labor force and a 1,000-person labor force. Finally, using a generous 20-year time span for a single generation of ruler(s), we calculated the number of workers necessary to complete the different construction units within this hypothetical 20-year generational span. The data readily show that massive work forces, numbering in the hundreds and possibly the thousands, were necessary to complete the mounds and other public works in a timely manner. Rapid construction would have been critical in order to ensure that mounds with complementary uses were up and functioning within a relatively short time. Support for short duration of construction comes from the second construction phase at the main mound of Sechín Alto. There, nine radiocarbon dates bracket the time of construction for the second phase between about 1500 and 1400 BC (Pozorski and Pozorski 2005, 148–154). Both the magnitude of construction and the requisite short duration for construction provide strong evidence for the presence of a well-defined social hierarchy with a governing elite capable of marshaling a large labor force to execute massive public works according to a clearly preconceived plan. Haas's (1987) research on chiefdoms helps us put Casma Valley construction in perspective because the ethnographic data concerning the monumental construction accomplishments of chiefdoms versus those of state societies reveals that no chiefdom has been documented to have built constructions much larger than 6,000 cubic meters. All ethnographic examples of truly monumental construction occur in the context of state-level political organization (Haas 1987, 31).

"Royal" Residence

The layout and internal characteristics of the Mound of the Columns at Taukachi-Konkán led us to conclude that this structure served as an elite residence housing the ruler of the Sechín Alto polity (Figure 13.3; Pozorski and Pozorski 1998, 1999a, 1999b). Most of the mound consists of very clean, well-built architecture that was likely formal or public in function. The front or eastern sector of the mound is accessible via a wide central staircase that leads into an ample atrium. From the atrium, more privileged visitors could be conducted into a more private audience venue formed by a square-room-unit variant with low wall niches that served as benches. A nearby square-room-unit room, complete with bar closure to restrict access, likely served as small-scale storage for goods given and received as the ruler interacted with others. Some 118 columns were regularly placed within the front sector of the mound to support a roof, and this mound's name was derived from this distinctive feature.

The actual living quarters of the leader are asymmetrical in plan and contain numerous large platforms that were likely reserved for sitting, eating, and sleeping. It is located at the rear of the mound, and this segment is accessed through a narrow corridor opening toward the south. Ample food remains were recovered from the residential sector, but there was no evidence of in situ food preparation. Immediately south of the main mound we discovered a structure with food remains, multiple hearths, subfloor storage chambers, a possible *pachamanka* (below-ground chamber for cooking on hot stones), and ample platforms that likely served as seating and as work surfaces. A narrow hidden side staircase leading south off the main mound would have allowed access from this food preparation area to the residential sector. This hidden staircase would also have allowed the ruler and other elites to come and go from the mound summit without using the more public central staircase.

Iconography

In their introductory chapter, Rosenswig and Burger suggest that a potential source of independent evidence for rulers is the society's iconography. Within the Sechín Alto iconography, the human representations that are most likely to represent leaders are the friezes that adorn Moxeke mound at Pampa de las Llamas-Moxeke.

The front of Moxeke mound was decorated with highly visible polychrome friezes that extended slightly around onto the sizes of the mound, thereby affording maximum visibility even to viewers at the edges of the large plazas between Moxeke and Huaca A. Tello exposed the set of friezes to the northwest of the central staircase (Tello 1956, 60–64). The friezes were set in a row of six shallow niches and applied to three intervening areas that formed a band across the front of the mound about 5 meters above the ground surface. Both colossal heads and full standing figures were depicted.

The four standing figures were in a group and were closer to the central staircase. Each completely filled a shallow niche and measured about 4 meters wide and likely least 3 meters tall. Preservation varies, but it is clear that all four standing figures wore skirts overlain by tunics with a scalloped border; three of the four depictions show pleated underskirts. North of the niches with the standing figures, and separated from them by approximately 6 meters of unadorned wall, are two smaller niches containing colossal heads. These heads were just over 2 meters wide and still stood about 1.5 meters tall. The more northern head has closed eyes and a slightly smiling mouth. The more southern figure has a grimacing mouth full of teeth. Its open eyes are accented by face paint consisting of a wide vertical band that descends from the eye area.

Both the standing figures and the isolated heads could represent culture heroes or generalized deities, perhaps creator gods. Alternatively, they may represent important people or distinct groups within the society. We prefer the latter interpretation because elements of the Moxeke iconography are also present at Cerro Sechín, where the figures are more humanlike than godlike. Specifically, the vertical band of face paint seen on one colossal head at Moxeke is also found on most Cerro Sechín warrior figures, and the victims on the carved-stone facade at Cerro Sechín are consistently clothed in pleated skirts overlain by scalloped tunics (Cardenas 1995, Figures 27, 30; Roe 1974, 34; Tello 1956, 60–64). If we view the Moxeke figures as actual persons or personages representative of high office, then the arrangement of the figures on the Moxeke facade may be significant. The full figures are nearer the entrance and the spaces between them are also adorned, suggesting that they had special significance at Moxeke or Pampa de las Llamas-Moxeke in general, perhaps serving as local leaders. The colossal heads are smaller, they are separated from the standing figures, they are located well away from the mound entrance, and they are surrounded by unadorned wall space. Although their presence on the Moxeke facade clearly reflects their importance, the context of the heads suggests that these personages had lower status among the elite—at least at Pampa de las Llamas-Moxeke.

Square-Room-Unit Architectural Element

Another feature of the Sechín Alto polity that argues for the existence of a well-developed social hierarchy is the repeated use of the square-room-unit architectural form in contexts that suggest that it functioned as a symbol of polity power and authority. Each module is freestanding and is characterized by rounded exterior corners, round or square interior corners, wall niches, and one or two entrances with raised thresholds, pilasters to narrow the passage, and sliding-bar closures to restrict access. This distinctive room type was first identified at Pampa de las Llamas-Moxeke, where it occurs in a variety of contexts (Pozorski and Pozorski 1994a). Square-room-unit modules cover the surface of Huaca A, where they served both to store goods and to restrict access to these goods. Immediately surrounding Huaca A are seven additional compounds formed of freestanding square-room units that likely more generally restricted access by controlling traffic to and from Huaca A. The central room of Huaca Moxeke is a large round-cornered room formed of immense granite blocks. Square-room units also form the centers of at least 85 intermediate-sized aligned mounds at Pampa de las Llamas-Moxeke. These mounds line both the edges of the site and the roads that afforded access to the site, and they are believed to have functioned administratively—perhaps to monitor traffic (roadside mounds) or to control production or procurement in off-site valley zones (aligned mounds) (Billman 1989; Pozorski and Pozorski 1991).

At Taukachi-Konkán, which has a layout very similar to that of Pampa de las Llamas-Moxeke, square-room-unit modules were excavated on the Mound of the Columns and within intermediate-sized mounds. On the mound summit, traditional square-room units likely served to store valuable goods given and received by the ruler and functioned to limit general access to these goods. Also on the mound top, a variant of the square-room unit with very low wall niches has been interpreted as an audience chamber because the low niches function well as benchlike seats (Pozorski and Pozorski 1999a, 1999b). Excavations within an intermediate-sized mound at Taukachi-Konkán confirmed that the central room there consists of a square-room unit, complete with wall niches and bar closures. Survey data suggest that similar square-room units formed the central room of other intermediate-sized mounds at the site, including examples along the road that enters Taukachi-Konkán from the north.

Excavations on the summit of the main Sechín Alto site mound were severely hampered by the later Early Horizon (1000–200 BC) occupation of the site, which destroyed most of the surface architecture pertaining to the last major Initial Period construction phase. Friezes were intentionally destroyed, stone was stripped from room walls and facades, and the conical adobe core was mined to secure raw material for later constructions. Nevertheless, limited excavations that penetrated 12 meters of fill of the second construction phase (Moxeke Phase B) encountered a partial square-room unit pertaining to the penultimate construction phase (Moxeke Phase A).

Published reports about Fuch's excavations at Sechín Bajo are not yet available, but our earlier surface reconnaissance at the site plus Internet images (McGuinness 2010) documented the presence of numerous symmetrically laid out square-room units. The successive round-cornered constructions at Cerro Sechín resemble square-room-unit modules and intermediate-sized mounds, and the bar-closure architectural element typically associated with such structures has also been observed at this site.

Finally, the square-room-unit architectural form is also known from the site of Bahía Seca, where it forms the center of a single intermediate-sized mound. This mound, surrounded by midden, residential architecture, and a single ventilated-hearth structure, is the main architectural feature at the site (Pozorski and Pozorski 1992, Figure 2). We believe it functioned administratively as part of the inland-coastal subsistence exchange system to monitor or control the procurement of marine resources and to ensure their delivery to the inland sites.

The pervasiveness and consistency of the square-room-unit architectural form within administrative contexts and other formal contexts at Sechín Alto polity sites suggests that this architectural element had come to have intrinsic meaning. This is especially evident on top of Huaca A at

Pampa de las Llamas-Moxeke because the mound surface is covered by freestanding square-room-unit modules in a manner that is clearly inefficient architecturally (Figure 13.3). Shared-wall construction would have used considerably less material and resulted in larger usable spaces. Clearly, meaning had become attached to this architectural form, and based on the contexts where it occurs, it seems likely that the square-room unit symbolized the power and authority of the ruling elite of the Sechín Alto polity.

Access Restrictions

Social hierarchy is also evident when access to special precincts is severely limited such that only a select few, the ruling elite, were able to enter certain spaces (Pozorski 1980). Restrictions on access were documented on all three of the main mounds we excavated: Huaca A at Pampa de las Llamas-Moxeke, the Mound of the Columns at Taukachi-Konkán, and the main mound at the Sechín Alto site. Fieldwork by Tello (1956, 54–60) at Moxeke suggests similar access restrictions were in effect there as well. All four of these mounds, especially Moxeke and Sechín Alto, face large plazas, suggesting that access through observation from ground level was appropriate for large numbers of people (Table 13.2). The size and position of the friezes that adorned Moxeke reflect the importance of public access at this level, and the plaza immediately in front of Moxeke is the largest in the entire Sechín Alto polity. With an area of over 185,000 square meters (Table 13.2), it could hold many times the actual population of the Sechín Alto polity, which has been estimated at about 23,000 (Pozorski and Pozorski 2005). In contrast, the smallest plaza is immediately adjacent to the Mound of the Columns at Taukachi-Konkán. This may reflect generalized access restriction, suggesting that relatively few citizens had access to the ruler at his residence or to any public-oriented events there. At both the Sechín Alto site and Taukachi-Konkán, plaza spaces tend to be smaller nearest the main mound, increasing in size with increasing distance from the main mound. This also may reflect some degree of access restriction among the citizens who observed public events.

All the mounds also have ample central staircases. However, these staircases either decrease in width as the top of the mound is approached (i.e., at Sechín Alto) or the visitor faces other restrictions (i.e., at Huaca A and the Mound of the Columns). Restricted access on the mound top is especially well documented on Huaca A. The main staircase is narrowed by large pilasters, a possible initial checkpoint. Once within the atrium, the visitor had to pass repeatedly through sliding-bar closure gates that blocked every entrance in order to move higher (in elevation) toward increasingly smaller rooms (Pozorski and Pozorski 1994a). On the Mound of the Columns, similar bar-closure barriers restricted access to the storage area and to the audience rooms and the elite residence was accessible only through a single narrow corridor. At the main Sechín Alto site mound, the central staircase narrows in segments from 17 meters wide at ground level to 5 meters wide at the entrance to the large mound-top room. A possible audience area on the south wing of the upper atrium may have served to screen visitors. From the large mound-top room, access to the sacred precinct was further restricted. This special area consisted of a rectangular room lined with friezed columns atop the conical adobe core, and it was reached via a corridor only 1.25 meters wide and 35 meters long (Pozorski and Pozorski 2005).

Clearly, access in general was strictly controlled within the Sechín Alto polity, and we can look further to examine what was being protected by the omnipresent access restrictions. At Huaca A, we see closely monitored multistage restrictions on access to comestibles and other stored goods. This reflects the importance of foodstuffs that were likely used to support the population in general and/or public works, especially when river flow was low and agricultural production decreased. On the Mound of the Columns, access restrictions limited access to the leader—both the total number of visitors and the number who could enter simultaneously (based on the capacity of the audience room). On the Sechín Alto main mound, only a select few were able to reach the *huaca* (mound) top and (especially) the more interior friezed chamber. Such varied objectives with respect to access restrictions both documents the presence of a corps of elite (who were able to gain access) and reveal that these Sechín Alto polity leaders exercised a high degree of control over many facets of the society.

Standardization of Architecture, Iconography, and Artifacts

An additional facet of the Sechín Alto polity that may reflect the presence of a hierarchical society and power exerted by the society's elite is extreme standardization that can be observed in the polity's architecture, iconography, and artifacts. With respect to architecture, the pervasive square-room unit is the best example. Its form remained amazingly consistent as it was used in a variety of administrative contexts. We also see a high degree of standardization with respect to other aspects of polity architecture. For example, the intermediate-sized mounds may vary in height, but they uniformly consist of a central square-room unit surrounded by a round-cornered platform with outer retaining walls and interior divisions into rooms. The fronts of intermediate-sized mounds are defined by lower atria accessed via a central staircase. This list of traits describes intermediate-sized mounds at Pampa de las Llamas-Moxeke, Taukachi-Konkán, the Sechín Alto site, Bahía Seca, and the interior constructions at Cerro Sechin—all the sites where such structures occur. The standardization of architecture at these Casma Valley sites is at least as uniform—if not more so—than the standardization seen in public architecture of later complex Andean cultures such as the Wari, Chimu, and Inka (Hyslop 1990; Schreiber 1992; Keatinge 1974).

With respect to iconography, the best evidence of consistency or standardization comes from the carved-stone facade at Cerro Sechín. In its totality, the iconography there can generally be described as a procession. Two near-identical standards, staffs with attached banners, occupy positions on either side of the central entrance. The standards are flanked by alternating warrior figures, who seem to emerge from the rear door and move toward the entrance, and victims, who are represented by either mutilated near-whole figures or body parts. Within this grisly scene, the figures are notably uniform. They also tend to face toward the entrance, resulting in mirror-image symmetry when the two sides are compared (Cardenas 1995, Figure 31). With the exception of one figure who might depict a leader (ibid., Figure 30[2]), the warriors are remarkably consistent in their dress and pose. Each is typically dressed in a loincloth-type garment decorated by possible feather elements. The only other clothing is a fezlike cap, sometimes with hair shown extending from the cap. The warriors' facial features typically consist of a grimacing mouth, D-shaped eyes with pendant pupils, and a single band of vertical face paint that crosses the eye area. Most figures hold short staffs or clubs with a stepped element at the top end and often a circular design with interior squares at the bottom end. Victims' clothing uniformly consists of a pleated skirt overlain by a scalloped tunic (Cardenas 1995, Figure 27).

Ceramic figurines comprise an artifact class that has numerous features and a high degree of standardization (Figure 13.5; Pozorski and Pozorski 1998). Over 150 fragments recovered from the Sechín Alto site, Taukachi-Konkán, and Pampa de las Llamas-Moxeke are remarkably consistent and similar. Typical examples are 12–15 centimeters tall, hand modeled from clay with relatively coarse temper, and slightly to moderately burnished.

Figure 13.5. Views of the front and back of an Initial Period solid figurine found at Sechín Alto Complex.

Individual features are created using a combination of incision, punctation, and appliqué. Eyes are formed by making a deep horizontal incision into which a bead of clay is inserted to form the eyeball. Then a deep round punctation is added to represent the iris. Ears are modeled or added as appliqué, and individual features are defined by three incisions in a C shape with a deep punctation for the earhole. Noses are modeled or added as appliqué, with two deep punctations forming the nostrils. Mouths consist of a series of deep horizontal punctuations. Two options for head treatment have been observed: fezlike caps and clearly defined locks of long hair applied as appliqué and further defined by incisions. Collars are uniformly present at the head-torso join. These are appliqué bands typically decorated by a combination of incision and punctation. Occasionally belt or loincloth-type clothing, defined by appliqué and/or incision, is present in the abdomen area. The upper torso is always bare; and the arms, added as appliqué, are folded across the torso. Hands with three to four fingers are defined by incision. Perforations in both armpit areas of most figures may have functioned to suspend the figurines or tie them to something. Figurine legs are uniformly conjoined and are defined front and back by deep incisions that may extend across the base of the figure to separate the feet. Three to four toes are defined by incision. Figurine bases are consistently flat or slightly concave, and the figures stand well.

We have included standardization of architectural elements, iconography, and artifacts as an indicator of social hierarchy because we believe that this standardization and the resultant uniform products reflect the nature of the power structure. We have argued that the square-room unit had intrinsic meaning as a symbol of power and authority, thereby attempting to account for its pervasive use. We also view both the highly consistent iconography of Cerro Sechín and the uniform features of the figurines as evidence that there was little latitude for artistic expression within the society. Elements that define the figurines can be related to the Cerro Sechín carvings (e.g., fezlike caps, well defined locks of abundant hair), and the content of the Cerro Sechín carvings can be related to the Moxeke friezes because the Cerro Sechín warriors have vertical bands of face paint and the victims at Cerro Sechín consistently have pleated skirts and scalloped tunics. These commonalities suggest that we might be dealing with depictions of leaders or distinct segments of society in both the iconography and figurines and that the form these depictions take was highly prescribed within the Sechín Alto polity.

Subsistence Base

There is no doubt that the Sechín Alto polity was supported by plant foods produced through irrigation agriculture coupled with marine products procured at coastal sites (Pozorski and Pozorski 1987). On the Peruvian desert coast, large inland settlements cannot be supported without irrigation agriculture, and this subsistence pattern is well documented to have begun in Preceramic times. The best evidence of the combined agricultural-marine subsistence base comes from actual remains of the foods consumed and from subsistence-related artifacts.

Middens at Pampa de las Llamas-Moxeke, Taukachi-Konkán, the Sechín Alto site, and the three coastal sites of Bahía Seca, Tortugas, and Huaynuná yielded ample remains of plants and animals (Pozorski and Pozorski 1986, 1987, 2002b; T. Pozorski and S. Pozorski 1990). The Initial Period food plant inventory expanded slightly compared to the species consumed during the Preceramic, and the remains are generally more abundant. Food and industrial plants used include cotton, gourds, squash, peanuts, potatoes, sweet potatoes, *achira,* manioc, common beans, lima beans, *Canavalia* beans, guava, *pacae, lúcuma,* avocadoes, and *cansaboca.* Maize is notably absent. Animal protein was supplied primarily by marine animals; however, deer were occasionally hunted. The most commonly consumed marine animals were anchovies and sardines as well as large mussels and clams. Fishhooks and especially looped and knotted netting are common artifacts; stemmed projectile points that were likely used in hunting deer and possibly sea mammals are found less frequently.

The Sechín Alto Polity

By examining various lines of evidence for social hierarchy within the Sechín Alto polity, we have also described many features of the polity and how it functioned. Nevertheless, it is difficult to explain how or why such a development occurred within the Casma Valley. Along the Peruvian desert coast, there are no readily apparent ecological differences among the valleys—at least none that could explain the magnitude of Casma's florescence relative to other similar Initial Period occupations in valleys to the north and south. We attribute Casma's Initial Period florescence to strong leadership with a preconceived plan. Likely with knowledge of earlier developments in the Norte Chico region, a charismatic leader emerged who was determined to create a similar settlement and economic system on a much larger scale. Ideas of structure symmetry, mounds with associated plazas, irrigation agriculture, and a coastal-inland subsistence exchange were likely derived from Preceramic antecedents. Intersite competition expressed as monumental construction of the type modeled by Ruiz, Creamer, and Haas (2007, 111–118) for the late Preceramic may help explain the magnitude of Casma Valley construction. Building on this Preceramic base, the Initial Period leader and associated elite added new ideas. The result was an intervalley polity centered in the two drainages of the Casma Valley system and comprised of precisely oriented sites with distinct but complementary functions. The importance of the Sechín Alto site, the polity's administrative center, is readily evident from its placement on prime arable land while other major sites are located outside the limits of early prehistoric irrigation. Precise planning is also evident within sites, and as a result of such planning, some sites closely resemble each other in layout (e.g., Pampa de las Llamas-Moxeke and Taukachi-Konkán). This overall plan was transmitted through several generations of rulers as evidenced at Pampa de las

Llamas-Moxeke, where rows of aligned mounds were constructed and gaps were filled in for the duration of the site.

The heavy hand of the Sechín Alto polity leadership is readily evident in their repeated use of the square-room unit both functionally in administrative and other nondomestic contexts and symbolically to represent their power and authority. Related to this is the standardization in architecture, artifacts, and iconography that also may reflect restricted societal norms with respect to artistic expression. The iconography may also give us clues about who these leaders were or at least how they looked and dressed. Taken collectively, the human depictions in the Moxeke friezes, the Cerro Sechín stone carvings, and the figurines document two types of important personages. One is represented by the standing figures that adorn Moxeke, the victims at Cerro Sechín, and possibly the bare-headed figurines. These wear pleated skirts and scalloped tunics and seem bare headed, albeit with long locks of hair. A second group is suggested by the warrior figures at Cerro Sechín, the figurines with hats, and possibly the colossal heads at Moxeke. These figures wear few clothes except for loincloths, collars, and fezlike hats. They commonly decorate their faces with large vertical bands of paint.

An additional important issue concerns how Sechín Alto polity leaders were able to exert and maintain control over Casma Valley society. Control of the subsistence system may have been key. The administrative structure at Bahía Seca and multiple intermediate-sized administrative mounds at Pampa de las Llamas-Moxeke suggest that production of foodstuffs was closely monitored. In addition, clear differences in magnitude between inland centers and coastal sites leave no doubt that power and authority resided with the elite of the inland sites. The restricted access to the Huaca A storage structure indicates that storage and distribution of comestibles was also controlled. Such centralization of food production, storage, and distribution could potentially have given Sechín Alto polity leaders tremendous leverage as they marshaled work forces for monumental construction. Despite clear evidence of social control, coercion was probably not the only motivating force operating within the polity. The huge plazas and public friezes at Moxeke and Sechín Alto site attest to the importance of community involvement and inspiration through observance of and possible participation in public events and ceremonies. The complementary functions of the major mounds and their associated populations would also have positively reinforced feelings of social identity and solidarity with the local community and polity as a whole. The net result was one of the most advanced civilizations in the New World for its time period.

At the apogee of its existence, the Sechín Alto polity was the most powerful political entity along the entire Peruvian coast. Given the size of the mounds built over relatively short periods of time and available ethnographic data on mound construction, it is quite likely that the Sechín Alto polity was an early state organization. The polity was ruled by a small group of elites who were able to organize large numbers of the general populace to construct numerous enormous mounds that served various complementary functions as central storage facilities, temples, a palace, and administrative facilities. They were able to have these mounds, their associated plazas, and nearby intermediate-sized mounds constructed in a very standardized and precise manner, and they were able to maintain this standard of size and precision over several generations of rulers spanning some 400 years.

It is probable that Sechín Alto polity monuments were built through the use of a corvée system of labor with the substantial agrarian portion of the population providing some 500 to 1,000 laborers each year in order to complete the tasks at hand. As was the case in the much-later *mit'a* system of the Incas, provisions and tools may have been supplied by the elite for the workers. In the case of the Sechín Alto polity, however, such provisioning may have been as simple as food allocations from stored comestibles, because most of the labor probably came from within the Casma Valley. Most of the workers could probably have worked on public projects while using their own homes as residences.

This chapter has demonstrated that the leaders of the Sechín Alto polity had considerable social control over their society. Control over the irrigation system, the distribution of the agricultural products derived from that system, and the distribution of marine products gathered at coastal sites probably enabled the elite to accomplish what they did in terms of the visible archaeological record. The locus of this control was likely the monumental architecture. Elites inhabited and worked from mound tops in positions that tangibly reiterated their elevated status. Access to mound summits and especially interiors was highly restricted, adding further to the perceived status and mystery of the elite.

Even under this scenario, however, the resultant society was probably more like a benevolent dictatorship than a totalitarian society. The number and size of plazas found at both Pampa de las Llamas-Moxeke and the

Sechín Alto site reflect a commitment to including the general population in public gatherings of both a religious and nonreligious nature, which would have given the common people a feeling of inclusion and social solidarity. This general sense of inclusion is also reflected in the midden remains excavated at various Sechín Alto polity sites. The variety of plant and animal remains is relatively uniform throughout these sites, indicating that no one was deprived of basic food resources. This contrasts with some later state organizations such as Teotihuacan in Mexico, where people living in the poorer parts of the capital city appear to have been denied much of the food that they themselves grew (Millon 1988, 143–146). We envision that as long as there was political and environmental stability, the common people were willing to be ruled by a strong-willed elite. This parallels the political dynamic in Old Kingdom Ancient Egypt, when the enormous stone pyramids were constructed. People were eager to participate in monumental construction projects (Johnson 1999, 58) because the conclusion of such projects brought a sense of pride to the communities involved and the subsequent public activities that took place reinforced a feeling of community involvement and solidarity.

Monumental construction was extremely important to the ruling elite of the Sechín Alto polity. The construction of enormous mounds for a predetermined purpose was a reflection of their social status both within and outside their own society. Archaeological data from the Initial Period, at least in the area around the Casma Valley, shows little evidence of status-laden artifacts. Pottery is relatively simple; its forms and decorative motifs are limited. No metal production is evident. A few textiles have complex designs, but most are undecorated cloth. Occasional beads and perforated disks or rectangles of shell and bone may be from jewelry or ornaments for clothing, but none is abundant or elaborate. This leaves monumental construction as the principal venue through which social status and power could be expressed. This is precisely what the elite did in a spectacular way—in the form of a palace of large proportions at Taukachi-Konkán, a temple at Moxeke perhaps containing the very images of the elite themselves, and large storage and administrative facilities at both Pampa de las Llamas-Moxeke and the Sechín Alto site. Along with their subjects, the Sechín Alto polity elite could take pride in their ability to bring about these construction projects. In addition, the resultant mounds and plazas were tangible evidence of the political power and conspicuous labor consumption that gave the Sechín Alto polity elite elevated social status both within and outside the Casma Valley area. These elites likely competed for prestige with leaders in other coastal valleys in a peer-polity fashion (see Haas and Creamer this volume), and any visitor to the valley would have been overwhelmingly impressed by the accomplishments of Sechín Alto polity leaders. Such information would have been transmitted via word of mouth to other coastal valleys, thereby spreading the news of Casma's greatness far and wide.

References Cited

Abrams, Elliot
1994 *How the Maya Built Their World.* University of Texas Press, Austin.
Alva, Walter
1986 *Las Salinas de Chao.* Materialien zur Allgemeinen und Vergleichenden Archäologie 34. Verlag C. H. Beck, Munich.
Billman, Brian
1989 Land, Water and Architecture: Political and Economic Organization of an Early Andean State. Unpublished M.A. thesis, Department of Anthropology, University of California, Santa Barbara.
Bird, Junius, and John Hyslop
1985 *The Preceramic Excavations at the Huaca Prieta Chicama Valley, Peru.* Anthropological Papers of the American Museum of Natural History 62, part 1. American Museum of Natural History, New York.
Bischof, Henning
1995 Cerro Sechín y el Arte Temprano Centro-Andino. In *Arqueología de Cerro Sechín,* vol. 2, *Escultura,* edited by Lorenzo Samaniego and Mercedes Cardenas, pp. 125–156. Pontificia Universidad Católica del Perú and Fundación Volkswagenwerk, Lima.
Cardenas, Mercedes
1995 Iconografía Lítica de Cerro Sechín: Vida y Muerte. In *Arqueología de Cerro Sechín,* vol. 2, *Escultura,* edited by Lorenzo Samaniego and Mercedes Cardenas, pp. 43–124. Pontificia Universidad Católica del Perú and Fundación Volkswagenwerk, Lima.
Chang, K. C.
1968 *The Archaeology of China.* Yale University Press, New Haven, Connecticut.
Chu, Alejandro
2008 *Bandurria: Arena, Mar y Humedad en el Surgimiento de la Civilización Andina.* Servicios Gráficos Jackeline, Huaura, Perú.
Collier, Donald
1962 Archaeological Investigations in the Casma Valley, Peru. In *Thirty-Fourth International Congress of Americanists,* pp. 411–417. Verlag Ferdinand Berger, Vienna.
Engel, Frederic
1957a Sites et Etablissements sans Céramique de la Côte Péruvienne. *Journal de la Société des Américanistes* 46(n.s.):67–155.
1957b Early Sites on the Peruvian Coast. *Southwestern Journal of Anthropology* 13:54–68.

1967   El Complejo El Paraíso en el Valle de Chillón Habitado Hace 5,500 Años: Nuevos Aspectos de la Civilización de los Agricultores del Pallar. *Anales Científicos de la Universidad Agraria* 5:241–280.

Erasmus, Charles
1965   Monument Building: Some Field Experiments. *Southwestern Journal of Anthropology* 21:277–301.

Feldman, Robert
1985   Preceramic Corporate Architecture: Evidence for the Development of Non-Egalitarian Social Systems in Peru. In *Early Ceremonial Architecture in the Andes*, edited by Christopher B. Donnan, pp. 71–92. Dumbarton Oaks Research Library and Collection, Washington, D.C.

Flannery, Kent
1998   The Ground Plans of Archaic States. In *Archaic States*, edited by Gary Feinman and Joyce Marcus, pp. 16–57. School of American Research Press, Santa Fe, N.M.

Fuchs, Peter
1997   Nuevos Datos Arqueométricos para la História de Ocupación de Cerro Sechín—Período Lítico al Formativo. In *Archaeológica Peruana 2: Arquitectura y Civilización en los Andes Prehispánicos*, edited by Elizabeth Bonnier and Henning Bischof, pp. 145–162. Sociedad Arqueológica Peruano-Alemana, Reiss-Museum, Mannheim, Germany.

Haas, Jonathan
1982   *The Evolution of the Prehistoric State*. Columbia University Press, New York.
1987   The Exercise of Power in Early Andean State Development. In *The Origins and Development of the Andean State*, edited by Jonathan Haas, Shelia Pozorski, and Thomas Pozorski, pp. 31–35. Cambridge University Press, Cambridge.

Haas, Jonathan, and Winifred Creamer
2004   Cultural Transformations in the Central Andean Late Archaic. In *Andean Archaeology*, edited by Helaine Silverman, pp. 35–50. Blackwell Publishing, Malden, Massachusetts.
2006   Crucible of Andean Civilization: The Peruvian Coast from 3000 to 1800 B.C. *Current Anthropology* 47:745–775.

Haas, Jonathan, Winifred Creamer, and Álvaro Ruiz
2004   Dating the Late Archaic Occupation of the Norte Chico Region in Peru. *Nature* 432(December 23):1020–1023.
2005   Power and the Emergence of Complex Polities in the Peruvian Preceramic. In *Foundations of Power in the Prehispanic Andes*, edited by K. J. Vaughn, D. E. Ogburn, and C. A. Conlee, pp. 37–52. Archaeological Papers 14. American Anthropological Association, Arlington, Virginia.

Hyslop, John
1990   *Inka Settlement Planning*. University of Texas Press, Austin.

Johnson, Gregory
1973   *Local Exchange and Early State Development in Southwestern Iran*. University of Michigan Anthropological Papers 51. Museum of Anthropology, University of Michigan, Ann Arbor.

Johnson, Paul
1999   *The Civilization of Ancient Egypt*. Harper Collins, New York.
Keatinge, Richard
1974   Chimu Rural Administrative Centers in the Moche Valley, Peru. *World Archaeology* 6:66–82.
Lanning, Edward P.
1967   *Peru before the Incas*. Prentice-Hall, Englewood Cliffs, New Jersey.
Maldonado, Elena
1992   *Arqueología de Cerro Sechín*. Vol. 1, *Arquitectura*. Pontificia Universidad Católica del Peru and Fundación Volkswagenwerk, Lima.
McGuinness, Tim
2010   The Mystery of the Nazca Lines: The Lost Cultures of the Peru and the Nazca Plateau. Electronic document, Nazcamystery.com/Casma_Sechin.htm, accessed May 14, 2011.
Millon, Rene
1988   The Last Years of Teotihuacan Dominance. In *The Collapse of Ancient States and Civilizations*, edited by Norman Yoffee and George Cowgill, pp. 102–164. University of Arizona Press, Tucson.
Moseley, Michael E.
1972   Subsistence and Demography: An Example of Interaction from Prehistoric Peru. *Southwestern Journal of Anthropology* 28:25–49.
1975   *The Maritime Foundations of Andean Civilization*. Cummings Publishing , Menlo Park, California.
2001   *The Incas and Their Ancestors*. 2nd ed. Thames and Hudson, London.
Pozorski, Shelia, and Thomas Pozorski
1979a   Alto Salaverry: A Peruvian Coastal Preceramic Site. *Annals of Carnegie Museum of Natural History* 48:337–375.
1979b   An Early Subsistence Exchange System in the Moche Valley, Peru. *Journal of Field Archaeology* 6:413–432.
1986   Recent Excavations at Pampa de las Llamas-Moxeke, a Complex Initial Period Site in Peru. *Journal of Field Archaeology* 13:381–401.
1987   *Early Settlement and Subsistence in the Casma Valley, Peru*. University of Iowa Press, Iowa City.
1989   Planificación Urbana Prehistórica en Pampa de las Llamas-Moxeke, Valle de Casma. *Boletín de Lima* 65:19–30.
1990   Reexamining the Critical Preceramic/Ceramic Period Transition: New Data from Coastal Peru. *American Anthropologist* 92:481–491.
1991   Storage, Access Control, and Bureaucratic Proliferation: Understanding the Initial Period (1800–900 B.C.) Economy at Pampa de las Llamas-Moxeke, Casma Valley, Peru. *Research in Economic Anthropology* 13:341–371.
1992   Early Civilization in the Casma Valley, Peru. *Antiquity* 66:845–870.
1994a   Multidimensional Planning at Pampa de las Llamas-Moxeke. In *Meaningful Architecture: Social Interpretations of Buildings*, edited by Martin Locock, pp. 45–65. Worldwide Archaeological Series 9, Avebury, Aldershot, UK.

1994b   Early Andean Cities. *Scientific American* 270(6):66–72.
1998   La Dinámica del Valle de Casma Durante el Período Inicial. In *Perspectivas Regionales del Período Formativo en el Peru,* edited by Peter Kaulicke, pp. 83–100. Boletín de Arqueología PUCP 2. Pontificia Universidad Católica del Perú, Lima.
2000   El Desarrollo de la Sociedad Compleja en el Valle de Casma. *Arqueología y Sociedad* 13:79–98.
2002a   The Sechín Alto Complex and Its Place within Casma Valley Initial Period Development. In *Andean Archaeology I: Variations in Sociopolitical Organization of the Central Andes,* edited by Helaine Silverman and William Isbell, pp. 21–51. Kluwer Academic/Plenum Publishers, New York.
2002b   Early Coastal Andean Formative. In *Encyclopedia of Prehistory,* vol. 7, *South America,* edited by P. Peregrine and M. Ember, pp. 78–97. Kluwer Academic/Plenum Publishers, New York.
2006   Las Haldas: An Expanding Initial Period Polity of Coastal Peru. *Journal of Anthropological Research* 62:27–52.
2008   Early Cultural Complexity on the Coast of Peru. In *Handbook of South American Archaeology,* edited by Helaine Silverman and William Isbell, pp. 604–631. Springer, New York.

Pozorski, Thomas
1980   The Early Horizon Site of Huaca de los Reyes: Societal Implications. *American Antiquity* 45:100–110.

Pozorski, Thomas, and Shelia Pozorski
1990   Huaynuná, a Late Cotton Preceramic Site on the North Coast of Peru. *Journal of Field Archaeology* 17:17–26.
1993   Early Complex Society and Ceremonialism on the Peruvian North Coast. In *El Mundo Ceremonial Andino,* edited by Luis Millones and Yoshio Onuki, pp. 45–68. National Museum of Ethnology, Osaka, Japan.
1996   Ventilated Hearth Structures in the Casma Valley, Peru. *Latin American Antiquity* 7:341–353.
1999a   Temple, Palais ou Entrepôt? La Centralisation du Pouvoir dans le Perou Prehistorique. In *Ville et Pouvoir en Amerique: les Formes de l'Autorité,* edited by Jerome Monnet, 87–110. L'Harmattan, Paris.
1999b   La Centralizacion del Poder en el Peru Prehispanico Temprano. *Revista del Museo de Arqueologia, Antropologia e Historia* 7:87–109. Universidad Nacional de Trujillo, Trujillo, Peru.
2005   Architecture and Chronology at the Site of Sechín Alto, Casma Valley, Peru. *Journal of Field Archaeology* 30:143–161.

Renfrew, Colin
1973   Monuments, Mobilization and Social Organization in Neolithic Wessex. In *The Explanation of Culture Change: Models in Prehistory,* edited by Colin Renfrew, pp. 539–558. Duckworth, London.

Roe, Peter
1974   *A Further Exploration of the Rowe Chavín Seriation and Its Implications for North Central Coast Chronology.* Studies in Pre-Columbian Art and Archaeology 13. Dumbarton Oaks, Washington, D.C.

Ruiz, Álvaro, Winifred Creamer, and Jonathan Haas
2007   *Investigaciones Arqueológicas en los Sitio del Arcaico Tardío (3000 a 1800 Años a.C.) del Valle de Pativilca, Perú*. Instituto Cultural del Norte Chico, Barranca, Peru.

Samaniego, Lorenzo
1973   *Los Nuevos Trabajos Arqueológicos en Sechín, Casma, Peru*. Larsen Ediciones, Trujillo, Peru.

Samaniego, Lorenzo, and Mercedes Cardenas
1995   *Arqueología de Cerro Sechín, Tomo II: Escultura*. Pontificia Universidad Católica del Perú and Fundación Volkswagenwerk, Lima.

Samaniego, Lorenzo, Enrique Vergara, and Henning Bischof
1985   New Evidence on Cerro Sechín, Casma Valley, Peru. In *Early Ceremonial Architecture in the Andes*, edited by Christopher B. Donnan, pp. 165–190. Dumbarton Oaks Research Library and Collection, Washington, D.C.

Schreiber, Katharina
1992   *Wari Imperialism in Middle Horizon Peru*. Anthropological Papers, Museum of Anthropology, University of Michigan 87. Museum of Anthropology, University of Michigan, Ann Arbor, Michigan.

Shady, Ruth
1997   *La Ciudad Sagrada de Caral-Supe en los Albores de la Civilización en el Perú*. Universidad Nacional Mayor de San Marcos, Lima.
2000   Sustento Socioeconómico de la Sociedad de Caral-Supe en los Orígenes de la Civilización en el Perú. *Arqueología y Sociedad* 13:49–66.
2001   *La Ciudad Sagrada de Caral-Supe y los Orígenes de la Civilización Andina*. Museo de Arqueología y Antropología de la Universidad Nacional Mayor de San Marcos, Lima.
2003   Los Orígenes de la Civilización y la Formación del Estado en el Perú: Las Evidencias Arqueológicas de Caral-Supe. In *La Ciudad Sagrada de Caral-Supe. Los Orígenes de la Civilización Andina y la Formación del Estado Prístino en el Antiguo Perú*, edited by Ruth Shady and Carlos Leyva, pp. 93–105. Instituto Nacional de Cultura, Lima.
2004   *Caral, la Ciudad del Fuego Sagrado*. Interbank, Lima.
2006   *La Ciudad Sagrada de Caral-Supe: Símbolo Cultural del Perú*. Instituto Nacional de Cultura, Lima.
2007a *The Sacred City of Caral-Supe: Cultural Symbol of Peru*. Instituto Nacional de Cultura, Lima.
2007b *The Social and Cultural Values of Caral-Supe, the Oldest Civilization of Peru and the Americas, and Their Role in Integrated Sustainable Development*. Instituto Nacional de Cultura, Lima.

Shady, Ruth, and Daniel Cáceda
2008   *Áspero, la Ciudad Pesquera de la Civilización Caral*. Instituto Nacional de Cultura, Lima.

Shady, Ruth, Jonathan Haas, and Winifred Creamer
2001   Dating Caral, a Preceramic Site in the Supe Valley on the Central Coast of Peru. *Science* 92(5517): 723–726.

Tello, Julio C.
1943 Discovery of the Chavín Culture in Peru. *American Antiquity* 9:135–160.
1956 *Arqueología del Valle de Casma, Culturas: Chavín, Santa o Huaylas Yunga y Sub-Chimú.* Vol. 1. Universidad Nacional Mayor de San Marcos, Lima.

Trigger, Bruce
1990 Monumental Architecture: A Thermodynamic Explanation of Symbolic Behaviour. *World Archaeology* 22:119–132.

Ugent, Donald, Shelia Pozorski, and Thomas Pozorski
1981 Prehistoric Remains of the Sweet Potato. *Phytologia* 49:401–415.
1982 Archaeological Potato Tuber Remains from the Casma Valley of Peru. *Economic Botany* 36:182–192.
1983 Restos Arqueológicos de Tubérculos de Papas y Camotes del Valle de Casma en el Perú. *Boletín de Lima* 25:1–17.
1984 New Evidence for the Ancient Cultivation of *Canna edulis* in Peru. *Economic Botany* 38:417–432.

Vega-Centeno, Rafael, Luis Villacorta, Luis Caceres, and Giancarlo Marcone
1998 Arquitectura Monumental Temprana en el Valle Medio de Fortaleza. In *Perspectivas Regionales del Período Formativo en el Perú,* edited by Peter Kaulicke, pp. 219–238. Boletín de Arqueología PUCP 2. Pontificia Universidad Católica del Perú, Lima.

Wendt, W. E.
1964 Die Prakeramische Seidlung am Rio Seco, Peru. *Baessler Archiv* 11:225–275.

Vallejos, Francisco
2008 Hallan la Edificación Más Antiguo del Perú. *El Comercio Online,* February 24.

Whalen, Andrew
2008 Ancient Ceremonial Plaza Found in Peru. Electronic document, http://www.physorg.com/news123316935.html, accessed May 14, 2011.

Wilson, David
1988 *Prehispanic Settlement Patterns in the Lower Santa Valley Peru.* Smithsonian Institution Press, Washington, D.C.

Wright, Henry, and Gregory Johnson
1975 Population, Exchange, and Early State Formation in Southwestern Iran. *American Anthropologist* 77(2):267–289.

Zoubek, Thomas
2006 Exploring the Cultural Identity and Relationships of Peru's North Coast Agricultural Societies during the Initial Period (c. 2100–1100 B.C.). Paper presented at the 25th Northeast Conference on Andean Archaeology and Ethnohistory, Philadelphia, Pennsylvania.

14

Monumental Public Complexes and Agricultural Expansion on Peru's Central Coast during the Second Millennium BC

RICHARD L. BURGER AND LUCY C. SALAZAR

> What looks large at a distance,
> close up ain't never that big.
>
> Bob Dylan

During the second millennium BC, monumental architecture proliferated along Peru's central coast on a scale rarely if ever equaled in the area's prehistory. Drawing upon investigations in the Lurín Valley, this chapter will explore the emergence of multiple U-shaped pyramid complexes and their relationship to the expansion of irrigation agriculture. By the end of the Initial Period (1800–800 BC) there were least nine public centers with monumental architecture in the lower and middle Lurín Valley. It will be argued that this monumental architecture developed in tandem with agricultural and demographic expansion on Peru's central coast and that the distinctive settlement pattern documented during the Initial Period in the Lurín Valley reflects factors other than the emergence of the archaic state and a hierarchically stratified society. The long-term impact of the unprecedented production of monumental constructions will also be considered.

Background

The production of monumental architecture on Peru's central coast began during the mid-third millennium BC during what is known in the archaeological literature as the Late Preceramic or Archaic Period. Examples of Late Preceramic public architecture are best known from the Chillón

Valley, particularly from the work of Frederic Engel (1966) and Jeffrey Quilter (1985) at El Paraíso in the lower valley. More recently, the investigations of Robert Benfer at Buena Vista (this volume) in the middle portion of the Chillón Valley has confirmed the presence of elaborate monumental architecture on the central coast during the third millennium BC and has begun to reveal its diversity and complexity.

The creation of large-scale public architecture by corporate groups on the central coast at this early time was not limited to Chillón, as shown by the investigations of W. E. Wendt at Rio Seco on the shores north of the Chancay drainage. While Late Preceramic monumental constructions have not yet been identified in all of the valleys of the central coast, the surveys of Thomas Patterson, Edward Lanning, and others have confirmed the importance of the Late Preceramic occupation on the shores and interior valleys throughout the region (Patterson and Moseley 1968; Moseley 1975; Wendt 1964).

Detailed study of floral and faunal remains from the multiple villages and centers of this time period document that fish and other marine fauna were the primary sources of animal food. Plant foods consisted of a mixture of cultivated items such as beans, squash, peppers, and local fruits and wild foods such as the roots of sedges and cattails (Cohen 1978, 1979; Meadors and Benfer 2009; Moseley 1972; Patterson 1971; Quilter et al. 1991; Reitz 1988). Maize was not yet significant from a caloric or nutritional perspective, and no other single crop high in calories seems to have constituted a dietary staple. The lack of pottery for cooking seems to have been linked to the continued reliance on a wide range of wild and cultivated foods that did not require boiling and other intensive cooking techniques.

The nature of this early episode of monumental construction remains poorly understood for most valleys on the central coast. Nonetheless, it has been established that the Late Preceramic constructions at El Paraíso covered some 58 hectares and that the two largest mounds each measured about 400 meters long. The construction of the 11 buildings at El Paraíso involved the movement of at least 100,000 tons of rock. Thomas Patterson has estimated that this investment would have required some two million person-days of labor. El Paraíso provides incontestable evidence of a precocious capacity to mobilize corporate labor on Peru's central coast before the introduction of pottery (Moseley 1975, 26; Patterson 1983).

Moreover, the U-shaped configuration at El Paraíso and the elaborate clay friezes recently uncovered at Buena Vista offer antecedents for the better known and more numerous Initial Period monumental complexes in

Chillón and the rest of the central coast that date to the second millennium BC. As in the case of the Initial Period large-scale constructions, the Late Preceramic architectural complexes appear to have been created as environments for ritual activity and other community activities rather than as funerary monuments or settings for more mundane purposes (Benfer this volume; Quilter 1985). There is also continuity in the construction techniques used in the monumental constructions, such as the popularity of building with rough stone and the use of disposable fiber bags (known as *shicra*) to hold stone fills.

Monumental Construction during the Initial Period

It was during the second millennium BC, a period that roughly corresponds to the Initial Period, that the creation of monumental architecture became widespread in the lower and middle valleys of Peru's central coast. In the four major central coast valleys of Chancay, Chillón, Rimac, and Lurín, at least 44 centers with monumental architecture were constructed, apparently all with similar architectural features. As first recognized by the Peruvian architect Carlos Williams (1971, 1985), the Initial Period monumental complexes of this region have a distinctive a U-shaped layout. It consists of a terraced flat-topped pyramid flanked by longer asymmetrical lateral terraced platforms. These three solid mounds surround a massive open rectangular plaza area that is defined by low stone retaining walls. A broad steep central staircase provided access to a central ritual environment set into the central pyramid and to the other buildings on the flat-topped summit. While the orientation of the U-shaped complexes varied between sites (13–64° NE), the open side of the ground plan consistently faces northeast toward the Andes and the source of water for farming.

The scale of these U-shaped pyramid complexes on the central coast is impressive. Thomas Patterson (1983, 1985) has estimated the volume of Huaca La Florida in the Rimac Valley as being over one million cubic meters, and he believes that its construction represents an investment of 6.7 million person-days. This calculation does not include the labor needed to level the terrain and to plaster and/or decorate the surfaces of the buildings. San Jacinto in the neighboring Chancay Valley appears to be even larger. According to Williams (1985), the central pyramid there reached 23 meters in height above the surrounding land surface, and he believed that the leveling of the 30-hectare open plaza area there alone would have involved the transport of two million cubic meters of fill.

The ubiquity on the central coast of the U-shaped monumental complexes is likewise startling. In the Chancay drainage within a 2.5-kilometer radius of the site of San Jacinto, there are five other centers with similar layouts (Williams 1985, 133). A comparable concentration of centers is true for all of the other valleys as well (Carrión 1998; Silva 1998). The monumental centers in the Chancay (n = 11), Chillón (n = 9), Rimac (n = 15), and Lurín (n = 9) drainages bear a strong formal resemblance to each other not only in terms of their layout but also with regard to other cultural elements, including iconography, figurines, aspects of the pottery style, subsistence systems, and settlement patterns. The culture responsible for creating these public complexes has been recently dubbed the Manchay culture (Burger and Salazar 2008).

The Economic Foundations of the Manchay Culture

The monumental constructions of the Manchay culture had their basis in a mixed agricultural and marine subsistence economy. The population acquired most of its protein from the sea in the form of fish and shellfish, although marine mammals birds were also consumed (Burger 1987; Burger and Salazar 1991; Gorriti 2009). Land animals such as deer and small birds were hunted but constituted only a tiny part of the diet. A stable exchange system existed that facilitated the provisioning of the inland populations of farmers with marine foods produced in shoreline villages, while the agriculturalists provided the residents of the Pacific shores with domesticated plants harvested from the lower and middle valley (Patterson 1971).

During the Initial Period, farming provided the bulk of vegetable foods, although wild plant foods and other materials continued to be harvested from the nearby fog oases (*lomas*) and the seasonally flooded river banks (Burger 1987; Cohen 1978, 1979; Umlauf 2009; Weir, Benfer, and Jones 1988). Recent isotopic research has suggested an increase in the consumption of plant foods as compared to marine foods during the Initial Period, although the former remained a major component of the diet both from a caloric and nutritional perspective (Meadors and Benfer 2009). Research on macrobotanical remains has confirmed the consumption of a wide range of food crops, including squash (three varieties), beans (three varieties), peanuts, hot peppers (two varieties), avocados, maize, and several types of fruit (*ciruela, lúcuma*, guava, *pacae*) (Chevalier 2002; Cohen 1978; Umlauf 2009). More recent analyses of starch grains left burned on the bottom of cooking pots from residential areas at Mina Perdida and Cardal in the Lurín Valley has yielded evidence of food plants high in complex carbohydrates, such as manioc, sweet potatoes, potatoes, *achira,* and maize (Victor Vasquez personal communication 2008 and 2009). This suggests a shift in the daily diet to starchy staples during the Initial Period, a change made possible by the widespread adoption of ceramics. While the presence of maize is noteworthy, skeletal, macrobotanical, and isotopic evidence all argue against this crop being an important dietary staple on the central coast during the Initial Period (Tykot, van der Merwe, and Burger 2006).

Given the extreme aridity of the central coast, where the average annual precipitation is only 15 millimeters, the shift to a more strongly agricultural regime would have required much more watered farmland than would have available from seasonal flooding of the small coastal rivers. Gravity canals have been documented on the north coast of Peru dating from about 5,400 years ago (Dillehay, Eling, and Rossen 2005), and small-scale canals may have already been present along the central coast during the Late Preceramic. The establishment of numerous large new centers throughout the lower and middle Lurín Valley during the Initial Period suggests the expansion of canal construction to funnel water from both natural springs (*puquios*) and the Lurín River. The expanding subsistence base in terms of high-caloric crops such as manioc combined with the growth in available farmland as a result of new canals apparently touched off a prolonged increase in the inland population of the central coast valleys that lasted throughout the second millennium BC (Cohen 1978; Moseley 1972; Patterson 1971). This general pattern was noted several decades ago by Patterson, Cohen, and others, but the evidence for it during the Initial Period is even more convincing now because of advances in archaeological research.

These changes, however, did not necessarily produce an improvement in the daily lives of these people or the quality of their health. In fact, a detailed study of the skeletal population from Cardal concluded that the people at this U-shaped center were smaller in stature and significantly less healthy than their Preceramic ancestors (Meadors and Benfer 2009; Vradenburg 2009).

Monumental Construction in the Lurín Valley

Despite the acknowledged presence of the Initial Period monumental complexes on the coastal plain surrounding Peru's capital, few centers of the Manchay culture had been studied in any detail prior to 1985. Therefore, a project was initiated in the Lurín Valley in order to better understand the

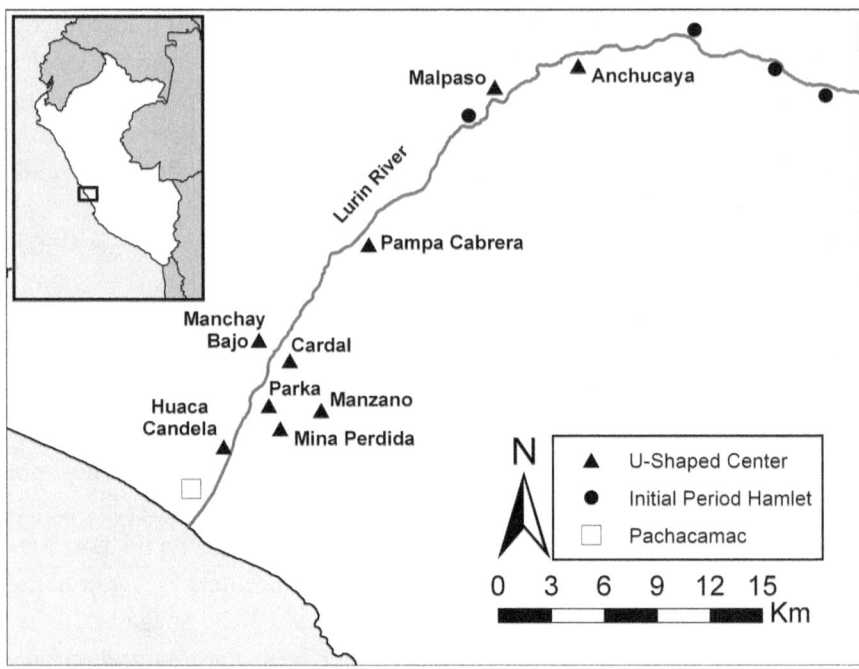

Figure 14.1. Location of U-shaped centers with monumental architecture in the middle and lower Lurín Valley. (Map by Chris Milan.)

nature of the society responsible for these monumental constructions and to determine the role of these centers. As the smallest (and southernmost) of the four valleys characterized by the Manchay culture, the Lurín Valley seemed to be best suited for a case study, particularly given the threat of impending destruction due to the urban expansion of Lima. Judging from survey and small-scale excavations by Patterson (Patterson and Moseley 1968), Harry Scheele (1970), Duccio Bonavia (1965) and others as well as the more recent efforts by archaeologists from the Pontificia Universidad Católica del Perú and the Universidad Nacional Mayor de San Marcos, there were at least seven U-shaped pyramid complexes in Lurín's lower valley and at least two more in the middle valley (Figure 14.1).

All of these centers are located on or adjacent to the narrow strip of irrigated farmland that borders the Lurín River. One of these, Parka, was located on a lower natural terrace below Mina Perdida (Figure 14.2) and has been completely destroyed; several others such as Huaca Candela in the lower valley and Anchucaya in the upper valley have been badly damaged by modern construction (Mesía 2000). At the present time, all of the surviving centers in the Lurín Valley continue to be at risk. Thus far we

Figure 14.2. Aerial photograph taken in 1947 showing the large U-shaped center of Mina Perdida and the now-destroyed U-shaped center of Parka. (Courtesy of Servicio Aereofotográfico del Perú.)

have carried out multiple field seasons at three of the centers: Cardal, Mina Perdida and Manchay Bajo.

The U-shaped complexes in Lurín vary substantially in scale. The largest of them, Mina Perdida, is located 8 kilometers inland at 100 MASL and covers some 30 hectares. Its U-shaped architecture features a central pyramid that rises to 22 meters (Burger and Gordon 1998; Burger and Salazar 2009). Other sites, such as Huaca Candela, Anchucaya, and Malpaso, are much more modest in scale, covering only a few hectares and with central pyramids less than 7 meters tall (Fajardo 1996; Mesia 2000; Scheele 1970). Centers such as Cardal and Manchay Bajo fall between these two extremes, covering about 20 hectares and having pyramids that rise to heights of 13 meters and 12 meters, respectively. We hypothesized at the outset of the project that all of these U-shaped complexes were constructed during the Initial Period, and all of the evidence recovered thus far is consistent with this hypothesis.

The presence during the second millennium BC of nine complexes with large-scale public architecture in a small valley such as Lurín is remarkable from a historical perspective. At no other time during the valley's prehistory was so much monumental construction carried out. During Chavin times, for example, little public construction was initiated (Dulanto 2009), and despite the establishment of the famous center of Pachacamac at the very end of the Early Horizon or the beginning of the Early Intermediate Period, large-scale complexes remained rare in Lurín until the Spanish conquest, with most major constructions concentrated at the site of Pachacamac. In late prehistoric times, there were never more than two or three monumental complexes in the valley after the Initial Period, despite the further expansion of the valley's irrigation systems, the growth of even denser agricultural populations, the reorganization of the valley into a complex polity, and its eventual incorporation into the Inca empire.

Why was monumental construction so common in the Lurín Valley during the second millennium BC, long before the establishment of a state-based sociopolitical formation? In order to respond to this question it is first necessary to establish the purpose that these monumental constructions served for the populations that built them. Fortunately, our excavations in Lurín have produced abundant evidence that indicates that the pyramids were mainly built to provide environments for religious rituals. The presence of clay friezes depicting religious iconography on the central pyramid and both lateral mounds at Cardal is perhaps the most dramatic testimony of this function (Fig. 14.3), but at Cardal and Mina Perdida we have also documented evidence of specialized summit altars, cached ritual paraphernalia, ceremonial offerings, and the discarded by-products of the rituals themselves (Burger and Gordon 1998; Burger and Salazar 1991, 1998, 2009; Salazar 2009).

The ceremonies on the summit of the platform mounds were carried out both in interior chambers not accessible to the general public and in open stage–like spaces that would have been highly visible from the plaza below (Burger 1987). The findings at the U-shaped centers in Lurín parallel earlier findings at U-shaped centers in other valleys on the central coast, such as Garagay in the Rimac Valley (Ravines 1984; Ravines and Isbell 1976; Ravines et al. 1984; Salazar and Burger 1983).

A substantial portion of the U-shaped architectural complexes were devoted to the open spaces or plazas, and considerable labor was invested to move fill and build retaining walls in order to formalize these spaces. The scale of the central plazas of U-shaped centers is immense and could have accommodated thousands of people without difficulty. At Mina Perdida, the open central space measures 400 meters by 340 meters and covers some 12 hectares. At Cardal, for the example, the enclosed rectangular central plaza measures 120 by 100 meters, a little over a hectare, but the entire open central space covers almost four hectares (Fig. 14.4). The massive scale of

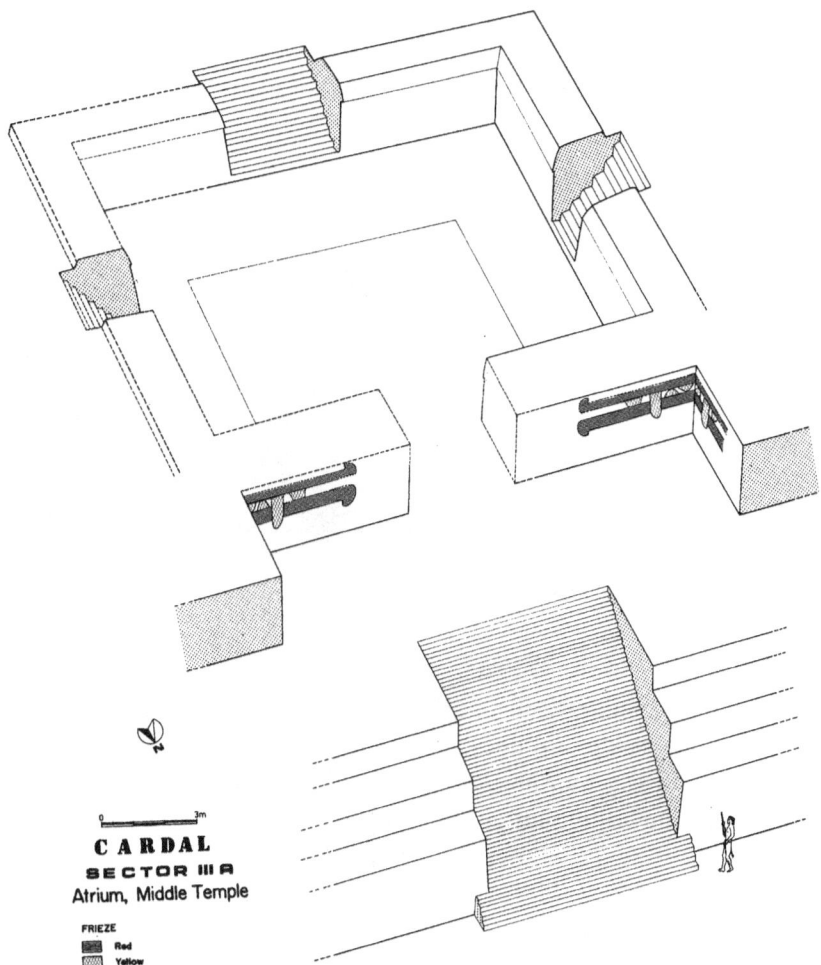

Figure 14.3. Isometric reconstruction of the main staircase and entrance into the atrium on the central mound of Cardal. (Drawing by Bernardino Ojeda.)

the plazas is actually comparable in scale to the plazas at Inca centers such as Huánuco Pampa and the plazas found among many tropical forest cultures. While direct evidence of the activities carried out in these spaces is very limited, it seems reasonable to suggest based on ethnohistoric and ethnographic analogy that they were used for community gatherings and ceremonial activities, including feasts, dances, parades, sports competitions and perhaps even ceremonial battles, much as they were in later prehistoric times (Burger 1987).

Figure 14.4. Low-altitude oblique photograph of Cardal showing U-shaped mounds and large central plaza area.

In some of the centers, such as Cardal, smaller-scale rectangular courts and sunken circular patios coexisted with the central plaza, and it is hypothesized that these may been used by social units smaller than the community itself, such as moieties, sodalities, or lineages (Burger and Salazar 1987). The cleanliness of the plaza and patio floors and the presence in the center of the circular patios of unusual elements such as a child's skull, a ceramic bottle decorated with double-headed snakes, and a T-shaped central hearth are consistent with the working hypothesis that the courts were used for group ceremonies (Burger 1987).

Archaeological surveys in the lower Lurín have repeatedly failed to encounter Initial Period sites without monumental architecture. In the middle valley, a small number of sites believed to correspond to hamlets were encountered in addition to two U-shaped centers (Scheele 1970). It is probable that similar hamlets lacking monumental architecture once also existed in the lower valley but have been destroyed or covered by river deposits.

We suggest that the U-shaped complexes constituted civic-ceremonial centers that served as the social and religious focus of life for dispersed agricultural populations living in hamlets and small villages. Despite their low visibility, residential populations dating to the final centuries of the

Initial Period (1100–850 BC) were documented adjacent to all three of the centers studied. Even during this time, these occupations must have housed only a small portion of the total support population. Moreover, there is no evidence of permanent occupation at the centers during most of the Initial Period (i.e., 1800–1100 BC).

The desire to create a central place for religious and civic activities by a dispersed rural population does not begin to explain either the size of the monumental architecture or the large number of centers in each of the central coastal valleys. However, excavations at the three Lurín centers point to a possible answer to these two basic questions. Each of the centers investigated was built using its own set of construction techniques and architectural features. For example, Mina Perdida used cubical adobes, Cardal used small ovoid adobes, and Manchay Bajo used large loaf-shaped adobes; all three of these sites are within a five-kilometer radius of each other. Comparable idiosyncrasies exist in the layout, such as the popularity of circular patios at Cardal, the pervasiveness of colonnades at Mina Perdida, and the taste for large vertically placed stone slabs at Manchay Bajo. The layout of the back staircases of the central mound similarly varies from site to site. When taken together, these elements give the public constructions at each center a unique identity, despite the existence of overarching conventions these sites shared with each other and with Manchay culture centers in neighboring valleys. At the same time, the activities carried out in each of the centers seems similar to those carried out at other nearby centers. In fact, there is no evidence of a hierarchy of sites in terms of site function or the resident populations, despite differences in the sizes of the mounds. Our working hypothesis is that each of the centers corresponds to a distinctive autonomous social group or polity.

This interpretation has received additional support from the study of the pottery assemblages. Preliminary analysis of the surface decoration and forms of the pottery indicates that each of the centers has a distinctive style with its own set of decorative preferences. A study utilizing neutron activation to characterize the clay component of the pottery from each of the sites confirmed that each center in Lurín was producing its own ceramics, although a small amount of exchange was occurring between the sites (Thorme 1999).

Thus the abundance of monumental architecture reflects the multiplicity of small-scale polities in the Lurín Valley during the second millennium BC. In our opinion, this organizational pattern may be a function of an irrigation network consisting of small gravity canals, each of which was independently constructed and operated (Burger 2009). In our model, each social unit or polity was responsible for the construction and maintenance of its own canal. If this is correct, the construction of a new canal system would have marked the birth of a new polity and the need for a new civic-ceremonial center where its population could come together to coordinate its communal activities and carry out rituals to ensure the adequacy of the water supply and the fertility of the crops. The iconography of the temple wall friezes at the complex reflects these common concerns and ritual goals.

While this model of sociopolitical organization may help to explain the presence of multiple autonomous centers within a single drainage of modest size, it does not account for the scale or monumentality of the public architecture in question. On the contrary, by positing that the pyramid complexes were built by small-scale social units with only weakly developed social stratification, it raises the question of how such societies could mobilize the labor necessary to build these huge public works. In order to begin to understand this, it is necessary to reconceptualize the monumental constructions. Most archaeologists and other modern visitors think of these mounds as ends in themselves. It would be more productive, however, to think of them as being the product of a long process of episodic construction that occurred over many centuries, usually without knowledge of what the final state of the centers would be at the time of their abandonment. In order to understand how these complexes were constructed, it is essential to study the life history of each of the monumental centers in question, without assuming that they were founded or abandoned at the same time.

The Episodic Construction of Monumental Architecture

Given the limited agricultural land suitable for irrigation in the Lurín Valley, it unlikely that any of the centers would have served a population of more than 1,000 people, some of whom would have been too elderly or young to participate in the building projects. How were the leaders at sites such as Cardal able to mobilize the labor to build massive complexes such as Mina Perdida? To begin to answer this question it is useful to consider labor mobilization patterns documented from later in prehistory and ethnography. In the Peruvian highlands, including the highlands above Lurín, labor mobilization was a fundamental feature of the most basic level of socioeconomic organization. Participation in communal labor projects was considered a requisite expression of community membership and thus was necessary in order to have access to the community resources essential for survival, most notably land and water. In Lurín and elsewhere on the coast, involvement in the annual repair and cleaning of canals was required in order to receive the water necessary to grow crops on the land that had been allocated to the family by the community. Failure to participate in the communal labor organized to maintain the canal system put access to water and other resources at risk and ultimately could result in ostracism from the community (Netherly 1984).

When cleaning and repairing canals, group labor was carried out in a festive context that often involved music, singing, the distribution of corn beer (*chicha*) and coca leaves, and sometimes religious rituals. The "father of Peruvian archaeology," Julio C. Tello, viewed this organization of communal labor for cleaning and repairing canals and reservoirs and the ceremonies associated with it as central to the success of Andean civilization, and he helped document one surviving case of it from Casta, at the headwaters of the Rimac Valley, linking these practices with local archaeological remains from prehistoric times (Tello and Miranda 1923). The ceremonies, like the actual repairs, were considered crucial for the success of the crops and the health of the community. It is important to emphasize that this type of communal labor was mobilized and organized without the intervention of the state or leaders with coercive tools such as the police or army. In these situations, the ultimate coercion was the threat of community approbation and the potential of losing access to land and water rights.

The remarkable ability of traditional Andean groups to mobilize communal labor also attracted the attention of Jose Maria Arguedas, arguably Peru's greatest ethnographer and novelist. To dramatize that power, he wrote that in order to achieve communal goals, local-level groups could mobilize enough communal labor to move mountains if necessary without the intervention of government authorities (Arguedas 1941).

We hypothesize that the ethnohistoric and ethnographic model of labor organization described above may shed light on how the U-shaped complexes were constructed. If each family that used lands watered by the community-built canal had to donate annual labor in the dry season not only to the cleaning and repair of the hydraulic system but also to the seasonal renovation of the civic-ceremonial center where they gathered and worshipped, then a reliable mechanism would have been set in place that guaranteed labor for as long as the community and its canal system remained intact. The drawback of such a system would have been that the labor it mobilized would have been unspecialized, limited in scale (no more than a few hundred people working each year), and limited in time to the winter months, when there is little water available and hence few agricultural demands. Such a model would be plausible only if the U-shaped centers gradually attained their final volume in small increments over long periods of time rather than over a few years or decades.

Naturally, it is crucial to examine how the U-shaped complexes in Lurín were actually built in order to see whether the construction processes are consistent with the proposed model. First of all, it can be observed that the techniques necessary for building the large constructions are rudimentary; there is little evidence of specialized skills or specialized labor. This central truth is often missed because of the size of the constructions or the encasing of the crude stonework in thick layers of clay plaster.

Second, in each of the three sites in the Lurín Valley studied thus far it is clear that what appear to be the huge monumental terraced platform structures are actually the accumulation of a multitude of superimposed buildings and fills. It is possible to identify three types of this incremental growth. In some cases, an architectural feature is covered completely with artificial fill and a new construction is built on top of it that recreates the architectural element found beneath it with only minor changes. This has sometimes been referred to as ceremonial interment or ritual burial. A classic case of this can be seen in the nine superimposed central staircases documented at Manchay Bajo. Because stairway after stairway was built in the same zone, the central mound gradually grew in width and height. At the same site, a similar pattern is visible in the vertical superposition of raised colonnades and associated patio areas adjacent to the summit atrium. The labor involved in such cases involves the transport and deposition of a layer of fill to cover the earlier structure and then the construction of a new element or building.

Perhaps the best-known instances of the pattern are the atria built into the summit of the central mounds. The sunken atria set in the summits of U-shaped temples such as Cardal or Manchay Bajo were only the last in a series of atria, the first of which may have required only a small amount of labor to construct. This idea was confirmed in the field most dramatically when a looter's trench at Mina Perdida allowed us to locate one of the center's oldest atria; it was set atop a platform only three meters (rather than 20 meters) high, but it occupied the same position as later atria. Similarly, work at both Cardal and Manchay Bajo revealed a series of superimposed atria in the central mound (Fig. 14.5).

This same repetitive process is evident in a second type of refurbishments at the U-shaped centers in which the original structure was left

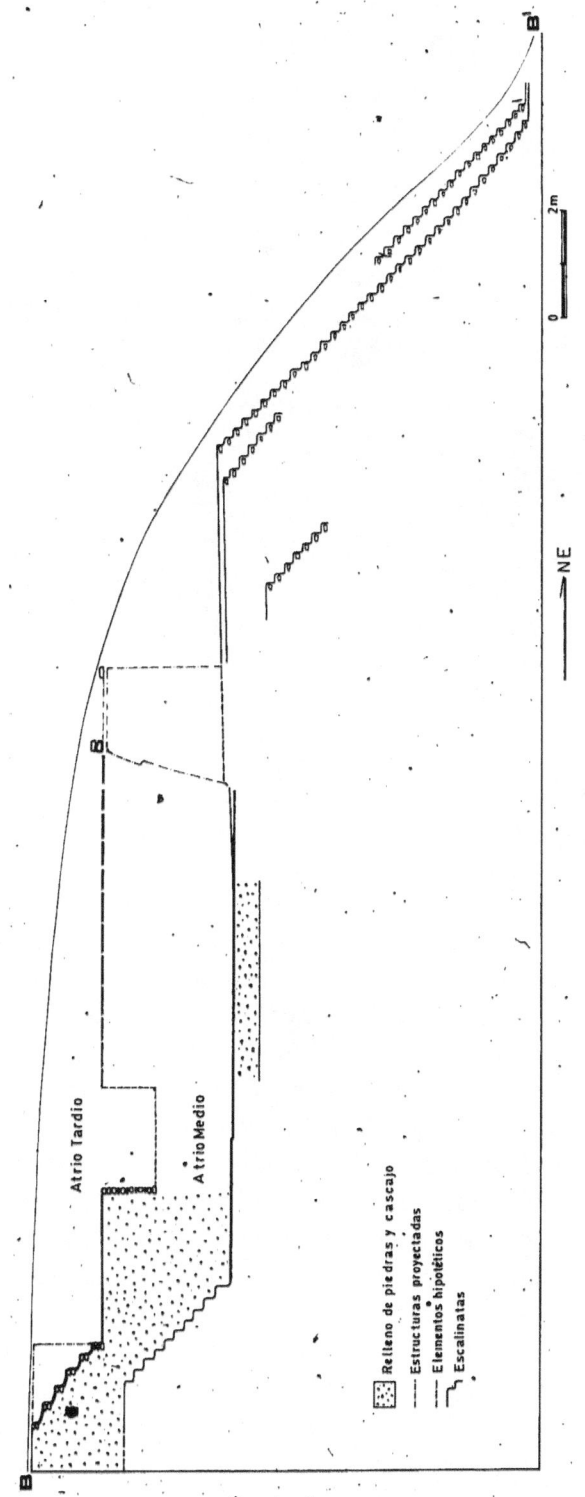

Figure 14.5. Cross-section showing superimposed atria at Cardal. (Drawing by Bernardino Ojeda.)

Figure 14.6. Balloon photograph of sunken circular patio with central ritual hearth at Cardal. Note evidence of two horizontal increments to original structure indicated by parallel retaining walls. (Photograph courtesy of James Kus.)

intact but its volume was increased horizontally by covering the exterior face of the outer wall with fill and then building a new retaining wall parallel to the earlier one, thereby encasing the original construction. At Cardal this technique of small horizontal increments was used to enlarge the narrow platforms surrounding sunken circular patios. In the case of Cardal's sunken circular patios, the structures studied show one, two, or even three such episodes of horizontal enlargement (Fig. 14.6). But this technique was not limited to the circular patios. In the 2008 excavations on Cardal's right arm, we were able to document how a decorated elevated platform on the summit was expanded incrementally to the north by a series of three-meter-high parallel retaining walls and fills. Each wall had been carefully plastered and painted (and in one case decorated by a new clay frieze), indicating that each increment constituted a completed task. As a result of these horizontal additions, the width of the platform would have increased by roughly 16 meters.

A third kind of construction process that occurred at the U-shaped centers was expansion through what can be referred to as modular increments. This practice was first noted at the site of Mina Perdida, where excavations on the left arm showed how the exterior face of the platform had been extended by a series of L-shaped retaining walls with their respective fills (Fig. 14.7); one extreme was anchored to the original platform face while the other was joined to the previous extension. Increments of the same size and shape were sequentially added to widen a small section of the second terrace, and each would have been plastered to hide the seams between them. Each of these segments featured a finished wall face that was perpendicular to the original platform wall, implying that it was designed to be visible at the time of its completion. As a consequence, the terrace face would not have been straight during this time but instead would have featured a part of the mound that had been broadened adjacent to the yet-unmodified original terrace wall. Our excavations revealed that the modifications to seven meters of a much larger terrace wall involved four separate and independent modular increments (Burger and Salazar 2009, 50). The widening of the entire terraces would have involved dozens of modular increments.

This same pattern was observed during the investigations of the back terraces of Cardal's main mound. It had been assumed that the terraces were expanded by the kind of "ritual burial" described above, but if that were the case, it would have constituted a massive labor project, given that the each back terrace runs for well over 100 meters. The excavations of the back terraces in 2008 revealed that expansion was accomplished by a series of modular increments. Approximately a dozen of them were documented along only 15 meters of rear terrace. Once again, each increment ended with plastered wall faces and, as at Mina Perdida, the seams between the increments were eventually plastered over, hiding this process.

Given the practice of ritual burial, horizontal increments, and modular increments, it is likely that a large center such as Mina Perdida involved hundreds of small-scale construction episodes, none of which would have required a massive labor force. Nonetheless, the sum total of this multitude of episodes over an extended period of time resulted in the monumental scale of the U-shaped centers.

Chronology and Monumental Construction

To assess how a small-scale society produces a monumental construction, it is essential to consider the issue of time. This is particularly true for the U-shaped centers of the Manchay culture. As noted, a rare insight into this problem was provided by the large looters' trench that was cut through the central pyramid of Mina Perdida, destroying most of the central staircase

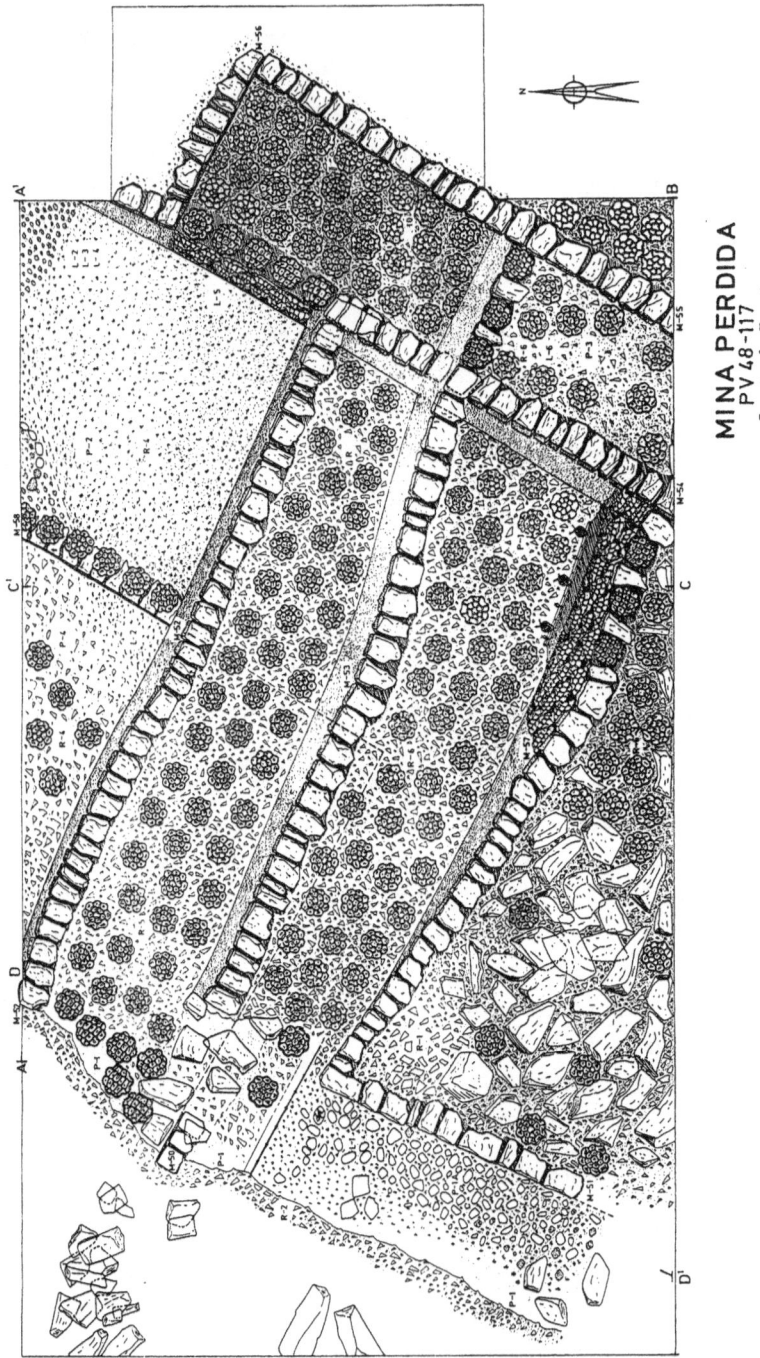

Figure 14.7. Drawing of modular increments made to expand the right arm of Mina Perdida. (Drawing by Bernardino Ojeda.)

and atrium zone. The cleaned profile of this trench permitted a unique view of the incremental growth of the massive central pyramid. As already noted, the initial construction, although identical in design and orientation to later constructions, consisted of only a three-meter-high platform with a modest eight-step central staircase (Fig. 14.8). This first complex was associated with a small number of pottery fragments and has been dated using ^{14}C to 3520±100 BP uncalibrated, or when calibrated approximately 2000 BC. It was only after 1,000 years of episodic superimposed constructions that the central pyramid reached its final height of 22 meters.

The Mina Perdida case illustrates that the scale of a monumental center was to some degree a function of the number of superimposed constructions that comprise it (Fig. 14.9), and this in turn was directly related to the length of time the center functioned. Other factors such as the number of people that could mobilized by a center and the type of construction techniques that were used (e.g., stone walls versus wattle and daub) were also relevant in determining scale but were probably less important than the amount of time the center flourished. For example, Cardal, whose central pyramid rises 12 meters, was only established around 1400 cal. BC, five or six centuries after Mina Perdida; Cardal appears to have thrived for only about 600 years. If this conclusion is correct, it would be predicted that the small U-shaped centers in Lurín such as Huaca Candela or Anchucaya were probably founded sometime after Cardal and likely flourished for only a few centuries.

In summary, the model suggested for the creation of Lurín U-shaped centers posits that Mina Perdida was the initial center established in lower Lurín and that at the same time a canal system would have been built. As the community thrived, its population grew in size until social friction and land shortages led a dissatisfied faction of families to branch off and establish a new canal system and its own civic-ceremonial center. This general pattern of population growth and the branching off of factions would have repeated itself on multiple occasions during the second millennium BC, until by 1000 BC there were at least nine centers with a shared ideology functioning simultaneously in the lower and middle valley. These small autonomous polities would have competed with each other for population and prestige but also would have interacted with each other to exchange goods and marriage partners. The heterarchical pattern of these autonomous polities proved to be remarkably stable for over a millennium, a historical reality at odds with the instability so often posited in theoretical writings on so-called chiefdoms (e.g., Earle 1991).

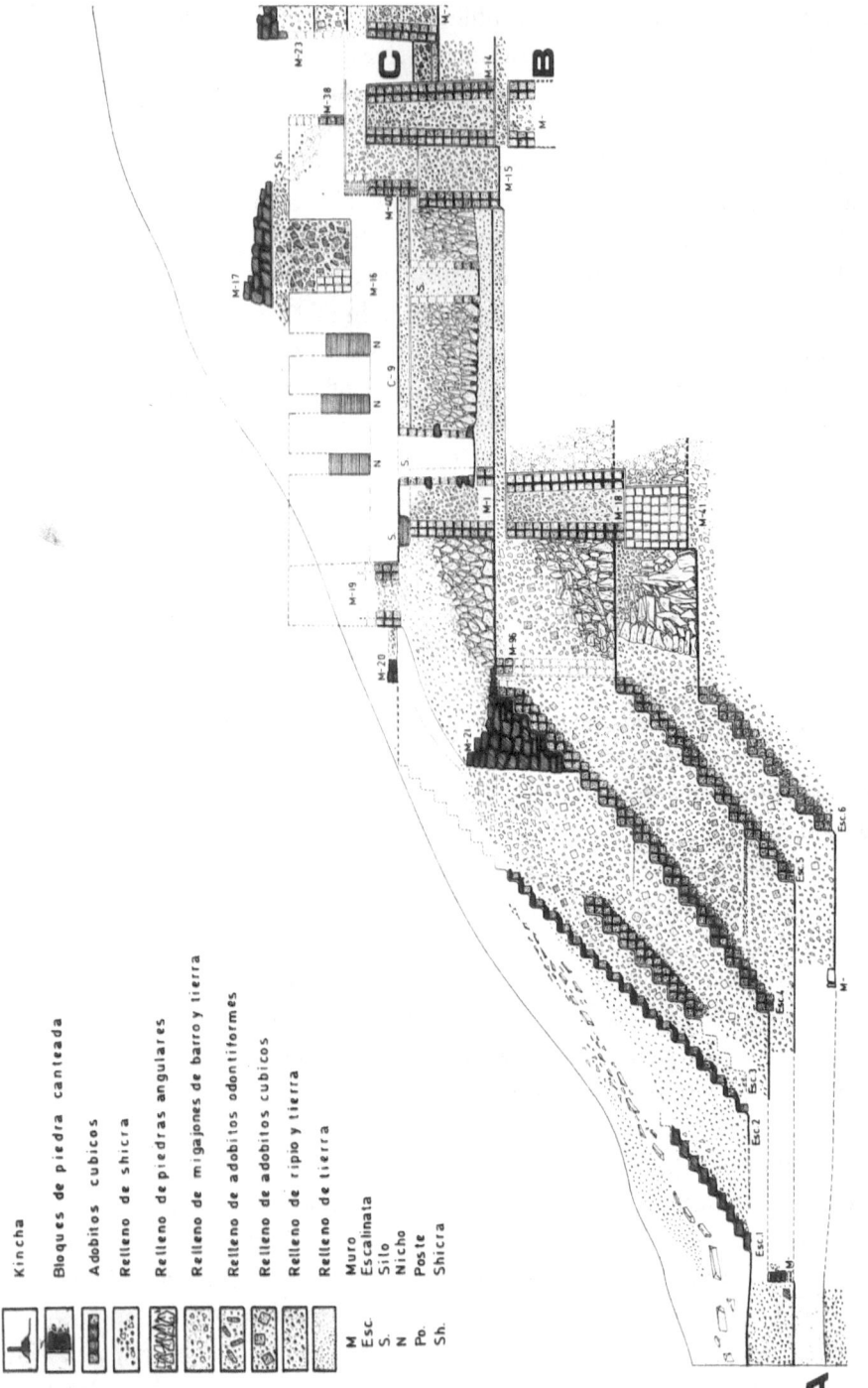

Figure 14.8. Profile of looters' cut in the central mound at Mina Perdida showing superimposed staircase, fills, and other structures. (Drawing by Bernardino Ojeda.)

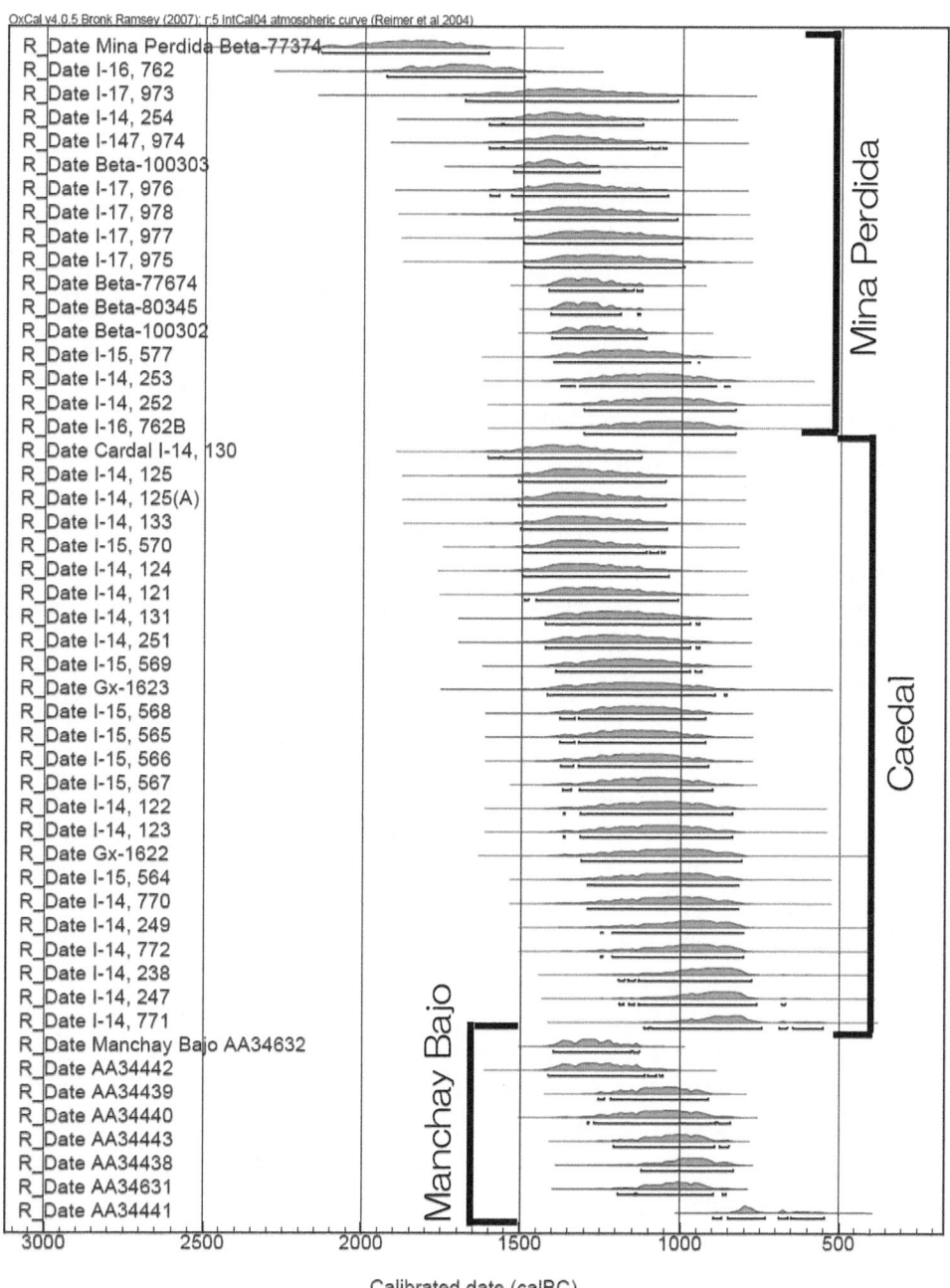

Figure 14.9. Calibrated radiocarbon measurements from Mina Perdida, Cardal, and Manchay Bajo.

Concluding Thoughts

In our view, the monumental scale of the Initial Period U-shaped complexes in the Lurín Valley and elsewhere on Peru's central coast was a byproduct of the long-standing patterns of mobilizing communal labor to provide suitable environments for ritual and other community activities. While most of these public constructions on the central coast date to the second millennium BC, their local antecedents can be found in the third millennium BC prior to the introduction of pottery. The expansion of monumental complexes throughout the valleys during the Initial Period and the increase in their number is hypothesized to have occurred in tandem with the expansion of canal systems and irrigated valley lands and with the accompanying demographic growth that resulted. These changes were associated with a mixed economy that combined the rich protein resources of the Pacific shores with a wide range of domesticated crops, including tubers high in caloric yield such as manioc, sweet potatoes, and potatoes. Most of these crops had been domesticated in other zones and became popular as foods on the central coast only after pottery use became widespread. There is no evidence that these constructions were created to memorialize powerful leaders or legitimize and/or reinforce their power. Evidence of mortuary and residential architecture casts doubt on whether such powerful leaders even existed during the Initial Period.

During the late second millennium at Cardal there is some evidence for emerging sociopolitical complexity, but this trend does not appear to have succeeded. Judging from the evidence available from Peru's central coast, the efforts to establish a more hierarchical society does not appear to be related to the process of the construction of monumental architecture, unless it was in some way related to their demise (Patterson 1983).

Similarly, the centers with large-scale public architecture on Peru's central coast do not seem to have been the focus of intensive interregional interaction. The interaction that did occur was more limited. Some of it was with adjacent highland cultivators and shoreline fisherfolk in order to obtain a more complete range of vertically arrayed foods and other resources. It is interesting that monumental architecture does not seem to have characterized these shoreline or highland communities, and thus it set the dwellers of the lower and middle valleys apart from their neighbors.

Interaction also occurred between the peoples of centers sharing the Manchay culture belief system either within a valley or between neighboring valleys as part of a regional ceremonial network. Both types of interaction would have been necessary for the nutritional and reproductive health of the small-scale autonomous polities that characterized the Initial Period on the central coast. Nonetheless, the evidence of subsistence and other goods at the U-shaped centers in Lurín suggests a relatively parochial society whose contacts only rarely extended beyond the limits of its small drainage. In this respect, it provides a sharp contrast with highland Chavin civilization.

Finally, the ability of these early agricultural societies to mobilize labor for the good of the community was perhaps the most remarkable quality of the Manchay culture. While a conspicuous application of this capacity was the construction of what some would consider to be large platform constructions with a ceremonial rather than a "practical" function, it is unlikely that the people of the Manchay culture would have shared this perspective. The power to mobilize community labor to build and renovate the U-shaped center was almost certainly viewed as a practical necessity that was no less important than the building, repair, and cleaning of gravity canals accomplished using the same mechanisms of labor mobilization.

The potential to mobilize labor—whether for "ideological" or "practical" ends—held the key to Manchay culture's success, and its existence allowed them to overcome the numerous disasters that must have occurred during the second millennium BC. One clear example of community labor mobilization being used for such "practical" ends is known from Manchay Bajo, where a huge stone wall was erected to protect the center against debris flows and floods coming from two dry lateral ravines (Fig. 14.10). This monumental wall or dam had a total length of 850 meters and a total volume in excess of 30,000 cubic meters. Excavation of the wall indicated that the original construction dated to the early phase of the site's occupation and that it was enlarged repeatedly during the following centuries (Burger 2003). The technology and scale of this wall is comparable to that involved in creating Manchay Bajo's central terraced pyramid, and it is likely to have been a product of the same social mechanisms and logic that produced the civic ceremonial center. More important, this product of communal labor succeeded in protecting the civic-ceremonial center of Manchay Bajo against the debris flows unleashed by repeated El Niño events.

Epilogue

As suggested in the introduction to this volume, the creation of monumental constructions has a long-term as well as a short-term impact, since

Figure 14.10. Monumental dam built during the Initial Period to protect U-shaped center of Manchay Bajo.

the production of such large structures with such powerful histories transforms the landscape forever. In the Lurín Valley, the time scales involved, as we have seen, are not adequately glossed with terms such as short-term and long-term, since in some cases, such as Mina Perdida, monumental architecture functioned as it was originally intended to do for close to a millennium without interruption—not exactly "short-term" in the normal sense. At the same time, the larger generalization that even after early monumental architecture was abandoned it continued to exercise power over the imagination and behavior of local residents is as true for the Lurín Valley as it is for the other cases discussed in this volume.

The valley floor of the lower and middle Lurín Valley is relatively flat, interrupted only occasionally by rocky spurs, and thus the massive terraced Initial Period platforms that rose 6 to 23 meters above the land surface remained as conspicuous features of the landscape long after their builders had moved away and the ceremonies had stopped. However, we must keep in mind that just as the monumental architecture built in the Lurín Valley during the Initial Period was not static during its use, it was also not unchanging after its abandonment, which took place between approximately 700 BC and 900 BC. Wind and water erosion from winter mist and the occasional El Niño event combined with the effects of salts deposited on the ruins from the ocean winds, and collectively these would have obliterated the bright red, white, and yellow pigments and clay friezes that covered the outer walls of these structures, colors that set them apart from the greens, grays, and tans of the nearby fields and desert. Similarly, the sharp angles of the pyramid terraces and flat-topped summits would have quickly taken on a more curved and natural appearance as exposed retaining walls and summit buildings collapsed, covering the structures with a rocky surface layer. A thick talus-like layer of rock and soil formed around the base of the constructions, obliterating their original footprint.

Another change that has occurred after the abandonment of the public architecture of the Manchay culture was the expansion of canal systems to higher elevations along the valley slopes. This created additional farmland and left the Initial Period pyramid complexes surrounded by cultivated land, thereby modifying their original location on the arid edges of tilled fields. In addition, the Lurín River sometimes shifted course and flooded some abandoned U-shaped centers, such as Manchay Bajo, dumping over three meters of alluvium on top of the plaza and adjacent areas (Burger 2003). At most sites, landslides deposited layers of earth, and rocky debris covered residential areas and modified the original land surface surrounding the mounds. The combined impact of these natural forces transformed the massive and conspicuous products of collective human labor into something resembling natural hills; indeed, today there are local residents who no longer recognize some of these prominences in the landscape as Pre-Hispanic ruins.

Nonetheless, there is ample evidence that the Initial Period centers of Lurín have had a long and varied history above and beyond their original use. At Cardal, the clearest evidence of later use occurs not on the summit but on the left arm of the U-shaped monumental architecture. During the 2008 excavations we encountered a series of stone line cists cut into the fill of the Initial Period summit architecture. The abundant coarse Ychsma-style pottery found scattered around the cists suggest a probable Late Intermediate Period date for the semi-subterranean features, particularly given the absence of Inca sherds. Some of the cists had unusual elements such as vertical *hunaca*-like stones or plastered walls and bottoms. Our tentative hypothesis was that local farmers chose the summit area for repetitive local religious rites that involved ritual activities including feasting in a spot that 2,200 years before had been the focus of public ceremonies by the Manchay culture.

At the nearby site of Manchay Bajo, across from Cardal on the north bank of the Lurín, our excavations of the main staircase of the central

Figure 14.11. Inca offering of Spondylus shell and metal sheet left along central axis at Manchay Bajo.

mound yielded a series of unexpected offerings that included whole Spondylus shells filled with seed necklaces and sheet metal artifacts (Fig. 14.11). These elaborate votive offerings occurred along the central axis of the site's main mound, despite the fact that the staircase had already been completely shrouded by eroded deposits from above and the layout of the site would not have been obvious. A small amount of associated pottery and an AMS ^{14}C measurement with a 2-sigma range of AD 1445–1651 (AA31150) made on the perforated seeds strongly suggested that the offering dated to the Late Horizon, the time when the Inca occupied the Lurín Valley and controlled the nearby ceremonial center of Pachacamac in the lower valley (Makowski and Vega Centeno 2004). The presence of Spondylus shells brought from the shores of Ecuador and their association with rare metal artifacts suggest the importance of the ritual offering. As in the case of Cardal, some sense of the Manchay Bajo's supernatural power appears to have survived into late prehistoric times, despite the likelihood that all memory of the Manchay culture and its distinctive U-shaped centers and ceremonies had long since vanished during a hiatus of over two millennia. During this hiatus at Manchay Bajo, the only evidence of continued use of the centers are the remains of Pre-Hispanic agricultural fields covering what once had been the site's central plaza. At the same time, the fact the archaeological ruin has been known since colonial times as Manchay Bajo is significant. The site name is taken from the Quechua word "*manchay*," a term that appears in the colonial dictionary compiled by Diego Gonzalez Holguin (1989 [1608]). The word is usually combined with others to suggest fear, awe, and terror. For example, *manchay manchay* is glossed as "*cossa espantable terrible temerosa*" (author's translation: a frightening and terribly fearsome thing). The very name Manchay Bajo suggests that some remnant memory of the monumental architecture's sacred power has somehow perdured.

From these anecdotal accounts, it would be easy to assume that the large scale of the U-shaped mound complexes make such associations likely if not inevitable, particularly in the Andes, where there is a long history of linking the hilltops, unusual rocks, and natural springs to mythical events and supernatural forces. In this light, the case of Mina Perdida is particularly curious. As the largest of all of the pyramid complexes it might be expected to have had the most impressive post-abandonment history of all. Yet our excavations suggest that this was not the case, at least not in Pre-Hispanic times. Investigations of the central mound yielded no evidence at all of such later activities.

However, on the upper terrace of the left arm of Mina Perdida, a small feature was encountered with well-preserved food remains and the lower walls of a modest house or hut, perhaps belonging to a farmer. The size of the peanuts and maize cobs was much larger than those associated with the Initial Period architecture, a fact soon explained by the recovery of a few Middle Horizon sherds from the feature. We concluded that some 1,600 years after the builders of Mina Perdida had abandoned their civic-ceremonial center, a local farmer decided that the clear view of the adjacent fields offered by the platform's upper terrace made it a fine location for building a temporary residence. His flimsy dwelling there may have been designed to discourage the theft of his harvest or to avoid having to return each day to the area from a more distant permanent abode. Apparently, Mina Perdida's fame as the oldest and largest of the Manchay culture complexes in Lurín had little impact on later Pre-Hispanic populations, even though the volume of its buildings remained an impressive feature of the landscape.

Paradoxically, it is the site of Mina Perdida that continues to live most vividly in the imagination of modern residents of the Lurín Valley. Among the agriculturalists today, virtually everyone knows the myth of the local farmer who saw a luminous glow, the telltale sign of a hidden treasure, when he was passing by the central mound of Mina Perdida. And they all know (and many believe) that this treasure was eventually uncovered late at night on the Fiesta de San Juan (perhaps in colonial or republican times) and that these illicit excavations revealed a golden litter studded with diamonds, pearls, and emeralds. According to the story, this treasure was uncovered, only to be buried again by a whirlwind when the *huaqueros* (looters) began to fight among themselves over the newfound wealth. This myth was so compelling that early in the twentieth century or in colonial times, according to Ducio Bonavia (1965), a powerful landowner ordered his workers to dig a massive trench through the center of the pyramid in search of this *"mina perdida"* (lost mine). From the perspective of many local farmers, even in the 1990s this myth offered the most plausible explanation for why we were willing to invest so much time and money in the investigation of this seven-story-high pyramid complex.

The long-term history of the monumental architecture in the Lurín Valley reflects fundamental shifts of attitude toward the massive and mysterious U-shaped mound complexes in the landscape. Despite these changes, even after more than a millennium, in Inca times they continued from being conceived of as the focus of supernatural power where appropriate offerings and communal rituals could bring the community health and successful crops. This was true despite the disappearance of any memory of the Manchay culture and its specific religious ideology. By modern times, this perception had almost completely shifted Although some of these monumental features were still associated with the supernatural, local myths saw them as offering the possibility of individual wealth if only the jealousy and dishonesty of fellow residents could be overcome.

References Cited

Arguedas, Jose Maria
1941   *Yawar Fiesta*. Editorial Losada, Buenos Aires
Bonavia, Duccio
1965   *Arqueología de Lurín (Seis sitios de ocupación en la parte inferior del valle)*. Instituto de Estudios Etnológicos del Museo Nacional de la Cultura Peruana y Universidad Nacional Mayor de San Marcos, Lima.
Burger, Richard L.
1987   The U-Shaped Pyramid Complex, Cardal, Peru. *National Geographic Research* 3(3):363–375.
2003   El Niño, Early Peruvian Civilization, and Human Agency: Some Thoughts from the Lurin Valley. In *El Niño in Peru: Biology and Culture over 10,000 Years*, edited by Jonathan Haas and Michael O. Dillon, pp. 90–107. Fieldiana, Botany new series No. 43. The Field Museum, Chicago.

Burger, Richard L., and Robert B. Gordon
1998   Early Central Andean Metalworking from Mina Perdida, Peru. *Science* 281(5391):1108–1111.
Burger, Richard L., and Lucy C. Salazar
1991   The Second Season of Investigations at the Initial Period Center of Cardal, Peru. *Journal of Field Archaeology* 18(3): 275-296.
1998   A Sacred Effigy from Mina Perdida and the Unseen Ceremonies of the Peruvian Formative. *Res* 33:28–53.
2008   The Manchay Culture and the Coastal Inspiration for Highland Chavin Civilization. In *Chavin: Art, Architecture, and Culture,* edited by William Conklin and Jeffrey Quilter, pp. 85–105. Cotsen Institute of Archaeology, University of California at Los Angeles, Los Angeles.
2009   Investigaciones arqueologicas en Mina Perdida, valle de Lurín. In *Arqueología del Periodo Formativo en la Cuenca Baja de Lurín,* edited by Richard Burger and Krzysztof Makowski, pp. 37–58. Editorial de la Pontificia Universidad Católica del Perú, Lima.
Carrión, Lucénida
1998   Excavaciones en San Jacinto, templo en U en el valle de Chancay. *Boletín de Arqueología PUCP* 2:239–250.
Chevalier, Alexandre
2002   L'exploitation des plante sur la cote péruvienne en contexte formatif. Unpublished PhD thesis, University de Geneva, Switzerland.
Cohen, Mark
1978   Population Pressure and the Origins of Agriculture: An Archaeological Example from the Coast of Peru. In *Advances in Andean Archaeology,* edited by David Browman, pp. 91–132. Mouton, The Hague.
1979   Archaeological Plant Remains from the Central Coast of Peru. *Ñawpa Pacha* 16:23–51.
Dillehay, Tom, Herbert Eiling Jr., and Jack Rossen
2005   Preceramic Irrigation Canals in the Peruvian Andes. *PNAS* 102(47):17241–17244.
Dulanto, Jalh
2009   Pampa Chica: Que sucedió en la coast central después del abandono de los centros en U? In *Arqueología del Periodo Formativo en la Cuenca Baja de Lurín,* Vol. 1, edited by Richard Burger and Krzysztof Makowski, pp. 377–99. Fondo Editorial de la Pontificia Universidad Católica del Peru, Lima.
Earle, Timothy
1991   The Evolution of Chiefdoms. In *Chiefdoms: Power, Economy, and Ideology,* edited by Timothy Earle, pp. 1–15. Cambridge University Press, Cambridge.
Engel, Frederic
1966   La complexe précéramique d'El Paraíso (Pérou). *Journal de la Societe des Americanistes* 55(1):43–95.
Fajardo, Fidel
1996   Centro cívico ceremonial de Piedra Liza: Implicancias durante el Formativo Medio. In *La Universidad Nacional Mayor de San Marcos y el VI Congreso Nacional*

de Estudiantes de Arqueología, edited by Gori Echevarría, pp. 57-64. Facultad de Ciencias Sociales, Universidad Nacional Mayor de San Marcos, Lima.

Gonzales Holguin, Diego

1989 [1608] *Vocabulario de la lengua general de todo el Peru llamada lengua Qquichua o del Inca.* Universidad Nacional Mayor de San Marcos, Lima.

Gorriti, Manuel

2009 Una primera aproximación al consumo de moluscos en el sitio formativo de Mina Perdida. In *Arqueología del Periodo Formativo en la Cuenca Baja de Lurín,* Vol. 1, edited by Richard Burger and Krzysztof Makowski, pp. 111-118. Fondo Editorial de la Pontificia Universidad Católica del Peru, Lima.

Makowski, Krzysztof, and Milena Vega Centeno

2004 Estilos regionales en la Costa Central en el Horizonte Tardío. Una aparoximación desde el valle del Lurín. *Bulletin de l'Institut Francais d'Etudes Andines* 33(3):681-714

Meadors, Sarah, and Robert Benfer

2009 Adaptaciones de la dieta humana a nuevos problemas y oportunidades en la coasta central del Peru (1800-800 a.C.). In *Arqueología del Periodo Formativo en la Cuenca Baja de Lurín,* Vol. 1, edited by Richard Burger and Krzysztof Makowski, pp. 119-159. Fondo Editorial de la Pontificia Universidad Católica del Peru, Lima.

Mesía, Cristian J.

2000 Anchucaya: aproximación teórica sobre un complejo en U en el valle medio del río Lurín. *Arqueológicas* 24:45-52.

Moseley, Michael Edward

1972 Subsistence and Demography: An Example of Interaction from Prehistoric Peru. *Southwestern Journal of Anthropology* 28(1):25-49

1975 *The Maritime Foundations of Andean Civilization.* Cummins Press, Menlo Park, California.

Netherly, Patricia

1984 The Management of Late Andean Irrigation Systems on the North Coast of Peru. *American Antiquity* 49:227-254.

Patterson, Thomas C.

1971 Population and Economy in Central Peru. *Archaeology* 24:316-321.

1983 The Historical Development of a Coastal Andean Social Formation in Central Peru. 6000 BC-500 BC. In *Investigations of the Andean Past,* edited by Daniel Sandweiss, pp. 21-37. Cornell University Latin American Studies Program, Ithaca, New York.

1985 The Huaca La Florida, Rimac Valley, Peru. In *Early Ceremonial Architecture in the Andes,* edited by Christopher Donnan, pp. 59-69. Dumbarton Oaks, Washington, D.C.

Patterson, Thomas C., and Michael E. Moseley

1968 Late Preceramic and Early Ceramic Cultures of the Central Coast of Peru. *Ñawpa Pacha* 6:115-134.

Quilter, Jeffrey

1985 Architecture and Chronology at El Paraiso. *Journal of Field Archaeology* 12:279-297.

Quilter, Jeffrey, Deborah Pearsall, Elizabeth Wing, John Jones, and Bernardino Ojeda
1991   The Subsistence Economy of El Paraiso, Peru. *Science* 251(4991):277–283.
Ravines, Rogger
1984   La formación de Chavín: imágenes y símbolos. *Boletín de Lima* 35:27–45.
Ravines, Rogger, H. Engelstad, V. Palomino, and Daniel Sandweiss
1984   Materiales arqueológicos de Garagay. *Revista del Museo Nacional* 46:135–233.
Ravines, Rogger, and William Isbell
1976   Garagay: sitio ceremonial temprano en el valle de Lima. *Revista del Museo Nacional* 41:253–275.
Reitz, Elizabeth
1988   Preceramic Animal Use on the Central Coast. In *Economic Prehistory of the Central Andes,* edited by Elizabeth S. Wing and Jane C. Wheeler, pp. 31–55. BAR International Series 427. British Archaeological Reports, Oxford.
Salazar, Lucy
2009   Escaleras al cielo: altares, rituales, y ancestros en el sitio arqueológico de Cardal. In *Arqueología del Periodo Formativo en la Cuenca Baja de Lurín,* vol. 1, edited by Richard Burger and Krzysztof Makowski, pp. 83–94. Fondo Editorial de la Pontificia Universidad Católica del Peru, Lima.
Salazar, Lucy, and Richard L. Burger
1983   La araña en la iconografía del Horizonte Temprano en la costa norte del Perú. *Beiträge zur Allgemeinen und Vergleichenden Archaölogie* 4: 213–253.
Scheele, Harry
1970   The Chavin Occupation of the Central Coast of Peru. Unpublished Ph.D. dissertation, Department of Anthropology, Harvard University, Cambridge, Massachusetts.
Silva, Jorge Elias
1998   Una aproximación al Periodo Formativo en el Valle del Chillón. *Boletín de Arqueología PUCP* 2:251–268.
Tello, Julio C., and P. Miranda
1923   Wallallo. Ceremonias gentílicas realizadas en la region cisandina del Perú central (disrrito de Casta). *Inca* 1(2):475–549.
Thorme, Trisha
1999   Trade Networks in the Lurin Valley Initial Period. Paper presented at the 64th Annual Meetings of the Society for American Archaeology, Chicago, Illinois.
Tykot, Robert, Nikolaas van der Merwe, and Richard Burger
2006   The Importance of Maize in the Initial Period and Early Horizon. In *Histories of Maize,* edited by John E. Staller, Robert Tykot, and Bruce Benz, pp. 187–198. Academic Press, New York.
Umlauf, Marcelle
2009   Restos botánicos de Cardal durante el Periodo Inicial. In *Arqueología del Periodo Formativo en la Cuenca Baja de Lurín,* Vol. 1, edited by Richard Burger and Krzysztof Makowski, pp. 95–110. Fondo Editorial de la Pontificia Universidad Católica del Peru, Lima.
Vradenburg, Joseph A.
2009   Biología osea de una población del Periodo Inicial Tardío:Cardal, Peru. In *Arque-*

ología del Periodo Formativo en la Cuenca Baja de Lurín, Vol. 1, edited by Richard Burger and Krzysztof Makowski, pp. 161–185. Fondo Editorial de la Pontificia Universidad Católica del Peru, Lima.

Weir, Glendon, Robert Benfer, and John Jones
1988   Preceramic to Early Formative Subsistence on the Central Coast. In *Economic Prehistory of the Central Andes,* edited by Elizabeth Wing and Jane Wheeler, pp. 56–94. BAR International Series 427. British Archaeological Reports, Oxford.

Wendt, W. E.
1964   Die prekeramische Siedlung am Rio Seco, Peru. *Baessler Archiv* 11(2):225–175.

Williams, Carlos
1971   Centros ceremoniales tempranos en el valle de Chillón, Rimac y Lurín. *Apuntes Arqueológicos 1:* 1–4. Lima.
1985   A Scheme for the Early Monumental Architecture of the Central Coast of Peru. In *Early Ceremonial Architecture in the Andes,* edited by Christopher Donnan, pp. 227–240. Dumbarton Oaks, Washington, D.C.

15

Agricultural Terraces as Monumental Architecture in the Titicaca Basin

Their Origins in the Yaya-Mama Religious Tradition

SERGIO J. CHÁVEZ

Dedicated to the memory of Karen L. Mohr Chávez,
who was and continues to be the intellectual author of this project.

A general reconnaissance of the Titicaca Basin shows that almost all of the landscape has been transformed by human activity into production zones, leaving basically no land in a pristine state. Such transformations are not uniformly present in the basin. Different strategies were used in diverse local environmental, climatic, and topographic conditions, including stone-faced terraces on slopes and steep hills (such as on the Copacabana Peninsula); cultivation on temporarily inundated areas among dispersed sod houses (Chávez 1998); agriculture on raised fields or platforms (e.g., Erickson 1988), agriculture on *qocha*, or artificial depressions (e.g., Flores and Paz 1985); and herding in *bofedales*, or artificially irrigated pasture lands (Palacios Ríos 1977). Many are associated with nearby archaeological settlements from different periods of time. Also, in the northwestern basin, radiocarbon dates on charcoal from excavated mounds associated with raised fields show a range of time between 1000 BC and AD 400 (Erickson 1988, 11), which would indicate their beginnings in the Yaya-Mama religious tradition (K. Chávez 1988, 25).

Among these various production strategies, terraces are the most impressive in terms of monumental scale, particularly those on the Copacabana Peninsula (Figure 15.1). Based on a priori assumptions, their origins have often been attributed to either the Tiahuanaco or the Inca, who had the power and organizational means to mobilize labor in a large scale.

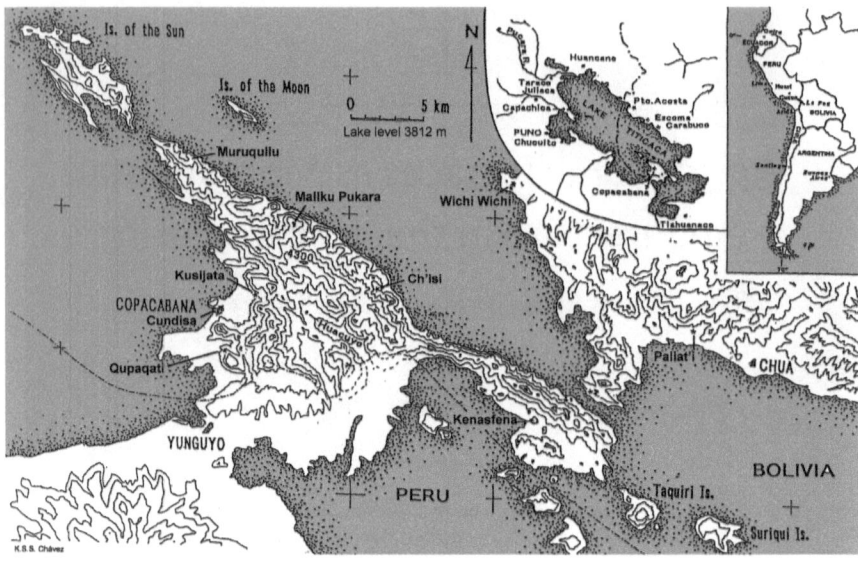

Figure 15.1. Map of the Copacabana Peninsula with an inset of the Lake Titicaca Basin showing all the temple sites mentioned in the text. Contour lines are at 100 meters. Drawn by Karen and Sergio Chávez based on topographic maps from the Instituto Geográfico Militar of Peru and Bolivia.

However, the results of our long-term research on the Copacabana Peninsula and beyond in the Titicaca Basin strongly support assigning the origin of terrace construction to the Yaya-Mama religious tradition—a basically egalitarian, sedentary, self-sufficient food-producing, noncentralized circumlacustrine tradition. This long-enduring tradition represents the first public architecture and the unification of diverse groups of people in the region, where the landscape was transformed into a series of sacred centers or temple domains (Figure 15.2), and the first organization of labor in the region to build extensive stone-faced terraces. Hence, our consideration of the social, political, and spiritual aspects associated with temples includes the practical dimensions of such temples in terms of controlling the outcomes of agricultural production. Many aspects of the tradition continued (with modifications) into the later Tiahuanaco empire (ca. AD 500–1100), particularly iconography in Huari culture (ca. AD 550–1000) and some architectural features (including terraces) in Inca times.

In the following sections I will present information about the magnitude of terrace construction, experiments with stone cutting, ethnographic studies, surface surveys, excavation on terraces, and analysis of relevant

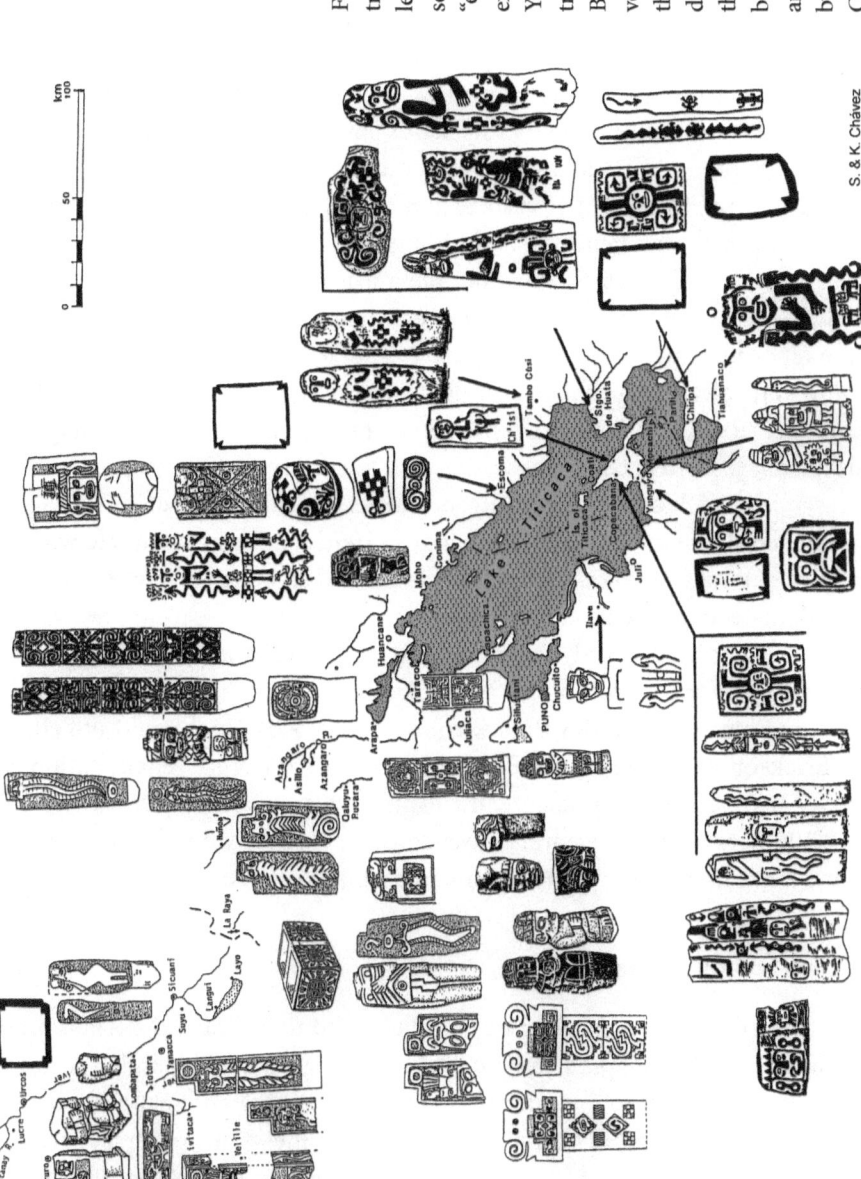

Figure 15.2. Distribution of a selected sample of stone sculpture showing the "early" and "late" co-existing versions of the Yaya-Mama religious tradition in the Titicaca Basin and the "late" version extending into the Cuzco Basin. The drawings are not at the same scale and are based on photographs and original rubbings by Karen and Sergio Chávez.

material derived from our excavations, which sought to define the Yaya-Mama tradition.

Magnitude of Terrace Construction

The stone-faced terraces range in width from one meter to more than 15 meters and are preserved in some areas to a height of three meters. Following the contour lines on the map shown in Figure 15.1, the distribution is continuous around the entire peninsula, including most areas of the islands of the Sun and Moon and several islands south of the peninsula. Terraces are interrupted only in areas with rock outcrops and steep hills.

Calculating the extent of vertical and horizontal distribution of terraces on the Copacabana Peninsula, including the time and labor involved, has been a most difficult task. For example, measuring on a topographic map only the first contour line of terraces near the lake beach and following that line all around the peninsula (Figure 15.1) gives a total of 100 kilometers. However, calculating the vertical distribution becomes more difficult because terraces meander into deep contours of steep hills of different heights, deep valleys lie in between these hills, and the valleys are interrupted by the presence of rock outcrops and rugged ridges. Additionally, satellite images are generally views with distorted angles. Hence, a formal estimate would require digitizing several topographic maps and creating a computer model to calculate area extent.

To my knowledge, only two published reports calculate the labor-intensive work on the Peruvian side of the basin, those dealing with rehabilitation by Ramos Vera and with new construction by B. Coolman (both cited in Erickson 2000, 332). The calculated estimate for terrace rehabilitation is 225–2,270 person-days/hectare; the estimate for new terrace construction is 2,500 person-days/hectare. However, these estimates do not include the hand labor involved in retrieving and making blocks using hammer stones.

Experimental Archaeology

It is clear that immense labor was used to build the stone walls. This labor includes roughly shaping the blocks; preparing the steeply hilled terrain from the lake shore to the summits of the hills; placing and securing blocks of different sizes in horizontal rows; adjusting the width of terrace walls, following the topographic contours; and filling the terraces with a thick

Figure 15.3. View from the Muruqullu temple site showing the distribution of stone-faced terraces to near the lake shore and a narrow terrace on the right used as a path for people and beasts of burden. Note in the background the other temple site of Mallku Pukara (4220 MASL), situated at two hours' walking distance away. (Photograph by Stanislava and Sergio Chávez.)

layer of gravel and then topsoil. Especially in areas where terraces are better preserved, such as at Muruqullu (Figures 15.3 and 15.4), the walls can reach up to three meters high, and some terraces have additional protruding slabs that were used as staircases and to facilitate access. Likewise, in areas where the sedimentary outcrops were not always close to the terraces, individual blocks had to be brought up to steep hills. In addition, general reconnaissance was conducted in and around rock outcrops to find the hammer stones used to carve and shape the blocks, and the only ones we could find were roughly rounded implements made of the same sedimentary rocks.

Therefore, experiments were carried out to help determine and understand the physical effort and time needed to remove and make blocks from the local sedimentary rock outcrops. One of the controlled experiments showed that four men were able to remove a piece from the outcrop and make a single roughly shaped rectangular block (about 60 × 30 × 20 centimeters) in about 40 minutes, using roughly rounded hammer stones of hard limestone. During the process, it was observed that flakes of different sizes were being generated (similar to the ones used as wedges in terrace walls) and that the most difficult task was separating the block from the natural rock cleavage. The use of bronze chisels would have greatly helped in the separation and shaping of blocks, but no such implements have been reported from surface or excavated contexts.

436 · Sergio J. Chávez

Figure 15.4. Satellite view of the excavated temple site of Muruqullu and surrounding steep hills and valleys extensively covered by terraces. (Photograph from Google Earth.)

Ethnographic Studies

Interviews of local farmers and direct observations have been carried out on the Copacabana Peninsula to document native agricultural practices, land management practices, terrace construction methods, soil and plant classification, the schedules of agricultural and related activities, recognition of and response to climatic changes, kinds of fuel and fertilizers used, and native maize terminologies. Such research confirmed our earlier observations about the extent of maize cultivation in the Titicaca Basin and enabled us to make comparisons with observations in the Cuzco Basin (Chávez 2004c; Chávez 2006; Chávez and Thompson 2006, 415–419; see also Chávez 2008). The results show that both European-introduced and native plants are cultivated in significant amounts on terraces and without irrigation, including maize grown at altitudes ranging from lake shores to 4,200 meters—the latter constituting the highest such cultivation in the Andes and perhaps in the world. Additional observations and interviews with local informants indicate that pastoralism is practiced on terraces during fallow periods (which range from four to seven years, depending on soil quality) and that most farming today is done on terraces because of problems related to heavy erosion on unterraced steep slopes. Furthermore,

Figure 15.5. View of the upper portion of stone-faced terraces near the excavated temple site of Huayllani. (Photograph by Stanislava and Sergio Chávez.)

terraces are rarely (if ever) maintained, and sometimes stones are removed for various private and communal construction projects. The extent to which the native people are exposed on a daily basis to the vertical challenge of walking through steep escarpments, valleys, and rugged ridges was also observed (Figures 15.3 and 15.5).

Surface Surveys on Terraces

Our ethnographic studies and direct observations show the practice of agriculture and pastoralism on terraces and how terraces were used for house construction, for drying agricultural products, and as paths for people and beasts of burden. Important and related artifacts are the bifacially flaked stone hoes of different sizes, made usually of a nonlocal basalt. Such implements are usually broken, have been excavated in all temple sites, and are also present in relative abundance in surface surveys, including on terraces. The frequent presence of such farming implements in excavations, especially at Yaya-Mama temple sites (where they are sometimes used as wedges in the construction of stone walls), prompted Karen Chávez to propose that such temples may also have functioned as centers of redistribution (Chávez and Chávez 1994).

Therefore, the possibility of the use of terraces and that they were first constructed and/or introduced during Yaya-Mama times had to be shown and documented through surface surveys and excavations on terraces around and beyond temple sites. Since the diagnostic forms, decorated sherds, and other special/ceremonial pottery (such as trumpets and ceremonial burners) so commonly present at temple sites are extremely rare or absent on terraces, we had to rely mostly on plain sherds. Karen Chávez made a study of the Yaya-Mama ceremonial utilitarian sherds that are frequently present in temple excavations, engaging in the tedious and painstaking work of identifying and documenting paste and temper constituents and related attributes on literally thousands of plain sherds (K. Chávez 2002). However, those retrieved from surface surveys and excavations on terraces were very small in size and quantity and were badly worn as a result of soil turning and harvesting over centuries. In addition, the absence of similar studies for Tiahuanaco and later plain pottery styles made their relative chronological association and/or identification even more difficult. With these caveats in mind, what follows is the result of intensive surface surveys conducted on terraces surrounding two Yaya-Mama temple sites, from the summits of the hills almost to the lake shore at Mallku Pukara and Kenasfena.

Beginning at the uppermost terrace immediately surrounding the Mallku Pukara temple at 4,220 meters, each of the 47 stone-faced terraces was surveyed. The results showed that the most common and abundant sherds were those pertaining to colonial or later styles. These were present on all the terraces but were less frequent near the top. Next in frequency are Yaya-Mama sherds (including some cream-on-red Chiripa-style fragments). These were overwhelmingly present on the seven upper terraces surrounding the temple and on several terraces in the middle of the hill and were very rarely present or were absent on the lower terraces. Tiahuanaco-style sherds were less frequent, although we found a cluster in the middle of the hill, a few near the temple, and none or very few in the rest of the terraces. Inca-style sherds were even more rare; they were mainly concentrated on the lower terraces and were very rare or absent on the rest of the terraces. Late Intermediate Period or pre-Inca sherds were almost absent and were present only on some lower terraces, and there only rarely. Consequently, it appears that Tiahuanaco were replicating or reusing the Yaya-Mama concentration on the uppermost and middle terraces, while Inca appear to have been present on (and perhaps expanded) the lowermost terraces.

At the temple site of Kenasfena (Figure 15.5), which is located on a top of a low hill (3,924 meters), the pattern on nine surveyed terraces to the lake shore is very different from those at Mallku Pukara. This time, the most abundant sherds were Yaya-Mama in style; these were distributed everywhere but were more heavily concentrated on the upper half of the terraces. Next in frequency were colonial and later styles, which had a distribution pattern similar to that of the Yaya-Mama sherds. Much less frequent were Tiahuanaco sherds; these were present only on the two uppermost terraces. Only two sherds of Late Intermediate styles and one Inca-style sherd were found on the first and second uppermost terraces, respectively. Therefore, at least at this site, it appears that Yaya-Mama may have built all the terraces. These terraces were subsequently used by Tiahuanaco but were not occupied by other peoples until colonial and later times.

We have also carried out surface surveys at other Yaya-Mama sites such as at Muruqullu and Pallat'i, which yielded much less material but had similar distribution patterns. In addition, we conducted surface surveys on the lowermost terraces and on the beach near the Muruqullu temple site; this work revealed the presence of several disturbed Tiahuanaco burials.

Therefore, the presence and distribution of Yaya-Mama sherds on many terraces at these sites supports the possibility that the first terraces were constructed during the Yaya-Mama tradition. More surveys and test excavations are needed to generate comparative data on terraces beyond temples to determine whether they were also built by the Yaya-Mama people or by later societies , which periods of time the terraces were expanded, and what role erosion played in displacing remains.

Excavation on Terraces

Surface surveys and excavations conducted at several sites on the Copacabana Peninsula and beyond show that many Yaya-Mama semi-subterranean temple complexes are surrounded by stone-faced terraces such as those at Muruqullu (Figure 15.4), Kenasfena (Figure 15.5), Mallku Pukara, Ch'isi (Figure 15.6), and Pallat'i. Therefore, our excavations were conducted in about the middle of a series of terraces facing the lake and below the previously excavated temple of Mallku Pukara. A site was selected corresponding to the wide and well-preserved terraces 11 and 12 (counted from the bottom), where a trench one meter wide and 12 meters long was dug along two consecutive terraces. The depth to bedrock varies from one meter to almost three meters at the edge of the second terrace. Remains of an

Figure 15.6. Satellite view of the excavated temple site of Ch'isi and surrounding hills and valleys extensively covered by terraces. (Photograph from Google Earth.)

older terrace were found buried inside the second terrace, about one meter behind the wall, containing a single Inca sherd in the fill, which could indicate that the Incas were responsible for the one meter terrace expansion. A small number of plain and eroded sherds that appear to be Yaya-Mama were present in the lower levels, and additional ones were present in the upper level mixed with Inca sherds.

Almost parallel to the excavated trench, a series of four contiguous units (2 × 2, 2 × 2, 3 × 3, and 3 × 4) was also excavated nearby on both terraces. These units had depths ranging from one to two meters and contained five to six natural levels. Such units also revealed wall foundations that appeared to predate the terraces, and consisted of an unusual stone structure one meter wide and six meters long beneath and perpendicular to the later terrace construction. It was extensively filled with rocks and gravel. Small amounts of plain sherds that appeared to be Yaya-Mama were recovered in almost all of the levels, but they were mixed with Inca and modern materials.

In conclusion, the handful of badly preserved plain sherds retrieved from the heavy rock fill and disturbed soil shows a possible Yaya-Mama affiliation. Inca-style sherds were even less frequent, and those for Tiahuanaco and intermediate styles were absent or could not be identified with any degree of certainty.

The Economic Basis

Based on the identification of 25,000 excavated specimens from Yaya-Mama contexts, Susan deFrance (deFrance 1997; Pearsall and deFrance 2002) has identified camelids, *Cavia*, deer, fowl, duck, and other lake species and fish in relative abundance. Likewise, based on the identification of 125 flotation samples and 572 carbon remains, Deborah Pearsall (Pearsall and Lee 1997; Pearsall and deFrance 2002) indicates an increased reliance on agriculture, including the native quinoa, *cañihua*, amaranth, local grasses, and wood and even carbonized freeze-dried potato and *oca*. One important agricultural product absent in the flotation list is maize—a plant that is extensively cultivated today in the region, including on ancient terraces (Chávez 2004c; Chávez 2006). Although assumptions about the lack of favorable conditions for maize cultivation in the Titicaca Basin prevailed and were widely accepted by scholars, especially in light of John Murra's verticality model (Chávez 2004c), maize phytoliths have been recently identified in food residues preserved on utilitarian sherds excavated at Yaya-Mama sites on the Copacabana Peninsula, including 247 samples from Ch'isi, Qhot'a Pata, Kusijata, Cundisa, and Qupakati (Chávez and Thompson 2006). In addition, three AMS dates directly obtained from such residues in sherds show a range of time (800–460 BC) within the early part of the Yaya-Mama sequence in the Early Horizon (Lusteck 2002; Chávez and Thompson 2006, 419). Hence, maize was consumed during Yaya-Mama times. It was likely grown on beach shores and terraces and was not a late or recently introduced crop in the basin.

Skeletal Analysis

A wide range of studies conducted by Dale Hutchinson (e.g., Hutchinson 1997) and Sara Juengst on over 200 skeletons excavated in different sites of the Copacabana Peninsula (most from Yaya-Mama times) found that mechanical trauma and systemic stress were common occurrences. Preliminary results show many cases of severe osteoarthritis of the joints, long bones, and vertebrae, including loss of cartilage and the resulting bone reactions, including eburnation (bone-to-bone contact that leaves shiny polished surfaces). Hutchinson also found cases of advanced degenerative disease in vertebrae that can be attributed to mechanical stress; this disease showed an increase from Yaya-Mama times (especially in females) to post–Yaya-Mama times (especially in males). Also, Sara Juengst found increasing frequency of cases of arthritis of the elbow joint during the Yaya-Mama times, especially at the site of Muruqullu (personal communication, July 2011). In addition to the vertical challenge observed today in the rugged and steep terrain of the peninsula, an important factor associated with such skeletal trauma and stress may be the physical demand related to the construction of terraces, including the repetitive and demanding work needed to remove and shape stone blocks, carry them across steep slopes, remove the vegetation, reshape the natural slopes, and build the continuous rows of terraces on a monumental scale.

The Cultural and Chronological Context

The Yaya-Mama religious tradition was first defined in 1988 by my late wife and colleague, Karen L. Mohr Chávez, based on seriation of a number of circumlacustrine stone sculptures lacking archaeological context (Chávez and Chávez 1975; Chávez 1982a; K. Chávez 1988), analysis of partially contemporary materials excavated earlier by Wendell Bennett at Chiripa and Alfred Kidder II at Chiripa and Pucara (Mohr 1966), and our excavations and surveys in the Titicaca and Cuzco basins (Mohr 1969; K. Chávez 1988). Based on our ongoing studies, we have concluded that the Yaya-Mama religious tradition (*yaya* meaning "father" and *mama* "mother," which we learned from a Quechua-speaker informant's reference to a stela with male and female personages) was a major long-enduring system that was indigenous to the high plateau of the Lake Titicaca Basin. Remains range from just above lake level at 3,812 meters to the summit of high peaks at 4,220 meters and date from ca. 800 BC to AD 200–300.

One of the four main archaeological indicators of the Yaya-Mama tradition are temple centers with sunken courts, stone-faced, unroofed structures that have a single entrance situated off center. The sunken court is about 15 meters on each of the four sides, dug down to bedrock or on artificial platforms, and the four walls are lined with stone to a depth of two meters. These temple constructions represent the first widespread public architecture in the region. They have been documented on artificial mounds, on hilltops, almost at lake level, at the base of impressive cliffs, and in island environments (Chávez 2004a, 73–74). Furthermore, temples are frequently surrounded by terraces, even in areas where terraces are otherwise rare or absent. For example, the temple site of Pallat'i is surrounded by terraced hills in an area where most hills are unterraced.

Excavations above and around the sunken courts also exhibit considerable variation. For example, excavations of peripheral features at the Chiripa and Pucara temples situated at both ends of the basin (Figure 15.2) show a series of bins containing basket impressions and food remains; these have been interpreted as temple storage facilities (K. Chávez 1988, 18–20, 22, Figures 2–3, 9). Those at Mallku Pukara temple on the Copacabana Peninsula include a series of corbel-vaulted structures, while those at the Ch'isi temple show a series of stone-lined and oblong human burials associated with modest remains of beads and sherds; a few include bronze pins and small spoon-like implements (Lechtman 2002; Chávez 2004a, 74, Figure 3.3). Dispersed between the burials are circular food offering pits, also dug into bedrock. The interpretation of these pits as food offering deposits derives from the identification of faunal remains that include fish, deer, guinea pigs, birds, and camelids and the botanical remains of charred native grains and root crops that include freeze-dried potatoes and *oca*. In addition, it should also be noted that except for these relatively modest temple architectures and egalitarian burials, there are no palaces or other significant residential structures. The only semi-subterranean structure showing greater elaboration is the one extensively excavated at Pucara in the northern basin, which includes four grave chambers with stepped-fret and double-jamb entrances housing single individuals (one associated with a small gold disk), situated in the middle of each of the sunken court walls (K. Chávez 1988, 22, Figures 9 and 12); a burial at the temple site of Huayllani containing a necklace with two small gold beads; and a Yaya-Mama multiple burial with two other gold beads at Muruqullu.

While our project expected to find only one or two distant temple centers (following a regional pilgrimage model), our work on the Copacabana Peninsula has revealed several temples at a walking distance of about two hours (Figures 15.1 and 15.3). It now appears that most of the temples were primarily local temples that serviced communities within their immediate domains. Only two residential structures have been identified and excavated around Ch'isi, and others may be lying under the modern house clusters. These local temple domains were linked with more distant populations that interacted with the Yaya-Mama network; such interactions were related to the procurement and distribution of obsidian from the southwestern Andes (Burger, Chávez, and Chávez 2000, 311–323, Figure 9); basalt for the elaboration of hoes, probably from 200 kilometers south on Poopó Lake (Ponce Sanginés 1970, 65, Figure 9); and coca leaves from the eastern slopes of the Andes (indirect evidence consists of miniature vessels containing calcium carbonate, which is used today in conjunction with coca chewing).

Temples with sunken courts continued, with some modifications, centuries later into Tiahuanaco times (Chávez 2004a, 74–75, Figure 3.5), and some architectural features such as trapezoidal and double-jamb doorways (seen in architectural models) were also repeated in Inca times. Additional evidence of an enduring sacredness was excavated inside the sunken court at the temple of Mallku Pukara, where Tiahuanaco offerings of Spondylus shell and silver foil figures were placed, as were Inca offerings at the Ch'isi temple consisting of male and female silver figurines and two gold llamas.

The other material indicator of the tradition are the stone sculptures, which depict supernatural images and geometric designs; some represent male and female personages and related motifs. They are usually associated with semi-subterranean temples and range in size from large (in one case almost six meters long and weighing 2.65 tons) to small and portable (15 centimeters). Based on associated dates, seriation, and degree of elaboration in the techniques and motifs, we have divided Yaya-Mama stone sculpture into an "early" variation that was distributed mainly on the southern basin and a "late" but partially contemporary variation found mainly on the northern basin and into the Cuzco region (Chávez 1989; Chávez 2004a, 75, 81; Chávez 2004b) (Figure 15.2). The latter is represented by the Pucara style, whose realism is unprecedented in Andean sculpture, including realistic statues with legs carved separately, some of which even have removable feet and pedestal portions.

Several pieces of Yaya-Mama/Pucara-style sculpture were found at the Tiahuanaco site associated with "classic" Tiahuanaco architectural remains, an indication of their continued sacredness and importance (Bennet 1934, 474; Chávez 1976; Chávez 1982b; Chávez and Jorgenson 1980).

Ritual paraphernalia, which directly imply music making, ceremonial burning, feasting, and other activities at Yaya-Mama temples, can be inferred from the relative abundance of pottery trumpets, a few statues that are holding a conch shell, fancy decorated vessels and miniature reproductions (some containing calcium carbonate), vessels that depict human heads and feline effigies, ceremonial burners, architectural models with trapezoidal double-jambed doorways (including a whistle representing a roofed house), carved slabs with supernatural images (or a formée cross outline) on one side that were used as grinding implements on the opposite side, and ceremonial utilitarian vessels (Chávez 2004a, 81–82, Figures 3.11–3.15,

3.18). Although almost all ritual objects and vessels are highly fragmentary (probably the result of deliberate ceremonial breakage), studies of form, decoration, and technique of manufacture show regional similarities and local differences (e.g., K. Chávez 1988, Figures 7, 11; Chávez 2004a, Figure 3.12). This variety is related to the widespread nature of the Yaya-Mama tradition in time and space. The tradition includes pottery styles in the south like those of Chiripa, Qalasasaya, and Qea (e.g., K. Chávez 2002; Steadman 1995; Steadman 2007; Chávez 2004a, 90–91) and other styles that are still being defined and styles in the north such as the Taraco and Pucara styles (e.g., Chávez 1992, 508–539). Likewise, differences in paste and temper suggest different sources of manufacture (K. Chávez 2002). Such diversity certainly implies a heterarchical pattern.

Finally, Yaya-Mama supernatural iconography portrayed in stone and pottery contains the first truly representational imagery in the Titicaca Basin, especially during the "late" Pucara version of the Yaya-Mama tradition. Yaya-Mama textiles are not preserved in the region, but there are some with Yaya-Mama iconography that lack archaeological context in coastal regions and include Pucara-related (e.g., Conklin 1983) and late Pucara or Provincial Pucara styles (e.g., Haeberli 2002, 116–128, Figure 30; Isbell and Knobloch 2009, 174–177, Figures 10–12). Examples of the circumlacustrine distribution of stelae, statues, and slabs corresponding to the southern "early" and northern "late" versions are presented in Figure 15.2. The few Pucara-style examples that have survived (Mujica 1990, Figures 125–126) suggest that many sculptures were also painted. Moreover, the emphasis on male and female personages, spotted felines, vertically divided eyes, and heads with rayed appendages has its direct antecedent in the southern "early" version of the tradition (Chávez 2004a, 90–92, Figures 3.11–15, 3.18).

The Pucara-style iconography portrayed on fancy polychrome and incised pottery vessels is not represented in stone. Such iconography features explicit detail, conventionalized rules, and complex depictions of two main themes aligned by sex/gender, each associated with specific motifs and geometric designs (e.g., Chávez 1992; Chávez 2002; see also Rowe and Brandel 1969–1970). The female personage (known as the Woman with Alpaca theme) is portrayed standing alone and in a frontal pose; she is leading an alpaca by a rope, is holding a staff, and is flanked by plants. Consequently, her clear association with the rainy season, agriculture, and pastoralism, including the meat- and wool-producing alpaca, can be interpreted as an intermediary role between the supernatural and natural forces that ultimately regulate production (Chávez 2002, 41–50, 64, Figures 2.2–6).

The other symbolic theme is known as the Feline Man, a clear contrast to the Woman with Alpaca. He is portrayed in profile and in a running stance, holding an axe and a severed human head in one hand and a segmented or striped staff in the other. This figure is depicted (with teeth and fangs) in pairs that either face or chase each other; sometimes they wear the pelt of a spotted feline. Therefore, the Feline Man is interpreted as representing conflict, competition, political dominance, and visual terrorism (Chávez 2002, 50–60, 64–66, Figures 2.11–19).

Many Yaya-Mama motifs, designs, and elements continued (with additional modifications and alterations and new associations) into "classic" Tiahuanaco and Huari times. For example, the male/*yaya* and female/*mama* personages with their own distinctive domains continued but with significant transformations that I have interpreted to reflect gender-role reversals at the ideological level (Chávez in press).

Discussion and Conclusions

The first unification of diverse groups of people in the Titicaca Basin began with the Yaya-Mama religious tradition through the introduction and establishment of temple domains, which were built in diverse locations using local materials. Those on the Copacabana Peninsula are relatively modest constructions, show different patterns of reuse, and are situated at about two hours' walking distance from each other. Despite the standard layout of sunken courts, the structures immediately above and around the sunken courts show considerable variability, including storage facilities, corbel-vaulted structures, and burials with modest remains associated with food offering pits. The diversity of attributes and styles derived from Yaya-Mama ritual paraphernalia, paste and temper constituents in pottery, and the "early" and "late" supernatural iconography also show a pattern of regional similarities and local differences.

Furthermore, except for the four grave chambers placed within the walls of the sunken court at Pucara and the rare presence of a few gold beads in some burials, there are no elite burials or especial structures. Likewise, there is no evidence for defensive architecture, weapons (except for a handful of projectile points at each site), or skeletons with signs of violence. I have argued elsewhere that the iconography depicting violent acts associated with the Feline Man theme suggests "social control by threat of force or visual terrorism to prevent some act or conflict . . . to warn by displaying terrorist imagery in the absence of, or as a substitute for widespread warfare or rule by force" (Chávez 2002, 65–66).

Therefore, temples were focused on servicing (in the material and spiritual sense) local communities, and the emphasis was on egalitarian relations, including interactions to procure and distribute basalt hoes, obsidian, and coca from distant sources. Such temple structures continued with modifications into "classic" Tiahuanaco times (including bringing to Tiahuanaco and/or reusing Yaya-Mama–style sculptures), while the sacredness and importance of Yaya-Mama temples was recognized by the placement of valuable offerings inside the ancient courts of Ch'isi and Mallku Pukara during Tiahuanaco and Inca times. Moreover, many other aspects of the Yaya-Mama tradition continued into Tiahuanaco times, as exemplified by the two symbolic themes aligned by sex and gender (along with their related motifs, geometric designs, and separate domains) that are so explicitly displayed on "late" Yaya-Mama polychrome pottery.

More than a powerful religious ideology, the tradition has been interpreted as constituting a system that had a ceremonial network that also involved integrative economic, political, and social activities and institutions above the household level and thus served in various ways to unify diverse groups of people for the first time. This network also made available resources (such as obsidian, basalt hoes, and coca) from faraway sources. However, very little evidence exists for any significant social ranking.

Regarding large constructions with a "practical" function, all Yaya-Mama temple and nontemple sites are adjacent to or directly associated with stone-faced terraces. For example, on the Copacabana Peninsula almost all the hills and slopes are extensively covered with a continuous distribution of terraces, ranging from lake level to sometimes above 4,000 meters. Although this type of large investment in labor has been attributed to later polities (such as the Inca) that had the organization to manage labor on a large scale, terraces may have grown through accretion over a long period of time. Hence, based on the identification and study of materials derived from surveys and excavations, ethnographic data obtained in the region, and experiments, we can safely propose its beginnings in Yaya-Mama times.

Limited excavated samples provide support for attributing the first construction of terraces to Yaya-Mama. The Inca have left a very limited presence (including a single sherd in the fill associated with terrace wall expansion) but no identifiable materials that can be securely assigned to

Tiahuanaco or intermediate styles. Surveys on a sample of terraces show an overwhelming presence of Yaya-Mama materials in the region (especially associated with temple domains), while those for Tiahuanaco, intermediate, and Inca styles are less frequent or even rare. Also, except for Tiahuanaco burials (which are present on lower terraces and near lake shores), there are no significant storage or residential structures or heavy occupations for Tiahuanaco, Inca, or other intermediate periods. Likewise, although pre-pottery projectile points sometimes show up in surveys and excavations in and around Yaya-Mama sites (including a few burials associated with late Preceramic projectile points at Muruqullu), there is no evidence for structures or any significant Preceramic presence/occupation in the region.

The diverse studies and strategies used to identify and date the initial and subsequent occupations of terraces, which are seen today on a monumental scale, also show strong lines of evidence for assigning the initial labor organization to Yaya-Mama times. Subsistence data show an increased reliance on cultivated root and grain crops (including maize) and camelid pastoralism supplemented with fishing and hunting. Hence, sustained self-sufficiency was achieved because of the exploitation of diverse lake resources. Local woods and grasses were also readily available and were used as fuel, and camelid and guinea pig dung may also have been used as fertilizers and fuel (according to observations and interviews).

The skeletal evidence of mechanical trauma and systemic stress, which has been identified mostly on Yaya-Mama skeletons, and experiments carried out to get an approximation of the time and effort involved in shaping a single block of stone both show that terrace construction is labor intensive. It likely required the participation of a large number of males and females; these workers were constantly exposed to the vertical challenges of the terrain in their labor to build, expand, and maintain terraces and to harvest the products they grew on terraces over the centuries.

In conclusion, large-scale terrace construction has often been attributed to the state-level societies of Tiahuanaco and Inca, which had the power to organize, administer, and mobilize centralized labor on a larger scale. However, all the lines of evidence point toward an egalitarian, self-sufficient, and noncentralized organization at a series of Yaya-Mama temple domains, where local leaders maintained local diversity but at the same time developed regional similarities. Such an interpretation is more in line with recent applications of the theoretical model of heterarchy (e.g., Crumley 1995; see also Roosevelt et al. this volume; Burger and Salazar this volume). In addition, although subsequent expansion of terraces likely occurred in later times, the range of time for Yaya-Mama presence in the basin (over 1,000 years) is far more extensive than the tenure of the Tiahuanaco (500 years) and the Inca (less than 100 years). It should also be noted that the monumental terraces observed today (especially on the Copacabana Peninsula), appear to reflect a uniform style and technique of construction. That is, even if massive expansions were made in the span of time between Tiahuanaco and Inca occupation, there are no recognizable changes in style of construction, such as more careful shaping of blocks, use of bronze chisels, or standardized hammer stones of harder rocks. This evidence indicates that each of these groups may have used the same locally available materials and ancient knowledge.

It is significant that the long-term built environment since the initial construction and use of terraces, the use of Yaya-Mama sculptures as objects of veneration, and the recognition of temple sites as sacred spots where valuable Tiahuanaco and Inca offerings were deposited (despite their subsequent collapse and abandonment) have all continued to the present despite different social, economic, and political contexts. In contrast to many other ancient monumental works, which served only one polity, one generation, or even one family/individual, the agricultural terraces in the basin have been used without interruption over three millennia. This remarkable achievement had its beginnings in the egalitarian, relatively modest, and self-sufficient Yaya-Mama religious tradition of the Lake Titicaca Basin.

Acknowledgments

I am most grateful to Richard Burger and Robert Rosenswig, who invited me to participate in their 2006 Society for American Archaeology symposium "Understanding the Origins of Monumentality in Latin America," where I presented many aspects of the arguments in this chapter. I also want to thank Michael Love and Kate Babbitt for their helpful editorial comments. Fieldwork was authorized by the Unidad Nacional de Arqueología in La Paz under the direction of several colleagues over the years, including Oswaldo Rivera Sundt, Juan Albarracin-Jordan, and Javier Escalante Moscoso. I wish to thank the specialists on our project who analyzed different remains from our excavations: Dale Hutchinson, Sara Juengst, Susan deFrance, Deborah Pearsall, Robert Thompson, Plinio Velazco Ayaviri, Heather Lechtman, and Alison Rautman. I also wish to thank Eduardo Pareja Siñanis for his decisive support as co-investigator of our project and

Rodney Kirk and Patricia Coen for many years of friendship and collaboration. Much appreciation and gratitude goes to my wife and colleague, Stanislava R. Chávez, for her intellectual support and helpful comments on the manuscript and her careful revision of fieldnotes. I am also grateful to the different *maestros* and *compadres* of our project, especially Pablo Ramos Nina, Celestino Nina López, Saturnino Ramos Quispe, Margarita Ramos de Nina, Eusebio Ylla Osco, Angel Nina Payi, Pedro Condori Quispe, Antonio Callisaya Mamani, Marcela Cuaquira Ramos, Pánfilo Tarifa Mamani, and Gabino Cuaquira. Over the years, our project (The Archaeology of the Yaya-Mama Religious Tradition in Bolivia) has received generous support from the National Science Foundation, the Wenner-Gren Foundation, the National Geographic Society, and the Foundation for Research and Conservation of Andean Monuments (Georgia de Havenon and Ron and Maxine Linde) and grants from the Faculty Research & Creative Endeavors program at Central Michigan University.

References Cited

Bennett, Wendell Clark
1934   Excavations at Tiahuanaco. *Anthropological Papers of the American Museum of Natural History* 34(3):359–514.
Burger, Richard, Karen L. Mohr Chávez, and Sergio J. Chávez
2000   Through the Glass Darkly: Prehispanic Obsidian Procurement and Exchange in Southern Peru and Northern Bolivia. *Journal of World Prehistory* 14(3):267–361.
Chávez, Karen L. Mohr
1988   The Significance of Chiripa in Lake Titicaca Basin Developments. *Expedition* 30 (4):17–26.
2002   Local Differences and Regional Similarities in Pottery of the Yaya-Mama Religious Tradition. Paper read by S. Chávez at the 67th Annual Meeting of the Society for American Archaeology, Denver, Colorado.
Chávez, Karen L. Mohr, and Sergio J. Chávez
1994   Archaeological Excavations of the Yaya-Mama Religious Tradition, Bolivia. Paper presented at the 22nd Annual Midwest Conference on Andean and Amazonian Archaeology and Ethnohistory, Ann Arbor, Michigan.
Chávez, Sergio J.
1976   The Arapa and Thunderbolt Stelae: A Case of Stylistic Identity with Implications for Pucara Influence in the Area of Tiahuanaco. *Ñawpa Pacha* 13 (1975):3–25.
1982a Notes on Some Stone Sculpture from the Northern Lake Titicaca Basin. *Ñawpa Pacha* 19 (1981):79–91.
1982b Notes on: Further Inquiries into the Case of the Arapa-Thunderbolt Stela. *Ñawpa Pacha* 19 (1981):189–191.

1988   Archaeological Reconnaissance in the Province of Chumbivilcas, South Highland Peru. *Expedition* 30(3):27–38.

1992   The Conventionalized Rules in Pucara Pottery Technology and Iconography; Implications for Socio-Political Developments in the Northern Lake Titicaca Basin. Unpublished Ph.D. dissertation, Michigan State University, East Lansing.

1998   Corbel Vaulted Sod Structures in the Context of Lake Titicaca Basin Settlement Patterns. *Andean Past* 5:357–408.

2002   Identification of the Camelid Woman and Feline Man Themes, Motifs, and Designs in Pucara Style Pottery. In *Andean Archaeology II: Art, Landscape, and Society*, edited by Helaine Silverman and William H. Isbell, pp. 35–69. Kluwer Academic/Plenum Publishers, New York.

2004a   The Yaya-Mama Religious Tradition as an Antecedent of Tiahuanaco. In *Tiwanaku: Ancestors of the Inca*, edited by Margaret Young-Sanchez, pp. 71–75, 81–85, 90–93. Denver Art Museum and University of Nebraska Press, Lincoln.

2004b   The Carved Slab of Copacabana. In *Tiwanaku: Ancestors of the Inca*, edited by Margaret Young-Sanchez, pp. 88–89. Denver Art Museum and University of Nebraska Press, Lincoln.

2004c   The Archaeology and Ethnography of Maize Cultivation in the Titicaca Basin. Paper presented at the 69th Annual Meeting of the Society for American Archaeology, Montreal, Quebec.

2006   Native Aymara and Quechua Botanical Terminologies of *Zea mayz* in the Lake Titicaca and Cuzco Regions. In *Histories of Maize: Multidisciplinary Approaches to the Prehistory, Linguistics, Biogeography, Domestication, and Evolution of Maize*, edited by John E. Staller, Robert H. Tykot, and Bruce F. Benz, pp. 623–629. Academic Press and Elsevier, New York.

2008   Integrating Local Communities in an Archaeological Project: Experiences and Prospects in Bolivia. In *Managing Archaeological Resources: Global Context, National Programs, Local Actions*, edited by Francis P. McManamon, Andrew Stout, and Jodi A. Barnes, pp. 257–275. Left Coast Press, Walnut Creek, California.

In press.   Identification, Definition, and Continuities of the Yaya-Mama Religious Tradition in the Lake Titicaca Basin. In *South Andean Iconographic Series*, edited by William Isbell and Mauricio Uribe. Cotsen Institute of Archaeology, University of California, Los Angeles.

Chávez, Sergio J., and David B. Jorgenson

1980   Further Inquiries into the Case of the Arapa-Thunderbolt Stela. *Ñawpa Pacha* 18:73–80.

Chávez, Sergio J., and Karen L. Mohr Chávez

1975   A Carved Stela from Taraco, Puno, Peru, and the Definition of an Early Style of Stone Sculpture from the Altiplano of Peru and Bolivia. *Ñawpa Pacha* 13:45–83.

Chávez, Sergio J., and Robert G. Thompson

2006   Early Maize on the Copacabana Peninsula: Implications for the Archaeology of the Lake Titicaca Basin. In *Histories of Maize: Multidisciplinary Approaches to the Prehistory, Linguistics, Biogeography, Domestication, and Evolution of Maize*, edited by John E. Staller, Robert H. Tykot, and Bruce F. Benz, pp. 623–629. Academic Press and Elsevier, New York.

Conklin, William J.
1983 Pucara and Tiahuanaco Tapestry: Time and Style in a Sierra Weaving Tradition. *Ñawpa Pacha* 21:1–44.

Crumley, Carole L.
1995 Heterarchy and the Evolution of Complex Societies. *Archaeological Papers of the American Anthropological Association* 6(1):1–5.

deFrance, Susan D.
1997 Vertebrate Faunal Use at Yaya-Mama Religious Tradition Sites on the Copacabana Peninsula, Bolivia. Paper presented at the 62nd Annual Meeting of the Society for American Archaeology, Nashville, Tennessee.

Erickson, Clark L.
1988 Raised Field Agriculture in the Lake Titicaca Basin: Putting Ancient Agriculture Back to Work. *Expedition* 30(3):8–16.
2000 The Lake Titicaca Basin: A Precolumbian Built Landscape. In *Imperfect Balance Landscape Transformations in the Precolumbian Americas*, edited by David L. Lentz, pp. 311–356. Columbia University Press. New York.

Flores Ochoa, Jorge A., and Magno Percy Paz Flores
1983 La Agricultura en Lagunas del Altiplano. *Ñawpa Pacha* 21: 127–152.

Haeberli, Joerg
2002 Tiempo y Tradición en Arequipa, Perú, y el Surgimiento de la Cronología del Tema de la Deidad Central. In *Huari y Tiwanaku: Modelos vs. Evidencias, Segunda Parte*, edited by Peter Kaulicke and William H. Isbell. *Boletín de Arqueología PUCP* 5:89–137.

Hutchinson, Dale L.
1997 Stability and Change: Stress and Disease Associated with the Yaya-Mama Religious Tradition. Paper presented at the 62nd Annual Meeting of the Society for American Archaeology, Nashville, Tennessee.

Isbell, William H., and Patricia J. Knobloch
2009 SAIS—The Origin, Development, and Dating of Tiahuanaco-Huari Iconography. In *Tiwanaku: Papers from the 2005 Mayer Center Symposium at the Denver Art Museum*, edited by Margaret Young-Sánchez, pp. 165–210. Johnson Printing, Boulder.

Lechtman, Heather
2002 Early Copper Artifacts from the Copacabana Peninsula. Paper presented at the 67th Annual Meeting of the Society for American Archaeology, Denver, Colorado.

Lusteck, Robert
2002 AMS Dated Maize at Tawa Qeñani. Paper presented at the 67th Annual Meeting of the Society for American Archaeology, Denver, Colorado.

Mohr, Karen L.
1966 An Analysis of the Pottery of Chiripa, Bolivia: A Problem in Archaeological Classification and Inference. Master's thesis, Department of Anthropology, University of Pennsylvania, Philadelphia.
1969 Excavations in the Cuzco-Puno Area of Southern Highland Peru. *Expedition* 11(2):48–51.

Mujica B., Elias
1990 Pukara: Une Societe Complexe Ancienne du Basin Septentrional du Titicaca. In *Inca–Perú: 3000 Ans D'Histoire*. Coordination et Rédaction Sergio Purín, pp. 156–177. Imschoot, Uitgevers, Belgium.

Palacios Ríos, Félix
1977 Pastizales de Regadío para Alpacas. In *Pastores de Puna: Uywamichiq Punarunakuna*, edited by Jorge A. Flores Ochoa, pp. 155–170. Instituto de Estudios Peruanos, Lima.

Pearsall, Deborah, and Susan deFrance
2002 Death and Dining: A Comparison of the Dietary Contribution of Plants and Animals in Yaya-Mama Ritual Contexts. Paper presented at the 67th Annual Meeting of the Society for American Archaeology, Denver, Colorado.

Pearsall, Deborah, and Midori Lee
1997 Paleobotanical Report of Five Yaya-Mama Sites from Lake Titicaca. Paper presented at the 62nd Annual Meeting of the Society for American Archaeology, Nashville, Tennessee.

Ponce Sanginés, Carlos, and Gerardo Mogrovejo Terrazas
1970 *Acerca de la Procedencia del Material Lítico de los Monumentos de Tiwanaku*. Academia Nacional de Ciencias, Publicación No. 21. La Paz.

Rowe, John H., and Catherine T. Brandel
1969–1970 Pucara Style Pottery Designs. *Ñawpa Pacha* 7–8:1–16 and Plates I–XVIII.

Steadman, Lee
1995 Excavations at Camata: An Early Ceramic Chronology for the Western Titicaca Basin, Peru. Unpublished Ph.D. dissertation, University of California. Berkeley.
2007 Ceramic Analysis. In *Kala Uyuni: An Early Political Center in the Southern Lake Titicaca Basin: 2003 Excavations of the Taraco Archaeological Project*, edited by Matthew S. Bandy and Christine A. Hastorf, pp. 67–112. California Archaeological Research Facility, University of California, Berkeley.

VI
CONCLUSION

16

A West Asian Perspective on Early Monuments

FRANK HOLE

Monumentality is commonly associated with "civilization," a tangible criterion of a state of advanced social/political/economic complexity. According to one historian, civilization (derived from *civitas*, or "city"), can be distinguished from the villages that came before by two criteria: monumental buildings and fortifications (Hallo and Simpson 1998, 30). An archaeologist writes that monuments "impose an artificial order on the use of space, they are often built on a massive scale, using enormous amounts of human labour, and they seem to have been constructed according to designs that were the expression of particular ideas about the world" (Bradley 2001, 70). The essays in this volume take a much broader view and illustrate that monuments occur in vastly different sizes and serve different purposes among societies that range from hunter-gatherers to states. It is clear from the essays in this volume that state-level society and physical coercion are not necessary to induce people to undertake monumental works. Moreover, they show that a rigid definition of monuments or monumentality does disservice to the concept. Monuments, it turns out, are in the eye of the beholder, quite literally when they consist of features constructed by humans on the landscape. It appears that few monuments in the Western Hemisphere were thrown up in a single act of construction and that their "monumentality" rose from humble beginnings but continually grew over a prolonged period. What we see today is the final product, but the process reveals insight into how and why they were built, often by small-scale community efforts.

The contrast with Western Asia is stark, both in the form of monuments and the processes by which some of them were constructed. We think immediately of the pyramids at Giza, which are among the largest constructions ever built by human labor (Lehner 2007). These were built in the course of single lifetimes, despite the enormous effort required to quarry, transport, and erect the tombs. This mobilization of human labor was on an unprecedented scale, in itself a monumental achievement. We cannot know what incentive was used to induce the laborers to work, but a clue about their organization is in the signs made by "gangs" of workers. It seems that work was subdivided among teams; possibly this is not dissimilar to the way some of the American monuments were built. We do not know how these gangs were recruited, whether their contributions were voluntary, or how long they may have been employed. We do know that they lived on site and were fed through state-run bakeries and breweries. Although the pyramids are monuments by any definition, they were meant to glorify individuals and to perpetuate the religious cults on which the livelihoods of the populace and the eternal well-being of the pharaohs depended.

The pyramids did not rise without antecedents. Earlier Egyptian rulers and officials (Dynasties 0 and 1) were buried in underground chambers that had little surface visibility; later they erected massive rectangular solid masonry *mastabas* with niched façades to contain the body. This style was transformed at the time of Djoser (Dynasty 3), whose architect Imhotep designed a large enclosure with the tomb, a *mastaba* that morphed into a nascent pyramid, inside the boundary walls at Sakkara (ca. 2700 BC). After this beginning there was an evolving sequence of ever-larger constructions that culminated in the pyramids at Giza. Monumental architecture in early dynastic Egypt consisted of pharaohs' tombs surrounded by all the necessities of an afterlife.

It is interesting to consider that the mobilization of labor for pyramid building established principles by which subsequent pharaohs could control peasant labor and perhaps their agricultural yield. While the great era of pyramid building lasted for only a century or so, the pace of state-run monumental construction projects, albeit geographically dispersed and to broader ends, especially smaller pyramids, temples, palaces and underground tombs, continued throughout Egyptian history. By the start of the third millennium BC, monumental constructions as well as domestic labor were performed by slaves. It is readily apparent that the pyramids and later monuments depended on the ability of peasants to produce agricultural surpluses, which ultimately fueled the work gangs through centralized provisioning. It is not known whether the cultivators became stonemasons or quarrymen in the off agricultural season, in effect paying themselves with the fruits of their agricultural labor.

Using the concept of monumentality in a different way, Simpson refers to the Narmar palette as "the major monument" of the reign of Menes (Dynasty 0), the legendary king who unified north and south Egypt (Hallo and Simpson 1998, 202, fig. 33). This palette, found in a temple at Hierakonpolis, established the pattern of representing the king as a military leader that remained unchanged through the millennia. The law code of Hammurabi (1792–1750 BC), a stela about the size of a man, evoked monumentality in the same way as the Narmar palette. This listing of offenses and judgments was erected in Babylon and was copied for some 2,000 years (Nemet-Nejat 1998, 225).

Monumentality in Mesopotamia took a different course than in Egypt, one with a much greater depth of time. The oldest monumental constructions in Western Asia reach back nearly 11,000 years, at the site of Göbekli in southern Anatolia (Schmidt 2001, 2006). Here, on the highest hilltop in the region, people quarried huge blocks of limestone from the bedrock to make pillars (often T-shaped) with carvings of animals and humans on their sides. These five- to seven-ton pillars, which were up to three meters tall, were erected in a circle. The excavator Klaus Schmidt sees them as open to the sky, like Stonehenge. While Schmidt argues that these are "temples" that were erected by hunter-gatherers, others see them as elaborate houses or community gathering places. What is noteworthy is that as many as 20 of these were erected, perhaps sequentially, and older ones were deliberately buried. There is no question that elaborate symbolism is associated with the pillars, which depict lions, leopards, foxes, vultures, spiders, snakes, and scorpions—all wild and dangerous—as well as vultures, ducks, and geese. The fauna from the site, in contrast, consists of gazelles, aurochs, red deer, pigs, goats, and sheep, all of which are morphologically wild. Because no domestic refuse with plant food remains, it appears as if the builders depended solely on gathered foods. A large series of bedrock mortars on the hill suggests that there was significant processing of cereals, whether wild or domestic.

It is well to underscore the age of this site. At 11,000 years old, it is some 6,000 years older than the earthworks of Giza and Stonehenge (3100–2000 BC) and more than 4,000 years older than the first small temples in Mesopotamia. A series of sites that were later than Göbekli have been located in Anatolia that were built during the early stages of the domestication of cereals. These have elaborate rooms, some of which have small carved pillars—perhaps rooms for community meetings and ceremonies (Hauptmann 1993, 1997; Hole 2000; Özdogan and Özdogan 1998). Nevertheless, none of these approaches the scale of Göbekli. It is worth noting, however, that Göbekli is not unique in southern Anatolia. Some years ago I visited another site with Schmidt that has the same kind of T-shaped pillars (which are as yet unexcavated) and numerous bedrock mortars on the surface. Similar carvings have also turned up during present-day construction projects and perhaps unauthorized digging at other possible sites; these can be seen in the museum in Urfa.

Göbekli stands atop the tallest hill in the region and overlooks (at a distance) the vast steppe of Syria. At the time the site was built it was in the midst of a rich ecotone for hunter-gatherers and incipient farmers. The quality of the environment for supporting nonagricultural people probably approached that of coastal dwellers in many parts of the world. One can make a case that agriculture started in this region, although harvesting wild stands of wheat was probably as productive as planting (Harlan 1992, 1967)

In southern Mesopotamia, the first large structures that stood above the landscape were temples dating to the mid-fifth millennium BC. Like the situation in the Lurín Valley (Burger and Salazar this volume), these started as simple rooms with a podium and through successive rebuildings gradually became larger, often encompassing earlier buildings, creating the form that came to be known as a *ziggurat*. These were stepped pyramids with a shrine on top that were named for the tutelary deity and were visible symbols of the power of the city. By the third millennium BC, all cities had a *ziggurat* whose temple was accessed via a stairway. Abundant cuneiform texts inform about the organization of labor and the meting out of rations, but we do not know the antiquity of the practice. By Late Uruk time (the late fourth millennium BC), lists with signs represented officials, priests, specialists, and common laborers, such as leather workers, herdsman, millers, and weavers (Nissen 1988, 80). While it is clear from third-millennium texts that labor, both human and animal, was provisioned from the surpluses generated by farmers and herdsmen, it has not been proven for Late Uruk times (ibid., 84). Nevertheless, it is likely that an elaborate system of accounting (perhaps similar to that of the Inca) ensured that work would be done and compensated. What may have been household and community effort in fifth-millennium Ubaid had changed to factory-like industrial production during the fourth-millennium Uruk period.

In both the Egyptian and Mesopotamian cases, the most visible monuments had a pyramidal form, but in Mesopotamia they held temples for the city god and were places for religious rites, where the populace could participate in or watch ceremonies. In Egypt, the pyramids and tombs were set apart from the settlements and presided over by priests. While religious rites were performed there, they were done out of the sight of commoners. In view of their central location in cities, there was a more of a public aspect to ceremonies at the monuments in Mesopotamia than in Egypt.

Mesopotamia, lying well outside of the zone of rain-fed agriculture, required irrigation. While irrigation systems began with small-scale gravity canals, over time they became of monumental scale, scarring the landscape for all subsequent time. Somewhat akin to the extensive terraces of the Andes, these were the backbone of sustainable subsistence. Because they served a rather mundane purpose, should these be considered monuments? In their own way, they were a national highway system, providing a means for efficient and inexpensive transportation of goods as well as providing irrigation water for the fields and domestic uses.

It appears that there are no analogues in Western Asia to the simple earth mounds so amply described in the chapters of this book or to the larger, more elaborate effigy mounds of Adena-Hopewell. This may have something to do with the nature of investigation, although that seems unlikely. It is often the case that archaeological sites in Western Asia consist of several mounds in close proximity, but in all cases that I know, each of the mounds consists of the remains of mud-brick buildings or other domestic refuse. After houses decay, they leave a mound on which later people often build. The practice in Mesopotamia is to build up rather than outward, so the mounds continue to grow in height. When the first temple mounds were built, they were the tallest structures on the horizon.

By the mid fourth millennium (Uruk period) there are numerous examples of a characteristic temple form that had antecedents in the fifth millennium (Ubaid period) in both southern and northern Mesopotamia. At the site of Uruk, the "world's first city," a series of cult or administrative buildings of stone construction date from 3600 BC. The city wall, encircling some 10 kilometers, may have been built during the time of Gilgamesh at the end of the fourth millennium BC. By any measure this wall would be considered monumental, but despite its immensity, it was razed by Sargon's soldiers around 2340 BC. Not all monuments last, and some are buried and forgotten.

We might also consider less-tangible monuments. Perhaps most important among these is the advent of writing, an Uruk-period phenomenon. Earlier, certainly by the seventh millennium, there was widespread use of tokens to denote type and quantity of goods (Kielt-Costello 2000; Schmandt-Besserat 1978, 1998). These prefigured an elaborate system of accounting that emerged during the fourth millennium (Nissen, Englund, and Damerow 1993)

We know little about the social context in which the oldest monuments were built. An extraordinarily rich environment in southeast Anatolia may have allowed bands of hunter-gatherers to congregate seasonally at Göbekli for communal hunts and celebrations. Despite the apparent wealth of food resources, it is hard to imagine hunter-gatherers building this site; such individuals were unlikely to have had previous experience in quarrying, erecting, and carving. At least in Western Europe there was a long tradition of building megalithic tombs and circular enclosures before Stonehenge was built over a period of several centuries. By contrast, Göbekli seems to have burst on the scene without antecedents, although structures continued to be erected there over some hundreds of years.

One thinks of the quarrying and erection of the great stone heads on Easter Island as a comparable physical challenge, or the enormous obelisks from Egypt that took all the mechanical skill of Roman workers to erect, even in the nineteenth century. Obviously the social systems behind these various enterprises were different, but they all depended largely on brute force manual labor. This raises the question of why.

In the case of Easter Island, it is thought that the stone heads depicted chiefs and signified competition between groups on the island. Still, that leaves unanswered why people chose the symbols that they did. Were the motives the same as those that inspired Olmec rulers to have great stone heads carved? In the Easter Island and Olmec cases, one could argue for aggrandizement of individuals. The Göbekli T-shaped columns with their strange carvings can hardly commemorate human individuals. Might they be purely decorative? Instead of hanging horns of bulls on the wall, did the pillars display much of the natural world of dangerous creatures as carvings? The specific iconographic significance may yet be discovered, but by virtue of their unique occurrence—in terms of age and subsistence base—they must be considered not only the oldest monuments in Western Asia but also the most enigmatic.

In later times one can fall back on religious fervor to explain the building of temples. People held a view that gods (of which there were many) had to be propitiated and were insatiable, so that enlargement and renewal of their shrines was a constant duty. At Susa a late fifth millennium site in southwest Iran, an enormous stepped platform was constructed (apparently very quickly) on virgin soil. Atop the platform rituals were conducted that featured offerings. The site was burned, rebuilt, and burned again before it was abandoned. I have argued that the platform was erected during a time of acute stress, as a final act of desperation before the Ubaid culture flamed out (Hole 1994, 2004, 2006, in press). The argument is that when things are going really badly, people turn to religion with greater zeal. Diamond made a similar argument concerning the end of monument building and the destruction of the monuments on Easter Island (Diamond 2005, 110). Lekson wrote of Pueblo Grande in Tucson, "Pueblo Grande's principal attraction seems oddly disjunct: monumental construction amid all that misery. The mound rose while babies died" (Lekson 2006, 784). This is also reminiscent of the Greenlanders, who continued to import luxury goods and adornments for the churches while their economy collapsed and their colonies died out (Diamond 2005, 275–276; McGovern 1994, 145).

These examples reinforce the point that monuments may have been (and are) erected for a variety of reasons. They are not confined to agricultural people or to states and they may exist for personal aggrandizement (as with Saddam Hussein's monument of crossed swords in Baghdad) or to supplicate the gods or to symbolize the power of the city or state or as arenas for competition, as with Mesoamerican ballcourts and our zeal for building ever-larger sport stadiums in America. Emulation or peer-polity competition may explain much of the proliferation of monuments in some regions.

What is a monument? We know one when we see one, but the more interesting questions are why people begin to erect monuments and what the kinds and scales of monuments say about the people and societies that constructed them. These are still matters for investigation, but the chapters in this volume provide expanded views on monumentality that will serve both as illustrations and cautionary tales.

References Cited

Bradley, R.
2001   The Birth of Architecture. In *The Origin of Human Social Institutions*, edited by W. G. Runciman, pp. 69–92. The British Academy, Oxford.
Diamond J.
2005   *Collapse: How Societies Choose to Fail or Succeed*. Penguin, New York.

Hallo, W. W., and W. K. Simpson
1998   *The Ancient Near East.* Harcourt Brace College Publishers, New York.
Harlan, J.
1992   Wild Grass Seed Harvesting And Implications for Domestication. In *Préhistoire de l'Agriculture: Nouvelles Approches Expérimentales et Ethnographiques,* edited by P. C. Anderson, pp. 21–27. Editions du CNRS, Paris.
Harlan, J. R.
1967   A Wild Wheat Harvest in Turkey. *Archaeology* 20:197–201.
Hauptmann, H.
1993   Ein Kultgebäude in Nevali Çori. In *Between the Rivers and Over the Mountains,* edited by M. Frangipane, H. Hauptmann, M. Liverani, P. Matthiae, and M. Mellink, pp. 37–69. Dipartimento di Scienze Storiche Archeologiche e Anthropologiche dell'Antichità, Università di Roma "La Sapienza," Roma.
Hauptmann, H. (editor)
1997   *Nevali Çori.* Vol. 4. Oxford University Press, New York.
Hole, F.
1994   Environmental Instabilities and Urban Origins. In *Chiefdoms and Early States in the Near East: The Organizational Dynamics of Complexity,* edited by G. Stein and M. Rothman, pp. 121–151. Prehistory Press, Madison, Wisconsin.
2000   Is Size Important? Function and Hierarchy in Neolithic Settlements. In *Life in Neolithic Farming Communities: Social Organization, Identity, and Differentiation,* edited by I. Kuijt, pp. 191–209. Kluwer Academic/ Plenum Publishers, New York.
2004   Symbols of Religion and Social Organization at Susa. (In Farsi.) *Bastanazhuhi* 12:48–61.
2006   Ritual and the Collapse of Susa, ca. 4000 B.C. In *Proceedings of the 5th International Congress on the Archaeology of the Ancient Near East,* edited by Joaquín Córdoba, Miquel Molist, Maria Carmen Pérez, Isabel Rubio, and Sergio Martínez, pp. 165–177. Universidad Autónoma de Madrid, Madrid.
in press   A Monumental Failure: The Collapse of Susa. In *Beyond the Ubaid: Transformation and Integration in the Late Prehistoric Societies of the Middle East,* edited by R. A. Carter and G. Phillip. The Oriental Institute of the University of Chicago, Chicago.
Kielt-Costello, S.
2000   Memory Tools in Early Mesopotamia. *Antiquity* 74:475–476.
Lehner, M.
2007   *The Complete Pyramids.* Thames and Hudson, New York.
Lekson, S. H.
2006   Review of Centuries of Decline during the Hohokam Classic Period at Pueblo Grande. *American Antiquity* 71:783–784.
McGovern, T. H.
1994   Management for Extinction in Norse Greenland. In *Historical Ecology: Cultural Knowledge and Changing Landscapes,* edited by C. L. Crumley, pp. 127–154. School of American Research, Santa Fe, New Mexico.

Nemet-Nejat, K. R.
1998   *Daily Life in Ancient Mesopotamia*. Greenwood Publishing Group, Westport, Connecticut.

Nissen, H. J.
1988   *The Early History of the Ancient Near East, 9000–2000 B.C.* University of Chicago Press, Chicago.

Nissen, H. J., R. K. Englund, and P. Damerow
1993   *Archaic Bookkeeping: Early Writing and Techniques of Economic Administration in the Ancient Near East.* University of Chicago Press, Chicago.

Özdogan, M., and A. Özdogan
1998   Buildings of Cult and the Cult of Buildings. In *Light on Top of the Black Hill: Studies Presented to Halet Çambel,* edited by G. Arsebük, M. Mellink, and W. Schirmer, pp. 581–601. Ege Yayinlari, Istanbul.

Schmandt-Besserat, D.
1978   The Earliest Precursor of Writing. *Scientific American* 238(6):50–59.
1998   *How Writing Came About*. University of Texas Press, Austin.

Schmidt, K.
2001   Göbekli Tepe, Southeastern Turkey. A Preliminary Report on the 1995–1999 Excavations. *Paléorient* 26:45–54.
2006   *Die bauten den ersten Tempel. Das rätzelhafte Heiligtum der Steinzeitjäger. Die archäologische Entdeckung am Göbekli Tepe.* C. H. Beck, Munich.

Contributors

David G. Anderson is professor of anthropology at the University of Tennessee, Knoxville. He has practiced archaeology for some 40 years, primarily in the southeastern United States.

Robert A. Benfer is Professor Emeritus at the University of Missouri. His research has largely been in the bioarchaeology and archaeoastronomy of Perú, related to the development of sedentism and monumental architecture. Recent articles include "La tradición religioso-astronómica en Buena Vista," *Boletín de Arqueología PUCP* 11 (2010): 53–102; and "Gourd and Squash Artifacts Yield Starch Grains of Feasting Foods from Preceramic Peru," *Proceedings of the National Academy of Sciences* 196 (2009): 13202–13206.

Bruce Bevan is a geophysicist and operator of the exploration firm Geosight. He is the author of "Archaeological Dating from Magnetic Maps: Some failures," *Journal of Environmental and Engineering Geophysics* 14 (2009): 129–144; and "Geophysical Exploration for Buried Buildings," *Historical Archaeology* 40, no. 4 (2006): 27–50.

Linda Brown is adjunct professor of anthropology at the University of Montana. She is a contributor to *The First Americans: The Pleistocene Colonization of the New World*, ed. Nina G. Jablonski (California Academy of Sciences, 2002) and coauthor of "Early Hunter-Gatherers in the Terra Firme Rainforests: Stemmed Projectile Points from the Curuá Goldmines," *Amazônica* 1, no. 2 (2009): 442–483.

Richard L. Burger is professor of anthropology at Yale University. He is an archaeologist specializing in the Central Andes and has carried out research in Peru for over three decades. He has directed excavations at Chavín de Huántar and Huaricoto in Peru's northern highlands and at Cardal, Mina Perdida, and Manchay Bajo on Peru's central coast. In Peru, Burger has taught on the archaeology faculties of Universidad Nacional Mayor de San Marcos and the Pontificia Universidad Católica del Perú. Burger also served as chair of the Senior Fellows of Pre-Columbian Studies at Dumbarton Oaks in Washington, D.C. Burger has written numerous books and articles on South American prehistory.

Sergio J. Chávez teaches archaeology and cultural anthropology at Central Michigan University. He is the director of the Interdisciplinary Yaya-Mama

Archaeological Project in the Lake Titicaca basin. He has conducted excavations in Peru (Cuzco and Puno regions), in Bolivia (Copacabana Peninsula), and in the United States (Michigan and New Haven). He has published several articles dealing with the four-field approach in Andean anthropology, including stone sculpture, iconography, pottery, ethnography, ethnohistory, linguistics, and applied anthropology.

Winifred Creamer is Distinguished Research Professor of Anthropology at Northern Illinois University. She has directed research on the development of social complexity, contact between indigenous and colonial cultures, and boundary formation in Peru, the American Southwest and Costa Rica. She is co-editor (with Jonathan Haas and Alvaro Ruiz) of *Archaeological Investigation of Late Archaic Sites (3000–1800 BC) in the Pativilca Valley, Peru* (Field Museum of Natural History, 2007).

Ann Cyphers is a senior research scientist at the Instituto de Investigaciones Antropológicas de la Universidad Nacional Autónoma de México. She has conducted research on the Preclassic period in Mesoamerica with emphasis on the Olmec culture. Her publications include *Escultura Olmeca de San Lorenzo Tenochtitlán* (UNAM, 2004).

Maura Imazio da Silveira is a researcher with the Emilio Goeldi Museum in Belém, Pará, Brazil. She received her Ph.D. from the University of Sao Paulo, Brazil.

John Douglas is professor of anthropology and department chair at the University of Montana. He is a contributor to *Hinterlands and Regional Dynamics in the Ancient Southwest,* edited by Alan P. Sullivan III and James M. Bayman (University of Arizona Press, 2007). His work has also appeared in *Latin American Antiquity.*

Francisco Estrada-Belli is Research Assistant Professor in the Archaeology Department at Boston University. Among his research interests are the beginnings of Maya civilization, remote sensing and GIS applications in archaeology. He is director of the Holmul Archaeological Project in Guatemala and a fellow of the Society of Antiquaries of London. He is author of *The First Maya Civilization: Ritual and Power before the Classic Period* (Routledge, 2011).

R. Jeffrey Frost is visiting lecturer of anthropology at California State University-Stanislaus. His research focuses on the organization and development of chiefdom polities in southern Central America. He has conducted archaeological investigations in Costa Rica, Peru, and throughout the Midwestern United States.

Jonathan Haas is adjunct professor of archaeology at the University of Illinois at Chicago and the MacArthur Curator of the Americas for The Field Museum in Chicago, Illinois. He is an anthropological archaeologist with over 30 years of field experience in both North and South America. His interests include the origins of war, the archaeology of the Southwest and Peru, the evolution of complex society, and museum anthropology. Haas has been at The Field Museum for 13 years and has been involved with development of numerous temporary and permanent exhibits, including *Chocolate*. He is the author of *From Leaders to Rulers* (Kluwer Academic, 2000); and the co-editor (with Michael Dillon) of *El Niño in Peru: Biology and Culture over 10,000 Years* (Field Museum of Natural History, 2003).

Frank Hole is Professor Emeritus at Yale. He also taught at Rice University for 17 years. He has been head of the Anthropology Division of the Yale Peabody Museum and C. J. MacCurdy Professor of Anthropology. He is a member of the National Academy of Sciences. Over a span of some 40 years, Hole has traveled and carried out archaeological, ethnographic, and land use research in the Near East, first in Iran and currently in Syria. His specialty is the history and development of agriculture and animal husbandry. Excavations at Ali Kosh and Chagha Sefid in Deh Luran, Iran, provided some of the first substantial evidence for the early stages of agriculture. His study of modern nomadic herders led to the excavation and interpretation of an 8,000-year-old herders' camp. In Syria, he has carried out a series of reconnaissance surveys and excavations ranging from the Neolithic to the Third Millennium. He has been co-principal investigator on NASA grants to study land use in Southwest Asia. Combining these land use studies with archaeological evidence, he is reconstructing a 9,000 year history of land use for the Khabur region of northeastern Syria.

Louise I. Paradis is professor at the Université de Montréal. She has directed research in Mexico, investigating the first Mesoamerican civilization in Highland Mexico and the ancient history of the Mezcala area in Guerrero. Her publications include *Histoires extraordinaires au pays des Balsas* (Université de Montréal, 1999); and "The Guerrero Region," in *The Archaeology of Ancient Mexico and Central America: An Encyclopedia*, edited by Susan Toby Evans and David L. Webster (Garland Publishing, 2001).

Thomas Pozorski is professor at the University of Texas-Pan American. He has conducted research primarily in the Andean area, investigating prehistoric irrigation and the origins of complex society on the Peruvian coast. His publications include *Early Settlement and Subsistence in the Casma Valley, Peru* (University of Iowa Press, 2006).

Joe W. Saunders is the regional archaeologist for northeast Louisiana and adjunct professor in Geosciences at the University of Louisiana at Monroe. His research is focused on the emergence of Archaic earthworks in the Southeastern United States. His publications on Archaic mounds include articles in *Science* and *American Antiquity*.

Shelia Pozorski is professor at the University of Texas-Pan American. She has conducted research in the Andean area, investigating early subsistence and the origins of complex society on the Peruvian coast. Her publications include *The Origins and Development of the Andean State* (Cambridge University Press, 2009).

Jeffrey Quilter is Deputy Director for Curatorial Affairs at the Peabody Museum of Archaeology and Ethnology (PMAE), Harvard University. His research projects in Peru and Costa Rica have tended to focus on issues of political organization. Recent publications include *The Moche of Ancient Peru: Media and Messages* (PMAE Press, 2010); and *Treasures of the Andes* (Duncan Baird, 2005).

Asa R. Randall is assistant professor at the University of Oklahoma. His work in Florida has focused on documenting the social conditions surrounding the emergence of monument construction among hunter-gatherer communities. His publications include "Remapping Archaic Social Histories along the St. Johns River, Florida," in *Hunter-Gatherer Archaeology as Historical Process*, edited by Kenneth E. Sassaman and Donald H. Holly Jr. (University of Arizona Press, 2011).

Robert M. Rosenswig is associate professor at the University at Albany–SUNY. He has directed research in Mexico, Belize, and Costa Rica, investigating the origins of agriculture and the development of political complexity. His publications include *The Beginnings of Mesoamerican Civilization: Inter-Regional Interaction and the Olmec* (Cambridge University Press, 2010).

Anna C. Roosevelt is professor of anthropology at the University of Illinois at Chicago. She is author of *Moundbuilders of the Amazon: Geophysical Archaeology on Marajo Island, Brazil* (Academic Press, 1991); and (with Egle Barone Visigalli) *Amaz'hommes: Sciences de L'Homme et Sciences de la Nature en Amazonie* (Ibis Rouge, 2010).

Lucy C. Salazar is the co-curator of the Machu Picchu exhibition and curatorial affiliate in anthropology at Yale University's Peabody Museum. She is an authority on Inca archaeology and the early prehistory of Peru. She is the co-editor (with Richard Burger) of *Machu Picchu: Unveiling the Mystery of the Incas* (Yale University Press, 2004); and (with Richard Burger) *The 1912 Yale Peruvian Scientific*

Expedition Collections from Machu Picchu: Human and Animal Remains (Yale University Publications in Anthropology, 2003).

Kenneth E. Sassaman is Hyatt and Cici Brown Professor of Florida Archaeology, Department of Anthropology, University of Florida. His field work on shell-bearing sites of the American Southeast has been situated in the Savannah and St. Johns river valleys, and now he is investigating this topic along the Florida gulf coast. He is the author or editor of eight books, including *The Eastern Archaic, Historicized* (AltaMira, 2010).

Judith Zurita-Noguera is in charge of the Phytolith Laboratory at the Instituto de Investigaciones Antropológicas, Universidad Nacional Autónoma de México. Her research field is paleoethnobotany, especially phytolith analysis, with a focus on Pre-Hispanic subsistence, traditional agricultural techniques, and paleo-landscape. Her publications include (with Ann Cyphers) "A Land That Tastes of Water," in *Precolumbian Water Management: Ideology, Ritual, and Power* (University of Arizona Press, 2006); and (with Ann Cyphers et al.) "Arqueología digital en la primera capital olmeca de San Lorenzo," *THULE* 25 (April/Octubre 2007–2008): 121–144.

Index

Page numbers in italics refer to illustrations

Abrams, Elliot, 9, 144, 379
Acatlán, Mex., 183
Acre, Ecuador, 279, 281
Agriculture: adaptations of, 153; calendars for, 212, 313, 321; and climate, 92, 153, 154, 319, 321, 403; cotton cultivation, 305, 319, 330, 367, 389; gourd cultivation, 305, 367, 389; grains/cereals cultivation, 151, 459–60; grasses cultivation, 441, 448; intensive, 16, 112, 113, 132, 152, 257, 258, 261, 264, 321; irrigation, 365, 366, 367, 368, 388, 399, 403, 420, 461; maize cultivation, 78, 84, 129, 151, 152–53, 154, 161, 270, 278, 279, 441; modern, 150, 153, 330, 436; and ocean currents, 319; and population levels, 84, 403; rituals related to, 410; and settlement patterns, 129, 152–53, 190, 258, 261, 269; and sociopolitical organization, 129, 151–52, 153, 155, 159, 193, 255, 257, 258, 278, 291; and soil quality, 153, 154, 261, 262; techniques and locations for, 141, 143, 144, 146, 154, 161, 202, 275, 279, 280, 281, 319, 431. *See also* Diet
Alaka culture, *256*, 264
Alenquer, Brazil, 273
Alexander Spring, 68
Altar de Sacrificios site, *199*, 201, 202
Alva, Walter, 314, 325
Amacuzac River, 177, 182
Amazonia: agriculture in, 261, 264, 279, 281; architecture in, 55, 264–69, 275; art in, 261, 262–64, 278, 280, 281; cosmology in, 270; diet in, 260–61, 262, 264, 267–68, 270–71, 279; exchange with, 280, 281; feasting in, 264; foraging in, 281; horticulture in, 270, 281; interaction with, 272; maps of, *256*; and migration, 263–64; modern, 267–68, 270, 271; monumentality in, 261, 262, 272, 278–79, 281; ritual activities in, 281; settlement patterns in, 261, 265, 278, 281; sociopolitical organization in, 261–62, 270, 280, 281
Amazonian Indians, 268, 275

Amazon River, *256*, 271, 272–73, 278, 279
Amenhotep, 347
Amuco Abelina, 177, 188, 192
Amuco de la Reforma, 175, *176*, 188–90
Ananatuba phase, 272, 273–75
Anatolia, 459–60, 462
Anchucaya, Peru, 404, 405, 417
Anderson, David G., 88
Andes: agriculture in, 322, 367, 436; architecture in, *290–91*, 303, 308, 322, 367, 386, 4 61; art in, 268, 444; central, 231, 236; children in, 322; climate in, 319; cosmology in, 318, 323, 346, 350, 353, 425; cultural development in, 299; diet in, 319, 322; exchange in, 367; feasting in, 305; health in, 321; interaction with, 443; labor in, 305, 411; public art in, 322; religion in, 314, 322; settlement patterns and population in, 303, 322; sites in, 268, 291–92
Andes Mountains, 401
Animals: vertebrates, 59, 61, 63, 64, 65, 70. *See also* Diet; Fish and shellfish; Iconography
Anita Grande, Costa Rica, 240
Arauquinoid phase/Tradition, 142, 271
Arboriculture, 152, 441, 448. *See also* Agriculture
Arc de Triomphe, 6
Arcelia, Mex., 188
Archaic period: agriculture during, 267; architecture from, 54, 70, 83, 114, 257, 264–67, 275; art from, 268; ceramics from, 267, 268; cultural patterns during, 233, 272; economy and diet during, 43–45, 262, 264, 267, 268, 271; group aggregation and interaction during, 95; maps of sites from, *79*; monumentality during, 8, 16, 54, 95; settlement patterns during, 42–43, 95, 217, 278; sites from, 26, 42–45, 79, 83; sociopolitical organization and status during, 8, 83, 84, 269. *See also* Late Preceramic
Architecture. *See* Mounds; Mounds, earthen; Mounds, shapes and types of; Mounds, shell; Patios; Plazas; Pyramids; Temples; Terraces

Architecture, mortuary. *See* Burials, cemetaries, and mortuary architecture
Architecture, square-room-unit, 382–84, 385, 390
Arco, Lee J., 144
Arguedas, José María, 411
Arkansas, 31, *34*, 40–41, 80
Arkansas River, 39, 41, 43
Arnold, Philip J., III, 161
Art, public, 313. *See also* Paintings; Sculpture
Artifacts: art, 268, 269; bannerstones, 30, 69; beads, 30, 31, *32*, 37, 69, 392, 443; biface reductions, 37; bronze, 443; carvings, 276; and cosmology, 213–14; decoration on, 339; earrings, 182; earspools, 123, 124; fired-earthen objects, 30, 32, 43; fishhooks and netting, 368, 389; gold, 443, 444; gourds, 339; gravel, 34; green stone, 123, 124, 182; imported, 123; Inca, *424*; jade, 200, 207, 213, 214, 217, 218; jewelry, 269, 392, *424*, 443; lithic fragments, 303; metal sheets, *424*; mica, 182; mirrors, 182; nonceramic figures and figurines, 444; obsidian, 217; ornaments, 182, 267, 268, 392; paleofeces, 59, 70; petroglyphs, 238; plaques, 182; points, 30, *31*, 37, 42, 43, 389, 446, 448; pollen, 92; ritual by-products and paraphenalia, 406, 444; serpentine, 182; shaped bone, 268; shells and shell fragments, 303, *424*, 444; silver, 444; skeletons, 207, 260, 261, 270, 271, 307, 321, 336, 403, 408, 441–42; and sociopolitical organization, 123–25, 217; speciality foods, 269; stela, 442; textiles, 392; weapons, 307. *See also* Ceramics; Paintings; Prestige goods; Sculpture; Tools
Asia Valley, 307
Aspero, Peru, *292*, 300, 326, 365
Astronomer-priests: activities of, 313, 318, 323, 341, 348, 349, 350, 351, 353; and monumentality, 313, 351; organization of, 352–53; and public art, 313; residences of, 330–31; and sun and moon rises and sets, 343
Astronomy: and architectural alignment, 324–27, 325–26, 328–29, 334, 341–50; calendar for, 313, 318, 321, 341; and constellations, 334, 342, 344, 345, 346, 348, 350; Egyptians and, 346; and events, 341, 350; Incas and, 351; instruments for, 313, 314, 323; and lunar cults, 352; modern, 351; and public art, 313;

and rituals, 350; sites associated with, 324; and solar cults, 352
Aten, Lawrence E., 67, 69
Aztecs, 130, 141, 183, 185, 214

Babylon, 459
Baghdad, Iraq, 463
Bahía Seca, Peru, 367, *370*, 375, 383, 386, 388–89, 390
Balsas River, 177, 190, 192, 194
Banana Bayou Mound, 27, *29*
Bandurria, Peru, *292*, 365
Barcelona, Spain, 304
Barrancoid phase, 276
Barriles, Panama, 235, 247
Basin of Mexico, 141, 182, 192
Bastrop, La., *34*
Bauer, Brian S., 328
Bayliss, Alex, 10
Bayou D'Arbonne (waterway), 39, 40
Bay West, 67
Béarez, L., 319
Belize, 201, 202, 203
Belmont Mound, 27, *29*
Benfer, Robert A., 319, 400
Bennett, Wendell, 442
Betton, Niederberger, 182, 188
Big Ben, 6
Blackman Eddy, Belize, *199*, 202
Blake, Michael, 114, 119, 125
Blue Spring, *55*, 64
Blue Spring state park, 57
Bluffton, Florida, *55*, 68–69
Bolivia, 142, *256*, 257, 272, 275–76, 279
Bolland, Thomas W., 9
Bonavia, Ducco, 404, 426
Boulder, Colo., 325
Brazil, 55, 142, *256*, 262–64, 265–67, 268, 275. *See also* Amazonia
Buena Vista, Peru: agriculture at, 319, 329–30; architecture at, 313, 314–18, 319, 327, 329, 330–41, 342–52; art at, 313, 339, 348, 400; astronomical alignment at, 338, 341–50, 351; climate at, 330, 344, 347; construction at, 328, 334–38; dating of, 314, 316–17, 329, 330, 336, 338; diet at, 319; extent of, 329; feasting and ceremonies at, 319, 331; location of, *16*, 329; modern incursions on, 336; occupation of, 328, 330, 331; population at, 319

Bull Brook, Mass., 80
Bullen, Ripley P., 67
Burger, Richard L., 11, 17, 255, 302, 319, 325, 326, 353, 364
Burials, cemetaries, and mortuary architecture: in Amazonia, 261, 264, 265, 269, 279, 280; in Arkansas, 80; Egyptian, 458; European, 462; in Florida, 81; in Guerrero, 175, 182, 190, *191*; in Intermediate Area, 235, 241, 242, 245, 246, 247, 248; looting of, 246; in Lower Mississippi Valley, *29*; Mississippian, 82; at Paloma, 321, 352; in St. Johns Basin, 54, 66, 67–68, 69, 80; in Titicaca Basin, 439, 443, 446

Caballete, Peru, *16*, *292*, *294*, 295, 298, 303
Caballo Muerto, Peru, 301
Cahal Pech, Belize, *199*, 202, 203, 217
Cahokia, Ill., *79*, 83–84, 85, 86, *88–89*, 90, 91, 92
Cahuacán River, 113, 115, 117, 119, 123, 131
Cahuaziziqui, Mex., 187, 188
Cajamarca culture, *290*
Calakmul, Maya Lowlands, *199*, 216
Caldwell, Joseph R., 26
California, 55, 269
Caney Mounds, La., 27, *29*, *30*, *34*, 41–42, *79*, 81
Cantileña swamp, 113, *114*, 118
Canto Grande, Peru, 327–28, 329, 330, 351
Cantón Corralito, Mex., 114, 115, 116, 117, 118, 122, 131
Cape Canaveral, Fla., 67
Capping events, 61, 66–69
Caral, Peru, *292*, 299, 300, 303, 365, 366. *See also* Chupacigarro/Caral, Peru
Cardal, Peru: architecture at, 300, 405, 406, *407*, *408*, 409, 412, 414, 415, 420; art at, 406, 414; astronomical alignment at, 325; ceramics from, 408, 409, 423; child's skull from, 408; construction at, 409, 414, 415, 420; dating of, 419; diet at, 402–3; establishment of, 417; health at, 403; lifespan of, 417; maps of, *404*; photos of, *408*, *414*; scale of, 405; sociopolitical organization at, 420; uses of, 408, 409, 423, 424
Cárdenas, Mercedes M., 325
Casa Blanca, El Salvador, 151
Casarabe, Bolivia, 276
Casma River, *370*
Casma Valley: agriculture in, 365; architecture in, 300, 364, 369, 376–80, 386, 389; artifacts from, 392; astronomical alignment in, 343; construction in, 377, 379; diet in, 365; drainages in, 389; economy in, 369, 390; interaction in, 369; labor in, 377, 391; location of, 364; maps of, *370*; settlement patterns in, 365, 369; sites in, 326, 367, 390; sociopolitical organization in, 11, 353, 364, 369, 375, 379–80
Casta, Peru, 411
Castalia, Lower Amazon, 275
Castanheira, Marajo Island, 272–75
Castells, Manuel, 12
Catholic Church, 304
Caves, 183–87, 190, 192, 262–63
Cemetaries. *See* Burials and cemetaries
Central America, 15, 241, 248. *See also* Intermediate Area
Central Valley, 241
Ceramics: and burials, 443; Chiripa-style, 438, 445; dating of, 61, 64, 65, 71–72, 202, 214, 272, 276; decoration on, 127, 182, 188, 202, 203, 204–5, 268, 272, 275, 276, 279, 313, 392, 408, 409, 438, 444, 445; Inca-style, 438, 439, 440, 447, 448; influences on, 247; and interaction, 217, 272; Late Intermediate, 438, 439; modern, 148, 267; Olmec-style, 188, 192; Orange, 71; Orange Incised, 65, 71, 72; Orange plain, 65, 71–72; origins and introduction of, 54, 113, 217, 233, 420; plain, 438; production of, 182, 268, 409, 445; Pucara-style, 445; Qalasasaya-style, 445; Qea-style, 445; quality of, 203; Ramirez Ware, 121, 123; and settlement patterns, 118, 267; and sociopolitical organization, 124, 445; St. Johns series, 72; styles of, 216, 278; Taraco-style, 445; tempers for, 78, 275; thickness of, 275; Tiahuanaco-style, 438, 439, 440, 447–48; uses of, 203, 204, 205, 217, 267, 444; Yaya-Mama, 438, 439, 440, 441, 448; and Yaya-Mama religious tradition, 445, 446; Ychsma-style, 423
Ceramics, forms of: architectural models, 444; bottles, 408; bowls, 203; ceremonial burners, 444; dishes, 203; effigies and effigy urns, 276, 444; figurines, 123, 182, 188, 192, 205, 276, 386–88; jars, 203, *213*, 214, *277*; plates, 203; pots, 267; ritual paraphenalia, 444–45; serving ware, 203; simple, 392; slabs, 444, 445; smoking pipes, *273*; stamps, *273*; statues, 444; trumpets, 444; vessels, 188, 201, 444
Cerro Blanco 2, Peru, *292*, 293–94

Cerro Lampay, Peru, *292*, 300, 305
Cerro Sechín, Peru: architecture at, 372, 375, 376, 386; dating of, 367; iconography at, 381–82, 386, 388, 390; as part of Sechín Alto Complex, 369, *371*, 375
Chalcatzingo, Mex., *176*, 183, 185, 192, 193, 215
Chancay Valley, 326, 400, 401, 402
Chang, K. C., 379
Chankillo site, Peru, 343
Chattahoochee River, 92
Chávez, Karen L. Mohr, 437, 438, 442
Chavín civilization, 330, 405, 421
Chavín de Huantar, Peru, *290*, 291, 339
Cheetam, David, 201, 205, 217
Cheniere Creek, 43
Chiapas, Mex., 201, 202, 214
Chicanel phase, 220
Chilapa, Mex., 183
Chilca River valley, 321–22
Chillón River, 319, 320, 329, 334, 344
Chillón Valley, Peru: agriculture in, 319; architecture, 330; architecture in, 400–401, 402; climate in, 319; and cultural similaries to other locations, 402; diet in, 319; and migration, 322; population in, 319; public art in, 313; sites in, 327–29, 341, 348, 399–400. *See also* Buena Vista, Peru; El Paraíso, Peru
Chilpancingo, Mex. *See* Coovisur, Mex.
Chimu culture, 386
Chiquito River, 142
Chiripa temple, Bolivia, 442, 443
Ch'isi temple, Bolivia, 439, *440*, 441, 443, 444, 447
Choctaw peoples, 91
Chontal groups, 143
Chupacigarro/Caral, Peru, 319, 326–27, 330, 331. *See also* Caral, Peru
Chuquitanta. *See* El Paraíso, Peru
Cival, Maya Lowlands: agriculture at, 218; architecture at, 204, 205–13, 215, 216, 217, 218, 219–20, 221; artifacts from, 203, 204, 212–13; astronomical alignment at, 212; cosmology and iconography at, 213–14, 215, 218, 220–21; founding of, 221; map of, *16*, *199*; rituals at, 213–14, 217; settlement patterns at, 211, 219, 220; sociopolitical organization at, 218, 219, 220
Clark, John, 114, 115, 119, 120, 161, 201, 205, 217, 297

Classic period: climate during, 157; cosmology and iconography during, 204, 213–14, 215, 218, 221, 299; ritual during, 204; sites from, 188; sociopolitical organization during, 219
Climate: and abandonment of mounds, 83; and agriculture, 153, 154, 321; changes in, 157, 159–60, 319, 320; and decline of San Lorenzo, 161; El Niños, 319, 320, 421, 422; and emergence of Mississippian culture, 92; flooding, 111, 119, 131, 141, 143, 145, 148, 150, 151, 153, 154, 160, 162n2, 273, 276, 334, 347; impact of, on architecture, 422–23; *islotes* and, 143, 159; in Mesopotamia, 461; and mound-building, 45; Olmec and, 162n3; rain, 403; and religion, 321; rituals related to, 410; and settlement patterns, 93; and sociopolitical organization, 92, 157; variations in, 162n2
Coatán River, 113, 114, 115, 116, 118
Coe, Michael, 121, 148, 153, 185, 298
Cofitachequi province, 82
Cohen, Mark, 403
Coles Creek culture, 84
Colombia, 231, 232, 233, *256*, 265, 275, 351
Columbus, Christopher, 232
Conchas phase: abandonment of sites from, 129–30, 133; agriculture during, 113, 132; architecture during, 17, 121, 122, 128–29; diet and food production during, 124, 125–28; feasting during, 129; iconography from, 127–28; maps of sites from, 114; settlement patterns during, 118–19, 131, 132; sites from, 116–17; sociopolitical organization during, 113, 116, 123–25, 129, 132
Conly mound, La., *29*, 32–33
Coolman, B., 434
Coosa paramountcy, 94
Coovisur, Mex., 175, *176*, 190, 192
Copacabana Peninsula: agriculture on, 436, 441; diet on, 441; health on, 441–42; interaction with, 443; maps of, *16*, *432*; sites on, 443, 446; temples sites on, 439; terraces on, 431–32, 434, 447, 449; terraces sites on, 439; Yaya-Mama religious tradition at, 432
Cornelison, John, 88
Cortez, Hernando, 130, 131
Cosmology and iconography: alpacas in, 445; and architecture, 200, 213–14, 216, 221, 240; Aztecs and, 214; bat-like figures in, 186; birds in, 187; Borgia, 214; centralized, 291;

Christian, 130–31; condors in, 339, 346; crocodiles in, 185, 190; ducks in, 459; and exchange, 192; foxes in, 347, 348, 349, 459; geese in, 459; gods and religious figures in, 156, 185, 204, 214, 215, 218, 221, 339, 352; and gold objects, 232; influences on, 247; and *islotes*, 156–57; jaguars in, 185, *186*, 187, 372; leopards in, 459; lions in, 459; lizards in, 185, 187, *277*; llamas in, 444; lunar and solar eclipses in, 343; maize in, 125, *127*, 214, 215, 218; Maya and, 204–5, 213–14; Mesoamerican, 192–93; Mississippian, 91; monkeys in, 276; and motifs, 204–5, 272; objects associated with, 200, 213–14, 215; Olmec, 156–57, 179, 183, 185, 186–87, 188, 190, 192, 193, 202; and paintings, 263, 280; scorpions in, 459; and settlement patterns, 138; snakes in, 459; and sociopolitical organization, 156, 220, 221, 248, 270, 381; solar eclipses in, 343; Vaticanus B, 214; vultures in, 459; and yaya, 447. *See also* Motifs

Costa Rica: architecture in, 235, 241; Atlantic region of, 241, 248; as border separating Intermediate Area sections, 233, 236; ceramics from, 241; chronology of, 232; goldworking in, 231; interactions in, 241; during late Formative period, 235; monumentality in, 231, 241, 248; scholarship on, 235, 241; sociopolitical organization in, 231, 235, 247; Southern Zone of, 241; Talamanca Mountain Range in, 233

Costa Rica Farm, Costa Rica, 240

Creamer, Winifred, 11, 302, 319, 322, 339, 353, 366, 389

Cuauhtémoc, Mex.: abandonment of, 119; architecture at, 119–23, 124, 128, 129, 132; artifacts from, 118, 123, 125–26, *127*, 132; communal activities at, 129; as Conchas phase center, 117; diet at, 124–27; elites at, 121, 122, 123, 124; feasting at, 121; function of, 117; geographic extent of, 119; iconography from, *127*; and La Blanca polity, 117, 119; labor at, 121–22; maps of, *16*, 114, 120; modern incursions on, 119; monumentality at, 113; occupation of, 113; scholarship on, 117–19, 132; settlement patterns at, 117–19, 122; significance of, 116, 117, 118; and sociopolitical organization, 123, 132

Cundisa, Bolivia, 441

Cunil complex, 202, 203

Curayacu, Peru, 323

Cuzco, Peru, *291*, 328

Cuzco Basin, *433*, 436, 442, 444

Cyphers, Ann, 11, 61, 146, 152, 154

Dalton culture, 80

Danta Pyramid. *See* El Mirador, Maya Lowlands

Dearborn, David S. P., 328

Debert, Nova Scotia, 80

DeFrance, Susan, 441

DeLeon Spring, 68

Denton Mound, 27, *29*

DeSoto, Hernando de, 82

Diamond, J., 463

Diehl, Richard, 148, 153, 308

Diet: *achira*, 305, 367, 389, 403; acorns, 33; agouti, 271; and agriculture, 268, 278, 322; alligators, 45; amaranth, 305, 441; anchovies, 389; aurochs, 459; avocadoes, 305, 367, 389, 402; beans, 305, 367, 389, 400, 402; birds, 145, 402, 443; camelids, 441, 443, 448; *cañihua*, 441; *cansaboca*, 389; cattail roots, 400; *Cavia*, 441; chilies and peppers, 305, 400, 402; *ciruela*, 402; coca, 329, 411, 443; condiments, 161; corn beer *(chicha)*, 411; crocodiles, 267; deer, 32, 44, 45, 389, 402, 441, 443, 459; duck, 441; ducks, 44; and food shortages, 150, 151, 154, 155, 159, 160; and foraging, 260–61, 270, 279, 281; fowl, 441; frogs/toads, 44; fruits, 264, 275, 279, 400; game, 260, 270, 271, 272, 275, 322; gazelles, 459; goats, 459; grains/cereals, 443, 448, 459; guava, 305, 389, 402; guinea pigs, 443; hickory nuts, 32; and horticulture, 270, 278, 279, 281; and interaction, 366, 420; invertebrates, 145; jicama, 305; legumes, 264; lima beans, 389; *lúcuma*, 305, 367, 389, 402; maize, 124, 125–27, 128, 132, 150, 151, 152, 153, 155, 261, 270–71, 278, 279, 305, 402, 403, 425, 441, 448; maize alcohol, 161; manioc, 260, 270, 271, 279, 389, 403, 420; in Mesopotamia, 459; mice/rats, 44; modern, 268, 270, 271, 330; nuts, 264, 279; *oca*, 441, 443; opossums, 32, 44; *pacae*, 305, 389, 402; palm fruits, 150; peanuts, 305, 389, 402, 425; pigs, 459; plants in, 319; potatoes, 367, 389, 403, 420, 441, 443; quinoa, 441; rabbits, 32, 44; raccoons, 32, 44, 45; and resource overexploitation, 155; root crops, 150, 152, 158, 160, 443, 448;

Diet—*continued*
   sardines, 389; sedge roots, 400; and settlement patterns, 268; sheep, 459; small animals, 264; snails, 32, 44, 45, 58–59, 64, 65; snakes, 44, 45; Solanaceae family, 305; squash, 305, 367, 389, 400, 402; squirrels, 32, 44; sweet potatoes, 367, 389, 403, 420; turkeys, 44; turtles, 32, 44, 45, 148, 150, 264, 267, 279; vegetables, 161. *See also* Agriculture; Fish and shellfish
Dillehay, Tom D., 162n3, 331
Diquís Delta, 248
Disease. *See* Health
Djoser (pharoah), 458
Dolfus, Olivier, 336
Don Hermelindo, Mex., 114, 116, 123

Early Archaic Period: economy and diet during, 25, 32–33, 45, 46, 262; food processing debris from, 323; group aggregation and interaction during, 80; settlement patterns during, 32, 46; sites from, *29*
Early Eb complex, 201, 203
Early Formative period: agriculture during, 125, 132, 151; architecture and construction during, 11, 16, 115–16, 120; artifacts from, 126; Bajío phase of, 146, 152, 159; Barra phase of, 114, 118; Cheria phase of, 114, 115, 118; Chicharras phase of, 146, 148, 152; climate during, 157, 161; Cuadros phase of, 114, 118, 131; diet during, 125, 151; *islotes* from, 146; Jocotal phase of, 114, 115–16, 118, 119, 120, 122, 128, 129; Locona phase of, 114, 117, 118, 119–20; monumentality during, 112, 175; Ocós phase of, 114, 117, 118; Ojochi phase of, 146, 147, 152, 157–58, 159; San Lorenzo A phase of, 146, 152, 159–60; San Lorenzo B phase of, 146, 152, 160; settlement patterns during, 118; sites from, *114*, 117, 118, 132, 141, 146, 175, *176*, 188; sociopolitical organization during, 123
Early Horizon: architecture and construction during, 175, 348, 406; ceramics from, 336; cultural change during, 236; economy during, 175; monumentality during, 175, 193; Olmec Horizon phases of, 175, 177, 182, 187, 188, 192, 193; at Sechín Alto site, 383; sites from, 327, 348, 406; sociopolical organization during, 175; Yaya-Mama sequence of, 441
Early Initial Period, 334

Early Intermediate Period, 236, 406
Early Preceramic, 330
Early Preclassic period, 217
Early Quimbaya period, 232
Easter Island, 462
Ecuador: ceramics from, 278; maize cultivation in, 270, 278; maps of, *256*; metalwork from, 278; mound complexes in, 272, 275, 276–78, 281, 295; shells from, 424
Egypt and Egyptians, 291, 346, 347, 392, 458–59, 462
El Bajio, Mex., 142
El Caño, Panama, 248
El Infierno, Mex., 114, 116, 117, 121, 122, 123
El Mesak, Mex., 115, 116, 119
El Mirador, Maya Lowlands, *199*, 200, 209, 216, 217
El Paraíso, Peru: architecture at, 306, 328, 330, 331, *333*, 334, 348, 349, 400; astronomical alignment at, 327, 328, 341–42, 348, 353; construction at, 297, 400; dating of, 329, 349; diet at, 319; location of, 329; occupation of, 331; scale of, 328; settlement patterns at, 331
El Remolino, Mex., 151
El Salvador, 201, 231
El Tigre, Maya Lowlands, *199*, 216
El Varal, *114*, 115
Endonino, Jon C., 69
Engel, Frederic, 322, 326, 331, 400
Era de Pando, *292*
Erasmus, Charles J., 143, 144, 379
Estero el Ponce, Mex., *114*, 115
Etowah, Ga., *79*, 86, 94
Eurasia, 264
Exchange, 190; Amazonia and, 280, 281; Andes and, 367; and cultural change, 236; decreases in, 93; Guerrero and, 175; and iconography, 192; during Initial Period, 367; during Late Preceramic period, 323; Maya Lowlands and, 214, 217, 218; Mesoamerica and, 190, 192, 193, 194, 232; Peru and, 323, 365; Peru's central coast and, 417, 420–21; during Preceramic period, 367–68; and sociopolitical organization and status, 83, 160, 218; Teopantecuanitlán and, 182, 183, 190
Exchange goods: basalt as, 443, 447; coca leaves as, 443–44, 447; condiments, 161; domestic crafted goods as, 161; foods and beverages as, 154, 155, 161, 183, 192; gold as, 232; green

stones as, 183, 190, 192; jade as, 218; obsidian as, 190, 192, 443, 447; prestige goods as, 280, 281; raw materials as, 161; ritual paraphernalia as, 161; seashells as, 183, 192

Faldas de Sangay, Ecuador, *256*, 276–78, 279
Feasting: equipment for, 204, 205, 217; evidence of, 71, 121, 305, 319, 444; and labor, 304, 305, 308; locations for, 407; remains of, 280; seasonal, 264; sites for, 121, 128, 265, 278, 407, 423; and sociopolitical organization, 83, 129, 159, 261, 280, 305
First Horizon phase, 193
Fish and shellfish: in Amazonia, 260, 264, 267–68, 270, 271, 275, 279; anchovies, 389; in art, 372; bass, 45; bony, 45; bowfin, 32, 44, 45; buffalo, 32, 44; bullhead, 32, 44; in Casma Valley, 368; catfish, 32, 44, 45; in central western Andes, 319; clams, 389; commonness of, 43–44; crappie, 44; crawfish, 32; dried, 143, 148, 149–50; drum, 32, 44, 45; as exchange goods, 368; finfish, 32; gar, 32, 44, 45; harvesting of, 145, 146, 150, 158; marine snapper, 148; modern uses of, 149–50; mollusks, 268; mussels, 32, 44, 45, 389; overexploitation of, 155; oysters, 182; at Paloma, 320; in Peru, 400, 402, 420; salted, 148; sardines, 389; shad, 45; shrimp, 150; small, 148, 149–50; smoked, 148, 149–50; sucker, 44, 45; sunfish, 32, 45; in Titicaca Basin, 441, 443, 448; in wetlands, 145. *See also* Animals; Diet
Fisheries, 147
Fishing and shellfishing, 269, 313, 319, 321, 366, 420
Florida: bodies of water in, 63; ecologic development in, 68; mortuary sites and practices in, 67–68, 80, 81; mounds and mound building in, 13, 53, 54, 67, 265; northeast, 53, 54. *See also* St. Johns Basin
Ford, James, 71
Formative period, 272–79; agriculture during, 268; architecture from, 111, 235, 257, 269; artistic industries during, 235; artwork from, 268; ceramics from, 268, 272, 273, *273*, 275; climate during, 157; culture during, 233, 275; diet during, 268, 271, 275, 279; forests during, 271; interaction during, 272; maize cultivation during, 270; monumentality during, 278–79; settlement patterns during, 235, 269,

272; sites from, 235; sociopolitical organization during, 131, 235
Fortaleza Valley, 292, 293–95, 298, 300, 303, 365
Frenchmand's Bend Mounds, La.: artifact density at, 41–42; dating of, 39; diet at, 45; features and topography of, 27, 37, 38–39, 40; layout at, 81; maps of, *29, 34, 38, 79*; modern incursions on, 37–38, 39
Fuchs, Peter, 326, 345, 372, 383

Garagay, Peru, 300, 406
Gaspar, Maria Dulce, 255
Gaudi, Antoni, 304
General Valley, 241
Geoglyphs, 327, 328, 353
Gibson, Jon, 8
Gilgamesh, 461
Giza, Egypt, 458
Global Climatic Optimum, 319
Göbekli Tepe, Turkey, 313–14, 459, 460, 462
Gonzáles Holguín, Diego, 425
Google Earth, 325, 327, 328, 332, 342
Greenlanders, 463
Grove, David, 184, 186, 188
Groves Orange Midden, *55*, 64
Guamuchal swamp, 113, *114*, 116, 118, 131
Guatemala, 113, 127, 201, 202, 204, 215
Guayabo de Turrialba, Costa Rica, 236–40, 243, 244, 247, 248
Guerrero, Mex.: agriculture in, 175; capitals of, 194; caves at, 183–87; dating of sites associated with, 192; and exchange networks, 175; funerary practices in, 190; iconography at, 187, 193; maps of, *176*; monumentality at, 175–76, 192, 193; Olmec iconography at, 183, 185, 186–87; paintings at, 183, *184–87*; sociopolitical organization at, 175, 183
Guianas, *256*, 271, 279
Guyanas, 142

Haas, Jonathan: on diet, 319; on Late Preceramic artifacts, 339; on Late Preceramic construction, 389; on Preceramic sites, 322, 366; on sociopolitical organization, 11, 351, 353, 380
Hammurabi code, 459
Harris Creek, Fla., *55*, 67, *79*, 81
Hartman, Carl V., 241
Health, 320, 321, 403, 441–42, 448

Hedgepeth Mounds, La., 27, *29*, *34*, 39–40, 41–42, *79*, 81
Hertenrits culture, 142
Hierakonpolis, Egypt, 459
Hodgson, John, 114
Hole, Frank, 18
Holmul, Maya Lowlands, 200, 201, 203–4, 215, 216, 217
Holmul K'awiil complex, 202
Holmul Pre-Mamom complex phase, *203*
Holmul River, 205, 217
Holocene period, 54, 80–82
Honduras, 29–30, 116, 128, 231
Hontoon Dead Creek (waterway), 58
Hontoon Dead Creek Complex, Fla.: architecture at, 58–61, 62, 63, 64, 81; and capping events, 66, 67, 68; dating of, 61; maps of, *16*, *55*, *59*, *60*, *79*; settlement patterns at, 61, 64; uses of, 66
Hontoon Island North, Fla., *55*, 63, 64
Hontoon Island state park, 57
Hopewell culture, 83
Hornsby Mounds, La., 27, *29*
Houston, Stephen D., 156
Huaca Candela, Peru, 404, 405, 417
Huaca del Sol, Peru, *290*
Huaca El Gallo/La Gallina, Peru, 367
Huaca Grande, Peru, *291*
Huaca La Florida, Peru, 401
Huaca Prieta, Peru, 323
Huaca Pucllana, Peru, *290*
Huacoy, Peru, 348
Huando, Peru, 326
Huanuco Pampa, Peru, 328, 407
Huapula River, 276
Huaral, Peru, 326
Huaricanga, Peru, *292*, 295, *295*, 303
Huari culture, *290*, 432, 446
Huaura, Peru, *292*
Huaura Valley, 292, 365
Huayllani temple site, 437, 443
Huaynuná, Peru, 326, 367, 368, *370*, 375, 388–89
Huayto, *292*, 295, 298
Hussein, Saddam, 463
Hutchinson, Dale, 441
Hyslop, John, 331

Ice Age, 262
Iconography. *See* Cosmology and iconography
Imhotep, 458
Incas: and architecture, 231, 233, 318, 331, 432, 444, 447, 448, 449; artifacts of, 444; and ceramics, 438, 439, 447, 448; and cosmology, 318; and labor, 391, 431, 447, 448, 460; and Lurín Valley, 406; offerings by, *424*; and public rituals, 351, 352; and roads, 6, 330; and sociopolitical organization, 351
Incised and Punctate Horizon, 272
Incised-Hachure Horizon, 274
India, 14
Initial Period: agriculture during, 402; architecture from, 17, 301, 325, 339, 341, 342, 353, 364–65, 368, 399, 400–401, 405, 408, 420, *422*, 423, 425; astronomical alignment during, 325–26, 329, 341, 342, 348; ceramics during, *387*, 392, 403; construction during, 302, 368; diet during, 319, 364–65, 388–89, 402–3, 420, 425; economy and exchange during, 367, 420; food production during, 17; health during, 321, 403; population during, 403, 420; regional differences during, 369; ritual and community activities during, 401, 408–9; sculpture from, 339; settlement patterns during, 399, 408–9, 421; sites from, 300, 301, 325, 326, 329, 330, 341, 342, 348, 365, 367, 370, 375, 383, 387, 408; sociopolitical organization and status during, 11, 17, 353, 364, 369, 389, 392, 420, 421; violence during, 372
Inka culture, 386
Instituto Geográfico Nacional, 329
Intermediate Area, 231–33, 234–35, 236, 238, 247, 248
Iran, 463
Iron Age, 14–15, 131
Islotes: architecture on, 61, 141, 147, 148, *149*, 151; artifacts from, 143; and climate, 141, 143, 145, 159, 160; construction of, 139, 143–44, 146, 158, 159, 160; and cosmology, 156–57; dating of, 146; images and maps of, *140*, *142*, *149*; locations of, 140, 141, 145–46, 162n1; modern occupation of, 143; and Olmec monumentality, 139; permanent, 151, 160; and property ownership, 146–47, 156, 158, 160; and settlement patterns, 146, 151; sizes of, 140, 144; and sociopolitical organization, 140, 151, 156, 157, 159; and subsistence resources, 145, 158–59; and trade, 160; and

transportation, 151; uses of, 139, 140, 141, 146, 147, 150–51, 155, 158, 159, 160
Izapa, Mex., 114, 117, 121, 123, 129, 130
Izapan culture, 200

Japan, 269
Jewelry. *See under* Artifacts
Jomon society, 264
Joyce, Rosemary A., 128, 130
Juengst, Sara, 441–42
Juxtlahuaca, Mex., 175, 185, 187, 188

Kanter, John, 14
Karnataka-Andhra Pradesh border, 14
Kelley, David H., 328
Kenasfena site, 438, 439
Key Marco, Fla., *79*, 82
Kidder, Alfred, II, 442
Kidder, Tristram R., 86
Kincaid, Ill., *79*, 86
King George's Island Mounds, La., 27, *29*, 42
Kirchhoff, Paul, 176
Kirker, Jennifer, 144
Knight, Vernon James, Jr., 86, 90–91
Kolata, Alan L., 162n3
Komchen, Maya Lowlands, *199*, 201
Kosak, Paul, 326
Kotosh religious tradition, 314, 322
Kuntur Wasi, Peru, *290*
Kusijata, Bolivia, 441

La Blanca, Guatemala: abandonment of, 117, 119; architecture at, 121, 128, 129, 132; artifacts from, 123, 132; labor at, 122; maps of, *16*, *114*, *199*; scale of, 116; scholarship on, 121, 132; settlement patterns at, 122, 129; significance of, 116; and sociopolitical organization, 117, 119, 123, 132, 193, 215
La Blanca polity: architecture from, 116–17, 129; artifacts from, 129–30; and diet, 124; duration of, 17, 117, 129; elites and, 121, 122; flourishment of, 119; locations of, 130, 131; and monumentality, 17, 114, 133; and settlement patterns, 122, 123, 129; sites associated with, 117, 121; and sociopolitical organization, 123–25
Labor: and agriculture, 153; calcuations of, 379; and community events, 411; and conspicuous consumption, 392; control of, 111; corvée system of, 391; as criterion for monumentality, 139; on Easter Island, 462; Egyptians and, 458–59, 462; estimates of, 8–9, 16, 87, 434–35; and feasting, 305, 308; and food production, 139; Incas and, 447; Mesopotamians and, 460; mobilization of, 3, 9, 91, 257–58, 259, 410–12, 421, 432, 448, 458, 460; motives for providing, 304–6; and mound building, 302, 303–4; and palisades, 92; and plazas, 91–92, 302; and power relationships, 91; and provision of resources, 305; recruitment of, 247; and religion, 304–6, 462–63; and rituals, 411; scholarship on, 86–87; as social act, 129; and sociopolitical organization, 11, 112, 160; supplies for, 391; Trigger on, 139; and Yaya-Mama religious tradition, 432
La Cabaña, 241
La Danta complex, Maya Lowlands, 216
La Florída, Peru, 329, 330
La Galgada, Peru, 300, 306
Lake George, 57, *63*
Lake Texcoco, 141
Lake Titicaca Basin. *See* Titicaca Basin
Lambayeque culture, *291*
La Montaña period, 232
Landscape archaeology, 13–14
Lanning, Edward P., 328, 400
La Pacifica, Peru, 328
Las Haldas, Peru, 367, *370*
Las Mercedes, Costa Rica, 240–41
Late Archaic period: architecture and sites from, *29*, 47, 113, *292*, 297, 298, 299, 300, 301–2, 303, 305, 306, 307, 308; cultural developments during, 300; economy and diet during, 25, 45, 47, 306; interaction and feasting during, 299, 305; labor mobilization during, 304–6, 308–9; settlement patterns during, 303; sociopolitical organization during, 299, 300, 301–2, 304–6, 308–9; trade during, 31–32; violence during, 306–7, 308
Late Bronze Age, 131
Late Classic period, 236
Late Formative period: architecture from, 117, 190; art from, 190; climate during, 157; diet during, 271; sites from, 117, 188
Late Horizon period, 424
Late Intermediate Period, 423, 438, 439
Late Neolithic period, 10
Late Pleistocene period, 80

Late Preceramic: architecture from, 11, 313, *315*, 316, 325, 330, 331, 336, 350, 399–401, 403; art from, 339; astronomer-priests during, 350; astronomical alignment during, 342, 348; children during, 322; climate during, 319; construction techniques during, 338, 401; cooking techniques during, 400; cosmology during, 318, 341; diet during, 319, 400; exchange during, 323; health during, 321; labor during, 400; religion during, 314, 322; ritual and community activities during, 401; settlement patterns during, 365; sites from, 313, 314, *315*, 319, 323, 326, 327–29, 330, 353, 399–400; sociopolitical organization during, 322

Late Preclassic period: architecture from, 205, *206*, 207–12, 215–16, 219; ceramics from, 203, 220; sculpture from, 204, 205, 320; settlement patterns during, 211, 219; sociopolitical organization during, 221

Late Uruk time, 460

Late Woodland period, 84

Latin America, 255, 269–70, 279. *See also* specific locations

La Tolita culture, 278

La Venta, Mex.: architecture at, 128, 156, 175, 179, 185; cultural developments at, 215; iconography at, 298; and interactions, 200; location of, 215; motifs found at, 185; mound complex at, 298; as Olmec capital, 141, 156, 192, 193; during Olmec Horizon II phase, 193; sculpture at, 298; and Veracuz-Tobasco, 193; wetlands near, 141

La Victoria, Mex., 121

La Zarca, Mex., 114, 116, 117, 121, 122, 123

Lekson, S. H., 463

Lewis, R. Berry, 13

Lima, Peru, *256*, 290, 404

Limp, W. Frederick, 145

Lindenmeier, Colo., 80

Little Egypt, Ga., *79*, 94

Little Ice Age, 93

Little Salt Spring (mortuary pond), 68

Live Oak Mound: capping events at, 66, 67, 68, 81; characteristics of, 61–62, *63*; construction of, 62, 64; dating of, 58, 62; maps of, *55*, *59*, *79*; modern incursions on, 62; uses of, 66

Llano de Mojos/Moxos, Bolivia, 142

Llanos de Mojos/Moxos, Bolivia, *256*

Loma Alta, Ecuador, 324

Lomeríos, 182, 188. *See also* Teopantecuanitlán, Mex.

Lorenz, Bernard, 345

Los Chimus, Peru, *370*

Los Naranjos, Honduras, 111, 130

Louisiana, 25–29, 31, 32, 33–45, 46, 298

Love, Michael W., 129

Lower Amazon, 257, 263, 264, 265, 268, 272, 275, 276. *See also* Amazonia

Lower Jackson Mound, La., 27, *29*, *34*, 41–42

Lower Mississippi Valley, 25–29, 31, 45–47

LSU Campus Mounds, 27, *29*

Lunagómez, Roberto, 146, 152, 154

Lurín River, 403, *404*, 423

Lurín Valley: agriculture in, 406, 411; architecture in, 17, 300, 399, 401, 404, 408, 417, 420, 460; astronomical alignment in, 325; ceramics in, 409, 420; construction in, 302, 405–6, 411, 412, 417, 420, 422; cultural similiarity in, 402; diet in, 403, 420, 421; exchange and interaction in, 417, 420–21; ideology in, 417; Incas and, 406, 426; labor mobilization in, 410–12, 420; modern incursions on, 404; population in, 406, 410, 417, 424; settlement patterns in, 399, 408; sites in, *404*, 408, 417; size of, 404; sociopolitical organization in, 17, 399, 406, 409–10, 417; Spanish conquest in, 406; topography of, 422

Mackie, E. W., 325

Macon Plateau, Ga., *79*, 94

Maize. *See under* Agriculture; Diet

Mallku Pukara temple, Bolivia, *435*, 438, 439, 443, 444, 447

Malpaso, Peru, *404*, 405

Malpass, Michael A., 330

Mamom complex, 202, 203, 220

Manchay Bajo, Peru: agriculture at, 424; architecture at, 405, 409, 412, 421, *422*, 423, 424; artifacts from, *424*; ceramics from, 409; construction at, 409, 412, 421; dating of, 419; flooding at, 423; labor mobilization at, 421; location of, *404*, 423; origin of name of, 425; scale of, 405; uses of, 409, 423–25

Manchay culture, 402–3, 415, 420–21, 423, 426

Marajoara phase, 273–75

Marajó Island, *16*, 142, 272

Marksville, La., *79*, 83

Marsh Arabs, 143
Martínez Donjuán, Guadalupe, 177, 179, 182
Maya (people): and architecture, 231, 233; and caves, 183; and cosmology, 156, 204–5, 213–14, 220, 221; and sociopolitical organization, 219
Maya Lowlands: agriculture in, 200, 202, 218; architecture in, 198, 201, 217, 218; ceramics from, 201–5, 216, 217, 220; ceremonial centers in, 218; climate in, 212; cosmology and iconography in, 218; craft specialization in, 214, 218; cultural change in, 219–20; exchange and interaction in, 205, 214, 217, 218; migration to, 200, 201, 202, 216; monumentality in, 198, 221; and Olmec, 200; settlement patterns in, 202, 205, 217, 218; sociopolitical organization in, 198–200, 216, 217, 218, 221
Maya region, 130–31, 298. *See also* Maya Lowlands
Mazatán estuary, 114
Mazatán zone: abandonment of, 116, 122, 123, 129, 131, 132; Early Formative sites in, 115; maps of, *114*; political centers in, 116, 117, 131; scholarship on, 114, 115; settlement patterns in, 118, 119; sociopolitical organization in, 123, 129
McAvoy, Fachtna, 10
Meador, Sara, 319
Medieval Warm Period, 92
Menes, 459
Mesoamerica: agriculture in, 175, 193; architecture in, 90, 141, 182; caves in, 183; cosmology and iconography in, 215; cultural change in, 236; diet in, 148; exchange and interaction in, 175, 176–77, 190, 192, 193, 194, 232; iconography in, 192–93; interactions in, 193, 217; and Intermediate Area, 231; monumentality in, 15, 16, 112, 174, 194, 221, 297, 298; pottery production in, 113; prestige goods from, 247; settlement patterns in, 193; sociopolitical organization in, 175, 193
Mespotamia, 459–61
Mexico, 55, 113, 138, 143, 215, 217, 298. *See also* Maya Lowlands; Soconusco, Mex.
Mexico City, Mex., 131
Mexico D. F., *176*
Mezcala-Balsas River, 182
Michoacan, Mex., *176*, 190, 192
Middle Archaic period: architecture and sites from, 26–30, 33–45, 46, 47, 68, 70, 113; artifacts from, 31, 32, *33*, 37, 41; economy and diet during, 25, 33, 41, 42, 43–44, 45; settlement patterns during, 32, 41–42; technology during, 26; trade during, 31, 39–40
Middle Formative Conchas phase, 113, 116, 128, 132
Middle Formative period: agriculture during, 127; architecture from, 112, 128, 132, 141, 190, 192; art from, 190, 192; Duende phase of, 114, 118; early, 116, 129; Escalón phase of, 114, 118; Frontera phase of, 114, 118; Guerrero sites from, 192; inconography during, 127; monumentality during, 175; settlement patterns during, 118–19; sites from, 112, *114*, 117, 128, 130, 141, 175, *176*, 188; sociopolitical organization during, 129, 132; tools from, 127. *See also* Conchas phase
Middle Horizon, 425
Middle Preceramic, 319, 320, 321, 330, 352, 353
Middle Preclassic Mamom phase, 203
Middle Preclassic period: architecture from, 201, 205, *206*, 207, *208*, 209, 211, 212; ceramics from, 203; cosmology and iconography during, 204, 214, 218; Cunil phase of, 203; Early Eb phase of, 203; Mamom phase of, 203; monumentality during, 221; sculpture from, 201; settlement patterns during, 211, 219
Middle Woodland period, 83, 84
Mid-Holocene period, 86
Milone, E. F., 328
Mina, Brazil, 264
Mina Perdida, Peru: architecture at, 405, 406, 409, 412, 414–18, 417, *418*, 422, 425; ceramics from, 409, 417; construction at, 409, 414–17, *416*; dating of, 417, 419; diet at, 402–3; labor at, 415; lifespan of, 422; location of, 405; looting of, 412, 415, *418*; maps and photos of, *404*, *405*; and modern mythology, 425–26; scale of, 405, 425, 426; uses of, 409, 425
Mission San Luis, Fla., 79, 82
Mississippi (state), 28, *29*, 31, 46, 69
Mississippian culture, 78, 79–80, 84–85, 91, 92
Mississippian period, 78, *79*, 82–83, 84, 87, 92–93
Mississippi River and Valley, 31, *34*, 81, 84
Moche civilization, 290, *348*
Moche Valley, 301

Moctezuma, 130
Monte Alban, Mex., *176*, 298
Monte Alegre, Brazil, *256*, 263, 271
Monte Sano Mounds, La.: artifacts from, *32*, 39; dating of, 39, 45; features and topography of, 39, 40; maps of, *29*, *79*; mentioned, 81; statistics for, 27
Monumentality: activities associated with, 95; and agriculture, 112, 113, 255; and astronomy, 313; beliefs associated with, 81; categories of, 174, 175; cave paintings as examples of, 183; and climate, 92; and conspicuous consumption, 4; critieria of, 156, 162; cross-cultural patterns of, 221; definitions of, 56, 57, 233–34; early examples of, 192, 194; as evidence of cultural change, 221; factors of, for study, 94; and funerary practices, 190; and interaction, 272; during Late Holocene period, 82; during Mid-Holocene period, 80–81; during Mississippian period, 94–95; and mortuary behavior, 81; origins of, 53, 198, 215, 219, 221; pervasiveness of, 91; and political institutions, 198; and power relationships, 91; process of, 94–95; purposes of, 123; rarity of, 289; regional patterns of, 300; and settlement patterns, 94–95, 262; and sociopolitical organization, 6–7, 56–57, 112, 122–23, 130, 132, 175, 219, 221, 255–59, 289–91, 364; symbolism of, 111; timing of, 93; uses of, 174; variations in, 95; and writing, 462
Moore, Clarence B., 54, 68
Morelos, Mex., *176*, 182, 193
Moseley, Michael E., 162n3, 318
Motifs: animal, 187, 459; anthropomorphic, 276; avian, 204, 215; biomorphic, 272; bloodletters, 203, 204; ceremonial clothes, 183; circular, 185; cleft, 179; clefts, 203, 204; comets, *263*; and cosmology, 204–5, 263, 272, 445; crosses, k'an, 203, 212–13, 214, 215; dignitaries, 183; double line-break, 188; double line breaks, 182; eclipses, 263; feline, 444; Feline Man, 446–47; flamed eyebrow, 203; foxes, 339; geometric, 185, 268, 272, 276, *277*, 444, 445, 447; headdresses, 183; heads with rayed appendages, 445; human, 459; human faces, *277*; humanoid, 444; human-reptile-feline, 182; hybrid beings, 187; incision, 276; interpretation of, 446; llamas, 339; Maize God, 204, 214, 215; male and female personages, 445; Mesopotamian, 459; moons, 263; music brackets, 203; from Olmec Horizon II phase, 182; parallel-line incision, 275; planets, 263; punctuation, 275; reptilian, 204; right hands, 185; smoking pipes, 272; spirit animals, 272; spotted felines, 445; Staff God, 339; stamps, 272; St. Andrew's cross, 179, 185; stars, 263; step-frets, 203; suns, 263; supernatural, 444; thrones, 183; vertically divided eyes, 445; were-jaguars, 184–85; Woman with Alpaca theme, 445; woven designs, 203; and Yaya-Mama religious tradition, 446; zoned incision, 275; zoomorphic, 268, 276, *277*
Mounds: characteristics of, 365; as complexes, 85–86; and conspicuous consumption, 392; construction and destruction of, 90–91, 93; construction of, 86–88, 91, 297, 302, 365, 368, 463; and cosmology, 248; dating of, 85; Eurasian Mesolithic, 264; layout of, 246, 297, 298, 367, 369, 372, 376; Lower Mississippi Valley, 26; maintenance of, 302; Mesopotamian, 461; Mississippian, 82, 90–91, 93–94; numbers of, 247; platform, 84; residential, 276; scale of, 272, 281, 301; and settlement patterns, 275; uses and functions of, 53, 128, 129, 238, 246, 247, 273, 300–301, 304, 372–73, 382; from Woodland period, 82
Mounds, earthen: abandonment of, 83; ages of, 25, 54; as burial sites, 69, 83; complex, 279; construction of, 279; dating of, 81; from Formative period, 257; images of, *239*; layout of, 279; roots of, 269; scale of, 128, 279; uses of, 26, 54, 128, 276, 279, 280; variation among, 46; from Woodland period, 83
Mounds, shapes and types of: animal forms, 276; circular, 241, 275; conical, 7, 17, 27–28, 29, 36, 40, 112, 116, 121, 124, 128, 129, 132, 273, 298; dome, 27–28, 36; effigy, 334, 348, 353, 461; geometric, 279, 280; human forms, 276; oval, 275; platform, 40, 85, 91, *293*, 297, 298, 302, 303, 313, 314, 318, *332*, 334–38; pyramid, 90, 91, 298; rectangular, 238, 276; ridge, 27–28; ring, 83; round, 273; stoneface, 238; U, 13, 65, 83
Mounds, shell: abandonment of, 83; ages of, 25, 54, 57, 58; agriculture at, 267; architecture associated with, 265, 267, 269; art associated with, 268; artifacts from, 265, 267, 269; burials at, 265, 267, 269, 278; capping events

at, 72–73; ceramics associated with, 268; composition and construction of, 53–54, 56, 68–69, 70–71, 81, 265, 275; dating of, 62, 70, 81, 264–65; destruction of, 54; diet at, 267; dimensions of, 58, 114; illustrations and maps of, *55, 114, 266*; life cycles of, 66; linear, 58; modern incursions on, 54, 64, 265, *266*; occupation of, 113–14; and settlement patterns, 70, 72, 265–67, 278; shapes of, 58, 64, 67, 71, 72; and sociopolitical organization, 71; subsequent occupation of, 275; symbolic context of, 68, 69, 70–72, 73; uses of, 54, 56, 57, 66, 70–71, 265, 268–69, 278; from Woodland period, 82–83

Moundville, Ala., *79*, 86, 94

Mount Taylor period: burials from, 65, 66, 67, 68–69; mound sites from, 58, 62; Orange period as outgrowth of, 64; settlement patterns during, 69–70; shell ridges from, 64; sites from, *55*

Mundo Perdido complex. *See* Tikal, Maya Lowlands

Muñoz, L. Miranda, 319

Murra, John, 441

Muruqullu temple site, 435, *436*, 439, 442, 443, 448

Muskogean peoples, 91

Nahua peoples, 156

Nakbe, Maya Lowlands, 198, *199*, 200, 201, 209, 216

Nan Choc, Peru, 295

Naranjo River, 113, 114, 119, 123, 131

Narmar palette, 459

Nazca, Peru, 327, 328

Neolithic period, 8, 14–15, 313–14, 323

Nicaragua, 231

Niederberger, Christine, 177

Nolan Mounds, La., 27, *29*

Norte Chico region, Peru: agriculture in, 305, 307, 366; architecture, 366; architecture in, 293–95, 297–98, 299–300, 306, 308, 323, 353, 368, 369; collapse of, 320, 323; dating of sites in, 322; diet in, 305, 366; economy in, 366, 369; feasting and public ceremonies in, 305, 308, 366; influence of, on other areas, 389; and interaction, 366; interaction in, 299, 308; labor in, 307, 308–9; locations making up, 292; population in, 302–3; residential architecture in, 303; settlement patterns in, 367, 369; sites in, *292*, 295, 296–97, 300–304, 305, 306; sociopolitical organization in, 11, 299–300, 305, 306, 307–9, 365, 366–67, 369; and violence, 306–7, 308

Oaxaca, Mex., *176*, 193

Oaxaca Valley, 204, 298

Ogeechee River, 81

Ohio, 83

Ojo de Agua, Mex.: architecture at, 128, *129*, 130; characteristics of, 117; location of, 116; maps of, *114*; significance of, 118; and sociopolitical organization, 122

Olmec: and agriculture, 151, 152–53, 154–55, 158; and arboriculture, 152; and architecture, 156; artifacts of, 190; and burials, 190; captials of, 192; and climate, 162n3; cosmology and iconography of, 156–57, 174, 176, 179, 186–87, 188, 190, 192, 193, 202; diet of, 148–49, 152, 158; and Maya Lowlands, 200; and monumentality, 138, 139–40, 156, 161; and mound construction, 298; and painting, 183, 184, 185, 186; and sculpture, 188, 201; and settlement patterns, 140, 141, 157–58; sites associated with, 190; and sociopolitical organization, 151, 462. *See also* Islotes

Olmec Horizon phase. *See under* Early Horizon period

Omitlán River, 182, 192, 194

Orange Mound, Fla., *55*, 68

Orange period, 63, 64, 71

Orinoco, 271

Ortega, Allan, 144

Ostra Site, Peru, 307

Oxtotitlán, Mex., 175, 183–88, 190, 192

Pacbitun, Belize, 202

Pachacamac, Peru, 341, 406, 424

Paintings: cave, 183–87, 190, 192, 262, 263; and cosmology, 218, 221, 263, 280, 313; dating of, 192, 263; locations of, 280; and migration, 263–64; and monumentality, 187; Paleoindian, 257, 263, 278; panel, *263*; photos of, *184, 186, 187, 263*; Preclassic Lowland Maya, 204; scale of, 263; and shamanism, 272; styles of, 280; symbolism of, 183, 185; in temples, 339

Paleoindian period: agriculture during, 264, 267; art from, 278; diet during, 262, 264, 267; group aggregation and interaction during, 81; paintings from, 257, 263; settlement patterns during, 262; shell mounds from, 264; sites from, 80
Pallat'i site, 439, 442
Palmar Sur, Costa Rica, 248
Paloma, Peru, 319, 321, 323, 324, 330
Pampa Chica, Peru, 327
Pampa de Cueva, Peru, 329
Pampa de las Llamas-Moxeke, Peru: architecture at, 300, 372, *373*, 376, 382, 383–84, 386, 389–90, 391, 392; ceramics from, 386–88; construction at, 377, 378; diet at, 388–89; iconography at, 381–82, 384, 388, 390, 392; labor calculations for, 377; layout of, *374*, 378, 389; map of, *370*; orientation of, 376; as part of Sechín Alto Complex, 375; restricted access at, 384–85; scale of, 377, 378–79; site planning at, 376
Pampa San Jose, Peru, *292*, 298
Panama, 231, 235, 241, 248
Panteón de la Reina. *See* Rivas-Panteón de la Reina complex, Costa Rica
Papagayo River, 182, 192, 194
Parka, Peru, *404*, *405*
Pasion region complex, 201–2
Paso de la Amada, Mex., 114–15, 116, 117, 120, 131
Patios: in Guerrero, 179; in Intermediate Area, 233, 238, 240, 245, 246, 247; in Maya Lowlands, 211; on Peru's central coast, 408, 409, 412, 414. *See also* Plazas
Pativilca Valley, 292, 295, 298, 300
Patterson, Thomas, 328, 400, 401, 403, 404
Pauketat, Timothy R., 85, 87, 92
Pearsall, Deborah, 441
Pedra Pinta do Panel do Pilao, 263
Peru: agriculture in, 319, 388; canals in, 403; central coast of, 399; coastal valleys in, 313; construction in, 420; cosmology in, 323, 343, 352; diet in, 323, 420; economy in, 318–19, 365; exchange in, 323, 365; fishing in, 319; geoglyphs in, 327, 328; highlands of, 410; Initial Period occupation in, 389; interaction in, 368, 420–21; introduction of ceramics in, 420; labor mobilization in, 410–11, 420; lunar alignments in, 343; maps of, *256*, *370*; monumental architecture in, 13, 16, 365, 420; monumentality in, 291, 352, 353, 365; mound complexes in, 298; Norte Chico region of, 291–92; Pacific coast of, 291; population in, 330; religion in, 314; sites in, 313, 314, 319, 324; sociopolitical organization in, 11, 17, 365. *See also* Norte Chico region, Peru
Peruvian Amazon, 271–72
Pino Matos, José L., 328
Pinson, Tenn., *79*, 83
Pinturas complex, Maya Lowlands, 216
Pitluga, Phyllis B., 328
Plazas: at Buena Vista, 316, 336; at Cardal, 325; in Casma Valley, 367, 368, 369, 377, 378–79, 381, 384, 389, 390, 391, 392; at Cival, 203, 204, 207, 209, 211, 212, 214, 215, 217–18; at Guayabo de Turrialba, 236, *237*, 238, *239*, 240, 247; at Homul, 203, 204; Inca, 407; in Intermediate Area, 233, 244; at La Cabaña, 241; longevity of tradition of creating, 80, 95; at Los Naranjos and Yarumela, 111; in Lower Mississippi Valley, 30; in Maya Lowlands, 200, 218, 220; and Mississippian culture, 78, 79, 82, 85; at Moundville, 86; in Norte Chico, 293, 297–98, 301, 302, 304, 305, 323, 368, 369; on Peru's central coast, 401, 406–8, 423, 424; photos of, *408*; at Rivas-Panteón de la Reina, 242, 245, 247; at Shiloh, 92; significance of, 13, 91–92; sizes of, 378; in Soconusco region, 117, 120; in Supe Valley, 336; at Tikal, 218, 219
Pleistocene period, 35, 36, 37, 38, 39, 43, 244
Plum Creek, La., *34*, *42*, 43–45
Polychrome Horizon, 272
Ponds, mortuary, 67–68
Ponta do Jauari, 272, 273
Pool, Christopher A., 154
Poopó Lake, 443
Porvenir, Peru, *292*, 295, 298
Postclassic period, 144
Pottery. *See* Ceramics
Pottery Archaic period. *See* Archaic period
Poverty Point, La.: architecture at, 70, 86, 91; construction at, 83–84, 88, 298; layout of, 298; as local phenomenon, 47; maps of, *29*, *34*, *79*; occupation of, 298
Poverty Point period, 25, 26, 32, 45, 47
Pozorski, Sheila, 11, 326, 330, 353
Pozorski, Thomas, 11, 301, 326, 330, 353
Preceramic period: agriculture during, 16, 368; and antecedents of Sechín Alto polity, 389; architecture from, 16, 62, 368, 369, 389; artifacts from, 448; burials from, 448; diet

during, 367–68, 388; economy during, 368; exchange during, 367–68; health during, 403; religion during, 318; settlement patterns during, 16, 367, 368; sites from, 366, 367; sociopolitical organization during, 366
Preclassic period, *199*, 200, 205, 220–21
Pre-Mamom: ceramics from, 199, 201–5, 214, 217, 220
Prestige goods, 235, 236, 247, 261, 280, 281, 392
Provincial Pucara styles, 445
Proyecto Arqueológio Norte Chico (PANC), 303
Pucara styles, 445
Pucara temple site, Peru, 442, 443, 446
Pueblo Grande, Ariz., 463
Pyramid of the Sun, 183
Pyramids: at Anchucaya, 405; astrologer-priests and, 351, 353; at Cardal, 405, 417; in Chancay Valley, 401–2; in coastal Peru, 399, 400, 403, 404, 410, 423; in Egypt, 291, 392, 458, 461; as examples of monumentality, 3, 12, 87, 111; at Huaca Candela, 405; in Lurín Valley, 406; at Malpaso, 405; at Manchay Bajo, 405, 421; in Maya Lowlands, 205, *206*, 207–9, 211, 212, 215, 217, 218, 219, 220; in Mesoamerica, 16, 90; in Mesopotamia, 460, 461; at Mina Perdida, 405, 415–17, 425, 426; Mississippian, 84–85, 91; Olmec, 299; in Peru, 314; in Rímac Valley, 401; in Soconusco, 112, 113, 121

Qhot'a Pata, Bolivia, 441
Quelccaya ice cores, 319
Quilter, Jeffrey, 319, 331, 341, 400
Quintero, Lauro Gonzáles, 190
Quipa, Peru, 323
Qupakati, Bolivia, 441

Randall, Asa R., 29, 297
Rapoport, Amos, 12
Real Alto, Ecuador, 295, 324
Real Xe, 202
Red River, 32
Reidhead, Van A., 145
Reilly, Kent, 128
Reitz, Elizabeth J., 320
Renfrew, Colin, 8, 15, 364
Republic Groves, Fla., 68
"Rey" (engraving), 183
Reyna Robles, Rosa, 177, 190
Rímac River, 319

Rímac Valley, 300, 328, 342, 401, 402, 406, 411
Río Buenavista, 241
Río Chirripó Pacifíco, 241
Río General, 241
Rio Huaura, *292*
Rio Jesus zone, 116, 123, 129
Rio Negro, 279
Rio Seco, 400
Riser Mound, La., 27, *29*
Rivas-Panteón de la Reina complex, Costa Rica, *16*, 236, 241–46, 247, 248, 248n1
Rocky Mountains, 325
Roosevelt, Anna C., 56
Rosenswig, Robert, 7, 255, 297, 364
Ruggles, Clive, 343
Ruiz, Alvaro, 339, 366, 389
Russo, Michael, 26, 45, 70–71

Sacnab, Guatemala, 201
Sacsaywaman, Peru, *291*
Sagrada Familia, 304
Sakkara, Egypt, 458
Salazar, Lucy, 11, 17, 302, 325, 326, 353
Salinas de Chao, Peru, 306, 314, 325, 330
Salinas la Blanca, Mex., 114, 115
Salisbury Plain, Eng., 8
San Bartolo, Maya Lowlands, 204, 216, 218, 221
Sandweiss, Daniel H., 255, 319, 321
San Francisco Bay area, 55
Sangay. *See* Faldas de Sangay, Ecuador
San Jacinto, Peru, 401, 402
San José Mogote, Mex., 192, 193, 298
San Jose phase, 204
San Lorenzo, Mex.: agriculture at, 151, 152, 153–54; architecture at, 112, 138, 153–54, 156, 160, 179, 185; construction at, 11, 138–39, 298; decline of, 161; labor at, 16, 112; map of, *16*; maps of, *142*; modern, 143–44, 149–50; monumentality at, 161, 174–75; motifs at, 185; as Olmec capital, 138; during Olmec Horizon 1 phase, 192, 193; and Olmec iconography, 193; population of, 144, 159–60; resources in areas surrounding, 145; sculpture at, 16, 112; settlement patterns at, 138, 139, 142, 152–53, 160; sociopolitical organization at, 138, 153, 155, 160, 192; and transportation, 161. *See also* Islotes
San Lorenzo polity, 16
San Lorenzo Tenochtitlán Archaeological Project, 143

San Pablo Nexpa, Mex., 182
Santarem, Brazil, 256, 271, 275, 276
Santarem culture, 279
Santarem phase, 275
Santa Valley, 307
Saqqara, Egypt, 291
Sargon, 461
Sassaman, Kenneth E., 29, 30, 297
Saunders, Rebecca, 26, 71
Savannah River, 81, 92
Schaan, Denise P., 142
Scheele, Harry, 404
Schmidt, Klaus, 353, 459, 460
Schmidt, Paul, 183
Scioto Valley, 79, 83
Sculpture: animal forms, 339, 347, 348; barro (mud plaster), 346–48, 349; bas-relief, 188; busts, 339; of chief-shamans, 279; dating of, 192; on Easter Island, 462; elements of, 188–90; of elites, 279; forms of, 179; human forms, 16, 348, 462; iconography of, 462; images of, 180; life-size, 235; low-relief, 313; "mask," 204; Menacing Disk, 339, 340, 346–48, 349, 350, 352; monumental, 174, 175, 179; and monumentality, 190; motifs on, 179, 182, 205; Olmec, 201, 298; Olmec style, 192; painted, 445; photos and drawings of, 189; as public art, 313; and Pucara style, 444, 445; sizes of, 444; and sociopolitical organization, 235; statues, 13, 444, 445; stone, 112, 138, 235, 238, 442, 444; three-dimensional, 313; and Yaya-Mama religious tradition, 433, 442, 444, 447
Sechín Alto, Peru: architecture at, 300, 384, 385, 386, 390, 392; astronomical alignment at, 326; ceramics from, 386–88; construction at, 377–78; dating of, 379; diet at, 388–89; function of, 370–72, 389; labor required at, 377, 378; layout of, 378; location of, 326, 345, 370; maps of, 371; materials used at, 376–78; occupation of, 383; as part of Sechín Alto Complex, 375; restricted access at, 384, 385; scale of, 326, 364–65, 376–77, 378–79; and Sechín Alto Complex, 369
Sechín Alto Complex, Peru, 16, 369–72, 375, 376, 380–81, 387
Sechín Alto polity: agriculture within, 389; architecture within, 367, 369, 382–84, 385–86, 389, 390, 391, 392–93; artifacts from, 390; characteristics of, 326; conspicuous consumption within, 378; construction within, 390; control within, 390–91; diet in, 388–89, 392; duration of, 389–90, 391; economy within, 389, 390; iconography within, 390; labor within, 391; leaders of, 380–82, 385, 388, 389–90, 391, 392–93; and Norte Chico region, 389; population of, 384; restricted access within, 385, 391; ritual and public gatherings within, 390, 392; significance of, 364, 391; site planning within, 376; standardization within, 385–88, 390; structure of, 11, 353, 372–73, 375, 390, 391
Sechín Bajo, Peru: architecture at, 367, 368, 375, 383; astronomical alignment at, 314, 326, 342, 353; function of, 372; maps of, 371; and Sechín Alto Complex, 369, 375
Sechín River, 369, 371, 378
Seibal, Maya Lowlands, 199, 201, 202, 218
Serra de Lua, Brazil, 263
Settlement patterns: and agriculture, 129, 152–53, 258, 261, 269; and architecture, 219–20; camps, 271; and ceramics, 267; and climate, 93; and cosmology, 138; and diet, 258, 268; and ecological change, 68, 73; elites and, 369; fishing villages, 265, 278, 307, 319, 322, 402; hamlets, 190, 271, 272, 408; hilltop, 205, 206, 211, 217, 219; and horticulture, 268; layout of, 265; and monumentality, 16, 262, 275, 279–80; nomadic, 16, 232, 278; nucleated, 276; Paleo-Indian, 233; permanent, 205, 217, 273, 278; residential, 25, 46; sedentary, 25, 261, 267, 269, 322, 366; semi-nomadic/semi-sedentary, 205, 217; and shell mounds, 265–67; and sociopolitical organization, 71, 72, 73, 124, 129, 193, 257; sustained or repeated, 69; urban, 261, 269; villages, 16, 123, 190, 202, 205, 217, 265, 267, 269, 272, 279, 280
Shady, Ruth, 303, 326, 331, 366
Sherwood, Sarah C., 86, 87
Shiloh, Tenn.: architecture at, 87, 88–90, 91, 92; construction of, 83–84, 86; images of, 90; maps of, 79; settlement patterns at, 94; uses of, 94
Sierra Madres, 113, 129
Silbury Hill, Eng., 10–11
Silver Glen Run Complex, Fla.: architecture at, 58, 62, 71, 81; artifacts from, 65, 71, 72; construction of, 65; descriptions of, 63–66;

layout of, 71; maps of, 55, 63, 79; modern incursions on, 63, 64–65; settlement patterns at, 64; and sociopolitical organization, 71
Simpson, W. K., 459
Sitio Conte Cemetary Complex, Panama, 248
Sloan, Ark., 79, 80
Smith, Adam T., 12, 131
Snarskis, Michael, 240
Society for American Antiquity, 17
Society for American Archaeology, 255
Sociopolitical organization, 198; and agriculture, 129, 151–52, 153, 155, 159, 193, 255, 257, 278; centralized, 255, 257, 262, 289, 375; chiefdoms, 8, 82, 84, 192, 231, 247, 281, 380, 417; complex, 151–52, 192, 232, 247, 255, 258, 261, 364, 365, 366, 375, 420; egalitarian, 190, 448; factors related to, 261; and hegemony, 299; and heterarchy, 255, 258–59, 351, 353, 417, 448; and hierarchy, 6, 9, 11, 17, 81–82, 217, 218, 221, 235, 240, 247, 248, 255, 257, 280, 291, 353, 366, 369, 375, 380, 384, 420; and kinship and lineage, 158, 190, 258; large-scale, 257; modern, 153; and monumentality, 112, 129, 130, 132, 175, 221, 302, 364; noncentralized, 448; nonhierarchical, 6; and persuasion, 258; priest-chiefs and, 280; ranked, 9, 190, 299, 322; states, 56, 131, 192, 198, 200, 217, 219, 221, 222, 232, 255, 257, 258, 259, 261, 262, 270, 278, 280, 281, 282, 299, 366, 380; tribes, 82; and Yaya-Mama religious tradition, 446. *See also* La Blanca polity; Sechín Alto polity
Soconusco, Mex.: agriculture in, 7; architecture in, 115–17, 120; ceramics from, 204; construction in, 298; food production in, 17; geographic characteristics of, 113; iconography in, 193; and La Blanca, 193; maps of, *114*; monumentality in, 113, 132, 193, 297; sites in, 115, 116–17; sociopolitical organization in, 17, 119, 123, 131
South America: agriculture in, 132; architecture in, 16–17; ceramics from, 71, 132; construction in, 15; cosmology in, 323; diet and food production in, 112, 148; goldworking in, 235; monumentality in, 132, 175, 291; sociopolitical organization in, 112, 132
South Carolina, 69
Southeast, U.S., 16–17, 53, 54, 83, 90, 112, 132

Southeastern Archaeological Conference, 90
Statue of Liberty, 6
St. Catherine's Island, Ga., 72
Stelly Mounds, La., 28, 42, 45
Stirling, Matthew, 235
St. Johns Basin, 53–54, 55, 56, 64, 67, 81
St. Johns River, 58, 62
Stonehenge, Eng., 459, 462
Stothert, Karen E., 330
Stout, Charles, 13
Suchiate River, 113, *114*, 117, 119, 123, 131
Supe Valley, 292, 299, 300, 365, 366, 367, 369
Suriname, 142, *256*
Susa, Iran, 463
Swasey/Bladen complex, 202
Symonds, Stacey, 146, 152, 154
Syria, 460

Tabasco, Mex., 143, 151
Tairona people, 232
Talamanca Mountain Range, 233, 241
Talamancan people, 240
Tapajós River, 265, 275
Taperinha, *256*, 264, 265–67, 275
Tatagapa River, 142
Taube, Karl, 127
Taukachi-Konkán, Peru: architecture at, 370, 372, *373*, 380–81, 382–83, 384, 385, 386, 392; ceramics from, 386–88; construction at, 377, 378; diet at, 388–89; labor calculations for, 377; layout of, 378, 389; materials used at, 378; restricted access at, 384, 385; roads at, 373; scale of, 377, 378–79; and Sechín Alto Complex, 369, *371*, 375
Tello, Julio C., 372, 384, 411
Temple of Talomeco, Cofitachequi, 82
Temples: Aztec, 130, 214; at Buena Vista, 314, 327, 331, *332*, 334, 335, 336–*37*, 338–39, 341, 342–43, 344–50, 351–52, 353; in Casma Valley, 326, 372, 392; in Chillón Valley, 341; Christian, 130; in coastal Peru, 353, 410, 412; Egyptian, 346, 459; at El Paraíso, 328, 331, *333*, 339, *340*, 341, 349, 351; historic descriptions of, 82; Inca, 233, 449; in Intermediate Area, 233; lack of, in Amazonia, 280; looting of, 331; Maya, 209, 215, 218, 233, 314; Mesopotamian, 459, 460; Mississippian, 85, 88; and non-utilitarian labor, 8; Old World, 353; in Sechín Alto polity, 391, 392;

Temples—*continued*
sociopolitical impact of, 6; Sumarian, 6; in Titicaca Basin, 432, *435*, *436*, 437, 438–39, *440*, 442–44, 446–47, 448, 449; wooden, 82; and Yaya-Mama religious tradition, 432, 437, 442, 446, 447
Templo Mayor, Mex., 214, 373. *See also* Tenochtitlán, Mex.
Tennessee, 67
Tennessee River, 92
Tenochtitlán, Mex., 130, 131, *142*, 148, 214, 298
Teopantecuanitlán, Mex.: and Amuco de la Reforma, 190; architecture at, 175, 177, *178*, 179, *180–81*, 182, 188, 192; artifacts from, 182; as capital, 182–83, 188, 192, 193, 194; ceremonial area of, 177, *178–79*, *180*, 182; and Coovisur, 190; cultural developments at, 215; dating of, 177, 182, 192; and exchange, 182, 183, 190; iconography at, 190; location of, *176*, 177; map of, *16*; modern incursions on, 177; monumentality at, 193; during Olmec Horizon 2 phase, 193; roads from, 192; sculpture at, 175, *180*; settlement patterns at, 177–79; sociopolitical organization at, 182–83
Teotihuacan, Mex., *176*, 183, 392
Tepila, Mex., 187, 188
Terminal Preclassic period, 215
Terraces: in Amazonia, 276; in coastal Peru, 401, 404, 414, 415, 421, 422, 423, 425; Incas and, 440, 447, 449; in Intermediate Area, 241, 242, 244, 245, 248n1; in Lower Mississippi Valley, 30, 35, 37, 38, 43; in Maya Lowlands, 209; in Norte Chico, 291, 293, 297; river, 241; at San Lorenzo, 16, 138, 160; and sociopolitical organization, 6; in St. Johns Basin, 59
Terraces, in Titicaca Basin: access to, 435; agriculture on, 441; ceramics from, 438–39, 440; construction of, 434–35, 438, 439, 442, 447, 448–49; dating of, 438, 448; images of, *435*, *437*, *440*; modern uses of, 436–37; as monumental architecture, 431; occupation of, 439; scale of, 434; stone-faced, 431, 432, 434, *437*, 438, 439, 447; styles of, 449; and temples, 442, 447; Tiahuanaco and, 449; and Yaya-Mama religious tradition, 438, 439, 447
Texas, 31
Texayac, Mex., 187, 188
Thebes, Egypt, 347
Thornhill Lake complex, Fla., *55*, 69

Tiahuanaco empire and people: and architecture, 431–35, 438, 439, 444, 447, 448, 449; artifacts from, 438, 439, 444, 448; extent of, 449; and iconography, 446, 447; precursors of, 432; and sociopolitical organization, 447, 448
Tick Island, Fla., 67
Tierra Caliente, Mex., 188
Tierra Colorada, Mex., 187
Tigris-Euphrates floodplains, 143
Tikal, Maya Lowlands: architecture at, 198, 201, 218, 220; ceramics from, 201, 203; construction at, 216; founding of, 218, 221; location of, 217; map of, *199*; Mundo Perdido complex at, 201, 216, 218
Tikuna Campo Alegre, Upper Amazon, 155
Tintal, Maya Lowlands, *199*
Titicaca Basin: agriculture in, 436, 441; artifacts from, *433*; dating of, 431; diet in, 441; excavations in, 439–40, 442; iconography in, 445; maps of, *432*; occupation of, 448; production zones in, 431; sociopolitical organization in, 432, 446; terraces in, 432; and Yaya-Mama religious tradition, 432, 442, 446, 449
Tiwanaku, Bolivia, 291
Tlacuachero, Mex., 114
Tlapa, Mex., 187
Tlatilco y Tlapacoya, Mex., 182
Tomoka, Fla., *55*, 69
Tools: agricultural, 127, 339; axes, 127, 213, 214, 218, 339, 352; celts, 214; drills, 37, 40–41; as exchange goods, 161, 443, 447; jade, 213, 218; manos, 125; manufactoring of, 31, 33; metates, 125–26; mortars and pestles, 125–26; shell, 61; sickles, 90; stone, 31, 33, 90, 125, 214, 238, 244, 276, 339, 437; in wetlands, 269
Tortugas, Peru, 367, 375, 388–89
Townsend, L. K., 90
Trigger, Bruce, 4–5, 111, 112, 114, 130, 133, 139, 174, 234, 364
Tucker, Bryan, 67
Tucson, Ariz., 463
Turkey, 313–14
Turrialba, Costa Rica, 236. *See also* Guayabo de Turrialba
Turrialba Volcano, 238, *239*, 240, 248
Tuxtlas, Mex., 149
Tuxtlas piedmont, 152–53

Uaxactun, Maya Lowlands, *199*, 201, 209, 216
Ubaid period, 460, 461, 463
Ucayali River, 272
Universidad Nacional Mayor de San Marcos U, 404
Upper Amazon, 257, 275
Upper Amazonia, 155
Upper Amazon River, *256*
Upper Xingu, 280
Urartian Empire, 131
Urfa, Turkey, 460
Urton, Gary, 346
Uruk period, 460, 461, 462
Uruk site, 6, 461

Van der Merwe, R., 319
Veblen, Thorstein, 4
Vega-Centeno, Rafael, 305
Venezuela, *256*
Ventanas complex, Maya Lowlands, 216. *See also* San Bartolo, Maya Lowlands
Vera, Ramos, 434
Veracruz, Mex., 138
Veracuz-Tabasco, Mex., 193
Vinto Alto, Peru, *292*, *295*, *296*
Virginia, 67
Virú Valley, 367
Voorhies, Barbara, 113

Wakna, Maya Lowlands, 209
Warfare, 306–7, 308
Wari culture, 386
Watson Brake (waterway), 35, 41
Watson Brake Mounds, La.: activities at, 37; artifacts and artifact density at, *31*, 34, 37, 41–42, 43; complexity of, 34; construction of, 36–37; dating of, 36–37, 43; diet at, 43–45; features and topography of, 35–36, 37, 40, 41, 43, 81; layout of, 298; location of, 35; manufacturing at, 37; map of, *16*; maps of, *29*, *35*, *42*, *79*; models of, *36*; resources at, 43; scale of, 298; settlement patterns at, 36, 41–43, 46; sites near, 41, 42; statistics on, 28
Webster, David, 144
Weeden Island culture, 84
Welch, Paul, 90
Wendt, W. E., 400
Wessex, Eng., 10
Wesson, Cameron B., 13
Western Asia, 458, 461
Western Europe, 462
Wetlands, 141–43, 232. *See also* Islotes
Wet sites, 269
Whittle, Alasdair, 10
Williams, Carlos, 326, 342, 401
Windover, Fla., *55*, 67, *79*, 80
Wing, Elizabeth, 148–49
Witz Monster, 156
Woodland period: architecture during, 25, 47, 82–83, 84; economy during, 47; sites from, *79*; sociopolitical organization and status during, 82, 83, 84
Wyman, Jeffries, 54, 64, 65

Xe phase, 202
Xingu, Brazil, 281
Xochipala, Mex., *176*, 177
Xunantunich, Belize, 202, 217

Yarumela, Honduras, 111, 130
Yates, Emily, 90
Yaxha, Maya Lowlands, *199*, 201, 217
Yaya-Mama religious tradition, 431, 432, 441–42, 445–47, 448

Zaña Valley, 295
Zeidler, James A., 324
Zoned Hachure Horizon, *273*
Zoned Incised Hachure Horizon, 272
Zurita-Nogura, Judith, 11

www.ingramcontent.com/pod-product-compliance
Lightning Source LLC
Chambersburg PA
CBHW021230300426
44111CB00007B/493